A Neo-Fatimid Treasury of Books

The Royal Asiatic Society was founded in 1823 'for the investigation of subjects connected with, and for the encouragement of science, literature and the arts in relation to Asia'. Informed by these goals, the policy of the Society's Editorial Board is to make available in appropriate formats the results of original research in the humanities and social sciences having to do with Asia, defined in the broadest geographical and cultural sense and up to the present day.

The Monograph Board

Professor Francis Robinson, CBE, DL, Royal Holloway, University of London (Chair)

Professor Tim Barrett, SOAS, University of London

Dr Barbara Brend, Royal Asiatic Society

Dr Evrim Binbas, Institute of Oriental and Asian Studies, University of Bonn

Professor Anna Contadini, SOAS, University of London

Professor Michael Feener, National University of Kyoto

Dr Gordon Johnson, University of Cambridge

Dr Firuza Melville, University of Cambridge

Dr Taylor Sherman, London School of Economics

Dr Alison Ohta, Director, Royal Asiatic Society

For a full list of publications by the Royal Asiatic Society see www.royalasiaticsociety.org

A Neo-Fatimid Treasury of Books

Arabic Manuscripts among the Alawi Bohras of South Asia

Olly Akkerman

EDINBURGH
University Press

Edinburgh University Press is one of the leading university presses in the UK. We publish academic books and journals in our selected subject areas across the humanities and social sciences, combining cutting-edge scholarship with high editorial and production values to produce academic works of lasting importance. For more information visit our website: edinburghuniversitypress.com

Edinburgh University Press Ltd
The Tun – Holyrood Road
12 (2f) Jackson's Entry
Edinburgh EH8 8PJ

First published in hardback by Edinburgh University Press 2022

Typeset in 10 / 12 Bembo by
IDSUK (DataConnection) Ltd, and
printed and bound by CPI Group (UK) Ltd,
Croydon, CR0 4YY

A CIP record for this book is available from the British Library

ISBN 978 1 4744 7956 1 (hardback)
ISBN 978 1 4744 7957 8 (paperback)
ISBN 978 1 4744 7958 5 (webready PDF)
ISBN 978 1 4744 7959 2 (epub)

Published with the support of the University of Edinburgh Scholarly Publishing Initiatives Fund.

Contents

Maps and Figures vii
Acknowledgements xii
Notes on Transliteration and Dates xv
Sources xvi

Prologue: Fatimid Encounters across the Indian Ocean xix

Introduction: Reading Sijistani in Gujarat: the Bohra Treasury of Books 1

Inside the Treasury of Books: Reflections on the Ethnography of Manuscripts 21

1 Community: Introduction to the Alawi Bohras 45
1.1 Shrine Custodians 47
1.2 Secret Manuscripts and their Social Lives 59
1.3 Everyday Documents and the Organisation of the *Da'wa* 72
1.4 An Indian Muslim Caste 86

2 Treasury of Books 98
2.1 Neither Library nor Archive: the *Khizana* as a Treasury of Books 105
2.2 A Lost Fatimid *Khizana* in Gujarat? 119
2.3 A Treasury of Books across the Indian Ocean 142
2.4 A Neo-Fatimid Treasury of Books in Baroda 146

3 Secret Universe 158
3.1 Bohra Spaces and their Modes of Access 162
3.2 Access I: A Profane Topography of the Bohra Universe 164
3.3 Access II: A Sacred Geography of the Bohra Universe 188
3.4 Gender, Etiquette and Access 202

4 Manuscript Stories 209
4.1 Secret *Khizana*, Social Manuscripts 218
4.2 Manuscripts of Alawi Provenance 220

4.3 Manuscripts of Non-Alawi Provenance 229
4.4 Practices of Borrowing, Lending and Appropriation 239

5 Materiality of Secrecy 249
5.1 Codicology of the Treasury of Books 251
5.2 Anatomy of Bohra Manuscripts: Paratexts from Head to Tail 272
5.3 Occult Paratexts: *Batini* Manuscript Culture 285
5.4 Magical Marginalia: *Zahiri* Manuscript Culture 290

6 Script and Scribal Politics 300
6.1 A Modern Isma'ili Manuscriptorium 301
6.2 Script and the Language of Secrecy 304
6.3 *Khizana* Scripts 312
6.4 Scribal Politics 328

Conclusion: A *Jihad* for Books 345

Epilogue: A Case for Social Codicology 351

Glossary 353
Bibliography 359
Index 374

Maps and Figures

All photographs taken by the author unless otherwise stated

Maps

I.1	Map of India	22
I.2	Map of Gujarat	22
2.1	Map of *khizana* sites in the Bohra tradition	120
2.2	Map of Yemen and the western Indian Ocean	130

Figures

I.1	His Royal Highness the late Dai, the Mazoon Saheb and the Mukasir Saheb and his entourage on their ceremonial procession to the *masjid*	27
I.2	The researcher with the royal women, including the Ma Saheba	37
I.3	Interior view of the Mazoon Saheb's office	39
I.4	Two *mu'minin* consulting the Mazoon Saheb	40
I.5	Jahangir's peacock throne	40
I.6	First page of the handwritten *khizana* catalogue, including the Mazoon Saheb's entry about the author in the community	41
I.7	Official *khizana* vignette	42
I.8	A written request to the Mazoon Saheb to take a photo, lying on a pile of manuscripts	43
1.1	Map in Gujarati of Bohra pilgrimage sites in *Ashab al-Yamin* in Yemen	46
1.2	Historic picture of the original grave of Sy. Ali Shamsuddin and Sy. Zakiyuddin	49
1.3	The invisible grave of Sy. Ali ibn Ibrahim	50
1.4	Devotees directing their prayer to the corner where Sy. Ali Shamsuddin is buried. Saraspur, Ahmedabad	50
1.5	Alawi Bohras in the *musafir khana*, waiting for the *thali* to be served. Saraspur, Ahmedabad	52
1.6	Folio from the *Diwān-e Ḥasan*, containing an Arabic poem in praise of the Mughal courtier of Jahangir and Shah Jahan, Shaa'istah Khan, the twenty-sixth viceroy of Gujarat under Shah Jahan	56

1.7 Diagram illustrating the transference of knowledge from God to believers, via the speakers, the Imams and the Dais 63
1.8 Gathering in the mosque, with the Dai seen surrounded by the Bhai Sahebs 77
1.9 The *chawri* (fly whisk) in action during a ceremony 79
1.10 The late Dai (middle) and the *hudud* wearing their ceremonial *ghagras, pagris, choris* and shawls 80
1.11 One of the historic registers of the community, read by the Mazoon Saheb and his assistant, Badruddin 81
1.12 The Mazoon Saheb reading a historic register of the community 82
1.13 A Dawoodi website for religious artefacts, advertising the sale of an *ʿalamat* plank 84
1.14 The late Dai blowing his *ruh* in the coconut during an engagement ceremony 87
1.15 *Nikah sehra* (veil) of the groom, with a beaded inscription that reads *Allah, Muhammad, Ali, Fatima, Husayn, Hasan* 89
1.16 The grave of the *shahid* parrot. Saraspur, Ahmedabad 95
1.17 Hussain feeding the peacocks, at the Saraspur graveyard, Ahmedabad 95
2.1 Marginal note, '*dalhī rutlām dāyrikt kār*', on the second flyleaf of manuscript no. 49075, Dar al-Kutub 99
2.2 The entrance of the royal *haveli* and the *khizana* 110
2.3 The Mazoon Saheb during his office hours, receiving believers in the treasury of books 112
2.4 The Mazoon Saheb standing in front of a manuscript cupboard 114
2.5 Manuscript preservation: *neem* leaf and pouch stuffed with rice 116
2.6 The Mukasir Saheb seen wrapping a cotton thread around a manuscript, and cotton envelopes protecting the fragile manuscripts 117
2.7 Genealogical *shajara* of the Alawi Bohras 123
2.8 Flyleaf of *Qaratis al-Yaman* with the title of the work, the dates of the letters, Hamdani owner stamp and *khizana* number 129
2.9 Fragment of *Qaratis al-Yaman* , the correspondence between al-Bharuchi and Moulai Raj Bin Moulai Hasan 136
2.10 The fortification of Thula, today a UNESCO heritage site, known as *Husn al-ghurab* 140
2.11 Historic photograph of the Alawi royal family, with Syedna Jiwabhai Fakhr al-Din b. Amir al-Din sitting in the middle 150
3.1 Girl from the city of Pune during her *ʿahd* ceremony 159
3.2 The girl's younger brother has taken a 'mini-*ʿahd*', his face decorated with garlands 161
3.3 Researcher's field sketch of Badri Mohallah 166
3.4 Badri Mohallah seen on a rainy day through the grills of the royal *haveli* 168
3.5 Entrance of the Noorani *masjid* 170
3.6 Façade of the Noorani *masjid* 171
3.7 Interior of the Noorani *masjid* 171
3.8 Spoons of salt on a communal *thali* plate symbolising the tears of Karbala 173
3.9 Bohra women finishing their communal *thali* in the *jamaat khana* 173

3.10 Life in the *jamaat khana* 174
3.11 An undated painting entitled 'Bohra Dastarkhan' by Abbas Batliwala, depicting a *thali* family meal 175
3.12 Bohra vernacular architecture 177
3.13 Art deco with an Islamic twist: a historic *manzil* in the *mohallah* 178
3.14 Wooden façade of a *manzil* 178
3.15 Another façade of a *manzil* 179
3.16 Entrance of *manzil*, with a *mu'mina*, her son and a goat, pictured during *eid* 180
3.17 Alawi Heritage Walk poster, with drawings of the traditional wooden façades of the Alawi *manzils* 181
3.18 *Topi* weaving in the *mohallah*, with the Ra's ul Hudood Saheb with a microphone in his hand 182
3.19 Painting entitled 'Telephoon' by Abbas Batliwala, depicting communication in the *mohallah* 184
3.20 The Dai is seen blowing his *ruh* into a coconut during the public royal birthday party of his grandson Luqman Bhai, held in the *jamaat khana* 198
3.21 Ladies' *majlis* in the *masjid* with the author sitting on the upper left of the 'royal' square 202
3.22 The researcher observing an all-male *ʿurs* commemoration at the *maqbara* in Baroda 205
4.1 Dissolving the sacred: pictures taken during the Ganpati Dussehra, 2013, in Baroda 222
4.2 Discarding sacred trash. Pictures of the Darul Shifa Jama Masjid and *roza* in Hyderabad 223
4.3 Hand-copied yet photocopied Jamea tus Saifiyah edition, including catchwords, pagination and footnotes 231
4.4 The personal archive of student identity cards of the Mazoon Saheb 233
4.5 Example of a Hamdani manuscript, dated 4th of *Rajab* 1306 (6 March 1889), with burgundy deer-leather binding and two library vignettes 236
4.6 Inside the same Hamdani manuscript is this first flyleaf with notes, including the title written twice 237
4.7 Preparation of the catalogue: social-codicological notes taken by the author on the second tome of a Hamdani copy of *Kitāb Jāmiʿ al-Ḥaqā'iq* 238
4.8 The private owner stamp reading *Sharafalisheikhmamujee Rangoonwala*, resembling an Ottoman *tughra* 238
4.9 Practices of erasure by previous owner in a copy of the *Daʿa'im al-Islam*, a Bohra manuscript of non-Alawi provenance 241
4.10 Practices of erasure by previous owner: Hamdani manuscript 242
4.11 Example of a non-Alawi manuscript, in which the history of its social life has been preserved beneath the intact colophon and the following folio 243
4.12 Alawi *khizana* stamps in English and Arabic 244
4.13 Example of blank spaces in a Bohra manuscript 245

4.14 Schematic overview of the transmission narrative of Bohra manuscripts 248
5.1 Text–codicology–social function triangle 256
5.2 The Mazoon Saheb proudly presenting a selection of small manuscripts in codex form 257
5.3 The Mazoon Saheb unrolling a scroll in his hands 259
5.4 Historic *waqf* scrolls 260
5.5 Single-sheet inheritance manuscripts laid out on the carpeted floor of the *khizana* 261
5.6 Further example of a modern single-sheet inheritance manuscript 262
5.7 Left, the Mazoon Saheb stores his *awraq*. Right, the handwritten talisman collection of the *khizana* 263
5.8 Royal ladies reciting poetry from the *awraq* in the *masjid* in honour of the Dai 264
5.9 A historic *waraq* held in the palm of the Mazoon Saheb 265
5.10 Left, book cover with *lisan* binding. Right, fore edge of a classical codex decorated with spray paint 268
5.11 Left, restorative paper book cover with hearts. Right, manuscripts with cloth covers 268
5.12 Left, Bohra watermarks. Right, a shield with three crescent moons dated 1875 271
5.13 Another watermark: *Extra Superfine Miftāḥ al-Hind* (Ar.; 'the key of al-Hind') with two interlocking keys 272
5.14 Two V-shaped colophons found in Bohra manuscripts 276
5.15 Standard Bohra incipit with marginal notes, royal *basmalas* and owner stamps 279
5.16 A sectarian overview of Bohra owner stamps, including the Alawi royal stamp and the Hamdani family *khizana* stamp 280
5.17 Ownership stamp, incipit 280
5.18 Reader notes 281
5.19 The codicological unit of the *juz'* of the text, mentioned throughout the manuscript on the upper left side of each folio 282
5.20 Material 'circumcision' of marginalia 283
5.21 Left, paratextual reading features found in a *zahiri* manuscript. Right, explanation of a Qur'anic verse on the recto folio 284
5.22 The 'Rosetta stone' of *kitab sirriyya*, reading *Abū Bakr laʿnahu Allāh* 286
5.23 The seal of Solomon written above a *buduh* square 287
5.24 *Ya kabikaj*: paratextual practice versus preservation practice 287
5.25 Ownership statement plus stamps and *kabikaj* formulae, followed by the formula 'I am faithful with God the all-giving from what he owns', and numerals 288
5.26 Picture of an official *daʿwa* invitation to the communal celebration of the birthday of a royal prince 289
5.27 *Abjad* values of the prophets Adam, Noah, Abraham, Moses and Jesus, written in Gujarati numerals 289

5.28 Diagram found in a *batini* manuscript 290
5.29 The paratexts: *ʿIlm al-fal* and *huruf* description written in blue and red pencil, and owner stamp, found in a *fiqh* manuscript 292
5.30 The social practice: *ʿilm al-fal* in action 292
5.31 The Mazoon Saheb is writing a *taʿwiz* in his office 294
5.32 The planetary pregnancy pie on the right folio, with a description in Persian above 296
5.33 Paratext on the miracles of a Bohra saint in Saraspur, written in *Lisan al-Daʿwa* 296
5.34 Various scribbled notes and writing exercises 297
5.35 Various marginalia on the final flyleaves of a *zahiri* manuscript 297
6.1 Marginal note found written on the end flyleaf of a *khizana* manuscript 300
6.2 Collation of *daʿwa* publications in *Lisan al-Daʿwa* and Gujarati, including a Gujarati translation of the *Daʿa'im al-Islam* 311
6.3 Writing samples of the late Dai Fakhr al-Dīn Jīwābhā'ī b. Amīr al-Dīn and the late Dai Ḍiyā' al-Dīn 313
6.4 The Yemeni and Indian book hands of Ms. 1458 320
6.5 Script sample of Sy. Burhanuddin b. Qutb Shah, *Risāla al-Waḍiyya* 322
6.6 Another script sample of Sy. Burhanuddin b. Qutb Shah 322
6.7 Script sample of the namesake of the community, Sy. Ali Shamsuddin b. Ibrahim 323
6.8 Script sample of Sy. Nuruddin b. Shaykhali 324
6.9 Nineteenth-century book hand 324
6.10 Further samples of nineteenth-century royal book hands 324
6.11 Sample of early twentieth-century royal book hand 325
6.12 Examples of late twentieth-century book hands 326
6.13 The Mazoon Saheb at work 332
6.14 Examples of historic cardboard *mistaras* 335
6.15 Preparing the paper: the making of lines with the *mistara* 336
6.16 Left: manuscript copying by the researcher from a photocopy. Right: corrections by the Mazoon Saheb 337
6.17 The *naskh* of the researcher with the royal *basmala* of the Mazoon Saheb 339
6.18 The colophon-exercise sheet of the Mazoon Saheb and the fresh manuscript copy in a booklet 342
7.1 *Qasida* verse, written in the hand of the 37th Dai, Sy. Ali Shamsuddin 346

Acknowledgements

This study is dedicated to the people of Badri Mohallah, who invited me into their homes and treated me as one of their own. Lending me their *ridas*, providing me with talismans and *tiffins*, sharing their *thalis* and *gulab jamun*, taking me on scooter rides, picnics, *pani puri* outings, *ziyara*, and passing the monsoon evenings on their swing beds, they have helped me in ways that I can only call humbling.

I wish to express my deep appreciation to Saiyedna Abu Sa'eed il-Khayr Haatim Zakiyuddin, the Dai of the Alawi Bohra community of Baroda and formerly known as the Mazoon Saheb, and his wife Bhu Saheba. It was through their painstaking efforts, and those of the Mukasir Saheb and the Rasulhood Saheb and their families, that I learned about the significance of the *khizana* and its rich manuscript collection. I thank them personally, and the community at large, for their trust, kindness, generosity and, most of all, patience. I hope this monograph in some way does justice to their world.

This monograph has benefited greatly from a broad and dynamic cacophony of teachers and academic supervisors. Manan Ahmed Asif, Léon Buskens, Beatrice Gründler, Verena Klemm, Sabine Schmidtke and Paul Walker should be mentioned in this regard. I am grateful to Manan, for pushing me out of my academic comfort zone, challenging my ideas without exception. I thank Léon, a fellow social codicologist in crime, for his thoughtful comments and conversations during our yearly dinners in Berlin, and Verena, for being a truly loyal mentor and 'Isma'ili rock star'. I am also indebted to Petra Sijpesteijn, for teaching me everything about ivory towers and beyond. I would also like to thank Paul Walker and Sabine Schmidtke for their help during my fieldwork. Finally, Samira Sheikh deserves a special thank you. Not only do I owe my entrance in the Alawi *da'wa* to her, but also my life. I am grateful to her to this day.

This study was generously funded by the Berlin Graduate School of Muslim Cultures and Societies (BGSMCS), the Dahlem Research School (DRS), and the Deutsche Forschungsgemeinschaft (DFG). The Graduate School was my academic *Heimat* for years, and its staff, P.I.s and doctoral candidates made it feel like home while at the same time forcing me to think outside the box. A heartfelt thank you goes out to Bettina Gräf, Gabrielle Freitag and Jutta Schmidbauer, who have been simply wonderful, and Gudrun Krämer, for her ever-present *irshad* and kindness.

I thank my fellow fellows at the BGSMCS for our epic friendships, the many office disco-choreographies, *mensa* luncheons, and a true sense of community, even though we are now dispersed all over the world: Nursem Aksay, Sarah Albrecht, Philip Bockholt, Samir Boulos, Eva Casal, Rosa de Castillo, Nadja Danileko, Muhammad Abdurrahman Eissa, Markus Fiebig, Chorshanbe Gobinazarov, Ahmad Fekri, Veronika Hager, Omar Kasmani, Razak Khan, Eva-Maria Kogel, Jasmin Mahazi, Kristina Mashimi, Katharina Muehlbeyer, Hana Nieber, Barbara Ogbone, Jasmijn Rana, Usman Shah, Neda Soltani, Masouda Stelzer, Torsten Wollina and Saud al-Zaid.

I was also most fortunate to benefit from the conversations, support and help of the following dear friends and colleagues: Iqbal Akthar, Michael Allan, Hasan Ansari, Christopher Bahl, Ingeborg Baldauf, Elisabetta Begnini, Gabrielle van den Berg, François de Blois, Gabriele vom Bruck, Giovanni Ciotti, Annabel Collinet, Michel Boivin, Farhad Daftary, Islam Dayeh, Maribel Fierro, Fred Donner, Ali Ashgar Engineer, Ulrike Freitag, Adam Gacek, Vineet Gupta, Nile Green, Heinz Halm, Abbas Hamdani, Shireen Hamza, Kerstin Hunefeld, Shamil Jeppie, Frederick de Jong, Nico Kaptein, Geoffrey Khan, Mahmood Kooria, Matt Melvin-Khoushki, Kai Kresse, Schirin Amir-Moazimi, Sepideh Parsapajouh, Christoph Rauch, Marina Rustow, Iqbal Surani, Rian Thum, Torsten Tschacher, Deniz Turker, Anne Regourd, Nir Shafir, Nur Sobers-Khan, Anne Stoler, Sarah Stroumsa, Annabel Teh Gallop, Tahera Qutbuddin and Jan Just Witkam. I thank Brinkley Messick for brainstorming over the title of this book in Rabat and Ravinder Kaur and Enseng Ho for their very insightful comments in Dar es Salaam. I am also indebted to my colleagues at the Institute for Islamic Studies at the Freie Universität, especially to Angela Ballaschk and Sonja Eising, and my students: it is a true privilege having you in my classroom. I would also like to thank Konrad Hirschler for his support and the many rounds of *Kaiserschmarrn*.

On an institutional level I wish to express my gratitude to the the Vadodara Heritage Trust, the Salar Jung Museum in Hyderabad, the Pir Muhammad Shah Library in Ahmedabad, the Dar al-Kutb al-Misriyya in Cairo, Tübingen University Library, Leiden University Library, the Staatsbibliothek zu Berlin, the School of Oriental and African Studies, the Royal Asiatic Society, the Department of History at Columbia University New York, the Sonderforschungsbereich Manuskriptkulturen in Asien, Afrika und Europa in Hamburg, the Netherlands Interuniversity School for Islamic Studies (NISIS), the Institute of Ismaili Studies in London, and the cluster Zukunfstphilologie at the Freie Universität Berlin.

I would also like to thank Haki Kapasi and the Reformist Bohras in Birmingham, the Bohra community on Lamu, my fellow Bohri travellers on the *Tawakal* bus in Kenya, Abdul Sheriff and Fatma Alloo, and Gulam Mohammad and Nilima Sheikh for their warm welcome in Dar and Zanzibar and Baroda. A special thank you to Ebtisam Aly Hussein and Raid al-Jamali.

I am also much obliged to the reviewers for their comments and suggestions, as well as to Alison Ottah at the RAS, Fiona Shipwright, and Louise Hutton and Nicola Ramsey at EUP for their editorial support, John Stewart Watson for preparing the maps and Shivani Pikle for sharing her beautiful drawing of the *mohallah* (Figure 3.17).

Finally, this book would not have been possible without the *yaysayers*, but certainly also not without *naysayers*, who, each in their unique way, and perhaps sometimes incomplicitly, have contributed to the journey of accessing manuscripts and writing this book.

After a decade of research on the Bohras, it is my family and close friends to whom I am most indebted. A big thank you to my dear parents for their love, patience, and curiosity for the world we share, to Quinten, Emma, Aleefa, Suki and Nargis, and to Sheila and Salim, for providing me with the space – and *kikapus* – to write.

These acknowledgements would not be complete without thanking Antonia Bosanquet, Fabiola Bierhoff, Lisa Bossenbroek, Julia Clauss, Willem Flinterman, Annemarie van Geel, Josefine Gelhar, Nick and Verena Gjorvad, Femke Groeneveld, Sarah Holz, Katja Jung, Victor Mireles, Eric van Lit, Wendy Mural Shaw, Moya Toennies, Nicola Verderame, Ruth Mas, Miri Ovadia, Maaike Voorhoeve, Denise Schinagl and Arjan Post. I am forever grateful for our friendships, which are majestic and phenomenal in each and every way.

Several of the already-mentioned friends joined me on the journey of writing this book, which, coincidentally, often took place on trains. I thank Faby and Eric for all our adventures. I thank Denise, who, once, more than a decade ago, courageously took a train with me to Birmingham to accompany me on my first interview with the Reformist Bohras, and, despite her deep fear of flying visited me in Chennai. With the exception of Samira, she was the only person outside the Alawi community who has seen me during my fieldwork, and she supplied me with everything I so sorely missed. I thank Femke, who, in each phase, was there, and accompanied me as my human talisman on what would become the first of many train rides to Berlin for my graduate school interview. And, speaking of historic train rides, I thank Zahir, my better half in every respect. Our Geisenheimer life is often nothing short of the *Lunatic Express*, dominated by our love affair with documents and manuscripts. Finishing two monographs at the same time while bridging so many different worlds: it is *academic romance* at its best. *Ib'atli jawwab wa thaminni . . .*

The book was heralded by a little boy named Taha Louis, who got here just in time. I am grateful for his lightness, and *baraka*, and most of all, for keeping us sane.

Notes on Transliteration and Dates

Transliteration

All Arabic terms, book titles, names and official titles are transliterated once according to the IJMES system, unless used otherwise by the Alawi Bohra clergy. After that, they are used without transliteration. The same goes for Gujarati, Hindi, Persian and Urdu.

Dates

All dates (including centuries), unless otherwise stated, are given in both the Hijri and the Gregorian calendar. The date belonging to the Muslim calendar precedes that belonging to the Gregorian calendar.

Places

Names of places (towns, cities, etc.) have not been transcribed unless stated otherwise. With the exception of the city of Vadodara – which was known as 'Baroda' under the British Raj and is still referred to as such by its Alawi Bohra inhabitants – cities in India are given by their post-colonial names (for instance, Bombay → Mumbai).

Sources

Sections and certain photographs of this monograph have been published in the following sources.

Parts of the Introduction in the article 'The Bohra Manuscript Treasury as a Sacred Site of Philology: a Study in Social Codicology': *Philological Encounters* 4 (2019): 1–21.

Parts of Chapter 1 in the article 'The Bohras as Neo-Fatimids: Documentary Remains of a Fatimid Past in Gujarat', *Journal of Material Cultures in the Muslim World* 1 (2020): 286–308.

Parts of Chapters 1 and 5 in the edited volume *Social Codicology: The Multiple Lives of Texts in Muslim Societies* (ed. Olly Akkerman). Leiden: Brill, 2022.

Figure 3.7 in *Muslim Matter. Photographs, Objects, Essays* (ed. Omar Kasmani and Stefan Maneval). Berlin: Revolver, 2017, 41.

To Taha Louis, and his first
footsteps into the world

Prologue: Fatimid Encounters across the Indian Ocean

Mombasa, Kenya

Overlooking the old harbour of Mombasa with its mangroves, fish market, and *dhows* from Kutch which have seen better days, one cannot fail to notice the contours of a particular building along its shores.

A historic mosque rises from the sea on a small cliff, its minaret marking the skyline of Mombasa, yet it is architecturally different from the 'Ibadi style of the neighbouring Mandhry mosque of the historic section of the city known as Old Town. Strikingly reminiscent of the Fatimid mosque of al-Hakim, the sight of the Burhani *masjid* brings one back to the medieval architecture of al-Mu'izz Street in Cairo. Yet we are in Mombasa, another centre of the Muslim world entirely, on the Swahili coast of the western Indian Ocean.

From both the seafront and the tiny alleyways of the Old Town, the Burhani mosque is built like an impenetrable fortress with its imposing gates and massive coral stone wall. The only way to observe this otherwise secluded space is from the other side of the canal, from the terrace of *English Point*: a trendy spot where well-heeled Mombasans and Nairobians alike visit the gym and meet for their sundowner. Observing the mosque from this distance, all one can see are its lanterns and chandeliers, which are lit at night for special occasions, such as Muharram. On these evenings small red flags are noticeable, blowing 'Ya Husayn' in the wind.

Moving to a very different part of Mombasa, to Old Town, one sees a different social stratum of the city reconvening every day on the seafront underneath one very large palm tree. It is the elders of Old Town, a colourful bunch of distinguished Swahili gentlemen, who come here for a cup of *kahwa* (coffee) or *tangawizi* (ginger infusion), to be enjoyed with some *halwa* (sweetmeat), while contemplating in silence over the horizon. This informal palm tree *baraza* (gathering) repeats itself every day in the late afternoon and takes place at a walking distance from the Burhani mosque. Yet despite its close proximity, not even the elders of the old town know what is going on inside this mosque. It is a world beyond their reach. That is how it is, they told me, and how it always has been.

The Burhani mosque in Mombasa, so secluded from its environs yet so present, belongs to the world of the Bohras. Inaccessible to the outside world due to an oath of secrecy, the Bohras are a small but vibrant Muslim community of Tayyibi Isma'ili Gujaratis. While the Bohras are dispersed all over the western Indian Ocean, the majority of believers live in Gujarat, India. As a historian and anthropologist, I myself was once part of the world of one of these Bohra communities in India while conducting ethnographic fieldwork. In fact, I was once referred to as the 'court historian' of the royal household of one of these groups, the Alawi Bohras of Baroda, who are at the centre of this book.

Throughout my East Africa travels, I encountered Bohras wherever I went, their colourful-laced *ridas* (Bohra traditional dress) blending in perfectly with the even more colourful *kangas* of the Swahili *mamas*. To my surprise, I observed that during these encounters in Nairobi, Lamu, Zanzibar and Dar es Salam, Bohras openly discussed and sometimes even criticised their community. This almost laissez-faire attitude seemed worlds apart from the tight-knit social control and strict dissimulation of one's religious identity practised by their subcontinental Bohra brothers and sisters in Surat, Mumbai and Karachi.

Encountering the diasporic Bohra community in East Africa, I experienced and observed them for the first time *from a distance* socially, temporally and spatially. While in Baroda the Bohras all knew me personally, or at least recognised my affiliation to the community through my *rida*, in the 'creole' context of the Swahili coast I was an outsider. What I could not have known at the time in India was that spending time in East Africa after my fieldwork was completed was crucial to my understanding of how the Bohras use their past to create a collective identity and, as such, negotiate their place in the larger Muslim world. I realised that the Fatimid dynasty, the Shi'i Isma'ili empire which ended roughly nine centuries ago in North Africa and the Arabic-speaking Middle East, was central to the Bohras' understanding of their past.

The Fatimid-style Burhani mosque of the Bohras in Mombasa was only one reference to the Fatimids that I encountered in East Africa. As I continued my travels along the Swahili coast of Kenya, Tanzania and Zanzibar, references to the Fatimids kept turning up in the most unexpected places. They were on the signs of bakeries, fishmongers, hardware stores, printing shops, and all kinds of other small businesses owned by Bohras. In Nairobi, I walked through the 'Fatemi' gardens, part of the recently opened Bohra university campus of the Jamea tus Saifiyah, the courtyard of which resembles architectural elements of both the al-Hakim and al-Azhar mosques in Cairo. In Dar es Salam, by accident, I found myself walking in a Fatemi Bazar, in which a picture of the al-Hakim Mosque was hanging next to a portrait of the *Dāʿi* (pl. *Duʿāt*), the community's spiritual head. I realised that the references to the Fatimids were not purely limited to the realm of Bohra architecture and commerce. Rather, 'Fatimid' was a term used by members of the community to refer to themselves, as the following anecdote illustrates.

Tanga, Tanzania

Earlier that summer, I was on my way from Tanga, Tanzania, to Mombasa on the famous *Tawakal* (Arabic for trust in the divine) bus line. The *Tawakal* bus was decorated with a colourful tiger motif and its passengers, young and old, reflected the cosmopolitan Indian Ocean world one reads about in academic textbooks. There were Gujarati Hindus, Khojas, 'up-country' Nairobians, Tanzanians, Somalis, Comorian Hadramis, Omanis and Zanzibaris. One group in this microcosm of the Indian Ocean could, of course, not be left out of the equation: the Bohras.

Fate had it that when I boarded the *Tawakal* bus I was seated next to two Dawoodi Bohras from Mombasa: Farida, a sous chef, and her younger brother Muhammad. While crossing the canal by ferry, Farida told me she was in the midst of preparing her wedding. For the Bohras in Mombasa, it was going to be the event of the year. The Dai would be flown in from Mumbai to lead the ceremony. When I told her about my contacts with the Dai of the 'other' Bohra group, the Alawi Bohras, she commented: 'Yes, the Alawis. We call them Fatemis.' Surprised I asked her, 'Are the Dawoodis not also Fatemis?' She said: 'Yes. We Dawoodis are Fatemis too.'

At the time, I did not make much of Farida's comment or why she identified the Alawi Bohras or her own community with the Fatimids (Fatemis). It was only later that I realised that these references to the Fatimids on the East African coast are not unusual. In fact, I also encountered them in Gujarat. They are striking examples of the way in which the Fatimid Imamate of Egypt sparks resonance among Bohras and other Isma'ilis today in these geographically removed contemporary local contexts. In addition, the *idea* of the Fatimid empire and its history highlights how, through trade, Bohra communities today are connected across the great expanse of the Indian Ocean, from East Africa to South Asia and the Gulf.

As we will see, Bohras claim what I call a distinctive 'Neo-Fatimid' identity as expressed through their communal politics, architecture and material culture. The most striking space, however, in which a Neo-Fatimid identity is negotiated is through the realm of books – handwritten manuscripts to be precise – and the sacred spaces in which they are enshrined, treasured and transmitted: the *khizānat al-kutub* (pl. *khizānāt*[1]), or treasury of books.

[1] Henceforth written as '*khizana*' in the singular, and '*khizanat*' in the plural.

Introduction
Reading Sijistani in Gujarat: The Bohra Treasury of Books

THIS BOOK IS ABOUT COMMUNITIES, manuscripts and their spaces of dwelling. It describes how people construct a sense of *togetherness* through books from the past, carefully enshrining and treasuring what is written.

It tells the story of one particular type of manuscript repository found all over the pre-modern Muslim world: the *khizanat al-kutub*, or treasury of books.[1] As a widespread social phenomenon, the *khizana* is part of a long tradition of keeping books. From Timbuktu to Xinjiang, *khizanat* were embedded in the daily lives of people: whether kept in the privacy of scholarly families in book chests or shelves at home, mentioned in *waqf* deeds, built in the walls of sacred vernacular architecture in *kutubiyyāt*, or institutionalised in the monumental royal palaces of ruling dynasties, such as the Fatimids, Mamluks, Safavids, Timurids and Ottomans.[2] The phenomenon of the *khizana*, the social act of treasuring books and the practices that surround this tradition of bibliophilia in the Muslim world continue to the present day.

This study describes how books that were once part of one of the biggest imperial book repositories of the medieval Muslim world, the *khizana* of Fatimid Cairo, ended up having a rich social life across the western Indian Ocean, starting in the mountains of Yemen and later in Gujarat. It narrates the story of how, under strict conditions of secrecy, over a period of several centuries, one *khizana* was turned into another, its manuscripts gaining new meanings in the new social realities they were preserved, read, transmitted, venerated and copied into. The result was the emergence of a new distinctive Isma'ili manuscript culture shaped by its Yemeni and later Gujarati local contexts in which these sacred books were enshrined in local *khizanat*.

For centuries, it was held that the Fatimid manuscripts that formed the basis of this Isma'ili manuscript culture had vanished after the fall of the Imamate. Scholars in Isma'ili studies argued that the Sunni Ayyubid conquest of Cairo in the late twelfth

[1] For a more detailed discussion of the term *khizana*, see Chapter 3 and the section 'Materiality of Secrecy' in this introduction.

[2] The *khizanat al-kutub* was not restricted to royal patronage and prerogatives: it was also found outside court circles; see Houari Touati, *L'armoire à sagesse: Bibliothèques et collections en Islam* (Paris: Aubier, 2003), 36–8, 178. On the *khizanat al-kutub* under the Mamluks, see Doris Behrens-Abouseif, *The Book in Mamluk Egypt and Syria (1250–1517): Scribes, Libraries and Market* (Leiden: Brill, 2018), 52–69, and for its reading practices see Konrad Hirschler, *The Written Word in the Medieval Arabic Lands* (Edinburgh: Edinburgh University Press, 2013), 125, 126. See also the discussion on *khizana* in Maaike van Berkel, 'Archives and Chanceries: pre-1500, in Arabic' and Astrid Meier, 'Archives and chanceries: Arab world', *E. I.*, 3rd edn.

century led, for ideological reasons, to the systematic destruction of the books held in the Fatimid *khizana* and other institutions.[3] The paradigm of the destruction of the Fatimid *khizana* and the vanishing of its cultural memory does not necessarily reflect historical reality.[4] This study is part of recent scholarship that has shown that Fatimid books continued to circulate, a process that is recorded in various historiographical works of the post-Fatimid period.[5] These works suggest that, rather than being systematically destroyed, the royal manuscript copies from the Fatimid imperial *khizana* reportedly 'flooded' the book markets of Cairo and Damascus and found their way into the private collections of scholars in Egypt and Syria, where they were consulted (and refuted) by scholars no less famous than Ibn Taymiyya (d. 662/1263).[6] Rather than a paradigm of destruction, it is therefore more accurate to speak of the dispersal of Fatimid manuscripts and the appreciation of their materiality as commodities with commercial value and cultural capital in the Islamic world.[7] As no Fatimid manuscript copies of Isma'ili treatises are known to exist at present, the fate of these manuscripts

[3] Farhad Daftary, for example, describes the destruction as follows: 'The immense treasures of the deposed dynasty were divided between Saladin's officers and Nūr al-Dīn. Saladin also caused the destruction of the renowned Fāṭimid libraries in Cairo, including the collections of the Dār al-ʿIlm.' Farhad Daftary, *The Ismāʿīlis. Their History and Doctrine* (Cambridge: Cambridge University Press, 2007), 253. Heinz Halm is more cautious, and suggests that Fatimid manuscripts were partly sold and partly destroyed Heinz Halm, *The Fatimids and their Traditions of Learning* (London: I. B. Tauris, 1997), 92, 93. It is important to note here that the sources that quote the historical event of the fall of the Fatimid empire are of a much later period, written from a Sunni and often polemic perspective, which, as Daftary describes in his introduction, is a larger problem in Isma'ili Studies, as no other sources are available. The narrative of destruction is very much alive among the various Isma'ili communities today.

[4] The fall of empires and the violent destruction of their manuscript libraries form a tantalising historical paradigm that is not restricted to the Fatimids. See Konrad Hirschler's remarks on the paradigm of library destruction in the medieval world in *The Written Word*, 130–2. For a strikingly similar account of the destruction of the Abbasid libraries of Baghdad after the Mongol conquest, and the afterlife of these libraries under the Ilkhanids, see Michal Biran, 'Libraries, Books, and Transmission of Knowledge in Ilkhanid Baghdad', *Journal of the Economic and Social History of the Orient* 62 (2019): 464–502.

[5] Fozia Bora explores these historiographical works in her article 'Did Salah al-Din Destroy the Fatimids' Books? An Historiographical Enquiry', *Journal of the Royal Asiatic Society* vol. 25, no. 1 (2015), 21–39. See also her book, *Writing History in the Medieval Islamic World: The Value of Chronicles as Archives* (London: I. B. Tauris, 2019). In reality, a great part of the Fatimid collection had already left the royal libraries in the mid-eleventh century following economic crisis and social unrest. According to Heinz Halm, the libraries were plundered after anarchy prevailed upon the empire when soldiers were unpaid. Halm, *Traditions of Learning* 77. Paul Walker describes a different scenario: the Fatimid government was forced to sell its valued manuscripts in order to pay the salaries of the military and civil servants. Paul Walker, 'Libraries, Book Collection and the Production of Texts by the Fatimids', *Intellectual History of the Islamicate World* vol. 4, nos 1–2, 2016: 7–21, 12. See also the description on the interchanging status of these manuscripts in Damascus from endowment to private property and vice versa in Hirschler, *The Written Word*, 132, 133.

[6] Konrad Hirschler, *Medieval Damascus: Plurality and Diversity in an Arabic Library: The Ashrafiya Library Catalogue*. Edinburgh: Edinburgh University Press, 2016, 34.

[7] Paul Walker describes how the Ayyubids carefully arranged and sold the library holdings of their predecessors, see P. Walker, 'Libraries, Book Collection', 13. See also Hirschler, *The Written Word*, 132, 133.

after their dispersal remains unclear.[8] This is where contemporary private collections, communal archives and libraries have the potential to shed new light.

Based on extensive archival and ethnographic fieldwork, this book argues that, despite the different temporal and spatial parameters, the manual transmission of Fatimid manuscripts is as much alive today as it was centuries ago. Fatimid authors such as Abū Ya'qūb al-Sijistānī (d. 361/971), al-Qāḍī al-Nuʿmān (d. 364/974) and Ḥamīd al-Dīn al-Kirmānī (d. 412/1021), as we will see, are read in Arabic in Bohra centres of learning in Surat, Baroda and Mumbai today. These Fatimid authors are enshrined in manuscript form in *khizanat* in Gujarat, where their texts have been manually copied for centuries under strict conditions of secrecy. These texts, and their presence in Gujarat, are foundational for Bohra Isma'ilism as it is practised today in South Asia and for the transmission of its knowledge system. Moreover, their material survival ultimately defines the Bohra community's identity and legitimises their position and authority in the larger Shi'i world and in the Muslim *umma* at large as heirs of the Fatimids.

The Bohras as Neo-Fatimids

The Bohras, or Musta'lī Ṭayyibī Isma'ilis, are a contemporary Shi'i Muslim merchant community of approximately 1.2 million believers residing in Gujarat.[9] While today the Bohras are divided into several sub-groups, notably the Dawoodis of Surat, the Alawis of Baroda and the Sulaymanis of Hyderabad and Yemen, they share the same past, read the same books, and treasure them in their royal *khizanat*. Historically embedded in the landscape of the Indian Ocean, all Bohras trace their clerical genealogy to medieval Yemen and their books to the royal libraries of Fatimid Cairo.

The Bohras consider themselves the heirs of the Fatimid Imamate, an empire that ruled over much of the Mediterranean and North Africa from the late third/tenth to the sixth/twelfth century.[10] Even though the days of Fatimid hegemony are long over, its sacred geography, Isma'ili knowledge system, *sharia* practices, calendar, royal titles,

[8] As for non-doctrinal Fatimid manuscript copies and the absence thereof, exceptions include Fatimid decrees and folios of the Qur'an, see Samuel M. Stern, *Fatimid Decrees: Original Documents from the Fatimid Chancery* (London: Faber & Faber, 1964), and Jonathan M. Bloom, 'The Blue Koran, An Early Fatimid Kufic Manuscript from the Maghrib'. Les Manuscrits du Moyen-Orient. Istanbul: Institut Francais d'Etudes Anatoliennes d' Istanbul, 1989. See for a more recent discussion, see Emily Neumeier, 'Early Koranic Manuscripts: The Blue Koran Debate', *Elements* no. 2 (2006). See for a surviving manuscript copy of a music dictionary from the Fatimid period: George Dimitri Sawa, *Ḥāwī l-Funūn wa-Salwat al-Maḥzūn, Encompasser of the Arts and Consoler of the Grief-Stricken by Ibn al-Ṭaḥḥān* (Leiden: Brill, 2021). In his article, Francois De Blois claims that the oldest Isma'ili manuscript in existence is a copy of al-Kirmani's *Kitāb al-Riyāḍ*, produced in Yemen during the Fatimid period (sixth/eleventh century). This dating, however, is based on his palaeographic analysis, and not on any date mentioned in the colophon. Nevertheless, it is an interesting article that gives us a rare glimpse of what Fatimid manuscripts might have looked like codicologically and palaeographically. Francois De Blois, 'The Oldest Known Fatimid manuscript from Yemen', *Proceedings of the Seminar for Arabian Studies* no. 14 (1984), 1–7.

[9] Tahera Qutbuddin, 'Bohras', *E.I.* THREE. This figure includes the *Makarima* in the Arabian Peninsula see Chapter 1.

[10] See, for example, Shainool Jiwa, *The Fatimids. The Rise of a Muslim Empire* (London: I. B. Tauris, 2017).

clerical hierarchy and manuscript tradition are central to Bohra communal identity. The study at hand therefore refers to the Bohras and their practices as 'Neo-Fatimid'.[11]

Bohra architecture, as the work of Paula Sanders and others has shown, is a striking example of the community's performance of a Neo-Fatimid identity.[12] Alongside the Nizārī Isma'ilis, the Bohras have been actively involved in the restoration of Fatimid monuments in the old city of Cairo and claim authority over sites that are considered part of their sacred heritage, such as the al-Hakim and al-Aqmar mosques. A more recent development is the 'revival' of Neo-Fatimid Bohra architecture across the western Indian Ocean, which includes newly built devotional spaces in the Fatimid style, such as mosques, *jamā'at khānas* (community centres), *musāfir khānas* (pilgrimage lodges), and *madrasas*. In this revival, the vernacular wooden architecture found across the western Indian Ocean, originally based on a *mandala* plan, is increasingly being replaced by Middle Eastern style Neo-Fatimid minarets and marble courtyards. Recent examples are the mosques in Mombasa and Malindi, Kenya, and the façade of the Zanzibar Bohra mosque.[13] In Nairobi, new elements, such as 'Fatimid' landscape architecture, have been added to the Dawoodi Bohra university complex.[14]

The Bohras, however, are not alone in tracing their genealogy to the Fatimids. Through material culture, architecture, heritage diplomacy, academic institutionalisation and other forms of communal politics, various Isma'ili communities, each in their own way, are competing for the same genealogy in the post-Fatimid modern era.[15] What makes the Bohra claim unique is the fact that they are the custodians of an Arabic manuscript tradition from the Fatimid past.

These manuscripts, one could argue, are the community's ultimate Neo-Fatimid assets and provide the basis for a claim that no other Isma'ili group, such as the Isma'ilis in the Pamir mountains of Tajikistan or in Salamiyya Syria, nor even Agha Khan I (d. 1298/1881) upon his arrival in India in the nineteenth century, is able to make.[16] This is not to say that these groups do not have their own manuscript cultures

[11] Paula Sanders was the first to coin this term in the context of a revival of Fatimid architecture. Paula Sanders, 'Bohra Architecture and the Restoration of Fatimid Culture', in Marianne Barrucand (ed.), *L'Égypte fatimide. Son art et son histoire* (Paris 1999), 159–65.

[12] Paula Sanders, 'Bohra Architecture and the Restoration of Fatimid Culture' and *Creating Medieval Cairo: Empire, Religion and Architectural Preservation in Nineteenth-Century Egypt* (Cairo: AUC Press, 2008). Sophie Blanchy, 'Le 'retour' des Bohras au Caire (Egypte): de l'état fatimide à la terre promise', in Boivin, Michel (ed.), *Les ismaéliens d'Asie du sud: gestion des héritages et productions identitaires* (Paris: L'Harmattan, 2007), 49–74.

[13] On Bohra vernacular architecture see Taibali Hamzali, 'The Architectural Heritage of the Lamu Bohra Mosque', *Kenya Past & Present* no. 40 (2012): 23–8, and Zahir Bhalloo, *A Brief Note on the Bohras in Malindi*, unpublished typescript, 2015.

[14] *The Jamea of Africa. A Millennium of Fatemi Learning Comes to Life in* Kenya, author unknown, 2 February 2018, https://www.thedawoodibohras.com/2018/02/02/the-jamea-of-africa-a-millenium-of-fatemi-learning-comes-to-life-in-kenya/ (last accessed 1 August 2019).

[15] Daniel Beben describes the place of the Fatimids in the communal memory of the Nizaris: 'The Fatimid Legacy and the Foundation of the Modern Nizari Isma'ili Imamate', in Farhad Daftary and Shainool Jiwa (eds), *The Fatimid Caliphate: Diversity of Traditions* (London: I. B. Tauris, 2017), 192–223. See also the Lawatiyya community in Oman and the construction of their Arab origins via the Fatimid Isma'ili emirate of Multan (fifth and sixth/tenth and eleventh centuries): Zahir Bhalloo, 'Construction et gestion identitaire chez les Lawatiya du Sultanat d'Oman, de Multân à Masqaṭ', *Journal Asiatique* vol. 304, no. 2 (2016): 217–30.

[16] Beben describes how the Nizari Isma'ili claim is rather a recent historical development that can be traced back to the eighteenth and nineteenth centuries. Beben, *The Fatimid Legacy*, 192.

and intellectual histories. For example, the Isma'ilis of Badakhshan have a rich Persian tradition of devotional texts attributed to Nasir Khusraw, and the Khojas of South Asia are known for their large repertoire of *gināns*, oral devotional hymns transmitted in Khojki.[17] Yet neither group possesses *khizanat* in which Fatimid texts play a central role in day-to-day religiosity.[18]

This study acknowledges the Bohra link to the Fatimids, demonstrating that a living Isma'ili manuscript culture continues to exist in Gujarat, where Fatimid titles are read and copied today, and are part of the construction of a Neo-Fatimid identity. Moreover, it explores how the Bohras use the Fatimid past to shape the present through their *khizana*. What this study does not do, however, is identify sought-after 'original' Isma'ili texts in Arabic that may or may not be present in Bohra treasuries of books. Rather than describe the content of the *khizana*, it examines the world that surrounds it.

This is because Isma'ili manuscripts, are, as I argue in this monograph, political. As objects of heritage and power, these manuscripts have become the social theatres around which modern Isma'ili identities are constructed, both internally on the level of community, as we shall see in the case of the Bohras, and vis-à-vis the Isma'ili other, such as the Nizari Isma'ilis. Unlike the Bohras, the Nizari Isma'ilis reconstituted their claim to the Fatimids in colonial South Asia through the presence of a living Imam, the Agha Khan.[19] In modern times, scholarly institutionalisation has become a powerful new way of reclaiming the Fatimid past. The creation of institutions such as the Institute of Isma'ili Studies and the Agha Khan University, which promote a new academic field of inquiry called 'Isma'ili Studies', has reinforced the claim of the Agha Khan to the political-religious authority of the Fatimids. The only possible challenge to this claim is posed by the *khizanat* of the Bohras in India, a problem that was circumvented recently by the Institute of Isma'ili Studies' acquisition of a number of Fatimid manuscript titles from reformist Bohra families, a trend that I examine in more detail at the end of this introduction. The material possession of Arabic Isma'ili manuscript collections, of whichever provenance, has become a new way of reconstituting authority over the Fatimid past and of bringing to the world a certain image of modern Isma'ilism. The Nizaris thus emerge in the modern period as the flag bearers of the Isma'ili heritage of Cairo, despite the fact that it is the Bohras, through their

[17] Beben, *Fatimid Legacy*, 192–223. Nourmamadcho Nourmamadchoev, *The Isma'ilis of Badakhshan: History, Politics and Religion from 1500 to 1750* (PhD diss., School of Oriental and African Studies, 2013). See, for the oral Isma'ili tradition in Badakhshan, Gabrielle van den Berg, *Minstrel Poetry from the Pamir Mountains: A Study on the Songs and Poems of the Isma'ilis of Tajik Badakhshan* (Wiesbaden: Reichert Verlag, 2004). For Khojki, see Zahir Bhalloo and Iqbal Akhtar, 'Les manuscrits du sud de la vallée de l'Indus en écriture khojkī sindhī: état des lieux et perspectives', *Asiatische Studien/Études Asiatiques* 72(2) (2018): 319–38. See also Daniel Beben, Jo-Ann Gross and Umed Mamadsherzodshoev, *Isma'ilism in Badakhshan: A Genealogical History* (forthcoming).

[18] An example in this regard, which will be explored in Chapter 1, is Isma'ili law. The Nizari and Tayyibi Bohra Isma'ilis historically share one *madhhab*, based on the Fatimid state compendium written by Qadi al-Nuʿman in the fourth/tenth century. While law for the Nizaris is based on the edicts of the living Imams, the Agha Khans, the Bohras continue to practise *fiqh* and *sharia*, transmitted both in print and manuscript form, to the present day.

[19] See Teena Purohit, *The Agha Khan Case: Religion and Identity in Colonial India* (Cambridge, MA: Harvard University Press, 2012) and Michel Boivin, *L'âghâ khân et les Khojah Islam chiite et dynamiques sociales dans le sous-continent indien (1843–1954)* (Paris: Karthala, 2013).

khizanat, who have for the last five centuries been the custodians of the Fatimid Arabic Isma'ili manuscript tradition.

Manuscripts and Mobility: A Treasury of Books across the Indian Ocean

While scholarship on Muslim contexts tends to favour the travel of manuscripts in urban settings and over land, the sea is a crucial element in the mobility of the handwritten word.[20] It is the movement of texts via the Indian Ocean that historically connects the Arabian Peninsula with the Indian subcontinent through trade ports such as Aden, Jeddah, Muscat, Zanzibar, Lamu, Surat, Cochin and Colombo in pre-modern times.[21] The Bohras, as we shall see, have been at the heart of this mercantile macrocosm – an Indian Ocean universe in which commodities, whether commercial or sacred, documentary or philological, were constantly on the move.[22] As one of the last vestiges of Isma'ilism in the post-Fatimid period, Yemen is a crucial axis in the mobility of Isma'ili books across the Indian Ocean, connecting Fatimid Cairo to Gujarat. This transmission history is not only crucial for the Bohras' Neo-Fatimid identity but also sheds light on the historical role of Yemen within the Indian Ocean. In this context, Yemen functioned as an export centre of Isma'ilism to Gujarat.[23]

As I argue in Chapter 2, the Isma'ili manuscripts that reached Gujarat from Yemen were powerful material symbols of authority as secret objects, carrying an aura of sacrality and opaqueness.[24] Stored in cupboards, chests, pouches and boxes, these secret *kitābs* (books) became part of repositories of mobile *khizanat*, which played a central role in the conversion of the local communities along the shores of Gujarat before their permanent transferral from Yemen to Gujarat.[25]

As manuscript repositories that travelled from Fatimid Cairo to the Arabian Peninsula, and onwards to the Indian subcontinent, Bohra *khizanat*, I argue, are *khizanat* of the sea *par exellence*. Thus far, analysis of the mobility of 'objects' within Indian Ocean

[20] On the travel of manuscripts and their codicological features over land see for example Graziano Kratli and Ghislaine Lydon, *The Trans-Saharan Book Trade: Manuscript Culture, Arabic Literacy and Intellectual History in Muslim Africa* (Leiden: Brill, 2011).

[21] See, for instance, Christopher Bahl, *Histories of Circulation – Sharing Arabic Manuscripts across the Western Indian Ocean, 1400–1700* (PhD diss., School of Oriental and African Studies, 2013) and Anne Regourd (ed.), The Trade in Papers Marked with Non-Latin Characters (Leiden: Brill, 2018).

[22] See Elizabeth Lambourn, *Abraham's Luggage: A Social Life of Things in the Medieval Indian Ocean World* (Cambridge: Cambridge University Press, 2018) and Sebastian Prange, *Monsoon Islam: Trade and Faith on the Medieval Malabar Coast* (Cambridge: Cambridge University Press 2018).

[23] Thus far, scholarship has mostly revolved around Hadrami diasporic networks, see Ulrike Freitag, *Indian Ocean Migrants and State Formation in Hadhramaut: Reforming the Homeland* (Leiden: Brill, 2003) and Engseng Ho, *The Graves of Tarim: Genealogy and Mobility across the Indian Ocean* (Berkeley: University of California Press, 2006).

[24] See for a similar phenomenon of legal texts in the Indian Ocean littoral Mahmood Kooria, 'Texts as Objects of Value and Veneration. Islamic Law Books in the Indian Ocean Littoral', *Sociology of Islam* 6 (2018): 60–83.

[25] On conversion in Gujarat see Samira Sheikh, *Forging a Region: Sultans, Traders, and Pilgrims in Gujarat, 1200–1500* (Oxford: Oxford University Press, 2010), 147–53.

studies has mainly focused on goods and documents and their commercial value in the western Indian Ocean economy.[26] The case of the Bohras highlights a larger historical phenomenon in the Indian Ocean that remains relatively undocumented: the movement of manuscript repositories. Moving beyond commerce and empire, an entire universe unfolds in which manuscripts and their spaces of domestication, such as libraries, archives, *genīzas*, *khizanat*, and other forms of keeping or storing books, are at the centre of the social life of communities, constantly shaping the social and political contexts around them.[27]

The Bohras are not alone in constructing their community through mobile manuscripts in the Indian Ocean. Other groups, such as the diasporic Hadrami Yemenis, Nizari Isma'ilis, Lawatiyya, Banias, Memons, Twelver Shi'i Khojas and Parsis are mercantile groups that share similar practices.[28] As Engseng Ho has recently noted, the textual repositories of these communities have the potential to offer new light on Indian Ocean history from a localised, communal, non-Eurocentric and non-imperial perspective.[29] Like the diasporic Hadramis, the Bohras use their manuscript repositories to construct a sense of *togetherness* through texts from the past, carefully enshrining the written word.

The textual content of Bohra manuscripts bears witness to their mobility across the Indian Ocean. The Bohras have preserved and transmitted an Arabic Yemeni Isma'ili tradition to the present day. It is also quite likely that the materiality of Bohra manuscripts and their scribal culture, scripts and book hands, readers' and owners' notes, storing practices, codicological features such as paper and bindings, and book formats are originally derived from Yemeni exemplars. This question will be discussed at length in the second part of this monograph.

[26] Exceptions in this regard in the context of manuscripts are the above-mentioned contributions of Ho, Kooria and Bahl. Moreover, Schlomotov Goitein has gone as far as demonstrating the movement of documents between Fatimid Cairo and the Indian Ocean in his study on Jewish merchant letters of the Cairo Geniza. The question of the brief Fatimid presence in South Asia has been the topic of debate between Bernard Lewis and Schlomotov Goitein. While Lewis argues that the Fatimid expansion into India took place prior to the settlement of Jewish merchants from North Africa and the Red Sea, Goitein claims that these merchants were the forerunners to Fatimid expansion in the region. In fact, he argues that their settlement in the Indian subcontinent led to the re-orientation of Fatimid politics – with Cairo focusing on the economic movement via the Indian Ocean, utilising this new route for its own interest, while relying on the Jewish communities. Shelomo Goitein, 'A Portrait of a Medieval India Trader. Three Letters from the Cairo Geniza', *Bulletin of the School of Oriental and African Studies* vol. 50, no. 3 (1987): 449–64. By the same author with Mordechai Friedman, *India Traders of the Middle Ages: Documents from the Cairo Geniza 'India Book'*, Leiden: Brill, 2007, 21–2 (for the counter argument). Bernard Lewis, *The Fatimids and the Route to India*, 1949.

[27] See for a more detailed discussion of the term *khizana* Chapter 3, and the section 'Materiality of Secrecy' in this introduction.

[28] See, for instance, Engseng Ho, *Graves of Tarim*, and Anne K. Bang, *Sufis and Scholars of the Sea: Family Networks in East Africa, 1860–1925* (Leiden: Brill, 2003), and Zahir Bhalloo, 'Le culte de l'imam Husayn chez les Khojas ismaeliens aga khanis a la fin du XIXe s', *Studia Islamica* (forthcoming). See, for the colonial period in South Asia, Nile Green, *Bombay Islam: The Religious Economy of the West Indian Ocean, 1840–1915* (Cambridge: Cambridge University Press, 2011).

[29] Instead of using the lens of empire and its subjects, Ho sees the Hadrami diasporic community as local yet cosmopolitan and mobile. Ho, *Graves of Tarim*, xxii.

Short Historical Introduction to the Bohras

The mobility of Bohra *khizanat* and the transmission of their manuscripts took place in two movements: first, from Cairo to Yemen in the twelfth century, and second, from Yemen to Gujarat in the sixteenth century. To understand the background to these movements it is necessary to provide a brief historical introduction to the Bohras.

Fatimid Cairo to Tayyibi Yemen

The Ṭayyibī Isma'ilis, or 'Bohras' as their followers later became later in India, see themselves as those who split off from the Fatimid dynasty before its downfall in Egypt, carrying on its intellectual tradition in secret until the present day. As one of the few Isma'ili communities to survive the fall of the Fatimid Caliphate in the late twelfth century, the Tayyibi Isma'ilis had already established an independent *da'wa* (community) in Yemen, following a schism in the Fatimid royal household.

The death of one particular Caliph-Imam towards the end of the empire, named al-Amīr (d. 524/1130), led to one of the biggest schisms among the Fatimid Isma'ilis: between the Hafizis and the Tayyibis. While the ideological, theological and political implications of this schism are beyond the scope of this Introduction, it is important to note that the Bohras consider themselves followers of al-Tayyib. The so-called Tayyibi Isma'ilis believed al-Amir's son al-Ṭayyib b. al-Amīr (d. unknown) to be the righteous heir of the Fatimid dynasty. However, his uncle al-Ḥāfiẓ (d. 544/1149) sat on the throne, and the Fatimid dynasty carried on without interruption until its fall in 566/1171. Followers of al-Tayyib's claim split from the Fāṭimids, who recognised al-Hafiz's claim to power and left the city of Cairo.[30]

According to Tayyibi tradition, Imam al-Tayyib was taken from Cairo to Yemen by his supporters and soon afterwards reportedly went into a state of *satr* (seclusion). In Yemen, a new Imamate was declared independently from the Fatimids, in the anticipation that a descendant of Imam al-Tayyib would return to the community as the *qā'im* ('the one who rises'). Instead of going underground, the Tayyibi Isma'ilis survived the Hafizi–Tayyibi schism by shaping a new community. It was in the highlands of Ḥarāz (north-western Yemen), under the patronage of a local dynasty, the Ṣulayḥids (r. 439–532/1047–1138), that the Tayyibis gained momentum politically as an Isma'ili Imamate separate from the Fatimids.[31]

A crucial element of the Bohras' narrative of their past is that, during the transition from Cairo to Yemen, Tayyibi Isma'ilis are said to have taken a substantial amount

[30] Daftary, *The Ismā'īlis*, 246–61. See also 'al-Ṭayyibiyya'. In *Encyclopaedia of Islam*, Vol. 2 and Fuad Sayyid, Paul Walker and Maurice A. Pomerantz, *The Fāṭimids and their Successors in Yaman: An Edition and Translation of 'Uyūn al-Akhbār* (London: I. B. Tauris, 2002).

[31] For more on the Ṣulayḥids see Chapter 1. See also Hussain Hamdani, *Al-Ṣulayḥiyyūn wa 'l-ḥaraka al-Fāṭimiyya fi 'l-Yaman* (Cairo, 1955).

of texts from the Fatimid royal *khizana*.[32] Even though the Tayyibis at times were forced to withdraw into the mountains of Haraz and practice *taqiyya* (dissimulation of one's religious identity), the production and transmission of scholarly treatises based on these texts from the Fatimid 'mother *khizana*' flourished in the late Fatimid and post-Fatimid period in Yemen.[33] We will leave the question of the transfer of Fatimid manuscripts to Yemen, including the selection of these texts and to what extent they represented the Fatimid *khizana* of Cairo, to the chapters that follow this Introduction.

In addition to the mobility of manuscripts, another relic from the Fatimid past is the organisation of the Bohra community today under a clerical hierarchy. This hierarchical structure derives from the organisation of the Fatimid state, and in particular from its extensive *daʿwa* network of Dais (missionary agents).[34] The institution of Fatimid *daʿwa* vanished gradually in the post-Fatimid Islamic world. In the absence of their hidden Imam, the Tayyibis in Yemen were the only Isma'ili community to preserve the hierarchies of the *daʿwa*, re-appropriating them to fit the new social and political order of the time. Almost simultaneously with the fall of the Fatimids and the death of the Sulayhid ruler, a Cairene Dai was appointed the new political and spiritual head of the Tayyibi community in Yemen.[35] The Tayyibi community, or *daʿwa*, was governed by a succession of Tayyibi Dais of Yemeni origin until the community moved to Gujarat in the tenth/sixteenth century.

The authority of these Tayyibi Dais was constructed around their spiritual and institutional link to the Fatimid Imams and, in particular, on the belief that the Dai was the only living individual who had contact with the hidden Imam al-Tayyib. Given this unique access, the Tayyibi Dais enjoyed a special status.[36] A long line of Tayyibi Dais transmitted and enriched the corpus of Isma'ili texts and created new syntheses of Isma'ili thought that integrated the works of Isma'ili authors from the East (mainly Iran). The result was a distinctive Tayyibi intellectual tradition with a strong focus on *ʿilm al-bāṭin*, the realm of the esoteric sciences.[37] Despite the Sulayhids' defeat by the Ayyūbids in 568/1173 and persecution by Zaydi political competitors, the Tayyibi community continued to exist in Yemen until the tenth/sixteenth century, when its clerical headquarters were transferred to Gujarat.[38]

[32] This is an event in Bohra history that is crucial to the Bohra Neo-Fatimid identity, as the Alawi Dai explained on several occasions in Baroda. See Chapter 1 for a more in-depth discussion. See also De Blois, *Oldest Isma'ili manuscript*, 1.

[33] Examples of this intellectual tradition are Ḥusayn al-Ḥamīdī's monumental *Kitāb Kanz al-Walad* (d. 577/1162), and Idrīs Imād ad-Dīn's (d. 872/1468) *magnum opus, Zahr al-Maʿānī*. Mustafa Ghalib, *Kitāb Kanz al-Walad* (Wiesbaden: Franz Steiner, 1971) and *Zahr al-Maʿānī* (Beirut: al-Muʾasassa al-Jāmiʿiyya li-al-Dirāsāt wa-al-Naṣr wa-al-Tawzīʿ, 1991).

[34] See Chapter 1 for a more detailed discussion of the various meanings of the term 'Dai'.

[35] The Dai Dhū'ayb (d. 546/1151) was the first official Dai of the Tayyibi Isma'ilis in Yemen. This lineage of Dais still exists today in the Tayyibi Isma'ili community in Yemen. The current Dai is number forty-four in the list. See for the complete list Daftary, *The Ismāʿīlīs*, 563.

[36] *Aṣḥāb al-Yamīn fī dhikr al-duʿāt al-muṭlaqīn al-yamāniyīn* (Gujarati and English). This is a historical account published by the Alawi Bohra *daʿwa*, 1432 AH, Baroda, 16–20.

[37] Daftary, 269–76. In academic literature this tradition is often referred to as 'Neoplatonic', a term that my Alawi and Dawoodi interlocutors, including the Alawi Bohra Dai, do not agree with.

[38] Daftary, 267.

Tayyibi Yemen to Bohra Gujarat

The regions of Gujarat and Sindh have known a long history of Isma'ili *da'wa* in the Indian subcontinent, dating back to as early as the ninth/fourteenth century.[39] Just as the Tayyibis had relied on pre-existing Fatimid relationships with the Sulayhids in establishing a new community, they also relied on networks that already existed with Gujarat to spread their interpretation of Isma'ilism. From Yemen, the Tayyibis successfully branched out eastwards through Indian Ocean networks overseas to Gujarat, reportedly converting large numbers of people (see Chapter 1). These converts were Hindus of the lower-middle Vaishya traders' caste, who referred to themselves as 'Bohras', a term deeply rooted in mercantile culture and derived from the Gujarati word *vehvar*, which means 'honest dealings'.[40]

From the ninth/fourteenth century onwards, the local Bohra community in Gujarat grew to such an extent that it outnumbered the Yemeni one, although believers in both Gujarat and Yemen recognised the authority of one single Dai in Yemen. For centuries, the Tayyibi Dais of Yemen travelled back and forth to Gujarat to govern the Indian community and collect the *zakāt* (alms).[41] In the in the year 946/1539, for the first time a Dai from Gujarat, named Yūsuf Najm al-Dīn ibn Sulaymān (d. 975/1567), was appointed head of both the Indian and the Yemeni communities.[42] As a result of political instability in Yemen, the religious and political headquarters of the new Bohra *da'wa*, including its treasury of books, was moved overseas to Sidhpur, Gujarat, and subsequently to Ahmedabad.[43]

In response to the new social, political and historical reality of early modern Gujarat, the Bohra clerical establishment gradually transformed into a sacerdotal royal family. As the new Indian temporal and spiritual leader of the community, the Dai became head of this royal household, taking on the role of the vice-regent of the hidden Imam and the guardian of the sacred *khizana* of the community. Under strict conditions of secrecy, the Bohra royal clergy preserved, copied, reworked and canonised Fatimid and Tayyibi Isma'ili heritage, thus creating a new Isma'ili intellectual canon that continued to be written in Arabic, along with new social practices that sacralised

[39] In fact, the advent of Isma'ilism to *al-Hind* brings us back to the Fatimids as they were the first to carry out *da'wa* missions to Sindh and Multan over land (fifth/tenth century). The Fatimid presence in Multan and Sindh might have been brief – the so-called Emirate of Multan only lasted two hundred years – but it was significant as it demonstrates that the travel of Isma'ilism to India was thus not an oceanic phenomenon per se. The political domination of Sindhi Isma'ilism lasted for a period of two hundred years: afterwards, the small Fatimid enclave was seized by the Ghaznavids in 400/1010. Ansar Zahid Khan, 'Isma'ilism in Multan and Sind', *Journal of the Pakistan Hist. Society* 23 (1975), 44. Sheikh, *Forging a Region*, 151, 152.

[40] Sheikh, Forging a Region, 149. Tahera Qutbuddin, 'The Da'udi Bohra Tayyibis: Ideology, Literature, Learning and Social Practice', in Farhad Daftary (ed.), *A Modern History of the Isma'ilis: Continuity and Change in a Muslim Community* (London: I. B. Tauris, 2011), 331.

[41] Mian Bhai Mullah Abdul Hussain, *Gulzare Daudi for the Bohras of India* (Ahmedabad, 1920), 22.

[42] No. 24, the first Indian Dai. The number refers to the number of the Dai in the lineage, starting with Shu'ayb Mūsā d. 546/1151, who reigned 530–546/1138–1151. See, for a detailed list of the Alawi Dais Daftary, *The Ismā'īlis*, 512, 513. See Chapter 1 for a more detailed description.

[43] Even though the headquarters of the *da'wa* were moved to India, a considerable number of believers still lived in Yemen. Interview with the Alawi Bohra Dai. *Ashab*, 41.

this tradition. In this new South Asian context, Bohra religious authority was shaped around and legitimised through these *khizana*, which continues to the present day.

In the centuries that followed, the community experienced turmoil caused by both internal and external threats. Following persecution at the hand of various Sunni local rulers in Gujarat, the community was forced to continue to exist underground and practice *taqiyya*.[44] It was in this period that the Bohra community and its *khizana* became scattered among different clerical families after experiencing internal communal conflicts, resulting in three Bohra *daʿwas* or communities: the Dawoodis, the Sulaymanis and the Alawis. It is the third community, the Alawi Bohras of Baroda, and their *khizana* that is the focus of the monograph.

As a merchant community originally descending from a Hindu merchant caste, it is not surprising that the Bohras had a world-view that extended far beyond Gujarat. Following the monsoon winds, the Bohras established businesses and *mohallahs* (quarters) from Jeddah to Rangoon and as far as East Africa and Madagascar. The mobility of Bohra manuscript *khizanat* beyond Gujarat is terrain that remains unexplored and is beyond the scope of this study.

The Materiality of Secrecy

Having had privileged access to the Alawi Bohra treasury of books in Baroda, I argue in this study that the Bohra *khizana* can only be understood through the community's own conception of secrecy. Secrecy in this context refers both to the esoteric content of the manuscripts kept in these *khizanat* and local understandings of the materiality of the manuscripts themselves. As such, this study is concerned with what I call the 'materiality of secrecy': that is, the physical appearance of the manuscripts and their social lives as secret objects.

This study gives special attention to the social practices that shape the treasury of books and the community at large, such as restricted modes of access to believers, traditions of transmission, and politics of identity construction in relation to the outside non-Bohra world, including practices of initiation, censorship and excommunication. These social practices, as we shall see, are legitimised through the question of access and non-access to the Bohra *khizana*, which is at the centre of the community yet inaccessible to the majority of believers. However, regardless of whether Bohra *mu'minīn* and *mu'mināt* (male and female believers) can access these manuscript repositories or not, 'their' *khizana* is also considered a sacred space: a sacred space which holds the material proof of the community's uninterrupted link to the Fatimids, to the Imams who came before them, and to the Prophet Muhammad and the *ahl al-bayt*. This therefore makes the manuscripts stored in the *khizana* not only secret but also sacred and untouchable by ordinary Bohra believers.

In addition, the Bohras' Indic Hindu roots – along with non-Islamic caste notions of ritual purity, social status and skin colour, and untouchability – and their relationship

[44] The most notorious of these rulers, at least in the collective memory of the Bohras, was the Mughal emperor Aurangzeb (d. 1119/1707). See Samira Sheikh, 'Aurangzeb as Seen from Gujarat: Shiʿi and Millenarian Challenges to Mughal Sovereignty', *Journal of the Royal Asiatic Society* 28 (2018): 1–25.

to their clerical sacerdotal 'royal' family impose an additional layer of secrecy to the manuscripts.[45] In this sense, the Bohras' composite *khizana* culture is a remarkable confluence of a Hindu-Indic caste structure and an Arabic Isma'ili manuscript tradition. This confluence is crucial for understanding why the *khizana* functions the way it does and the Bohras' positionality vis-à-vis its sacred materiality.

By focusing on the *khizana* in its entirety instead of individual texts, authors or periods, this study attempts to write from the bottom up. Instead of thus taking the *khizana* as a historical reality set in stone, this monograph carefully deconstructs the agency attributed to it, humanising its custodians and giving a voice to the people who have the ceremonial right to access the *khizana* and those who do not: those who write, read, collect, collate, venerate and consume the sacred materiality of its manuscripts. It thus aims at giving the community a voice instead of operating via the standards of academia and academic understandings of knowledge production, manuscripts and repositories of knowledge.[46] As such, this book does not refer to the *khizanat al-kutub* as a 'library' or an 'archive', employing instead the term used by the community to refer to this space. In this regard, this study differs from recent scholarship on archives and libraries in Muslim contexts, which tends to apply these modern categories to describe historical or contemporary manuscript repositories.[47] This does not mean, however, that the *khizana* is essentialised as a historical reality. Rather, the objective is to deconstruct its use by the Bohras and bring to light what Anne Stoler calls 'the uncertainties of the archive', in this case its Neo-Fatimid narrative.

The Bohras as Subject of Study

Because of the Bohras' practices of secrecy up to the present day, their communities and manuscript repositories remain shrouded with mystery to the outside world. As mentioned, until recently it was widely assumed that the fall of the Fatimids meant the end of its rich Arabic Isma'ili intellectual tradition in the Muslim world. In the last few decades, however, this paradigm changed after several reformist-minded Dawoodi Bohra individuals donated their private family collections to academic institutions in India and Europe.[48] Disenchanted with the clerical establishments of their respective communities, they thus broke with a long tradition of secrecy that kept the esoteric

[45] See Marc Gaborieau, on *sayyids* taking the place of Brahman priests among Muslim castes in South Asia: 'Typologie des specialists religieux chez les musulmans du sous-continent indien, les limites d'islamisation', *Archives des sciences sociales des religions* 29 (1983): 29–52.

[46] See for this perspective also Brinkley Messick, *Sharia Scripts. A Historical Anthropology* (New York: Columbia University Press, 2018).

[47] See Messick and Hirschler. For a larger discussion on the terminology regarding *khizana*, and whether terms such as 'library' and 'archive' are applicable, see Chapter 2.

[48] These donations include the Zahid Ali and, most recently, Hamdani collections to the IIS in London. The first private collection, however, was donated by Asaf Fyzee to Mumbai University. Delia Cortese, *Arabic Ismāʿīlī Manuscripts: The Zāhid Alī Collection* (London: I. B. Tauris, 2002). Francois De Blois, *Arabic, Persian and Gujarati Manuscripts: The Hamdani Collection* (London: I. B. Tauris, 2011). Muhammad Goriawala, *A Descriptive Catalogue of the Fyzee Collection of Isma'ili Manuscripts* (Bombay: Bombay University Press, 1965).

content of these manuscripts hidden from the outside world.[49] Even though these private collections only represent a fraction of Bohra Tayyibi manuscripts, their donation has been immensely important for the field of Isma'ili Studies, as it led to the rediscovery of this intellectual tradition. As a controversial act of *gift giving* to the outer, non-communual domain, these donations highlight the tension that is inherent in the encounter between people and manuscripts, clerics and believers and the questions of ownership rights, heritage, agency and access.

Research on Bohra Manuscripts

On the basis of these donated manuscript collections, Bohra Tayyibi Isma'ili treatises have become the subject of academic study, resulting in contributions that are bibliographical in nature or intellectual histories.[50] However, Bohra manuscripts have been mostly used to study older periods and historical contexts, either the Fatimid period or, in some cases, the Yemeni Tayyibis, but are not studied as part of the Bohra intellectual tradition. These manuscripts are thus removed from their context and dislocated from the Bohra *khizanat* they come from. The dislocation of Bohra manuscripts and its effects is discussed at length in Chapter 4.

Studies based on these individual manuscripts on intellectual history, theology, *adab* and historiography are carried out from the comfort of the library armchair; they do not take into consideration or reflect on the role of Bohra manuscripts in the community.[51] As important as these studies are in their own right, they do not provide a full picture of the Bohra philological tradition or canon: we still know so little about what was read, transmitted, commented upon, stored and enshrined. Nor do these studies address the social context that gives meaning to these philological traditions as secret texts. The main reason for this lacuna in the existing scholarship is that no researcher until now has been able to access and study the manuscripts with the Bohras *in situ*. Because of traditions of secrecy, the social meaning of Bohra manuscripts has not been understood.

The social embeddedness of philological traditions, however, is not merely of interest to social historians or anthropologists. It is crucial to understanding how canons, textual corpora and manuscript repositories *work* and what meaning they have in local contexts. According to my observations among the highest clerical circles of the Alawi Bohras, manuscripts cannot be read only as academic sources: as isolated,

[49] What these manuscript donors could have not foreseen is the fact that, in some cases, access to these collections remains restricted, either due to insurmountable administrational challenges or for other reasons.

[50] Ismail Poonawala's monumental *Biobibliography of Isma'ili Literature* deserves special mention in this regard (Malibu: UCLA Undena Publications, 1977). See also Farhad Daftary's *Isma'ili Literature: A Bibliography of Sources and Studies* (London: I. B. Tauris, 2004).

[51] The dislocation of manuscripts is a larger problem within the field of manuscript studies, codicology, palaeography, documentary practices, museum and library studies and philology, which, in my opinion, is often not addressed sufficiently. Discussing the provenance of manuscripts not only is important for political reasons in the post-colonial age we live in, but also matters in terms of understanding these texts. See, for a larger discussion of this argument, my article 'The Bohra Manuscript Treasury as a Sacred Site of Philology: A Study in Social Codicology', *Philological Encounters*, 4 (2019): 182–201.

single texts from which one can mine information, taken from a library shelf. This is not how texts are read in Bohra *khizanat*, where each title is surrounded by ritual and is part of a hierarchy of knowledge, subdivided into periods and genres, compendia and commentaries. The manuscripts are arranged according to textual hierarchies of secrecy, to which one has to be initiated physically, intellectually and spiritually by the Dai: this process takes years and includes the taking of oaths of allegiance, memorisation and manual copying. Looking at Bohra manuscripts through the perspective of the community, it becomes clear that the function of these texts in their social context of producers and users has been overlooked, as have the rituals that surround these manuscripts, the spiritual guidance they offer, and the particular conditions of accessing the secret *khizana*. This study fills those gaps.

Ethnographies on the Bohras

Providing an understanding of the social context of things and people is where the ethnographer comes into play. As much as the issue of access has hampered historians and philologists in their studies on texts, anthropologists too have struggled with the Bohras' long-cultivated and self-imposed tradition of secrecy. Due to persistent practices of *taqiyya*, very few anthropologists have had access to the closed-off lived worlds of Bohra believers.

Jonah Blank and Denis Gay's monographs are exceptions in this regard. Their works on the Dawoodi Bohras in Mumbai and Madagascar are foundational for what we know about Bohra lived religiosity, both in the centre of Dawoodi clerical authority (Blank) and on the periphery (Gay).[52] My own ethnographic observations, which will be central throughout this study, were made almost entirely among the Alawi Bohra community in Baroda. The positionality of the Alawis in relation to the smaller community of Dawoodis, already highlighted in the prologue, is vital in understanding these communities in the present and will be discussed at length in the following chapters. This book thus breaks new ground in the field of 'Bohra Studies', because it is about the Alawi Bohras, who have hitherto not been studied.

Blank and Gay's access to the Dawoodi Bohra community is remarkable, yet they did not have access to the *khizana* of the community. On the basis of my own ethnographic observations, I argue that understanding the Bohra treasury of books requires an understanding of how the Bohras perceive the *ʿilm* (knowledge) that is materialised in their *khizanat*. Bohras consider their community 'the *daʿwa*': a universe with a lived Islam that is distinctly Bohra, local, inaccessible to the outside world yet transnational, with its own unique social and *khizana* practices, rituals, clerical hierarchy (each discussed in

[52] Jonah Blank, *Mullahs on the Mainframe: Islam and Modernity among the Dawoodi Bohras* (Chicago: Chicago University Press, 2001). Denis Gay, *Les Bohra de Madagascar. Religion, commerce et échanges transnationaux dans la construction de l'identité ethnique* (Berlin: Lit Verlag, 2009). See also Christelle Brun, 'De la caste marchande gujarati à la communauté religieuse fatimide: construction identitaire et conflits chez les daoudi bohras (ouest de l'Inde)' (PhD diss., Toulouse University, 2013). For an insider's perspective see the following contributions: Hussain, *Gulzare Daudi*, Ali Asghar Engineer, *The Bohras* (New Delhi: Vikas, 1980), Roy Shibani, *The Dawoodi Bohras: An Anthropological Perspective* (Delhi: D.K. Publishers, 1984) and Noman Contractor, *The Dawoodi Bohras* (Pune: New Quest Publications, 1980).

Chapter 1) and spatial particularities (see Chapter 3). *Ilm* in this universe, I learned, has an exoteric, *ẓāhirī*, and an esoteric, *bāṭinī*, meaning. The exoteric interpretation of practices, sacred texts and rituals is open to all believers, as Blank and Gay have mapped out extensively in their ethnographies on the Dawoodis. The hidden, esoteric interpretation, also known as the *ḥaqā'iq* or eternal truths, by contrast, is a world not easily accessible to the anthropologist because it is revealed through the initiation and embodiment of certain *batini* texts.

Access to these texts, as we see in Chapter 2, is a highly restricted and gendered affair for men only. It requires taking secret oaths and undergoing passages of initiation and is considered a sacred privilege and royal right. What makes this esoteric *ilm* even more inaccessible is the fact that it can only be found in handwritten manuscripts, stored in the Bohra *khizanat*, and copied manually. Putting the esoteric into print, as discussed in Chapter 6, is out of the question, as the sacred materiality of handwritten texts is considered as important as their content. The philological world of manuscripts and *khizanat*, central to the Bohras yet at the same time inaccessible to most believers, has traditionally been out of reach of the anthropologist.

In short, scholarship on the Bohras is not complete, because anthropologists and philologists are not in dialogue with one another: individual *batini* texts are studied out of their social context; although the daily life of the Bohra *mohallah* (quarter) and its *zahiri* affairs have been documented, the central role of Bohra *khizanat* and its *batini* manuscripts is missing in these ethnographies. The exoteric *zahir* and the esoteric *batin* thus remain artificial and separate realms in scholarship, even though, according to my observations, they are not mutually exclusive and are equally important to believers in their daily lives.

Social Codicology

Examination of the above-discussed lacuna demands a new methodological perspective in which the observant eye of the ethnographic, the archival and the codicological are in conversation. In this book I offer the contours of what such an interdisciplinary perspective may look like through the lens of *social codicology*.[53] As described elsewhere in more detail, social codicology is the study of the encounter between the philological – in this case, the world of manuscripts and their repositories – and people. As a study in social codicology, this monograph investigates the tension inherent in this encounter – 'what people do with texts', whether printed or handwritten, and how the social informs the philological, and vice versa.[54]

In focusing on the particular localised social life of the *khizana*, the present study moves beyond the frequently articulated idea that manuscripts are inert objects of material culture, imprisoned in the histories of their creation. I argue, instead, that manuscripts have a rich social life through their interaction with people and communities over time and space. This monograph thus shifts the focus on manuscripts

[53] Olly Akkerman (ed.), *Social Codicology: The Multiple Lives of Texts in Muslim Societies* (Leiden: Brill, forthcoming).

[54] Olly Akkerman, 'A Study in Social Codicology'.

entirely from their study as material objects to the social framework in which they gain meaning through their interaction with readers, communities and archives of knowledge. Through social codicology it thus coins a new disciplinary practice, which humanises the people who write, use and venerate manuscripts in a living understanding of Islam as a local human experience.

As a study in social codicology, it demonstrates that manuscripts continue to play a central role in Muslim contexts. Through questions of gender, agency, veneration and identity formation, this study thus engages with the larger question of how Islam functions as a localised practice through texts, manuscript culture, secrecy and community. In short, it is a book about a *khizana* that is inaccessible, yet one that is *at work*, maintaining a collection of secret manuscripts with, as we will see, very rich social lives.

The actor- and agency-oriented approach of social codicology documents the many facets of a South Asian diasporic community's locally lived Shi'i, Isma'ili and distinctly Arabic Indian Ocean experience of Islam. Approaching the Bohra *khizana* from this perspective allows us to imagine how Islam functioned across the western Indian Ocean before the emergence of external factors, such as colonialism, the introduction of print, and more recent universalising Wahhabi Sunni, Twelver Shi'i or Nizari Isma'ili political and legal understandings of Islam, grounded in uniform social and textual practices.

Through the lens of social codicology, we thus disentangle the local social meaning of a *khizana* that is secret yet central to the community's Neo-Fatimid identity of togetherness. The notion of an inaccessible *khizana* and its reproduction through the continued practice of manual copying, I argue, plays a central role in the legitimisation and strengthening of the Bohras' communal identity and its clerical hierarchy.

Gender in the Treasury of Books

Despite the digital age we find ourselves in, physical archives, libraries and other book dwellings remain the most important repositories of historical inquiry. *Going to the archives*, involving long waits, the exchange of formalities and the building of trust, is a nuisance to some and a sacred ritual to others. Yet the process is rarely seen as a social practice that, ultimately, determines the histories that are written. Whether private, communal or state-regulated, archives are sites of power where access often depends on personal relationships and social hierarchies. Recognising these repositories as sites of power, one cannot get around the social and thus gendered nature of archival research. Gender, as this monograph demonstrates, shapes the nature of research itself: in the access we have and the kind of work we end up publishing. Yet there has hardly been a conversation on how gender affects the historical research we do, especially in the context of libraries and archives in the global south.

Our gender, as well as many other factors relating to our positionality such as skin colour, sexuality, age, nationality, ethnic and socioeconomic background, is what shapes our experiences, archive stories and library journeys; in many cases these factors determine the fate of our research through enabling or preventing access. Following the so-called reflexive turn in cultural anthropology, reflecting on these factors has become standard in ethnographic writing. Yet among philologists, historians and codicologists, gender is often overlooked, taken for granted, deemed irrelevant, rarely discussed or abandoned to an anecdote in the margins of scholarship.

This is not surprising given that, historically, scholarship on books and people in Muslim societies belonged to the realm of male scholars. In other words, there was no need to address the question of gender as being male was a given. However, the unique access that scholars such as Snouck Hurgronje, Vladimir Ivanov, Ignace Krachkovsky or, more recently, Brinkley Messick and Engseng Ho had in Mecca, Aceh, Pakistan, India, Damascus, or Ibb and Tarīm (Yemen), was directly shaped by their gender.[55] Had they been women, their stories and thus their scholarship would have been different. Access to archives and libraries in Muslim contexts in the global south remains challenging. As we will see in the reflexive section, access to book repositories and manuscript collections in living communities is always personal, as access is determined by personal characteristics or personal relationships. The encounter between people and their books, as described earlier, needs to be addressed and reflected on to fully understand the social meaning of the historical sources we deal with.

In addition to starting an interdisciplinary discussion on the social lives of manuscripts and their spaces of dwelling through social codicology, this monograph proposes a critical reflection on gender in 'the archive'. More precisely, it brings in gender in scholarship on manuscripts, archives and libraries. It discusses gender in the context of the hierarchies of otherness, power, privilege, discursive practices of knowledge production, questions of access, agency, ritual and honour and engages with larger themes such as coevalness, orientalism and (post)colonialism. As such, this study aims to start a conversation on gender while doing the work that we do as philologists, historians and ethnographers of whichever gender: going to the archives, observing manuscript cultures, cataloguing collections, recording scribal practices and studying libraries.

This monograph therefore includes a detailed analysis of the author's entry into the community and male-dominated inaccessible space of the *khizana*: a realm that has never been accessed before by the majority of believers, let alone by an outsider, and especially not a woman. Being subject to a wide range of limitations and rituals of access, this book tells the story of how I was able to pursue this path *despite*, but at the same time *because of*, my gender. The subjectivity of my otherness, I argue, including my ethnicity, socioeconomic and religious background, marital status and academic capital, is what *defined* access; after months of intense negotiations in the field, this subjectivity allowed me to write this monograph, which, as a printed book, will have its own social life in academia and, more importantly, in the *khizana*.

55 Snouck Hurgronje, *Mekka* (The Hague: Het Koninklijk Instituut voor de Taal-, Land- en Volkenkunde van Nederlandsch-Indië te 's-Gravenhage, 1888–9). Vladimir Ivanow, *A Guide to Isma'ili Literature* (London: Royal Asiatic Society, 1933). See for his memoirs: Farhad Daftary, *Fifty Years in the East: The Memoirs of Vladimir Ivanow* (London: I. B. Tauris, 2015). Ignace Y. Kratchkovsky, *Among Arabic Manuscripts: Memories of Libraries and Men* (Leiden: Brill, 1953). Messick, *Sharia Scripts* and *Calligraphic State*. Ho, *Graves of Tarim*.

Chapters of the Book

The book consists of six chapters, followed by a short reflexive epilogue. In each chapter, I make anthropological observations, supplemented by short thick descriptions, interview quotations alongside philological readings, codicological analyses and manuscript histories. The social-ethnographic and the codicological-archival come together in the Conclusion.

Chapter 1, 'Community', is devoted to the Alawi Bohra community in Baroda. It is preceded by a reflexive section, titled 'Inside the Treasury of Books', which focuses on my entry into the community as a philologist and historian. It tells the story of how, through unanticipated anthropological experiences, I negotiated access to the treasury of books. Through the lens of these experiences, of my gaining access to the closed, male-dominated realms of the royal household, I introduce the reader to the community and its 'Faatemi way of life': its social discourses, rituals of secrecy, orthopraxy, clerical hierarchies, caste structures, documentary practices and courtly protocol. The Alawi Bohra community, as we will see, functions on its own as a universe, carefully constructed around what I call the 'Neo-Fatimid' narrative of historical continuity: a community closed both in a bordered socio-geographical sense, spatially embedded in a *mohallah* in Baroda, and in an esoteric-philosophical sense, through the Bohra reading and embodiment of the Fatimid-Isma'ili knowledge system.

The second chapter, 'Treasury of Books', focuses on the social role of the *khizana* in the Alawi Bohra universe as a manuscript repository of strictly secret texts. I discuss the meaning and usefulness of notions of archive, library and *khizana* within the context of the community's Neo-Fatimid narrative and reconstruct its collection history and the politics of enshrinement through its manuscrips and documents. Tracing back the Alawi *khizana* over the Indian Ocean to Tayyibi Yemen, I argue that, as a consequence of several historical events, an evident process of '*taqiyyafication*' (increase of secrecy as both a social and a textual practice) of Bohra scholarship has taken place: it has not only resulted in the monopolisation of knowledge production and reproduction by the clerics but, more importantly, has also shaped the Bohra treasury of books into a secret *khizana* in the contemporary community. I conclude that, in contrast to the community's closed narrative of the *khizana* as a static royal-clerical institution, it is an instrument of its custodians as it legitimises and cultivates clerical hierarchies and the organisation of the community at large. The chapter ends with a discussion of reactions in the community to my presence as a participant observer in the *khizana* and how its social life was changed.

The third chapter, 'Secret Universe', focuses on the politics of access. More precisely, I address specific questions of space, access, secrecy and *khizana*. In order to understand the community's multi-layered practices of secrecy, I walk the reader through the Alawi Bohra quarter, entering its different realms through two modes of access. 'Access I' is a profane geographical mode, in which I highlight the architectural topography of the *mohallah*. 'Access II' is a conceptual sacred geography, mapping out the various sacred spaces of the Alawi Bohra universe. I demonstrate that the *khizana*, as such, functions as two spaces in one: as the administrative headquarters of the clerics, which is the public ceremonial space where all religious and communal affairs are adjudicated, and as the treasury of books, which functions as a sacred, inaccessible space. This perspective not only helps us understand the social discourse of the Bohra *khizana* but also explains why I, as a non-believer, woman and non-cleric, was able to successfully access the *khizana* through the mode of 'access I', respecting the restricted content of these texts.

Working with the assumption that, as 'things', manuscripts have social lives and life cycles, the following three chapters document the social lives of *khizana* manuscripts, the social practices that surround them, and the local meaning of their materialty: from their birth through sacred copying rituals and scribal politics; to social usage, consumption and appropriation; to the demise and afterlife of manuscripts and their immaterial qualities of talismanic healing.

Chapter 4, 'Manuscript Stories', centres around the individual biographies of the manuscripts in the treasury of books, studied through their paratexts and oral histories. In this chapter, we look at the question of how the mobility of manuscripts from Fatimid Cairo and Tayyibi Yemen continued in India among the three Bohra communities from the lens of the Alawi *khizana*. In doing so, I extend the notion of the social lives of manuscripts even further by making the argument that, textually and paratextually, there is a traceable parallel between the private lives and family histories of the royal family and the manuscripts. I demonstrate that, through their materiality, *khizana* manuscripts have unique stories to tell that expand beyond the notion of a restricted *khizana*. These manuscripts contain traces of rich social lives outside the treasury of books – of cultural and local appropriation; of material demise and social practices of discarding and even ingesting the written word; of material 'circumcision'; and of travel, exchange and circulation across time and space and highly contested political borders of communities.

In Chapter 5, 'Materiality of Secrecy', I analyse the social life of marginalia that characterise the Bohra *khizana*. I argue that, unlike other manuscript cultures in the Muslim world, glosses and commentaries are doctrinally prohibited. At the same time, marginalia on Bohra manuscripts are often the basis of dealings with members of the community who seek guidance. As objects, the manuscripts of the Bohra treasury of books thus have a 'public-inaccessible' function for the community, as believers see the objects but cannot access them. Mapping out the localised paratextual practices of the *khizana*, I demonstrate that even marginalia have social lives: esoteric manuscripts contain marginalia, such as spells, curses, secret scripts and alphabets, that contribute to their inaccessibility to the uninitiated reader, and exoteric manuscripts contain traces of magic and popular occult traditions that are still practised today in the *khizana*.

The final chapter, 'Script and Scribal Politics', introduces the reader to Bohra philology *in action* as it documents the living manuscript tradition of the Alawi Bohras and explains the importance of the handwritten word for the continuing existence of the community and its Neo-Fatimid *khizana*. Bohra manuscripts are considered the material manifestation of the Isma'ili 'eternal' esoteric truths, or *haqa'iq*, which form the basis of the Bohra interpretation of Isma'ili thought. Because of this, the closed collection of esoteric texts and scripts in Baroda is still manually copied by hand by Bohra clerics. This secret practice, which I participated in myself as a scribe through what I call *codicological participant observation*, is considered a *jihād* or spiritual struggle and can only be carried out according to strict scribal rituals by the highest clerics of the community. By thus writing 'against' print culture (which is prohibited), I argue that the circulation of these sacred objects is restricted to the Bohra *khizana*. Additionally, I analyse the dialectics between, script, secrecy and scribal agency, making the argument that, in the specific social context of the Alawi Bohras, Arabic and its scriptural form *naskh* have been elevated to a hegemonic language and script of secrecy.

The monograph ends with a short conclusion and epilogue, titled 'A Jihad for Books', in which we return to the question of the emergence of Neo-Fatimidism among the Bohras. In addition, it includes my personal reflections on writing an ethnography of the *khizana* several years after returning from the field, discussing challenges in the preservation of the community's endangered cultural memory and the sacred materiality of its manuscripts in the digital age. Finally, it examines the introduction of a new addition to the Bohra *khizana* collection, represented by this monograph that is dedicated to the rich social life of this unique treasury of books.

Inside the Treasury of Books: Reflections on the Ethnography of Manuscripts

Baroda, Gujarat

In the middle of the old bustling city of Vadodara, famous for its pearl carpets and its Gaekwad and Mughal architectural splendor, and home to the largest handwritten Qur'an in the world, resides a small Muslim community, known as the Alawi Bohras.[1] Vadodara, or Baroda as it is still referred to by its inhabitants, has been the home of the Alawi Bohra community for more than three centuries.

The city, located on the banks of the Vishwamitri River and named after its majestic banyan trees, is the third most populated city in the western Indian province of Gujarat (see Maps I.1 and I.2).[2] The Alawi Bohras are not the only merchant community, or 'caste' as they call themselves, in Baroda. Baroda's strategic location close to the Gulf of Cambay made it an important trading centre linking Gujarat's hinterland to the wider world of the Indian Ocean.[3] Baroda has historically been inhabited by a large variety of religious denominations, such as various Hindu castes and Sunni and Shi'i Muslim, Jain, Parsi, Sikh, Christian and Buddhist communities, each with its own *mohallah* in the old city.[4]

Characterised by an eclectic mix of pastel-coloured, decaying art-deco colonial houses, surrounded by sweet shops, pharmacies, perfumers and *jalebi* sellers, the Alawi community is confined to one neighbourhood in the old Mughal city of Baroda, known as 'Badri Mohallah', or simply the 'Bohra lane', as it is referred to by outsiders. In addition to the community's Neo-Fatimid Indian Ocean identity, Alawi Bohras also proudly consider themselves Barodian Gujaratis. The 'Bohra lane' is known to residents throughout the city. In this historic *mohallah*, the community functions as its own microcosm, a parallel universe that seemingly operates completely independently from wider Indian society through a well-oiled network of its own schools, hospitals, shops and religious infrastructure. Like the Dawoodi Bohra sister community, the

[1] On the Qur'an see http://zeenews.india.com/news/nation/partly-restored-229-year-old-quran-back-in-baroda-mosque_628785.html

[2] Vadodara is the city's name after independence; Baroda is its old colonial name. As the Alawi Bohras, and many other inhabitants of the city, still refer to it as 'Baroda', I will do so as well in this monograph. It has a population of around 1.4 million inhabitants.

[3] See Ho, 'The Two Arms of Cambay: Diasporic Texts of Ecumenical Islam in the Indian Ocean', *Journal of the Economic and Social History of the Orient* 50 (2007): 347–61.

[4] Samira Sheikh, *Forging a Region*, Introduction.

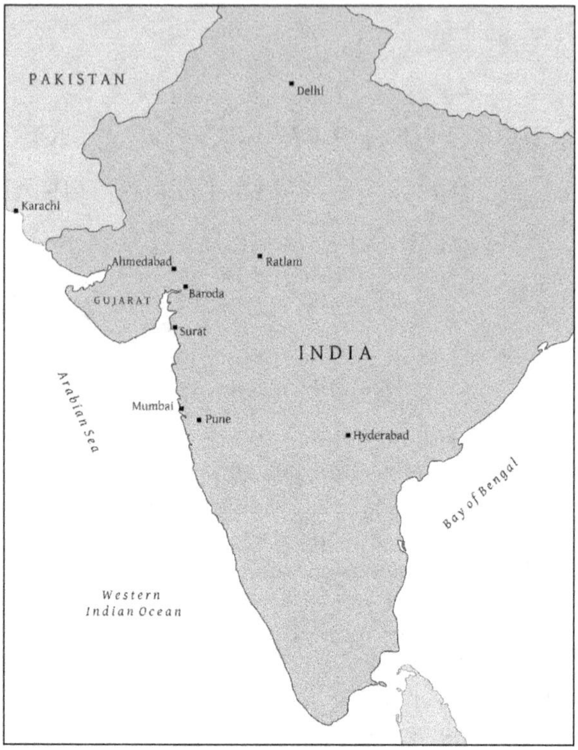

Map I.1 Map of India.

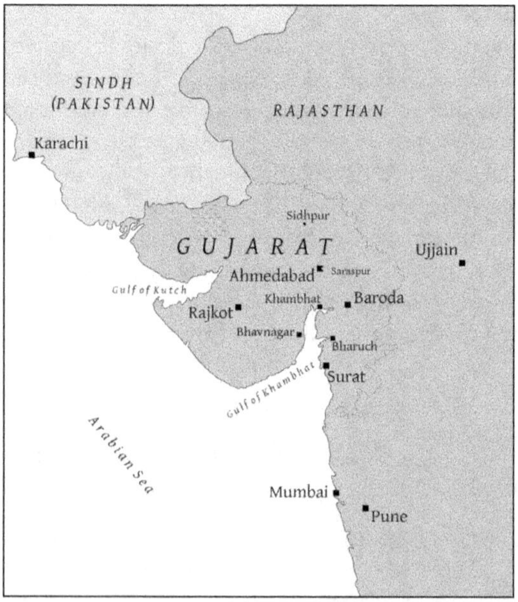

Map I.2 Map of Gujarat.

Alawi Bohras practise *taqiyya* (see Chapters 1 and 2), which refers to the community's social practice of secrecy. Believers will never answer questions from outsiders about their faith, always referring them to their clerics. Unless one is part of the Alawi Bohra universe, it is difficult to know anything about the community or even set foot in the Bohra lane.

Through a series of accidental events, however, I became part of this universe. What started as 'going to the archives' led to my appointment as 'court historian' of the Alawi Bohra royal family and finally to my role as 'accidental ethnographer' of the community and its treasury of books. This reflexive chapter describes the story of my attempts to gain access to the Alawi Bohra treasury of books. An intense and at times challenging process, it resulted in success after many months, despite my being denied access many times during the process. I have written down my attempts to access the *khizana* chronologically – from my arrival in Baroda, to physically entering the Alawi Bohra *mohallah*, to gaining authorised permission to enter the treasury of books, to becoming part of the daily life of the treasury of books as a cataloguer and scribe.

On 'Going to the Archives'

Going to the archives is a social practice so fundamental to historical research, yet one that is rarely the subject of reflection. Every researcher does it, yet we rarely talk about what it is that we do when 'going to the archives', why we do it, how we do it, and how our positionality, including our gender, affects the scholarship we produce.[5] Whether we are dealing with the bureaucracy of state archives or preserving endangered archives in the intimacy of private collections or community libraries, the question of access remains sensitive, especially in the global south. The success or failure of archival research depends on building personal relationships and trust, a complex process that often involves navigating local notions of hierarchy, social status, gender and power. No matter how historical or philological one's academic interests are, the encounter with *the social* is inevitable.

As this study argues, the social encounter with librarians, shrine caretakers, custodians of mosques, archivists, antique dealers and collectors is crucial to our understanding of the archival sites and collections we study. As such, this monograph is an argument in favour of taking these social encounters seriously. Moreover, it advocates incorporating these encounters or archive stories in academic writing as part of an ongoing reflection on the social practice of going to the archives, archiving and cataloguing. By acknowledging the importance of our archive stories, we move beyond the frequently articulated idea that archives and libraries are inert sites that store dusty objects from the past. Instead, archives, libraries and other repositories of texts have rich social lives through their interaction with people and communities over time and space. I propose therefore in the following section to reflect on positionality in the archives by exploring the encounter between the researcher, the community and its treasury of books, in this case the Alawi *khizana* in Baroda.

5 An exception in this regard is Antoinette Burton (ed.), *Archive Stories. Facts, Fictions, and the Writing of History* (Durham, NC: Duke University Press, 2006).

From Accidental Ethnographer to Social Codicologist

Bohra *khizanat* and the manuscripts they store are notoriously difficult to access, which is precisely what makes them so fascinating. In their communities, Bohra manuscripts are considered sacred objects that are not supposed to be touched, read or possessed by any member of the community other than the royal family. Interestingly, I was subjected to the social practices of keeping these books secret long before I observed these manuscripts in their social context and learned about their sacred status. Early on in my career, I discovered that the world of Isma'ili manuscripts is complex, as its politics transcended their respective communities, a process I discussed in the Introduction. Experiencing these layers of communal politics was interesting as much as it was challenging, as I was left with no texts to work with.

In a final attempt to access Isma'ili manuscripts, I decided to travel to Baroda to visit the private *khizana* belonging to the royal family of the Alawi Bohras. Against all odds, I was granted an audience with the Alawi Bohra Dai after expressing my interest in the *khizana* via email. It felt like a small window of opportunity, and in the autumn of 2012 I travelled, with little preparation, to Baroda, expecting to be refused at the door. My original plan of *going to the archives* for two weeks, however, turned into an intense ethnographic experience of four months, which fundamentally changed the way I understood books, people and the encounter between them. It also changed the character of this study: the archive became a treasury of books, inhabited by real scribes, readers and custodians whom one usually only gets to know in the colophons and marginalia of manuscripts. Now, however, they were living people with stories, personalities and royal titles. The sterile university libraries I was so used to work in made way for a *khizana*, a site of power with strict rules of access, surrounded by ritual and royal protocol, oaths of secrecy and other rites of initiation. It was a communal yet private and undisclosed space that had never been accessed before by the majority of the community, let alone by an outsider; it was also a space that was off-limits to women.

The obstacles I encountered as an outsider, and the uncertainties and ethical dilemmas that came with it, are described in detail in this chapter. I narrate these stories not for the sake of the ethnographic anecdote, but because they reveal the unwritten rules of the community that are self-evident to believers and explain the complex process of access. I was subject to these unwritten rules and rituals of access, while embedding myself in the community as a somewhat accidental participant observer. Understanding the gendered nature of my access is crucial in this regard. This chapter therefore analyses how I was able to pursue this path *despite*, and at the same time *because of*, my gender. The subjectivity of my complete otherness, I argue, including my ethnicity, socio-economic and religious background, marital status and academic capital, is what *defined* access and, after months of intense negotiations in the field, allowed me to write this study.

Even though unintentional at first, conducting archival fieldwork within the Bohra community and accessing and cataloguing its *khizana* became an exercise in ethnographic observation. For the codicologist, trained to work with perfectly preserved manuscripts in special collections reading rooms, where manuscripts were ordered by filling out a library form and opened on cushions while wearing gloves, the world of a living South Asian Bohra manuscript *khizana* at work in Badri Mohallah was completely alien. At the same time, I was certainty alien to the community. This reflexive section is thus also a personal account of how these initially unintentional anthropological experiences, the encounter with *the social*, the people of Badri Mohallah, not only were my entry in the community but also changed my entire understanding of their treasury of books. It thus describes the process of transformation from accidental ethnographer to social codicologist of the treasury of books.

The Community

Scattered across South Asia and the larger western Indian Ocean, the Bohras instantly stand out in the streets of Baroda, Karachi or Colombo. Bearded *Bohri* men wear spotless white *kurtas* and golden *topis*; women dress in bright pink, orange and purple *ridas* – burqa capes, decorated with patterns of lace – and matching long skirts. The *rida* does not resemble what women wear in South Asia, the Gulf or East Africa. It is clearly distinguishable from a colourful *sari*, *shalwar kameez* or *kanga*, and it certainly does not look like a black *hijab*, *abaya* or *bui-bui*. Having once worn a fluorescent fuchsia *rida* oneself, one immediately realises that outside the walls of the Bohra *mohallah* it is impossible to go around unnoticed. The *rida* highlights communal boundaries in neon colours: one is either a Bohra or not. As such, wearing the *rida* is a social act: a strong sartorial statement in the public sphere and a form of social control among believers.[6]

Despite their sartorial visibility in the public domain, the Dawoodis, Alawis and, to a certain extent, the Sulaymanis are virtually unknown in the societies they live in.[7] As a gentleman in Islamabad once said to me humorously after I gave a lecture at Quaid-i-Azam University: 'The only thing we know [in Pakistan] about the Bohras is that we do not know anything about them. We do not know what happens in their *mohallahs*, we do not know what happens in their *jamaat khanas*. They are a complete mystery to us.'[8] Inaccessible to the outside world due to an oath of secrecy, the Alawis, Dawoodis and Sulaymanis are the ultimate *other* in South Asia, in the larger Muslim *umma*, and even to each other following the schisms within the Bohra community.

While the Dawoodi Bohra community has recently become more visible in the political arena, the other communities remain off the radar. Smaller in number and less politically influential or affluent than the Dawoodis, the Alawis are especially unknown to others. They are the second-largest Bohra community (an estimated 10,000 persons) after the Dawoodis (an estimated one million); the Sulaymanis (an estimated 8,000 believers) form a considerably smaller community.[9] Each of these

6 In her article on the the Dawoodi Bohras in East Africa, Eva Paul agrees that the *rida* is a form of social control. Paul, Eva (2006) *Die Dawoodi Bohras – eine indische Gemeinschaft in Ostafrika* (PDF). Beiträge zur 1. Kölner Afrikawissenschaftlichen Nachwuchstagung.

7 I was told that the Sulaymanis do not always wear the traditional Bohra dress in daily life.

8 Quaid-i-Azam University, Islamabad. 16 March 2014.

9 See, for a more detailed description, Tahera Qutbuddin's *E.I.* article. She estimates there are one million Dawoodis, 8,000 Alawis and 8,000 Sulaymanis. This figure excludes the *Makārima* in the Arabian Peninsula; see Chapter 1. According to the Alawi Bohra clerical headquarters, the Alawi community includes 10,000 believers.

Bohra groups follows a separate genealogy of spiritual leaders, known as Dais. Royal in social status and considered almost infallible spiritually, the Dais are the absolute sovereigns of their communities and the custodians of Bohra *khizanat*. Despite their shared history in Yemen, Gujarat and beyond, today the three Bohra *daʿwas* are three separate communities. As such, they do not recognise each other and hold their headquarters in separate centres in India: the Dawoodis in Surat and Mumbai, the Sulaymanis in Hyderabad and the Alawis in Baroda. Built around these centres are the historic Bohra *mohallahs*, which in some cases form larger *Bohrwads* (neighbourhoods of several *mohallahs*).[10]

Badri Mohallah, as mentioned, is the centre of the Alawi Bohra *daʿwa*, with Syedna Abū Saʿīd al-Khayr Ḥātim Zakī al-Dīn Ṣāḥib as its present, forty-fifth Dai.[11] Syedna Abu Sa'eed il-Khayr Haatim Zakiyuddin is the head of the community's sacerdotal royal family and clerical establishment. He is the community's spiritual, political and temporal replacement for the hidden Imam and is popularly referred to as *Syedna* (from the Arabic '*Sayyidnā*', 'our lord/Sayyid', usually abbreviated as 'Sy.'). Next in line in the clerical hierarchy are the Dai's brothers and sons; the Mazoon Saheb (from the Arabic *Ma'dhūn*, the governor of the community), the Mukasir Saheb (Ar. '*Mukāsir Ṣāḥib'*) and the Ra's ul Hudood Saheb (Ar. '*Ra's al-Ḥudūd Ṣāḥib'*), followed by the lower ranks of the *daʿwa*. Members of the royal family bear the titles 'Bhai Saheb' (prince) and 'Bhu Saheba' (princess). The Bhu Sahebas have important functions in the organisation of the *daʿwa*, especially among the *mu'minat*, as we see in Chapter 1.

Members of the royal Alawi Bohra clerical family have a semi-infallible status among the community's *mu'minin* and *mu'minat*. Their special status is based on the belief that their genealogy can be traced back to the Fatimid Caliph-Imams, ʿAlī and the Prophet Muḥammad. The powerful status of the royal family is not based on wealth, for they are supported by the community, but on spiritual ancestry. The royal family can be recognised easily by their sartorial practices, royal attributes and pious demeanour (see Chapter 1). The Dai, Bhai Sahebs, and often also the Bhu Sahebas, appear in public very rarely and mostly during official functions. On such occasions, they are accompanied by a large entourage of *mullahs* and helpers, who are the go-betweens between the sacerdotal royalty and the *mu'minin* and *mu'minat*.

Mu'minin and *mu'minat* depend on the royal family for spiritual guidance and must ask permission for all important life decisions such as marriage, the upbringing of their children, travel, education and the like. Every member of the clerical hierarchy is responsible for a particular organisational facet of the community, starting with the Ra's ul Hudood Saheb, followed by the Mukasir Saheb and the Mazoon Saheb, who is at the head of all ceremonies and acts as an intermediary between the Dai and the community (Figure I.1). At the very top of the hierarchy is His Royal Highness the Dai, who only manifests himself in public at great ceremonial functions such as

[10] See Madhavi Desai, *Traditional Architecture: House Form of Bohras in Gujarat* (Delhi: National Institute of Advanced Studies in Architecture, 2008).

[11] http://alavibohra.org/history.htm (last accessed 9 January 2018).

Figure I.1 His Royal Highness the late Dai (middle), the Mazoon Saheb (left), and the Mukasir Saheb (right) and his entourage (note the royal umbrella and the different turbans) on their ceremonial procession to the *masjid*.

Ramadan and ʿAshūra (commemoration of the death of Imam Husayn; see Chapter 1). It is the Dai who is the custodian and sole heir of the treasury of books, a royal right and privilege that comes with great responsibility.

The royal family of Badri Mohallah constitute only a small minority within the community. The majority of the quarters' inhabitants are the *mu'minin* and *mu'minat*. Just as the Dai, Bhai Sahebs and Bhu Sahebas have certain privileges, codes of conduct and a protocol to follow, believers must adhere to certain social codes of their universe. As we see in Chapter 3, these social codes, which specify how one behaves and presents oneself, are linked to access to the spaces of Badri Mohallah: from the spaces that are open to all, such as the mosque and the graveyard, to places that can only be accessed on special occasions, such as the royal palace or *haveli*, to sites that are off-limits to *mu'minin* and *mu'minat*, such as the treasury of books.

These social codes are, first and most importantly, bound to credentials and reputation; they address initiation, piety, sex, class, caste, marital status, family (and *their* reputation), wealth, property and connections. Secondly, there is a set of specific etiquettes that address: appearance – bodily cleanliness, dress codes (religious dress) and hairstyles (men, minimal or short hair plus beard; women, long hair, dyed with *henna* and worn in a French braid); conversation – language and speech (humble); and ethics – ritual purity, spiritual purity, and so forth.

The Question of Access

In the complex matrix of social codes of Badri Mohallah and its invisible barriers, rituals and reputation, how did I – a non-Bohri, non-Muslim, non-Indian, European, single (but considered beyond marriageable age), academic, white woman – fit into the Alawi Bohra universe? How was I to access the community in the first place and gain their trust, transcending barriers of *taqiyya*? How was I to communicate and connect with the Bhai Sahebs and earn their trust? How was I going to inform the clerics that the thing I was most interested in was the *khizana* and the sacred objects it held, including possible undisclosed secrets of the community? How was I to access and handle the sacred objects held in the *khizana*, respecting the unwritten rules and regulations of the *daʿwa*, without knowing what they entailed? And finally, how was I, as a woman, going to navigate in this milieu of pious men, finding the space I needed to do my research?

I left for Baroda with all these concerns and questions at the back of my mind. While not receiving access at all would have proven my hypothesis of the inaccessibility of Isma'ili *khizanat*, at the same time it would have meant a catastrophic end to my research. After a very long process of negotiations with the Bhai Sahebs and the Dai, and drinking litres of *karak chai* with piping-hot *samosas*, I was not only granted authorised access to the community but I also became a part of it, living in Badri Mohallah and participating in every community ritual and religious gathering, wearing a *rida*, not talking to anybody outside the community (*taqiyya*), going on *ziyāra* (pilgrimage), and even performing the *ma'tam* (self-flagellation, only performed very mildly by women) during Ashura.

Even though becoming part of the community was necessary to build trust among the Bohras – which itself was needed to access the *khizana* – it also complicated my position, as my status as a non-Bohri and unmarried woman of unknown credentials was unclear. Even after the community took me in as one of them, the Bhai Sahebs still had to find a justification for granting me access to the *khizana*. It took many more rounds of deep discussions, audiences and *thālis* (a traditional Gujarati meal served on a big round plate made for sharing) before I was given that access. I soon, however, realised that access to the physical space of the *khizana* did not necessarily mean access to its manuscripts.

From Outsider to Court Historian

My initial contact with the Alawi Bohras was made earlier that year from afar via email. Interestingly, making initial contact went along the same hierarchical lines that any believer would have to follow. This meant that my official communication with the Bohra clerical establishment started with the lowest clerical rank of Ra's ul Hudood Saheb, who in turn brought my request to the Mukasir Saheb and the Mazoon Saheb. As soon as they decided that I could visit their community, special permission had to be granted by the Dai, who honoured my request and hence gave his blessings for my visit to Baroda. What exactly my project entailed at that time was not clear to any of the involved parties, least of all myself, but as long as I would work according to the restrictions and regulations of the *da'wa* (what this meant nobody could tell me exactly either), I was welcome. For a long time, I wondered why the Bhai Sahebs were so eager to correspond with me. Why did they not observe the usual *taqiyya*? My attempts to work with other Bohra groups, the Dawoodis and the Sulaymanis, had been unsuccessful. In fact, my previous communications via official channels with these communities had always been rejected quite brusquely.

After a few emails it became clear that there were different motives for approving my rather unusual stay with the community, depending on the Bhai Saheb I corresponded with. Some of the Bhai Sahebs felt that their community and history had never received the scholarly attention it deserved, being one of the smaller Bohra communities, and they were therefore looking for what they called a *court historian* who would record their past. The late Dai and the Mazoon Saheb seemed more interested in preserving the spiritual heritage of the community, the manuscripts, and seemed open to the idea of somehow involving me in the *khizana*. Even though I was mostly interested in documenting rare Isma'ili manuscript titles at the time, I felt I was not in the position to make any demands. Despite the surprisingly forthcoming attitude of the Dai and the Mazoon Saheb regarding their *khizana*, it remained a delicate topic and I pushed it to the background at first.

Trust and Control

I arrived in Baroda to find the city partly flooded by the yearly monsoon. My luggage (including all my official documentation, diplomatic gifts, university letters, malaria pills and, most importantly, *ridas* and other pious garments) had not reached India, and thus I had no clothes to wear, my bank accounts were blocked, and I was covered in mysterious termite bites that I had caught on the train to Baroda from Mumbai. To make matters worse, it turned out that all the Bhai Sahebs were out of town for *ziyara*. The only person I was able to contact from the community was the wife of the Mazoon Saheb, who only spoke Gujarati, a language that was completely alien to me at the time. This is how my fieldwork started. The circumstances were hardly ideal for an audience with the Dai and my introduction to the community.

It was in this chaotic situation that I had my first meeting with the *entire* clerical establishment who, without warning – and to the great astonishment of the hotel manager – showed up with their entourage in full regalia in the lobby of my tiny hotel. It was only then that I understood the true meaning of the phrase they had used earlier on the phone: 'Don't look for us; we will come to you.' The meeting was almost jovial; cordialities were exchanged, and in between formalities the Mazoon Saheb took out several manuscripts from a small pouch, describing these books as 'something to read on the way', as if it were the most natural thing in the world.

The atmosphere could not have been more different the next day when I was picked up by the royal mini-van of the *da'wa* and dropped off at the clerical headquarters in the middle of Badri Mohallah. I remember my initial shock at how modest the living conditions were, especially in comparison to the Dawoodi Bohras *mohallahs* I had visited in the past. My first official *majlis* (audience or gathering, pl. *majālis*) with the clerics could not have been more different from the informal meeting the day before. The *majlis* took place in the royal *haveli* (mansion), and the three Bhai Sahebs – the Mazoon Saheb, Mukasir Saheb and Ra's ul Hudood Saheb – were present. I was taken aback by the fact that, before anything was said, I was asked to take an oath of trust on the spot. In this oath I swore not to write anything without the permission of the Bhai Sahebs and not to talk with anyone about my research either within the community or in India.[12] The Bhai Sahebs made it very clear that I had to abide by their rules and regulations at all times and that it was my place to listen, instead of asking questions. I was told that the content of the *khizana* was extremely secret and that I was under no circumstances allowed to 'roam around' or even 'know what was there'. Manuscripts were not to be touched, copied or photographed unless they allowed me to do so; for every photograph I had to ask special permission. As I took 3,000 photos one can imagine what a lengthy process this was. At first, anything I would record, document or note down was considered suspicious and needed to be approved by the clerics.

Before I could start with my research (whatever that entailed), the Bhai Sahebs made it very clear that since I was an outsider I had to win their trust. I soon learned that reputation is everything in the Bohra community and that any mistake on my part or cause for suspicion would be a reason to 'expel' me. Through social media the Bhai Sahebs had already 'screened' me before they had extended their invitation to Baroda. During the first week of my stay, however, they interrogated me about many details of my private life. They wanted to speak to my father and they emailed my academic supervisors (who mercifully responded); they checked my CV and academic pedigree, official documents and references, to which countries I had travelled, to which conferences I had gone, to whom I had talked, and so forth. Not only the Bhai Sahebs but also the Bhu Sahebas and other women of the community suddenly took a very strong interest in the intimate details of my private life. Control was the magic word, and it was therefore decided that I was going to live in a small room right across from the house of the Mazoon Saheb. Even though I never intended to stay in the *mohallah*, I realised that living in the Mazoon's proximity would give me extraordinary insight into the day-to-day life of the community.

The initial weeks of 'screening' were intense and felt overwhelming. It became clear to me that I desperately needed some distance from the community. However, I realised that if I left the *mohallah*, I would never gain the trust of the Bhai Sahebs, which I needed to access the collection of the *khizana*. There was simply no other way. Privacy, personal space and going outside the *mohallah* for a coffee were out of the question and seen as suspicious behaviour. During my four-month stay in the *mohallah*, I left the Bohra lane three to four times in total. There was no space to breathe (sometimes quite literally due to the *tuk tuk* traffic), no distance, no comfort zone: everybody observed each and every move I made. After some time, I learned that I was not the only one who suffered from this closed system of communal togetherness. The inhabitants of the entire *mohallah* seemingly suffered from the lack of privacy, yet they were the same people who kept its social conventions in place.

[12] I took the oath and have done my very best to honour it ever since. The content of this monograph has been discussed prior to publication. See the discussion on ethics in the section 'On Documenting the *Khizana*: Ethics of Disclosure'.

The social control was suffocating at times and very different from anything I have ever encountered during fieldwork in other parts of the world. My immediate neighbours, for instance, made it a habit to report the most bizarre details of my personal life to the Bhai Sahebs, hoping to gain *baraka* (blessings). The interesting part was that often the information was so insignificant that even the Bhai Sahebs did not understand the point of this practice. Given my status as the ultimate other, the people in my street were either fascinated by my behaviour or felt they had to be. So even though I did not live with the Mazoon Saheb and his family, they were aware of every move I made – where I was, with whom I had talked that day, what time I would go to bed, when (how often and how long) I took a bath, whether I had eaten toast or cereal that day, and so on – and would comment on it. For instance, if I took a shower in the evening, the Mazoon Saheb would phone me immediately, asking me why I did so; was I not aware of my reputation? Or when I went to bed a little later than usual, the phone would ring with the question why I was not sleeping. There were times when I had more than eighty missed calls on my mobile in one evening; not answering the Bhai Sahebs was out of the question. While I tried my best to conduct myself in the most pious possible way, often I had no idea what this entailed in the specific context of Badri Mohallah. As a result, I made many faux pas.

Among the Royal Family

Living in the Bohra *mohallah* meant I could not only observe but also actively participate in all community rituals, functions, activities and festivals because they took place right outside my room. From day one, I found myself sitting in crowds of weeping men and women at graveyards for the death anniversary of the Imams; sharing *thalis* during the massive communal dinners in the *jamaat khana*, observing the royal processions in the *mohallah* with its musicians and firecrackers; attending marriage ceremonies and celebrations; watching believers taking oaths and divorcing; repenting during official audiences; and going on picnics with the Dai and his family. Despite the hardships of living in the old town of Baroda, I discovered that it was something that I greatly enjoyed.

For the main communal events I was always kept under the umbrella of the Bhu Sahebas; for the smaller gatherings I usually joined my neighbours at their homes or in the *jamaat khana*. As mentioned, the royal Bohra family enjoys a sacred status in the community, and it is therefore a rare occasion for believers to see them in public. By contrast, I was in the fortunate position of having been taken under the wing of the Bhai Sahebs and Bhu Sahebas, and the Dai to a certain extent, and I developed a fondness for the Bhu Sahebas and their extended families. My close contact with them meant I had access to the private life of the religious authorities of the community, the Dai in particular, whom I observed in full regalia not only during processions in the *mohallah* and the *jamaat khana*, but also while he watched television in his royal villa, where I stayed from time to time when life in the *mohallah* would get overwhelming. This was not always understood or appreciated by believers, and as a result rumours spread about my contact with the royal family.

My physical closeness to the Bhai Sahebs also complicated my fieldwork, as the boundaries of official and unofficial, formal and informal became blurred. For example, I had *chai* with the Bhai Sahebs every day, during which they would discuss their health and family affairs with me at length. Yet, if I saw them walking in the streets of the *mohallah*, it would be considered the most egregious faux pas to greet them (which I, of course, initially did not realise).

The Mazoon Saheb, with whom I spent most of my time in Baroda, and I developed a relationship of master and disciple (see Chapter 4). At that time, his father the Dai was very old, and so it was the Mazoon Saheb who was in charge of the *khizana*, a responsibility he considered his life's work. He taught me everything I know about the community, the treasury of books and Bohra manuscripts – from how to sit in the mosque, to the art of reciting the *marsiyya* (Ar. '*marthiyya*', religious poetry in honour of Imam Husayn) to how to copy a manuscript. As interesting as it sounds, it was hard work. He was a stern and disciplined teacher. It was a perfectly normal situation to be scolded by him for being sluggish and lazy and then to gossip over a *thali* in pyjamas and watch *Who Wants to Be a Millionaire* with the young Bhai Sahebs like nothing ever happened. Initially, I found the code switching between the personal, informal – being part of the family – and the impersonal, formal: the never-ending suspicion, mistrust and harsh attitudes very challenging. Remarkably, the Mazoon Saheb could read me like a book. I never had to tell him when he or the other Bhai Sahebs had set too many conditions on me; he would know it before I realised it myself. One afternoon, when I had had enough of the trust issues and the social control, the Mazoon Saheb said to me:

> Ollybehn [sister], don't you see why we are so harsh on you and scold you all the time? We trust you with our most secret, undisclosed texts, our history. No one except for me, my father [the Dai] and my brothers, have ever seen, let alone touched these texts and they never will. Never in history has a woman seen this, not even my wife. I know it is hard for you and I am sorry for it, but we have to be very strict with you, I don't have a choice. But never forget, this, you being here studying our texts and community, is your personal *jihād*, it is a good thing and God will – *inshallāh* – give you *sawab* [*thawāb*; reward].

I felt validated by the Mazoon Saheb's characterisation of my fieldwork being my personal *jihad*, which is exactly how I experienced it at times, as I continued to participate in the daily life of Badri Mohallah.

Accessing the Treasury of Books

Even though I thus slowly gained the trust of the community and became familiar with its complex social structures, *daʿwa* rules, regulations and etiquette, I still had no clue how I was to access the most sacred space in the *mohallah*, the *khizana*. How was I to work with these sacred manuscripts, respecting the unwritten rules and regulations of the *daʿwa*, even though these rules and regulations would limit my fieldwork extensively?

After my 'induction period' in the community was over and I had settled in the *mohallah*, the time had come to express my research interest in the *khizana*. When I finally found the courage to discuss my research, my conversation with the Bhai Sahebs happened to be interrupted by a young boy who was brought into the Mazoon Saheb's office by his parents to take the *ʿahd* (the oath of allegiance, discussed in Chapter 2). During the ceremony the boy was told that now that he had become a man and responsible *mu'min*, he was strictly forbidden to share any information about his faith with outsiders under *any* circumstances. I remember one of the Bhai Sahebs saying, 'When people ask, just tell them that you belong to the Bohri caste and that it is *ḥarām* [forbidden] to talk about your faith'. There it was: *taqiyya* implemented live in action. But this boy was only told to keep standard religious knowledge to himself; he was not initiated into the esoteric aspects of his faith.

How was I supposed to gain access to the *undisclosed* if the *disclosed* was already taboo? After the family left, I very hesitantly brought up my interest in studying esoteric *batini* texts again, expecting to be rejected immediately. To my great surprise, however, my request did not seem to be a problem at all. In fact, it turned out that the Mazoon Saheb and his brothers were happy to grant me access. Against all odds, I was initiated into the highest levels of *batini* knowledge of the *khizana* during my first weeks in Baroda, taking private sessions with the Bhai Sahebs as if it were the most normal thing in the world.

The reply of the Bhai Sahebs had struck me by surprise. Were these texts not supposed to be secret and undisclosed and only to be read by the top ranks of the clerical establishment? What about the inaccessible nature of the *khizana*? Did this mean that the *batin–zahir* paradigm – of inaccessible, esoteric knowledge versus accessible, exoteric knowledge – no longer applied? What about the *ʿahd* and practices of *taqiyya*? When I cautiously asked the Bhai Sahebs, they explained that the *batin–zahir* paradigm did exist, but it was just not applicable to me as a non-Bohri. Since I had sworn that I would not reveal my knowledge to community members, they entrusted me with the esoteric. They joked that even if I did reveal these secrets, Bohris would never believe me because the content of these texts was too complicated and far away from any Islamic discourse they would be familiar with. Besides, they argued, no Barodian was ever going to read (meaning access) my work anyway. As is often the case in ethnographic fieldwork, being the ultimate outsider was thus as beneficial for the research as it was an obstacle: it was a truly double-edged sword.

The Bhai Sahebs were hence content to shed light on their reading of *batini* texts, an interpretation of Ismāʿīlī esoteric knowledge that was very different from the Neoplatonic lens academic scholars have used so far to analyse this genre. They were thus willing to share information on the content of their treasury of books, information that normally would not have been shared with anyone. The challenge remained in what particular way and how. The 'how' question turned out to be difficult for both parties. I had to figure out ways to get access via various indirect – but ethically sound – routes. The Bhai Sahebs, meanwhile, were unsure what to do with me: how to interact with me, where to seat me, and so forth. The biggest challenge on their side was how to stretch the rules to grant me access while at the same time legitimising these changes to themselves, the rest of the community, and his holy highness the Dai.

My relationship with the Mazoon Saheb was that of a pupil, not of a researcher. I was seen as a student and had no authority whatsoever. The fact that I was not a man complicated communication in every possible way (more about this later). My gender certainly did not enhance my position in the bargaining process. In their eyes, I had no agency whatsoever, and I was thus not in a strong position to negotiate. The Mazoon Saheb and I, however, soon discovered our shared passion for manuscripts. Codicology and palaeography became the language through which we were able to communicate. Moreover, the Bhai Sahebs had great respect for my (mostly male) professors. I soon learned that I could make my research requests via their authority. Playing the academic card worked. In fact, it was the *only* thing that worked.

'We don't entertain people. If we do something for you, we want something in return!' This was one of the first things the Mazoon Saheb said to me when I entered his office. I learned very early on that everything, even (or perhaps especially) my gender, was negotiable as long as I was able to offer something in return. My request was clear: permission to access the *khizana*, scrutinise its manuscripts, and catalogue and photograph them for further study. But what could I offer in return? Share my academic network (which enabled the Bhai Sahebs to exchange manuscript copies for books) or contribute some rare books and manuscript scans? These were, after all, quite limited options that would not give me access to, or an ethically sound excuse to work with, the manuscripts.

Cataloguing the Treasury of Books

As mentioned before, the sense of *da'wa* or community is extremely important for the Alawi Bohras, especially because of the community's marginalised position vis-à-vis other Muslim groups in Baroda and Indian society at large. I observed that there was a great fear among those who represent and guide their community that one day their strong social cohesion will come to an end, the community will fall apart, and its sacred heritage will be destroyed, disappear or turn into dust. This anxiety, which was clearly present among the Bhai Sahebs, is not totally unjustified in the context of Gujarat, which has yearly monsoon floods and a recent history of communal riots.

Preservation and conservation seemed to be the magic words in the eyes of the Bhai Sahebs. So, to safeguard the *khizana* for future generations and keep it in better shape, I offered the Bhai Sahebs my knowledge concerning manuscript restoration and preservation. Since my knowledge on the subject was fairly limited, especially regarding local conservation techniques used in the Indian subcontinent, I decided to travel to several major libraries in India to speak with experts in the field to gain as much knowledge as I could. I was fortunate to meet the librarians of the Salar Jung Museum in Hyderabad, the caretakers of the Mohammad Reza Pir Library in Ahmedabad, staff members of the National Mission for Manuscripts Initiative in Delhi and caretakers of several small private libraries in Chennai, Ahmedabad and Hyderabad.

In addition to supporting the community in the preservation of their treasury of books, I wondered what other knowledge or skills I had to offer. Analysing the Mazoon Saheb and the Dai's own positionality vis-à-vis their *khizana*, I realised that, in a way, they were the community's living manuscript catalogue: they were the only two people who actually knew what was inside the treasury of books and, more importantly, where to find a given manuscript or document. The Mazoon Saheb always said half-jokingly, 'I am James Bond, licence to kill! If I tell you our secrets, I have to kill you.' If something were to happen to either one of them, all their knowledge would perish. I thus sensed that there was a strong desire to record the manuscript collection of the *daʿwa*, meaning that the manuscripts had to be catalogued, numbered and photographed, which was exactly the kind of practical skills I could offer as a young codicologist.

Through this process the Bhai Sahebs and I finally came to a compromise: I would prepare an academic catalogue authorised by the Alawi Bohra *daʿwa*. This catalogue would be strictly private and under no circumstances published; after all, a *khizana* would not be secret if the community (or the academic community) could know its content. Cataloguing manuscripts meant that I had to fully scrutinise the material, which gave me the opportunity to study these undisclosed esoteric texts in as much detail as I wanted, which in turn would enable me to write a monograph. The monograph, in its turn, would give the community the academic attention that believers felt their community deserved. The negotiations had finally come full circle, or at least I thought so. I soon learned, however, that I had been given permission for the *idea* of accessing the *khizana*, not the actual practice. The next obstacle in accessing the treasury of books caught me off-guard, as it was non-negotiable: my gender.

Gender Trouble: 'The female properties of a lady scholar'

The fact that I was a 'lady scholar' in the male-dominated space of the *khizana* was controversial and caused heated debates. Gender trouble had arrived in the treasury of books. The conversations the Bhai Sahebs and I had on what they called the 'female properties of a lady scholar' were rather personal. As uncomfortable as these conversations were, I have consciously included them in this study because they are crucial to understanding how the Alawi Bohras relate to their manuscripts as material objects. Moreover, it shows how truly gendered the affair of access is – not only in the specific context of Badri Mohallah and for me personally but also in the larger framework of gender and archival fieldwork. It illustrates how positionality shapes the scholarship we produce: had I been male, my story of access, and thus the monograph that I ended up writing, would have been completely different.[13]

Problems regarding my gender in the treasury of books, the Bhai Sahebs explained to me, were mostly related to ritual purity according to the Bohra interpretation of Islamic law. *Ṭahāra* (ritual purity) is considered one of the seven pillars of faith and is deeply embedded in the daily life of believers. Every facet of ritual purity has its own place and time in the Bohra life, year, week and day and is practised accordingly. Nails, for instance, are to be clipped at a particular hour after the Friday prayer, from right to left.

[13] Leon Buskens is one of the few anthropologists to describe how his positionality affected his access to manuscripts in the context of manuscript trade in Morocco as a *Nesrani*, a Christian (non-Muslim). See 'From Trash to Treasure: Ethnographic Notes on Collecting Legal Documents in Morocco', in Maaike van Berkel et al. (eds), *Legal Documents as Sources for the History of Muslim Societies Studies in Honour of Rudolph* Peters (Leiden: Brill, 2017), 180–207.

Women, in particular, must observe these rules since they are considered to have a latent 'quality' of bodily impurity, due to the fact that they menstruate and are able to give birth. It is believed that during childbirth and menstruation women are vulnerable and can fall under the spell of *jinns*, evil spirits that are attracted by impure body fluids. During my stay in Badri Mohallah I witnessed several cases where women underwent exorcism to free them from evil spirits. For the same reason it is considered *ḥarām* to enter places of worship or to participate in other sacred acts – in my case, entering the *khizana* and, more importantly, touching sacred objects such as manuscripts – while menstruating. Interestingly, while the clerics explained the community's rituals on bodily purity and the touching of sacred artefacts through the lens of Islamic law, similar practices exist among various Hindu-Indic castes in Gujarat (see Chapter 1).

According to the Bhai Sahebs, the problematic aspects of my gender were related to touching manuscripts due to my impurity; to make matters more complicated, according to the Bohra interpretation of Islamic law, I was only worth half a man. As often was the case during my stay in Badri Mohallah, topics that were usually seen as taboo among its inhabitants did not seem to apply to the outsider. It thus happened that something as intimate as my menstrual cycle became the topic of days of discussion with the Bhai Sahebs.

Eventually we came to a pragmatic solution that allowed me to enter the *khizana* and touch its manuscripts, except on the days when I had my period, which would thus protect the sacred materiality of the manuscripts. Even though this meant that my research was interrupted once a month for several days, when I had to stay in my room, I accepted this decree. After all, manuscripts were seen as sacred objects, and it was believed that they would be corrupted if I touched them during these intervals. What was harder to deal with was that, again, nothing during my stay in Badri Mohallah was private, and so my menstrual cycle became a subject of great speculation not only among the Bhai Sahebs and their wives but also the entire *mohallah*. Apparently, this issue was considered so important that my laundry and even my garbage were checked regularly to see whether I was respecting the agreement we had made.

As unsettling as these new developments to my fieldwork were on a personal level, the gender trouble in the *khizana* did not end there. As part of the negotiations, I was informed that all Bohra women are fully circumcised as soon as they reach a marriageable age. I discovered that contrary to Sunni and Shi'i *fiqh*, female genital mutilation (FGM) is an important part of Isma'ili *fiqh* among the Bohras and considered an integral part of *tahara*. In fact, the practice is promoted actively by Bohra clerics and practised in all Bohra communities.[14] Even though circumcision would never have been part of my initiation into the Bohra community (as it would be for female converts), it *did* play a role in the discussion of whether I was suitable to work with the manuscripts. Strangely enough, these topics never seemed to be taboo in any kind of way among the clerics, and to my horror yet again, the entire *mohallah* discussed it.

[14] In past years the issue of FGM has become the cause of heated debate both within and outside the Bohra communities. See the following newspaper articles: 'Bohra Women Go Online to Fight Circumcision Trauma', http://www.hindustantimes.com/mumbai/bohra-women-go-online-to-fightcircumcision-trauma/article1-779782.aspx; and 'Uproar over Female Genital Mutilation: Bohra Muslim Woman Activist Launches Campaign on Facebook to Ban Practice', http://www.npwj.org/content/Uproar-over-Female-Genital-Mutilation-BohraMuslim-Woman-Activist-Launches-Campaign-Facebook

After weeks of negotiations, the Bhai Sahebs decided that I was allowed to 'work with' the manuscripts. After all, my work would also benefit the *khizana* and thus the community. The only minor detail was that I was still not allowed to touch the manuscripts, an impossible condition both for me as the researcher and for the clerics, because it would prevent me from scrutinising the codices properly and the Bhai Sahebs simply did not have the time to sit with me all day. It was also not an option to appoint one of the younger Bhai Sahebs to turn the pages of the manuscripts because these texts were not *supposed* to be seen by any other member of the community. In addition, the Bhai Sahebs reasoned that, as an unmarried woman, I could not be left alone with a man unattended. After all, any type of rumour would be fatal, both for the position of the Bhai Sahebs and the researcher. In the end, it was decided that I was allowed to touch the manuscripts under the strict supervision of the Mazoon Saheb, except on the days I had my period.

The new arrangement felt like a small victory on my side, as if I had been upgraded from 'the woman folk', as the Bhai Sahebs would refer to the women of the community, to somewhere in between the realm of men and women. My new gender-transcending position did not mean, however, that I could behave like a man. I still had my honour and reputation to take into account. Nevertheless, it allowed me not only to take part in the 'lady spaces', such as the committee of pious ladies, the kitchen, the beauty salon, and so forth (Figure I.2), but also to roam around in circles

Figure I.2 The researcher with the royal women, including the Ma Saheba (on the right).

that are considered exclusively for the 'gentlemen', such as most Bohri ceremonies and official functions, the streets and shops of Badri Mohallah, the mosque, the office of the Mazoon Saheb, *ziyarat* and the *madrasa* (see Chapter 3). Strikingly, the men of the *mohallah* never had any problems with my presence in these spaces (they were simply told that the Bhai Sahebs had approved of my presence and that was enough). The majority of the women, by contrast, did not always appreciate my movement in the 'gentlemen' spaces (see Chapter 3).

In addition to being able to move between different hierarchical layers (clerical–nonclerical) or mutually excluding spaces (men–women, royal–non-royal), my gendered presence in Badri Mohallah had another major advantage. The Mazoon Saheb explained that if I were a man I would never have had the opportunity to enter the community the way I had. Since I belonged to the 'women folk', the Bhai Sahebs felt responsible for my security and well-being and adopted me into their family as their self-appointed guardians. If I were a man, they told me, they would not have felt responsible for me, nor could they have trusted me among the women of the community.

Jahangir's Peacock Throne

My passage into the *khizana*, the sacred space of the community, consisted of four stages: my entrance into the *mohallah*; access to the physical space of the *khizana* itself; authorised permission to 'work with the manuscripts', which in a way meant being employed by the Alawi Bohra *daʿwa* to catalogue their *khizana*; and finally, the Bhai Sahebs' consent to work with the codices in a physical sense, including authorised permission to touch, scrutinise and, more importantly, catalogue the material semi-independently from the Bhai Sahebs.

I was stationed in the Mazoon Saheb's office (Figure I.3), virtually next to the Mazoon Saheb himself, who would go on with his usual daily routine – receiving his constituents (Figure I.4), discussing *daʿwa* matters with his brothers, preparing his sermons and playing with his grandchildren from time to time. Within the hustle and bustle of the Mazoon Saheb's office I had been assigned my own little corner (next to the fan underneath the portrait of the late Dai), where I would work my way through piles of manuscripts. Cataloguing these manuscripts manually, day in and day out; writing codicological descriptions from the peacock throne; surrounded by heaps of manuscript leaves, scrolls and sometimes talismans, the only research tools available to me were a simple ruler, a notebook, a pencil and my *rida*. I felt extremely honoured by the fact that I had become part of the 'furniture' of the headquarters of the Alawi Bohra *daʿwa*, especially being the only woman in the office.

What was even more extraordinary was the fact that I was the only person in the room sitting on a chair (and thus was literally higher than the Bhai Sahebs). This was not just any chair (chairs are not at all a common thing in Badri Mohallah households because most people cannot afford any furniture and people prefer sitting on the floor): it was the royal ceremonial chair belonging to Ma Saheba, the late Dai's wife and spiritual mother of the community, on which she would sit during religious functions in the mosque. Despite the Bhai Sahebs' serious appearance, sometimes they would fall out of their character as stern clerics. In this case they

Figure I.3 Interior view of the Mazoon Saheb's office.

Figure I.4 Two *mu'minin* consulting the Mazoon Saheb (one kneeling on the ground and one paying his *salams* to the Mazoon Saheb). The third person in the picture is the Mazoon Saheb's secretary, Mr Attarwala Bhai.

thought it was hilarious that I was sitting on this ceremonial chair, and they would joke around, calling me the 'Saheba of Jahangir's peacock throne' (Figure I.5).[15] Believers who would visit the Mazoon Saheb for an audience were very confused by my presence in his office, let alone the fact that I was sitting on Ma Saheba's throne. The confusion was mutual; I had no idea how to conduct myself, feeling incredibly clumsy in my too small a *rida* while sitting on this extravagant chair. Many of the Mazoon Saheb's visitors had never seen any strangers, especially not in a *rida* reading secret manuscripts, which led to many humorous and at times embarrassing interactions.

A day in the life of the *mohallah* would start as follows. I would wake up, put on my *rida* and report to the Mazoon Saheb's office. By the time I arrived, his office was already in full swing, with believers coming in and out and phones ringing. I would get seated in my corner where the Mazoon Saheb had already carefully selected a pile of manuscripts that were waiting to be catalogued. In addition to the daily daunting pile of manuscripts, a booklet was waiting for me, in which he had prepared a list of

Figure I.5 Jahangir's peacock throne (on it: piles of manuscripts with photo requests (on little notes), a ruler, official *daʿwa* stickers, the researcher's handwritten catalogue, a *daʿwa* vignette).

[15] Jahangir's peacock chair is a common cultural reference in South Asia.

the manuscripts. Over time, this booklet turned into a fascinating codicological unit: it became the handwritten catalogue of the *khizana* in which the Mazoon would write down my 'manuscript homework' for the day, and I would jot down the manuscript entries by hand in it, including drawings, and detailed codicological descriptions. The handwritten catalogue was thus a living philological conversation, a log book of some sort, between the Mazoon and me. The first page of this booklet, which includes a description penned by the Mazoon Saheb of my first day as a cataloguer, dated 2 September 2012, is shown in Figure I.6.

At the end of every day the Mazoon Saheb would perform his *maghrib* prayer right next to me, and afterwards we would sit for an hour or two and discuss my findings. It was during these informal chats that the Mazoon Saheb would share the more private stories behind the manuscripts I had scrutinised that day. He would tell me how the manuscripts had travelled, who had previously owned them, what role these texts played in his childhood and how these texts had been the subject of schisms, intrigues, secrets and even murder (see Chapter 4). After discussing my findings with the Mazoon, I had to fill out an official *da'wa* library vignette titled '*AD-DAWATUL HADIYYATUL ALAVIYYAH*', for each manuscript (Figure I.7), number it, and paste it inside the binding. Even though I was personally against writing or pasting

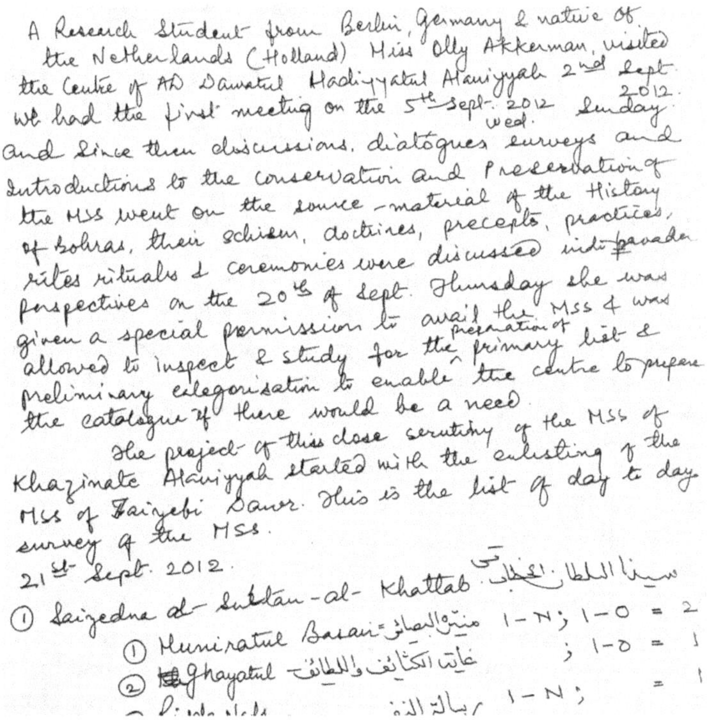
A Research Student from Berlin, Germany & native of the Netherlands (Holland) Miss Olly Akkerman, visited the Centre of AD Dawatul Hadiyyatul Alaviyyah 2nd Sept 2012.
We had the first meeting on the 5th Sept. 2012 Wed. Sunday.
And since then discussions, dialogues surveys and introductions to the conservation and Preservation of the MSS went on the source-material of the History of Bohras, their schism, doctrines, precepts, practices, rites rituals & ceremonies were discussed ind-pavada perspectives on the 20th of Sept. Thursday she was given a special permission to avail the MSS & was allowed to inspect & study for the preparation of primary list & preliminary categorisation to enable the centre to prepare the catalogue if there would be a need.
The project of this close scrutiny of the MSS of the Khazinate Alaviyyah started with the existing of the MSS of Zaizebi Sawr. This is the list of day to day survey of the MSS.
21st Sept. 2012.
① Saiyedna al-Sultan-al-Khattab سيدنا السلطان الخطاب 1-N; 1-O = 2
① Muniratul Basair منيرة البصائر ; 1-O = 1
② Ghayatul غاية التكاليف والطائف = 1
Risala ... رسالة الذ... 1-N;

Figure I.6 First page of the handwritten *khizana* catalogue, including the Mazoon Saheb's entry about the author in the community.

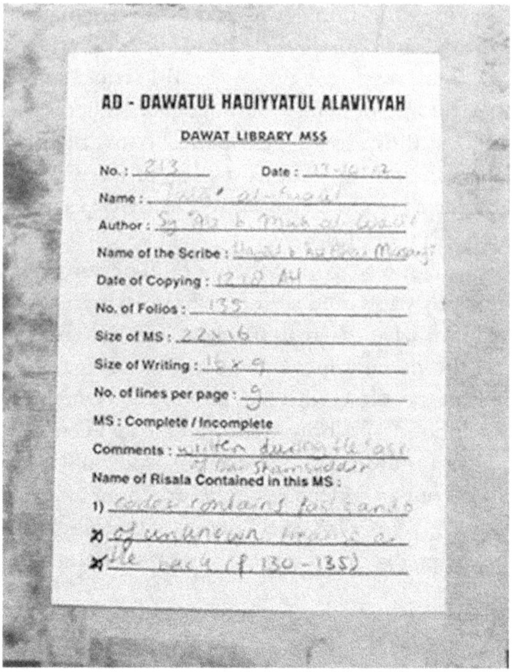

AD - DAWATUL HADIYYATUL ALAVIYYAH

DAWAT LIBRARY MSS

No.: 213 Date:

Name:

Author:

Name of the Scribe:

Date of Copying:

No. of Folios: 135

Size of MS: 22x16

Size of Writing:

No. of lines per page: 9

MS: Complete / Incomplete

Comments:

Name of Risala Contained in this MS:

1)

2)

3) (f 130 – 135)

Figure I.7 Official *khizana* vignette (filled in and glued into the manuscript by the researcher; the name of the author and treatise were erased in this picture for reasons of confidentiality).

anything in the manuscripts, this was the wish of the Bhai Sahebs, and thus unintentionally my work was thus literally pasted into the *khizana*. Despite the trust I had built, it was strictly forbidden to roam through the stacks of the *khizana* freely. Moreover, I had to make written requests to the Mazoon Saheb to gain his permission to take every photograph (Figure I.8). Through this daily practice I developed a routine in the *khizana*. It was only towards the end of my stay that I was allowed to be alone with the manuscripts. In fact, at a certain point I was handed the key of the *khizana* for the afternoons when the *mohallah* would take its afternoon nap.

After some time, I developed a certain intimacy with the manuscripts of the *khizana*, becoming familiar with their dusty smell, the soft touch of their deerskin covers and handmade Gujarati paper, and the sound of spines and bindings falling apart. Many books I encountered were in poor material condition (see Chapter 4), and while cataloguing the collection I discovered a large diversity of tropical flora and fauna living inside the manuscripts – rotting, crawling, jumping and nesting. I also learned about using botanical species to repel them. More often than not, I found myself covered in the dust of these manuscripts, discovering little pieces of sacred script between the layers of my *rida* at home. Unfortunately, on several occasions the termites that had nested in manuscripts also found their way into my *rida*, and not even the protective spells found in the margins of the manuscripts could protect me.

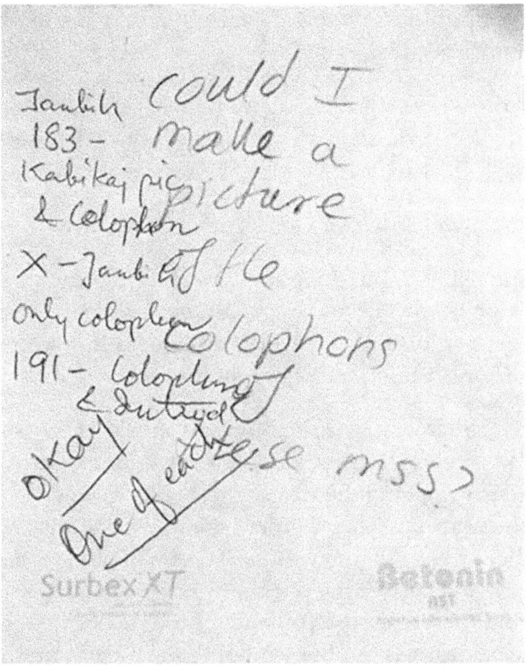

Figure I.8 A written request to the Mazoon Saheb to take a photo, lying on a pile of manuscripts.

Witnessing the proceedings of the *daʿwa* office while sitting on Jahangir's peacock throne was a very symbolic *passage*, both in the process of accessing the *khizana* and in my personal relationship with the Mazoon Saheb; it represented the tiny little space I had conquered in the *daʿwa*'s headquarters after long negotiations, and it was a symbol of the royal authorisation of my presence in Badri Mohallah in a larger sense. What I did not anticipate, however, was that sitting on Jahangir's peacock throne for days on end gave me an opportunity to see the community from an entirely different perspective.

Jahangir's peacock chair forced me out of my academic comfort zone and made me realise that I had to let go of the idea of the *khizana* and its books, and the *daʿwa* and its people, as two separate realms: *the khizana was the community*, and *the community was the khizana*. In other words, the social-anthropological and the codicological-archival worlds were interdependent and equally important in understanding the other. Slowly it dawned on me that the treasury of books was not just a private manuscript collection but also functioned as the religious headquarters of the community: the living, devotional, almost sacrosanct semi-open space where religious gatherings are held, justice is administered and people pay their *salāms* (respect) to their charismatic clerics. I did not see it at first. I needed to sit on Jahangir's peacock throne for a while to realise what was actually happening right in front of my eyes: the treasury of books was the beehive of the community, full of social activity. The following conversation with the Mazoon

Saheb was crucial in this understanding. After two months in the *khizana* completely focused on the manuscripts, I asked him:

> So I noticed all these people paying their *salams* to you, presenting their new-born babies and asking for permission to get married, but where do the *mu'minin* and *mu'minat* go to ask legal advice, where is the *sharia* court, and who are the *qadis*?'

The Mazoon Saheb answered with a radiant smile on his face:

> Ollybehn, let me tell you one thing: *I am the qadi* And this, my office where you have been working from your peacock chair, *this is the sharia court!* This is the place where people get permission to get married, where they come to ask advice on financial matters, or get punished or repent for their mistakes.

The Mazoon Saheb's answer came to me as a shock. How could I have been so ignorant? I made an intervention in my fieldwork and decided that, from that day onwards, along with cataloguing the treasury of books, I would note down *everything* that happened in the Mazoon Saheb's office: from how the Bhai Sahebs solved complicated legal conflicts, to the starching of turbans by the Bhu Saheba, to the way the *daʿwa*'s accountant would answer the phone, to how manuscripts were copied. I thus dedicated my work to observing the daily life of the treasury of books, and an entire new world unfolded. I learned to observe during the quieter moments and started to notice that, in both their presence and absence, manuscripts played a major social role in the busy social life of the *khizana*.

From that moment onwards, I could not look at a manuscript in the same way. The social encounter had changed the path of my research on the Alawi Bohras for good: from a philological edition of a secret Arabic Isma'ili text to an ethnography of manuscripts: a 'social codicology' of the Alawi Bohras and their treasury of books.

Obituary

Upon my finishing writing this monograph, the sad news reached me that His Royal Highness Sayyidnā Abū Ḥātim Ṭayyib Ḍiyā' al-Dīn b. Nūr al-Dīn Yūsuf, Dai of the Alawi Bohra throne in Baroda since 1974, passed away on 23 May 1436/2015. My sincere condolences go out to the royal family and the community at large, who have lost their father, grandfather and 'Sayyidna'. *Naṣṣ* (meaning that the seat of the Alawi Bohra throne was transferred) was bestowed upon Abū Saʿīd al-Khayr Ḥātim Zakī al-Dīn Ṣāḥib, formerly known as the Mazoon Saheb and a central figure in this book, as the forty-fifth Dai of the community.

Chapter 1

Community: Introduction to the Alawi Bohras

Haraz, Yemen

Scattered across Gujarat are polished-marble tombs decorated with colourful lights, situated in the middle of bustling cities such as Khambhat, Jamnagar, Ujjain and Surat. These green, peaceful and spotlessly clean oases are known to the Bohras as *qabaristān* (graveyards). The *qabaristan* are the final resting places of the physical remains of the communities' legendary missionaries and founding fathers, the Dais. These sacred sites of *ziyara* are frequented by Bohras young and old, male and female, rich and poor. The *qabaristan*, along with the burial tombs they enshrine and their rituals of commemoration and mourning, are as much spaces of togetherness as they are of contestation.

On the other side of the western Indian Ocean, in the mountainous regions of Haraz in western Yemen, another sacred land is claimed by the Bohras through a network of white burial tombs, some of them dating back as far as the sixth/twelfth century, belonging to the Dais of Yemen, also known as *Aṣḥāb al-Yamīn*.[1] The Bohras may trace themselves and their books to Fatimid Cairo spiritually, but it is in Yemen that the Bohra clerical genealogy of Dais and Tayyibi Isma'ili teachings crystallised. It was also from Yemen that Fatimid missionaries and later Tayyibi Yemeni Dais set foot on the Indian subcontinent, known as the *Jazīrat al-Hind*.

Within the larger context of the western Indian Ocean and the Red Sea, and the movement of things and people in it, the Bohras historically connected the geographies of Haraz and Gujarat through networks of trade, conversion, books and pilgrimage. Throughout history, the burial tombs of former Dais found in Yemeni villages such as al-Ḥuṭayb, Zabīd and Jibla were frequented by Bohras until the recent war in Yemen (Figure 1.1). As I was once told by one of my Yemeni students, the 'flooding' of these burial tombs by mysterious crowds of Gujarati *rida*- and *topi*-wearing pilgrims was 'quite a phenomenon' for the locals of these villages.[2] A small number of Dawoodi Bohras resided in Aden and Haraz permanently, and several Yemeni tombs

[1] The term *Ashab al-Yamin*, literally meaning 'people of the right hand', is a Qur'anic expression that finds great resonance in Sh'i Isma'ili thought. It is mentioned in the Qur'an six times and according to Bohra tradition refers to the genealogy of their Dais. *Ashab al-Yamin* is also the title of the official history of the Yemeni Dais published by the Alawi Bohra *da'wa*. Sayyidna wa Mawlana Abu Hatim Tayyib Diya al-Din Sahib, *Aṣḥāb al-Yamīn fī dhikr al-du'āt al-muṭlaqīn al-yamāniyīn* (Gujarati and English). Historical account published by the Alawi Bohra *da'wa*, 1432 AH, Baroda.

[2] See also Nafeesa Syeed, 'Learning Gujarati in Yemen', *Wall Street Journal*, 24 September 2012, https://blogs.wsj.com/indiarealtime/2012/09/24/learning-gujarati-in-yemen/ (last accessed 1 December 2019). See also Hare, 56, f. 59.

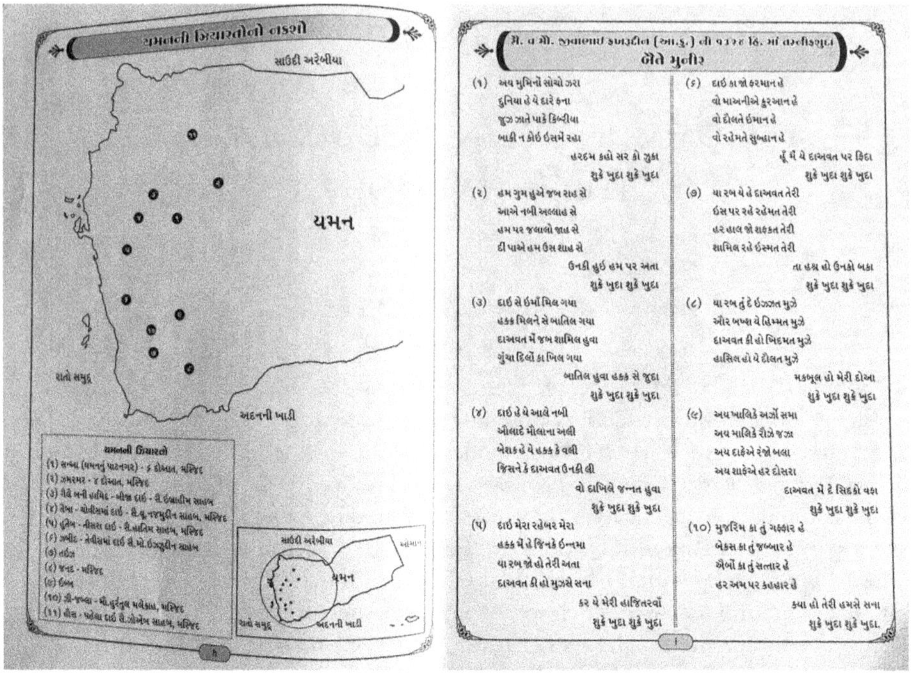

Figure 1.1 Map in Gujarati of Bohra pilgrimage sites in *Ashab al-Yamin* in Yemen.

have been restored by the Bohras.[3] While the Indian, mostly Dawoodi, Bohras were evacuated from Yemen in 2015, the Yemeni Sulaymani Isma'ilis, of Arab origin, can still be found in the several villages of the Haraz region and in Najrān, Saudi Arabia, where they live in relative isolation.[4] Despite the fact that the sacred land of Yemen is currently inaccessible to the Bohras due to the war, the mountain cliffs of Haraz and other places continue to be present in the minds and rituals of Bohra believers in India

[3] J. Moncelon, 'La Da'wa fatimide au Yémen', 1995, 9. According to Jean Moncelon, 5,000 Dawoodi Bohras still resided in the Haraz Mountains in the 1990s. Jean Moncelon,. 'La Da'wa fatimide au Yémen', *Chroniques yéménites* 3, http://cy.revues.org/79; DOI: 10.4000/cy.79, 1995. In her article on the mobility of Indians between Yemen and Ethiopia, Dominique Harre mentions the historic presence of the (Dawoodi) Bohras in both countries and their involvement in the Red Sea boom of the late nineteenth century. She also briefly describes the Bohra mosque and community hall in Aden. Dominique Harre. 'Exchanges and Mobility in the Western Indian Ocean: Indians between Yemen and Ethiopia, 19th–20th Centuries' *CmY* special issue: *From Mountain to Mountain: Exchange between Yemen and Ethiopia, Medieval to Modern* 1 (2017), 54. On the restoration of Yemeni tombs see Paula Sanders, *Creating Medieval Cairo*, 135.

[4] Whereas Farhad Daftary estimates the community to number 200,000–300,000 believers, Jean Moncelon mentions 70,000 (this number includes the 5,000 Dawoodi Bohras in Yemen). Daftary, *The Ismā'īlis*, 298. Moncelon, 9. Harre describes how this isolation is not practised in the context of migration movements in the Horn of Africa, which brought Yemenis to Eritrea and Ethiopia, where Yemeni Isma'ilis and Indian Bohra families mixed and intermarried. Harre, 55. See for a more detailed study in the community see T. Gerholm, *Market, Mosque and Mafrag* (Stockholm, 1977).

and beyond, through photographs and other memorabilia of the shrines of Yemen, which are kept in their homes and spaces of worship.[5]

In this chapter, we see that the shrine-scape of Bohra *qabaristan* across Yemen and the Indian subcontinent is as complex as the sectarian history of its communities. As the 'other' Bohra group still residing in Gujarat, but with no keys to any of these shared sites of pilgrimage, the Alawi Bohras consider themselves marginalised in relation to the other Bohra communities, especially the Dawoodis. The community's subaltern position is enhanced by the fact that, thus far, only the Dawoodis have received attention in academic scholarship, something the Alawi clerics in particular are very much aware of. As a result, Alawis are relegated to the margins of the already small field of Bohra Studies.

Yet the Alawi Bohras, following the lineage of Sy. Ali Shamsuddin and having resided in Baroda for more than three centuries, have their own unique history and identity, organisation, rituals, traditions, dress, *khizana* and manuscript culture. Like the roots of the *banyan* trees after which the city of Baroda was named, all these facets together form a universe, which the Alawis refer to as the *da'wat al-hādiyya al-'Alawiyya* (lit. 'the guided Alawi *da'wa*', but often translated as the 'holy mission'). Central to the *da'wat al-hadiyya* is the community's treasury of books, through which the Alawis legitimise their genealogical claim as heirs of the Fatimids. Yet the *khizana* and its manuscripts are not the only links through which the community cultivates its Fatimid past. In this chapter, we explore how the Alawi Bohras practise their Neo-Fatimid identity in everyday life through doctrine, clerical hierarchy, jurisprudence and ritual, and how they express their 'Faatemi way of life' through sartorial practices, documentary culture and ceremony. It is impossible to write about the everyday life of the community without coming across its *kutub*: books, documents, talismans and other written materials. We encounter them in many material forms and formats, as I demonstrate how they play a central role, often in remarkable ways, in the lives of believers, despite their quality of being secret.

1.1 Shrine Custodians

We start our introduction to the Alawi Bohra universe at the location foundational to where the community came into being: the *qabaristan* of Saraspur, Ahmedabad. Saraspur is part of the larger shrine-scape of Bohra *qabaristans* across Yemen and the Indian subcontinent; it had a complex development given the sectarian history of its communities.[6] As a result, some shrines are shared by the Alawis, Dawoodis and Sulaymanis (Yemen), while others, dating from the post-bifurcation period in India, are strictly separate (Gujarat, with the exception of Ahmedabad). The fragmented nature of Bohra pilgrimage culture makes the annual *ziyara*, which is obligatory to all,

[5] Yemen is currently off-limits to the Bohras, especially after a small population of Dawoodis residents were among the Indians evacuated by the Indian government in 2015. See Aarefa Johari, 2015. 'India's Bohra Muslims Are Back Safely from Yemen but Have Many Reasons To Still Be Anxious', online: https// scroll.in/article/719205.

[6] I should mention here that Bohra shrines also exist outside Gujarat in the Indian subcontinent, in Madhya Pradesh, Uttar Pradesh and Rajasthan, and in the Punjab, Pakistan. The shrines outside of Gujarat are beyond the scope of this monograph. Daftary, *The Ismā'īlis*, 277, 299. See also Blank, Mullahs on the Mainframe, 139.

a complex affair. As I immersed myself in the world of the Alawis, I learned that these *qabaristan* are as much spaces of presence and remembrance as of collective amnesia, depending on who holds the keys to the shrines.

The last Bohra *qabaristan* in history to be shared by the Alawis, Dawoodis, and Sulaymanis in Gujarat is the graveyard of Saraspur (also known as Bibipur), situated in the middle of a *dalit* neighbourhood on the outskirts of Ahmedabad. According to my Alawi informants, the graveyard of Saraspur dates to the tenth/sixteenth century, when the first Indian Dai, Sy. Jalāl Shamsuddīn b. Ḥasan (no. 25, d. 975/1567), was buried in Ahmedabad. I was told that before the thirteenth/nineteenth century when the British constructed roads in Ahmedabad, the graveyard was considerably bigger in size, because 'each and every believer had a grave there'. At present, only Dawoodi royal family members are buried in Saraspur, with the exception of the community's last two Dais, the late Sy. Muhammad Burhanuddin (no. 52, d. 1435/2014) and Sy. Tahir Sayfuddin (no. 51, d. 1385/1965): they are buried in the recently constructed Rawdat Tahera mausoleum in Mumbai. In the architecture of Saraspur, and even more that of Rawdat Tahera and the Bohra mosques and *jamaat khanas* across the Indian Ocean and beyond, one can clearly observe an architectural evolution from the old South Asian vernacular style of the tombs (Mughal architecture) to a new Neo-Fatimid architecture, as Paula Sanders has shown.[7] The Alawi Bohras have followed suit in this architectural development, with the construction of their newly built Saiyedi Musanji Masjid mosque in Mumbai.[8]

While the Saraspur *qabaristan* is administered by the Dawoodi Bohras and most of the more recent tombs are of Dawoodi provenance, the complex is nonetheless considered a sacred space for all three Bohra communities. For the Sulaymanis from Yemen, the small black-and-green-marbled mausoleum of Sy. Sulayman b. Ḥasan (no. 27, d. 1005/1597) is situated in Saraspur, built in an architectural style very different from the polished Dawoodi Taj Mahal-esque shrines. Perhaps even more than for the Sulaymanis, however, Saraspur is an important site of remembrance for the Alawi Bohras and the foundation of their community.

Sy. ʿAlī Shamsuddīn (no. 29, d. 1046/1637) is the namesake and first Dai of the Alawi community after the Alawi–Dawoodi schism in 1034/1624–1625. To the Alawis, he is considered a martyr, and his burial tomb in Saraspur was the last Alawi grave that was ever built in Ahmedabad, as the community was allegedly forced to move to Baroda after the split. The status of Sy. Ali Shamsuddin's grave is precarious, because his tomb, which also used to house the graves of his father and grandfather, was recently destroyed by the Dawoodis (Figure 1.2). My interlocutors claim that the tomb was destroyed by the Dawoodis in 1996 under the pretence of needing the space to build a new mausoleum and describe the real purpose of the demolition as follows: 'to remove the signs of spiritual attachment of Alavis from the Bohra cemetery on the behest of some envious

7 Paula Sanders, *Creating Medieval Cairo*, 126–32. See also the Prologue to this study.

8 The mosque, which contains elements of the façade of al-Aqmar's mosque in Cairo, was inaugurated on 23 Sha'baan 1440/28 April 2019. See *Inauguration of Saiyedi Musanji Masjid*, https://www.alavibohra.org/Inauguration%20of%20Saiyedi%20Musanji%20Masjid%201440.htm (last accessed 30 May 2019).

Figure 1.2 Historic picture of the original grave of Sy. Ali Shamsuddin and Sy. Zakiyuddin prior to its destruction. Credits: Alawi *da'wa.*

anti-Alawi elements in the Da'wat hierarchy of Dawoodis'.[9] Not only was the shrine of Sy. Ali Shamsuddin demolished, believers informed me, but the tomb of another Dawoodi Dai was also built directly on top of the old grave (Figure 1.4). The Alawi shrine has thus become an invisible and, therefore, a liminal space, only existing for the Alawis who visit it. The destruction of the tomb caused great dismay among the Alawis, who felt they 'have been targeted in their very foundation', and worsened already tense relations between the two communities.[10]

Undaunted, however, by the absence of a burial tomb, the Alawis continue to perform their annual *ziyara* in Saraspur. As the Bohra 'other', the Alawis are likely not received warmly in Saraspur, yet their presence is tolerated. Their modest *musāfir khāna* (pilgrim lodge, see figure 1.5), however, is situated outside the plot. Except for visiting the grave of Sy. Ali Shamsuddin, all Alawi rituals and commemorative gatherings are only allowed to take place outside the walls of the graveyard. The Alawis' contested presence at the *qabaristan* is characteristic of how the three Bohra communities relate to one another.[11] The relationship of the Sulaymani Bohras with the other groups seems to be relatively cordial, because they govern the local shrines in Yemen, and believers from all the groups rely on their goodwill.

The Alawis' relationship with the Dawoodis, however, remains contested. On numerous occasions, Alawi Bohras describe the Dawoodi community as excelling in 'the four m's' in comparison to their own community: 'manpower (the number of

[9] *The Unfortunate Event in the History of Alavi Bohras: The Demolition of the Holy Graves*, https://www.alavibohra.org/introduction%20files/intro%20-%20The%20Unfortunate%20Event%20in%20the%20History%20of%20Alavi%20Bohras.htm (last accessed 14 May 2020).

[10] Ibid.

[11] And to a certain extent the Sulaymanis. I was told that they have a good relationship with the even smaller Indian Sulaymani community who practise their Bohra identity less strictly.

Figure 1.3 Devotees directing their prayers to the corner where Sy. Ali Shamsuddin is buried (underneath the current Dawoodi tomb). Saraspur, Ahmedabad.

Figure 1.4 The invisible grave of Sy. Ali ibn Ibrahim (underneath the shrine of a Dawoodi Dai).

believers), money (economic wealth), management (the organisation of the *daʿwa*), and muscles (both in terms of the power of their political lobbying and physique)'. To understand the complexity of this relationship and the Alawis' at times self-imposed subaltern position, we must go back to the seventeenth-century schism that divided the two communities and tell its story through the eyes of the Alawis.

The Materiality of Naṣṣ

The stories that surround the martyrdom of Sy. Ali Shamsuddin and the schism between the Alawi and Dawoodi Bohras are remembered and performed during the community's annual visit to Saraspur for the *ʿurs* (death commemoration). Several months into my ethnographic fieldwork, I was allowed to travel with the men of the Alawi community to Saraspur. This was an honour, as the *ʿurs* was traditionally only carried out by the male *mu'minin*, and not the female *mu'minat* of the community, who stayed at home in Baroda with their families. Special arrangements therefore had to be made, given that, as an unmarried woman, I could not stay at the *musafir khana* nor travel on the specially designated *ziyara* bus to Ahmedabad. Although the Alawis felt a sense of unease because they were unable to offer me their hospitality, travelling on my own was a welcome break from the *mohallah*: I had not been able to move outside the Alawi quarter freely, nor had I enjoyed the luxury of hot water or a constant supply of electricity for months.

After my arrival in Ahmedabad, I immersed myself in the life of the *musafir khana*, which by now was full of believers, all dressed in white. I observed the community in the various sections of the concrete building and its outdoor spaces, including its massive, tented pop-up soup kitchen, the quarters of the royal family, and the courtyard where prayers were conducted and ceremonies were held (Figure 1.5).

On the auspicious night of the ʿurs, the commemorative gathering slowly moved from the *musafir khana* to the *qabaristan*. To the outsider, the scene was odd, as the 'ya Husayn' lamenting crowd, while crossing the street, was met with street *faqirs*, *sadhus*, and other mendicant holy wanderers, asking for donations. To my surprise, within the *qabaristan* the Alawis gathered inside a shrine that had been dedicated to a Dawoodi Dai (Figure 1.3). I observed how the group commemorated the death anniversary of their Syedna through the recitation of the *marsiyya* and self-flagellation led by the Mazoon Saheb in a tomb that was no longer theirs. These rituals in themselves were nothing out of the ordinary, as I had observed them on several occasions at the *qabaristan* in Baroda. What was unusual, however, was the fact that these lamentations were not sung in honour of the Dawoodi Dai who was buried here. Instead, the believers all directed their prayers and pious invocations towards one particular nondescript corner of the already very crowded Dawoodi shrine, standing in line to kiss the marble floor and covering it with rose petals. This small corner was the space that once was the grave of Sy. Ali Shamsuddin: to the outsider it is completely invisible, yet to the Alawis it is a sacred space (Figure 1.3).

While I observed how the rhythmic lamentations intensified, and crying turned into shrieking, I realised that the believers were not only mourning the death of Sy. Ali Shamsuddin and the hardship that followed, but also the destruction of the tomb itself,

Figure 1.5 Alawi Bohras in the *musafir khana*, waiting for the *thali* to be served. Saraspur, Ahmedabad.

which somehow contributed to his status as a martyr. In this brief moment in time, the shrine dedicated to the Dawoodi Dai was thus transformed into a liminal Alawi-only space where the marble grave of the Dawoodi Dai who was buried on top of Sy. Ali Shamsuddin and his ancestors, who were also buried here, did not seem to exist. The absence of a physical tomb, in its current immaterial form, thus made the ritual more powerful. As intense as the ceremony was, the entire *ʿurs* gathering lasted no longer than ten minutes, and the Alawis left as swiftly and quietly as they had arrived.

Upon their return to the *musafir khana*, a *majlis* was held in honour of this auspicious night. The believers, around two hundred of them, sat on their knees on the floor of the neon-lit courtyard around the Mazoon Saheb and his brothers, the Mukasir Saheb and the Ra's ul Hudood. It was the yearly *majlis* dedicated to the story of the succession of Sy. Ali Shamsuddin, conducted in the language of the community, known as *Lisan al-Daʿwa* (see Chapter 5). Despite the late evening hour, the uncomfortable seating arrangement on the concrete floors, and the unbearable heat that the fans in the courtyard did little to relieve, there was a general atmosphere of excitement and anticipation. Something exceptional was about to happen.

The Mazoon, who had seated himself on a plastic chair decorated with golden garlands and who was wearing his ceremonial turban and matching golden spectacles, had brought along a leather handbag. The handbag carried a mysterious object of utmost significance, which was about to be revealed to the crowd. Because it was an object from the *khizana*, I already knew what it was: a *sijill* (pl. *sijillāt*), an official *daʿwa* document in the form of a *rotulus* or vertical roll, which had been carefully photocopied and framed in a plastic golden frame.[12] This *sijill* was a secret document, and its public display among believers was to be a historic moment. I therefore waited with everyone else in anticipation, eager to observe the reaction of the believers.

As a book format, the *sijill* has had a long historical presence in the Bohra and earlier Tayyibi Isma'ili communities and their *khizanat*. It was the preferred codicological form both for documentary practice, through letters and contracts, and in social usage as ritual objects used during communal services and ceremonies (see Chapter 5). Contemporary sources mention *sijillat* as forms of official caliphal correspondence between Fatimid Cairo and Yemen as early as the fourth/tenth century under the reign of Caliph-Imam al-Muʿizz (d. 364/975), as well as the transmission of these rolls from Yemen to Gujarat as early as the tenth/sixteenth century.[13] We do not know what these historic *sijillat* looked like, as their content was only transmitted in later texts in the form of a codex.[14] What is certain, however, is that the tradition of writing on the *sijill* format of the roll continues to the present day among the Alawis, as we will see in the next chapter.

The particular *sijill* that was about to be revealed by the Mazoon Saheb in Ahmedabad, however, was not just any historical document from the treasury of books, nor just any *sijill*: it was the much-disputed document that formed the basis of the schism between the Alawis and the Dawoodis. Dating from the period of the bifurcation, this eleventh-/seventeenth-century roll, written in Arabic, was the officially designated *sijill*, which, to the Alawis, was the material proof for Sy. Ali Shamsuddin's receiving *naṣṣ* (the divine designation of succession) as the twenty-ninth Dai of the community.

The question of *nass* is a highly complex matter among the Bohras. According to Bohra tradition, it is the Dai alone who is responsible for designating his successor; he traditionally bestows *nass* upon the person of his choosing, a member of his family, under the divine guidance of the hidden Imam. The *manṣūṣ* (chosen successor), I was told, is without exception a learned individual, male, and is often the brother, cousin or eldest son of the Dai. The Alawi clerics explained to me that the identity of the *mansus* is manifested to the Dai through the direct *ilhām* (inspiration) coming straight from God through the hidden Imam. It is thus not through reason, but through divine revelation, that the Dai appoints his successor.

The *nass* of the 'seat of *daʿwa*' is either transferred orally in private or is documented in a special type of sealed *sijill* that is traditionally kept undisclosed until after the demise of the current Dai. Analysing the designation *sijill* on a codicological level, royal seals ensure the protection of the bifurcation rolls from being opened too early. Historical sources from the Tayyibi period provide unique insight into the materiality of these *nass* documents. An example is *Qarāṭīs al-Yaman* (see Chapter 2), a collection of official correspondence between *daʿwa* officials in Gujarat and Yemen between the

[12] For a further discussion of its terminology and social practice, see Olly Akkerman, 'The Bohras as Neo-Fatimids: Documentary Remains of a Fatimid Past in Gujarat', *Journal of Material Cultures in the Muslim World* 1 (2020): 286–308.

[13] Ibid. Hollister, *The Shi'a of India*, 212. *Aṣḥāb al-Yamīn*, 131.

[14] Akkerman, 'Documentary Remains of a Fatimid Past in Gujarat'.

ninth/fifteenth and the eleventh/seventeenth centuries.[15] The *Qaratis* mentions a *nass* document ('*nuskhat naṣṣ*') in which the twenty-fourth Dai, Sy. Yusuf (d. 974/1567), bestows *nass* upon the twenty-fifth Dai, Sy. Jalāl Najm al-Dīn (d. 975/1567). It reports that the document was composed in the company of no fewer than seven witnesses, and was transcribed in golden ink and lapus lazuli.[16]

In *nass sijillat*, the name of the *mansus* is concealed palaeographically through what is known as *kitāb sirriyya*, a secret and encrypted alphabet that is only decipherable by the Dai and his close confidants.[17] Through the scholarship of Strothmann and DeBlois, we now know that several variants of these secret scripts exist and that their characters somewhat resemble ancient alphabets of South Arabia found in Yemen.[18] The survival of these secret scripts in the *khizana* could indicate another palaeographical linkage of the Bohras and their scribal practices to Yemen. In the *sijill* genre, the tradition of concealment of the identity of the *mansus* is thus multi-faceted: it can not only be observed through social practice but can also be traced through the materiality of the scripts and seals of *sijill* rolls. Because the *mansus* functions as the testament of the *da'wa*, the encrypted nature of its identity, which is built into these documents on so many levels, has led to various practical problems. What does one do when several candidates claim to be *mansus* at the same time, basing this on the existence of different versions or even forgeries of the same document? It is therefore not surprising that the Bohra tradition of the propagation of *nass* and the secrecy around the designation of *mansus* have led to several crises of succession. It also explains why Bohra historiography and the history of Shi'ism are characterised by so many schisms.[19]

The political history of the Bohras and the legitimacy of its ruling royal families are therefore not without controversy. Recent schisms aside, the two major bifurcations that characterise Bohra historiography are the Sulaymani schism in 999/1591 and the Dawoodi–Alawi schism in 1034/1624.[20] The Alawis, Dawoodis, and Sulaymanis have each developed a detailed narrative on the schisms that occurred and their divinely designated *mansus*. One can devote an entire monograph to these perspectives and claims, which is not, however, what this study intends to do. What the bifurcations among the Bohras *nass* cases have in common, however, is that they involved petitions

[15] See n. Ch. 2, n. 58 for more detailed information on the surviving manuscript copies.

[16] *Qarāṭīs al-Yaman*, MS Ma VI 330, Tübingen University Library, 46r–47v.

[17] See Chapter 5 for a more detailed description. François de Blois, 'The Oldest Known Fatimid Manuscript from Yemen', *Proceedings of the Seminar for Arabian Studies* vol. 14 (1984), 1–7, 5. f 11. R. Strothmann, *Gnosis-Texte der Isma'iliten. arabische Handschrift Ambrosiana H 75* (Göttingen: Vandenhoeck u. Ruprecht, 1943).

[18] According to De Blois, these scripts are 'doubtless of Yemenite origin', as they share a superficial similarity with Ancient South Arabian (ASA) writing. De Blois, 5 f 11. Earlier work by Strothmann shows a possible combination of ASA letters, Indian numerals, and Arabic letters given arbitrary values. Strothmann describes various variants: Rudolf Strothmann (ed.), Gnosis-Texte der Isma'iliten (Göttingen: Vandenhoeck & Ruprecht, 1943), 60, 61. Akkerman, 'Documentary Remains of a Fatimid Past in Gujarat', 300.

[19] The notion of *nass* is also an important concept in Twelver Shi'ism before the great occultation of the twelfth Imam; see Rodrigo Adem, 'Classical Nass Doctrines in Imāmī Shī'ism: On the Usage of an Expository Term', *Shii Studies Review* 1 (2017) 42–71.

[20] See for a detailed description Daftary, *The Ismā'īlīs*, 280–2. See, for the Nagoshias, the final section of this chapter.

and juridical battles that were played out in the courts of Mughal emperors. These stories are richly documented in Bohra *khizanat* and in Mughal imperial records.[21]

Moreover, these *nass* histories are significant because they resulted in the spatial relocation of the Bohra communities. The Sulaymanis moved back to Haraz, Yemen, in the late tenth/sixteenth century, the Alawis to Baroda in the mid-eleventh/seventeenth century, and the Dawoodis to Jamnagar and Ujjain a few decades later.[22] I was told by the Ra's ul Hudood, with whom I had a special session on the history of the bifurcation, that the Alawi community was forced to move to Baroda in 1110/1699 to escape 'persecution and bullying'. The Alawis, he told me, chose Baroda as their new spiritual home because it was the city where Sy. Ali Shamsuddin was born before he joined his father in Ahmedabad at a young age. The 'bullying' that the Ra's ul Hudood mentioned referred not only to inter-communal tension and violence but also to persecution under Mughal rule, which, according to Abdul Husayn, turned the Bohras into a *taqiyya*-practising 'society of trading nomads', a development that ended with the colonial period.[23] The Dawoodi–Alawi split and its aftermath, which I briefly describe in the following section, lasted several decades before the two communities officially parted ways and moved to different cities.

These bifurcations occurred at the highest layers of the clerical establishment within branches of different royal families, each with their own allegiances, rituals, and etiquette, and coming from different cities. I was told that, in this context, the death of a Dai would mean the end of these political allegiances and sometimes even marriages, the shift of centres of power and royal palaces, and the scattering of royal possessions, such as funds, treasuries, and shared intellectual property. On the level of the treasury of books and its scholarly collection, the historic bifurcations among the Bohras were catastrophic, as we see in Chapter 2.

Among the Alawis, the schisms that formed the three Bohra communities are preserved and transmitted in different forms: orally, in epigraphy, and through manuscripts and printed books. The rich oral traditions that narrate the bifurcation stories include the *bayān* (reports) and the yearly recurring *majalis* held by the Bhai Sahebs. As we will see, these sermons are surrounded by protocol, rituals, and ceremonial performance. The bifurcations can also be traced in the material culture of the Alawis in Arabic epigraphy found on gravestones and mausoleums and in what the Alawis refer to as the '*kutub* of the *naṣṣ*'. Although some *kutub* are published in printed form in *Lisan al-Daʿwa* and are meant to be read by all believers, the majority are only available in Arabic manuscript form in the Alawi *khizana*. Genres range from lamentation poetry on the death of Sy. Ali Shamsuddin, to *rasā'il* (epistles, s. *risāla*) to *ta'rīkh* (historical) works, to *diwāns* (poetry anthologies), to *nass sijillāt*, documents, and references related to the court cases.

[21] See Samira Sheikh, 'Aurangzeb as Seen from Gujarat', 10.

[22] The Dawoodis would eventually move to Surat in the late twelfth/eighteenth century. See Mian Bhai Mulla Abdul Husain, *Gulzare Daudi for the Bohras of India* (Surat: Progressive publication, 1920), 28–30.

[23] Husain, *Gulzare Daudi for the Bohras of India*. See, for a detailed description of persecution of the Bohras under the Mughals, Samira Sheikh, 'Aurangzeb as Seen from Gujarat', 9–13.

A famous *diwan* collection in the Alawi tradition is the *Diwān-e Ḥasan*, written in Arabic by the thirty-first Alawi Dai, Sy. Hasan Badruddin (no. 31, d. 1090/1679; see Figure 1.6). The *diwan* is a collection of poems written in praise of influential political actors and courtiers in order to win their support for the Alawi cause. While many of the poems are addressed to local *nawabs* (viceroys) and governors, some of these political actors included personages no less than the Mughal emperors, such as Jahangir, Shah Jahan and Aurangzeb. *Diwān-e Ḥasan*, which is only available in manuscript form, demonstrates the Dai's network of influence that included Mughal personalities, and it deserves further study. What is fascinating is its use of eloquent Arabic panegyric poetry, showing that Sy. Hasan Badruddin adopted the courtly norms and protocol of the Mughal court. According to the Ra's ul Hudood, the poems were addressed during the 'hostile situation' in Ahmedabad when followers of Sy. Ali Shamsuddin were the victims of violent attacks by the other Bohra camp, which later would be known as the Dawoodis (see later discussion).

Sy. Hasan Badruddin compiled several other Arabic accounts in prose describing in detail the question of the *nass* of Sy. Ali Shamuddin and the events that followed. *Kitāb Ithbāt al-Naṣṣ ʿalā Sayyidnā ʿAlī b. Ibrāhīm al-Shahīd wa Ḥujja al-Mutaghallib* is the best-known account, which, according to the Mazoon Saheb, was written in 1050/1641.[24] Not all accounts and epistles falling in the category of *nass* literature, however, were written by members of the royal family. For example, *Risāla fī Ithbāt al-Naṣṣ ʿalā Sayyidnā ʿAlī Shamsuddīn b. Ibrāhīm* was compiled by one of the followers of Sy. Ali Shamsuddin in 1030/1621 and, in a similar style to the *Diwān-e Hasan*, addressed the local ruler Ya'qub b. Nizām al-Dakhānī of Nadiad, a city between Ahmedabad and Baroda.

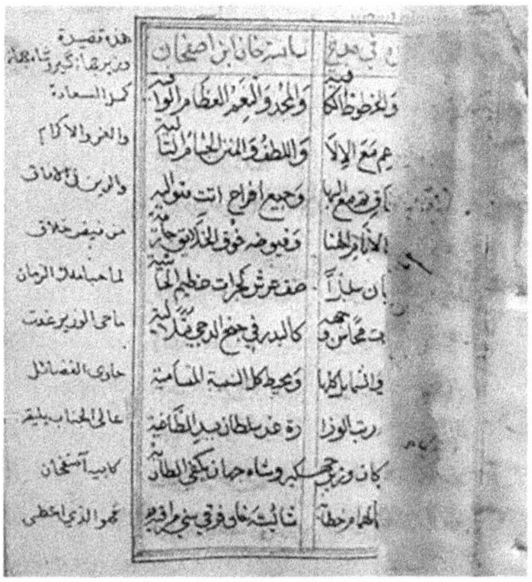

Figure 1.6 Folio from the *Diwān-e Ḥasan*, containing an Arabic poem in praise of the Mughal courtier of Jahangir and Shah Jahan, Shaa'istah Khan (d. 1105/1694), the twenty-sixth viceroy of Gujarat under Shah Jahan (1646–8). It is a unique and original autographed copy written between 1048 and 1080 (1638–69) in Ahmedabad. Marginal notes, written in the hand of the Mazoon Saheb, contain the missing text that vanished when the manuscript was restored. Credits: Alawi *daʿwa*.

24 This treatise too is only available in manuscript form in Baroda.

The Sulaymanis and Dawoodis, too, have a rich tradition of texts in Arabic and *Lisan al-Daʿwa* in which the Sulaymani and Alawi–Dawoodi (in the case of the latter) bifurcations are discussed at length, and the question of *nass* in particular. Thanks to Poonawala's *Biobibliography*, we can trace the *nass* literature throughout Bohra collections.[25] Given the polemical nature of this genre, the intertextuality of these works is fascinating, as they describe the same events through different sectarian lenses. One such text is the lithographed *Mawsim-e Bahār fī Akhbār al-Ṭāhirīn al-Akhyār*, written in *Lisan al-Daʿwa* by Muḥammad ʿAlī b. Mullā Jīwābhāʾī Rāmpūrī (d. 1315/1897). *Mawsim-e Bahar* is a historiographical work, which discusses not only Bohra bifurcations from a Dawoodi perspective but also the community's entire genealogical history, starting with the Prophet Muhammad, and reaching to the Fatimids and the Tayyibis in Yemen (vol. I), and to the history of the community on the Indian subcontinent and their Dais (vol. II).

The Alawis strongly disagree with the perspective of the *Mawsim-e Bahar*, as it repeats the Dawoodi narrative found in many primary sources and academic scholarship: it asserts that *nass* was bestowed on Sy. ʿAbd al-Ṭayyib Zakī al-Dīn (no. 29, d. 1041/1633), who would later become the twenty-ninth Dawoodi Dai, instead of Sy. Ali Shamsuddin. According to Rampuri, Sy. Ali Shamsuddin initially obeyed Sy. Abd al-Tayyib Zaki al-Din's order to apologise at Jahangir's court. He then describes how Sy. Ali Shamsuddin's *nafs* (soul) was persuaded by the *shayṭān* (devil) to break the *bay'a* (oath) he took at Jahangir's court and to subsequently declare himself the next Dai.[26] The Alawis naturally do not accept that their Dai was seduced by the devil, but also claim that Sy. Ali Shamsuddin never protested nor went against the judgement of Jahangir. According to the Ra's ul Hudood, he kept his word and sent his Mukasir Saheb, the earlier-mentioned Hasan Badruddin, to the Mughal imperial courts to seek refuge following atrocities committed by the Dawoodis. While his first visit to Jahangir's court in Lahore in 1031/1622 seemingly helped lower the tensions, during his second petition to the court of Shah Jahan in Kashmir in 1046/1637 sectarian violence flared up again and Sy. Ali Shamsuddin was killed.

A more recent work of Dawoodi provenance that deals with the events surrounding the schism is a *risāla* written by the Dawoodi Dai Tahir Sayf al-Din (no. 51, *ʿaṣr* from 1915 to 1965): it is titled *Ḍaw' al-Nūr al-Ḥaqq al-Mubīn*. The work is the first *risāla* of a series of forty-nine highly popular epistles, titled the *Risāla al-Ramaḍāniyya*, written by Tahir Sayf al-Din in prose in the early twentieth century.[27] In this Arabic treatise, we see the same narrative as in *Mawsim-e Bahar*. Tahir Sayf al-Din refers to Sy. 'Ali Shamsuddin as insubordinate, and to his followers, the Alawis, as the '*firqa al-ʿalīliyya*' (the weak or defective sect).[28] So far as I am aware, no response was written by the Alawi *daʿwa* to the epistle.

[25] Poonawala, *Biobibliography*.

[26] *Mawsim-e Bahar fī Akhbār al-Ṭāhirīn al-Akhyār*, lithographed (Bombay: Maṭbaʿat Ḥaydarī Ṣafdarī, 1884–93), 3 vols (in Gujarati written in Arabic script), vol. 2, 264–9. Interview with the Ra's ul Hudood.

[27] Tahir Sayf al-Din, *Risāla al-Ramaḍāniyya: Ḍaw' al-Nūr al-Ḥaqq al-Mubīn* (Mumbai: Tayyibi Da'wat Publications, 1335/1917). See, for a description of the *Risāla al-Ramaḍāniyya*, Traboulsi, 'Transmission of Knowledge and Book Preservation in the Ṭayyibī Ismāʿīlī Tradition', 30–4.

[28] Traboulsi, 'Transmission of Knowledge', 165.

On the basis of this great variety of accounts, anthologies, and oral traditions, Bohra *nass* texts can be seen as a literary genre on their own, yet they remain entirely unstudied. Through interactions between the Dawoodi and Alawi clerical leadership and Mughal officialdom, the Bohras emerge as a visible and identifiable community in the Mughal period, not only in their own communal records through accounts such as the *Kitāb Ithbāt al-Nass* and the *Mawsim-e Bahar*, but also through the petitions included in the empire's imperial records.[29] Samira Sheikh showed that sectarian disputes in Gujarat often played out in the imperial Mughal courts.[30] In the context of Isma'ilism in South Asia, however, the Bohras' presence in the courts does distinguish them from other Isma'ili groups, such as the Khojas.

To the Bohra communities, the material evidence that forms the basis of *nass* texts as a literary genre, is, of course, the *nass sijill*, which is at the centre of what I call 'the materiality of *nass*': through *nass* texts' material survival in modern times, they have become the object of ritual. A central trope in these bifurcation narratives is the claim that their designations as *sijillat*, and the seals, stamps, signatures, and secret alphabets they contained, were forged. This is because various rolls circulated at the same time, and each party claimed to possess the original.[31] While today the Alawis have circumvented the issue of *nass* by publicly appointing the *mansus* during the Dai's lifetime, through what is known as the *naṣṣ al-jālī* (explicit *nass*), contestations continue among the Dawoodis, as their most recent schism has shown, following the death of Sy. Muhammad Burhanuddin in 2014 (no. 52, *'aṣr* from 1965 to 2014).[32] As in Mughal times, this conflict was brought to the Indian courts, and the judgement is still pending. A new development, however, is the fact that expert advice was requested from various academic scholars to validate the claims to the Dawoodi throne through the authentication of the *sijillat* and other documents.[33] As the schisms in Bohra historiography show, the *sijill* is thus much more than a historic document: it is a living relic of the community and the object of heated political debate and polemics.

Returning to Ahmedabad, the crowd that had gathered in the *musafir khana* was patiently waiting for the Mazoon Shaheb to start the *majlis*. After reciting the *fatiha* through a crackling microphone, the Mazoon slowly and diligently started to narrate every detail of the bifurcation saga in Ahmedabad: from the death of Sy. Shaykh

29 I have seen copies of family petitions in Bohra family collections dating from the early twelfth/eighteenth century.

30 Samaria Sheikh, 'Aurangzeb as seen from Gujarat'.

31 Oral narrative of the Alawi *da'wa*.

32 The crisis is due to a conflict over *nass*, which was claimed to be bestowed in secret upon the half-brother of the late Dai and former Mazoon Saheb, Khuzaima Qutbuddin. Instead, the *nass* was taken over by the son of Sayf al-Din, Mufaddal Saifuddin, who proclaimed Qutb al-Din's assertion invalid and excommunicated him. At present, both clerics have claimed and taken the *daiship*, leaving the community divided and continuing the battle in the High Court of India.

33 Whether it is through the possession of manuscripts (as I argued in the Introduction) or the opinion of scholars in succession disputes, there is a strong tendency among the Bohra clergy to legitimate their existence through academic scholarship. See for instance 'Plea in Bombay HC on leadership of Dawoodi Bohra Sect: American Expert Examined'. *The Indian Express*. 29 November 2019, https://indianexpress.com/article/cities/mumbai/plea-in-bombay-hc-on-leadership-of-dawoodi-bohra-sect-american-expert-examined-6141871/an (last accessed 1 May 2020).

Ādam Safīuddīn b. Ṭayyibshāh (no. 28, d. 1030/1621) and the crisis that followed, to how the case was brought to the Mughal courts as far as Lahore and Kashmir, to the inter-communal tensions and violence, to the house arrest and persecution of the community by Mughal rulers, who, according to the Mazoon Shaheb, were bribed by the Dawoodis; and, finally, to the martyrdom of Sy. Ali Shamsuddin. Just as during the visit to the *qabaristan* earlier that evening, the atmosphere in the *musafir khana* turned from excitement to collective gloom.

When the Mazoon reached the climax of the story, his leather bag was brought to him, from which he revealed to the audience a fragment of the framed *sijill*. The crowd was in awe; some people began to weep, and others listened carefully to the words of the Mazoon Saheb, waiting for an explanation of the significance of the mysterious object. The Mazoon, whose voice had become stern, continued his account, explaining that the very *sijill* he held in his hands was the one and only authentic *nass* document that proved the legitimacy of Sy. Ali Shamsuddin's position as the twenty-ninth Dai of the community. In detail, he narrated that that Sy. Shaykh Adam Safiuddin b. Tayyibshah, Sy. Ali Shamsuddin's predecessor, had explicitly and clearly written down the *laqab* (title) of Shamsuddin in the last lines of the document in *kitab siriyya*, which was definite proof of his *nass*. The Mazoon continued by stressing Sy. Ali Shamsuddin's many qualities, including his truthfulness and patience during the difficult times that followed, which he used as an argument to emphasise the validity of his *nass*. The tone of his voice became more polemical as he juxtaposed the qualities of Shamsuddin with those of his contemporaries, who illegitimately claimed *nass* on the basis of a forgery of the original *sijill*. After the crowd uttered eulogies in remembrance of Sy. Ali Shamsuddin, the *sijill* went back into the handbag, and a communal *thali* was served. The day of the *ʿurs* had been long, and soon after the kulfi ice cream was served, all the believers went to their modest accommodations to sleep.

1.2 Secret Manuscripts and their Social Lives

Of all the rolls and charts, tomes and volumes, secret scripts and talismans and other material manifestations of writing I encountered during my observations in the treasury of books, no exemplar showed me more clearly the social role of secret manuscripts among the Alawis than the Ahmedabad *sijill*.

As I removed my polyester *rida* from the back of the *riksha* that drove me from the *musafir khana* back to the centre of Ahmedabad, I reflected on the events I had just witnessed. The bifurcation roll the Mazoon had just revealed was considered one of the most secret, and therefore most inaccessible, texts of the *khizana*. Despite its inaccessibility, it was displayed to the entire community present at the ceremony. Revealing this *sijill* in Ahmedabad and not at home, in Baroda, had special significance. Ahmedabad, after all, was where the schism and all the events that followed had occurred. Yet this did not explain why the *mu'minin*, who usually do not have access to books from the *khizana*, were allowed to see the bifurcation roll. Why had the Mazoon Saheb chosen to reveal this document? And in the process, had it lost its divine aura of being secret?

Having been taken out from the *khizana*, the *sijill* had been presented to the crowd from a distance and was not shown in full; in any case, believers were certainly not able to read the handwritten Arabic, let alone the secret script it contained. The experience of witnessing a document as a sacred object is different from reading it, but can be as powerful. As we know from other contexts, merely catching a glimpse of a sacred text that has strong healing powers attributed to it, such as the *Qaṣīda al-Burda* by the seventh-/thirteenth-century poet al-Būṣīrī, can have restorative and cathartic effects on believers.[34] The *mu'minin* were certainly moved by seeing the bifurcation *sijill*; however, what was significant in this context was not its healing powers but rather its role as the founding document of the community, legitimising its right of existence. Yet from what I observed, I felt that, in addition to it having a social function as a political document and sacred text, there was more at stake.

Perhaps the *sijill* was shown to the public not *despite* its quality of secrecy but precisely *because of* it. With its aura of mystery and inaccessibility, the *sijill* needed to be seen, witnessed and experienced by the believers so they would know of its existence and to be aware of what they do not have access to.[35] In hindsight, observing the *ʿurs* in Ahmedabad was crucial in my understanding of how the Alawi community, and its treasury of books, *works*. I deliberately choose a present-tense verb to describe this relationship, because it is something that is active, happening as we speak, and constantly in flux. In other words, the *khizana* and its books, through their social interaction with the community as secret objects, are very much alive. Books from the *khizana*, I learned, no matter how secret, have a social role to play in the daily lives of believers. To outsiders, this might sound like a contradiction in terms, yet to the Alawis it is normal. To believers, the Dai embodies the secrets of the treasury of books, which, as we will see in this chapter, are vital for leading the community both in the here and now and in the afterlife. It is therefore the Dai, and the Dai alone, who is the divinely ordained custodian of the treasury of books. In this capacity, he is thus the gatekeeper of the treasury of books, the treasurer of the material *kutub* of the *daʿwat al-hadiyya* and its documents on the organisation of the *daʿwa*, and the guardian of the doctrine that is transmitted in its manuscripts.

The bifurcation history of the Bohras may have resulted in separate genealogies and ruling royal families, yet the Alawis, Dawoodis, and Sulaymanis continue to follow the same doctrinal principles. As Shi'i Isma'ili Tayyibis, the Bohras follow a unique interpretation of Islam, which forms the foundation of what the Alawis refer to as their 'Faatemi way of life'.[36] The books of the Alawi *daʿwa* describe this way of life as follows:

> The Alawi Bohras form part of the world Muslim Ummah. They comprise of followers of the Faatemi Imaams who founded the kingdoms, fostered noble traditions

[34] See, for instance, Suzanne Pinckney Stetkevych, 'From Text to Talisman: Al-Būṣīrī's "Qaṣīdat al-Burdah" (Mantle Ode) and the Supplicatory Ode', *Journal of Arabic Literature* vol. 37, no. 2 (2006), 145–89; and *Burda. The Mantle Odes. Arabic Praise Poems to the Prophet Muhammad* (Bloomington: Indiana University Press, 2010).

[35] This practice is unique to the Alawi Bohra *daʿwa*. The case of the Dawoodis, as Jonah Blank describes, is different. Blank, Mullahs on the Mainframe, 97.

[36] The Dawoodi Bohra also published a pamphlet in the 1980s titled *The Fatimi Tradition*. See B. H. Zaidi, *The Fatimi Tradition* (Mumbai: Dawat-e Hadiyah, Department of Statistics and Information, 1988) Pamphlet, 5.

> of thought and philosophy, produced and guarded an immense wealth of literature, and established a splendid civilization and the wise way of Islaam as the bedrock . . . In this way the impact of the Faatemi traditions, culture, and heritage became impressed on the history of many continents and lands and in each of these a considerable followers settled to carry on the traditional Faatemi way of life.[37]

The Bohras' Faatemi way of life is based on an identity that is distinctly Shi'i: its first and most important pillar is devotion to the *ahl al-bayt* (the family of the Prophet), the teachings of the 'pure' Imams, and the commemoration of the tragic death of Imam Husayn. Yet at the same time it is also deeply entrenched in Isma'ili thought and traditions covering both esoteric and exoteric dimensions of existence in which the Fatimids and their Imams are central. Finally, the Faatemi way of life includes a messianic component, as Tayyibi communities continue to await the return of Imam al-Tayyib while following unconditionally the spiritual and political hegemony of his vice-regent, the Dai, in his absence.

In what follows, we briefly explore the Bohra episteme as practised in the Alawi Bohra community, transmitted in the books of their *khizana* in Baroda, and continued through Fatimid traditions and institutions. The relationship between the community and the *khizana* and its books, as we will see, is of an osmotic nature: it is impossible to understand one without the other.

Doctrine and Books

To the outsider, unravelling the Bohra knowledge system is a daunting task: it is a highly complex and multi-layered system of beliefs, a world of souls and intellects, of divine knowledge, covenants, and initiation. It should be noted that, as a prerequisite to my initiation into the Bohra episteme, I took an oath of secrecy in the presence of the Dai and the Bhai Sahebs before they transmitted their knowledge orally and in writing. This monograph aims to respect this oath. I therefore made the conscious decision not to disclose certain aspects of Bohra esoteric thought, which are to be remain hidden. If the reader wishes to do so, he or she can become acquainted with these aspects in the established academic literature on the topic.[38] As an ethical intervention in my writing, I therefore base this discussion on Alawi Bohra sources that are freely accessible, including the official website of the *da'wa* and conversations with believers. I have therefore disclosed no information without the permission of the community.

Given the practical constraints of this study, I only highlight aspects that, on the basis of my observations, are foundational to the Alawis' understanding of knowledge and organisation of their *da'wa*. These include the following: the distinction between *batini* (esoteric) and *zahiri* (exoteric) sciences; the concept of *satr* (concealment) and

[37] Alawi Bohra *da'wa* publication titled *Da'wat Faatemiyah*, 59–60.

[38] See, for instance, the work of Daniel de Smet, Farhad Daftary and Samer Traboulsi. See for a short overview Daftary, *The Ismāʿīlis*, 269–76. See, for a deeper analysis of Tayyibi thought, Daniel De Smet, *La philosophie ismaélienne. Un ésotérisme chiite entre néoplatonisme et gnose* (Paris: Cerf, 2012) and Samer F. Traboulsi, 'The Formation of an Ismāʿīlī Sect: the Ṭayyibī Ismāʿīlis in Medieval Yemen' (PhD diss., Princeton University, 2005).

kashf (manifestation); *taqiyya* (precautionary dissimulation); and, finally, Isma'ili law as codified under the Fatimids. Regarding the orthopraxy of the Alawis Bohras, Isma'ili law is especially relevant for understanding what it means to be part of the *'Alawi Faatemi da'wa'*. Yet as we will see, the Faatemi way of life also includes rituals, ceremonies, and practices which are specific to the vernacular, Gujarati context and which coexist side by side with Fatimid-inspired beliefs and practice.

When writing from the perspective of the community, the way in which the Alawi Bohras live and interpret their belief system does not, in some cases, necessarily correspond with current academic scholarship on Isma'ili history, historiography, sources, and hermeneutics. The tension between the lived experience of Tayyibi Isma'ili Shi'ism of the Alawi community in Gujarat and classical Isma'ili doctrine as reconstructed by academic research will be investigated, including my own role as an academic in the field navigating these worlds.

Secrecy, Seclusion and Esotericism

Earlier in this chapter, I specifically referred to the Alawi Bohra *da'wat al-hadiyya* as a universe: a community in a bordered socio-geographical sense, confined to the streets of Badri Mohallah in Baroda. Yet the notion of a 'universe' in this context can also be understood in an esoteric-philosophical sense, in which time and space are embedded in a narrative that is not linear but cyclical. We need to understand this *Weltanschauung* first before venturing into aspects of orthopraxy – such as *'ibadāt* (devotions) and *mu'amalāt* (transactions) and questions of what is *ḥarām* (forbidden) or *ḥalāl* (permissible) – because it explains how the Bohras see the world and their place in it.

During my initiation into the Bohra knowledge system in Baroda, I learned that the kernel of what the Mazoon would refer to as 'the Fatimid Isma'ili *'aqā'id* (principles, s. *'aqīda*)' is that everything in the Alawi universe has an outer, *zahiri*, and a deeper, inner, *batini* meaning.[39] The Mazoon Saheb explained that 'our life has two facets: that which is external, open, and evident, we call it *zahir*, and that which is veiled, internal, and secret, we call it *batin*'. He explained that *'ilm al-zahir* is considered knowledge belonging to the 'outer' exoteric sciences, meant for the general believers so they can practise daily aspects of the religion. *'Ilm al-batin*, in contrast, is seen as the 'inner' esoteric knowledge that is considered secret and only accessible to, and comprehensible for, the initiated.[40] The Mazoon emphasised that this division of knowledge is not dualistic: all *zahiri* matters can also be interpreted on a *batini* level, and vice versa. However, he stressed, only those initiated into the spheres of *batin* possess the ability to see that there is no discrepancy between the two.[41]

According to the Alawi Bohra narrative, *'ilm al-batin* has been present in all pre-Islamic religions through God's divine revelation, a notion that can also be found in

[39] It should be noted that the *zahir–batin* paradigm is also present in the context of Imamic esotericism, Sufism and Isma'ili intellectual histories. See, for the Imamic tradition, the oeuvre of Mohammad Ali Amir-Moezzi, in particular *Le Guide divin dans le shi'isme originel. Aux sources de l'ésotérisme en Islam* (Paris: éd. Verdier, coll. Islam Spirituel, 1992).

[40] Halm, *The Fāṭimids and their Traditions of Learning*, 41, 49.

[41] See also Daftary, *The Ismā'īlis*, 242–5.

Isma'ili and Imami theology.[42] *ʿIlm al-batin* is thus considered timeless, eternal and universal, as it was handed down from God to humankind through the prophets, called the *nuṭaqā'* (speakers, s. *nāṭiq*; see Figure 1.7). It is the responsibility of the *nutaqa'* to translate this esoteric essence to the people, simplifying its message into *ʿilm al-zahir* through rules and regulations applicable to the time.

According to this model of transmission, *ʿilm al-batin*, considered eternal and never changing, was kept to the prophets, who subsequently transferred it to a lower category of messengers, the so-called *awṣiyā'* (receivers, s. *wāṣī*). ʿAlī b. Abī Ṭālib, the grandson of the Prophet and Muhammad's deputy according to the Shi'is and Isma'ilis, was one such *wasi*. 'Saiyedna Ali', as Bohras refer to him, in his turn revealed *ʿilm al-batin* to the

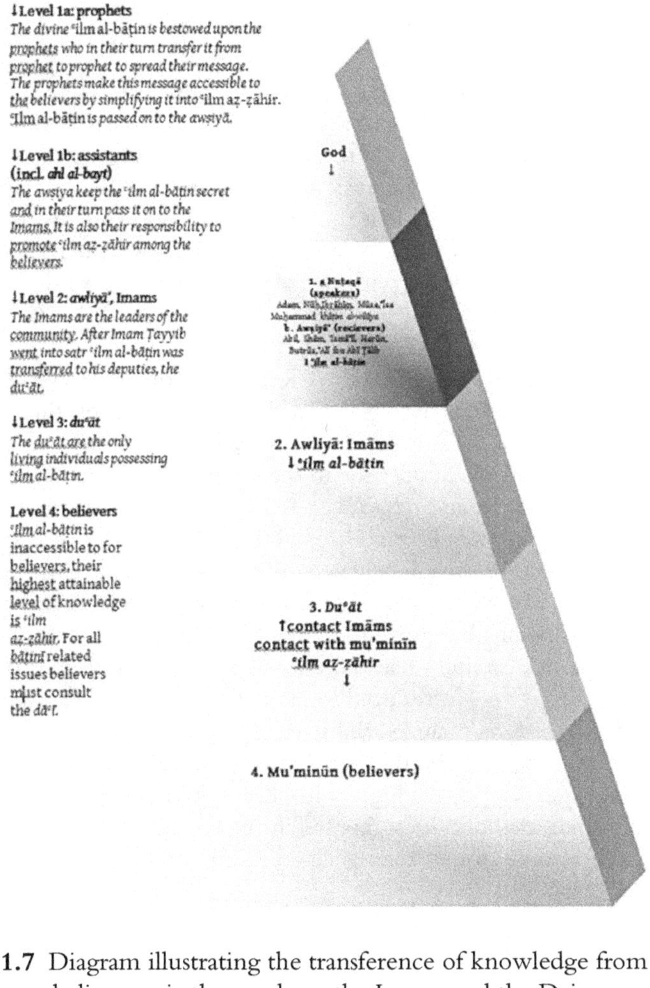

Figure 1.7 Diagram illustrating the transference of knowledge from God to believers via the speakers, the Imams and the Dais.

[42] Ali Amir-Moezzi, in particular, *Le Guide divin dans le shi'isme originel.*

rest of the *ahl al-bayt*, the family of the prophet, and the pure Imams, who are referred to as the *awliyā'* ('friends of God', s. *wālī*). It was the *awliya'* who were responsible for governing the *umma* after ʿAli's death and who passed on this knowledge to each other for generations.[43] To the Bohras, these *awliya'* include the first seven Imams and the later Fatimid Imams.

The model of the transmission of esoteric knowledge, and the place of the Bohras in it, is seen as a cyclical process that will restart after the appearance of a new prophet. Each *natiq*, prophet, *wasi*, receiver and *wali*, Imam has subsequently manifested himself in one cycle of *kashf* (manifestation), followed by his death, or in the case of the Imams, *satr* (seclusion). According to the cyclical model of manifestation and seclusion, the Bohras currently find themselves in the cycle of Muhammad, as he is considered the final *khāṭim al-wilāya* (the seal of the prophecy), followed by 'Ali as his *wasi*, and ending with the teachings of the Fatimid Imams and the seclusion of the last Imam, al-Tayyib in Yemen.

While the Nizari Isma'ilis currently follow a lineage of living Agha Khan-Imams, Twelver Shi'is believe that their Imam is *ghayba*.[44] The difference between *ghayba* and *satr* is that the *ghayba* model is based on the idea that the Imam is not living in this world but is residing in another dimension. In contrast, the Bohras, who believe in the concept of *satr*, are convinced that the descendants of Imam Ṭayyib are still alive and are *mastūr* (hidden) at a secret location in this world.[45] Whether Shi'ite Imams are in *ghayba* or *satr*, there is consensus with regard to the view that they both will return to their communities as the *mahdī* (for the Twelvers) or the *qā'im* (Seveners) at the end of times.

The Fatimid Imams are central in the cyclical cosmogony (the science of the origin of the universe) of the Bohras: it is believed that it was through their progeny that the *zahiri* Isma'ili doctrine was revealed openly in history. This doctrine was meant to elucidate facets of the Isma'ili doctrine to the common believers and is the basis for *fiqh* (law), *kalām* (theology), and *tafsīr* (exegesis) and is still followed by the Bohras.[46] However, the esoteric layers of Fatimid Isma'ili thought, it is believed, were kept concealed from the majority of Isma'ili believers. We have seen that in the Fatimid period the Imams were not in concealment but fulfilled an active role in the community as Caliphs. As Caliph-Imams they were the only individuals who had access to *ʿilm al-batin*. Only the Imam's carefully selected entourage – the *duʿāt* (missionary officers) and the *quḍāt* (judges) – were introduced to the outer layers of *ʿilm al-batin*. During the Fatimid period, *ʿilm al-batin* included the sciences of *ḥikma* (wisdom), *ta'wīl* (exegesis on a deeper and more secret level than *tafsir*), cyclical hiero-history, eschatology, cosmology, astrology and *ḥaqā'iq*, the highest level of esoteric knowledge.[47]

Academic sources describe how this system of thought, with its components of secrecy and cyclical time, found resonance among Isma'ilis in Yemen and the later

43 Lecture titled 'Isma'ilism and Neoplatonism', Alawi daʿwa. See also Daftary, *The Ismāʿīlis*, 17.

44 See for more information Daftary, *The Ismāʿīlis*, Chapters 6 and 7.

45 Asef Fyzee, *Compendium of Fāṭimid Law* (Simla: Indian Institute of Advanced Study, 1969), XIVIII.

46 Halm describes how the Fatimids legitimised the power of the Caliph-Imams through this model of transmission. It was necessary for the Fatimids to reveal *ʿilm al-zahir*. Halm, *Traditions of Learning*, 17, 18, 41–55.

47 See for more information Halm's chapter 'Sessions of Wisdom' in *Traditions and Learning*, 28–30.

Bohra communities in Gujarat, as well as in other parts of the Muslim world, as conveyed by missionaries and books.[48] The Bohras, however, believe that it was baby-Tayyib, in his capacity as the legitimate heir of the Fatimid throne, who brought *ʿilm al-batin* to Yemen. While the line of Fatimid Imams continued to reign from Cairo until the demise of the empire in the late sixth/twelfth century, the Tayyibi Isma'ilis in Yemen added an extra category to the model of knowledge transmission after Tayyib's seclusion in 524/1130. This extra layer was the category of the Dais, formerly missionary officers under the Fatimids who, under the Tayyibis, became the sole chain between the hidden Imam and the community. According to the books of the Alawi *daʿwa*, this additional layer was institutionalised in the year 532/1138, under the auspices of Malika al-Hurra, eight years after Tayyib's seclusion.

The institution of this *Dāʿī al-muṭlaq* (lit. 'absolute dai'), as the Ra's ul Hudood would stress on many occasions, 'continues spiritually without interruption up to this day as the seat of *daʿwa*'.[49] Through their exclusive contact with descendants of Imam al-Tayyib, only the Dais have access to *ilm al-batin*, including information on their state of *satr* (concealment). This new, unique position of the Dais and their personal connections with the hidden Imam enhanced their power and status in the community.[50] We can thus conclude that in the Tayyibi Yemenite context, through the hidden Imam, *ʿilm al-batin* was extended to the legitimisation of the power and the position of the Dai.

As we see in Chapter 2, in addition to the canon of Fatimid and other Isma'ili sources that the Bohras have preserved, the intellectual history of the Yemeni phase can be characterised by an expansion of the *batini* and *haqa'iq* genres by Tayyibi authors. After the concealment of Imam Tayyib, the Tayyibi Isma'ilis in Yemen made the following changes to earlier doctrinal ideas. The Tayyibi notion of *satr*, which belongs to the highest level of *ilm al-batin*, is not only reflected in Tayyibi Bohra historiography but also shaped it in its entirety. The Bohra past, present, and future consist of cycles or *adwār* (Ar. sing. *dawr*) of *kashf* or *ẓuhūr* (a period of manifestation) and *satr* (a period of concealment). According to Tayyibi history the first *satr* comprised the early Isma'ili period, up until the advent of the Fatimids. This period was followed by a period of *kashf*, notably the Fatimid period, where the Imams were openly ruling the *daʿwa* or community. This period of *kashf* was followed by the current period of *satr*, in which the contemporary Bohra community exists and in which Imam Tayyib disappeared as the last and twenty-first Imam.[51]

The position of the Dai in the Tayyibi community in Yemen was legitimised by the belief that he was the only individual on earth who was in personal contact with the Imam. As noted, the historical missionary figure of the Dai thus became the link between the hidden Imam and the community. The Tayyibi Isma'ilis went even further by stating that, without the existence of the Dai, the community would lose contact with the Imam and would be doomed. This rhetoric can be found in contemporary

48 Traboulsi, 'Transmission of Knowledge and Book Preservation in the Ṭayyibī Ismāʿīlī Tradition'.

49 See also *Da'wat-e-Faatemiyah*, https://www.alavibohra.org/Dawat-e-Faatemiyah%20and%20Spiritual%20Lineage.htm (last accessed 15 May 2019).

50 Daftary, *The Ismāʿīlīs*, 275, 13.

51 Ibid., 238–9.

sources, such as in the treatise *Tuḥfat al-Qulūb*, written by the Yemenite Dai Ḥātim b. Ibrāhīm al-Ḥāmidī (no. 2, d. 595/1199).[52] The idea that the Dai thus had access to the hidden Imam was not only a means of legitimisation of power in medieval Isma'ili Yemen but also continues in present-day Bohra communities. The historical development of the office of the Dai is of vital importance to understanding the organisation and institutionalisation of the contemporary Alawi Bohra community, which will be discussed at length in the following sections of this chapter.

The *batini* sciences have been described throughout the ages by well-known Isma'ili authors from both Iran and North Africa in the pre-Fatimid, Fatimid and post-Fatimid Tayyibi periods, such as the earlier-mentioned Abū Yaʿqūb al-Sijistānī (d. 360/971) and Ḥamīd al-Dīn al-Kirmānī (d. 411/1020). These well-known treatises, as we see in the next chapter, are enshrined in the *khizana* in Baroda as part of the Alawi *batini* canon. The Alawis also attribute texts to their *batini* tradition that are not necessarily ascribed to Isma'ili authors in academic scholarship. Let us, for example, take the *Rasā'il Ikhwān al-Ṣafā'* (Epistles of the Brethren of Purity); its provenance is much debated in academic sources and is often attributed to the anonymous fourth-/tenth-century 'Brethren of Purity' of Basra.[53] According to the Alawis, the *Rasā'il* were written by the ninth Imam Aḥmad al-Mastūr (*satr* unknown), who was leading the 'progeny of Maulaatana Faatemah', the underground Fatimid Isma'ili community, during the reign of Abbasid Caliph al-Ma'mūn (d. 218/833).[54] To the dismay of the Alawis, modern intellectual historians have described the *Rasā'il* and other Isma'ili titles that focus on *batini* concepts, such as *ʿaql* (intellect), the migration of the *nafs* (soul), *sūra* (form) or the *aflāk* (spheres), as 'Neoplatonic' and 'Aristotelian'.[55] From the perspective of the Mazoon Saheb, the fact that the beliefs of his community are associated with philosophy and the '*shuyūkh al-Yunān*' ('the sheikhs of Greece': Aristoteles and Plato) is highly problematic and incorrect, because these esoteric truths are transmitted from God to the Prophet via the uninterrupted chain of Imams. To blame for this association are not, he said, modern historians, but rather the Abbasids, who

52 Hussain Hamdani, 'The Dāʿī Ḥātim Ibn 'Ibraḥīm al-Ḥāmidī and His Book Tuḥfat al-Qulūb'. Oriens 23–4 (1974): 258–300. Abbas Hamdani (ed.), *Tuhfat al-Qulub, The Precious Gift of the Hearts and Good Cheer for Those in Distress. A Critical Edition of Risālat tuḥfat al-qulūb wa-furğat al-makrūb* (London: Dar-al-Saqi, 2012).

53 Nader el-Bizri (ed.), *The Ikhwan al-Safa and their Rasail: An Introduction* (Oxford: Oxford University Press in association with Institute of Isma'ili Studies, 2008).

54 According to the Alawi narrative, the 53 epistles of the *Rasā'il* were written in seclusion by Imam Ahmad but became so popular that the Abbasid Caliph al-Ma'mun tried to discredit them. Lecture by the Mazoon Saheb titled *Rasaa'il Ikhwaan is-Safaa wa Khullaan il-Wafaa. The Reasons behind its Compilation by the Ninth Fatemi Imam Maulaana Ahmad il-Mastoor (as)*, No. 38, 115–19. Blank confirms the same narrative, yet less detailed, among the Dawoodis, Mullahs on the Mainframe, 23. The late Abbas Hamdani has shown the Isma'ili authorship of these *rasā'il* in his paper 'An Early Fatimid Source on the Time and Authorship of the Rasa'il Ihwan al-Safa', *Arabica* 26 (1979): 62–75. Note how he describes it as 'an early Fatimid source'. See also Mas'ud Habibi Mazaheri and Farzin Negahban, 'Aḥmad b. ʿAbd Allāh al-Mastūr', in *Encyclopaedia Islamica*, Editors-in-Chief: Wilferd Madelung and-Farhad Daftary. Consulted online 8 March 2020.

55 Netton 'Foreign Influences and Recurring Ismâʿîli Motifs in Rasâ'il of the Brethren of Purity', in *Seek Knowledge: Thought and Travel in the House of Islam* (London: Routledge Curzon, 1996), 108; 'Private Caves and Public Islands', in M. Elkaisy-Freimuth and J. M. Dillon (eds.), *The Afterlife of the Platonic Soul: Reflections of Platonic Psychology in the Monotheistic Religions* (Leiden: Brill 2009), 107–20.

during their translation movement misinterpreted these texts and were unable to unify them with the deeper meanings of the Qur'an and the *sharia.*[56]

Fatimid Jurisprudence

While *batini* knowledge may seem too esoteric and abstract to ordinary believers, *fiqh* (jurisprudence) is something people in the Alawi community relate to, and identify with, in their daily practice of religion. The Alawis, as the other Bohra communities, follow a separate school of jurisprudence referred to as the Fatemi *maddhab*. I argued earlier that the Neo-Fatimid identity of the Alawis and their Faatemi way of life are strengthened and legitimised through their *khizana* and clerical hierarchy. In addition, this identity is practised in day-to-day life by believers through *fiqh*.

The Fatimid school of law, also known as the Isma'ili school of law in academic sources, was codified during the early years of the Fatimid Empire by the jurist Qāḍī al-Nuʿmān (d. 363/974). Al-Nuʿman served as *Qāḍī al-quḍāt* (chief justice) under various Fatimid Imams and was commissioned to compose an official code of law under the auspices of Imam al-Mu'izz li-dīn Allāh (d. 364/975).[57] This compendium, titled *Daʿā'im al-Islām* (The Pillars of Islam), was accepted as the official code of conduct of the Fatimid Empire in the year 349/960. Based on seven pillars, the *Daʿa'im* is considered a single authoritative source on *fiqh* by all Isma'ilis today.[58] The Bohras, however, are the only Isma'ili community still practising Fatimid jurisprudence. For the *mu'amalat*, a vernacular genre exists of *fiqh* literature for believers in Gujarati and *Lisan al-Daʿwa*.

The *Daʿa'im* is the earliest official source on Isma'ili doctrine, containing regulations concerning *imāmat* (the absolute sacred and political status of the Imam) and *walāya* (believers' devotion to the Imam). The treatise is divided into two volumes; in the first volume the *qadi* deals with *ʿibadat*, whereas in the second volume the *mu'amalat* are discussed. Nuʿman describes the seven *arkān* (Ar. 'pillars', sing. *rukn*), which are obligatory for all believers, as follows:

1. *Walāya*: loyalty to the Imam, his *imāmat* and, in the Bohra interpretation, his representative in the community, the Dai. *Walaya* is considered the most important *rukn*, and it is also known as the Isma'ili *shahāda*.

[56] *Isma'ilism and Neoplatonism*, https://www.alavibohra.org/Isma'ilism%20and%20Neoplatonism.htm (last accessed 24 February 2019).

[57] Asaf A. A. Fyzee, 'Qadi al-Nuʿman the Fatimid Jurist and Author', *Journal of the Royal Asiatic Society of Great Britain and Ireland*, No. 1 (January 1934), pp. 1–32. F. Dachraoui, 'al-Nuʿmān', in P. Bearman, T. Bianquis, C. E. Bosworth, E. van Donzel and W. P. Heinrichs (eds), *Encyclopaedia of Islam*, 2nd edn, http://dx.doi.org/10.1163/1573-3912_islam_SIM_5977 (last accessed 28 February 2020). Devin Stewart, *Disagreements of the Jurists: A Manual of Islamic Legal Theory* (Library of Arabic Literature) (New York: New York University Press, 2017).

[58] Instead of five pillars in Sunni Islam. See Ismail Poonawala, 'Al-Qaḍī al-Nuʿman and Ismāʿīlī Jurisprudence', in F. Daftary (ed.), *Mediaeval Ismāʿīli History and Thought* (Cambridge: Cambridge University Press, 1996), 117–43. Daftary, *The Ismāʿīlis*, 242–5. For more information see Sumaya Hamdani, *Between Revolution and State: The Path to Fatimid Statehood* (London: I. B. Tauris, 2006).

2. *Ṭahāra*: ritual purity, which plays a central role in every miniscule aspect of the daily life of believers (see the final section of this chapter).
3. *Ṣalāt*: prayer, also known as *namāz*, which starts by asking the *ahl al-bayt* and the Fatimid Imams for divine assistance. Bohras perform the five prayers divided over three sessions daily (with a short pause between *ẓuhr* and *ʿaṣr* and *maghrib* and *ʿishā'*), in a posture sitting sideways (praying on the right knee, with the legs to the left).
4. *Zakāt*: the religious obligation of paying alms. The Bohras have a complex system of paying alms in addition to the 2.5 per cent of the *zakat*, which finances the *daʿwa*. There are various financial contributions for special occasions and celebrations, such as the the birthday of the Dai and marriage and funeral ceremonies; special taxes per household; the *nazār al-maqām*, alms paid for the absence of the hidden Imam; and the *khums* (alms amounting to one-fifth of an unexpected income, such as an inheritance).
5. *Ṣawm*: fasting, which is performed not only during Ramadan but also during special ceremonial days, such as Muḥarram and death commemorations of the Fatimid Imams and the Dais.
6. *Ḥajj*: pilgrimage to Mecca. Part of this *rukn* is also obligatory *ziyara* to holy places in India, Yemen, Iraq, Egypt, Israel and Syria.
7. *Jihād*: struggle. As the seventh pillar, *jihad* refers to the struggle of the *nafs* (soul or ego). In addition to this big, bodily *jihad*, there is also the small *jihad*, which is the obligation to fight the holy war for the cause of the Imam. In his absence during the *dawr al-kashf*, the small *jihad* is not permissible.

Because all of the seven *arkan* have a strong *zahir* practical component, there is also an allegorical *batini* side to *tahara*, *walaya*, *jihad*, *sawm*, *hajj*, *salat* and *zakat* for those who have the power to grasp its deeper esoteric meaning. For instance, from a *batini* perspective, meditation supplements *namaz*; *zakat* is considered not merely a material but also a spiritual donation of knowledge; fasting represents the hunger and thirst for esoteric eternal knowledge and the spiritual guidance of the Dai; *hajj* is an inner spiritual journey to God; *jihad* and *tahara* both represent man's struggle against the *nafs* (ego); and, finally, *walaya* refers to the deep spiritual dedication to the Dai.[59]

'*Uṣūl al-fiqh* (sources of jurisprudence) in Fatimid law include the Qur'an, the *sunna*, the corpus of *aḥadīth* of the *ahl al-bayt*, and the *sunna* of the seven Imams (Jaʿfar al-Ṣādiq and Muḥammad al-Bāqir in particular) and the Fatimid Caliph-Imams.[60] Historical judgements of the Dais are not included in the juridical canon of the Bohras. Even though largely unstudied, compendia and commentaries on *fiqh* by Bohra authors do indeed exist, such as the works by the eleventh-/seventeenth-century Dawoodi scholar and jurist Amīnjī b. Jalāl b. Ḥasan (d. 1010/1602).[61] While the Ja'fari-Twelver and the Fatimid-Sevener schools of law partially share the same roots of *fiqh*, several

59 Hollister, *The Shi'a of India* 257–69. Blank, Mullahs on the Mainframe, 168.

60 Fyzee, *Compendium of Fāṭimid Law*, XIVIII.

61 Poonawala, *Biobibliography*, 185, 186. Another, much more recent example in this regard, which proves that Bohra scholars still actively wrote on jurisprudence in the 1950s, is *Kanz al-Fiqh*, written by Mullah Qurban Godrawala (d. 1372/1952). Poonawala, 236.

discrepancies exist relating to family law, such as the practice of *nikāḥ al-mutʿa* (the marriage of enjoyment), which is considered *haram* according to Fatimid law; *wuḍū'* (see *tahara*); and polygamy and divorce (which are both discouraged in Fatimid law).[62]

As the vice-regent of the hidden Imam, the Dai is the highest *qadi* of the community, and he enjoys a position similar to that of the *marja' taqlīd* among the Twelvers as the most learned *faqīh* (jurist) of his time. Historically, the Bohras have functioned extra-judicially, as can be reconstructed from the internal legal documents held in the various *khizanat* and in the private collections among believers. Yet, for conflicts that could not be resolved within the community, such as disputes about *nass* or in cases involving Bohras and non-Bohras, petitions were filed externally at the courts of rulers, such as the Mughals and the British in colonial times. Similarly, today the Alawi community continues to function extra-judicially from the Indian state. I witnessed several cases in the realm of inheritance and family that were heard in the *khizana* in the presence of the Dai. It is the Dai, in his capacity as the vice-regent of the hidden Imam, who has the royal right to judge and make decisions about every aspect of the lives of believers, which they are obliged to follow. These decisions, as we see in the following sections, reach far beyond law as they affect the personal lives of believers.

The absence of the hidden Imam, however, has legal implications in the realm of *fiqh* and *sharia*. For instance, I was told that since Imam Tayyib was the only individual who was allowed to lead the *khuṭba* (Friday sermon), this practice has been temporarily abolished since his *satr*. For the same reason, a *minbar* (pulpit) has reportedly been absent from Bohra mosques ever since. Moreover, the *ḥudūd* scripturally prescribed punishments have been abolished, and other legal requirements, such as the obligation of the small *jihad* (holy war) and *daʿwa* (conversion), have become void.[63]

An aspect of Islamic law, which is of relevance in the absence of Imam Tayyib, is *taqiyya*. *Taqiyya* can best be described as dissimulating one's religious identity in times of danger. It is a well-practised tradition in all Bohra communities, which, as we will see throughout this monograph, shaped, defined, and continues to give shape to the Alawi Bohras' religious identity and historical narrative. The history of the Bohra community is dominated by a narrative of persecution, conflict, and concealment: from fighting the Zaydi Imams to being under the hegemony of the Ottomans or, in Yemen, the Gujarat Sultanate (809–981/1407–1573) and Mughal emperors (see the later discussion).

Taqiyya is considered legitimate in Shi'i milieux of the Seveners and the Twelvers at all times and under all conditions in the absence of the Imam during the period of *ghayba* (Twelvers) or *dawr al-satr* (Seveners).[64] The scriptural basis for this conviction

[62] See for a more detailed comparative analysis between the Sunnī, the Ja'farī and the Fatimid schools of law: Agostino Cilardo, *The Early History of Isma'ili Jurisprudence. Law under the Fatimids: A Critical Edition of the Arabic Text and English Translation of al-Qadi al-Nuʿman's Minhaj al-Fara'id* (London: I. B. Tauris, 2012).

[63] The point of conversion does not, of course, fit the Bohra narrative of conversion in Gujarat by the Tayyibi Dais.

[64] Strothmann, R. and Djebli, M., 'Taḳiyya', in P. Bearman, T. Bianquis, C. E. Bosworth, E. van Donzel and W. P. Heinrichs (eds), *Encyclopaedia of Islam*, 2nd edn (Brill Online, 2015), http://referenceworks.brillonline.com/entries/encyclopaedia of islam-2/takiyya-SIM_7341 (last accessed 21 March 2014. For recent scholarship on *taqiyya* see Daniel Beben, 'Reimagining *Taqiyya*: The "Narrative of the Four Pillars" and Strategies of Secrecy among the Ismāʿīlīs of Central Asia', *History of Religions* vol. 59, no. 2 (November 2019): 83–107.

lies in *fiqh* works of the Fatimid and Ja'fari schools of law, which are based on sayings of Ja'far al-Sadiq and Muhammad al-Baqir, who argued, *'Inna taqiyya min dīnī wa dīn ābā'ī'* (Taqiyya is part of my creed and the creed of my forebears).[65] On the basis of this *hadith*, the Tayyibi Isma'ilis and the Bohras managed to maintain an apolitical stance – through scripture and practices – towards the local sectarian politics of medieval Yemen and Mughal India throughout the ages, surviving to the present day by seeming to live the life of Sunni Muslims to the outside world. The Bohra narrative of suffering under Sunni persecution came to an end during the colonial rule of the subcontinent. Nevertheless, the Bohra practice of *taqiyya* was strictly maintained, so that up until the present day, outsiders to the community, let alone researchers, only rarely have had access to the *daʿwa*. I address the concept of *taqiyya* as a social practice and its specific relation to the treasury of books in Chapter 3. It should be mentioned that, just like the earlier-mentioned *nass* roll, law books – manuscript copies of 'the *Daʿa'im*' in particular – have a very rich social life in the Alawi *khizana* both through their content and their marginalia. I explore these marginalia and how they are used during ceremonies at length in Chapter 5.

Another aspect of the Bohra interpretation of Fatimid jurisprudence is the importance of *tahara* (more on this later). As entrepreneurs, the Bohras have historically proven to be masters in finding niches in mercantile trade that are considered unworthy by Hindus (such as the selling of soap, hardware, glassware, paint, stationary and spices), without violating the laws of *tahara*, such as butchering and cleaning.[66] During my stay in Baroda, Alawi Bohra clerics often stressed the specific Alawi 'kind and tactful' trade ethics: 'We always start a business after considering the aspects of *halal* and *haram* in it. To keep our words and accomplish the undertaken tasks is in our blood.' Historically, each Bohra community has specialised in a specific mercantile niche, running shops and businesses in that niche. Whereas today the Dawoodis are known for the import and export of hardware, silk, horns, garments, glass and leather and are active in larger industries and banking, the Alawis have a monopoly in Gujarat on 'specs' (glasses) and the framing business.[67]

Rituals of the Fatimid Calendar

The influence of Fatimid traditions on the contemporary Bohra community is not restricted to doctrine and the organisation of the *daʿwa*, but also, as we have seen, extends to space and time, which according to *batini* sources are embedded in a cyclical narrative. The *dawr* which the Bohras consider themselves to be in today also has a linear history in *hijra* years. Time is measured according to the Fatimid calendar, which is referred to by the Bohras as the *miṣrī* (Egyptian) calendar. Years and dates are

[65] Translation, Poonawala, 77. Ismail K. Poonawala and Asef. A. A. Fyzee, *The Pillars of Islam: A Translation of al-Qādī An Nuʿmān's Daʿā'im al-Islām* (Oxford: Oxford University Press, 2002). al-Qādī Al-Nuʿmān, *Daʿā'im al-'Islām wa dhikr al-ḥalāl wa 'l-ḥarām wa 'l-qaḍāya wa 'l-'aḥkām* ed. Asaf b. Ali Asghar Fyzee (Caïro: Dār al'Aḍwā', 1991), 60.

[66] This was especially the case in the colonial period. Blank, *Mullahs on the Mainframe*, 47. See also Nile Green, *Bombay Islam*.

[67] Abdul Hussain, Gulzare Daudi for the Bohras of India, 75. Blank, *Mullahs on the Mainframe*, 40.

therefore not written in *hijri* but in Fatimid years.[68] The Fatimid calendar is not a lunar calendar, as commonly used by Sunnis and Twelver Shi'is; instead it is based on Fatimid astrological calculations. In practice, this means that religious days such as *Ashura*, the *Hajj* and *Ramadan* start several days earlier or later than in the rest of the Muslim *umma*.

The Bohra ritual calendar is arranged according to the twelve Islamic months. *Ramadan*, the *Hajj* and *Ashura* are the most important 'holy' events of the Bohra year. Each month of the *hijrī* year has its specific religious celebrations and commemorative days; some are shared Sunni and Shi'i traditions, such as the practice of fasting during Ramadan and the following *ʿĪd al-fiṭr* and *ʿĪd al-aḍḥā*, whereas others are strictly Shi'i holy days, such as *Ashura* and *Ghadīr khumm*.

Finally, there are celebrations, commemorative days and ceremonies that are specific to the Bohra community. The majority of these holy days are devoted to the earlier-described death anniversaries of the Dais of the community, the *ʿurs*, and the days of birth, known as the *milād*. Furthermore, the birth of Imam Ṭayyib is celebrated, which is referred to as *Rabbīʿ al-ākhir*, following the tradition of *Rabīʿ al-awwal*, the celebration of the birthday of the Prophet Muhammad.

In addition to the *ʿurs* anniversaries, there are two recurring communal gatherings: the *wāz* (the weekly Friday sermon) and the *majlis* (the sermon given on the first day of every month). These ceremonies are led by the Dai in the *masjid* in a very elaborate style (with a lot of weeping and '*ya Hussain!*'), while he is seated on a special royal throne that is golden in colour and is known as the *takht*. The Dai's oldest son, the Mazoon Saheb, is seated on a smaller throne on his right-hand side; the rest of the men of the royal family are standing behind the *takht*. The Dai is often accompanied by his wife, who is seated on a smaller throne left of the Syedna. The additional 'womenfolk' of the royal household and their entourage are seated in a designated royal square around the *takht* (unless the ceremony is segregated). As part of these ceremonies, the younger believers (boys) of the community fan the Dai with a royal ceremonial *chauri* (fly whisk).

Attending Bohra ceremonies is an extraordinary experience for the observant outsider. Before these official gatherings begin, a procession takes place in which the royal family ceremonially leaves the royal palace and strides to the *masjid* (a distance of less than forty metres; see Figure I.1). At the head of the procession is the Dai, followed by his sons and grandsons, who are escorted by their personal helpers and bodyguards, who hold a royal ceremonial umbrella over the head of the Syedna. The extended male royal family and their entourage are next in line, followed by the royal women and their entourage. Finally, the believers, who are awaiting the procession to pass by their houses, are the last in the ceremonial march to reach the mosque. The royals and their entourage wear various robes of honour, turbans, and royal head attire of a number of colours and shapes, depending on their rank in the *daʿwa* (see the final section of Chapter 1 on sartorial practices). Important aspects of these processions are not only what believers experience in terms of seeing (the ceremonial spectacle of the parade), smelling (the scent of incense) or feeling (the powerful emotions prompted by the occasion) but also their awareness of the street's soundscape, which is changed

[68] Fatimid English Date Converter, https://www.alavibohra.org/calendar/alavi%20taiyebi%20calendar/fatimid-english%20date%20converter.php (last accessed 20 January 2020).

entirely from the mundane. The procession is accompanied by *tablas* (ceremonial drums), devotional poetry is recited and firecrackers are let off, all in anticipation of the Dai's emergence from his palace. It is during these processions that believers have the rare occasion to witness the royal family, their helpers and the Dai in public and to ask for *duʿā* (supplication prayers).

1.3 Everyday Documents and the Organisation of the *Daʿwa*

In the previous section, I described how Bohra doctrinal manuscripts play a unique social role in the Alawi community as secret books. Like manuscripts, documents, in whichever form, are central to the life of Badri Mohallah and its people. In fact, I argue that the best way to understand the Alawi *daʿwa* and how it works is through its documentary culture: its contracts, letters, registers, talismans and other forms of writing. Whereas manuscripts are kept in the *khizana* under lock and key, documents form part of the contingent, day-to-day life of the community; they play important roles in the ceremonies that are central to the personal lives of its believers and in the structure and institutions of the *daʿwa*. In what follows, we will reconstruct these and other organisational aspects of the Alawi community through reading its documents and observing their social meaning.

The Spiritual Hegemony of the Dai

Hitherto I described the *daʿwa* as a universe, a community in an esoteric-philosophical sense, as well as one being spatially confined to Badri Mohallah. The Bhai Sahebs, however, describe their meaning of 'the *daʿwa*' and their own role in it as follows:

> In the collection of Da'wat books, the word 'Da'wat', wherever it is mentioned, is described in conjunction with the words of guidance, advice, manner and conduct . . . This Da'wat is not merely meant for spiritual ascension but also for the regulation and control of social and cultural customs and practices. Da'wat-e-Haadiyah guides and directs in each and every aspect of the life of a mumin. Saaheb-e-Da'wat serves to the mumineen and mankind as a symbol of benevolence and kindness sent by Allah through which they make people recognize their ranks and status (darajaat). Indeed, Da'wat is the divine light and a ray of hope in this period after the satr of Imaam uz-Zamaan (AS).[69]

Instead of focusing on its linguistic meaning – the idea of historical continuity or communal togetherness – in their explanations of *daʿwa*, the Bhai Sahebs emphasise nouns that are related to normative orthopraxy, such as 'manners', 'conduct', 'customs', and 'practices'. As the *Saaheb-e-Da'wat*, they stress that it is their duty to regulate this code of conduct through 'control', 'guidance', and 'direction' of the community in the post-*satr* period. The *mu'minin* and *mu'minat* have to acknowledge

[69] See https://www.alavibohra.org/Taiyebi%20rasm%20-%20nisbat.htm. Rasm-e-Taiyebi (online article) (last accessed 12 May 2019).

'their ranks and status' in the community's *darajāt* (s. *dajara*), the clerical hierarchy. The quotation illuminates how the Alawi Bohra clerics position themselves within the community – as omnipresent, giving both guidance and regulating social and cultural customs. This omnipresence, according to Blank, is unique to the Bohras. In his ethnography he describes exactly what I observed among the Alawis: no aspect of personal life is treated as a purely private affair, and the guidance and blessing of the Dai are considered fundamental to community members.[70] It should be mentioned that the hegemonic position of the Bohra Dai is not without its controversies, as we will see in the following chapter.

Throughout this monograph, I use the terms 'clerical establishment' and 'sacerdotal royal family' to refer to the hegemonic position of the Bohra Dai and his spiritual entourage. Yet these terms do not adequately describe the extraordinary hegemonic structure of the Bohra *darajat* or *ḥudūd* (s. *ḥadd*): the spiritual ranks of the Bohra clergy. Jonah Blank describes the position of the Dai and his spiritual hegemony in the Dawoodi community as an extraordinary phenomenon, which cannot be compared to a 'single member of the Sunni or Shi'i *ulama* and is fundamental to Bohra identity as 'the strongest barrier against the assimilation to the mainstream Indian Islam'.[71]

The spiritual hegemony of the Dai in Bohra communities is unparalleled in Muslim communities for a reason: the structure and institutions of the contemporary community are a remnant of the Bohras' Fatimid past in Yemen. As mentioned in the Introduction, the Fatimid Caliph-Imams sent off the Dais to faraway places, including Yemen, to spread the Isma'ili message. In his article 'The Organisation of the Fatimid Propaganda', Vladimir Ivanow was the first to reveal the complicated hierarchical structure of the *daʿwa* missionaries under the Fatimids and to point out that this structure has indeed been preserved by the Bohras up to the present time.[72] After months of participant observation at the Alawi clerical establishment I can affirm his claim.

Let us have a look at the organisation of the Alawi Bohra *hudud*. At the head of the Bohra universe is the Dai or Syedna, whose official title is *dāʿī muṭlaq* (Ar.; 'absolute Dai'). He is considered the sole spiritual, temporal and political head of the community in the absence of the hidden Imam.[73] As we have seen, to all Bohras the existence of the Dai is essential, for without his physical and spiritual presence the hidden Imam will not be able to return to the community. On a higher, *batini* interpretation, the Dai is also responsible for the continuation of the process of cyclical time and space by transferring the souls of believers to the afterlife (see Chapters 3 and 4).

As the spiritual, temporal and political head of the community, the Dai not only has the special power to communicate with the hidden Imam as his representative but is also considered semi-infallible in his actions and deeds. While Twelver Shi'is and Sevener Isma'ilis believe that the hidden Imam (and all Imams who went before him) are *maʿṣūm* (infallible), the Bohras distinguish a sub-category of spiritual perfection, *ka 'l-maʿṣūm* (Ar.; 'like infallible'): the Dai is seen as 'semi-holy', for he is in close

70 Blank, *Mullahs on the Mainframe*, 69.

71 Ibid., 174.

72 Vladimir Ivanow, 'The Organisation of the Fatimid Propaganda'. *Journal of the Bombay Branch of the Royal Asiatic Society* (1939) 15: 1–35.

73 http://alawibohras.com/ (last accessed 10 March 2015).

contact with the hidden Imam. Interestingly, the Alawis hold that their Dai is allowed to make mistakes.[74] Yet the Dai, 'His Highness', not only is regarded as the absolute authority of the community on worldly and divine matters, but is also a charismatic spiritual leader for believers. I observed time and time again that believers are willing to do whatever is possible to be in close proximity to the Dai, both in a *zahiri* sense of physical closeness and a *batini* sense of spiritual closeness or *walaya*.

The Dai's absolute hegemony is legitimised by his unique thread of contact with the hidden Imam. There is, however, also a material reason for the Dai's undisputed authority: he is the custodian and the sole heir of the Fatimid Tayyibi esoteric heritage: *ʿilm al-batin* and the earlier-described *haqa'iq*, as transmitted and materialised in the form of Arabic manuscripts stored in the *khizana*. On the basis of the Syedna's knowledge of the realm of *ʿilm al-zahir* and his embodiment of the highest levels of esoteric truths, it is believed that the Dai instinctively knows what is best for the community, both in its entirety as a *daʿwa* and in terms of each individual believer. The Dai is omnipresent in the lives of believers. Believers are obliged to ask the Dai for spiritual guidance and permission, known as *raza*, for all significant life decisions, such as getting married, naming a child, and choosing an education, profession, and even investments. The Dai's *raza* is legally binding, and disregarding his permission is considered a transgression that can lead to excommunication.

The foremost requirement of the Dai is that, as the *mansus*, the *nass* of his predecessor is bestowed on him. The position of the Dai, however, is not simply inherited: the ideal Dai needs to have a very specific set of qualifications, which can only be acquired through spiritual initiation and training from childhood. The Mazoon Saheb explained to me once that these qualities are a combination of skills that can be learned and personal characteristics. The skills, he explained, included royal *adab* or etiquette, being extremely learned and knowledgeable, learning by heart the *kutub al-daʿwa* (the books of the *daʿwa*), being fluent in its languages (Arabic, Gujarati, Persian, Urdu) and knowing how to disseminate knowledge. Personal characteristics that a Dai should have are the following: charismatic without being fearful or fierce, intelligent, amicable, easy to approach (while keeping the appropriate distance), humble, disciplined, pure of heart, compassionate and merciful, morally and ethically 'safe and sound', able to read the minds of the people, understanding what is going on in the community, and, finally, having a beautiful and pure voice. The Mazoon Saheb summed it up as follows: 'He should speak one word against a thousand words; he should speak that word which is the same at night and in the morning; his word should be code of law of justice.'

Furthermore, the Mazoon Saheb argued, the Dai should be well-versed in 'the politics of the time', and he should be 'omnipresent' in the governance of the *daʿwa* on all levels. According to the Mazoon Saheb, there are four levels of governance:

- *Siyāsat al-khāṣṣa*: governance of the self. The Dai should be morally and ethically sound at all times, given the fact that he has a representative and exemplary function.

[74] Based on a personal interview with the Mazoon Saheb. A progressive Dawoodi article on the matter can be read here: *Fatimid Literature: Creation, Preservation, Transfer, Concealment and Revival*, http://dawoodibohras.com/news/66/97/Doctrine-of-infallibility-in-Islamilitradition/d,pdb_detail_article/ (last accessed 10 March 2015).

- *Siyāsata al-ʿāmma:* governance of the common believers. The Dai should guide the community to stay on the right path by safeguarding the *sharia* and taking care of their spiritual, social and economic needs.
- *Siyāsat al-hamma*: governance over his own private household. The Dai should know the politics in his own royal residence, but should never favour people from his own family. The Dai should under no circumstances mix the *siyāsat al-hamma* and *ʿāmma*.
- *Siyāsat al-lamma:* governance of the collective and the checks and balances of *daʿwa* in its entirety.

Interestingly, these exact categories of governance (with the exception of *siyasat al-lamma*) and the personal qualities of the Dai, as described by the Mazoon Saheb, are addressed in a Fatimid genre known as *adab al-dāʿī* (etiquette of the Dai), such as al-Naysabūrī's *Risāla al-Mūjaza* mentioned earlier in this chapter.[75] Again, it becomes clear that the Alawis understand their Neo-Fatimid identity and the structure of the *daʿwa* through contemporary Fatimid sources. This is not surprising, given the fact that the *Kitāb al-Himma* and *Risāla al-Mūjaza* are part of the Alawi Bohra *kutub al-daʿwa* (more about this in the next chapter). What is remarkable is that these sources, written, respectively, in the late fourth/tenth and the fifth/eleventh centuries in Fatimid milieux that politically, geographically, culturally and linguistically could not be more different from contemporary Gujarat, are still of great relevance in contemporary times.

The Organisation of the Daʿwa

As noted in the Introduction, in the socio-political reality of medieval Gujarat, the local Bohra scholarly elite was transformed into the sacerdotal royal family as it is known today. The sacerdotal Alawi royal family is also referred to by the honorary title '*bayt al-zaynī*' (house of the righteous), and as we have seen, its members bear titles such as 'Prince' (Bhai Saheb) and 'Princess' (Bhu Saheba). The wife of the Dai is referred to as 'Ma Saheba', revered mother. While there is a distinction within the Dawoodi royal household between the 'upper royals', the *Qaṣr ʿAlī* (the castle of ʿAlī), and the rest, there is no such internal royal social hierarchy in the Alawi royal family, which is much smaller.

The current royal Alawi family residing in Baroda is originally from Ahmedabad. In total, the Alawi *bayt al-zayni* has brought forth nineteen generations of Dais in Baroda since its bifurcation from the Dawoodis. According to the Mukasir Saheb, there is a demarcation between two types of families in the community: families who

[75] Verena Klemm, *Die Mission des Fatimidischen Agenten Die Mission des fāṭimidischen Agenten al-Mu'ayyad fī ad-dīn in Shirāz* (Frankfurt: Peter Lang, 1989). Verena Klemm and Paul Walker, *A Code of Conduct: A Treatise on the Etiquette of the Fatimid Isma'ili Mission* (London: I. B. Tauris, 2011). The late Ali Asghar Engineer discussed the *Risāla al-Mūjaza* in relation to the modern Bohra community in his article *Dai and His Qualifications*, http://dawoodi-bohras.com/news/68/97/Dai-and-his-qualifications/d,pdb_detail_article_comment/ (last accessed 18 January 2015). Another source in this regard is al-Qāḍī Nuʿmān's *Kitāb al-Himma fī adab al-a'imma*. Muḥammad Kāmil Ḥusayn (ed.), *Kitāb al-himma fī ādāb atbāʿ al-aʾimma* (Silsilat makhṭūṭāt al-Fāṭimiyyīn, 3) (Cairo: Dār al-Fikr al-ʿArabī, 1948). Ivanow describes and analyses both sources in his Organization of the Fatimid Propaganda.

descend directly from those who supported the claim of Sy. ʿAli ibn Ibrahim 350 years ago, 'the original people, who were there with Sy. Ali', and 'other' families: outcasts and Alawi families who intermarried with outsiders to the community; 'they are second grade, and not pure, they have a different recognition'. Then, he continued, there are the royals who, as a class, again are divided into two grades: first grade, the nuclear family of the Dai, and second grade, the 'families that go back three generations or more, we consider them royals'. When I asked him how the royal family of the Dai differs from other families, he told me, 'We are not like the people of Badri Mohallah; we have our own royal etiquette and family discipline; we are more aristocratic, our children and us; we have a certain charisma, discipline, and taboo.'[76]

Returning to Figure 1.7, which depicts the transmission of knowledge from God through the prophets, the *awsiya* and the *nutaqa*, we see that the Dai is on the receiving end of the influx of eternal truths (he is the third layer from the prophets). This process of transmission, however, does not end with the Dai. In fact, under the wing of the Dai there are three ranks or *hudud* who assist the Syedna in the governing of the community. As argued earlier, these three *hudud* are – together with the office of the Dai – remnants of the Fatimid missionary hierarchy, carrying on these historic titles.

Alawi Believers not only fully depend on the personal spiritual guidance of the Dai but also rely on the advice of the three *hudud*. Every rank is responsible for a particular organisational facet of the Alawi government or *wizārat*. The *wizarat* starts on the lowest level with the Ra's ul Hudood Saheb, the youngest son of the Dai, who is in charge of worldly matters, such as guidance on 'non-spiritual' matters, education and healthcare. The Ra's ul Hudood pursued a career in medicine and therefore also runs the communal homeopathic *daʿwa* clinic. His elder brother and peer, the Mukasir Saheb, is responsible for larger worldly affairs, such as the organisation of *ziyara* and the *Hajj*. Furthermore, the Mukasir Saheb grants permission for marriages, the naming of children, and all other important earthly decisions in Bohra life. The highest *rank* is that of the Mazoon Saheb, who is the Dai-in-command, and therefore is responsible for all spiritual affairs, such as leading the *waz* and *majlis*, spiritual healing and maintaining the *khizana*. As mentioned, at the time of my fieldwork, the late Sy. Tayyib Diya' al-Din was still the Dai of the community. His eldest son, Abu Sa'eed il-Khayr Haatim Zakiyuddin, fulfilled the rank of Mazoon Saheb and *mansus*; he is the community's Syedna at present. Currently the posts of Mukasir and Ra's ul Hudood Saheb are carried out by his younger brothers. Often these offices are also held by the brothers, half-brothers or cousins of the Dai.

The royal Alawi women of the community, including the wives, sisters, mothers and cousins of the Dai and the three *hudud*, fulfil similar public *daʿwa* roles to their husbands', but in the realm of the women of the community. Regardless of the high educational level of Bohra women and their free movements prior to marriage, public life in the Alawi Bohra community is strictly segregated according to the notion of *purdah*, the segregation of the sexes.[77] The royal women are responsible for various health committees, school camps and, most importantly, matrimonial matchmaking.

[76] Interview with the Mukasir Saheb, 28 November 2013. By 'hav[ing] a certain . . . taboo' the Mukasir refers to respecting taboos and honour-related matters and adhering to ritual purity.

[77] Blank, *Mullahs on the Mainframe*, 365.

Furthermore, the Bhu Sahebas, together with their children, accompany their husbands during celebrations and religious ceremonies.

While the community relies upon the royal family for spiritual guidance, in return the royal family is fully dependent on the revenues of the *zakat*. According to my observations, the Bhai Sahebs and the Bhu Sahebas live very modest and quiet lives, devoid of luxury or excesses, contrary to what people often assume. The Alawi *daʿwa* is considerably smaller than that of the Dawoodis, who are known for their multi-layered institutionalisation of the *daʿwa*; therefore, its organisational structure is very clear.

Apart from the Dai, the *hudud*, and 'their womenfolk', the royal family consists of Bhai Sahebs of lower ranks, who assist the men in these royal offices. These positions are honorary, and people often have jobs, as well as exercising their Bhai Saheb privileges. In addition, non-royals can obtain the title *mullāh* as a reward for their *khidma* (services) to the community. Finally, there is the position of *ʿāmil*: a deputy cleric who is responsible for the administration of *mohallahs* outside of Baroda. Blank describes how there is no social mobility within the royal family, let alone between the royal and non-royal classes. Interestingly, this is not in accordance with my observations in Baroda: there, several men who were very high up in the clerical hierarchy married non-royal women, and various community members with more modest backgrounds became close associates or confidants of the Dai. We will get to know these community members, and many others, in Chapter 3.

Figure 1.8 Gathering in the mosque, with the Dai seen surrounded by the Bhai Sahebs. Note the small partition dividing the *khassa* from the *ʿamma*.

Ceremonies and Sartorial Practices

As I spent my days being part of the private household of the Dai and his royal family, I gained unique insights into the courtly culture of the Alawis and its sartorial practices. I noticed that while in daily life the male and female royals dress modestly in accordance with the rest of the community – in white *kurtas* and *sherwanis* with a white-golden *topi* (skullcap) on the head (see Chapter 3) – differences in social class become very apparent during official religious ceremonies. Because royal Alawi men have a more public function than their wives, male ceremonial attires are more elaborate.

Specific courtly ceremonial gowns are worn for specific occasions. For ceremonies of a more common nature there is the very long white Middle Eastern-inspired gilt or diamond-edged *jalabiyya*, which is set with imitation golden cuff-links and is covered by a white overcoat, worn with a special royal *topi*. For special occasions, such as Muharram, there is a dress that resembles the Mughal ceremonial gown known as the *ghaghra* (Figures 1.8–1.10): a voluptuous gathered white skirt is tied at the waist with cotton strings, and attached to it is a white *chori*, a top that is tied asymmetrically and diagonally on the right side of the chest. The attire is covered by an opulent shawl, which is loosely wrapped around the chest (Figure 1.10). The colour white is meaningful in this regard as it is seen as the dynastic colour of the Fatimids, who were believed to wear white in opposition to the Abbasids, who wore black.[78]

The courtly attire is accessorised with ceremonial objects such as rings with seals; off-white gold gilded shawls, which are worn in a folded fashion over the right shoulder; a *tasbīḥ* (prayer beads) made of silver or semi-precious stones (held in the right hand); and a folded handkerchief (held in the left hand). The Mukasir Saheb confided in me that he and his brothers have special 'specs' (glasses) 'for each and every ceremonial occasion'. Finally, no royal attire is complete without the *pagri*, which is a turban wrapped around a *topi*. Each rank within the royal family has its own *pagri* model: from the *mullahs* who, as non-royals, have the privilege of wearing a modest golden turban, up to the Dai, the three *hudud*, and their entourage, who wear stiff cotton *pagris* made of metres of white cotton and cardboard. The wife of the Mazoon Saheb, who bears the honorific title 'Bhu Saheba', is in charge of making the *pagris* by hand for the entire Alawi Bohra court; she has a small *pagri* workshop in the attic of the royal palace. For the royal 'ladies', hennaed hands and feet are a religious obligation, and gold is worn excessively (bangles in particular, which are never made of glass) to accessorise the Bohra *rida* dress and the most impressive feature of all: the royal Guajarati nose ring (see Figure I. 2).[79]

[78] For white as the dynastic colour of the Fatimids, see Jane Hathaway, *A tale of Two Factions. Myth, Memory, and Identity in Ottoman Egypt and Yemen* (Albany: State University of New York Press, 2003), 97. Irene Bierman, *Writing Signs: The Fatimid Public Text* (Berkeley: University of California Press, 1999), 21, 36, 105, 120. Sanders, *Creating Medieval Cairo*, 31, 88–9, 196f. Heinz Halm, *Empire of the Mahdi The Empire of the Mahdi: The Rise of the Fatimids* (Leiden: Brill, 1996). 186, 414.

[79] For an interesting history of the *rida*, see this newspaper article: 'Bohra women cut from the same cloth', http://tribune.com.pk/story/602497/bohra-women-cut-from-the-same-cloth/

Figure 1.9 The *chawri* (fly whisk) in action during a ceremony.

Ceremonial objects are also used during the rituals, such as the *chawri*, which is a ceremonial fly whisk made of *yak* hair from Ladakh (Figure 1.9). The purpose of this *chawri* is not to keep the Dai cool. Instead, the Mazoon Saheb explained, 'It is his *rasm*; it is his ceremonial right'. Another object to which the Dai has a ceremonial right is the *chamal*, the royal umbrella (Figure I.1). There are three variants of the *chawri* and the *chamal*, two silver ones and one golden one; they are kept in a special safe and are used only for special occasions. The Mazoon Saheb explained that the *chawri* and the *chamal* are not only the ceremonial objects reserved for the Dai: they are also part of his personal hereditary possessions, which also include 'his books, his *sayf* (sword), his golden *sabīl* (water vessel), his Quran, all belongings when he sits on pulpit, such as the *tāj* (crown) behind the pulpit, the *takht* (throne), each and every royal *dupatta*'.

While it is by no means the focus of this study, certain aspects of the sartorial courtly culture of the Alawis, such as the ceremonial *ghaghra*, the *pagri* and the waving of the *chawri*, show striking similarities with Mughal court culture as portrayed in Mughal miniatures paintings and drawings.[80] The Mazoon Saheb confirmed this when I asked him about these ceremonial attributes and practices. He said, to my surprise,

[80] See illustrations 29–31 in my dissertation, *The Bohra Dark Archive and the Language of Secrecy*.

Figure 1.10 The late Dai (middle) and the *hudud* wearing their ceremonial *ghagras*, *pagris*, *choris* and shawls. Note the eye-glass frames, handkerchiefs and silver rosaries. Credits: Alawi *daʿwa*.

'No, these are not from Gujarat; people say they are Mughal; it has nothing to do with local Gujarat or Islamic tradition.' The presence of these objects and practices indicates that, throughout history, the community was not as closed as the Bohra narrative likes us to believe. In fact, it indicates that relations certainly existed between the local Mughal courts of Gujarat.

Alawi Documentary Culture: Fatimid Leftovers and Other Documents

Observing the life of the *khizana* from my peacock chair, I witnessed the omnipresent position of the Dai and the Bhai Sahebs in the daily lives of believers through their persona, and through documents. As the *qadi* of the community, the Dai was responsible for issuing decisions on legal affairs and settling conflicts. While these legal verdicts were generally expressed orally, without exception they involved manuscripts (used as reference works) and the writing, registering and exchange of documents related to inheritance, property and divorce. Given his capacity as *qadi*, the Dai's verdict was unequivocal and his signature sacred. There is thus nothing in the *daʿwa* that would take place without his signature, which functioned as a royal seal.

The *daʿwa* has kept a detailed handwritten register of the community since its move from Ahmedabad to Baroda in the eleventh/seventeenth century, recording the

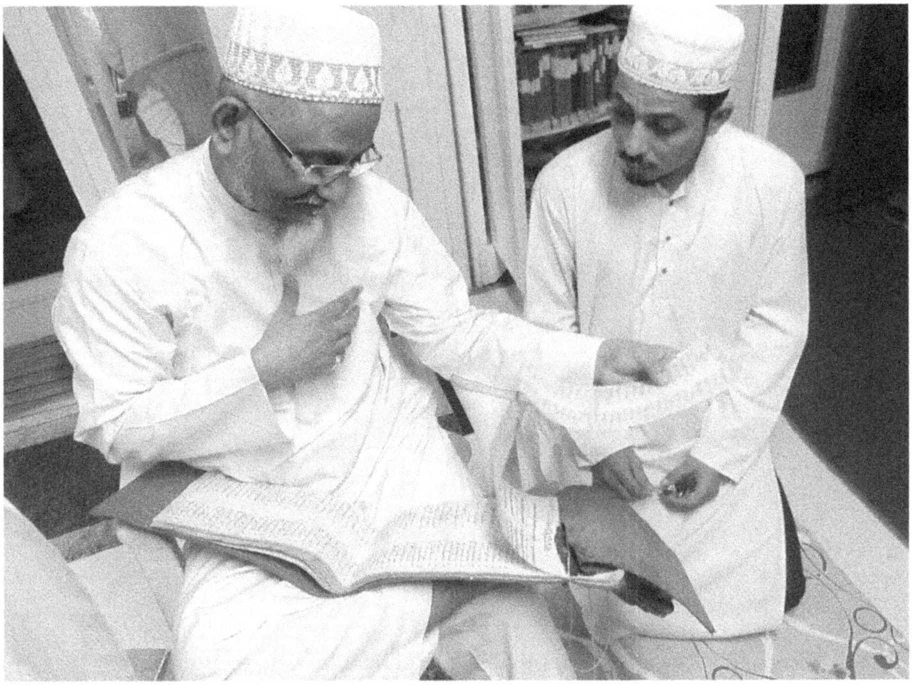

Figure 1.11 One of the historic registers of the community (nineteenth-century), read by the Mazoon Saheb and his assistant, Badruddin.

names, birth dates, whereabouts and deaths of its believers. The Bhai Sahebs record every event that takes place in the lives of believers in registers dedicated to marriages, pilgrimages, births and deaths. These registers (Figures 1.11 and 1.12) are historic documents in themselves and reveal much of the social history of generations of Alawi families. According to these registers, the community started with fifty to sixty community members (three to five families) post-bifurcation. The census that was taken seventy-five years ago mentions 1,285 believers in total. According to the current register, 2,500 community members are residents of Baroda and its surrounding areas. The Mazoon Saheb told me that the rest of the community resides in Mumbai, across the Indian Ocean, Australia or the USA, together totalling around 10,000 believers worldwide. Despite the historic (Indian Ocean) and more recent (North America and Australia) globalisation of the community, today the Bhai Sahebs exert hegemony and social control among believers, even from afar through active management of social media.

The register shows that the community experienced a baby boom in the thirteenth/nineteenth century, which led to a practical problem: an absence of family names (surnames). Prior to this sudden expansion, children would bear the name of their father or mother (for instance, 'son of Ali'). As a consequence, family names were introduced that are based on one's profession. Interestingly, a similar but larger-scale development occurred among the Dawoodis, who adopted English professional names,

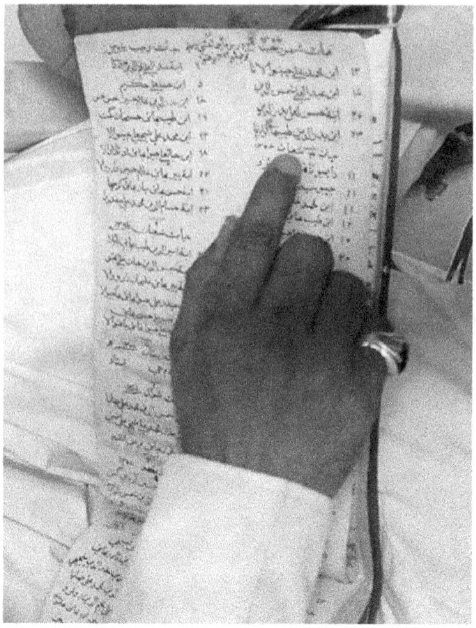

Figure 1.12 The Mazoon Saheb reading a historic register of the community (nineteenth-century).

such as Contractor, Doctor, Merchant, or Engineer, reflecting the skills of the family.[81] Alawi families chose composite names in Urdu, Hindi or Gujarati, such as the Attarwalas (*attar* = perfume + *wala* = man = perfume seller), the family who owned the building I lived in; the Kitabwalas (bookseller); and the Sabziwalas (vegetable seller). These names were meant for the common believers. The royal households historically had the privilege of bearing honorary Islamic titles, such as Badruddin (moon of the religion), Shamsuddin (sun of the religion), and Ziyauddin (splendor of religion) in the case of the Alawis, and Burhanuddin (proof of religion) or Sayfuddin (sword of religion) in the case of the Dawoodis. Furthermore, clerics and royal family members receive a new honorific Islamic title for every move up the clerical ladder.

The letters of each of these honorific titles correspond to a numerical value, which is considered auspicious and is linked to certain rituals and supplications. Given the Dai's almost infallible character and his charisma in the Bohra communities, he is present in the lives of believers not only spiritually through his guidance but also visually and materially. Whereas Blank describes how photographic representation is the norm among the Dawoodi Bohras as a means of making their devotion and affiliation known, the Alawis rely on the written word of the Dai and the Bhai Sahebs, to which a certain sacred materiality is attributed.[82] The Alawis hence have a wide variety of

[81] Blank mentions a few rather eccentric Dawoodi Bohra names, dating from the colonial period, such as Lightbulbwala, Electricwala and Africawala. Blank, *Mullahs on the Mainframe*, 138.

[82] Blank, *Mullahs on the Mainframe*, 173.

documentary practices that go far beyond the realm of jurisprudence to establish a relationship between believers and their clerics.

Since documents, such as accounts, letters and invitations, are objects that are likely to be discarded, it is common practice to write the *basmala* together with the name of the Dai using their numerical values written in Gujarati. This is a fascinating example of social codicology, as discarding a document bearing the name of God or the Dai is considered an act of profanity.[83] We discuss this, in light of *'geniza'* practices, in Chapter 5. In addition to writing the name of the Dai, the actual handwriting of the Dai and Bhai Sahebs is seen as a medium with talismanic powers for guidance and blessing. Examples in this regard are writing practices related to the mercantile-oriented character of the community. For example, at the beginning of the new fiscal year (staring with Diwali), the shopkeepers of the community are granted a visit to the royal *haveli* to have their account books signed by the Dai. This practice is known as *rasm al-Tayyibi* (which roughly translates as 'the sign of the *daʿwa*'), and is another example of social codicology, where the link between the social usage and materiality of the document is evident. The Dai writes several qur'anic verses, including the *basmala* and the *ḥamdala*, on the first page of the new account books of each year as a blessing for prosperity and a successful business. This documentary practice has an interesting parallel in Islamic eschatology. In addition to evoking auspiciousness in business, the practice symbolically refers to the 'spiritual account book' of good and bad deeds that, according to Islamic tradition, God keeps of all believers.[84] The Alawis, like all Muslims, pray a special yearly *du'a* on the fifteenth night of the month of Shaʿbān for forgiveness and prosperity, and for the 'clearance' of the 'spiritual account books'.[85]

Another common documentary practice among the Alawis embedded in the mercantile traditions of the community is the ceremonial writing of the Dai's *ʿalāma* (pl. *ʿalā'im*), or calligraphic signature. Upon opening new shops, businesses or factories, the Dai gives the new establishment his royal seal of approval by performing various rituals, which include the recitation of several qur'anic verses – the *abyāt* (poetic verses of the *daʿwa,* s. *bayt*) of the *daʿwa* and the *dhikr ahl al-bayt* (praise of the family of the prophet) – followed by the writing of a protective qur'anic *taʿwiz* (Ar. *taʿwīdh,* talismanic text which is attached to the wall.[86] This writing practice, which can also be found among the Dawoodis, is known as the *ʿalama.*[87] *ʿAla'im* are without exception handwritten by the Dai, and the script they carry are considered to bring *baraka* (blessings) and *rizq* (prosperity). The seal of the Dai, as I observed on a daily basis, can also have powerful qualities in its immaterial form. As a medium, water is commonly used to dissolve the *ʿalama*, or written verses of the Qur'an, that marks the inauguration of shops, offices or businesses by the Dai.[88]

Whereas the Alawis have their *ʿalama* inscribed on a simple piece of paper, the Dawoodis use special wooden planks as a writing medium. Yet, as sacred objects,

83 Jonah Blank describes a similar practice among the Dawoodis. Blank, *Mullahs on the Mainframe*, 173.
84 https://www.alavibohra.org/taiyebi%20rasm%20-%20alaamat.htm (last accessed 20 May 2019).
85 Interestingly, mid-Sha'ban is when Twelver Shi'is remember the *ghayba* of the *mahdi.*
86 https://www.alavibohra.org/taiyebi%20rasm%20-%20alaamat.htm (last accessed 14 March 2020).
87 Blank, *Mullahs on the Mainframe*, 174.
88 https://www.alavibohra.org/Taiyebi%20rasm%20-%20Dhaaru.htm (last accessed 14 March 2020).

ʿala'im are sought-after items in the Alawi community, being worth hundreds of rupees on the black market.[89] The Dawoodis have managed to commercialise the practice even further. Websites such as bohrashopping.com offer devotees 'Good Quality Wooden Plank for Alamat Sharifa by Aaqa Maula TUS [the Dawoodi Dai] to be framed and Hanged at your Homes (on sale)' (Figure 1.13).[90] One can thus speak of a commodification of the *ʿalama* practice, which, in Dawoodi circles, has become a service and therefore has a hefty price tag attached to it.[91] Interestingly, the banner of the website, which sells a wide variety of devotional Bohra objects, contains the *ʿalama* of Sy. Sayfuddin on its upper right-hand side. Aesthetics, in this context, are important and are linked to the social practice. The *basmala* looks like a humble scribble, and not a beautifully calligraphed piece, because it is not supposed to: it has to look as though it were written during a busy congregation in a mosque. After all, the powers from the *ʿalama* are not derived from its beauty, but from the sacred materiality that is attached to the book hand of its scribe: the Dai.

The usage of the term *ʿalama* in the context of the calligraphic signature of the Dai is significant in relation to the Alawi Bohras' documentary past and Neo-Fatimid identity in the present.[92] As an imperial documentary practice, the *ʿalama* was the distinctive signature used in the medieval Muslim worlds of the Abbasids, Mamluks

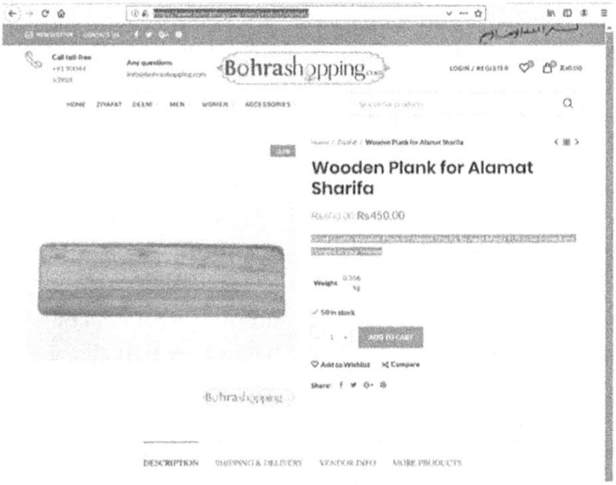

Figure 1.13 A Dawoodi website for religious artefacts, advertising the sale of an *ʿalamat* plank; note the Dai's *basmala*. Credits: https://scontent-ort2-2.cdninstagram.com/v/t51.2885-15/e35/70133508_103266584382342_3128866380520241793_n.jpg?_nc_ht=scontent-ort2-2.cdninstagram.com&_nc_cat=106&_nc_ohc=_-fg3H9rCN0AX_kXKMw&oh=8906ff485edffb6a045d19eef55b2c8d&oe=5E9012B4

89 See also Chapter 6 in relation to the opening *basmalas* and *hamdalas* in manuscripts.

90 https://www.bohrashopping.com/product/alamat/

91 Blank, *Mullahs on the Mainframe*, 154.

92 Akkerman, 'Documentary Remains of a Fatimid Past in Gujarat'.

and the Fatimids to authenticate official documents.[93] These imperial *ʿala'im* consisted of a personalised pious expression or motto, instead of sultanic names or titles. After all, a name was superfluous as there was only one Caliph, or Caliph-Imam in the case of the Fatimids, and if anyone's signature was known, it would be his. The Fatimids were known to use the *hamdala*, *al-ḥamdu li-llāhi rabbi 'l-ʿālamīn*, as their *ʿalama*, which was written right under the *basmala* on decrees and other diplomatic documents.[94]

Just like the Alawis' preservation of the *sijill* that I described at the beginning of this chapter, the *ʿalama* too, is a possible Fatimid documentary leftover that has survived to the present time, as I have argued elsewhere.[95] I suggest that it is not unlikely that the Fatimid imperial *ʿalama* evolved into what the Bohras today refer to as the ritual of the *ʿalama*. Through the lens of social practice, we see that its inscription continues to fulfil the same function as the Fatimid *ʿalama*: as a royal seal of the *daʿwa* meant to authorise *something* officially. In the absence of an Imam in modern times, it is the Dai, and not the Caliph-Imam, who provides his royal seal of approval in the community through his signature. As a proper *ʿalama*, the Dai does not sign with his name, but with the *basmala*, often paired with the *hamdala*. He writes *ʿala'im* not only on the occasion of the new fiscal year but also throughout the year. Believers seek his blessings through the inscription of the *ʿalama* in all life events, from moving into a new home, to solving legal conflicts, to naming a baby. The *ʿalama*, I witnessed, thus functions as a royal decree to believers. Whereas the Bohras have ritualised this documentary practice through ceremony and protocol, one can thus speak of a continuity in the *hamdala* as a signature *ʿalama* from the Faṭimid period. However, a seeming discontinuity, or novelty, is the *basmala* as an authenticating practice, which was never part of the original Fatimid *ʿalama* protocol. We return to the *ʿalama*, the *sijill*, and other documentary practices of the community in the following chapter.

The writing of the *ʿalama* is only one of the many services the Bohra clerics provide. The majority of believers, I observed, requested an audience with the Dai to seek what they called 'spiritual guidance'. Spiritual guidance, I learned, came in many forms, the most practised form being healing rituals. In front of my own eyes, babies were blessed, fathers would get magic cords with blessed knots (in which the Dai's breath was blown) meant for their pregnant daughters to tie around the belly to safeguard the pregnancy, and men and women would enter the office with empty bottles to get holy water to calm down temperamental family members. In the last case, the Dai would write little notes containing qur'anic verses mixed with purified water meant to be eaten. On other occasions, quarrelling families would come and seek the Dai's assistance to intervene or would ask for legal advice concerning financial issues such as inheritance or dowry; they would ask for permission for the son or daughter to get engaged, and then receive the blessing through coconuts (which are used on

[93] Samuel Stern traced this practice of sealing documents back to as early as the Abbasid period; it continued until the early Mamluk period. S. M. Stern, *Fatimid Decrees: Original Documents from the Fatimid Chancery* (London: Faber & Faber, 1964), 123–65.

[94] The pairing of the *basmala* and the *hamdala* can be seen in Stern, *Fatimid Decrees*, plate 17. Marina Rustow, *The Lost Archive: Traces of a Caliphate in a Cairo Synagogue* (Princeton: Princeton University Press, 2020), 268.

[95] See Akkerman, 'Documentary Remains of a Fatimid Past in Gujarat'.

various occasions, such as weddings).[96] Finally, the Dai and Mazoon Saheb would read qur'anic omens, a popular practice I discuss in Chapter 5. Most of these rituals or ceremonies were intimate and often emotional affairs; this was especially true for occasions when families would pressure excommunicated members to repent and to ask the Dai for mercy. Some believers came alone to seek guidance on very private matters; others, it seemed, brought along the entire *mohallah*.[97] The Dai's office was no larger than twenty-five square metres and was crowded with believers from morning until evening.

Just as believers would experience an audience with the Pope or the Dalai Lama as a once-in-a-lifetime occasion, to my neighbours and friends in Badri Mohallah these moments of closeness to their Dai were very special. Talismans, in particular, but also other documents that contained his written word were carefully kept and treasured for ever at their homes or in special pouches. The sacred materiality of the Dai's book hand was considered as important as the content of these documents dealing with legal affairs of the mundane. As such, I realised, the Dai's authority is thus inscribed in believers' lives from birth to death through documents.

The documentary culture of the Alawis is, of course, not restricted to written texts meant for the community, nor is it a one-way affair. Time and time again I witnessed how believers would hand (or throw) their written requests for *du'a*, wrapped in rupee notes, to the Bhai Sahebs and their entourage during official gatherings, hoping to reach the Dai. The modest size of the Alawi community makes the distance between common believer and Dai relatively small and rather personal, notwithstanding royal etiquette. This close contact would be unthinkable in the much larger Dawoodi context. Reaching the royal family via *du'a* notes or having the Dai present at one's wedding or other ceremonies has become costly, only affordable by the happy few. In addition to its manuscript corpus, the *daʿwa* also keeps and produces a wide array of documents for internal usage. I discuss these documents and their codicology and social usage, including the Dai's personal notes, lectures and sermons, in Chapter 5.

1.4 An Indian Muslim Caste

The Alawis see their universe and Faatemi way of living as strictly adhering to an identity that is Indian, Fatimi Tayyibi Isma'ili, Shi'i and, most importantly, Muslim. Yet without exception, my interlocutors would refer to their community as the Alawi 'caste'. To them, there seemed no discrepancy between their Muslim identity and seeing their community as a caste. In fact, they addressed all other communities in Baroda, such as the Parsis, the Khojas, the Memons or the Jains, in a similar manner. I wondered whether this was merely a linguistic matter or whether there was more at stake.

The longer I immersed myself in the everyday life of Badri Mohallah, the more I noticed how the community integrated various local customs of Gujarat – and South Asia at large – into their rituals and ceremonies. For instance, coconuts,

96 The coconut is a popular symbol in the context of ritual practice in Gujarat among communities of various denominations and is commonly used during weddings and other ceremonies.

97 I describe my presence and positionality during these private sessions in Chapter 3.

flower petals and garlands would always be present during festive occasions, such as birthdays, the *niṣbat* (engagement) and the *nikah* as symbols of fertility, prosperity and auspiciousness. During these celebrations the Dai himself would ritually bless fresh coconuts with his *rūḥ* (spirit): he would blow his breath into the coconut and wave it over the heads of the believers (from right to left, three times; Figure 1.14). Afterwards, the blessed coconut would be broken into pieces and consumed by the family or distributed along with the wedding invitation (in the case of an engagement). Sweets have a similar symbolic meaning. For instance, it is customary that when families arrange the engagement of their son or daughter, the Dai blows his *du'a* on a plate of sugar cubes brought by the father of the bride. These sugar cubes, which have taken on a function as a talisman, are distributed among family members. In addition to edible condiments, the Dai also infuses water with verses of the Qur'an with his *ruh*, transforming it into *ba barakat* (holy water, lit. 'with baraka') water, which is either used for ingesting in case of illness or is evaporated in the believer's home or business.[98]

Figure 1.14 The late Dai blowing his *ruh* in the coconut during an engagement ceremony.

[98] https://www.alavibohra.org/Taiyebi%20rasm%20-%20Dhaaru.htm (last accessed 14 May 2019).

In the context of Alawi Bohra ritual and ceremony, the materiality of simple objects, such as a bottle of water, a string, a coconut or a coin, can thus acquire new sacred qualities through the mediation of the Dai by acts of touching, writing or even breathing. The objects being such, their social life as 'things' thus changes radically from having no special meaning to becoming artefacts of veneration, consumption and healing. Even though the manuscripts of the *khizana* do have a specific meaning already attached to them as sacred objects only accessible through ritual and initiation, in a similar vein their social lives, as we shall see in the following chapters, are also subject to change. As such, secret manuscripts can thus become objects of veneration, consumption and healing as much as coconuts and sugar cubes can.

Marriage ceremonies are another example of a practice where local Indic rituals, known as the *shadi*, and Muslim traditions, the *nikah*, meet. I happened to be in Baroda during the marriage season and was privileged enough to observe both ceremonies, which take place separately. While living in a small *mohallah* such as the Alawi one, it is impossible not to observe the *shadi*: the procession of the groom is an extremely loud affair. Mian Bhai Abdul Hussain, a Dawoodi Bohra scholar, described the experiences as follows: '*Like Hindus they take out the bridegroom to bride's house in procession on horse with music, tomtom, fireworks, and in case of rich persons, with illumination* (fireworks).'[99] The *shadi* rituals, which are a standard feature of most Bollywood films, take place separately in the future bride's and groom's family homes before the procession. They include the decoration of the bride with *henna* and *haldi* (turmeric) and the performing of *ārthī* (an Indic *puja* ritual of burning ghee and singing Bohra devotional songs). The *nikah*, in contrast, is a public occasion where relatives and friends of both the bride and groom attend the wedding ceremony, which takes place at the clerical headquarters. Its rituals include the personal consent of the Dai and of the bride and the groom, the presence of a *walī* (guardian), and the segregation of the sexes during the ceremony, which is followed by the blessing of the Dai and the exchange of the *mahr* (dowry). Whereas it is customary in the Dawoodi community for the *mahr* to consist of the symbolic number of 786 rupees (the numeral equivalent of the Arabic letters resembling the *basmala*), in the Alawi community the *mahr* was recently fixed by the Bhai Sahebs as 1,000 rupees.[100] Again, we see that objects play an important ceremonial role. In addition to coconuts, sweets and flowers, ceremonial *nikah* objects are the *sehra*, a beaded veil worn by the groom, and the *rakhi*, a golden piece of cloth under which the groom and the father-in-law interlace fingers under the ceremonial eye of the Dai to seal the bond between the two families (Figure 1.15).

The various other ceremonies that are central in the lives of believers, such as birth ceremonies, taking the oath of allegiance in front of the community (see Chapter 3) and funerals, are carried out according to a similar choreography. An essential part of these ceremonies is the communal *thali* that is consumed in the *jamaat khana*. Having shared many rounds of mutton biryani and kulfi ice cream, I learned that the *thali* is much more than sharing a meal together. It creates a social bond and, through ritual

99 *Gulzare Daudi for the Bohras of India*, 73. It should be noted that this study was published over a hundred years ago, yet I observed many of the rituals the author described in Baroda.

100 Blank, Mullahs on the Mainframe, 55.

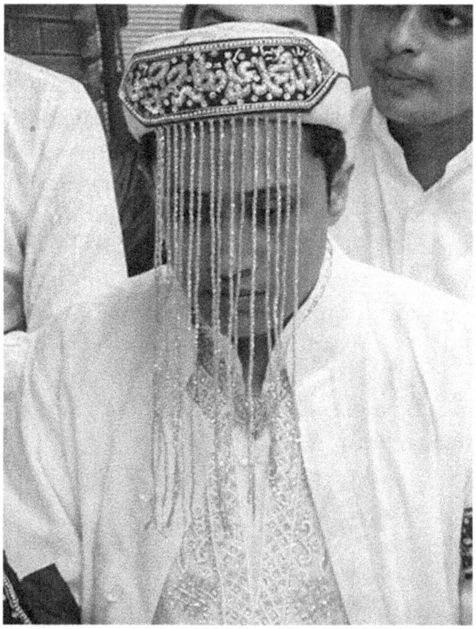

Figure 1.15 *Nikah sehra* (veil) of the groom, with a beaded inscription that reads *Allah, Muhammad, Ali, Fatima, Husayn, Hasan.*

and etiquette, has an aura of religiosity attached to it, such as sitting in the modest 'Bhai Saheb' posture (sitting on the knees) and observing ritual purity. According to Blank, this habitus is based on Gujarati Vaishya traditions that have been transferred to an Islamic context.[101]

Another example in this regard is the Alawis' belief in auspicious and inauspicious days for carrying out certain acts, events or ceremonies; they are calculated through astrology and must be taken into account before proceeding. For instance, it is considered bad luck to buy a house or get married on a day that is inauspicious. Blank describes this tradition, which he considers to be a Fatimid–Gujarati confluence, as follows:

> Among the Gujarati folk beliefs common at this time was ascription of auspiciousness to the performance of certain tasks on certain days of the week: Sunday was said to be good for naming a child, eating a new dish, wearing new clothes, tilling land, or learning a new skill, but bad for buying a house or setting out on a journey; Monday was good for laying the foundation for a house, sending a bride to her husband's home, or bartering an animal; Tuesday, lucky for business or for taking a bath after an illness; Wednesday, good for shaving, changing residence, or learning a new lesson, but bad for buying a cow.[102]

[101] Ibid., 214.

[102] Ibid., 54. Blank considers the astrological aspect of it, especially, to be of Fatimid origin. See also Abdul Hussain, Gulzare Daudi for the Bohras of India, 83.

Similarly, the Alawis consider omens to be crucial factors in determining the auspiciousness or inauspiciousness of dates and times for making personal decisions and investments, travelling, or celebrating religious ceremonies. Omens are generally taken from the Qur'an (see Chapter 5) or from non-religious sources; for example, the appearance of certain animals, such as birds. Furthermore, the Alawis practise various popular rituals to ward off the evil eye and malevolent spirits, such as lighting firecrackers, playing loud musical instruments during processions, engaging in practices of exorcism, tying magical knots, reading astrological charts and tables, burning incense, eating a pinch of salt before dinner and wearing lucky coins. As a woman in the community, I also observed various rituals during menstruation, such as self-isolation and gender segregation, and rituals regarding the disposal of personal hygiene items (which are believed to attract evil spirits). Other aspects influenced by local Gujarati traditions, such as cuisine, the *rida*, living conditions, architecture, aesthetics and language, are discussed separately in Chapters 2, 3 and 6.

Are Bohras Brahmins?

Following processes of colonialism and globalisation in the late nineteenth and mid-twentieth century, the Bohras, alongside the Khojas, went through several waves of reform that focused on Islamisation and the elimination of practices and traditions of a Hindu past.[103] Despite these reforms, many Gujarati traditions remain central to the Bohra communal identity today, whether in the Alawi, the Dawoodi or even the Suleymani context.[104] It is a unique confluence of practices, rituals and references which to the Alawis, whether they are Fatimid, Yemeni or Gujarati, are in no way in conflict with one another, nor seen as 'syncretic': they constitute what it means to be Bohra.

The question of caste origins, however, and the community's conversion from Hinduism, remain controversial, especially in the current political climate of India. In fact, this is the subject of heated debate, as many theories exist yet very few contemporary historical accounts are available. Two sources should be mentioned in this regard: *Muntazaʿ al-Akhbār*, written in Arabic by the Dawoodi Bohra Quṭb al-Dīn Sulaymānjī Burhānpūrī (d. 1241/1826), and the earlier-mentioned *Mawsim-e Bahār* written in *Lisan al-Daʿwa*.[105] Interestingly, instead of focusing on the Fatimids, the dominant narrative in these sources revolves around the Yemeni Dais, and the notion that, prior to conversion, the majority of Bohras were Gujarati Hindus of the Vaishya mercantile caste, who converted en masse as early as the Fatimid period when

[103] For example, Jonah Blank mentions that, prior to the reign of Sy. Muhammad Burhanuddin and his reforms of Islamisation, Bohras followed Hindu inheritance law. Blank, *Mullahs on the Mainframe*, 8, 93. See also Michel Boivin. 'Institutions et production normative chez les ismaéliens d'Asie du Sud', *Studia Islamica* 88 (1998), 158, 159.

[104] I draw here on my own observations, as well as Blank's numerous descriptions in his ethnography (see previous notes).

[105] Quṭb al-Dīn Sulaymānjī Burhānpūrī, ed. Samer F. Traboulsi (Beirut: Dār al-Gharb al-Islāmī, 1999). *Mawsim-i bahār fī akhbār al- ṭāhirīn al-akhyār*. See also Poonawala, *Biobibliography* 217. For a short historical overview see my thesis, Chapter 1.

Caliph-Imam al-Mustanṣir (d. 497/1094) sent his Dais to Gujarat from Yemen.[106] Tahera Qutbuddin mentions that certain Bohra families, including that of the Dawoodi royal family, claim that their ancestry can be traced to clans of the Rajput caste.[107] Even though the Alawi royal family does not distinguish itself in terms of caste, it does consider itself to be of a separate, aristocratic class. As I described earlier, the Alawi community is divided into different classes, depending on the ancestry of one's family, a notion that is undoubtedly linked to caste heritage. For instance, Alawi families who intermarried with outsiders to the community (of different castes) have a different status, as they are considered impure. This statement, once made by the Mukasir Saheb, already indicates that the community is not as homogeneous as the theory of mass conversion of the Vaishya mercantile caste makes us believe.

Scholarship on Hindu–Muslim conversion in Gujarat has shown that throughout history waves of conversion occurred, and that multiple castes, including *dalits* (members of untouchable communities), joined the initial Muslim converts.[108] Michel Boivin and others have demonstrated that, contrary to the community's narrative, the Khojas were derived from multiple artisanal and agricultural castes that came together as late as the nineteenth century under the new religious dispensation of the Agha Khan.[109] We could hypothesise that, in what Samira Sheikh calls the 'religious marketplace' of Gujarat, agricultural and artisanal castes were converted by the original Dais from Yemen forming the basis of the original Bohra community, which, in later centuries, increased in size as new waves of converts joined the *da'wa*.[110] In this religious market-place, she describes how Isma'ili groups and their traditions are sites of internal contestation, a process that continues throughout history to the development of modern religious identity.[111] Although not outwardly acknowledged, today these assimilative processes continue to operate within the Alawi community, as non-Bohra Muslim women from other parts of India intermarry in the community.

The question of the caste origins of the Bohras, and of Muslims in Gujarat in general, has recently become the subject of speculation and political discourse in India. When searching for 'Bohras' online, surprisingly, one of the first suggested hits on Google and various social media accounts is 'Are Bohras Brahmins?'.[112] Members of the Rashtriya Swayamsevak Sangh (RSS), a right-wing Hindu nationalist party in India

106 *Muntaza' al-akhbār fī akhbār al-du'āt al-akhyār*, ed. Samer F. Traboulsi. On the *da'wa* to India: Daftary, *The Ismā'īlis*, 276, 277. Hollister, *The Shi'a of India* 267–71. Hamdani, Husain F., 'The Letters of Al-Mustanṣir bi'llāh', *Bulletin of the School of Oriental Studies*, University of London, vol. 7, no. 2 (1934), 308. On the Bohras' Vaishya descent: Qutbuddin, E.I. three. Blank, *Mullahs on the Mainframe*, 14. Annemarie Schimmel, *Islam in the Indian Subcontinent* (Leiden: Brill, 1980), 70. See also Abu Zafir Nadir, 'The Origin of the Bohras', *Is. Cul.*, 8, 639. Sheikh, *Forging a Region*, 149. R. E. Enthoven, *The Tribes and Castes of Bombay* (Mumbai: Governmental Press, 1920), 197.

107 Qutbuddin, 'The Daudi Bohra Ṭayyibīs', 345. Blank, *Mullahs on the Mainframe*, 14.

108 Michel Boivin, *Les âghâ khâns et les Khojah: Islam chiite et dynamiques sociales dans le sous-continent indien (1843–1954)* (Paris: Karthala, 2013). Samira Sheikh, *Forging a Region*. Dominque-Sila Khan, *Conversions and Shifting Identities: Ramdev pir and the Isma'ilis in Rajasthan* (New Delhi: Manohar, 1997).

109 Michel Boivin, *Les âghâ khâns et les Khojah*, 44. See also *La Renovation du Shi'isme Ismaelien en Inde et au Pakistan. D'après les Ecrits et les Discours de Sultan Muhammad Shah Aga Khan* (London: Routledge, 2003).

110 Sheikh, *Forging a Region*, 162.

111 Ibid., 153.

112 Google, consulted 23 February 2020.

that has the re-conversion of Muslims to Hinduism on its agenda, recently claimed that that the Bohras originally were Nagar Brahmin families who were forced into conversion. As a result, the RSS has reportedly implemented a programme of re-conversion of Muslims in Gujarat, especially targeting Bohras due to their alleged Brahmin roots.[113] The theme of re-conversion seems to spark resonance inter-communally, as Mufaddal Saifuddin, the current Dai of the Dawoodis, urged the Alawis to re-convert to the Dawoodis in one of his speeches five years ago. So far as I was able to find out, no Alawis 're-converted' to the 'Dawoodi caste' or 'back' to Hinduism.

The specifics of the caste origins of the Bohras may remain ambiguous, yet what is clear is that a Hindu past of some sort is reflected in many characteristics of their *daʿwas* that go far beyond the earlier-mentioned occasional rituals. The position of the clerical sacerdotal royal family among the Alawis is the most striking example. Marc Gaborieau argues that there were limits to the conversion to Islam in South Asia, as he describes how Muslim *sayyids* took over the position of Brahman priests among *dalits* who converted to Islam. He argues that the Brahmans, with Sanskrit as their sacred language, were replaced by Muslim religious experts for the performance of rituals chanting verses in Arabic.[114]

In the Bohra context we see a similar structure where the Dai is the sole custodian and interpreter of the sacred texts. The recitation or chanting of these sacred texts is referred to as *chalisa*, a term that in Hindu practice has the sense of a devotional hymn. Through protocol and guidance, it is the Dai who is the mediator between the divine – personified in the messianic figure of the hidden Imam – and believers. His omnipresent position and spiritual hegemony in believers' lives, based on an uninterrupted and what is seen as an unpolluted bloodline, are fully ritualised through traditions of initiation. On the one hand, the *daʿwa* follows the principle of egalitarianism where every believer is equal, thus going against Hindu laws of caste hierarchy. Yet at the same time the *daʿwa* consists of different clerical ranks which believers have to adhere to, of which some are inaccessible to believers. As I described earlier, these *darajat* are embedded in rites of passage and through practice, the most striking being the practice of the *qadam-bosi*, or the kissing of the feet of the Bhai Sahebs by believers as a sign of showing respect.

These ideas seem to reinforce our earlier discussion on the mercantile orientation of the Bohras and how their identity is a continuation of what Jonah Blank calls 'the pre-Islamic Vaishya ethic'.[115] Interestingly, my shopkeeper neighbours told me that, although the holy month of Muharram is seen as the religious New Year, Diwali is used as the start of their fiscal year.[116] In addition to trade customs, the central importance of practising *tahara*, which permeates the smallest details of believers' daily lives, such as dining and sartorial practices, was already briefly discussed in this context. I was told that all Alawis do not mix in any possible way with any other Muslim (Sunni or Shi'i), Hindu or Jain 'caste': they do not interact with, inter-marry with, eat food

[113] https://economictimes.indiatimes.com/news/politics-and-nation/sanghs-ghar-wapsi-event-in-full-swing-in-gujarat/articleshow/45611337.cms (last accessed 23 February 2020).

[114] Gaborieau, *Typologie des specialists religieux chez les musulmans du sous-continent indien*, 29–52.

[115] Blank, *Mullahs on the Mainframe*, 203.

[116] Blank reports a similar practice among the Dawoodis. Blank, *Mullahs on the Mainframe*, 174.

prepared by or dine with Hindus, or wear clothes made or washed by non-Bohris. In fact, as a *mohallah* in the old Mughal city of Baroda, the Alawi Bohra universe functions in such a way that it does not need to: it is remarkably self-sufficient, and believers only interact with the outside world when required to mix. Adhering to the laws of ritual purity, including in culinary practices, is thus one of the basic requirements of community. The Alawis faced a schism in the late twelfth/eighteenth century, when a group of believers, calling themselves Nagoshiyyas (no-meat eaters), left the community following their excommunication by the Dai in 1204/1789. The Alawi Nāgoshiyyas, of which today I was not able to trace any followers, were a messianic movement, which claimed that the *dawr* (cycle) of Muhammad had ended, and they practised various Hindu traditions related to ritual purity, such as vegetarianism.[117]

The Alawis' emphasis on ritual purity, and its link to class, culinary practice, skin colour and other physical features, is another striking link to local Hindu notions of caste. According to Blank, the Bohras' notion of *tahara* is a combination of Fatimid doctrine and Vaishya standards of ritual cleanliness.[118] Among the Alawis I observed that the laws of ritual purity apply especially in the realm of personal hygiene, aesthetics and morality. For instance, it is a religious obligation to perform an extra *ghusl* (ritual ablution) before prayer and to dress in white while doing so. Female genital mutilation (FGM) is a highly sensitive but widely practised tradition among the Bohra communities, including the Alawis, and is seen as a religious obligation as part of 'our *tahara*'. The challenges I faced while working in the *khizana*, and issues relating to my personal *tahara* as a non-Bohra woman, were already mentioned in this regard.

Finally, ritual purity is of special significance in relation to how the Alawis position themselves vis-à-vis the materiality, and untouchability, of the sacred objects of their *daʿwa*. The Dai, as we have seen, is the sole custodian of the *khizana* and its sacred manuscripts, which can only be accessed by a small number of the highest clerics, after strict protocols of rituals purity and initiation (see Chapter 6). Not only is the *khizana* inaccessible to non-clerics, but also its sacred manuscripts can under no circumstance be touched by the ritually uninitiated and impure. The Dais, like the Brahmans, are the only individuals in their community who have the ceremonial right to touch, read and initiate. To the Bohras, their Imams, and thus indirectly their Dais, are considered the most pure in terms of intellect, heart and deeds, and therefore they are always referred to as the *'a'imma al-ṭāhīhrīn* (pure Imams). The difference in this regard from Brahmanic notions of touching sacred objects is that common believers are considered impure. Aniket Jaaware describes how, in the context of caste and untouchables, regulations on touching things were transposed – through convenient metonymies – onto people.[119] A parallel can certainly be drawn here between the untouchability of the manuscripts of the *khizana* and that of the Dai and Bhai Sahebs, with whom believers can only come in physical contact through kissing or touching the feet, the least pure part of the body.

[117] According to the Mazoon Saheb, all Nagoshiyya families eventually converted back into the Alawi community. See also Poonawala, *Biobibliography* 13 and Daftary, *The Ismāʿīlis*, 282.

[118] Blank, *Mullahs on the Mainframe*, 172.

[119] Aniket Jaaware, *Practicing Caste. On Touching and Not Touching* (New York: Fordham University Press, 2019), 164.

Through these special modalities of access to the *khizana*, the hegemonic position of the clerics is legitimised and enforced through their own exclusiveness as royals, while at the same time communal cohesion is enhanced. Kala Shreen has described very similar patterns among the Nagarathar Vaiyshas in Tamil Nadu and their relationship to material sacred material culture.[120] The social practices that surround the Alawi *khizana* and its manuscript culture should thus be seen as a confluence of a Hindu-Indic caste structure and an Arabic Isma'ili manuscript tradition. This confluence is crucial for understanding why and how the treasury of books works, and the Bohras' relationship with its inaccessible collection, as I explore further in the next chapter.

Final Notes to Chapter 1: Shrine of a Parrot Saint

This chapter began with a discussion of the materiality of the Ahmedabad *nass* roll of Saraspur and the significance of its existence as a secret manuscript with an important social life as the founding document of the Alawis. The city of Ahmebadad, however, had something else in store for me. It shed light on another aspect of the Alawi community that I could not have understood properly without having spent more time in its *qabaristan* in Saraspur.

My experience of the Saraspur graveyard the morning after the remembrance of the martyrdom of Ali Shamsuddin could not have been more different from the tense atmosphere I sensed during the *ʿurs*. In broad daylight, the graveyard turned out to be a surprisingly peaceful, lavishly green and spotlessly clean space inhabited by peacocks and other tropical birds, parading through what seemed to be a sea of white, polished-marble shrines. While exploring the many burial tombs of Saraspur, I was chaperoned by Hussain, a young and rather shy Ahmedabadi Alawi who was instructed to show me around but was too embarrassed to talk to me and therefore decided to focus on the birds instead. While feeding the peacocks, we stumbled upon a section of white graves marked by red stars. Husayn told me that this was a special section devoted to Bohra *shuhadāʾ* (martyrs), who were killed or tortured under Mughal rule.

Next to the majestic mausoleums of the Dawoodi Dais, one martyr's grave caught my attention. It was a small white shrine with a red star built in the wall, overgrown with money plants (Figure 1.16). The grave it enshrined was very small, about the size of a shoe-box, and was covered with fresh rose petals. Given its size I suspected this was the grave of a young child. Hussain, however, informed me that this was a very special grave, which was indeed devoted to a martyr of the community, but not a believer (Figure 1.17). Here lay the remains of the legendary 'holy parrot', he told me, belonging to one of the Dais of the eleventh/seventeenth century. Legend has it that this parrot was not merely the beloved pet of the royal family. In fact, the parrot was a *ḥāfiẓ* (memoriser of the Qur'an), having been part of the most learned scholarly family of the community. According to the tradition, the bird had memorised the Qur'an by heart and was thus able to eloquently recite the *suras* of the holy Qur'an in the quarters of the royal family. The bird's life came to an end after it was brutally killed under

[120] Kala Shreen, 'Socio-cultural Dimensions of Ritual Objects: Nagarathar Rites of Passage', *International Journal of Interdisciplinary Social Sciences* vol. 5, no. 5 (2010).

Figure 1.16 The grave of the *shahid* parrot. Saraspur, Ahmedabad.

Figure 1.17 Hussain feeding the peacocks at the Saraspur graveyard, Ahmedabad.

the reign of Mughal emperor Aurangzeb (d. 1119/1707), together with its master, the Dawoodi Dai Sy. Quṭub Khān Quṭbuddīn (no. 32, d. 1058/1648), also referred to as Qutubuddin al-Shaheed (Qutbuddin the Martyr), after charges were levelled against him of apostasy.[121] This, I was told, is how the parrot became a martyr and was buried at the *shahīd* section of the *qabaristan* of Saraspur. The fame of the *hafiz* parrot continued far beyond its allegedly tragic end. Throughout the centuries, the parrot became a patron saint for children with speech impediments and hearing problems, and its grave was turned into a modest shrine. As such, it became a sacred space for prayer and *du'a* for parents and families, a tradition, Hussain told me, that continues to this day.

The symbolism of the martyr-parrot as a saint for the mute and deaf is significant. Parrots, I learned, are considered sacred animals in South Asia as they are associated with Hindu deities and appear in devotional literature. Due to their auspicious character, parrots are popular pets in Gujarat and across the Indian Ocean, and they are found in textiles, such as the *patola patan* (a local *ikat* weave), and vernacular architecture, and on the structures of ships.[122] The heads of parrots are also common motifs on the busts of the Dhows from Kutch and decorate the wooden façades of historic houses in Gujarat and East Africa.[123] Moreover, pet parrots feature in tales and popular stories, such as the earlier-discussed *Rasa'il Ikhwan al-Safa*, the Persian *Tutinameh* (The Parrot Book), Sanskrit *Sukasaptati*, the fables of *Kalīla wa Dimna* (Persian literature) and *Alf Layla wa Layla* (Thousand and One Nights). In these stories the birds appear as messengers of love, good fortune and morals; as storytellers; and even as astrologers.[124]

I came across manuscript copies of these popular stories in the *khizana* and various private Bohra collections, not knowing that, in the *Tutinameh*, a speaking parrot is the protagonist, who describes himself as a faithful Muslim, wearing green (the colour of the Prophet) and reciting the Qur'an as *hafiz*.[125] Pious pets parroting holy verses, I learned, is also is a trope in Hindu devotional literature, where talking parrots reportedly chant the Vedas in Sanskrit.[126] The Bohras are thus not alone in integrating this South Asian trope into their local shrine culture in Ahmedabad.

The parrot, however, was also a beloved symbol of a civilisation on the other side of the western Indian Ocean, so highly revered by the Bohras: the Fatimids. The Mamluk historian al-Maqrīzī (d. 845/1442) describes how Caliph-Imam al-Ẓāfir

[121] See, for a detailed account of the trial and execution of Sy. Qutub Khan Qutbuddin, and the persecution of the Bohras under Aurangzeb, Sheikh, 'Aurangzeb as Seen from Gujarat', 9–13.

[122] See the example of the dhows from Kutch, named Kotia. John H. A. Jewell, *Dhows at Mombasa* (Nairobi: East African Publishing House, 1976), 49, and *The Life of the Red Sea Dhow: A Cultural History of Seaborne Exploration in the Islamic World* (London: Bloomsbury, 2019), 168.

[123] Jay Thakkar, *Naqsh: The Art of Wood Carving in Traditional Houses of Gujarat* (Ahmedabad: Research Cell, 2008), 58, 59, 131, 143.

[124] Richard Lenn E. Goodman, *The Case of the Animals versus Man Before the King of the Jinn* (Oxford: Oxford University Press, 2009), 17, 180, 269, 272.

[125] Richard Foltz, *Animals in Islamic Traditions and Muslim Cultures* (London: One World Publications, 2006), the parrot book.

[126] Alf Hiltebeitel, *Rethinking the Mahabharata: A Reader's Guide to the Education of the Dharma King* (Chicago: University of Chicago Press, 2001), 269, f. 53. Somadeva Bhaṭṭa (trans.) *Kathasaritasagara* (New Delhi: Penguin, 1994), 149. See also David Pinault, *Notes from the Fortune-telling parrot: Religious Pluralism in Pakistan* (London: Equinox, 2008).

(d. 549/1154) kept a white parrot in his royal palace, which would recite short qur'anic *suras*.[127] 'Parrot' or '*babaghā*' was a common nickname for the favourite *wazirs* of the Caliph-Imams, and the colourful birds were a beloved theme in Fatimid material culture, such as in cast bronze scent bottles, incense burners, ceramics, textiles, and the famous rock crystal ewers.[128] Commissioned by the Caliph-Imams and carved out of a single piece of flawless rock crystal, these ewers were so costly that they were stored in the Fatimid royal *khizana*.[129]

One could argue that a crystal carafe from medieval Egypt and a parrot saint from Mughal Ahmedabad might not necessarily have anything in common. After all, as objects they were created in socio-political and historical contexts that could not be more different, nor could their social usage differ more. Yet, in the universe of the Bohras, these worlds might not be as far apart as they seem. As a symbol, the parrot is a powerful signifier that represents the confluence of the many worlds that the Alawi Bohras bring together in their universe: the worlds of a Muslim community of Shi'i Isma'ilis originating from Yemen, organised along (caste) structures reminiscent of a distant Hindu past, crystallised in a Neo-Fatimid identity, represented in a small shrine of a *hafiz* parrot martyr of the Dai from Gujarat. The Alawis' Faatemi way of life, we have seen so far, comprises a set of beliefs and practices that are deeply rooted in the intellectual traditions of the Fatimids and their successors in Yemen – through jurisprudence, the notion of cyclical time, the 'presence' of a hidden Imam and the spiritual hegemony of the Dai, and the organisation of the *da'wa*. Their Neo-Fatimid identity, as I have argued, is thus practised in everyday life through jurisprudence and ritual and expressed through sartorial practices, documentary culture, and ceremonies in which the Fatimid Imams are honoured. Sceptics may say that the doctrinal beliefs, traditions and practices of the Bohras described in this chapter are modern reconstructions, not unknown to other Isma'ili groups. Yet as we move on to the next chapter, we see what material evidence the treasury of books enshrines, which forms the material evidence for the Fatimid–Gujarati link.

127 Taqī al-Dīn Abū al-'Abbās Aḥmad ibn 'Alī ibn 'Abd al-Qādir ibn Muḥammad al-Maqrizi. Muhammad Abd al-Qadir Ahmad Ata (ed.), *Itti'āz al-Ḥunafā' bi-Akhbār al-A'immah al-Fāṭimīyīn al-Khulafā'* (Beirut: Dar al-Kutub al-Ilmiyya, 1996) Vol. 1, 273.

128 Anna Contadini, *Fatimid Art at the Victoria and Albert Museum* (London: V&A Publications, 1998), see Chapter 1: 'Rock Crystal: Rock Crystal Pieces in the V&A'.

129 The Fatimid ewers led to a landmark sale for auction house Christies in 2008, see https://www.christies.com/presscenter/pdf/09102008/11133.pdf (last accessed 24 February 2020).

Chapter 2

Treasury of Books

Dar al-Kutub, Cairo, Egypt

In search of Fatimid manuscripts as a student, I found myself in the dusty Cairene reading rooms of a *khizana* very different from the one I would observe in Baroda many years later. I had come to *Dar al-Kutub*, the National Library of Egypt, housed in the historic Khedivian building of *Bab al-Khalq*, to consult copies of a treatise I discussed previously, Qadi al-Nuʿman's *Daʿa'im al-Islam*. Access to *Dar al-Kutub*'s manuscript collection, I had learned, was a notoriously painstaking process and was therefore almost considered a rite of passage that all philologists, historians and manuscript enthusiasts had to undergo at least once.[1] Prepared for the ritual of providing the librarians with the required letters and stamps and then sitting out the long wait that would follow, I was pleasantly surprised when a rather stern-looking woman informed me that the manuscript would be ready by the following morning.

Manuscripts, without fail, have surprises in store for their scholarly admirers. After all, they are not printed books but are handwritten and therefore unique objects: no manuscript is the same, even if the copyist tried to produce an identical copy. Over the years, I have learned that someone can consult a manuscript with a certain purpose in mind, yet traces of its past social lives will inevitably take the reader into completely different realms and directions. In this respect, manuscripts can be a revelation, leading to unexpected finds and moments of euphoria, but can also lead one down a rabbit hole, as one is faced with much more than one bargained for. Before the scholar knows it, the research takes unexpected turns as marginal notes, inventories, scribbles, stains and other fascinating peculiarities take hold. Resistance is futile.

This is exactly what happened to me in *Dar al-Kutub*. Upon my return the next day, my excitement instantly faded away when I was confronted with another rite of passage of going to the archives: the collective disappointment that codicologists experience when being provided with a microfiche instead of a physical codex. Making sense of the intricate details of the social lives of manuscripts on a microfiche machine is far from ideal, as codicologists crave the materiality of the codex. As I made myself familiar with the creaking microfiche machine and scrolled through the folios of the *Daʿa'im*, I soon realised this manuscript was not the Fatimid unicum I had hoped for. Its book hand, written in Arabic *naskh*, seemed erratic and curly, and to my surprise its marginalia were written in Gujarati (owner statements), Persian (poetry), Arabic

[1] See Jan Just Witkam for a vivid but dated account of working with manuscripts in *Dar al-Kutub*: Jan Just Witkam, 'Manuscripts & Manuscripts. Research Facilities for Manuscripts in the Egyptian National Library', *Manuscripts of the Middle East 2* (1987), 111–15.

(*du'as*) and English (vocabulary exercises). A rather strange-looking phrase in Arabic caught my attention on the second flyleaf, '*dalhīrutlām dāyrikt kār*', yet I was not able to understand its meaning (Figure 2.1).

As I read on, I discovered that this manuscript, which had been authorised by someone as *ṣāḥiḥ* (Ar.; 'correct') on the first flyleaf, belonged to a gentleman named Lakhbhai Shaikh Abdulhussein Rampuri. It began to dawn on me that, instead of a Fatimid copy, what I had in front of me was an Indian exemplar of the *Da'a'im al-Islam*, dating from the twentieth century. The provenance of the manuscript was clearly Indian, and Bohra, as it was written in *madḥ* (praise) of a certain Dai, whose name curiously was erased. As I became familiar with the book hand, I suddenly realised what the Arabic phrase meant: *dalhīrutlām dāyrikt kār* stood for *Delhi-Rutlam direct car*, which indicated that Rampuri had undertaken a journey, most probably a train ride, taking the manuscript with him from Delhi to Rutlam, a city in western Madhya Pradesh situated not far from the neighbouring state of Gujarat.

At the time, I was not aware of the geography of Gujarat and Madhya Pradesh, let alone the Bohras' link to a Fatimid past. My only encounter with Bohras had been in *shāri'at al-Mu'izz* (Mu'izz street) in Cairo and its heavily restored al-Hakim Mosque, where I had observed several Dawoodi Bohra women praying behind a curtain a few days earlier.[2] There were many questions I wanted to ask them, but since they were practising *taqiyya*, as I later found out, no one felt comfortable talking to me. The only Dawoodi woman I managed to make contact with in the polished marble courtyard of the mosque turned out to be deaf and mute, as her brother informed me.

Despite my lack of success with my Bohra interlocutors at the al-Hakim Mosque, the Bohras, through manuscripts and microfiches, continued to appear on my horizon in Cairo. As I scrolled through the folios of Ismaili *fiqh* on microfiche, I became aware

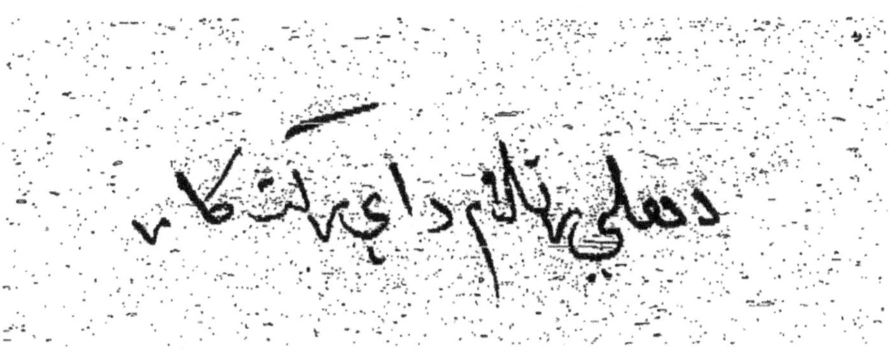

Figure 2.1 Marginal note, '*dalhī rutlām dāyrikt kār*', written on the second flyleaf of manuscript no. 49075, Dar al-Kutub. Credits: Dar al-Kutub al-Misriyya.

[2] The al-Hakim Mosque, among several other historic buildings dating back to the Fatimids, was restored heavily by the Dawoodi Bohras in the 1980s. See for a detailed analysis, and reception by the international community, Sanders, *Creating Medieval Cairo*, 118–29.

of the paradoxical situation of the social life of the *Da'a'im*. After all, Cairo had been the city where Qadi Nu'man had composed the *Da'a'im* more than a thousand years ago as the state compendium of law of Fatimid Egypt, after which his treatise was copied for over a millennium throughout its journey to Yemen, Gujarat and the Indian Ocean littoral up until the present day. Despite its significance for Egypt's intellectual and political history, the libraries of *Dar al-Kutub*, al-Azhar, Cairo University, or any other Egyptian institution for that matter, do not hold physical manuscript copies of the *Da'a'im* nor any other Ismaili works in their collections.[3]

The Bohras, alongside the Nizari Isma'ilis, have invested heavily in their reconstruction of Neo-Fatimid architecture in the city. Paula Sanders writes, 'Fatimid Cairo, to the Bohras, is neither Egyptian nor medieval . . . It remains "Fatimid Cairo". . . an Ismaili site that finds it meaning in the present. Its proper context, then, is the living Fatimid tradition.'[4] Although the old city of Cairo is full of examples of this living tradition through Fatimid or perhaps (re)claimed Neo-Fatimid architecture and inscriptions, the only traces of the written literary word of Fatimid Ismailism in Egypt are a handful of microfiches of manuscripts of Indian provenance.[5]

Scattered over several Egyptian universities and institutions, these microfiches have fascinating social lives themselves. They were donated by the late scholar and *Da'a'im* specialist Asaf A. Fyzee, who, as a Sulaymani Bohra, was the first Pakistani cultural counsellor of Egypt and later a professor of Semitic Philology and Persian at al-Azhar University and Cairo University; he also served as the Indian ambassador to Egypt in the 1950s.[6] In the introduction to this study, I discussed the power and politics of manuscript endowment, gift-giving and ownership. Although Fyzee is best-known for endowing Mumbai University with his private manuscript *khizana*, his donation of these microfiches to Cairene institutions was as meaningful, at least symbolically.[7] For the first time in eight centuries, Egypt's Fatimid intellectual heritage had returned to Cairo, the city of its origin, and home to what once was the *khizana* of all *khizanat*: the Fatimid royal treasury of books.

The story of the Fatimid *khizana*, however, does not end in the dusty reading rooms of *Dar al-Kutub*. In fact, what Sanders calls the living Fatimid tradition, as we have established, continues to flourish elsewhere in a different social and cultural environment. My search for treasures from the Fatimid *khizana* in Cairo led me to the Indian subcontinent, to the world of the Bohras, and their continuation of the Fatimid *khizana* tradition in Gujarat. More specifically, it led me to the universe of the Alawi Bohras, where Isma'ili manuscripts from Egypt and Yemen continue to be at the centre of the community's Neo-Fatimid identity in the present. To the Alawi

3 See also Ismail K. Poonawala, 'Isma'ili Manuscripts from Yemen', *Journal of Islamic Manuscripts* 5 (2014), 221, i2.

4 Sanders, *Creating Medieval Cairo*, 138.

5 For a thorough description on manifestations of the Fatimid public text, especially inscriptions on Fatimid architecture, see Irene A. Bierman, *Writing Signs: The Fatimid Public Text.*

6 See, for a biography of Hamdani, De Blois, *Arabic, Persian and Gujarati Manuscripts*, xxxiii.

7 The donation included 186 manuscripts in total, which are currently difficult to access. Muhammad Goriawala, *A Descriptive Catalogue of the Fyzee Collection of Ismaili Manuscripts* (Bombay: Bombay University Press, 1965).

Bohras, the Fatimid *khizana* of Cairo is the archetypical mother *khizana* of their intellectual tradition, an intellectual tradition that is seen as sacred and possesses an aura of evanescence.[8]

In Chapter 1, we examined how the Alawi Bohras practise their Neo-Fatimid identity today through their doctrinal beliefs, clerical hierarchy and rituals, and how they express their unique Gujarati 'Faatemi way of life' through ceremony, sartorial practices and documentary culture. I argued that, whether it be in the form of secret manuscripts that are ceremoniously revealed, popular talismans that protect, or the Dai's seal of authorisation, the Bohra clergy inscribe their authority through what Ann Stoler calls 'the force of writing', thereby asserting their status of omnipresence in the lives of believers through writing practices.[9]

This chapter is devoted to the space that domesticates, produces, preserves and enshrines this force of writing in the Alawi community: the Neo-Fatimid treasury of books. The Alawis, I argue, constitute their Neo-Fatimid identity through their treasury of books and the material existence of its manuscripts, which embody the community's uninterrupted link of manuscript transmission with the Fatimids. It would be a mistake, however, to think of the *khizana* as an inert repository of texts or a shrine, frozen in the history of its creation. On the contrary, in describing the social role of the *khizana*, we will see the community *at work*. Through this lens, it becomes an institution in which power relations are inscribed, social order is maintained, and custodians and community members become actors rather than passive caretakers and visitors. As the epicentre of the community, the treasury of books is thus very much alive, constantly in flux, and its social role is subject to change and negotiation, as it is contingent upon time and space.

As my experience of accessing, cataloguing, documenting, and simply being present in, the treasury of books was so deeply rooted in the world of the Alawi Bohras, this chapter, even more so than the rest of this study, is written from an emic perspective. Rather than relying on existing external notions of manuscript libraries and archives, I am interested in how the Alawis see their *khizana*. That is why the first part of this chapter focuses on the idea of the Neo-Fatimid treasury of books as I explore how the community constructs a sense of togetherness through the *khizana* and its collection: how believers relate to this sacred, inaccessible space; how it functions as an institution in their daily lives, despite its inaccessibility; and how the community derives its Neo-Fatimid identity through the *khizana* and its manuscripts.

The second part of this chapter documents the history of the Alawi *khizana* and the mobility of its manuscripts; as we will see, this is in fact a history of several treasuries of books that historically were connected with one another in Yemen and Gujarat. We investigate how these *khizanat* came into being after schisms, the fall of empires and

[8] Whereas the term *khizana* was used for all kinds of repositories in Fatimid Egypt, such as for robes of honour, banners and flags, books were stored either in one of the wings of the royal palace library or in the library of *Dār al-ʿilm*. See Halm, *The Fāṭimids and their Traditions of Learning*, 73, 77, 91, 92 and Aḥmad ibn al-Rashīd Ibn al-Zubayr, *Book of Gifts and Rarities*, Ghādah Ḥijjāwī Qaddūmī (trans.) (Cambridge, MA: Harvard University Press, 1996), 16.

[9] Ann Laura Stoler, *Along the Archival Grain: Epistemic Anxieties and Colonial Common Sense* (Princeton: Princeton University Press, 2009), 1.

the establishment of new communities, and how their collections travelled and were reconstituted as *treasuries of books* across the Indian Ocean. We focus on the presence of Gujarati Bohra actors in Tayyibi Yemen and their active role in the mobility of manuscripts from Yemen to Gujarat. Their involvement, as we will see, was crucial, as these manuscripts would form the basis of Bohra *khizana* culture in Gujarat and enable the continuation of a Fatimid manuscript tradition among the Alawis. We end the chapter by looking into what manuscripts from this Indian Ocean transfer have survived in the Alawi *khizana* in Baroda today. Can we indeed speak of a lost Fatimid, or perhaps Tayyibi-Fatimid, *khizana* in Gujarat on the basis of manuscripts and documents present in the Alawi treasury of books? And if so, what makes it a 'Neo'-Fatimid *khizana*?

On Documenting the *Khizana*: Ethics of Disclosure

Archives, libraries and other repositories of things written, as I argued earlier, have rich social lives through their interaction with people and communities over time and space. As a social codicologist, I gained a rare insight from being immersed in the microcosm of the Alawi Bohra community, the *khizana* and the intimate private lives of its custodians: an insight that was a privilege, yet one that had to be earned and, once earned, inevitably came with responsibility. As an argument in favour of reflecting on 'going to the archives' and taking the social encounters that are inherent in archival fieldwork seriously, I start this chapter by discussing this responsibility and the ethics of writing about a *khizana* that is seen as secret.

While I managed to document the Alawi Bohra community and its *khizana* with relatively few restrictions in Baroda, upon my return to Europe I had to impose limits on myself, while at the same time finding a balance in detaching myself from my involvement in the community. Having been initiated into the community's treasury of books, cataloguing its manuscripts and observing its social importance as a Neo-Fatimid *lieu de mémoire* was one matter, yet writing about it, and documenting the practices of secrecy that surrounded it, was another.

Post-Baroda, I instinctively wanted to treat the *khizana*, and the Alawi community, as a sacred, untouchable shrine, applying self-censorship in my writing. Doing so, however, would turn the community and its *khizana* into a monument, frozen in time and space, which is exactly the opposite of what I observed in Baroda and what constitutes the argument of this monograph. Like so many ethnographers working within constraints of secrecy who went before me, I was tormented by the ethical elephant in the room. How does one write about objects one observes, sacred spaces one has been part of, and secret teachings one has been initiated into that are carefully and purposefully shrouded by mystery and are inaccessible to the uninitiated, outside world? Should it be done at all? And if so, is it even possible to say something meaningful about it as a complete outsider? Or as Hugh Urban describes it, if one 'knows', one cannot speak; and if one speaks, one must not really 'know'.[10] And, finally, the classic question: I having been a white, privileged European woman doing fieldwork

[10] Hugh B. Urban, 'The Torment of Secrecy: Ethical and Epistemological Problems in the Study of Esoteric Traditions', *History of Religions* vol. 37, no. 3 (February1998): 209–48.

in the Global South, staying with the community for months, had there been an unevenness in our exchange?

Reflecting on the ethics of writing a monograph that is essentially about people, books and secrecy, I struggled with these questions. I had taken an oath of trust, vowing not to disclose anything about the *khizana* without the consent of the community, yet the more the private and often intimate lives of the Alawi royal family and myself became intertwined, the more these lines became blurred. Moreover, I felt I had a moral responsibility to tell the story of the community, its sacred manuscripts and its *khizana*, without losing my academic integrity or betraying the trust of the people of Badri Mohallah.[11] As a social codicologist, I wanted to provide insight into their agency by writing about the *khizana* through their perspective and by documenting the experience of the people who enshrine, write, read and venerate its manuscripts.

The Alawis may trace their spiritual lineage back to Cairo and Yemen, yet in their day-to-day lives they are Gujaratis, a 'traders' caste' as they would often describe themselves, and therefore masters in the art of negotiating. When I arrived in Baroda, the clerics were perhaps slightly reluctant at first, yet later they were surprisingly willing to accommodate my interest in their *khizana*, despite their practice of secrecy. We each had our own interests, yet we found a way to navigate around and through the borderlands of our differences without losing our integrity. Even though the *khizana* was secret and inaccessible to the community, the clerics strongly felt the need to share their inaccessible but available heritage with me. Moreover, the Mazoon Saheb and his brothers wanted me to be the court historian of their community, the *da'wat al-hadiyya*, and its stories and manuscripts.

My access to the community, and eventually to the *khizana* and its manuscripts, was not the result of luck or generosity or of bribing the Bhai Sahebs, as some community members believed. From my arrival in Baroda, reciprocity and exchange were the common denominators between the Mazoon Saheb and his brothers, the Bhai Sahebs, and me. Establishing reciprocity, however, as I described in the reflexive chapter, was a long process that required the building of relationships and trust. It was the result of a long and carefully choreographed series of negotiations, starting from the exchange of one book for another, to the sharing of my academic network, to offering manuscript preservation advice, and, finally, preparing a catalogue in return for my presence in Badri Mohallah and my documentation of the social role of the manuscripts. The more useful I proved to be for the community and the more I was willing to immerse myself in it, the more I was allowed to see and the more access I gained.

My complicated status as a 'lady scholar', as I described in the reflexive chapter, had provided me with an unexpected entry into the community. Yet what gave me agency in my negotiations with the Bhai Sahebs was not my gender, socio-economic background or ethnicity, although these factors may have played a role, but my positionality as an academic. Even though I was a PhD student at the time, I had practical

11 For a discussion on the ethics of disclosure in the context of the book market and post-colonial book collecting in Morocco, see Léon Buskens, 'Paper Worlds: A Nesrani Ethnographer Entering the Manuscript Trade in Morocco', in M. Almoubaker and F, Pouillon (eds),*Pratiquer les sciences sociales au Maghreb. Textes pour Driss Mansouri* (Casablanca: Fondation du Roi Abdul-Aziz Al Saoud pour les Etudes Islamiques et les Sciences Humaines, 2014), 239–65.

skills to offer, which the Bhai Sahebs needed. Moreover, the prospect of academic attention and a future monograph on their community, they reasoned, would take the community out of its (self-perceived) position of marginality as the Bohra 'other'. My title of 'court historian' was therefore not randomly chosen: the Bhai Sahebs wanted me to write about their past, they wanted their perspective to be recorded, and they wanted a book on their community on the shelves of their *khizana*. As my work moved in the direction of the Alawi *khizana* tradition, I realised that, indirectly and unintentionally, this book also became part of the story of how the Alawis negotiate themselves as Neo-Fatimids through their *khizana*. Yet as much as I was self-critical of this position and became wary of the danger of seeing links to the Bohras' Fatimid pasts, the texts spoke for themselves.

In conclusion, The Bhai Sahebs and I thus developed a reciprocal relation, based on mutually satisfactory arrangements. Buskens summarises the delicate balance of exchange and reciprocity in the context of post-colonial book collecting in Morocco as follows: 'all parties involved have a certain agency, they all have good reasons, partly economical, partly of a different nature, to be involved in these exchanges'.[12]

Respecting the trust of the Dai and the Mazoon Saheb, there are certain matters that I consciously decided to omit from this study, even though some of this information would have been crucial to my argument. For example, during my stay in Baroda I prepared a private catalogue of manuscripts for the Dai. This catalogue will not be published because its content is considered to reach the highest level of secrecy. Preparing the catalogue did, however, give me free access to the *khizana* and its manuscripts. The permission I received to access the *khizana* was based on trust, which was articulated in an oral contract, an oath of allegiance, in which I made a vow that I would not write about anything without the permission of the Bhai Sahebs, except for the following themes we both agreed upon: manuscript culture, manuscript preservation and copying, the history and analysis of the *khizana* as an institution, the history and analysis of the community (which included attending all ceremonies and gatherings), the role of Arabic as a non-vernacular language in the community, and, finally, the initiation into and study of the Isma'ili knowledge system, including *'ilm al-haqa'iq*. The detailed content of the *khizana* and the exact manuscript titles the *khizana* enshrines, by contrast, would not be disclosed in this study.

Even though this chapter touches upon the collection of the *khizana*, it is not my aim to reveal possibly hidden Fatimid manuscript titles that may be stored in the *khizana*. The Bhai Sahebs did, however, grant me permission to write about observations of a more general nature. I will therefore dedicate sections to the history and holdings of the *khizana*, focusing on manuscript authors (and thus, with some exceptions, not providing information on the titles) who are considered canonical by the Alawi clerical establishment.

I refrained from listing manuscript titles because they are not of direct interest to this study. As I mentioned in the previous chapter, the intellectual content of most treatises found in Baroda and other Bohra communal and private *khizanat* have already been studied in great detail. What thus far has received no attention, however, is their

[12] Buskens, 'Paper Worlds', 263, 264.

social significance, or what John Dagenais calls their 'horizon': how these texts are used today, how they are implemented in the daily life of believers as undisclosed texts, how they speak the law and rule the community, how they travel, and how they are transmitted and preserved.[13]

This study is therefore primarily concerned with what people, in this case the Alawi Bohras, do with books, manuscripts and documents and their spaces of dwelling. Whereas philologists are mostly interested in reading, in the chapters that follow I argue that manuscripts can also play different social roles that do not concern reading at all. I am thus interested here in the traditions and practices of secrecy that shroud these manuscripts in mystery, the regulations of access and the rituals of initiation, and less in the secret content itself. Through this lens, in which the emic perspective of the community is central, the secrets enshrined in the *khizana* thus remain intact.

2.1 Neither Library nor Archive: the *Khizana* as a Treasury of Books

As a community dispersed over the Indian Ocean throughout its history, the Alawi Bohras embody a lived Shi'i, Isma'ili, and distinctly South Asian Arabo-Gujarati experience of Islam. The Alawi Bohra *daʿwa*, its clerical hierarchy and day-to-day understanding of orthopraxy, I argue, cannot be fully understood without a reference to an institution intrinsic to the community: its treasury of books.

The Alawi Bohra *khizana*, housed in the middle of Badri Mohallah, is the epicentre of the community. For outsiders to the Alawi quarter, its social role might be hard to understand. It is a space that is considered secret and inaccessible, yet at the same it is heavily frequented by the community. The *khizana* is the central space where the community's books from the past are stored and documents are accumulated by generations of Dais; yet it is not a library per se, nor is it exactly an archive. Whereas in our modern, secular and Western understanding archives and libraries store either documents or books, as separate, discursive traditions, the Alawis make no such distinction. Instead, it is the act of treasuring that has significance in defining the *khizana*, rather than the object or tradition that is treasured. It is for this reason that, in this study, instead of defining the *khizana* as an 'archive' or 'library', I remain faithful to the terminology used by the community.

What ultimately characterises the *khizana* from an emic perspective, I observed, is the fact that it is considered a sanctuary of books and other forms of writing. Similar to the *qabaristan* in Gujarat and Yemen I described in the previous chapter, it is a repository of something sacred, yet instead of the remains of holy people it is the books of the community that are enshrined, venerated and remembered. In other words, the *khizana* is a treasury of books that functions like a communal shrine with books as its relics. In this sense it thus functions differently from the practice of donating books to publicly-endowed spaces of shrines of Muslim *sayyids* or Imams and other institutions where books are added to shrines, as we see for instance in the shrines of the eighth

[13] John Dagenais, *The Ethics of Reading in Manuscript Culture: Glossing the Libro de Buen Amor* (Princeton: Princeton University Press, 1994), xiv.

Imam in Twelver Shi'ism, Imam 'Alī al-Riḍā (d. 203/818) in Mashhad, and of Shaykh Ṣafī al-Dīn Khānegāh in Ardabil (d. 735/1334).[14] It is a highly ritualised sacred space which, just as the *qabaristan*, requires a certain habitus, including dress code, etiquette, and specific conditions of access. As in the case of the *qabaristan* in Saraspur, which is administered by the Dawoodi clergy and can only be visited collectively for special occasions after gaining the Dai's permission, the Alawi treasury of books too can only be accessed after gaining special authorisation. It is precisely because of these conditions of access that the treasury of books plays such an important role in the community, not only for those who have access to it, but even more so, as we will see, for those who do not.

The divide between those who have access to the treasury of books – the Alawi royal family who represent the highest layers of the clerical establishment – and those whose access is restricted, the lay people or *mu'minin* and *mu'minat*, becomes apparent from the way in which the people of Badri Mohallah refer to it. The uninitiated believers, who form the great majority of the community, refer to the *khizana* as 'the centre'. The treasury of books owes this name to the fact that the space of the treasury of books is housed within the *haveli* of the royal family, and it also simultaneously functions as the headquarters of the Mazoon Saheb. To the outsider, the way the space of the *khizana* and the Mazoon's office is organised seems impractical, if not contradictory. Yet the significance of this particular spatial arrangement, as we see later, should not be overlooked.

In contrast to the majority of the community, the Dai and his immediate clerical family use the term *khizanat al-kutub*, or *khizana* of *kitab*, which translates from Arabic into 'treasury of books', to describe this space. The Mazoon Saheb explained that there are four Arabic terms that are used to refer to treasuries: *dafīna*, which is used to refer to treasures buried in the ground;[15] *zakhīra*, a collection of 'objects' that can be stored anywhere, such as a printed book collection; *kanz*, a treasure in the sense of curiosities of any kind that one inherits from one's forefathers, such as jewellery or china; and *khizana*, which Bohra clerics describe as a treasury in the form of a storehouse, containing any kind of rare items that are – as the Mazoon Saheb would repeat – 'kept under lock and key'. The Mazoon Saheb explained the importance of the *khizana* as follows: 'The Dai considers *'ilm* and books the greatest holdings of the world and the hereafter. There is nothing more costly and more important in his eyes than the *khizana* of *kitab*.'[16]

The importance of the *khizana* also becomes apparent from the many adjectives used by the clerics to describe it, ranging from those that highlight its inaccessibility, such as *al-khizānat al-maknūna* ('the guarded' *khizana*), *al-khizānat al-khāṣṣa* ('the

[14] Zahir Bhalloo, 'Archival Practice in Safavid Iran: The View from the Shrine', in P. Sartori (ed.), *Cultures of Documentation in Persianate Eurasia. Handbook of Oriental Studies* (Leiden: Brill, forthcoming). See also Mahdieh Tavakol's MIDA (Mediating Islam in the Digital Age) research project, Traveling Manuscripts, Freie Universität Berlin.

[15] On the practice of burying manuscript collections in the ground in Afghanistan, see Ahmad Azizy's forthcoming dissertation *Briefkultur in Afghanistan* (Humboldt University Berlin), and, in Dagestan, Rebecca Gould's Endangered Archives Project, *Digitizing Dagestan's Manuscript Heritage: Manuscripts from the Library of 'Alī al-Ghumūqī (1878-1943)*, https://eap.bl.uk/project/EAP957 (last accessed 1 July 2020).

[16] Conversation with the Mazoon Saheb, Badri Mohallah, interview, 16 November 2013.

special' *khizana*) and *al-khizānat al-sharīfa* ('the exalted' *khizana*) to those emphasising its devotional character and royal status, such as *al-khizānat al-mubāraka* ('the blessed' *khizana*), *al-khizānat al-'amīra* ('the royal' *khizana*), or simply *al-khizānat al-ʿAlawiyya* (the Alawi *khizana*).

That the Alawis use distinctly Arabic terms for their treasury of books is significant in the context of South Asia. One would expect a Persian term, such as *kitabkhana* (library, lit. 'storage of books'), originating from the royal libraries of the Timurids and the Safavids; it is commonly used among Muslim communities who speak Hindi, Urdu and Farsi on the subcontinent.[17] Yet all Bohra communities use the term '*khizanat al-kutub*'. In fact, I was told that Dawoodis and Sulaymanis use the same adjectives mentioned earlier for their treasury of books. Among the Dawoodis, the designated caretaker of the treasury of books is known as the *khizanjee* ('*khizana* caretaker'), an honorary title I encountered on several occasions in marginalia of Dawoodi manuscripts and was made aware of while interviewing Dawoodi interlocutors. Moreover, the Alawi community has used the term *khizana* throughout the centuries to refer to their treasury of books, as I was able to reconstruct on the basis of its documentary practice of producing book inventories (*fihrist*).

In the Alawi community, those who refer to the treasury of books as the *al-khizanat al-mubaraka*, *al-amira* or *al-maknuna* are considered the spiritual guardians of its collection. Spiritual guardianship means that only the Bhai Sahebs – the clerics – are privileged to access the *khizana* and read, consult, transmit and produce its manuscripts and other written artefacts. Through their mandate over the treasury of books, the Dai and, to a lesser extent, the Bhai Sahebs enjoy the status of absolute rulers of the community, in matters of both the sacred and the profane, and in the political, religious and spiritual domains. Through their mastery of Isma'ili *fiqh* and *sharia* manuscripts kept in the *khizana*, they 'speak' the law and maintain social order in the community in the absence of the hidden Imam.

For believers, there is no distinction between the Bhai Sahebs and the treasury of books. The Dai, in particular, represents, carries and transmits the Bohra interpretation of the Isma'ili knowledge system; because he is the embodiment of the eternal truths the treasury of books enshrine, he can be seen as the living *khizana*.[18] The Bhai Sahebs are the intermediary between the common believers and the Dai and his *khizana*. They are responsible for the delicate balancing act of translating the esoteric truths enshrined in the treasury of books to the daily lives of believers in small doses, while at the same time protecting what should remain undisclosed: the sacred Isma'ili esoteric tradition. The transmission and preservation thereof, as Traboulsi confirms, are constrained by restrictions imposed by the state of *satr* of the Imam.[19]

The Alawi treasury of books enshrines this esoteric tradition in the material form of manuscripts. As I describe in more detail in the following section, the *khizana* contains hundreds of *batini* and *zahiri* Isma'ili manuscripts, in addition to a unique collection of

17 Touati, *L'armoire à sagesse*, 38.

18 Theologically, there is an interesting parallel here with the notion of the Imam as the speaking Qur'an. See Mohammad Amir-Moezzi, *Le Coran silencieux et le Coran parlant. Sources scripturaires de l'islam entre histoire et ferveur* (Paris: CNRS Éditions, 2011).

19 Traboulsi, 'Transmission of Knowledge and Book Preservation', 22.

documents and other forms of writing, which are handwritten by generations of Alawi Dais and Bhai Sahebs. The majority of these manuscript titles belong to the highest level of esoteric knowledge, the *haqa'iq*, and contain complex and multi-layered systems of thought coded in a very specific Arabic vocabulary, shrouded in secret alphabets, and protected by curses and spells (see Chapter 6). Initiation into the various levels of this esoteric tradition is restricted to the royal male offspring of the community, the young *mansus* and, to a lesser extent, the sons of the Mukasir Saheb and Ra's ul Hudood, and it involves a lifelong ritualised process of manuscript reading and copying. The esoteric tradition of the *khizana* is not accessible to the royal women of the community.

The *batini* Isma'ili tradition is thus carefully enshrined in the treasury of books through language, manuscript culture, and social practices of access, rites of passage and levels of initiation. As noted, the identification and analysis of this knowledge system have already received scholarly attention in academia. However, these ideas are completely unknown to Alawi *mu'minin* and *mu'minat*, who remain uninitiated for their entire lives. Its esoteric discourse, I observed, could not be more different from the believers' exoteric *zahiri* day-to-day understanding of Isma'ili Islam. The Bhai Sahebs expressed the idea that they actively cultivate this division, keeping *batini* 'behind lock and key' because its secrecy is prescribed in the authoritative texts of the *khizana*.

In addition to what is prescribed in the authoritative texts of the *khizana*, there is also a more practical motive for keeping undisclosed the *batini* tradition of the *khizana*. The Bhai Sahebs confided in me that they fear that if they were to introduce believers to the complex levels of the esoteric knowledge system, it could be misinterpreted as un-Islamic or *bid'a* (an undesired religious innovation). As one cleric put it, a potential threat could be that the Bohra *da'wa* could lose their *mu'minin* and *mu'minat* to the successful Wahhabi *tablīgh* disseminated in Baroda by missionary organisations from Pakistan and Iran. His fear is not entirely unjustified, since preachers from both schools are active in the old Mughal city of Baroda, and both an Iranian- and a Saudi Arabia-funded mosque were recently constructed right behind Badri Mohallah. As a result of these developments, some Alawi families have indeed converted to either Sunni or Twelver Shi'i schools of Islam.

Whereas *batini* manuscripts could be misinterpreted by uninitiated readers, the Bhai Sahebs stressed that, in their interpretation of these manuscripts, there is no discrepancy between *zahir* and *batini* knowledge. Instead, as pointed out in Chapter 1, the two spheres complement one another. The Mukasir Saheb clarified this point as follows:

> Whether one is a schoolteacher or a Bhai Saheb, each and everyone has a function in the community, and every function comes with different *'ilm* [knowledge], we don't want to bother people with unnecessary *'ilm*. A schoolteacher simply needs *'ilm* on the outer parts of the Bohra faith, for instance, *'ilm* on how to perform prayer and ablution. We [Bhai Sahebs] need to understand *batini 'ilm*, because we deal with the esoteric aspects of life.

While I refrain from disclosing esoteric truths from the *khizana* out of respect for the community, with the permission of the Bhai Sahebs there is one aspect I would like to highlight here, as it is paramount in understanding the role of the treasury of books as a sacred and inaccessible *khizana* in theology and social practice. When I asked the Mukasir Saheb what was the purpose of knowing the esoteric aspects of life, to my surprise he answered, 'Because we are responsible for the salvation of souls of the *mu'minin* in the afterlife'. The Mukasir Saheb explained that, as Bhai Sahebs, they have the important responsibility of keeping believers on the right path not only from the cradle to the grave but also from the here and now until the hereafter. The *mu'minin* and *mu'minat* believe that it is the Dai and the *hudud* (the Bhai Sahebs) who take care of their souls after death, and that by following them, their place in heaven is guaranteed. According to the self-understanding of believers, without the infallible Dai there is no afterlife, no life in the present time, no *daʿwa*, no universe. By embodying the esoteric knowledge of the *khizana*, the Bhai Sahebs are thus able to carry out this important task.

As a treasury of the *haqa'iq* over time and space, the *khizana* thus is seen as a crucial element in the eschatological discourse of the Alawis. It is not only in the personal interest of believers that the collection of the *khizana* is kept intact and its conditions of access are respected; the process of what is considered the 'migration' of souls to the hereafter also has implications for the *daʿwa* in its entirety. The Alawis are currently waiting for the return of their *qa'im* or hidden Imam, and it is believed that the *khizana* plays an important role in this process. *Batini* sources from the treasury of books report that the *qa'im*'s return can either be accelerated, through the increase in the number of souls of believers when they reach heaven, or hampered, if the flow of souls to the hereafter stops. The latter would be a catastrophe for the community, as the *qa'im*, personified in the descendant of Imam Tayyib, is believed to restore justice on earth and stop the process of cyclical time. Interestingly, when the hidden Imam reveals himself, the distinction between *batin* and *zahir* becomes void, and thus the *khizana* and its *haqa'iq* will become accessible to all. In other words, as long as the hidden Imam is in seclusion, the books of the *daʿwa* should remain undisclosed in the treasury of books. Through the lens of the community, the *khizana* becomes a shrine of sacred esoteric truths, a treasury of books with the Bhai Sahebs as its divinely appointed custodians, rather than a library or archive.

In addition to its central role in eschatology and *batini* esotericism, the *khizana* also functions as the centralised space in the community for the administration of all *zahiri* affairs in the here and now. Upon entering the building of the royal *haveli* (Figure 2.2), the building that houses the *khizana*, one encounters two signs on its façade. One neon-green sign, which is lit at night, reads '*al-daʿwat al-hādiyya al-ʿAlawiyya*' (the rightly-guided Alawi *daʿwa*) written in calligraphed Arabic with a transcription into Gujarati below it. Underneath it, is a blackboard for public announcements; on it, the Arabic expression '*al-wizārat al-'Alawiyya*' (the Alawi ministry) is transcribed into Gujarati. Both terms, *daʿwat al-hadiyya* and *wizara*, hold great significance in the history of Isma'ilism, as I will discuss in the following section. *Al-wizarat al-'Alawiyya* indicates that we are dealing with a place of governance. As a treasury, the *khizana* functions as an institution where the community is governed and legal guidance and religious services, such as marriage ceremonies, legal opinions and blessings, are offered. As an institution of the law, the space of the *khizana* functions as a court of arbitration and settlement. As a *wizara*, the treasury of books thus is an office of power, a ministry, and the community's main department of domestic communal affairs in which, as I argued in the previous chapter, authority is inscribed.

Figure 2.2 The entrance of the royal *haveli* and the *khizana*.

As an institution of power, the treasury of books divides the community between the believers and the royal Bhai Sahebs, while legitimising the absolute hegemony of the latter. Through the institution of the *khizana* a hierarchical relationship is created between those who have access and those who do not, those who are the custodians of its manuscripts and are initiated to esoteric knowledge and thus have the right to govern versus those who are not. In other words, the *khizana* is a shrine of books and power. Through its manuscripts, it forms a structure that keeps the social order and the clerical hierarchies of the community in place. It legitimises the Dai and the Bhai Saheb's powerful position in the community, and everything and everyone around them. The social hierarchies of the community and their modes of access and non-access to the *khizana* were so self-evident to the believers that, when I would ask them what this inaccessible space meant to them, none expressed discontent or a hint of protest against their lack of access. My interlocutors would answer that, as *mu'minin* and *mu'minat*, it would not be their place to access it, that such are the rules and regulation of the *daʿwa* and they should be respected out of loyalty to the Dai, and that was the end of the matter.

At first, the believers' loyalty and obedience to the Dai surprised me. Yet the more time I spent in Badri Mohallah, the better I understood what the Dai really meant to people. To the community members, his status of semi-infallibility and his charisma were no less powerful than that of the Pope or the Dalai Lama. As mentioned, the believers understand that without the Dai there is no salvation, no afterlife, no life in the present time, no *daʿwa*, no Alawi Bohra universe. It sometimes seemed as if people believed that the Dai actually *was* the universe. Only very rarely did I encounter mild criticism among believers (mostly internationals) concerning the authority of the Bhai Sahebs, but this criticism was directed at logistical aspects of the *da ʿwa*; it was never related to the position of the Dai or the inaccessibility of the *khizana*.

In contrast to the Dawoodis, for whom the inaccessibility of the *khizana* is a source of discontent among the critical intelligentsia, Alawis seemed to share an acceptance of the inaccessibility of the *khizana* and its undisclosed holdings. Interlocutors told me that they were aware that these manuscripts were secret objects, but because they did not have a command of Arabic they lost interest, because 'everything' that had something to do with Arabic was considered 'difficult'. *Mu'minin* and *mu'minat* receive minimal training in Arabic in *madrasas* and are discouraged by the clerics from pursuing further studies, let alone those needed to access Arabic manuscripts. The few people who pursued studies in Arabic often received education via non-Bohra channels (either at university or via institutions of other Muslim 'castes', such as the Sunni Tablighi Jamaat, or Iranian-funded mosques) and were therefore considered outcasts from the community. I observed also that a lack of access was not seen as problematic, for the simple reason that the people of Badri Mohallah were far more preoccupied with the struggles of their daily lives, such as managing to feed their families, keeping them healthy and safe, and finding spouses for their daughters and sons.

'Are community members never curious about the books of the *khizana*?' I asked the Mazoon Saheb. 'Don't they ever transgress limits of *batin* and *zahir*?' He replied: 'They sometimes are and they sometimes do. Sometimes, but only very rarely, we raise a small corner of the veil to satisfy them; this is harmless for it is only a drop from an ocean of knowledge.' 'Raising a small corner of the veil', I observed, takes place in various ways in the *da ʿwa*. In one of his lectures, the Mazoon Saheb describes how small portions of esoteric knowledge are taught 'in the form of lectures among small groups of deserving students'. He stresses, however, that most of this knowledge 'is kept in strict supervision and obscurity'.[20] Purposefully obscuring what should remain undisclosed, yet at the same time offering believers a glimpse, I witnessed, also occurred in subtler and less direct ways. Understanding the particular spatial arrangement of the *khizana* and how it simultaneously functions as the headquarters of the *da ʿwa* is important in this regard. As we will see in the following sections, the Mazoon Saheb's cushioned throne is literally surrounded by cupboards storing the *da ʿwa*'s collection. These iron cupboards have no locks or keys and could theoretically be opened by anyone. Time and time again I would observe that the manuscripts he would be working with prior to his office hours would, despite their secret content, not be returned to their iron cupboards. Instead, they would be casually placed on one of the small stands next to the Mazoon's cushion or stacked in piles on the floor (Figure 2.3).

When believers would visit 'the centre', they are thus made aware indirectly of the *khizana*'s manuscript collection. They would see the manuscripts yet have no access to their content. Even though *batini* manuscripts would often be lying on the floor within arm's reach, believers would never touch them. After all, it was not their place

[20] Private written lecture of the Mazoon Saheb titled 'The Occurrences of the Episodes of Arab History in Isma'ili Literature' (unpublished).

Figure 2.3 The Mazoon Saheb during his office hours, receiving believers in the treasury of books. A manuscript is casually placed on the floor in the foreground among various printed books.

in the *daʿwa* to do so. Yet the act of witnessing what is available yet not accessible is crucial. After all, the idea of something secret and undisclosed only functions if people know about it and witness it. Had the manuscripts of the *daʿwa* been stored somewhere outside the city at an unknown location, believers would never have come into contact with what they are not allowed to see.

In other words, I believe the community needs to see their clerics use these secret objects right in front of them, to see that *batini* manuscripts indeed do exist, to see what they cannot access, and, more importantly, to actually witness that the Bhai Sahebs, who are responsible for the fate of believers not only in the here and now but also in the afterlife, know and embody the secrets of their esoteric tradition. Through their material presence, it is thus not only the institution of the treasury of books but also its manuscripts that play a crucial role in legitimising power dynamics in the Alawi Bohra universe, an idea that is developed further in this study.

Khizana Practices and Collection

We have established that the *khizana* is both a shrine of books in the Alawi community, where manuscripts are venerated as sacred objects, and an institution of power where the community is administered. Its collection consists of more than 450 Arabic manuscripts; a small collection of non-Isma'ili titles in Urdu, Persian and Hindi; and a collection of documents written in Arabic and *Lisan al-Daʿwa*.[21] The manuscripts that are part of the *khizana* are referred to as *kutub* (books), *makhṭūṭāt* (manuscripts) or *nuṣkhāṭ* (copies). The *makhtutat* are stored in traditional iron cupboards to keep them safe from theft and protect the codices against termites.

The manuscripts of the *khizana* are classified and stored according to time period and then by genre. As discussed in the previous chapter, Tayyibi Isma'ili historiography divides the Bohra past into periods of *satr* (concealment) and *kashf* or *zuhur* (manifestation), and manuscripts are arranged accordingly. The first group of manuscripts are titles first produced in the *zuhur* period, which is the Fatimid period that lasted until the Tayyibis split from the Fatimid Empire (297/909–534/1130); this group includes all works attributed to the Fatimid Caliph-Imams and Dais from Egypt, North Africa, and Iran. The second group contains all manuscript titles belonging to the *satr* era during which the Imams were in hiding, starting with the seclusion of Imam Tayyib. This period is divided into the Yemenite (524/1130–946/1539) and Indian (946/1539–present) periods and includes all treatises written by the Tayyibi and Bohra Dais. Manuscript copies of Fatimid titles are stored in one cupboard dedicated to the works of the Caliph-Imams, their Dais and other contemporary authors. Handwritten copies of manuscripts by Yemeni authors cover the first and second stacks of the second cupboard, while the rest of the stacks of the second cupboard contain manuscripts (both copies and original works) written by Indian Dais.

Manuscripts are arranged chronologically according to the age in which the author lived (and not the date of copying). The authority of a manuscript copy, however, depends on when it was copied – the older, the more authoritative – and on the identity of the copyist; for instance, royal versus non-royal. A sloppy manuscript copy of an unknown copyist from the early eighteenth century may be considered less authoritative than a late eighteenth-century exemplar copied by the Dai. This notion was also very present during my interaction with the Mazoon Saheb. For instance, my daily allotment of manuscripts was always presented to me in chronological order, no matter what the topic; yet royal copies were always stacked on top of my pile of the day.

The treasury of books also holds a small collection of popular non-Isma'ili manuscript titles that are consulted by the Bhai Sahebs. Among these titles are works of both Sunni and Shi'i provenance, which are stored separately, as well as *Diwans* and popular works of *adab* in Arabic and Persian. As works 'alien' to the canon of the treasury of books, these manuscripts enjoy a lesser status than those of Bohra Tayyibi Isma'ili provenance. They are not considered sacred books, yet nonetheless are carefully stored, preserved and enjoyed as rare books and curiosities. Their presence in the *khizana* is important, as it gives us insight into the collecting practices of the Alawi royal family and their literary preferences. It demonstrates that, in the case of the Alawi royals, their traditions of bibliophilia were not merely restricted to preserving the devotional canon only. Interestingly, other Dawoodi manuscript collections from Gujarat and other parts

[21] See also http://www.alavibohra.org/introduction%20files/intro%20-%20Vadodara%20City-%20A%20centre%20of%20Dawat.htm (last accessed 17 September 2012).

of South Asia contain very similar Arabic titles. The collecting practices of the previous Dais of the Alawi community are not always easy to reconstruct, as many manuscripts of the *khizana* did not survive the intense monsoon climate of Gujarat. The collection was also built on the practice of manuscript exchange, through family donations and diplomatic gift giving, which demonstrates the social role of manuscripts as commodities. As I describe in Chapter 4, these 'manuscript transactions' can be retraced through donation statements and erased ownership notes. A non-Isma'ili title that illustrates the function of manuscripts as commodities is a copy of the *Tuḥfat al-Kirām* (The Gift of the Nobles), written by the eighteenth-century Sindhi historian Mir Ali Shir Qani (d. 1202/1788). This richly illuminated and lavishly gilded rare Persian manuscript was allegedly given to one of the Alawi Dais by a *wazir* of the Mughal court as a diplomatic gift.[22]

Finally, there are several cupboards storing official and private handwritten documents, such as the private notes and sermons of the Mazoon Saheb; *taʿwīdh* (*pl. taʿwīdhāt,* henceforth written *taʿwiz*) (see Chapter 5); official *daʿwa* documents, such as *nikah* and *zakat* registers and account books that are bound in traditional Gujarati 'box books'; rolls known as *sijillat* (both volumen and rotulus); tables of inheritance; *waqf* documents; and, finally, *ʿahd* (initiation) rolls (see the next chapter). Depending on their material form, documents are either stacked horizontally on top of each other (Figure 2.4) or are stored in specially designated boxes. As I have already argued elsewhere, in the *khizana*

Figure 2.4 The Mazoon Saheb standing in front of a manuscript cupboard.

[22] See for a description and picture of this manuscript 'Preserving Culture for Posterity', *Times of India*, date unknown. http://alavibohra.org/images/photographs/akhbar/culture.jpg

no distinction is made in status between documents and manuscripts.[23] As both discursive traditions are copied and sealed or authorised by the Dai, it is primarily the sacred materiality of his book hand, and not the type of written artefact, that gives it meaning. Even though the usage and social practices that surround documents and books may differ entirely, their practices of enshrinement in the *khizana* are the same.

It is for this reason, as I argued earlier, that, in the context of the treasury of books, an academic distinction between 'archive' and 'library' would be artificial. In fact, as I describe later, notions of what constitutes a document and what is a manuscript are fluid, as I encountered manuscripts that enshrined documents, and vice versa. There are also, of course, differences between the manuscript culture and documentary culture of the *khizana*, such as social practices and language.

In addition to manuscripts and documents, printed books also form an important part of the *khizana* collection. Several cupboards are filled with printed books: lithographs and academic publications and reference works on Islamic Studies in English, Arabic, Persian, Gujarati, Urdu and Hindi. Moreover, the *khizana* contains a large collection of printed books on Isma'ili Studies: virtually any work that was ever published on anything remotely Isma'ili is present in Baroda. Printed critical editions in particular, including rare titles printed in the Middle East and India, take up a large portion of the cupboards for printed books. As we shall see in Chapter 6, these printed editions are crucial for editing and preserving the manuscript collection. In addition, there is a cupboard for storing photocopies of manuscripts that are not (yet) in the collection of the *khizana*. These photocopies are used to create copies of manuscripts and can therefore be seen as the in-between world for the text in transition from one manuscript to another. Finally, a cupboard holds all popular *da'wa* publications in Gujarati and *Lisan al-Da'wa*.

Manuscripts of the *khizana* are stored according to the classical Middle Eastern tradition of keeping books, which means that instead of standing upright they are laid horizontally above one another. Manuscripts were traditionally stored in this fashion because their titles were written on the fore edge instead of on the cover or the spine, as famously depicted in al-Ḥarīrī's *Maqamāt* (The Assemblies).[24] Interestingly, even though this is rarely the case with the *makhtutat* in Baroda, the codices are still stored in this fashion (Figures 2.4 and 2.6).

Even though the community does not have access to sophisticated conservation equipment and techniques, the Bhai Sahebs have developed their own vernacular preservation practices for the collection. Cupboards are stuffed with mothballs to repel termites and with pouches stuffed with rice and cloves, which guard against mould and fungi (Figure 2.5). At the level of manuscript and scribal culture, *khizana* books are protected through *kabīkaj* formulae (see Chapter 5) and magical squares that are written in the incipits. The botanical Indian equivalent of the *Kabikaj* plant is the *Azadirachta Indica* or *neem*, whose leaves are kept between manuscript folios to protect the paper.[25] Supposedly these leaves have such a bitter aftertaste that they repel anything that comes

[23] Akkerman, 'Documentary Remains of a Fatimid Past in Gujarat', 286–308.

[24] Jonathan Bloom, *Paper before Print: The History and Impact of Paper in the Islamic World* (New Haven: Yale University Press, 2001), 113.

[25] Akkerman, 'The Bohra Manuscript Treasury as a Sacred Site of Philology', 195.

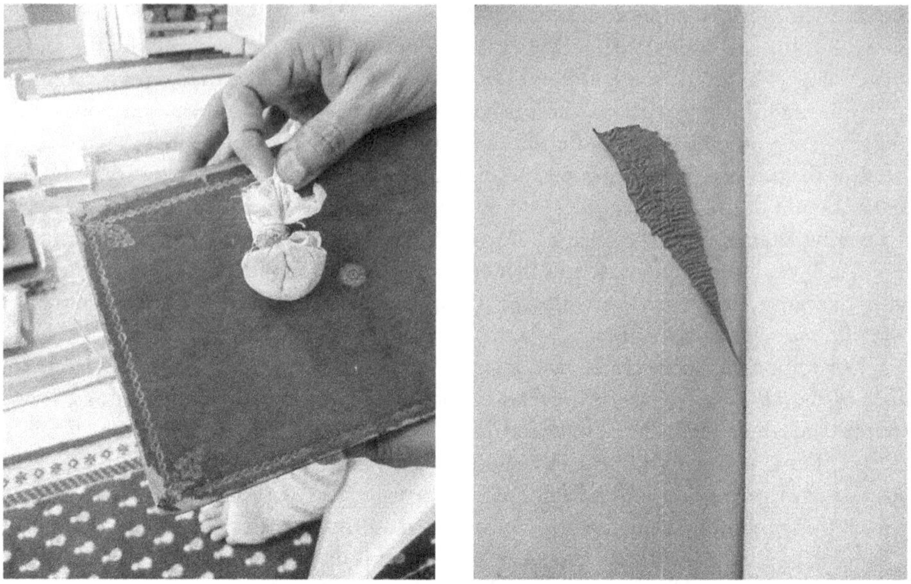

Figure 2.5 Manuscript preservation: *neem* leaf (right) and pouch stuffed with rice (left).

near, including termites, insects and fungi. The entire manuscript collection is dusted on a weekly basis and is thoroughly searched for these unwanted inhabitants. As termites prefer to nest in and thus eat away the spines of the manuscripts, many exemplars have been re-bound with a cloth binding, which is held together with a little white cotton string (more about this later). Extremely old or fragile manuscript copies are kept in cotton envelope-shaped pouches.

The question of ownership is an interesting one in the context of the Alawi *khizana*. I came across a marginal note in Persian, jotted down on the first flyleaf of a rather poor copy of the *Da'a'im al-Islam* by an anonymous reader, which read, 'One who claims that this book is mine is wrong, it belongs to the *da'wa*. If you will go to the court of any *pāshā* he will be the judge of that.'[26] This statement is followed by the name of the owner and several magical protective *budūḥ* squares. What the author of the marginal note means is that in the Alawi Bohra *da'wa*, the concept of legal ownership of a manuscript does not exist; he even refers to external authorities, the court of any *pasha*, as endorsing this concept. One can be a manuscript's temporary guardian and, as if it were a monument, write one's name in it as a *memento mori*, yet ultimately, it still belongs to the *da'wa* and thus its *khizana*.

It is for this reason that the tradition of making a manuscript into a *waqf* (a pious institution) and donating it to a shrine or *madrasa* does not exist in Bohra manuscript culture. After all, all *da'wa* manuscripts are stored in their own pious institution, a designated shrine of books where, theoretically, they remain for the rest of their material

[26] The text is followed by the name of the owner and several magical *budūḥ* squares. Manuscript copy of the *Da'a'im al-Islam* by Qadi al-Nu'man, Alawi *khizana*, Baroda.

Figure 2.6 The Mukasir Saheb seen wrapping a cotton thread around a manuscript (top), and manuscripts stacked onto each other horizontally (bottom).

existence and where they can only be accessed by those who are authorised to do so. Yet through the stamps and seals that *khizana* manuscripts contain (see Chapter 5), interesting parallels can be found with exclusionary practices found in *waqf* seals in, for instance, Iran and Central Asia, that restricted readership to certain types of people, such as philosophers.[27] Even though not stated explicitly, in the Bohra *khizana* context, the stamp of the *daʿwa* imposes a similar restriction: this manuscript should not be read by any individual other than the officials of the *daʿwa*.

[27] I thank Zahir Bhalloo for drawing my attention to the existence of these *waqf* seals.

Each Bohra *khizana* has its own, unique official *da'wa* seal. The manuscripts of the Alawi collection contain this seal and an official *khizana* sticker. Some manuscripts, which reached the treasury of books from outside the Alawi community, also contain the original *ṣaff* (shelf) and *khāna* (cupboard) number of their previous *khizana*; this is in contrast to the traditional way Alawi manuscripts were arranged and labelled. Even though the content of the *khizana* has always been secret, there is a tradition of recording the holdings of the *khizana* in handwritten inventories or *fihrists*. Paratextual features reveal that in earlier times when the collection was small, these lists were written on the first flyleaves and end leaves of manuscripts. However, once the collection grew extensively, these inventories were recorded on separate rolls and, at a later stage, in traditional Gujarati accounting books.

As transmission practices such as reading, memorising and copying the manuscripts of the *khizana* take place among such a select circle of scholars, *ijāzāt* (reading certificates) and *sama'āt* (hearing certificates) – meant to popularise the readership of religious texts to the masses in pre-modern bookish Muslim societies – are unnecessary. After all, the genealogy of the lineages of transmission between Dai, the *mansus* and perhaps the Mazoon Saheb and the Ra's ul Hudood is short; the names are known to all in the community and need no further legitimation.

The Mazoon Saheb has been the custodian of the *khizana* for more than twenty-five years (since he was appointed to the position), and he has made it his personal quest to 'complete' the collection of the *da'wa* as much as possible (more about this in the second part of this chapter). The Mazoon Saheb alone is responsible for preserving and restoring the manuscripts, and under his strict supervision the *makhtutat* have been (partly) listed and labelled (with stickers and with a vignette containing a small handwritten description of each work and its codicological and palaeographical features). As part of my project of cataloguing the *khizana*, As discussed previously, I was asked to continue labelling the manuscripts while preparing the catalogue. As discussed previously, I felt uncomfortable pasting stickers in the flyleaves of what were often very old manuscripts and inserting my own hand in them through these vignettes, yet this was the way the collection was identified and organised, and I could not go against the orders of the *da'wa*.

The Khizana as a Modern Manuscriptorium

In the Introduction to this study, I described how the Bohras' treasury of books is part of a larger social-historical phenomenon of bibliophilia in the Muslim world. Manuscript repositories and social practices of book keeping, collecting and treasuring, I argued, have long been part of the daily lives of individual book lovers, scholarly families, communities and rulers alike.

The Alawi treasury of books in Baroda offers us a glimpse into the past of a world long gone: one where manuscripts were copied manually by professional scribes, bookbinding and paper making were considered arts, and the handcrafted materiality of the codex was the norm, rather than the generic template of the industrially mass-printed book. It was a world where manuscripts were exchanged to be treasured and borrowed to be copied, and where the material life span of a handwritten book may have been shorter than that of its printed counterpart, yet through the tradition of *ijazat* and *sama'at*, the genealogy of its oral and manual transmission could go back for centuries.

The *khizana* is thus a remnant of the world of bookish communities and societies before print. Whereas the manual transmission of manuscripts in Muslim milieux on the subcontinent and beyond was interrupted by the advent of print, such as among the Khoja Ismailis and the Twelver Shi'i seminaries in Uttar Pradesh, the Bohra communities refrained from this technological invention, preserving the sacred practices and materiality of their *khizana* culture instead.[28] I discuss the ideological reasons for the Bohras' attitude to print in detail in Chapter 6.

The *khizana* tradition of the Bohras in Baroda has thus survived in South Asia, despite external factors such as the introduction of colonialism, inter-communal bifurcations, persecution and book confiscation, and the introduction of more recent universalising political and legal notions of Islam.[29] Had it been left to the termites of Gujarat, the treasury of books and its manuscripts would have long ago turned into dust. Yet, notwithstanding the climatic challenges of the monsoon season, the treasury of books continues to exist as a living *khizana*, a modern manuscriptorium where books are preserved and copied tirelessly by hand in a race against the elements. It survived, as I argue in this chapter, not because it was a forgotten manuscript repository from the past nor by accident, but for a very specific reason.

As much as keeping the *khizana* tradition alive in the Alawi and other Bohra communities has historically been a practice of the clergy, in the context of medieval Gujarat, I argue, it became an instrument of power. Following schisms and the centralisation of communities under their clerical authorities, manuscripts were used to create and maintain a new social order. In other words, each community needed a clerical family and its own books to survive. I argue that recently the Bohra *khizana* has come to play a more central role in the community as a signifier of a new Bohra identity: the Bohras as Neo-Fatimids. To understand the development of the Bohra *khizana* tradition through a *longue dureé* perspective, however, we must first start at the origins of the community's narrative.

2.2 A Lost Fatimid *Khizana* in Gujarat?

> It was one of the wonders of the world, and it was said that in all the lands of Islam there had been no greater library than the one in the palace of Cairo. Among the astonishing things is the fact that there were 1,200 copies of al-Tabari's chronicle and many others! It is said that there were 1,600,000 volumes in it.[30]

[28] See, for two in-depth studies on the introduction of print in Muslim communities in South Asia, Michel Boivin, *The Sufi Paradigm and the Makings of a Vernacular Knowledge in Colonial India: The Case of Sindh (1851–1929)* (Cham: Springer, 2020), 63–93, and Justin Jones, *Shia Islam in Colonial India: Religion, Community and Sectarianism* (Cambridge: Cambridge University Press, 2012), 58–66.

[29] See for book confiscation under the Mughals among the Bohras, Sheikh, 'Aurangzeb as Seen from Gujarat', 9–13.

[30] Translation Halm, *The Fāṭimids and their Traditions of Learning*, 92.

Map 2.1 Map of *khizana* sites in the Bohra tradition.

This is how the Syrian chronicler and poet Ibn Abī Tayyi' (d. 625/1228) described the Fatimid palace library. These numbers may have been exaggerated; the earlier-mentioned Egyptian historian al-Maqrizi and his contemporaries mention that the palace *khizana* collection comprised 200,000 manuscripts.[31] Even though the great historians of Egypt and Syria may not have agreed about the size of its collection, they were of the same opinion – that for the bookish societies they were part of, it was indeed one of the wonders of the world. By the time they wrote their accounts, however, the chambers of the palace library had been converted into a hospital wing, and its manuscripts had been partly destroyed, sold on the book market, or entrusted to al-Qāḍī al-Fāḍil (d. 597/1200), the head of Saladin's chancellery.[32]

On the basis of contemporary Fatimid documents, we know that the palace library was indeed referred to as the *khizanat al-kutub*, and it carried the name of the ruling Caliph-Imam, together with the epithet '*al-sharīfa*' (the exalted), which, as we have seen, is still in use among the Bohras. For instance, in a record in which a Fatimid *amir* is granted a book from the *khizana* in 537/1142, the treasury of books of Imam al-Ḥāfiẓ (r. 527–544/1132–1149) is referred to as the '*khizānat al-kutub al-Ḥāfiẓiyya al-sharīfa*'.[33] Whereas earlier, according to Geoffrey Khan, the administration of the

[31] Al-Maqrīzī, *Itti'āẓ al-ḥunafā'*, ed. Ayman Fu'ād Sayyid, vol. 3, 393. Halm, *The Fāṭimids and their Traditions of Learning*, 92. Geoffrey Khan, *Arabic Legal and Administrative Documents in the Cambridge Genizah Collections* (Cambridge: Cambridge University Press, 1993), 442. See also Paul Walker, 'Libraries, Book Collection and the Production of Texts by the Fatimids', 7–21.

[32] Halm, *The Fāṭimids and their Traditions of Learning*, 93.

[33] I am grateful to Geoffrey Khan for drawing my attention to this important document, 441–2. Khan, Arabic Legal and Administrative Documents in the Cambridge Genizah Collections, document no. 116, 442.

khizana fell under the responsibility of a highly-placed government official, from the year 517/1123 the *Dāʿī al-Duʿāt* (the chief missionary) was appointed to this position.[34] This information sheds new light on the historical legitimation of the Dai as the custodian of the *khizanat al-kutub* in modern times, especially in the absence of the hidden Imam in the Bohra community.

The Fatimid royal *khizana*, which was one of the largest of its kind in the medieval Islamic world, is seen as the mother library of all Bohra *khizanat*. As an institution of knowledge, it is considered the sacred model to which the Bohras trace their manuscript tradition and authority through textual transmission. It also serves as a template for their own treasury of books, both in terms of its canon and collecting practices designed to make the *khizana* as 'complete as possible' and through maintaining certain hierarchies of knowledge, conditions of access, and spatial arrangements (see Chapter 3). 'We take great pride in our Faatemi [*sic*] past with our *khizana*.' With this short one-liner, the Mazoon Saheb summarised the argument of what would later become the basis of this monograph. It contained all the elements of the community's identity as heirs of the Fatimids in modern times: pride, the Fatemi past, and 'our *khizana*'. Even though the collection of the Alawi *khizana*, or any other Bohra collection, is considerably smaller in size and only contains a micro-fraction of the collection of its Cairene mother *khizana*, it enshrines what the community considers to be its sacred Fatimid-Tayyibi heritage.

To the self-understanding of the community, the past, present and future, as discussed previously, are embedded in a narrative of the cyclical history of the universe and humankind that forms the basis of the Bohra Tayyibi Isma'ili knowledge system. According to the Bohra narrative, it was during the cycle of the Prophet Muhammad and during the manifestation of the Fatimid Caliph-Imams that the foundations were laid for this system of divine thought in a fixed and closed canon. This sacred canon of what is seen as 'high literature' or '*daʿwa* literature' was recorded by the Fatimid Caliph-Imams and their Dais in their famous institutions of learning and science, such as *Dār al-ḥikma* or *Dār al-ʿilm*, with Arabic as the Fatimid *lingua franca* of the empire.[35]

Tahera Qutbuddin writes: 'The Ṭayyibis [i. e. the Bohras] believe the entire corpus of their scholarly canon possesses a sacred nature as well as authoritative force . . . All Tayyibi writings are based on mother texts produced in the Fatimid period.'[36] What Qutbuddin is implying is a notion that is prevalent among all Bohra communities today: Bohra-Tayyibi manuscripts found in the *khizanat* of the different communities represent an uninterrupted chain of manuscript transmission from Fatimid Cairo to modern-day Surat or Baroda.

This does not mean, however, that all manuscripts present in Baroda, or other Bohra *khizanat* in Gujarat, necessarily date back to the twelfth century or are of

[34] Khan, *Arabic Legal and Administrative Documents in the Cambridge Genizah Collections*, 441–2.

[35] Heinz Halm, *The Fāṭimids and their Traditions of Learning*, 17–29, 41–55, 71–8. See also for the Dawoodi Bohra perspective: http://dawoodi-bohras.com/news/77/97/Fatimid-Literature-Creation-preservation-transfer-concealment-andrevival/d,pdb_detail_article_comment/ (last accessed 7 March 2014).

[36] Qutbuddin, 'The Da'udi Bohras', 338.

Egyptian provenance. Rather, it means that the texts of Fatimid-era authors and the Caliph-Imams, together with the corpus of Tayyibi-Yemeni authors, have been transmitted for centuries by generations of Bohra scholarly families and are read, copied and venerated today. Some of these copies may date back to the Tayyib-Yemeni period, whereas others, the 'millennial copies' as I liked to categorise them in the catalogue, dated from as late as the 2010s. As a matter of fact, manuscript copies of Fatimid and Tayyibi authors are currently being copied in the Barodian treasury of books. On a regular basis, the Dai proudly sends me pictures of his latest scribal achievements via WhatsApp. Does this make these manuscripts less authoritative? Academic circles, who discuss the living manuscript tradition of the Alawis, often discard these manuscripts: how could they be taken seriously when they were not even half a century old? And besides, as I was often asked condescendingly, do 'these clerics' even have the slightest idea what they are copying?

To the community, the constant re-copying of the *khizana* is not only the life's work of the Dai and considered his greatest act of piety, which brings *baraka* to the community; it is also seen as crucial for the continuation of the cyclical and linear conception of history. Through the labour of manual manuscript copying, which historically often occurred under challenging circumstances, the Bohras thus see themselves as the ultimate saviours of the Fatimid tradition. This grand narrative, which has been reproduced by scholars in Isma'ili studies, almost has an apocalyptic element to it: it is held that without the Tayyibi Bohras, as I discussed in the Introduction, the Fatimid tradition would have disappeared.[37] Whether there is truth to this claim will be further explored in this chapter by taking a closer look at the Alawi *khizana*'s provenance. Does it indeed reveal an uninterrupted chain of manuscript transmission from medieval Cairo to modern-day Gujarat? And if so, can we speak of a lost Fatimid *khizana* in Gujarat? We must first, however, investigate the Alawis' self-understanding of the history of their *khizana*, their grand narrative of historic continuity, and, essentially, of themselves.

The Alawi Bhai Sahebs distinguish different phases in the historiography of their community, based on the genealogy of people – the Prophets, the Imams and the Dais – and the transmission of books, including the mobility of *khizanat* between communities. The Fatimid period is seen as the period of revelation and the transfer of the Imamate and its manuscripts from Cairo to Yemen; this is followed by the periods of the concealment of the hidden Imam, which include the Yemeni period and the relocation of the community and its *khizana* to Gujarat; and finally, the Bohras in Gujarat, the history of the bifurcations, and the survival of the Alawi *da'wa* and the relocation of its headquarters-cum-*khizana* to Baroda.

The Fatimid era, however, is not the starting point in the genealogical *shajara* or tree of the Alawis and other Bohra communities. Instead, it is through the Fatimid Imams that they trace their genealogy to the divine, starting with Imam Tayyib as their twenty-first Imam and ending with Husayn and Hasan as the first two Imams, preceded by Ali b. Talib, the Prophet Muhammad, and the prophets that came before him (Figure 2.7). *Walaya*, or devotion to the Fatimid Imams, is deemed so important

[37] Poonawala, 'Isma'ili Manuscripts from Yemen', 220.

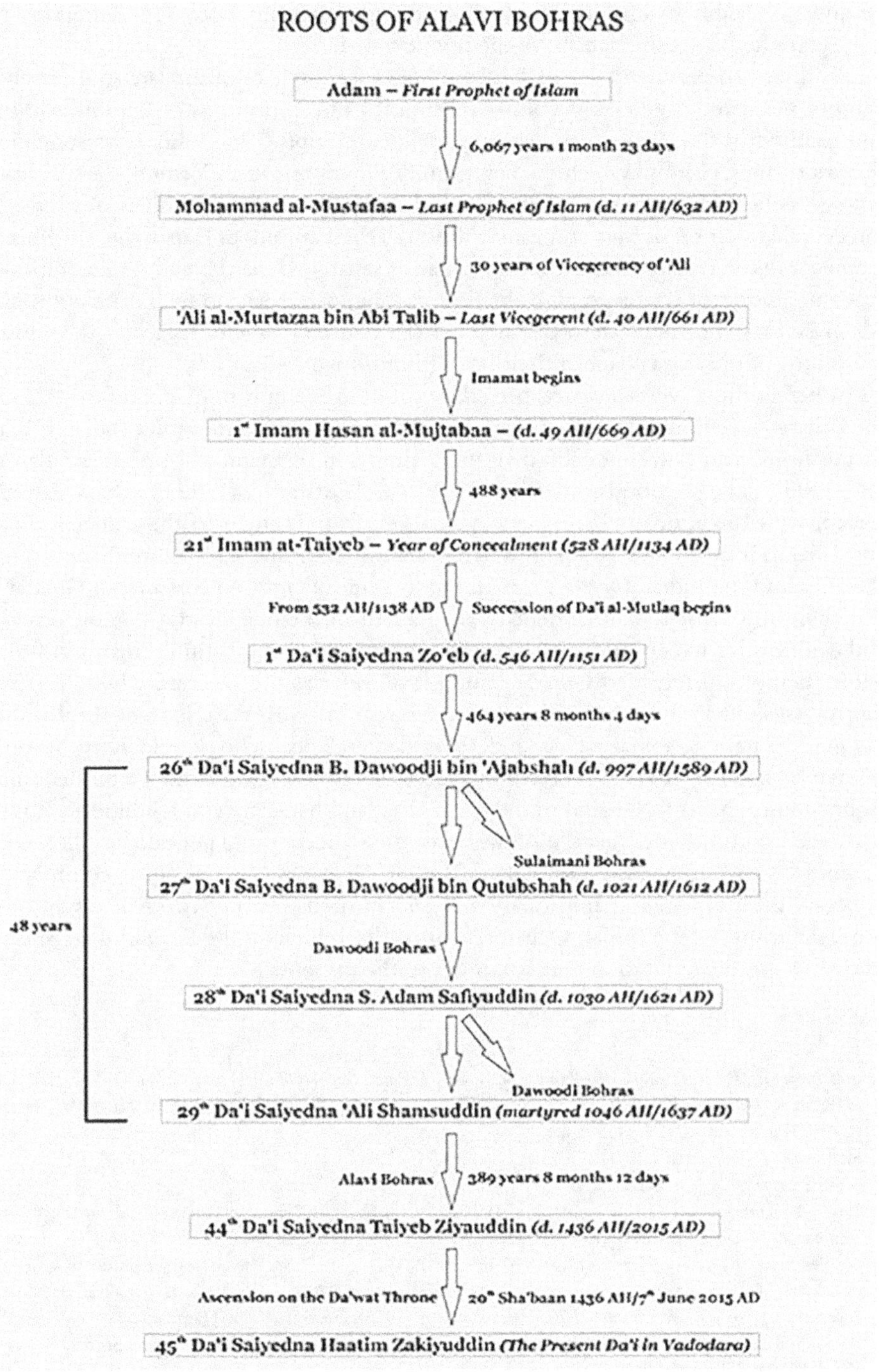

Figure 2.7 Genealogical *shajara* of the Alawi Bohras. Credits: Alawi *daʿwa*.

because, as Caliph-Imams, they were the last living Imams in history, and their teachings were the last manifestations of the divine word.[38]

As discussed previously, the fall of the Fatimid Caliphate in the late sixth/twelfth century marked the end of its culture of libraries and institutions of Isma'ili learning and resulted in the alleged destruction of its manuscripts.[39] In Bohra historiography, this is a turning point in which the community's predecessors in Yemen, the Tayyibis, emerge as both the survivors of the Fatimid dynasty and the custodians of its sacred intellectual tradition of *batin* and *zahir*. Although the Fatimids of Cairo, the Tayyibis of Yemen and the Bohras in India are described as separate dynasties and communities in academic works of reference, in Bohra historiography there is no such distinction: the Alawi Bohras are the modern-day heirs of the Fatimid-Tayyibi legacy as they await the return of the descendant of their last Fatimid Imam.

Whereas the Tayyibi-Fatimid period is crucial in the historiography of the Alawis, the Bohras trace their genealogical link to the Fatimid Imams via earlier Indian Ocean connections, which were established under the reign of Imam al-Mustansir Billah in 486/1093.[40] The previously-mentioned *Sijillat al-Mustansiriyya* refer to official Fatimid missionary expeditions, which were undertaken from Yemen to the *jazirat al-Sindh* and *Hind* to found a new *da'wa*, as well as establish maritime trade routes between the Red Sea and the Indian Ocean through the strategically located coastline of Gujarat.[41] For these missions, Indian students were trained in Yemen by the highest officials and clerics, after which they were formally introduced to the Fatimid Imams in Cairo before being dispatched to Gujarat, Sindh, and as far as the Deccan, where, according to *Ashab al-Yamin*, 'they enlightened the regions with the Noor of the Fatimid *Da'wa*'.[42] These legendary Dais and their descendants, who would later become known as the *Walī al-Hind*, successfully converted Hindu traders and established small Bohra communities in Gujarat in the cities of Khambhat, Patan and Sidhpur.[43] It is to these early communities that the Alawis trace their ancestry and genealogical link with Fatimid Cairo through the networks of Indian Ocean *da'wa* and *tijāra* (commerce). Whereas the networks of missionary activities turned into networks of *ziyara* over time, the routes of the Indian Ocean remained the vehicle of the Bohras' engagement in overseas trade, a tradition that continues to the present.

[38] It is therefore the first pillar of Qadi al-Nu'man's *Da'aim*. See *Kitāb al-Walāya* in al-Qaḍī al-Nu'man, *Da'ā'im al-'Islām wa dhikr al-ḥalāl wa 'l-ḥarām wa 'l-qaḍāya wa 'l-'aḥkām* (ed. Asaf b. Ali Asghar Fyzee) (Caïro: Dār al-'Aḍwā', 1991), 3–84.

[39] Halm, *The Fāṭimids and their Traditions of Learning*, 94.

[40] See for instance *Ashab al-Yamin*, 12–14.

[41] Samer F. Traboulsi, 'Lamak ibn Mālik al-Ḫammādī and Sulayhid-Fāṭimid Relations', *Proceedings of the Seminar for Arabian Studies*, Vol. 30, Papers from the thirty-third meeting of the Seminar for Arabian Studies held in London, 15–17 July 1999 (2000): 221–7, 224, 225. The region of Sindh was already under brief Fatimid sovereignty in the third/ninth century; see Ansar Zahid Khan, 'Ismailism in Multan and Sind', *Journal of the Pakistan Historical Society* 23 (1975): 35–57. Abbas Hamdani, *The Beginnings of the Ismā'īlī da'wa in Northern India* (Surat: Hamdani Institute of Islamic Studies, Islamic Studies Series, 1 (Cairo: Sirovic Bookshop, 1936).

[42] *Ashab al-Yamin*, 15.

[43] Ibid.

As the last historic vestige of Isma'ilism in the post-Fatimid period, Yemen plays a central role in the community's narrative of its uninterrupted link to the Fatimids. Yemen, as *Ashab al-Yamin* reports, 'is considered more auspicious than any other regions in the world . . . we cannot imagine the Da'wat of Allah without the role of Yaman'.[44] The Bohra notion of an uninterrupted chain to the Fatimids that carries on to the present is legitimised on two levels: through the genealogy of Dais who represented the hidden Imam during his occlusion and through the mobility of books over the Indian Ocean. It is this mobility of manuscripts and the *khizana* practices of the community that I am reconstructing in this section.

In my attempt to retrace the Alawis' *khizana* practices throughout history, the only *khizana* reference the Mazoon Saheb mentioned was that of Malika al-Arwā (d. 532/1138), the head of the Sulayhid dynasty, who allegedly had one of the biggest private *khizanat*, which was kept in her palace. In *Ashab al-Yamin* she is praised for being 'an open book of Fatemi literature, history, jurisprudence, and esoteric knowledge from a young age'.[45] Yet I was not able to find details on the transfer of books from Fatimid Cairo to Sulayhid Yemen in the historic sources of the *khizana*, nor were the Bhai Sahebs able to give me any information in this regard. In an unpublished lecture, the Mazoon wrote, 'Till now it was believed that the Isma'ili literature was totally destroyed and confiscated by their adversaries at the fall of Faatimid [*sic*] Egypt but a considerable amount has been preserved still in the Isma'ili Musta'alavi Taiyebi Community [i.e. the Bohra community]'.[46]

Yet his narrative does not tell us anything about the mobility of Isma'ili manuscripts from Cairo to Yemen. This was not surprising, because I later found out that, despite the immense importance of these manuscripts, the process is barely recorded in contemporary Tayyibi or later Bohra sources. The Bhai Sahebs credit one single Yemeni Dai as the 'flag-bearer' for keeping the 'Faatemi tradition alive' by sending manuscripts from Cairo to Yemen roughly a century prior to the fall of the empire. This flag-bearer, who in *Ashab al-Yamin* is referred to as the 'the one who performs *jihad* with the pen', was the Sulayhid chief *qadi* Lamak b. Mālik al-Hammādī (d. 491/1097).[47] As is recorded in the *Sijillat al-Mustansiriyya*, Lamak b. Malik was sent to the court of Imam al-Mustansir in Cairo as the official emissary of the Sulayhids in 454/1062. He spent five years in the company of another central figure in Bohra historiography, the Fatimid Dai and poet Mu'ayyad fī Dīn al-Shīrāzī (d. 470/1078).[48] While awaiting his audience with Imam al-Mustansir, Lamak b. Malik received his initiation into the esoteric sciences under the personal supervision of Mu'ayyad fi Din.[49] According to

[44] *Ashab al-Yamin*, a.

[45] Ibid., 16.

[46] Unpublished written lecture of the Mazoon Saheb titled 'The Occurrences of the Episodes of Arab History in Isma'ili Literature'.

[47] The story of Lamak's stay in Cairo is also narrated in several historiographic sources, such as Idrīs Imād al-Dīn's *'Uyūn al-Akhbār*. Traboulsi, 'Lamak ibn Mālik al-Ḫammādī', 222 (decrees no. 55 and 61).

[48] Hamdani, 'The Letters of al-Mustansir bi'llah', *Bulletin of the School of Oriental (and African) Studies* 7 (1934): 307–24, 308 (two letters, no. 42 and 54). See also Ḥātim al-Ḥāmidī, *Risālat tuḥfat al-qulūb wa-furğat al-makrūb* , 105–6, and Ḥusain Fayḍ Allāh al-Hamdānī, 'Some Unknown Ismā'īlī Authors and their Works', *Journal of the Royal Asiatic Society*, 1933, 361–2.

[49] Hamdani, *History of Isma'ili Da'wa*, 135. Hollister, *The Shia of India*, 241.

Hussein Hamdani, upon his return to Yemen Lamak b. Malik carried a substantial amount of manuscripts from the Fatimid palace *khizana* in Cairo, including works composed by Mu'ayyad fi Din.[50] Hamdani makes this claim on the basis of the *Sijillat*.[51] I, however, was not able to find any reference to the transfer of books from Cairo to Yemen in relation to Lamak b. Malik or any other Dai in the *Sijillat* al-Mustansiriyya. All that the decrees demonstrate, according to my reading, is that the contact between the two Dais did indeed exist. Whereas Bohra scholars such as Hamdani and Poonawala credit Lamak b. Malik for his heroic role in rescuing Fatimid manuscripts, Traboulsi suggests that, instead, Lamak b. Malik would later transmit this knowledge to the Sulayhids on the authority of Mu'ayyad fi Din and Imam al-Mustansir. In other words, he suggests that the knowledge transmission occurred orally, rather than through physical books carried from Cairo to Yemen.[52] This more plausible view corresponds with a tradition narrated from Imam al-Mustansir in *Ashab al-Yamin* in which he commanded, 'Oh Lamak b. Malik . . . Whatever you have learned from Saiyedna Mo'aiyad ash-Sheeraazi (aq) for five years in Egypt, shower it on the *mumineen* of Yaman and fill their hearts with the life of Faatemi knowledge so that the Noor of Imaamat remains in the land of Yaman.'[53] Another scenario of transmission could be that the movement of books was a more gradual process, which was simply not recorded in official decrees after the Tayyibis had pledged their allegiance to Imam Tayyib, rather than to the lineage of the ruling Caliphs in Cairo.

Whether orally or in the form of physical books, which texts were transferred and how they were selected are unknown. It is most likely that, while in Cairo, Lamak b. Malik and the Tayyibi Dais who came before him simply collected whatever was available, instead of selecting a homogeneous corpus of treatises representing the Fatimid intellectual tradition. As Traboulsi demonstrates, it is not at all certain whether Lamak b. Malik or any other Tayyibi scholar actually had access to the Fatimid *khizana* or any other libraries for that matter. In practice, the transfer of this literary corpus (whatever it entailed) from Egypt to Yemen caused much confusion among later Tayyibi scholars who were not able to consult the original Fatimid mother *khizana* any longer, as the texts were 'confusingly scattered'.[54]

Due to a lack of (accessible) sources, the question of whether and under which conditions physical Fatimid manuscripts from the royal *khizana* made their way to Yemen cannot be answered in this study. What is certain, however, is that Bohra *khizanat* today have preserved substantial amounts of Fatimid *zahiri* and *batini* literature. Not only have these manuscripts been preserved but they are actively read, copied and memorised; they form the basis of the Bohra knowledge system, including the practice

[50] Hamdani, *The Letters of al-Mustansir bi'llāh*, 308 (two letters, no. 42 and 54). Traboulsi, 'Lamak ibn Mālik al-Ḫammādī', 225. See also Hollister, *The Shia of India*, 317.

[51] Hamdani, *The Letters of al-Mustansir bi'llāh*, 308.

[52] Traboulsi, 'Lamak ibn Mālik al-Ḫammādī', 225. The transfer of manuscripts from Fatimid Egypt to Yemen is further discussed by Hamdani, *Al-Ṣulayḥiyyūn*, 175–83; Ayman Fu'ād Sayyid, *Tārīḫ al-maḏāhib al-dīniyya fī bilād al-Yaman ḥattā nihāyat al-qarn al-sādis al-hiǧrī* (Cairo: Dār al-miṣriyya al-lubnāniyya, 1988), 130–8; Poonawala, *Al-Sulṭān al-Khaṭṭāb: Ḥayātuhu wa-shiʿruhu* (Beirut: Dār al- ġarb al-islāmī, 1999, 2nd edn), 10–14.

[53] *Ashab al-Yamin*, 14.

[54] Traboulsi, 'The Formation of an Isma'ili Sect, 154, 155, 157 i56.

of jurisprudence. Moreover, the presence of these manuscripts, together with a corpus of treatises of later Tayyibi and Bohra authors, forms the basis of the Bohras' identity as Isma'ilis and their claim as heirs of the Fatimids.

What is fascinating is that the Tayyibis and Bohras not only preserved Fatimid manuscript titles but also enshrined Imamic Fatimid documents in their tradition. As I describe later, these documents were either preserved in the form of manuscripts or incorporated into other works by Tayyibi Dai scholars. Two examples in this regard are: (1) the earlier-mentioned Imamic diplomatic correspondence, the *Sijillat al-Mustansirriya*, and the documentary practices that eventually evolved from them; and (2) the tradition of preserving the orations of the Fatimid Caliphs during ceremonies, festivals and processions, which are also mentioned in the *Sijillat al-Mustansirriya*. These sermons are also documented in the historical multi-volume work *'Uyūn al-Akhbār* (The Choicest of Reports) by Idrīs Imād al-Dīn (d. 872/1468, no. 19) and are described in Ḥātim b. Ibrāhīm al-Ḥāmidī's (d. 596/1199) *Tuḥfat al-Qulūb* (The Precious Gift of the Hearts).[55] On the basis of the presence of Fatimid Tayyibi manuscripts and the *khizana* practices and manuscript culture that preserve this tradition, one could indeed speak of a 'lost' Fatimid treasury of books or, at least, fragments of it in Gujarat.

One could raise the question of how archetypal contemporary Bohra manuscript collections are in relation to the intellectual tradition of the Fatimids. Bohra *khizanat* do contain a large amount of Fatimid scholarship that was transferred to Yemen, but it should be taken into account that the transfer was most likely more haphazard than Bohra or academic narratives would like us to believe. Bohra *khizanat*, as well as family collections, give us a unique insight into texts that survived the Fatimids, but their holdings are certainly not exhaustive. Analysing anthologies and chrestomathies written by Tayyibi and Bohra scholars, it becomes clear that certain Fatimid titles simply did not survive the Tayyibi period, such as the nineteenth Dai Idrīs Imād al-Dīn b. al-Ḥasan's (d. 872/1468) historical work *Nuzhat al-Afkār* (The Excursions of Thoughts), which refers to lost sources and documents, and Ḥasan b. Nūḥ b. Yūsuf b. Muḥammad b. Ādam al-Bha'rūchī's (d. 939/1533) anthology *Kitāb al-Azhar*.[56] It is very possible that other abridged Fatimid treatises have indeed survived in Tayyibi manuscript corpora but have not yet been identified as such.

Critical inquiry about the archetypal nature of Bohra *khizanat* and their Fatimid collection may be interesting from an academic point of view, yet it is of no relevance to the Bohras, which explains why I could never find answers to these questions from the clerics nor in the books of their *khizana*. From the perspective of the community, the treasury of books *is* the lost Fatimid *khizana*. As a sanctuary of books, protected from the outside world in the absence of the hidden Imam, it continues to enshrine the eternal Fatimid esoteric and exoteric truths in an uninterrupted chain of transmission.

[55] Abbas Hamdani, *Tuhfat al-Qulub*. Paul Walker, *Orations of the Fatimid Caliphs: Festival Sermons of the Ismaili Imams* (London: I. B. Tauris, 2009), *Sayyid, Walker and Pomerantz, The Fāṭimids and their Successors in Yaman: An Edition and Translation of 'Uyūn al-Akhbār.*

[56] Samer Traboulsi, 'Sources for the History of the Ṭayyibī Ismā'īlī Da'wa in Yemen and its Relocation to India', *Journal of Islamic Manuscripts* 5 (2014): 246–74.

Devotees from a Distant Land: The Bohras in Tayyibi Yemen

The story of the lost Fatimid *khizana* in Gujarat and the question of the mobility of Fatimid manuscripts across the Indian Ocean can only be understood through the history and *khizana* practices of the Fatimids' successors in Yemen: the Tayyibi Isma'ilis. Whereas the study of the intellectual history of Isma'ilism in Yemen has gained momentum in the last decade, I approach this period with a focus that remains relatively explored: the active involvement of Gujarati Bohras in Yemen and their role in the mobility of manuscripts from Tayyibi *khizanat* in Yemen to Gujarat, where they would form the basis of all later Bohra *khizana* collections.

Historically, Tayyibi Yemen and Bohra Gujarat have been treated as separate geographic, social, political and linguistic worlds that were only connected through Indian Ocean trade routes and missionary expeditions until their religious headquarters merged in the sixteenth century. Apart from the Bohras' being reliable taxpayers and devout seekers of knowledge, their participation in the political, diplomatic, economic and intellectual history of medieval Yemen has hitherto been neglected. Two sources, however, shed a different light on the matter. The first is the earlier-discussed biographical-historiographical work, *Ashab al-Yamin*, which is written from the perspective of the modern-day Alawi community. The second is *Qarāṭīs al-Yaman*, a corpus of official correspondence in Arabic exchanged between *daʿwa* officials in Gujarat and Yemen between the early ninth/fifteenth and the late eleventh/seventeenth centuries. Essentially, *Ashab al-Yamin* is a biographical work on the traditions of the lives of the Tayyibi Dais based on the books of the Alawi *khizana*; it refers to the *Qaratis al-Yaman* on many occasions.

Original copies of the *Qaratis al-Yaman* have, to the best of my knowledge, not survived, yet similarly to the *Sijillat al-Mustansiriyya*, its letters were preserved in manuscript form in Bohra collections (Figure 2.8).[57] Reading the *Qaratis*, one gets the impression that the letters were preserved in a haphazard fashion: they are not in strict chronological order, some are not dated, and sentences and formulaic openings and endings are missing.[58] Yet, despite these shortcomings and the heavy editorial hand of later copyists, the letters of *Qaratis al-Yaman* are invaluable.[59] They demonstrate how

[57] Three manuscript copies are known of the *Qaratis*: (1) Tübingen University Library, MS Ma VI 330 (containing letters from 906 to 1199/1500 to 1688, dated 19th century). This manuscript was originally part of the *khizana* of the Hamdani family (and bears its original family seal). (2) Institute of Isma'ili Studies, No. 5, Adam Gacek, *Catalogue of Arabic Manuscripts in the Library of the Institute of Ismaili Studies* (London: Islamic Publications, 1985), 2. (3) Hamdani Collection Manuscript, donated to the IIS and originally part of the Hamdani family *khizana*, thus far not catalogued (containing letters from 800 to 1100/1397 to 1688, dated 19th century). Unfortunately, I only had access to the Tübingen manuscript, which covers a slightly shorter period than the copy catalogued by Gacek. See for further details Traboulsi, 'Sources for the History of the Ṭayyibī Ismāʿīlī Daʿwa in Yemen and its Relocation to India', 256–9; Traboulsi, 'The Ottoman Conquest of Yemen: The Isma'ili Perspective', in J. Hathaway (ed.), *The Arab Lands in the Ottoman Era* (Minneapolis: University of Minnesota Press, 2009), 45; and Poonawala, *Biobibliography*, 403.

[58] Traboulsi agrees and adds that the letters have been edited heavily, 'Sources for the History of the Ṭayyibī Ismāʿīlī Daʿwa', 256.

[59] For instance, the years on the flyleaf of Figure 2.8 do not respond with the dates cited in the actual letters.

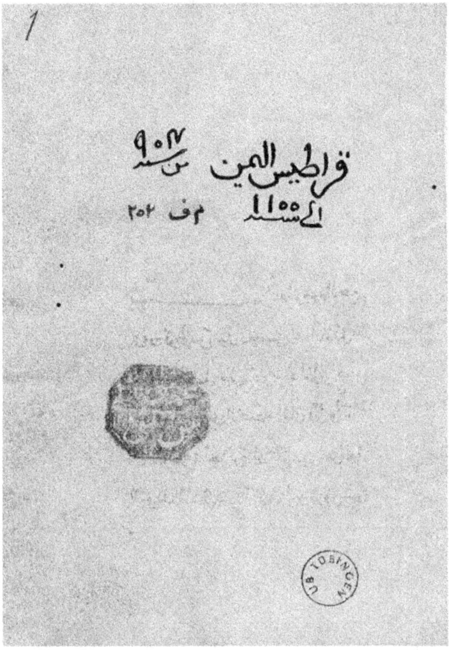

Figure 2.8 Flyleaf of *Qaratis al-Yaman* (folio 1v, MS Ma VI 330-Tübingen University Library) with the title of the work, the dates of the letters (from 954 to 1155), Hamdani owner stamp and *khizana* number. We will see the same owner stamp in manuscripts of the Alawi *khizana* (Figure 5.16). Credits: Tübingen University Library.

Indian Bohra merchants, *da'wa* officials, scholars and students, who were known in Yemen as the *muhajirūn*, actively participated in Yemeni Tayyibi society and its clerical milieu; they were no strangers to the political affairs of the *da'wa* or to its *khizana*. These letters, which were written before the Tayyibis' transoceanic transfer of their headquarters to Gujarat, thus give a voice to the Indian *muhajirun* in Yemen. The *Qaratis* reveal the active involvement of these Gujarati Bohras in the transmission of knowledge in Yemen, document their role in the safeguarding of the Tayyibi *khizanat* from looting and confiscation, and, as we see, record how these strangers from a distant land facilitated the gradual movement of Isma'ili books across the Indian Ocean.

Before we delve into the world of the *Qaratis*, let us first become acquainted with the Tayyibi Isma'ili community and its traditions of manuscript preservation and transmission. We may not know much about the movement of books from Fatimid Cairo to Tayyibi Yemen, yet what is certain is that in their new geographic and political context, the social meaning of these manuscripts changed from objects of splendor preserved in the imperial palace libraries to books belonging to a sectarian Fatimid Isma'ili community that continued to exist in secrecy, secluded in the mountainous Haraz region of Yemen. From their mountain fortresses and citadels in Thūla, Shibām and Masār, the Tayyibis thus preserved fragments of the intellectual tradition of an

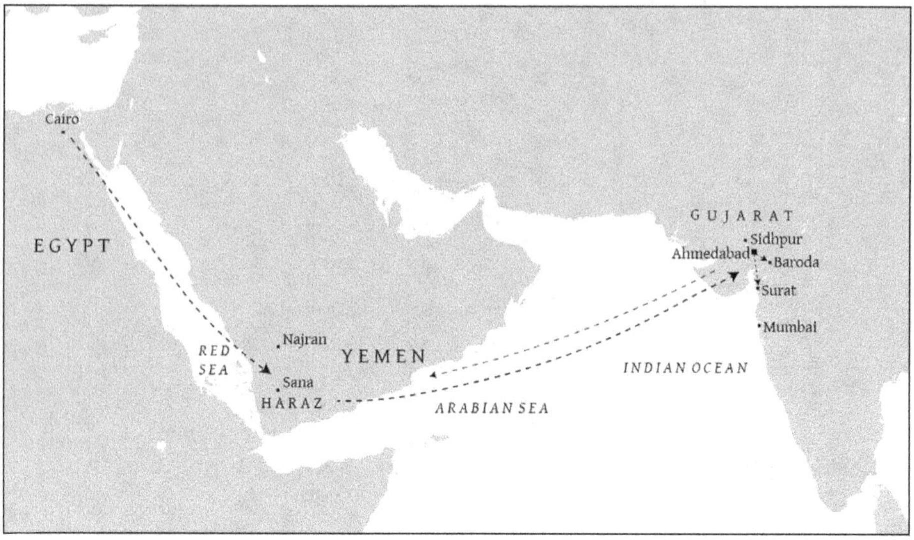

Map 2.2 Map of Yemen and the western Indian Ocean.

empire that had fallen into ruins and reshaped it as generations of Dais and their students preserved and expanded it (see Map 2.2).

Traboulsi has reconstructed the Tayyibis' traditions of transmission of knowledge, and much of what he describes corresponds to the modern Alawi *khizana* practices of access and concealment. Restrictions of access to *batini* manuscripts were imposed after the concealment of the last Fatimid Imam.[60] Fu'ad Sayyid paints a similar picture, as he acknowledges the existence of a central *khizana* belonging to Sy. Idris Imad al-Din, to which 'no historian outside of these religious circles associated with the Tayyibi *da'wa* in Yemen could possibly have had access to'.[61] What is remarkable, however, and does not have a place in the Bohras' modern *khizana* culture, is that, in addition to the community's central *khizana*, Tayyibi scholars initiated into the various *batini* levels of knowledge had their own private collections, a tradition that still survives among the Sulaymani Tayyibis in Yemen today.[62] Private *khizana* practices and a strong Tayyibi tradition of learning and manuscript transmission thus also existed outside clerical circles among scholarly families.[63] After taking an oath of allegiance, students were first taught a basic curriculum in the *zahiri* sciences, which included the memorisation and copying of exoteric manuscripts. As a form of tuition, these manuscripts would be donated to the master's *khizana*, a practice, I was told, that still continues among the

[60] Traboulsi, 'Sources for the History of the Ṭayyibī Ismā'īlī Da'wa', 248. See also Poonawala, 'Isma'ili Manuscripts from Yemen', 229.

[61] Sayyid, A. et al., *The Fāṭimids and their Successors in Yaman*, 8.

[62] Traboulsi, 'Sources for the History of the Ṭayyibī Ismā'īlī Da'wa', 251–6. See also Poonawala's account of his quest to find Isma'ili manuscripts among the Salaymanis in Yemen and Saudi Arabia: Poonawala, 'Isma'ili Manuscripts from Yemen', 235–7.

[63] Traboulsi, 'Sources for the History of the Ṭayyibī Ismā'īlī Da'wa', 248.

Dawoodis. Just like today, the novices had only limited access to the *batini* levels of religious literature. In contrast to contemporary Bohra communities, however, it was possible for scholars outside clerical circles to be initiated into the study of *batini* texts.[64]

As part of these restricted conditions of access to *batini* manuscripts, Traboulsi describes the introduction of an 'abridgement culture' in the Tayyibi and later Bohra tradition. Instead of being initiated into entire treatises, students only had access to excerpts from esoteric texts through anthologies and chrestomathies. He describes that, through this censored reading practice, students were made aware of the existence of certain *batini* texts without fully accessing their content. Looking at this development through the lens of social codicology, the circulation of the altered format of the original hefty *batini* tomes, he further argues, also made these manuscripts more manageable and less costly, which contributed to their survival and preservation.[65] The culture of abridgement can still be traced in Bohra *khizana* collections today and was carried on by Bohra scholars in Gujarat, such as by Ismāʿīl b. ʿAbd al-Rasūl al-Majdū' (d. 1184/1770) and his *Fihrist al-Kutub wa'l-Rasā'il* (Bibliography of Books and Treatises).[66] In the modern-day Alawi community, the abridgement culture of translating bits and pieces of the esoteric to a larger audience can be observed in sermons, in which the Dai occasionally refers to the *batini* books of the *khizana*. In the Dawoodi community the earlier-mentioned *Rasa'il al-Muhammadiyya*, meant for the religiously educated elite, fulfils a similar role of lifting a small corner of the veil of esoteric knowledge.[67]

Despite the fact that the Tayyibi milieu of esoteric learning was sequestered from the outside world, promising Bohra students from the overseas community in Gujarat, as is recorded in the *Qaratis* and the *Ashab al-Yamin*, would cross the western Indian Ocean to pursue studies in *daʿwa* literature. Some of these students, as we see later, would become famous scholars, contributing to the Tayyibi-Fatimid tradition.[68] *Ashab al-Yamin* mentions the special status of the Indian students in Yemen, who were welcomed personally by the Dai and were allowed to sit in his assembly above the *hudud* (ranks) of the *daʿwa*. It reports that Sy. Idris Imad al-Din once said, 'The Indian students are superior to the *mu'mineen* from Yaman because of their steadfastness and strong belief of Da'wat, which brought them all the way from India facing hardships and difficulties of journey'.[69] The students from India, the *Ashab* reports, who would be selected by the *Wali* in India, would cross the Indian Ocean

[64] Traboulsi, 'Transmission of Knowledge and Book Preservation in the Ṭayyibī Ismāʿīlī Tradition', 26, 27.

[65] Ibid.

[66] Al-Majdu' was a Dawoodi Bohra scholar from the city of Ujjain, Madhya Pradesh, who infamously was given the nickname 'al-Majdu' (Arabic for 'The one with the disfigured nose') after his nose was cut off, following his support for the separatist Hebtiya movement. The Hebitya movement was led by his son, who claimed to be in contact with the hidden Imam. Poonawala, 'MAJDUʿ, ESMĀʿIL', *Encyclopædia Iranica*, online edition, 2015, http://www.iranicaonline.org/articles/majdu-esmail (last accessed 22 September 2015); Daftary, *The Ismāʿīlīs*, 285.

[67] See for a complete list, Traboulsi, 'Transmission of Knowledge and Book Preservation in the Ṭayyibī Ismāʿīlī Tradition', 33–4.

[68] *Ashab al-Yamin*, 116.

[69] Ibid., 101.

together in cohorts to Yemen, where they received a full training in the *ʿulūm al-daʿwa* (the sciences of the *daʿwa*). Upon completion of their studies, the *muhajirun* would return to their respective home towns, after receiving the *raza* of the Dai to work in the *khidma* (service) of the *daʿwat al-Fatimiyya* in India.[70]

It was not unusual for an individual to undertake several voyages across the Indian Ocean in his or her life, as the *daʿwa* networks of Isma'ili learning were intrinsically linked to the community's commercial networks of *tijara*. In fact, many of these scholars and students were Indian Bohra traders who commuted between Gujarat and Yemen with their goods; they either stayed in Yemen seasonally, awaiting the change of the monsoon winds eastwards, or settled there permanently. These Indian Ocean networks also enabled the movement of other professional seafarers, such as captains, middlemen and slaves. The lives and trajectories of many of these ordinary individuals, which have come to light through the study of trade documents in recent years, are rarely mentioned in Tayyibi Bohras sources.[71] There is one narration, however, about a common man in the *Ashab*, which revolves around an Indian *bhishti* (water carrier) from Gujarat who travelled to Yemen with a group of Bohra students during the time of Sy. Idris Imad al-Din. Upon his arrival in Aden, the *Ashab* reports, the *bhishti* was received with open arms by Dai Idris Imad al-Din in Shibam, who, to the great dismay of the other *hudud* of the *daʿwa*, decided to test the loyalty of his followers by inviting the water carrier to sit in the *majlis* above the Yemeni *mu'minin*. Following the great unrest that prevailed among the Yemeni believers, the Dai decided to put the Indian community to the same test, with the aim of proving that, as believers, they were more loyal and obedient to him than their Yemeni brothers.

On the orders of the Dai, the *bhishti* was sent back to Gujarat at once, carrying gifts and two official decrees to be handed over to the *Wali al-Hind* of the Bohras. In the first decree, Idris Imad al-Din ordered the instalment of the *bhishti* as the new *Wali* with immediate effect. To his great surprise, upon his arrival the *Wali* kissed the decree and immediately obeyed the order of Idris Imad al-Din. The *bhishti*, according to the story, was made the most powerful authority of the Indian *daʿwa*, replacing the former *Wali* Mawlā Ādam (fl. ninth/fifteenth cent.). As he was not Muslim, the *Ashab* reports that the water carrier was taught to pray and recite the Qur'an. After he had completed the *maghrib* prayer, following the instructions of Idris Imad al-Din, the second decree was opened, which congratulated Mawla Adam for passing the test and confirmed his reinstatement as the *Wali*. The decree, according to the story, furthermore stated that the *bhishti* was ordered to return back to Yemen to report to Idris Imad al-Din and to hand over the official letters written by Mawla Adam that proved the Indian community's absolute obedience to the Dai. Pleased with the outcome, Idris Imad al-Din addressed the Yemeni community,

70 *Ashab al-Yamin*, 102. The phrase '*fī khidma daʿwat al-Fāṭimiyya*' can be found throughout the *Qaratis* when referring to the services that *da'wa* officials carried out.

71 See, for instance, Amitav Ghosh, *In an Antique Land: History in the Guise of a Traveler's Tale* (New York: Vintage, 1992); Goitein and Friedman, *India Traders of the Middle Ages*; Lambourn, *Abraham's Luggage*; Fahad A. Bishara, *A Sea of Debt: Law And Economic Life In the Western Indian Ocean* (Cambridge: Cambridge University Press, 2017).

including its *huhud* and *mashāyikh* (s. *shaykh*), in an assembly with the following devastating words:

> Oh mumineen of Yemen, look at the submission and loyalty of the mumineen of India. Very soon that land will nurture the Noor of Da'wat. The blessings of the Da'wat will go away from here. Brothers of India who have sacrificed their lives and wealth for the Da'wat will raise the flags of Faatemi Da'wat on their land.[72]

The theme of the clever Dai putting his followers to the test through trials and tribulations recurs often in the *Ashab*. I have thus far not been able to retrace this particular story of the water carrier, which obviously favours the Indian community, in the *Qaratis* or any other sources. In addition to the fact that in the Alawi narrative the land of Gujarat is destined to raise the Fatimid flag, the story highlights two other important features: the ethnic rivalries and tensions between the Gujarati Indians and the Yemeni Arabs within the *daʿwa* and the mobility of people between the two continents.

Please Send Books: Qaratis al-Yaman

Within the Isma'ili networks of the Indian Ocean, the commercial interests of the Gujarati Bohras by no means excluded the spiritual pursuits of seeking knowledge, which occasionally even led to scholarly careers in the ranks of the *daʿwa*. One such Indian Bohra scholar, who appears throughout the *Qaratis* as both an author and recipient of the letters and is praised continuously in the correspondence of others, was Hasan b. Nuh al-Bharuchi.

Al-Bharuchi, who was commonly referred to in Yemen as '*al-Hindī*' (the Indian), was a prominent Indian Ocean trader from Khambhat, Gujarat, with businesses reaching as far as the Arabian Peninsula, the Levant and Egypt.[73] Due to his affluent position as a merchant tycoon, al-Bharuchi was in the privileged position of receiving his education directly from two Yemeni Dais in Masar and Shibam, Ḥasan b. Idrīs (d. 918/1512, no. 20) and Ḥusayn b. Idrīs (d. 933/1527, no. 21); after completing his education, he dedicated himself to the *khidma* (service) of the *daʿwa*.[74] He is famous for his seven-volume chrestomathy of Isma'ili literature, *Kitāb al-Azhar* (The Book of Flowers), in which he not only preserves many works that otherwise would have perished but also describes the curriculum and progress of his studies.[75]

Al-Bharuchi became a powerful, if not an omnipresent, figure in the Tayyibi *daʿwa*. In addition to his scholarship, *Ashab al-Yamin* reports that he funded the education and

[72] *Ashab al-Yamin*, 101–3.

[73] Ibid., 108. Poonawala, 'al-Bharūchī, Ḥasan b. Nuḥ', in Kate Fleet, Gudrun Krämer, Denis Matringe, John Nawas and Everett Rowson (eds), Encyclopaedia of Islam, Vol. 3,, http://dx.doi.org/10.1163/1573-3912_ei3_COM_25156 (last accessed 25 August 2020).

[74] Ibid.

[75] Not to be confused with the Zaydi *fiqh* compendium of the same title by Imam al-Mahdī Aḥmad b. Yaḥyā al-Murtaḍā (d. 841/1437), Messick, Sharia Scripts, 62–4. Poonawala, 'al-Bharūchī. Ḥasan b. Nūḥ'; al-Bharūchī, *Kitāb al-azhār wa-majmaʿ al-anwār al-malqūṭa min basātīn al-asrār*, ed. ʿĀdil al-ʿAwwā (Damascus: Muntakhabāt Ismāʿīliyya, 1958).

lodgings of the Indian students, became the main adviser and close confidant of several Tayyibi Dais, negotiated on behalf of the community with Zaydi Imams and Ottoman officials, and was responsible for the appointment of the Tayyib *daʿwa's Mawālī al-Hind* (the *Walis* of India) overseas and the financial accounts of the community.[76] At the height of his career, al-Bharuchi took on the role of mentor and teacher of another central figure of the *Qaratis* as he prepared him to assume the post of Dai: Sy. Yusūf b. Sulaymān (d. 974/1567, no. 24), the first appointed Indian Dai, who ruled the *daʿwa* from the village of Ṭayba, Wadi Dhahr, from 946 to 974 (1539–67). Al-Bharuchi died in the fortress of Masar in Yemen, where he was buried, yet as befits a cosmopolitan of the Indian Ocean, a lesser-known second shrine, which is still frequented by the Bohras for his *ʿurs*, is located in Khambhat.[77]

The sources agree that, as an intermediary between both Indian Ocean worlds, al-Bharuchi proved his worth in gold (or books) in Yemen. The tenth/sixteenth century was a tumultuous period for the Tayyibi community, which struggled to survive several internal *fitnas* (splits and conflicts), while it was simultaneously involved in constant battles with the Zaydi Imamate.[78] The Tayyibis had historically relied on a centralised state in the lowlands of Yemen, under the Ayyubids, Tahirids and Ottomans, to avoid persecution under the Zaydi Imamate in the highlands in the north, which continued until the Ottoman conquest of Yemen in 913/1507.[79] During al-Bharuchi's lifetime, the Tayyibi community was forced to leave one of its main strongholds in Wadi Dhahr, which was taken over by the Zaydis in 931/1525, and move to join the other Tayyibis in Haraz. Towards the end of his life, al-Bharuchi negotiated on behalf of his community with the Zaydis, financed the Tayyibi *jihad*, and helped to bail out high officials of the community on several occasions.[80] After his death, the *Ashab* reports, Yemen sank into anarchy and chaos.[81] The Tayyibis were defeated by the Zayids once again, and their fortresses in Shibam, Masar and other places were taken over. The Dai was imprisoned, shrines were destroyed and manuscript *khizanat* were looted.[82]

The political power of the Tayyibis in Yemen weakened considerably, which resulted in the strategic appointment of the first Indian Dai in Yemen in 946/1539, Sy. Yusuf b. Sulayman, a *muhajir* from Sidhpur, Gujarat. The final chapter of *Ashab Yamin* is dedicated to Sy. Yusuf. It reports that, in addition to the political turmoil, the Yemeni *mu'minin* had drifted away from their faith and loyalty to their Dai and that the *nass* should therefore be bestowed on a devotee from the Indian followers.[83] The letter of *nass*, together with *kutub al-daʿwa* and 'treasures', were sent from Yemen to Sidhpur. Upon receiving the letter of *nass*, Sy. Yusuf accepted his responsibility. The news was conveyed to every Bohra *mohallah* in Gujarat, and Sy. Yusuf subsequently

[76] *Ashab al-Yamin*, 108–9.
[77] Ibid., 109.
[78] The Zaydi Imamate was founded in 284/897 and continued to rule large parts of Yemen until 1962. See Messick, *Sharia Scripts*, 11–19.
[79] Traboulsi, 'The Ottoman Conquest of Yemen', 42, 43.
[80] Ibid., 48.
[81] *Ashab al-Yamin*, 131.
[82] Ibid. Traboulsi, 'The Ottoman Conquest of Yemen', 41–60.
[83] *Ashab al-Yamin*, 130.

sailed to Aden disguised as a merchant.[84] The *Ashab* explains that 'the disciples from India' had to conceal their identities to avoid persecution. Sy. Yusuf's cover proved to be unsuccessful, as he was arrested in Yemen and his possessions, including books, were confiscated.[85]

Despite the short intervals of prosperity and peace that came with the advent of Ottoman rule in Yemen, Traboulsi argues that under Sy. Sulayman the *daʿwa*'s authority in Yemen slowly crumbled, and the Indian Dai struggled to govern the community and its Yemeni tribal factions; this led to conflicts between the tribes and the *daʿwa*, rivalries between the Indian and Yemeni believers, and extortion from Ottoman officials (see the later discussion).[86] The Tayyibis relocated the headquarters of the *daʿwa*, including its followers, clerics and *khizana*, overseas to Ahmedabad in 974/1566. The transoceanic move could not have come at a better time, as Haraz was plagued by a pandemic and under siege by the Zaydis, which had disastrous consequences for the Tayyibis who remained in Yemen.[87] Al-Bharuchi was an eyewitness for most of these historic events, which would eventually transform the *daʿwa* and its centres of learning for good. He may not have lived long enough to witness the transoceanic move of the community's headquarters, yet the *Qaratis* reveal that he was anticipating and possibly even making arrangements for this relocation to ensure the survival of the *daʿwa* and its manuscripts.

Let us return to the year 910/1509. The Tayyibi community is headed by Sy. Hasan b. Idris, who, at an old age, has entrusted al-Bharuchi with the affairs of the *daʿwa*, including its official correspondence with Gujarat. In Aden, on the eighteenth month of *safar* (7 June), al-Bharuchi, who is referred to by the copyist in the margins as 'Sayyidi Hasan b. Nuh', writes to Sayyidi Rāja b. Ḥasan Walī al-Hind Shāja' al-Dīn, the *Wali al-Hind* of Gujarat, in response to an earlier letter from Ahmedabad, which has not been preserved.[88] The addressee of the letter, Sayyidi Raja b. Hasan Wali al-Hind Shaja' al-Din (d. 925/1519), was not just any *daʿwa* official: as the eighth *Wali al-Hind* of Ahmedabad he was the head of the Bohra community in Gujarat. In Bohra historiographical sources he is known as Moulai Raj Bin Moulai Hasan. Today, his grave in Saraspur is frequented by believers as he is seen as 'the champion of the Fatimid da'wa in India'. The *Ashab* describes how, ten years after his correspondence with al-Bharuchi, the Indian *daʿwa* experienced a *fitna* within the community. Moulai Raj Bin Moulai Hasan, it reports, was forced to operate underground, disguising himself as a beggar while visiting the houses of the *mu'minin* at night and bringing them back to their Fatimid *imān* (faith). These nightly missions would eventually lead to his martyrdom, as he was allegedly chopped into pieces by his opponents on the market square of Ahmedabad.[89]

Before his violent death, however, Moulai Raj Bin Moulai Hasan frequently corresponded with al-Bharuchi regarding the affairs of the Indian *daʿwa*. Despite the fact that the correspondence took place between two native Gujaratis, the letters, like all

[84] Ibid., 131, 132. Traboulsi, 'The Ottoman Conquest of Yemen', 48.

[85] *Ashab al-Yamin*, 134.

[86] Traboulsi, 'The Ottoman Conquest of Yemen', 51, 52. *Qaratis al-Yaman*, 44r–46v.

[87] Ibid., 52.

[88] Qaratis al-Yaman, 9r.

[89] *Ashab al-Yamin*, 116, 117. See for a detailed account on the Ja'fari schism: Daftary, *The Ismāʿīlis*, 278, 280.

the other *Qaratis*, are written in Arabic, the official language of correspondence of the *da ʿwa*. After exchanging formalities and updating Moulai Hasan on the latest political developments in Yemen, al-Bharuchi writes:

> Concerning the two manuscript titles [you requested], '*al-Zīj fī 'l-Tanjīm*' and '*al-Malīḥa fī 'l-Taqwīm*', I sent the messenger to al-Ḥaql and a [positive] reply came from the eminent scholars. We ordered a copyist to prepare a flawless copy of both '*Zīj fī Tanjīm*' and '*al-Malīḥa fī Taqwīm*'.[90] As for the other book which has been requested previously,[91] it is not present in the *khizāna*. I kept insisting on the manuscript copies of the '*Zīj fī Tanjīm*', and '*al-Taqwīm*'; however, the messenger returned before the procession of the caravan, neither with [a copy of] one work nor the other. After the movement of the caravan, I subsequently traveled to al-Ḥaql myself and brought the two copies along. I also searched for the book you mentioned in the *khizana* which, God willing, I will be able to send in the future. (Figure 2.9)[92]

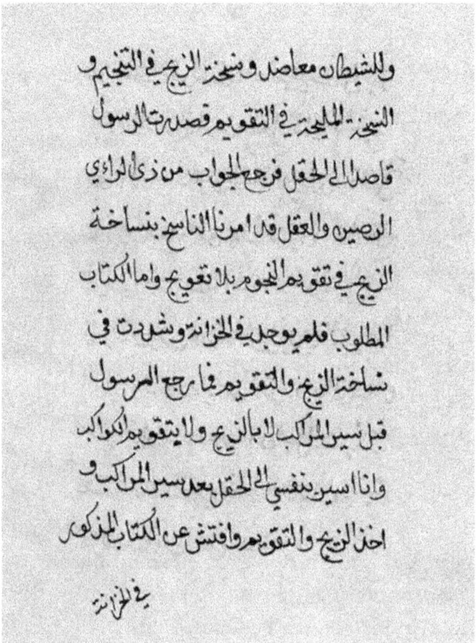
وللشيطان معاصد ونسخة الزيج في التنجيم و
النسخة المليحة في التقويم قصدت الرسول
قاصد الى الحقل فرجع الجواب من ذوى الراى
الرصين والعقل قد امرنا الناسخ بنساخة
الزيج في تقويم النجوم بلا تعويج واما الكتاب
المطلوب فلم يوجد في الخزانة وشددت في
نساخة الزيج والتقويم فما رجع الرسول
قبل سير المراكب لا بالزيج ولا بتقويم الكواكب
وانا اسير بنفسي الى الحقل بعد سير المراكب و
اخذ الزيج والتقويم وافتش عن الكتاب المذكور
في الخزانة

Figure 2.9 Fragment of *Qaratis al-Yaman* (folio 8v, MS Ma VI 330-Tübingen University Library), the correspondence between al-Bharuchi and Moulai Raj Bin Moulai Hasan. Note the catchword '*fī 'l-khizāna*' ('in the *khizana*'). Credits: Tübingen University Library.

[90] The scribe has copied the text here as *al-Zīj fi 'l-Taqwīm wa 'l-Nujūm* and later as *al-Zīj wa 'l-Taqwīm*.

[91] The book Moulai Raj Bin Moulai Hasan requested earlier is a polemical work mentioned in f. 7v., which was collated by the Dai and written against someone (*fulān*) who was against the Tayyibis, who are referred here to as the *ahl al-ḥaqq*.

[92] *Qaratis al-Yaman*, f. 8r–9v.

From the section of the letter, we can conclude that the two had engaged in an earlier exchange about a request for manuscript copies made by Moulai Raj Bin Moulai Hasan. The casual yet businesslike tone of the letter, as well as of several other letters in which others made similar book requests, seems to indicate that it was not uncommon to order books overseas, which were transported by Bohra merchants from Aden to Ahmedabad and other towns in Gujarat. Through the corpus of *Qaratis*, we can thus reconstruct a practice of overseas book collecting, copying and exchange. The *Qaratis* that have come down to us are certainly not complete and provide only a tantalising glimpse of these practices. Nevertheless, the transfer of Tayyibi-Fatimid manuscripts across the Indian Ocean from Yemen to India was a gradual process that took place over decades and perhaps centuries, which, contrary to what has been assumed previously, preceded the official transfer of the community in 974/1566. It did not occur as a sudden relocation of the entire Tayyibi *khizana*.

Why was the *Wali al-Hind* requesting manuscripts from Yemen? Was he building his own private *khizana* or ordering these astrological treatises for his own scholarly interests? Perhaps. Was there a shortage of Arabic manuscripts among the Bohras? Probably. Were the books used as commodities and diplomatic gifts of exchange, being part of the constant negotiations between the two *daʿwa*s? Most likely. These may all have been factors that played a role in Moulai Raj Bin Moulai Hasan's manuscript request to al-Bharuchi. However, it is my hypothesis that there was more at stake and that the manuscript order of the *Wali al-Hind* was part of a larger development. Through al-Bharuchi, the Indian *daʿwa* was gradually building its own *khizana*. This effort was not merely the pursuit of gathering knowledge for scholarly interests; more importantly, it was done to prepare the Indian *daʿwa* for its new leading role as the headquarters of all believers, led by an Indian Dai from Gujarat. In describing the role of the *khizana* in Bohra theology, we established that without a *khizana* there is no *daʿwa*, as its *kutub* are essential in order for the Dai to govern the community and, in the long term, for the return of hidden Imam to the community. Establishing a central *daʿwa khizana* in Ahmedabad was thus crucial for the success of the Indian community in its future role in governing believers in both al-Yaman and al-Hind. Al-Bharuchi, who was familiar with both worlds, was instrumental in this process of gradual manuscript relocation. His involvement demonstrates that the Indian *muhajirun* in Yemen were not merely visitors or passive students. On the contrary: they were at the centre of the Tayyibi community and its affairs.

Locating the requested manuscripts, the letter reveals, was not an easy task. Al-Bharuchi describes the 'hunt' he undertook to find the titles that Moulai Raj Bin Moulai Hasan requested, after previous failed attempts to send a courier to locate them. He personally travels to al-Haql, a small town south-east of San'a, where he consults 'the *khizana*' and is able to locate the first two manuscript titles. As for the third, untitled manuscript, which his messenger was initially unable to find in al-Haql, the letter is unclear about whether al-Bharuchi was able to retrieve it and whether it was located in the same *khizana* in al-Haql or elsewhere. Interestingly, the titles that Moulai Raj Bin Moulai Hasan requested are astronomy works of non-Isma'ili provenance. It is thus possible that al-Bharuchi's search led him into the territory of Sunni, Mu'tazili or perhaps even Zaydis libraries. If this were the case, the letter would illustrate an early example of scientific exchange, despite the strong sectarian tensions between the communities. The '*khizana*' he refers to towards the end of the letter could also have been a Tayyibi Isma'ili collection, yet this is difficult to confirm.

The reply to this letter has not been preserved, and thus we do not know whether the manuscript copies ever reached Moulai Raj Bin Moulai Hasan, and if they did, whether he was pleased with them. In the letters that follow in the *Qaratis*, Moulai Raj Bin Moulai Hasan's successors continue to correspond with al-Bharuchi from Ahmedabad about the exchange of gifts and goods[93] and praise him for his supervision of the affairs, guidance and education of the *da'wat al-hadiyya* in Yemen, Hind and Sindh.[94]

Even though we remain in the dark about many aspects of the letter, Moulai Raj Bin Moulai Hasan's book request is significant, as the mobility of the manuscripts he requests, as well as of many other manuscripts that were dispatched to Gujarat, made possible the development of later Bohra *khizana* collections. Remarkably, the practice of manuscript exchanging, gifting or requesting copies between communities, cities and states, as I observed, still continues between the Bohra *da'was*, despite strained relations. In fact, as I argue in Chapter 4, this practice forms the basis of how *khizana* collections are built and continue to function and survive today.

In another letter from Yemen to Gujarat,[95] al-Bharuchi is in contact with a certain Miyān Nūḥjī b. Ādam concerning the request of books and textiles. I was not able to identify Miyan Nuhji b. Adam in Bohra sources, which could indicate that he was a *da'wa* official of lower rank in India.[96] This letter, as so many in the *Qaratis*, is not dated, and given the fact that the chronological arrangement of the letters is sometimes unclear, we cannot be certain that this letter was indeed written after the letter shown in Figure 2.9. Al-Bharuchi writes to his colleague Miyan Nuhji b. Adam:

> As for the book which we ordered, if a time occurs when you are free, let it be copied and sent along with other items, such as textiles from Ahmedabad, Cambay, Surat, and Bharuch. I would like to know what books you have, and I will let you know which books I have and we can order. Please sign the letters that are with you so that we know what is with you and what is with us, in order that if we need something, we can order it from you, God willing.

Whereas, in the first letter, it was the Indians who ordered manuscripts to be copied from Yemen, in this piece of correspondence al-Bharuchi himself requests manuscript copies to be sent from the centre of the Bohra community in Ahmedabad to Yemen. This letter illustrates how the transport of books was facilitated, as they were sent along with other trading commodities (textiles) from Surat and the coastal trading towns Khambhat and Bharuch. Through this short statement, the letter thus supports the earlier argument that the networks of *tijara* and the spiritual affairs of the *da'wa*

93 *Qaratis al-Yaman*, 9r.

94 Ibid., 17r.

95 *Qaratis al-Yaman*, 34v.

96 The title of this official 'Miyan' is interesting, as it is a Mughal title. This does not mean the *da'wa* official was Mughal, but rather indicates that the Bohras were influenced by Mughal court culture (see Chapter 1) as Adam Nuhji is a typical Bohra name. It shows how the Bohras copied Mughal hierarchies and notions of the clerics being 'royals' (see discussion in Chapter 3, section 3.4).

were intimately linked. In fact, similarly to how the community's Dais would cross the Indian Ocean incognito, Tayyibi Bohra esoteric manuscripts possibly may have been transported disguised as trading goods. The passage also gives us an insight into the documentary practices of the *qaratis* tradition between Yemen and Gujarat, as al-Bharuchi specifically asks his colleague to sign the letters upon receipt. Al-Bharuchi not only orders books from overseas but also requests an inventory of what manuscripts are available in Gujarat. In return, he offers Miyan Nuhji b. Adam a list of manuscripts available in Yemen. Unfortunately, these lists have not survived in the *Qaratis*.

In this letter, it is thus al-Bharuchi's turn to request manuscripts from Gujarat, which suggests either that new manuscripts were available in Gujarat or that certain titles were no longer obtainable in Yemen. This is surprising, as during al-Bharuchi's lifetime Yemen was still home to the Tayyibi-Fatimid headquarters and its centres of learning. To understand why the community's epicentre had to be supplied with manuscripts from India, we need to briefly address the local political and social circumstances of the Tayyibis and the Bohras at the time this letter was written. Although it is not dated, we can assume that it was written no later than 939/1533, the year of al-Bharuchi's death, and, if we follow the order of the letters of the *Qaratis*, it was composed sometime between 910/1509 (the date of the previous letter) and 939/1533.

While they lived in Yemen, the Tayyibis were constantly at war and suffering persecution by the Zayids. In contrast, except for internal conflicts and some periods of persecution, in Gujarat, the Bohras enjoyed relative freedom in the tenth/sixteenth century and were able to store books in several central locations in Ahmedabad and Surat.[97] Over the lifetime of al-Bharuchi, Bohra *khizanat* in India flourished. After all, students who had visited Yemen for generations brought with them their own manuscript copies after completion of their *madrasa* training or transmitted them orally upon their return to India. According to the Mazoon Saheb, by the tenth/sixteenth century, a central Bohra manuscript *khizana* in India was stocked by the *Mawali al-Hind* and the *muhajirun* with books they had secured on their travels to Yemen. Although this *khizana*, or perhaps *khizanat*, undoubtedly stored a substantial portion of manuscripts of Yemeni provenance, the Bohras started copying their own exemplars in Gujarat; as we can trace in the development of book hands and marginalia (see Chapters 4 and 6), this was the beginning of a new, local Bohra-Gujarati manuscript culture. Al-Bharuchi was instrumental in this development, not only by sending manuscripts but also, more importantly, by facilitating the network of mobility and learning of the Indian students to Yemen. By the end of al-Bharuchi's life, the Bohra community in India was prospering through trade and a local manuscript, and a *khizana* culture had emerged.

The position of the Tayyibis, however, had become precarious as the Yemeni highlands were retaken by the Zaydis, and the community was plagued by various kinds of misfortune. It was especially after the death of al-Bharuchi, who, during his lifetime, had been able to keep the Zaydis at bay to some extent by offering them bribes, that the Tayyibis' situation deteriorated.[98] Fragments from the *Qaratis* written after his death provide insight into the crumbling of the authority of the *da'wa* under the reign of Sy. Yusuf b. Sulayman, the last Dai in Yemen. A series of letters, dated 969/1561, were

[97] Traboulsi, 'The Ottoman Conquest of Yemen', 45.
[98] Ibid., 48.

written between Sy. Sulayman, the earlier-mentioned first Indian Dai in Tayba who is referred to as 'Sy. Yusuf', and an Indian *daʿwa* official named Sy. Da'ūdjī in Gujarat. One particular letter, compiled by Sy. Yusuf, reports a *fitna* between the *ahl al-daʿwa* in Haraz and a certain local *amir*, and that the people in Haraz wrote a petition to the Ottoman *pasha* to intervene in the matter.[99] As we have seen previously, asking for the support of Ottoman officials and middlemen did not always end well, as it resulted in extortion. In the folios that follow, Sy. Yusuf reports on the fate of the books of the *daʿwa*, which were previously stored in the citadel of Tayba:

> It is said in the *Fihrist of kutub*, that the books which were in Tayba, Haraz, which were under the supervision of Abdallah b. Hasan, were brought by Miyan Ahmad b. Ajabshah after the death of Sy. Yusuf – may God sanctify his spirit – to Tayba, where they remain under his supervision in the citadel (Hisn) of Thula.[100]

Following social unrest (*fitna*) within the community, the letter reports the relocation of books from the citadel of Tayba to another Tayyibi stronghold, the fortress of Thula, a small village fifty kilometres south-east of Sana'a (Figure 2.10). As for *khizana* practices, interestingly, Sy. Yusuf mentions a *fihirst* (inventory) of books in which this relocation is mentioned. Even though it is not stated explicitly, his letter seems to indicate that the books of the *daʿwa* were transported to Thula to safeguard them from destruction.[101]

Another letter, written in 977/1569, provides insight into how the situation continued to deteriorate two years after the death of Sy. Sulayman. It mentions how the Zaydis attacked the fortress of the *daʿwa*, captured the tribal leaders and notables and

Figure 2.10 The fortification of Thula, today a UNESCO heritage site, known as *Husn al-ghurab*. Credits: http://whc.unesco.org/en/tentativelists/1719/.

[99] *Qaratis al-Yaman*, 40r.
[100] Ibid., 46v.
[101] Ibid.

imprisoned the *shaykhs* and *amirs*, and explicitly mentions the confiscation of the books of the *da'wa* by the Zaydis. It is recorded that the Zaydis continued to loot the *kutub al-da'wa,* 'until God plotted against them'.[102] The letter reports that one Tayyibi *amir* managed to escape, and fled to the region of Tahāma, from where he managed to get the Ottoman troops on his side against the Zaydis, joining them in their conquest of San'a and establishing contact with the various tribes.[103] The looting of Tayyibi books by the Zaydis in the tenth/sixteenth century seems to have been occurring systematically, as the *Qaratis* and other Tayyibi historical sources report. The *Qaratis* reports that, on several occasions, the Zaydis 'took apart' Tayyibi manuscripts and 'dispersed them over their various forts'.[104] Traboulsi describes how the Tayyibi historiographic work titled *'Ibrat al-Labīb* by Jābir b. al-Faḥd al-Makramī (fl. eleventh/seventeenth century) reports the looting by the Zaydis of a sizeable collection of manuscripts in Shibam, which they transferred to Sana'a in 944/1537.[105]

What is interesting about this source is that it clearly states that, despite the fact that the Zaydis followed a *madhhab* different from the Tayyibis, they did not destroy the books they confiscated, but transported them instead to their headquarters in Sana'a. This might be explained by the fact that, according to the Zaydi tradition, their Imams are expected to be well-versed in other schools of law in addition to their own. It is thus therefore very plausible that these Tayyibi manuscripts gained an entirely new social life as they were not only stored in Zaydi book repositories but also became part of the Zaydi *khizana* tradition as books of other *firaq* (sects) and were re-copied as such. I have come across such a Zaydi-Tayyibi manuscript, which was an Ismaili treatise on *fiqh* copied by a nineteenth-century Zaydi-Imamic book hand.[106] Thus, the tradition of Isma'ili manuscript confiscation by Zaydi Imams continued well into the early twentieth century, as Eugenio Griffini and Abdallah al-Jarafi mention.[107]

In conclusion, by the time al-Bahruchi wrote his letter to colleagues in Gujarat towards the end of his life, the *da'wa* in Yemen was already in serious decline, as its *khizanat* were under threat and its manuscripts became displaced following looting. Because the Tayyibi *da'wa* could not function without a well-stocked *khizana*, his inquiry for manuscript lists and titles from Gujarat is not surprising. Sending manuscripts from India to Haraz, however, would have been in vain, given that the *da'wa* and whatever was left of its *khizanat* were to be relocated to India about thirty years after his death. Despite the relocation and the schisms that followed, letters of the *Qaratis* corpus continued to be written between *da'wa* officials in Yemen and Gujarat well into the twelfth/seventeenth century.[108] As we see in the next section, the tradition of correspondence between what had become Tayyibi Yemen and Bohra Gujarat and the mobility of manuscripts over the Indian Ocean also continued.

102 Ibid., 48v.

103 Ibid.

104 Ibid., 46v.

105 Traboulsi, 'The Ottoman Conquest of Yemen', 48.

106 Akkerman, 'An Isma'ili Manuscript in the Hand of a Zaydi Imam' (forthcoming).

107 Eugenio Griffini, 'Die jüngste ambrosianische Sammlung arabischer Handschriften', *Zeitschrift der Deutschen Morgenländischen Gesellschaft*, vol. 69 (1915), 84. 'Abd Allāh b. 'Abd al-Karīm al-Jarāfī, *al-Muqtaṭaf min tārīḫ al-Yaman* (Cairo, Dār iḥyā' al- kutub al-'arabiyya, 1951), 233.

108 The last *qirtas* in the Tübingen manuscript is dated 1199/1688.

2.3 A Treasury of Books across the Indian Ocean

Tayyibi-Fatimid manuscripts, in their back-and-forth journeys between Yemen and Gujarat, were certainly not the only objects that were shipped over the Indian Ocean as commodities. On the basis of recent scholarship on Indian Ocean trade and the mobility of goods, documents and people, one could raise this question: what was so special about the manuscript mobility mentioned in the *Qaratis*? After all, the Tayyibis and Bohra *muhajirun*, as I discussed in the Introduction to this study, were certainly not the only community in this regard. As a community that, by the sixteenth century, was essentially dispersed over South Arabia and the Indian subcontinent, the *daʿwa* functioned through very specific Indian Ocean networks that were restricted to Tayyibi Bohra *only*. These networks, as we have seen, went far beyond mercantile interests and the occasional missionary official who was sent to the *jazirat al-Hind*. Instead, the Indian Ocean networks of the *daʿwa* were exclusive and multi-layered, as they catered to the small Tayyibi-Bohra cosmos. This cosmos included the education of Bohra *madrasa* students and *daʿwa* officials in Yemen, systems of overseas taxation and the funding of holy war in Yemen, overseas pilgrimage, the appointment of local authorities and building of a religious infrastructure in India, and, finally, as we have seen, book exchange and *khizana* building in Gujarat. The networks of this Indian Ocean cosmos were so powerful that, eventually, they facilitated the relocation of an entire community of Tayyibi Yemenis and Indian *muharijurn* overseas to Gujarat.

The history of the Bohras and its *khizana* thus gives us a unique insight into an Indian Ocean world that is entirely different from the perspectives and aspirations of the great imperial naval powers, whether the Europeans, Ottomans or the Omanis, or even from other local communal perspectives such as the Hadramis' or the Jews'. Those communities, of course, also carried their books and documents over the Indian Ocean, as we have seen earlier in the work of Bahl, Goitein and Ho, to satisfy the interest in Arabic books in the Indian subcontinent.[109] Yet what is unique about the Tayyibi-Bohra networks is that they facilitated the mobility of manuscripts, which came to play a central role in Gujarat as they became enshrined in *khizanat*, which would today form the basis of the Bohras' Neo-Fatimid claim.

Contrary to the case with other Isma'ili communities, it is the sea routes of the Indian Ocean, and not the routes over land, that are central to the Bohras' transmission history of Tayyibi-Fatimid-Isma'ili manuscripts, and, as we see, to a certain extent also the Fatimid-Tayyibi Imamic documentary tradition. Paradoxically, despite the community's practices of *taqiyya*, this transmission is characterised by constant mobility between networks of people, goods, and communities overseas. Yet these networks were very specific communal *daʿwa* networks of Bohra traders and students. A Jewish merchant from the world of Amitav Ghosh's *In an Antique Land* might have come in contact with these networks and traded in textiles with the Bohras.[110] It

[109] A special interest in the trans-regional reach of Arabic among Indian Ocean communities has emerged in recent years: Ho, *The Graves of Tarim*; Bahl, *Histories of Circulation*; Ronit Ricci, *Islam Translated: Literature, Conversion, and the Arabic Cosmopolis of South and Southeast Asia* (Chicago and London: University of Chicago Press, 2011).

[110] Amitav Ghosh, *In an Antique Land*.

would be highly unlikely, however, that, as a non-Bohri, he would be entrusted to ship books of the *daʿwa*. In this sense, the Bohra involvement in the Indian Ocean, and the story of the movement of the manuscripts that would form the basis of future Bohra *khizanat*, is unique. It is part of the cosmopolitan world of the Indian Ocean and the movement of goods in it, yet at the same time it follows a very specific Bohra agency and trajectory that, as it often operated incognito, remained undisclosed to the non-initiated outside world.

The fall of the Yemeni *daʿwa*, as Dai Idris Imad al-Din had predicted in the story of the water carrier, did indeed happen. A transfer of the Tayyibi community to Gujarat became inevitable, and in the year 974/1567 the *flags of Faatemi Da'wat*, to use the symbolic words that were attributed to him, were raised on Indian soil.[111] What influence did the relocation of the *daʿwa* headquarters have on the newly merged Tayyibi-Fatimid-Bohra community in Gujarat? More specifically, what effect did this transoceanic move have on Bohra *khizana* practices and manuscript culture? And as objects of transfer over the Indian Ocean, how did the mobility of these Tayyibi-Fatimid books reshape their social, and perhaps even political, role as objects, creating new narratives of togetherness and social order?

In Yemen, the Tayyibis were constantly at war with the Zaydis and suffered from persecution and looting. Nonetheless, after the relocation of the *daʿwa* to India, a Tayyibi-Fatimid *khizana* tradition was perpetuated among the so-called Sulaymanis. After following three Indian Dais (of whom two lived in Ahmedabad and one in Yemen), the Sulaymanis separated from the clerical headquarters in India towards the end of the tenth/sixteenth century following a dispute that was brought to the courts of the Mughal Emperor Akbar.[112] This schism divided the community between a Yemeni branch that would eventually settle in Najran, Saudi Arabia, and accepted Sulaymān b. al-Ḥasan's *nass* (d. 1005/1597), and an Indian Dawoodi branch that accepted the claim of Dā'ūd b. Quṭbshāh (d. 1021/1612).[113] Much remains unknown about the effect of this schism and its aftermath on the Isma'ili *khizanat* collections of Yemen and Gujarat and awaits further research.

In Gujarat, as the letters of al-Bharuchi and his contemporaries have shown, Tayyibi-Fatimid books from Yemen had already arrived in waves long before this official transfer and the schism that followed, resulting in a local Bohra *khizana* culture in India. Yet the official relocation of the Tayyibi *daʿwa* from Yemen to Gujarat was a turning point in Bohra history. Gujarat became a central *qutb* of the entire community, frequented by students from Yemen for their *'ulum al-daʿwa* studies. The relocation of the *daʿwa* changed the contours of the community into an Indian Ocean, Gujarati, Fatimid-Tayyibi community, in which clerical authority and books acquired a newly ritualised centrality.

The meaning of books of the *khizana*, I argue, changed in the new social, political and linguistic reality of medieval Bohra Gujarat. Whereas Traboulsi describes how in

111 *Ashab al-Yamin*, 135. See for the practice of raising Fatimid banners in foreign lands: Verena Klemm, *Memoirs of a Mission: The Ismaili Scholar, Statesman and Poet, Al-Mu-ayyad Fi'l-Din Al-Shirazi* (London: I. B. Tauris, 2004), 92.

112 Daftary, *The Ismāʿīlīs*, 280–2.

113 See for more information on the modern-day Sulaymani community: Daftary, *The Ismāʿīlīs*, 295–300.

the Tayyibi context books were seen as only a medium for preservation, I argue that in the Gujarati Bohra milieu books gradually became sacred objects that were enshrined and venerated. This development can be traced in the rich marginalia found in both Alawi and Dawoodi manuscript culture. In the Alawi *khizana*, I observed that manuscripts dating back to the period of the transfer and a century afterwards contained no marginalia, whereas manuscripts copied in the centuries that followed were full of them. The emergence of these new marginal traditions indicates another important development in the Bohra community at large: the transformation of clerical authority.

The new ritualised role of books, I argue, cannot be seen as separate from the metamorphosis of clerical authority in the Indian Bohra *da'wa*, a development that is still not fully understood. What is certain, however, is that in the context of medieval Gujarat, the main figure of authority, the Dai, was transformed from the head of the Tayyibi clerical-scholarly hierarchy into a nearly infallible spiritual and regal persona. The Dai became a 'royal', the head of a newly constructed sacerdotal royal family with its own unique notions of social order and divine sovereignty, ritualised through courtly culture, sartorial practice and traditions of kinship. In this new narrative of community, the sacerdotal royal class of Bhai Sahebs and Bhu Sahebas legitimised their indisputable position of power, as we have already seen, by tracing their genealogy overseas to the Fatimids via the Yemeni Dais and their *khizana* tradition. They being absolute custodians of the Indian *da'wa*, over time, the Tayyibi-Fatimid books that had reached Gujarat through the network of the *muhajirun* in Yemen would become their sacred, monarchical property.

The transformation from the Tayyibi clergy into a royal family in the eleventh/sixteenth and twelfth/seventeenth centuries needs to be studied in more detail through the lens of Gujarati sources, which is beyond the scope of this study. What can be said, however, is that the court rituals, sartorial practices, ceremonial attributes and other symbols of royalty among the Alawi discussed previously seem to mirror local empires and dynasties in South Asia, such as Rajput culture and the courtly culture of the Mughals: these cultures have survived among the Alawis despite, or possibly as a reaction to, colonial hegemony in South Asia.[114]

In this new manifestation of clerical authority influenced by local Gujarati traditions, all objects associated with or touched by the royal family attained an aura of exclusivity and evanescence. The handwritten word of the Dai in particular, as we saw in the previous chapter, began to play an important role in the community, whether through documentary practices or through the copying of untouchable *batini* manuscripts. Whereas Yemeni-Tayyibi scholars took on the role of copyists, transmitters of knowledge and authors, in the Indian context the hand of the Dai attained a sacred status, through which books and other 'things' were turned into blessed objects and sacred artefacts through his physical touch.

The transformation of the social meaning of the written word from the context of Tayyibi Yemen to Bohra Gujarat, and the differences between the two contexts in present times, are illustrated by the following event. In 1431/2010 the late Dawoodi Dai Muhammad Burhanuddin inaugurated the dome of the shrine of Dai Idris Imad

[114] Certain Bohra narratives also claim Rajput descent. See Vineet Gupta's forthcoming work.

al-Din in Shibam, which was recently renovated by the Dawoodis.[115] In this ceremony, which went unnoticed in Yemeni media and was only recorded through Dawoodi channels, the Dai 'inscribed', or rather engraved, his sacred '*alama*, a *basmala* in calligraphic gold, inside the dome of the mosque. While this display of inscribing authority on objects, documents or buildings is common among the Bohras in the context of Bohra Gujarat, this highly ritualised practice is entirely alien to the Yemeni context and among the Sulaymanis who still live in Shibam and its surroundings.

Following the transoceanic relocation of the *daʿwa*, the Bohra community in Gujarat would transform itself to such an extent through new narratives of community, notions of clerical authority, social order and caste that it became unrecognisable to its Sulaymani Tayyibi brothers who had remained in Yemen. The only link with Yemen, and through Yemen with Fatimid Cairo, which remained, and which was carefully preserved throughout history, and through which authority was exercised, was the sacred chain of transmission of books. Manuscripts, over time, became exclusively associated with the *daʿwa* and its sacerdotal royal family. A far more recent phenomenon is the Bohras' architectural intervention and restoration of Tayyibi shrines and mosques, which has become significant for the Bohra's construction of their identity.

In the ongoing reshaping of new forms of authority and the sacralisation of books, it was inevitable that the social meaning of another institution was transformed: the Tayyibi *khizana*. The Tayyibi *khizana* changed from a library or storage space for books, which was often private and in the possession of generations of scholarly families, into a centralised shrine of sacred manuscripts: it became a guarded treasury of books with specific conditions of access depending on one's social status in the Bohra *daʿwa*. The Dai became the sole custodian of the treasury of books, as the fate of his community was put into his scribal hands. The *khizana* and the Tayyibi-Fatimid manuscripts it stored in India in turn legitimised and reinforced his authority and structures of clerical hegemony. Over the following centuries, the undisputed authority of the Dai, as we have seen, would become the subject of several schisms, resulting, as is discussed in the next section, in separate treasuries of books, and separate manuscript and *khizana* cultures.

Despite being dispersed into different *khizanat* in modern times, the Fatimid-Tayyibi Bohra intellectual tradition and its manuscripts remain intrinsically connected with each other – not only because they belong to the same Fatimid tradition but also in the literal sense. The Alawi *khizana* may enshrine a certain collection of *kutub* at present, some of which are considered precious or rare copies, whereas other titles consist of many exemplars. Its collection, however, as we see in Chapters 4 and 6, is constantly subject to change and much more in flux than one would think. Some *kutub* outlive generations of Bhai Sahebs, whereas others do not survive the climate of Baroda, which is becoming increasingly manuscript-unfriendly due to the effects of global warming in Gujarat.

More than five centuries after its composition, the world of the *Qaratis* and the Bohras' presence in Yemen have by no means vanished. Until the civil war in Yemen

115 *September 28. Qubba of Syedna Idris Imaduddin RA (Shibaam-Yemen).* Qutbibohras.blogspot.com/2014/09 (last accessed 16 May 2020). Interestingly, the online newsletter in which this event was described is called '*Sijill*'.

that began in 2014, a population of modern Bohra *muharijun* were still residing in Yemen, where they were actively involved in the restoration of Tayyibi shrines and, as I have been told, in consulting Sulaymani manuscript collections to complete their *khizanat* in Gujarat. Yet, despite the community's deep historical and intellectual ties with the Yemeni highlands, the Gujarati Bohras remain strangers from a distant land.

On the other side of the Indian Ocean, an unofficial Tayyibi-Fatimid manuscript copying network continues to exist among clerics from various communities, despite deep inter-sectarian tensions. Exactly as is described in the *Qaratis*, manuscript titles are requested from other *khizanat* and collections for copying. After the establishment of the Fatimid mother *khizana* in Cairo, the routes of manuscript copying and *khizana* collecting may have changed, yet the practice of manuscript exchange, modes of Isma'ili knowledge transmission and scribal networks remain, continuing to shape and keep alive the living *khizana* culture of the Bohras.

2.4 A Neo-Fatimid Treasury of Books in Baroda

From the Indian Ocean world of al-Bharuchi and the *Qaratis al-Yaman* we move to Baroda, Gujarat, in which we find the Alawi treasury of books. What manuscripts have survived in the Alawi *khizana* in Baroda? Can we indeed speak of a lost Fatimid or perhaps Tayyibi-Fatimid *khizana* in Gujarat on the basis of manuscripts and documents present in the treasury of books? And if so, what makes it a 'Neo'-Fatimid *khizana*?

To the anthropologist these questions may be of little relevance, as it is the emic perspective that counts. Through their *khizana* and the genealogy of the Dais, the Alawi Bohras claim their position as heirs of the Fatimids in modern times, which is expressed through shop names in the *mohallah*, sartorial practices that are seen as 'Faatemi', and the ritualised practice of faith. According to my observations, these and other modern non-textual elements, such as architecture and interior design, are as central to the cultivation of the Alawi's Neo-Fatimid identity as the *khizana* and its manuscripts. Focusing on the *khizana* itself, the Alawis' link with the Fatimid past is not only reflected in its content but also – as we see in the next chapter on access and space – in its interior and the *haveli* of the royal family as a monumental sanctified space.

As much as the emic perspective is central in this study, as a social codicologist, I am also interested in the histories and material evidence that complement, or perhaps problematise, the Alawis' claim as heirs of the Fatimids. This section discusses the Alawi *khizana* tradition, including its history on the subcontinent and its collection. I describe the collection of the treasury of books in a way that does not compromise my oath of secrecy or disclose the tradition's esoteric secrets. The list I provide is therefore by no means exhaustive. It does, however, give the reader an idea of the authors whom the clerics consider canonical to their treasury of books; in other words, what is read and what is not.

History of the Alawi Khizana

The treasury of books in Baroda, which houses a substantial amount of Fatimid, Tayyibi and Bohra literature, dates to the late eleventh/seventeenth century when the Alawis migrated from Ahmedabad to Baroda in 1090/1679. According to the Ra's ul Hudood, several Bohra *mohallahs* already existed within the walled city of Baroda at that time. As noted, the Alawi and Dawoodi Bohras had already bifurcated into two communities after a dispute over succession. Their *khizana* was subsequently split into two: the Alawi *khizana* in Baroda and the Dawoodi *khizana* in Surat and later Mumbai.[116]

Very little is known about the history of the pre-bifurcation *khizana* in the Indian subcontinent. A *khizana* was established shortly after the headquarters of the Tayyibi *da'wa* moved from Yemen to Gujarat in the late tenth/sixteenth century. According to the Mukasir Saheb and the Ra's ul Hudood, this pre-bifurcation *khizana* was housed in the graveyard area of Saraspur in Ahmedabad.[117] This *khizana*, I was told, was managed by five generations of Dais over a period of nearly fifty years – from Sy. Sulayman (no. 24), the last Dai in Yemen, to Sy. Sheikh Adam Sayfuddin (no. 28, d. 1030/1620) and ended with the bifurcation in 1030/1620. On the preservation and the copying of manuscripts in this period, the Mazoon Saheb mentions the following in a lecture:

> The task of transcription of MSS between the periods of 24th Da'i up till the time of 28th Da'i was chiefly carried out by the pupils who enjoyed the tutelage of the Da'i and were imparted education in Isma'ili History, Philosophy, Jurisprudence and Occult Sciences.[118]

This statement indicates that during the formative stages of the Bohra *da'wa* in India the right of copying manuscripts was not limited to the Dai and the *hudud* but was also given to 'pupils' who contributed to the collection in a similar fashion to the Bohra *muhajirun* in Yemen. Bohra manuscripts thus must have also circulated among non-clerical younger scribes in the eleventh/seventeenth and twelfth/eighteenth centuries. Even though not much is known about these networks or the number of manuscripts that were available, the earlier-mentioned *Fihirst* of manuscripts by al-Majdu' gives us an idea of the corpus of manuscripts that were available in India during his lifetime. The multi-volume *Fihrist* is surprisingly extensive as it mentions 250 titles. According to Poonawala, this is considerably more than the number of titles in book lists from the Tayyibi period, such as the earlier-mentioned works by Idris Imad al-Din and al-Bharuchi.[119]

I was told that, in addition to being held in a clerical treasury of books, manuscripts were kept in several central *da'wa* locations in Sidhpur and Surat, as well as in private *khizanat* of pupils and scholars. We are able to reconstruct the process of building these private, non-clerical *khizanat* and Bohra treasuries of books in the pre-modern period on the basis of the oral histories of Bohra family collections. The oral histories, books and manuscript cultures of these scholarly family collections, as we see in Chapter 4, are of importance for the Alawi *khizana* and its collection.

[116] The Dawoodi *khizana* is in fact not one *khizana* but consists of several *khizanat*.

[117] It is interesting that the *khizana* was housed in a graveyard; the idea of disposing of sacred texts in graveyards is further discussed in Section 4.2.

[118] Private written lecture of the Mazoon Saheb (unpublished).

[119] At the same time he also mentions titles that could not be fully copies because copies were not available any more. Poonawala, 'Isma'ili Manuscripts from Yemen', 229: Traboulsi, 'The Ottoman Conquest of Yemen', 45.

One such collection is the *Khizānat al-Muḥammadiyya al-Hamadāniyya*, which belongs to the learned Tayyibi Yemeni scholarly family of the Hamdanis of Haraz. As part of the efforts to build a new *daʿwa khizana* in Gujarat, the Hamdanis were invited by the Dawoodi Dai Ibrāhīm Wajīḥ al-Dīn (no. 39, d. 1168/1754) to migrate with their large *khizana* to Surat in the twelfth/eighteenth century.[120] Even though the Tayyibi-Fatimid *daʿwa* had migrated to the Indian subcontinent two centuries earlier and the Sulaymani community had become independent soon after, the mobility of the Hamdanis shows that the close contact between the two communities continued, as scholars and their manuscripts travelled between the two continents. The Hamdanis descended from a long line of renowned scholars, authors and calligraphers. Their arrival in Surat led to a new influx of Yemeni Isma'ili and non-Isma'ili manuscripts in Gujarat that, in turn, led to an increase in the number of *ḥalaqas* (studying and copying circles; see Chapter 6), in which manuscripts were copied, as well as the construction of a large Hamdani *khizana* in Surat.[121] Even though the Hamdanis' migration to Surat enabled them to escape their difficult circumstances in Yemen, the flourishing of their *khizana*, however, was not foreordained in Gujarat. In the centuries that followed, Hamdani manuscripts became dispersed over various manuscript collections, including the Alawi *khizana*, following the centralisation and confiscation of Bohra family collections by the Dawoodi clergy.[122] The modern heirs of the *Khizanat al-Hamadaniyya* include the late scholars Hussein Hamdani, whom we encountered in Cairo at the beginning of this chapter, and his son, the late Abbas Hamdani, who spared no efforts to reunite the books of his family *khizana*.[123]

The centralisation and confiscation of family *khizanat* into clerical 'royal' treasuries of books with restricted conditions of access marked a radical change in Bohra *khizana* culture. Abbas Hamdani notes that among Bohra milieux in medieval Gujarat, manuscripts were actively accessed and used by a class of *ulama* and *shuyūkh*.[124] The transcribing of these manuscripts was carried out by students who donated their copies to the private libraries of their teachers in lieu of tuition fees. These private book treasuries, he contends, were often in the possession of generations of learned scholars and were thus not restricted to the royal Dai family. According to Hamdani, this 'open access' tradition of manuscript study, transmission and ownership continued until the mid-fourteenth/twentieth century, when the entirety of Dawoodi Bohra literature – including family *khizanat* – was confiscated by the late Dai Burhan al-Din and his father Tahir Sayf al-Din from learned families.[125] As a result of this rigid policy, all 'royal' *daʿwa khizanat* were closed to a non-clerical audience, and the class of learned *ulama* and their students lost their authority.[126] Interviews with Dawoodi Bohras confirm

[120] De Blois, *Arabic, Persian and Gujarati Manuscripts*, xxvi. Poonawala, 231, 232.

[121] Ibid., xxvi.

[122] Ibid., xxvii.

[123] Currently, the majority of the books of the *Khizānat al-Muḥammadiyya al-Hamadāniyya* are housed in the library of the Institute of Ismaili Studies where they were donated by the late Abbas Hamdani.

[124] Abbas Hamdani, '*Fatimid Literature: Creation, Preservation, Transfer, Concealment and Revival*', http://dawoodi-bohras.com/news/77/97/Fatimid-Literature-Creation-preservation-transfer-concealment-and-revival/d,pdb_detail_article_comment/ (last accessed 2 July 2017).

[125] Poonawala, 'Isma'ili Manuscripts from Yemen', 230.

[126] Hamdani, '*Fatimid Literature: Creation, Preservation, Transfer, Concealment and Revival*'.

that manuscript confiscation, especially following the death of a family member, is still practised today and is required in order to obtain permission for the recitation of the *fatiha* for the departed soul of the deceased.[127]

The Mazoon Saheb and his brothers confirmed this change in Dawoodi Bohra *khizana* culture and assured me that similar practices did not occur in the Alawi community. It seems that the Alawi *khizana* has always been inaccessible terrain for non-clerics since the bifurcation with the Dawoodis. This tradition can be explained by the fact that the Alawis hid their manuscripts from the outside world out of fear of confiscation by the Dawoodis. According to the self-understanding of the community, from its inception, the Alawi clerical establishment was forced to practise *taqiyya* and at times literally go underground (the Dais resided in underground dwellings) with their *khizana*. It is this tradition that I call the '*taqiyyafication*' of the *khizana*. Moreover, the process of the *khizana* becoming a guarded space explains the policies of access that are still adhered to vigorously. However, as we see in Chapter 4, the Alawi *khizana* also contains manuscript copies, which reveals cracks in this narrative and indicates that, perhaps on a smaller scale, similar practices of manuscript confiscation occurred.

To return to the Alawi *khizana* in its post-bifurcation period, how does one rebuild a *khizana* collection from scratch following disaster and bifurcation? According to the Alawi clerics, the community remained in Ahmedabad for three generations of Dais, and it was during this period that their manuscript collection was reportedly confiscated by the Dawoodis and other 'non-Isma'ili' communities. Perhaps as a result of the looting of the manuscripts, the Alawi Dais, who were forced to live incognito, 'had ample time to copy books in heaps and heaps', as the Ra's ul Hudood's oral history contends. Nobody knows, however, what happened to these magical heaps of books. The Ra's al-Hudood suggested:

> The works must have been lost or damaged during the transportation of the *jamaat* from Ahmadabad to Baroda. Books were brought in wooden boxes and there were no bridges [at that time], they had to be transported through rivers in the boat, because when you come from Ahmedabad to Vadodara there are two rivers. Yes, indeed, putting in boat, water might have seeped in, or lightning or termites.

Even though the circumstances under which the Alawi *daʿwa* and its treasury of books survived the schism remain unclear, what is certain is that a new Alawi Bohra *daʿwa* was established in the year 1090/1679 after the Alawi royal family and the community moved to Baroda. According to the Mazoon Saheb, around three hundred manuscripts were housed in the centre of the *daʿwa* in the area of Badri Mohallah. Marginalia in Alawi manuscripts, such as inventories mentioned in the flyleaves displayed earlier, show that, over the course of the history of the *khizana*, several Dais were especially committed to preserving and expanding the collection of their new treasury of books, whereas others seem to have played no such role. The Dais Shams al-Dīn Shaykh ʿAlī b. Shams al-Dīn (no. 37, d. 1248/1832) and Jīwābhā'i Fakhr al-Dīn b. Amīr al-Dīn (no. 41, d. 1347/1929, see Figure 2.11) are particularly honoured for transcribing and repairing damaged manuscripts. Their efforts can be

[127] See for more details, Poonawala, 'Isma'ili Manuscripts from Yemen', 230 i33.

Figure 2.11 Historic photograph (dated 1315/1898) of the Alawi royal family, with Sy. Jiwabhai Fakhr al-Din b. Amir al-Din sitting in the middle. Source: Alawi *daʿwa*.

traced in the margins, colophons, incipits and first flyleaves of those manuscripts that mention reader and copying statements in their name and hand. I have seen many of these statements of these two Dais, which are recognisable by their sophisticated, neat and clean *naskh* hands. It is because of their scribal efforts that we can trace a wave of manuscript copying in the collection during the nineteenth and twentieth centuries. Their scribal activities and interventions should not be seen as merely a scholarly endeavour: the lifespan of paper manuscripts in Gujarat is short, and their efforts thus safeguarded the survival of the *khizana*. As a result, manuscripts from the pre-bifurcation period of Gujarati provenance and even copies of Yemeni provenance have survived in the *khizana*.[128]

Contemporary sources also report many adverse events that threatened the existence of the *khizana*. For example, during the year 1350/1931 several heavy floods destroyed the *khizana*, and termite attacks damaged the collection greatly.[129] The Bhai Sahebs told me that some manuscripts of this period were damaged so seriously that manuscript copies of the Dawoodi and Sulaymani communities had to be borrowed

[128] Due to my oath of secrecy I am not able to mention these titles. For a list of the oldest extant manuscripts of Yemeni provenance in Bohra collections, including pictures, see Poonawala, 'Isma'ili Manuscripts from Yemen', 239, 240; De Blois, 'The Oldest Known Fatimid Manuscript from Yemen'.

[129] Private written lecture of the Mazoon Saheb (unpublished).

for the restoration process, an undertaking that is continued by the Mazoon Saheb (see Chapter 4). Via one individual community's own clerical *khizana* network, I observed, new manuscript titles are copied into other communities' collections, and, in the case of the Alawis, into their treasury of books, where they are appropriated and enshrined (see Chapter 5). In addition, there are manuscripts that are alien to Alawi manuscript culture yet at the same time part of the larger Fatimid Tayyibi tradition that come to the *khizana* via different, unconventional and sometimes unexpected routes and places (see Chapter 4). The printed books of the *khizana* and the publication of academic sources, such as critical editions of Isma'ili manuscripts, enable the Mazoon Saheb and his brothers to preserve the collection by restoring missing folios and passages; they lead to an influx of new works. In other words, no efforts are spared to restore the Fatimid treasury of books or, at least, fragments of its sacred tradition to its former glory.

The Alawi Khizana Tradition: Manuscripts and Documents

The majority of manuscripts that are held in the *khizana* are categorised by its custodians as 'Tayyibi-Fatimid literature'. The focus of this section is not the dates of these manuscripts but the *Alawi khizana tradition* itself: Which titles and authors are canonical, and which are not? Technically speaking, most of the Bohra Tayyibi-Fatimid corpus was written by Dais who were not part of the Fatimid *daʿwa* in North Africa, because these texts were written before the advent of the Fatimids, or because some such texts, such as the treatises of the Persian Isma'ili scholars, were never commissioned by them. Moreover, a very large part of the Bohra scholarly canon was produced in the post-Fatimid period in Yemen under the Tayyibis. Yet, as we saw earlier in this chapter, to the Alawis this chronology poses no challenges because there is no such thing as 'post-Fatimid'. On the contrary, returning to the genealogical tree of the transmission of esoteric knowledge, these periods, authors and the communities they belonged to, including the present, are all connected and essentially seen as 'Fatimid'. To make a distinction between the Fatimid Imamate that ruled Egypt and North Africa and its imperial aspirations, I use the term 'Neo-Fatimid' to refer to the modern-day, apolitical Bohra communities, their uniquely Yemeni-Gujarati *khizana* practices, and other expressions through which they refer to their Tayyibi-Fatimid past.

The Alawi *khizana* tradition includes authors from a over very wide timespan and broad geographical area – from the early Isma'ili Dais in Khorasan, Yemen and North Africa; to authors of the Fatimid period in Egypt; to treatises ascribed to Fatimid Imams; to authors of the Tayyibi period in Yemen; to the Bohra tradition that flourished in Gujarat. In this case, 'attributed to' means that autographed manuscript copies have not survived some of these periods, and the majority of exemplars are copied by Indian Bohra hands.

The great majority of manuscripts of the *khizana* are treatises that can be characterised as *ʿilm al-batin* and *haqa'iq* manuscripts, followed by *fiqh* and *ʿaqa'id* works. The Bhai Sahebs describe the holdings of the treasury of books as follows in an official statement on their website:

> He (the late Dai Ziya' al-Din) meticulously preserved those manuscripts and maintained this legacy for posterity. There are also autograph copies chiefly transcribed by the Alawi missionaries (Dais) making it a unique treasure house and a rich traditional heritage. These manuscripts are mainly on Faatimi [*sic*] jurisprudence (*fiqh*), history (*akhbar*), doctrines (*'aqa'id*), facts and realities (*haqa'iq*), lectures (*majalis*), succession in Prophets and their progeny with propagation of *nass* (inheritance), refutation of false sects, religious sciences, poetry, biographies, admonitions and prayers and on comparative studies.[130]

The description does not, however, correspond to the tradition in which the *khizana* collection is organised. As we have seen in section 2.1, Bohra manuscripts and their authors are arranged according to the periods of *kashf* and *satr*. According to the Mazoon Saheb, authors from the *kashf* period include all Dais from the early Isma'ili and Fatimid period and titles attributed to Fatimid Imams. In the Baroda *khizana*, the most prominent authors of the *kashf* period are as follows:

Composer(s) of the *Rasā'il Ikhwān al-Ṣafā'* (Epistles of the Brethren of Purity) (*ʿilm al-batin/haqa'iq*, attributed to the ninth Imam Aḥmad al-Mastūr, fl. second/eighth century, see Chapter 2.2).

Abū Ḥātim al-Rāzī (d. 322/934, *ʿilm al-batin/haqa'iq*, *ʿaqa'id*).

al-Qāḍī al-Nuʿmān (d. 363/974, *fiqh* and *ʿilm al-ta'wil*).

Abū Yaʿqūb al-Sijistānī (d. 393/1003, *ʿilm al-batin/haqa'iq*).

Aḥmad b. Ibrāhīm al-Nisaybūrī (fl. fifth/eleventh century, mostly *ʿilm al-batin/haqa'iq*).

Ḥamīd ad-Dīn al-Kirmānī (d. 411/1020, *ʿilm al-batin/haqa'iq*).

Mu'ayyad fī Dīn al-Shīrāzī (d. 470/1077, *ʿilm al-batin/haqa'iq*).

Abū 'l-Barakāt (fl. sixth/twelfth century, *ʿilm al-ta'wil*).

Treatises attributed to Qadi al-Nuʿman are especially numerous in the collection, taking up almost an entire cupboard in the *khizana*. Copies of *Daʿa'im al-Islam* are his most popular work, followed by *Kitāb al-Ṭahāra* (The Book of Purity) and *Kitāb al-Himma fī Ādāb Ittibāʿ al-A'imma* (A Code of Conduct for the Followers of the Imam) and other standard Isma'ili works on exoteric sciences, such as *Kitāb Iftitāḥ al-Daʿwa* (The Book of the Commencement of the Mission) and *Ta'wīl al-Daʿā'im* (Exegesis of the *Daʿa'im*).

The *kashf* period is followed by the period of *satr*, which is divided into a Yemeni and an Indian period. The Yemeni period includes titles attributed to Dais who were

[130] https://www.alavibohra.org/introduction%20files/intro%20-%20Vadodara%20City-%20A%20centre%20of%20Dawat.htm

at the head of the Tayyibi community Yemen (twenty-three in total), preceding their Indian Bohra successors in the sacred pedigree of Syednas. These authors are (the number refers to the number of the Dai in the community's sacred geneology):

1. al-Dhu'ayb b. Mūsā al-Wādi'ī (d. 546/1151, *'ilm al-batin/haqa'iq*).
2. Ibrāhīm b. al-Ḥusayn al-Ḥāmidī (d. 557/1162, *'ilm al-batin/haqa'iq*).
3. Ḥātim b. Ibrāhīm al-Ḥāmidī (d. 596/1199, *'ilm al-batin/haqa'iq*).
4. 'Alī b. Ḥātim al-Ḥāmidī (d. 605/1209, *'ilm al-batin/haqa'iq*).
5. 'Alī b. Muḥammad b. al-Walīd (d. 612/1215, *'ilm al-batin/haqa'iq*), also known as Ibn al-Walīd.
6. Idrīs b. al-Ḥasan b. 'Abd Allāh b. al-Walīd (d. 872/1468, *'ilm al-ta'rikh*), also known as Idrīs Imād al-Dīn.

With the exception of Idris Imad al-Din, the great majority of the Tayyibi-Fatimid corpus in the *khizana* in Baroda was produced by the first five Dais in the fifth/eleventh and sixth/twelfth centuries. The Mazoon Saheb stressed the importance of treatises attributed to the first five Dais. Idris Imad al-Din, composer of the famous compendium on *haqa'iq*, titled *Zahr al-Ma'ānī* (The Flower of Meanings), and the earlier-discussed historical account *'Uyun al-Akhbar*, is considered of lesser importance as an Isma'ili author. This is reflected by the few manuscript copies of his works in Baroda in comparison to treatises attributed to the first five Yemenite Dais. Thus, authors from earlier times are considered more authoritative and therefore take precedence over authors of works composed in later times. Comparing authors from the *kashf* and the *satr* period, it becomes apparent that – with few exceptions – the ideological focus of the philological tradition of the Tayyibis post-*kashf* shifted from the *zahir* to the *batin*, with a strong emphasis on *haqa'iq* treatises.

The second part of the *satr* period covers the Indian era in which the Tayyibi-Fatimid philological tradition was transferred from Yemen Gujarat, a process we explored at length in the following chapter. The Indian period is divided into two eras: the pre-bifurcation era, in which only one Dai was recognised by all Bohras, and the post-bifurcation era, resulting in a Dawoodi and an Alawi royal pedigree. The first category includes treatises written by Indian Dais in the period before the bifurcation (1030/1621). These Dais are (the numbers refer to the Dais' place in the community's sacred geneology):

24. Yūsuf b. Sulaymān (d. 974/1567).
25. Jalāl b. Ḥasan (d. 975/1567).
26. Dā'ūd b. 'Ajabshāh (d. 997/1589).
27. Dā'ūd Burhān al-Dīn b. Quṭbshāh (d. 1021/1612).
28. Shaykh Ādam Ṣafī al-Dīn b. Ṭayyibshāh (d. 1030/1621).

One can argue that for the Indian period, at least in the formative period, works that are considered canonical are mostly written by non-Dai authors. Examples are al-Bharuchi's earlier-mentioned *Kitab al-Azhar* and one of the very few Bohra commentaries on *fiqh* titled *Kitāb al-Ḥawāshī* (The Book of Commentaries), written by

Amīnjī b. Jalāl b. Ḥasan (d. 1010/1602). In addition, a substantial amount of official *da'wa* documents were produced in this period.[131]

The second era of the Indian period covers post-bifurcation literature produced in the Alawi community. Qutbuddin argues that the Dawoodi Bohra community witnessed a renaissance of Tayyibi literature in the nineteenth and twentieth centuries, resulting in a rich tradition of *Risalas*, *Diwans* and *Hafti* (prayer books).[132] The opposite occurred in the Alawi Bohra community. The political turmoil in the community is reflected in the very sparse literary output of the Alawis: few manuscripts and documents of this period are present in the *khizana*. Alawi titles are mostly of a polemical nature, refuting the Dawoodis, followed by official *da'wa* documents, and poetry *Diwans* composed by the Alawi Dais. Alawi treatises on *haqa'iq* seem to be absent from the collection. Although Alawi Bohras do not recognise the 'Daiship' of the Dawoodis, I observed that the Bohra *khizana* also holds a substantial amount of Dawoodi historical literature, which is considered authoritative because these texts are based on similar sources. Finally, a selection of poetry *Diwans* composed by Dawoodi Dais is present in the *khizana* in Baroda.

Comparing the Indian *satr* period to the *kashf* and *satr* periods in Yemen, it becomes clear that the number of works produced among Bohra scholars in Gujarat is small. This is, however, not specific to the Alawi scholarly tradition. Dawoodi collections such as the Fyzee, Zahid Ali and Hamdani collections reflect a similar trend in Bohra literary production.[133] Over the last few centuries, Bohra scholarship has mostly been occupied with the reproduction of knowledge and manuscript copying, instead of esoteric knowledge production, which is seen as the task of the hidden Imam. The question of why Bohra scholarship is focused on knowledge reproduction instead of production is tackled in Chapter 6. As we have seen in the first chapter, the Bohras are not the only Twelver Shi'i or Isma'ili community in Gujarat. It should be mentioned that literary traditions produced in other Isma'ili milieux in Gujarat, respectively the Nizari, the Khojas or the Satpanth, are not part of the *khizana* tradition of the Alawis.

In addition to handwritten copies of Isma'ili treatises, the collection of the *khizana* also holds manuscripts of non-Isma'ili origin. With the exception of Persian poetry volumes, the great majority of these Sunni and Twelver Shi'i titles are written in Arabic, even though these texts are available in India in vernacular languages. Though treatises from Shi'i intellectual milieux are closer to the Isma'ili literary tradition from a theological point of view, the Bhai Sahebs by no means consider these texts to be more authoritative than the works of Sunni authors. In fact, according to my inventory, twice as many Sunni works are present in the *khizana* as Shi'i works.[134] These Sunni titles include popular compilations on the sayings of the prophets (Sunni authors), such as the *Qiṣṣaṣ al-Anbiyā'* (Stories of the Prophets, various authors), and traditions of the *ahl al-bayt* (Shi'i authors), such as *Nāhj al-Balāgha* (The Way of Eloquence), compiled by Sharīf al-Raḍī (d. 442/1015), and *Arba'ūna Ḥadīthan* (Forty Hadith, better known

131 See Poonawala, *Biobibliography*, 184–250.

132 Qutbuddin, 'The Da'udi Bohras', 339.

133 Cortese, *Arabic Isma'ili Manuscripts*; De Blois, *Arabic, Persian and Gujarati Manuscripts*; Goriawala, *A Descriptive Catalogue of the Fyzee Collection of Ismaili Manuscripts*; Poonawala, *Biobibliography*.

134 See for a description of non-Isma'ili works in the Barodian *khizana* my thesis, 130–6.

as *Kitāb Arbaʿīn*) by Bahā' al-Dīn al-ʿĀmilī (d. 1031/1622). As for standardised Sunni *ḥadīth* literature and prophetic traditions, one would have expected to find titles such as *Ṣaḥīḥ Muslim* or *Ṣaḥīḥ Bukhārī*. These works, however, are not present, which is because Bohras have their own hadith literature corpus.

It is not entirely clear how these particular works were selected or how they made their way into the *khizana*. The presence of non-Isma'ili Islamic literature does, however, show the importance of these texts in Bohra circles, and it proves that these texts circulate outside the Sunni and Shi'i milieux in which they are usually read. This raises the question of how these texts are used and treated. The Mazoon Saheb did not have an answer. He suspected that 'before his time' these manuscripts were part of the Bhai Saheb's curriculum of teaching *shiʿr* (poetry) in the *daʿwat-e hadiyya* classes (classes for clerics). He is certain that they were not used for reading in the *majlis*. Today, the Mazoon Saheb and his brothers use these Sunni and Shi'i texts for personal study. The Mazoon Saheb said: 'Now and then I read these works, and I have also written many lessons from in my personal notes used for preparing the *majlis*.' It should be noted that non-Isma'ili doctrinal works, as well as literature, are present in all Bohra manuscript collections.[135]

What does the presence of non-Isma'ili manuscripts in the *khizana* signify? Could it indicate that Isma'ili manuscripts were at times so rare that the Bohras were forced to read popular Sunni works (which must have been more widely available)? According to the Mazoon Saheb it is the other way round: the presence of these manuscripts proves that at other times the collection of the *khizana* must have been 'complete'. He reasoned: 'Why otherwise would one make the painstaking job of copying a non-Isma'ili work if there are plenty of Isma'ili works to be copied?' The copying of an Isma'ili work thus precedes the copying of a non-Isma'ili work. 'First', he said, 'you make your collection complete; right now I have twenty-seven Xerox copies waiting to be copied (and fading away so it should be done fast).' It should be noted that Sunni and Shi'i works are also available in printed form. However, because some of these works were once copied by what are considered the sacred hands of Bohra Dais, Sunni and Shi'i manuscripts are thus also considered sacred objects and therefore treated as such. Therefore, it is the sacred materiality that has importance over the non-Isma'ili content of these manuscripts (see Chapter 6). At present the collection of the Bohra *khizana* in Baroda is not 'complete'. The Mazoon said that he has no time to copy these works, but he stressed that if he did have the time, he would devote his life to it.

Finally, there is a category of literature that I call 'hybrid' religious literature: literature that is neither purely Isma'ili nor Sunni nor Shi'i, is written by anonymous authors, and is actively part (meaning read and copied) of the *khizana* tradition. What surprised me was that the possible non-Isma'ili provenance of these texts was not considered very important by the Bhai Sahebs. After all, 'manuscripts are manuscripts', they argued. The Mazoon Saheb, to my surprise, was in constant correspondence with scholars over the authenticity of these manuscripts, while closely following their publication. This exchange not only demonstrates the fluidity of categories of Bohra

[135] See the catalogues of the Fyzee, Zahid Ali, and the Hamdani collection mentioned above, as well as Gacek's *Catalogue of Arabic Manuscripts*, and Cortese's *'Ismāʿīlī and other Arabic Manuscripts*.

literature in practice but also shows the engagement of the Bhai Sahebs in the international scholarly discourse on Isma'ili literature. This engagement has two aims. The Bhai Sahebs are interested in what is published in the field and, being trained in Islamic Studies themselves, want to be part of it. This engagement is also a pragmatic way to keep tabs on and at times influence scholarly debates in the field.

Final Notes to Chapter 2: A Lost Fatimid Treasury of Books?

Today, the Alawi *khizana* in Baroda is an institution. It is a treasury of books where manuscripts are enshrined and esoteric truths are kept. The Bhai Sahebs are its sole custodians and treasurers. It is a sacred space where the authority of the clerical hierarchy is legitimised, where the law is spoken, and through which social order is maintained. Its existence and the material transmission of its manuscripts, as we have seen, are crucial to the community's self-understanding, both of its eschatology and of the here and now.

The Alawis consider themselves heirs and saviours of an uninterrupted chain of transmitted Fatimid and Tayyibi manuscripts, and it is because of this that their *khizana* tradition is considered closed, fixed and sacred. Under the influence of several historical events that occurred within the community in Ahmedabad, mainly the bifurcation of the Bohras, an evident process of *taqiyyafication* of Alawi Bohra scholarship took place: this process not only resulted in the monopolisation of knowledge production and manuscript ownership, but, more importantly, it also shaped the Alawi *khizana* into the treasury of books it is today. This process of *taqiyyafication*, however, should not be seen as a development that is limited to history and books only. Instead, as we see in the next chapter, it is an ongoing process that is present in the culture of the *khizana* and the manuscripts it holds; it is also a social practice that is deeply rooted in the Alawi community at large.

On the basis of the manuscripts preserved among the Alawis in Baroda, we can indeed argue that fragments of the Fatimid-Tayyibi *khizana* have been preserved in their treasury of books. As legendary as this almost millennium-old chain of manuscript transmission may sound to an uninitiated non-Bohra audience, authors such as al-Sijistani, Qadi al-Nuʿman, Idris Imad al-Din and al-Bharuchi are indeed read and copied in manuscript form in Arabic in Baroda today. Despite their inaccessibility and enshrinement in inaccessible treasuries of books, these authors and titles of the Alawi and other Bohra *khizana* traditions are foundational for Bohra Isma'ilism as it is practised today in South Asia. Their material survival into modern times ultimately defines the Alawi's communal identity and legitimises their position and authority in the larger Shiʿi context, and the Muslim *umma* at large, as heirs of the Fatimids. To the Bohras, these manuscripts are thus a crucial, if not the central, element in the community's Neo-Fatimid identity.

A philological link between the Bohras and the Fatimids has hitherto been acknowledged through the mobility and preservation of these manuscripts. Through the *Qaratis al-Yaman* we know that Fatimid-Tayyibi manuscripts did indeed physically move between Yemen and Gujarat and vice versa, and have continued to do so up until today. Through these letters, it is clear that the Gujarati Bohras were actively involved in the affairs of the *daʿwa* in Yemen and in the gradual transfer of its headquarters and manuscript *khizana* to Gujarat. We learned about the existence of private collections in both Yemen and, later, the Indian subcontinent, and how this culture changed through bifurcations, persecution and manuscript confiscation in the Dawoodi community, which resulted in the centralisation of the *khizana* around the figure of the Dai. Sulaymani family libraries in Yemen seem to be the exception in this regard.

In addition to manuscripts, an important element of Alawi *khizana* culture that suggests links with a Fatimid past, and has thus far remained unexplored, is the world of documents. Elsewhere I suggested that practices from the Fatimid chancery continued in Yemen and Gujarat in the post-Fatimid world and continue to survive today in the Bohra community's ritualised documentary culture, such as the writing of the *ʿalama* and the usage of the *sijill* for ceremonial purposes.[136] Furthermore, documents from the Fatimid chancery, such as the letters of *Sijillat al-Mustansiriyya*, the *Qaratis al-Yaman*, and fragments of documents containing the orations of the Fatimid Imams, have survived in manuscript form in the Alawi and other Bohra *khizanat*.

On the basis of the presence of these Fatimid-Tayyibi manuscripts and documents, as well as the survival of certain ritualised writing practices, one can indeed speak of a 'lost' Fatimid treasury of books, or, at least, fragments of it, in Gujarat. The world of Fatimid documents may have vanished to the outside world and been rediscovered only recently by scholars working on the Cairo Geniza. Yet to the Bohras, it was a world that was never considered lost to begin with.

[136] Akkerman, 'Documentary Remains of a Fatimid Past in Gujarat', 286.

Chapter 3

Secret Universe

Pune-Baroda

THE ART OF MAKING AN *entrance* in the Alawi community is an initiation in itself. It was my first week as an accidental ethnographer in the Alawi *daʿwa*, and I had been dropped off by motorbike by one of the Bhais to a neighbourhood outside of Badri Mohallah. It was the monsoon season, and thus my attempts to dress appropriately in my brand-new salmon-pink *rida*, accessorised with peacock motif bangles and freshly hennaed arms and hands, seemed futile as I sheltered from the heavy rainfall and mud on the parking lot underneath a rather grim-looking concrete apartment block.

As the honourable guest of the Dai, I had come to this otherwise unremarkable part of the city to witness the oral ceremony of the *ʿahd* or *mīthāq*, or oath of allegiance, which is popularly referred to as the '*bay'at*' or '*misaq of Dai-e Zaman huzratali*' (Ar. *ḥuḍur ʿAlī*: the holiness of *ʿAlī*, also known in South Asia as '*hazratali*'). The *ʿahd* is taken by all Bohra boys and girls during adolescence and can be seen as a spiritual initiation into the community, during which they swear absolute loyalty to the Dai. The *ʿahd* is considered one of the most important rituals of Alawi Bohra life. Even though Bohra boys and girls receive basic religious education in the so-called Tayyibi *madrasa*, they can only officially become *mu'minin* and *mu'minat* by taking an oath of loyalty to the Dai.

The *ʿahd* that day involved the daughter of a middle-class Alawi family from Pune, a city in the neighbouring state of Maharashtra, who had come to Baroda for the ceremony. While the *Punekars* (the people from Pune) nervously waited in their apartment upstairs with their relatives and friends, the Dai's entourage, the Mullahs and Bhais, dressed in their white ceremonial attire and wearing *pagris* (turbans), were slowly arriving in *rikshaws* at the driveway of the apartment block. The wide variety of *pagris* they proudly wore, some like gold turbans, others made of white starched cotton wrapped around green and red *topis*, represented their official rank in the *daʿwa*. Little did I know that I would become well-acquainted with this group of around twenty men, young and old, with perfectly manicured beards and spotlessly white kurtas, as I would accompany them on pilgrimage and observe them during every event in the community in the months that were to follow. We get to know some of these gentlemen more closely in this chapter.

As more of the Dai's clerical entourage arrived, the smell of aromatic *oudh* (agarwood) intensified. While I continued to struggle with the cape of my *rida* while holding an umbrella, the mud and rain did not seem to bother the Bhais as they had an important task to fulfil: to receive their Syedna. Suddenly, ceremonial umbrellas appeared, and three non-Bohri musicians, dressed in blue, started to play their *dholak* drums and bamboo *bansuri* flutes, and firecrackers were lit: the Dai was to about to arrive.

One of the younger Bhais dramatically lifted his palm as a shiny grey Toyota entered the driveway. Within a split second, the Dai, the Mazoon Saheb, the Mukasir Saheb, and his two grandsons Murtaza and Mujtaba descended from the car as their entourage gathered, trying to kiss their feet, and a small but carefully choreographed procession followed them into the apartment block. Somewhat bewildered, and staying at an appropriate distance, I followed the procession upstairs. We entered a modestly sized apartment, which was heavily decorated with fresh flower garlands and was already filled with Alawis up to the hallway. I was squeezed in with the women next to the silver aquarium in the family's living room. This was a prime spot, it turned out, from which I could observe the Dai and his relatives who were seated on couches. The Dai's youngest grandson was sitting on his lap, and the rest of the Bhais were on the carpeted floor around him.

As soon as the three generations of royals were seated, one of the older Bhais recited the *fatiha* and started reading aloud a printed text in *Lisan al-daʿwa*, officially announcing the ceremony to the audience and informing the taker of the *ʿahd* about what was about to come. The girl from Pune, who must have been no older than sixteen and was wearing a beautiful golden-white *dupatta*, was brought into the room with her mother, and they were seated in front of the Dai on the floor (Figure 3.1).

As we have seen previously in Ahmedabad during the *ʿurs* of Sy. Ali Shamsuddin, books from the *khizana* are occasionally taken out of their state of concealment for the

Figure 3.1 Girl from the city of Pune during her *ʿahd* ceremony, with her parents to her left, and the Syedna, Mazoon Saheb and Mukasir Saheb to her right.

community to see. On this communal occasion too, a manuscript from the treasury of books was taken out of the *khizana*. In this case, however, it was not used as historic documentary evidence. Instead, its social role was that of being a ceremonial object for this initiatory rite of passage: it played an instrumental role in the public reading of the oath.

What I encountered in the neon-lit living room was another case of the public revealing of an official *sijill*, a manuscript in the form of a vertical roll. In this case, the *sijill* contained the formula of the *ʿahd* in *Lisan al-Daʿwa*. The object had been folded, to make it easier to handle, and laminated, as it was torn due to heavy usage. As the Dai was about to read aloud the formula from the *sijill*, the oath giver, and the oath receiver, the girl, were connected to one another through the *raki*, a golden cloth that both parties held in their hands. In front of what felt like the entire community, who had squeezed into the living room, the Syedna carefully opened the *sijill* on his lap and started reciting the formula of the oath aloud. After each sentence, the girl, who clearly had trouble understanding *Lisan al-Daʿwa*, hesitantly said, '*Naʿam*' (Ar.; 'yes') as an oral agreement to what was asked of her. Slowly and diligently, the Dai read out the entire text as the *sijill* unfolded like a paper snake on the floor. After the girl agreed with a final '*naʿam*', the ceremony, which had not lasted longer than thirty minutes, came to an end; the Bhai Sahebs were then offered gifts and left as swiftly as they had arrived. When the girl was congratulated by her relatives who crowded around her in the small space of the living room, I discovered that her younger brother had also undergone a 'mini-'*ʿahd*' for children, for which his face was decorated with flower garlands in honour of his circumcision (see Figure 3.2).

The ceremony marked the girl's official initiation, and thus her transition into the universe of the *daʿwa* as a *mu'mina*, and from girl to woman. This new status should not be taken lightly. Before taking the oath, Bohra adolescents are considered children without religious responsibilities, whereas after entering into this oral contract with the Dai they have spiritually become part of the Alawi *daʿwa*. As such, they are expected to behave according to the '*aḥkām of the sharīʿa*' (rulings of the sacred law): they must observe religious laws, become available for marriage and conform to gender segregation norms. The most important responsibility they assume upon entering into the oral contract, however, which marks their birth into a new world, is to keep these *ahkam*, and all the other *ʿilm* of their universe, undisclosed to the non-initiated, outside world and to pledge absolute loyalty to the Dai in the absence of the hidden Imam.

In this chapter, we focus on the question of secrecy and access, both to the community itself and to their treasury of books. It is through the oral ceremony of *ʿahd*, I argue, that the Alawis and other Bohras institutionalise the social practice of *taqiyya* in their community and create boundaries between the sacred geography of their *daʿwa* and the outside world. As is the case with numerous Bohra practices, rituals and institutions, the ceremony of the *ʿahd* is a tradition that is historically rooted in the early Isma'ili and Fatimid period, especially in the context of conversion. As such, the ritual of the *ʿahd*, the practice of *taqiyya* and other traditions of secrecy, including the dissimulation of esoteric knowledge and the inaccessibility of their *khizana*, are seen as central to their 'Fatemi' and Tayyibi way of life. According to the Alawis, even during the Fatimid period, esoteric knowledge was only disclosed to those who were initiated by the Imam,

Figure 3.2 The girl's younger brother has taken a 'mini-ʿ*ahd*', his face decorated with garlands.

and access to the palace *khizana* was thus restricted. The Tayyibis in Yemen, as we have seen, continued this tradition and, after enduring years of persecution, closed their *khizana* to the outside world. In the absence of the hidden Imam, how do these traditions of the dissimulation of esoteric knowledge translate to the social reality of Badri Mohallah?

The way in which the Bohras give expression to these traditions is deeply rooted in their Gujarati caste identity through a wide variety of unwritten etiquette rules, traditions and rituals that directly relate to access: access to the community, to the various spaces of the *mohallah*, and to the *khizana*. These various spheres, which together constitute the community's spatial narrative of their *mohallah*, fulfil different functions in the Alawi universe, each with its unique modes of access. It is through these *rites of passage* that modes of access are established and cultivated, and spaces transform from city to the universe of the *mohallah*, from outside to inside, from communal to royal, from open to secret, from library or archive to treasury of books, and from dusty books to sacred artefacts.

In this chapter, these different modes of access and their accompanying rites of passage will be explored, mapped out and walked through. What are the spatial features of secrecy in the Alawi community? How is the inaccessibility of the *khizana*, and the Alawi universe at large, built in the architecture of the *mohallah*? What makes these spaces sacred for the Alawis? How is the sacred enshrined, guarded and cultivated? These questions will be tackled by focusing on two spatial narratives of Badri Mohallah: the profane, physical narrative and the narrative of sacred geography.

3.1 Bohra Spaces and their Modes of Access

The spatial modes of the profane and physical versus the sacred and spiritual can best be explained by the story of the *ʿahd* ceremony of the girl from Pune. As that showed, one can be born into the Alawi Bohra community without being initiated into the realm of the *mu'minin* and *mu'minat* and thus without being spiritually part of the community. Similarly, as an outsider one can walk through Badri Mohallah and observe its architecture, spatial arrangement and aesthetics, and even see its *khizana* and its sacred books, without being part of the community and its sacred geography. In other words, one can be physically present in the *mohallah* without grasping the emic perspective of what it means to be part of the Alawi universe and its unwritten rules and regulations.

It is these unwritten rules and regulations, I observed, that give shape to the geography of the Alawis and keep undisclosed what should remain hidden to the uninitiated outside world: the *sacred*. From the Alawi emic perspective, the sacred is spatially manifested in Badri Mohallah, its traditions, rituals, etiquette and esoteric truths, which are materially manifested in Fatimid-Tayyibi books and are guarded by the Dai in the *khizana*.

Earlier in this study, the reader was introduced to the various esoteric layers and cyclical dimensions of the Bohra Fatimid Isma'ili interpretation of the concept of 'universe'. In this section, I translate this multi-layered system of the universe into the here and now by identifying the different Bohra spaces and their modes of access. The Bohra universe is divided into various kinds of spaces: domestic spaces; workspaces; devotional spaces that have a communal ceremonial function (the *jamaat khana*, the *qabaristan*, the *madrasa* and the mosque); spaces of governance (the offices of the Mazoon, Mukasir and Ra's ul Hudood Sahebs); royal domestic spaces (the royal *haveli* or palace); and, finally, spaces that should remain undisclosed (the treasury of books). The majority of these spaces are accessible to the entire community, and therefore they are referred to as *ʿāmma* (Ar.; 'common') spaces. *ʿAmma* spaces include all communal devotional spaces of Badri Mohallah; the *jamaat khana*, the mosque, the *madrasa* and the *qabaristan*.

Opposed to *ʿamma* spaces are the *khāṣṣa* (Ar.; 'special') spaces, notably the *khizana* and the royal *haveli*, which can only be accessed after obtaining the special permission of the Dai. In reality, the term '*khassa*' is used as a synonym for the royal family. What should be noted is that *ʿamma* and *khassa* spaces do not necessarily exclude each other, at least not spatially, as we have seen with the *khizana*, which is situated in the office of the Mazoon Saheb. Instead, they coexist and transcend the spatial geography of the office of the Mazoon Saheb. Also, there are in-between spaces that are neither *ʿamma* nor *khassa*, such as the offices of the Mazoon, Mukasir and Ra's ul Hudood Sahebs, which are accessible to the people of Badri Mohallah, but only with special permission and according to specific rules, regulations and rituals.

Clerical and non-clerical spaces in Muslim cultures and societies are often conceptualised and analysed through the lens of private and public spheres, on the basis of the idea that social spaces are accessible for everyone in society as discursive spaces of social gathering and the transformation thereof.[1] Among the Alawis, we encounter the exact opposite phenomenon: the discursive tradition of *not* having access to certain spaces *because* they are explicitly secret, esoteric and inaccessible. The reflexive chapter, in which I described my personal story of accessing the Bohra universe, should make it clear that Western conceptions of public and private spheres are not relevant to understanding spaces such as the Bohra *masjid* or the *khizana*, because the notion of 'public space' does not exist in the Bohra community. For the world outside of Badri Mohallah, *al-khārij* (Ar.; 'the outside'), everything is private. Badri Mohallah is not an open social space accessible to whoever wants to go there: it can only be accessed by people initiated into the community, and, as we have seen, even within the *mohallah* not all spaces are necessarily accessible to all believers.

In fact, as with the treasury of books, some spaces in Badri Mohallah are explicitly and intentionally inaccessible, without evoking any protest from those who cannot access these '*khassa*' spaces. It is thus a discussion not of public versus private, but of the Bohra universe and *al-kharij*, the non-Bohra 'outside other'. An emic perspective is critical for making sense of the multi-layered spatial narrative of Badri Mohallah and its complex modes of access, both from a royal *khassa* perspective and through the eyes of the *mu'minin* and *mu'minat*, the *ʿamma*; and, finally, for understanding the rationale behind my personal story of access to the *khizana* and its untouchable manuscripts.

I suggest here two modes of access. The first mode, hereafter known as 'access I', focuses on the profane, physical structure of the community, the *mohallah*, and its vernacular architecture. At the other end of the spectrum, 'access II' is a mode of access where the sacral is central, and one through which we will transcend the walls, doors, basements and locks of Badri Mohallah and focus on the sacred geography of the Alawi universe and its *khizana*. These two modes of access are not dichotomies but complement each other as different realms: a profane topographical and architectural realm (access I) and a sacred spiritual realm (access II).

The Bohra interpretation of the Fatimid-Tayyibi knowledge system, both in daily practice and as sacred scripture, serves as the bridge between the two modes. Access II gives a sacred meaning to the geographical space of access I, and the physical features of access I explain why the sacred space of access II looks the way it does. Access II transforms the spatial geography of Badri Mohallah (access I) into a universe of cyclical time and space, where the clerical establishment is not merely a hierarchy of clerics and librarians but a semi-infallible royal family and representatives of the hidden Imam. The royal family, in turn, being at the head of the Alawi Bohra clerical establishment, gives materiality (access I) to the Bohra universe through the *khizana* and its manuscripts by safeguarding the rituals of access and initiation that surround it.

[1] See, for instance, Birgit Meyer and Annelies Moors, *Religion, Media, and the Public Sphere* (Bloomington: Indiana University Press, 2005) and Dale F. Eickelman and Jon W. Anderson, *New Media in the Muslim World: The Emerging Public Sphere* (Bloomington: Indiana University Press, 2003).

Applying the categories of access I and access II not only helps us grasp the significance of the *khizana* and its a central role in the larger sacred geography of the Alawi Bohra universe but also explains why I, as a female researcher and foreigner so alien to the Alawi universe, was granted authorised access to the treasury of books, transcending social conventions applicable to the *mu'minin* and *mu'minat*. Even though the sacral importance of the *khizana* and its manuscripts, as well as the necessity of invisible barriers, was stressed by the clerics time and time again, these barriers did not apply to me because I was merely part of the profane structure of the *mohallah*, and not of the sacred Bohra universe as a believer. The idea underlying these modes of access is that a space comes into being only when a person moves through it and attributes certain qualities of 'the sacred' to it.[2] There is thus a difference between being present in the *mohallah* geographically and being embedded in it spiritually.

Accessing the community and its treasury of books was thus possible through the mode of access I. Spatially, I was among the Alawis; I lived in Badri Mohallah for months, ate their *thalis*, participated in their ceremonies, offered my curatorial services to the Dai, and made friends – yet spiritually I was never part of it, nor fully initiated into their universe. My position is not unique for cultural anthropologists in the field or for women in particular, as the work of Lila Abu-Lughod and others has shown.[3] It did, however, help me understand my unique position in Badri Mohallah and my authorised presence in the *khizana*. For instance, the sacred truths of the *haqa'iq* were perhaps stored in my brain, but were not, as they would be in a true Bohra cleric, embodied in my *ṣadr* (chest).

Through the mode of access I, I could thus enter the *khizana* and other sacred Bohra spaces without converting or taking the proper oath of allegiance (even though a special version was designed for me as an oath of trust); more importantly, I was able to touch the manuscripts as a ritually impure woman. Had I been a Bohri, my status would be highly problematic, as the hierarchies of the *daʿwa* would not grant me any of the privileges I had as an outsider. Had I been a male outsider, the clerics confided in me, I would have never gained the access to the community I did, as they would not have felt responsible for my safety. While other limitations and challenges applied to me as an outsider and as a woman, operating under access I allowed me to negotiate the invisible barriers and rituals of access mentioned earlier. It was exactly for this reason that the Bhai Sahebs saw me as their confidante and would occasionally confide in me their own secrets, fears and disappointments in life.

3.2 Access I: A Profane Topography of the Bohra Universe

Let us start with exploring Badri Mohallah through the lens of access I. The *mohallah* is not protected by guards, special doors or gates: anyone in Baroda can walk through it, and it can be located on maps. Similarly, the treasury of books and its cupboard

2 See Aike Peter Rots, 'The Rediscovery of "Sacred Space" in Contemporary Japan: Intrinsic Quality or Discursive Strategy?', in Liu Janhui and Sano Mayuko (eds), *Rethinking 'Japanese Studies' from Practices in the Nordic Region* (Kyoto: International Research Center for Japanese Studies, 2014), 31–50.

3 Lila Abu-Lughod, *Veiled Sentiments*, Ch. 1, 'Guest and Daughter', 1–38.

of manuscripts have no locks or keys, and its space is not a heavily armed or guarded palace or citadel, such as was the case in Fatimid and Tayyibi times. Through the lens of access I, the *khizana* is located in a house in the middle of the Alawi *mohallah* that is visible to the outside and – in theory – can be entered by anyone who wishes to do so. From the access I perspective, it is merely a repository of historical texts, an archive-cum-library, managed by the Mazoon Saheb as its caretaker.

Considering the topography of Badri Mohallah, from an architectural point of view there is no difference between *ʿamma* and *khasssa* spaces: the *masjid*, the *jamaat khana*, the *qabaristan* or the *khizana* are all physical spaces with doors that can be opened and rooms that can be entered. The key question for an analysis of the *khizana* through an access I perspective is the following: what is the relationship between the *mohallah* and its environment? In other words, what is the spatial particularity of the *mohallah* in the geography of the city? To answer this question, we will map the *ʿamma* and *khasssa* spaces of Badri Mohallah, its vernacular architecture, focusing on the dynamics between the Bohra house as an inhabited domestic space and the universe to which it belongs, and the dialectics of inside and outside. The chapter sections essentially provide a stroll through Badri Mohallah, starting from the outside and ending at the treasury of books. On this tour we access its rooms, cupboards and staircases; its spaces of worship and of governance; royal domestic spaces; and, finally, the physical space of the *khizana*.

An Alawi Enclave in the City: Badri Mohallah from the Outside

Situated in the middle of the historic city, Badri Mohallah looks like any other quarter of Baroda. It consists of around eighty *havelis* (mansions) and *manzils* (houses) in total (Figure 3.3). Compared to the historic Dawoodi Bohra quarters in other cities in Gujarat, such as Surat, Sidhpur, Godhra, Khambhat, Ahmedabad, Palanpur and Bhavnagar, where several *mohallahs* together form larger areas known as *Bohrwads*, Badri Mohallah is a quite small enclave by Bohra standards.[4] It has one central alley that is known to all as the 'Bohra lane'. The Bohra lane is considered the sacred space of the *mohallah*, hosting the devotional infrastructure of the community: its spaces of worship such as the mosque and the *jamaat khana*, the private domains of the clerics, the royal *haveli*, and the *khizana*. All devotional practices and commemorations – prayer, religious ceremonies, celebrations and processions – take place in the Bohra lane. From a topographical point of view, the Bohra lane is enveloped by its surroundings, Jahangir Lane and Joghandi, where many Alawis live or have their shops. Together, these streets, along with the Alawi graveyards, which are situated outside the city, make up the Alawi Bohra physical universe.

A large part of the Alawi community does not reside in Baroda, either because families moved elsewhere to start businesses or because they felt safer there: many believers have moved away from Badri Mohallah since the Gujarat riots of 2002, which turned the quiet Bohra lane into a sectarian battlefield. According to my interlocutors,

[4] See Madhavi Desai, *Traditional Architecture: House Form of Bohras in Gujarat* (Delhi: National Institute of Advanced Studies in Architecture, 2008).

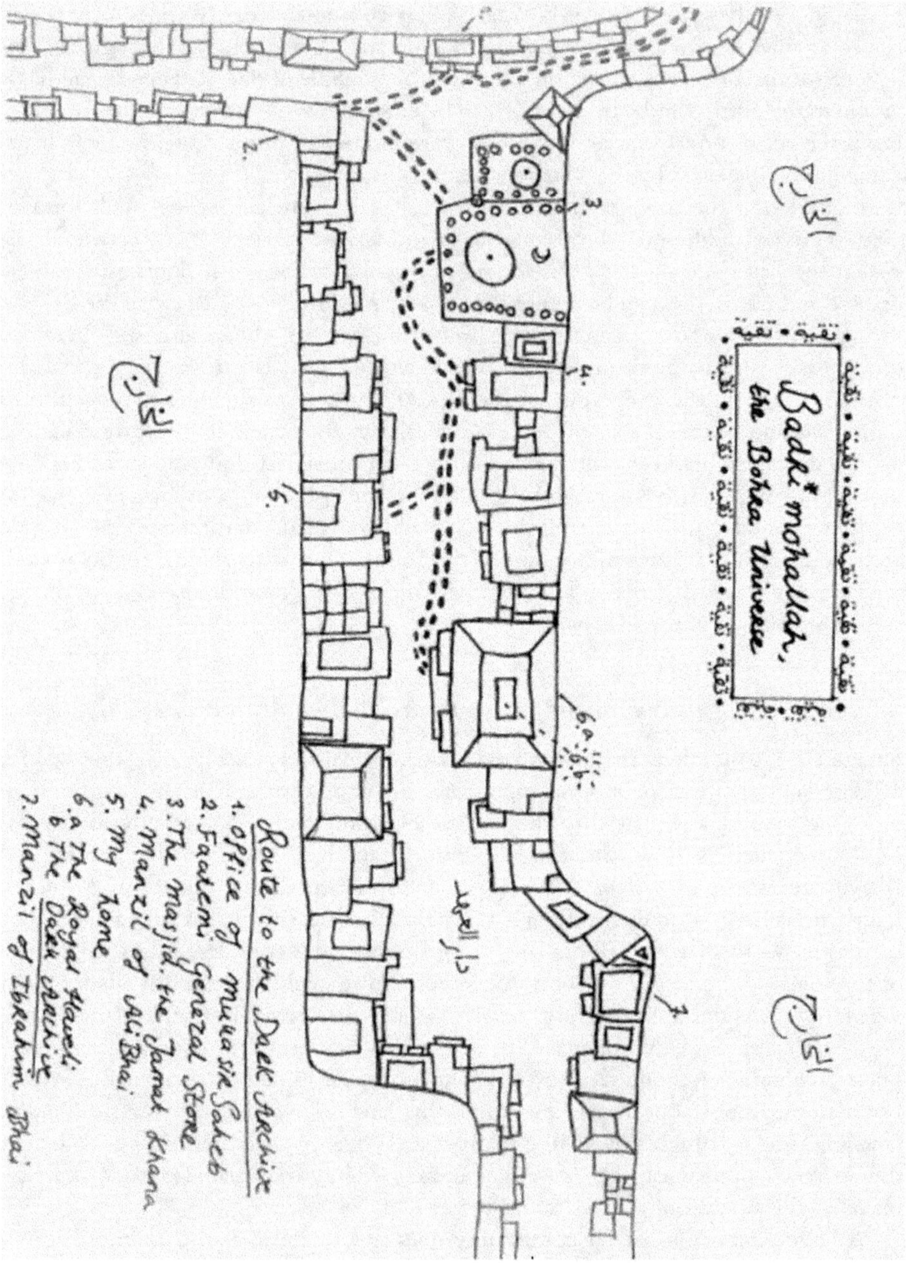

Figure 3.3 Researcher's field sketch of Badri Mohallah.
Note: 'dark archive' is used here to refer to the *khizana*. See my thesis, *The Bohra Dark Archive and the Language of Secrecy*, 139.

there is not a single believer in the *mohallah* who has not lost a family member or experienced violence during the riots. Believers who decided to stay in Badri Mohallah, close to the Dai and the rest of the royal family, confided in me that they always have their suitcases ready in case of future inter-communal violence. Sadly, in the current political climate in India, these anxieties are not unfounded, as anti-Muslim sentiments in Gujarat are on the rise.

Even though Badri Mohallah is not a guarded or gated community, it functions as a self-sufficient and secluded universe, as is reflected in the architectural structure of the Bohra lane. According to my observations, outsiders rarely entered the *mohallah*, and *rikshawalas* often had no idea where Badri Mohallah was located or would refuse to take me there. Yet, Badri Mohallah is a crowded noisy place in the midst of the busy city life of Baroda. Its narrow alley, covered by a canopy of electricity wires, is constantly crowded with Bohra *rikshawalas*, motorcycles, *sabziwalas* (vegetable sellers), *faqirs*, a great variety of religious processions, wedding bands, playing children, livestock (mainly goats), and holy cows from the Hindu lane attracted to the piles of waste in the street.

The streets around Badri Mohallah are occupied by Hindu, Tablighi and Twelver Shi'i Muslim communities, who reside in neighbouring alleys that are referred to as the 'Hindu lane', the 'Wahhabi lane' and the 'Shia lane' respectively.[5] Even though these *mohallahs* are not gated, the daily lives of these communities are absolutely segregated; my interlocutors assured me that one does not interact with someone from another religious 'caste', and shrines and temples, which are often common spaces of multi-religious worship in other regions of India, are in this case not shared under any circumstances.

Segregated or not, the Hindus, Jains, Sunnis, Shi'ism and Bohras share the intense soundscape of the old city of Baroda. The acoustic environment of Badri Mohallah is not challenging only because of its many *rikshaws*, street vendors and cattle. The soundscape, which continues day and night, is also multi-religious: bells of Hindu temples and the monthly processions compete with the great variety of daily *azaans*, which are either highly Persianised, in the case of the Twelver Shi'is who routinely curse the rightly-guided Caliphs, or in an Arabised style for the Tablighis; and finally, there is the Bohra *azaan*: like the *azaan* of the Twelver Shi'is, the Bohra *azaan* is only performed three times per day and is characterised by a strong Gujarati pronunciation.

The riots of 2002 led to inter-communal tension and suspicion among these different communities. During Muharram and various Hindu festivals, Badri Mohallah and all other 'Muslim lanes' are completely closed off with barricades for days by the Baroda police. The only movement between the different *mohallahs* that I noticed was the daily migration of the Langur monkeys, which would jump over the roofs at dawn, the strolling of holy cows, and the wondering *faqirs* who would come to the alleys of the old city after the *ẓuhr* prayer shouting '*yā ʿAlī madād!*' (Twelver Shia) or '*yā Muḥammad rasūl Allāh!*' (Sunni) or '*yā a'immat aṭ-Ṭāhirīn!*' (Bohra), depending on the *mohallah* they happened to pass through.

[5] Bohra clerics consider all Muslim communities who actively perform *tablīgh* in the old city Wahhabis.

Entering the Bohra Universe

Now that we have an idea of the soundscape of Badri Mohallah and its embeddedness within the old city of Baroda, let us start mapping out the Bohra lane from the outside in. Even though the Bohra lane has no road signs, it is clear on entering it that one is among Bohras: *saris* turn into *ridas* and the names of shops change. At the corner of the lane is a very small grocery shop that sells ice cream, known as the Fatemi General Store. It is a gathering place where elderly Alawi gentlemen sit with their grandchildren while exchanging the latest gossip. The name of the grocery shop clearly refers to the Alawis' identification with their Fatimid roots. Right across the small grocery is a very small and inconspicuous office, facing the beginning of the Bohra alley. This is the office of the Mukasir Saheb, who is in charge of all communal affairs.

It is no coincidence that the office of the Mukasir Saheb is situated near the entrance to Badri Mohallah; literally every movement from and into the street is registered from the office of the Mukasir Saheb by his secretary and personal assistant Amina. Despite her modest background, Amina is the 'mover and shaker' in the Alawi universe: she is rarely seen, yet she is always present, running from one place to another to 'do the needful'. The Ra's ul Hudood's office, which also functions as a homeopathic clinic, is situated one block away from the entrance to the neighbourhood. The locations

Figure 3.4 Badri Mohallah seen on a rainy day through the grills of the royal *haveli*.

of the offices of the three brothers – the Ra's ul Hudood Saheb, the Mukasir Saheb and the Mazoon Saheb – represent the hierarchy and political power of the clerical establishment very clearly in proximity to the *khizana*; from outside the *mohallah* (Ra's ul Hudood) to just inside (Mukasir), to the royal *haveli* itself (Mazoon).

The Dai has no office in Badri Mohallah, first because he rarely concerns himself with earthly matters, and second because he would not need a physical space in the *mohallah* as he *is considered* the *mohallah*: he gives materiality to this world and is thus omnipresent in the geography of Badri Mohallah. According to the narrative of the community there is no universe, past, present or future, without the Dai, and therefore His Royal Highness must be kept safe at all costs. Several attempted attacks on the Dai and his family occurred during the riots of 2002; ever since, the Dai has lived in a quiet and safe villa far outside the *mohallah*, which bears the very fitting title '*Dār al-Salām*' (House of Peace), offering His Royal Highness privacy and earthly *satr*.

The Masjid without Minbar

The most striking example of Bohra architecture in Baroda is the large white marble mosque at the entrance to Badri Mohallah, known as the *Noorani majsid*. The Alawi *masjid* was constructed by the late Dai Nūr al-Dīn Yūsuf b. Badr al-Dīn (no. 43, d. 1394/1974) and it is the architectural hallmark of the community. Its architectural features are unusual, as it was built before the trend of Bohra Neo-Fatimid architecture in South Asia in the last several decades and, more recently, with the Dawoodi mosque in Mombasa in East Africa.[6] This Neo-Fatimid turn in architecture can be observed in the Alawi Bohra community too; for example, in the recently inaugurated Alawi Badri Masjid in Mumbai. Even though less pronounced in comparison to the Dawoodis, it is the first example of Alawi architecture to combine Neo-Fatimid architectural features and ornaments.[7]

The Noorani *masjid*, however, is the most prominent *ʿamma* space in the *mohallah* and was built in the 1970s. Architecturally, it combines features reminiscent of Mughal architecture, such as the marble dome of the Taj Mahal – a style that was common in Bohra devotional architecture before it was mixed with Neo-Fatimid features – and a 1970s variation on modernist architecture resembling Le Corbusier's straight lines. The marble entrance of the *masjid* is very grand; it has imposing wooden doors and the upper part of the entrance is decorated with gilded Qur'anic verses (Figures 3.5 and 3.6).

From the inside, the *masjid* resembles a typical mosque in South Asia, with its golden chandeliers (still covered in plastic), oriental carpets, plastic chairs and fans. Apart from the *takht* (throne) of the Dai, which is the centre-piece of the space, and the names of the *ahl al-bayt* that are carved in Arabic on the wall, there is nothing distinctly Bohra about the *masjid*. As opposed to Sunni and Shi'i mosques, Bohra

6 Sanders, *Creating Medieval Cairo*, 127–32.

7 *Badri Masjid*, Mumbai, https://www.alavibohra.org/Badri%20masjid%20-%20mumbai%20darajaat%20e%20tameer.htm (last accessed 7 November 2020).

Figure 3.5 Entrance of the Noorani *masjid*. Picture taken during the Alawi Heritage Walk. Credits: Vadodara Heritage Trust.

spaces of prayer have no *minbar* (pulpit); the right to give the Friday *khuṭba* (Friday sermon) is reserved for the hidden Imam.

The *majsid* consists of two floors. The ground floor contains the space of prayer, which is divided in sections for *mu'minin* and *mu'minat*; they are separated by a wall with classical Arab lattice work in the South Asian style, known as *mashrabiyya*. Both sections have separate entrances (women enter through the back). These women-versus-men spaces are flexible when it comes to the *waz* or *majālis* (s. *majlis*, a religious gathering other than for prayer). For instance, on many auspicious days 'ladies only' *majalis* are organised in the *masjid*, such as during the recitation of the *marsiya* sessions, which are held every afternoon during the month of Muharram. During shared *majalis* the women often participate while sitting on the *mashrabiyya* marble balconies on the first floor (while observing the men), which during weekdays serve as the *Madrasa al-Tayyibiyya*. The balconies on the first floor give the best views of the ceremonies (Figure 3.7).

Figure 3.6 Façade of the Noorani *masjid*. Picture taken during the Alawi Heritage Walk. Credits: Vadodara Heritage Trust.

Figure 3.7 Interior of the Noorani *masjid*, picture taken during a *majlis*.

The Jamaat Khana and the Tears of Karbala

The *jamaat khana*, which is directly connected to the *masjid*, is the community's most important *ʿamma* space of togetherness. Although communal affairs in Muslim societies often take place in the *masjid*, among the Bohras, business, gossiping, matchmaking and, above all, eating take place in the *jamaat*. It is thus in the *jamaat khana* and not the *masjid* where *mu'minin* and *mu'minat* spend the majority of their communal lives.

The *jamaat khana* is a very spacious but simple marble space equipped with fans, water tabs and neon lights. There is no furniture present in the *jamaat khana*. In fact, I would argue that, except for the *takht* of the Dai, the peacock throne of Ma Saheba, some plastic chairs for the elderly ladies in the *masjid* and the Gujarat swing beds, there is almost no furniture anywhere in the entire *mohallah*. As with all devotional and social spaces in the Bohra universe, the *jamaat khana* is not open to outsiders.

The historiography of Isma'ilism is dominated by polemical literature replete with mysterious myths and stories around the *jamaat khanas* of the Bohras and other Isma'ili communities.[8] I was surprised to learn that the narratives of some of these stories still widely circulate in India and Pakistan today. There is one particular story that was recounted to me several times in Ahmedabad, Lahore and Islamabad by non-Bohris about mass marriage ceremonies. According to this myth, brides lie en masse face-down on the floor in the *jamaat khana* with their hair spread out, upon which the Dai (in the case of the Bohras) or the Agha Khan (in the case of the Nizaris) walks with his bare feet. This caricature must have its roots in the Bohras' practice of secrecy, which prevents outsiders from learning about their rituals.

The main activity of the *jamaat khana*, as I observed, does not revolve around indecent or 'un-Islamic' rituals but around the sharing of food. After every *majlis*, no matter how long or short, big or small, all community members (who sometimes number thousands of believers) consume a communal meal known as the *thali* (Figures 3.8 and 3.9). The *thali* is a very large round metal plate on which a great variety of Bohra Gujarati culinary dishes are presented – all kinds of non-vegetarian dishes with goat meat prepared in *ghee*. The family, usually around eight to ten people, sit on the floor, and the *thali*, placed on a tripod, is placed in the middle of them.[9] The family members eat the curries, *biryanis*, sweets and savouries with their hands while sitting on the floor. Whereas the practice of the communal dinner in the *jamaat khana* can be found in other communities, what is unusual about the Bohras is that the food is consumed from the same *thali* (Figure 3.9).[10] Dawoodi interlocutors in Blank's ethnography hold that this practice was introduced in Bohra milieux in medieval Gujarat as an egalitarian answer to Hindu exclusivism.[11] In the Alawi *jamaat khana*, the huge communal dinners are distributed by the young volunteers of the communities (adolescent boys),

[8] Daftary, *The Ismaʿilis*, 7–10. Blank, *Mullahs on the Mainframe*, 24.

[9] Several cookbooks have been devoted to Bohra cuisine in India. See for instance Normal Rangwala's *With a Pinch of Salt: An Expression of Bohra Culture & Cuisine* (Mumbai: Create Space Independent Publishing Platform, 2011). As for academic studies, see Zoe Goodman, 'Tales of the Everyday City: Geography and Chronology in Postcolonial Mombasa' (PhD diss., SOAS University of London, 2018).

[10] A similar practice exists among the Twelver Khojas.

[11] Blank, *Mullahs on the Mainframe*, 150.

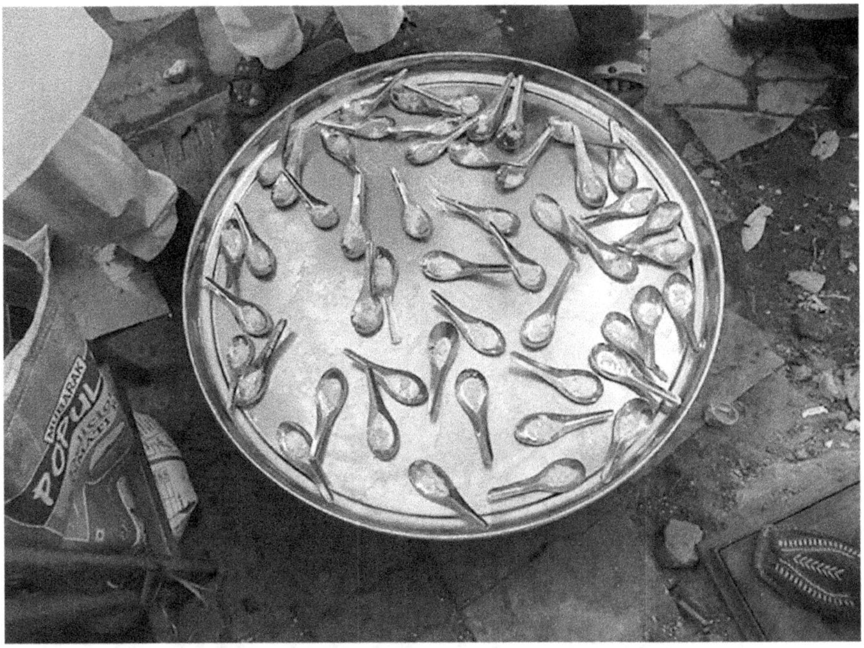

Figure 3.8 Spoons of salt on a communal *thali* plate symbolising the tears of Karbala.

Figure 3.9 Bohra women finishing their communal *thali* in the *jamaat khana*.

who, as part of their *khidma*, are responsible for distributing the rice, *dals* and *rotis* from very large buckets (Figure 3.10). At *jamaat khana* gatherings the royal family eats from special *khassa thalis* in a separate space. *Mu'minin* and *mu'minat* also dine separately.

Through participant observation during many communal dinners, I learned that the *thali* is about more than feeding the body. As mentioned in Chapter 1, it is considered a sacred ritual with a beginning and an end that can only be carried out according to a specific set of rules (and etiquette) that go far beyond discussions of what is *halal*

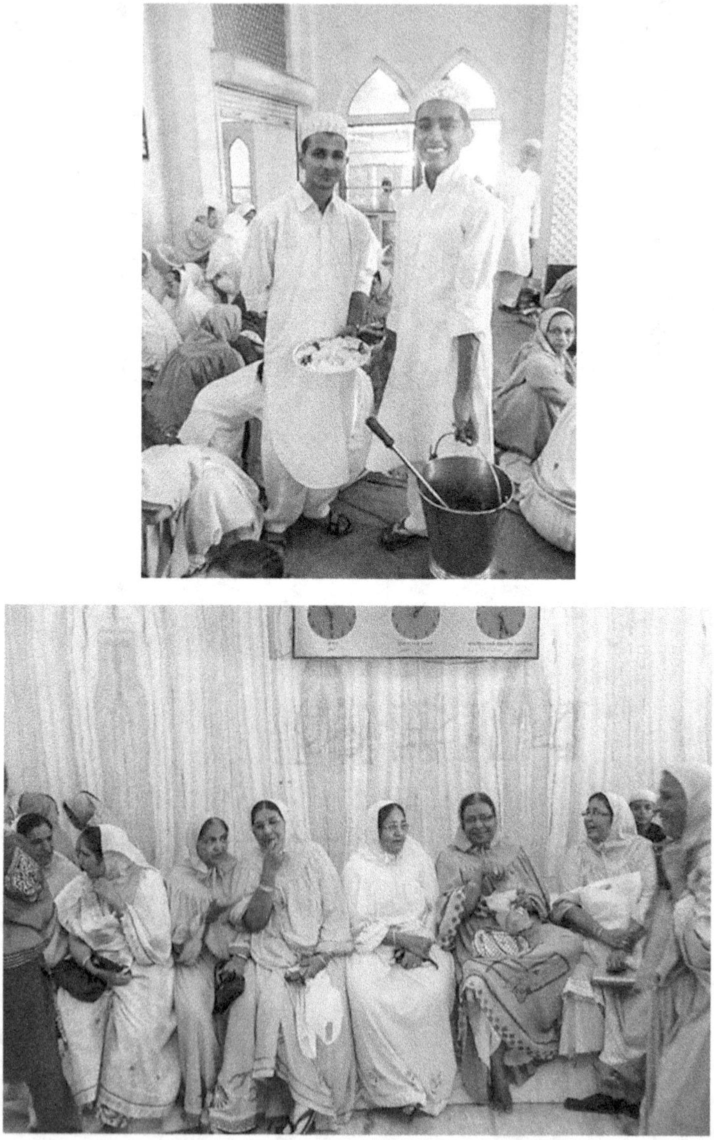

Figure 3.10 Life in the *jamaat khana*.

and *haram*. The *thali* ritual starts with eating a pinch of salt before every meal, which is symbolic of tears for the martyrdom of Imam Husayn (Figure 3.8); then the *basmala* is whispered silently and the meal is consumed (at very high speed). There are special recipes for special days, both auspicious and inauspicious, which are mentioned in the stories of Imam Husayn in Karbala. An example of this would be *shīr kurma*, a vermicelli pudding prepared with cardamom, dates and nuts that must be consumed after the slaughtering of the goats at *eed* (*ʿīd al-fiṭr*; feast of the breaking of the fast). The ritual ends by finishing the *thali* with something sweet, symbolising good fortune and auspiciousness, which in the *jamaat khana* is always *kulfi* ice cream. The ritual of consuming the *thali* is not only confined to the space of the *jamaat khana* but is also the way families eat in the privacy of their homes (Figure 3.11).

Emotions, food habits, orthopraxy and rituals are strongly connected among the Alawis. This is especially the case with cooking, as I was told by the Bhu Saheba once when she had her hair oiled by Amina while rocking on a swing mattress. She explained that women (responsible for the cooking in the community) are encouraged to cry during cooking, reminding themselves of the suffering of Imam Husayn and his

Figure 3.11 An undated painting entitled 'Bohra Dastarkhan' by Abbas Batliwala, depicting a *thali* family meal. Credits: https://www.dawoodi-bohras. com/news/1311/107/An-artist-true-to-himself-true-to-his-soil/d,pdb_detail_article_comment.

family in Karbala.[12] I observed, however, that the ritual of crying is not restricted to the space of the kitchen and is certainly also not a gendered practice.

According to the Mazoon Saheb's interpretation of the *Daʿa'im*, there are five categories of crying, ranging from crying out loud, to lamenting, to wailing, to sobbing, and finally to weeping uncontrollably. Each category of crying has a specific purpose and is considered *farḍ* (mandatory), and is used for both joyful and sad occasions, depending on the time, place and date. For instance, crying out loud, or 'stylized sobbing' as Blank calls it, is considered obligatory during Muharram and the *ʿurs*, and during weddings; 'less' stylised sobbing is only allowed during cooking, whereas weeping is considered acceptable for personal matters only.[13] Coming from a cultural background where crying in public is considered weak, embarrassing and unmasculine, I was surprised to find the Bhai Sahebs cry in public on several occasions, and not only to commemorate the death of Imam Husayn, which is usually combined with loud screaming, heavy breathing and open-hand *ma'tam*. I often encountered public crying in the *masjid* in relation to personal matters. Once, I witnessed the Dai burst out in tears in the *masjid* during a very emotional speech in honour of Ma Saheba (his wife). It was at her public birthday celebration, during which he informed the audience that he was so grateful that his wife was still able to celebrate her birthday after her recent heart surgery. This display of emotion took place in front of thousands of believers, who had come from all over the subcontinent to pay their respects to Ma Saheba. As a result, the Bhai Sahebs and the entire public cried (myself included), and this time it had nothing to do with the story of Karbala.[14]

Heritage beyond Books: Bohra Vernacular Architecture

The *jamaat khana*, *masjid* and the office of the Mukasir Saheb together constitute the religious infrastructure of Badri Mohallah designed for the *ʿamma*. There is one very important *ʿamma* space in the Bohra universe that has not been covered yet: the domestic space. Alawi Bohra vernacular domestic architecture is very different from the majestic Bohra *masjid* style. It is dominated by colourful and lavishly decorated but somewhat deteriorated *havelis*, referred to as 'Bohra *manzils*'. These *manzils* are three- or four-storey traders' houses, dating from the late nineteenth and the early and mid-twentieth centuries. The *havelis* together form the tightly-knit Badri Mohallah.[15]

There are two types of Bohra *havelis*, the traditional colonial-style Bohra dwellings dating from the nineteenth century and more recent homes built in the 1940s and 1950s. The traditional Bohra residences are constructed of wood and stand out from every other kind of architecture in the old city of Baroda because of their intricately decorated façades and use of Arabic calligraphy for Qur'anic verses. These facades are not just a treat for the eye. The traditional Bohra *havelis* are built in such a way that

[12] Badri Mohallah, television room of the royal *haveli*, 14 November 2012.

[13] Blank, *Mullahs on the Mainframe*, 148.

[14] Badri Mohallah, *masjid*, on the occasion of the birthday of Ma Saheba, 11 November 2012.

[15] See for an in-depth study of Bohra *mazils* in Sidhpur: Madhavi Desai, *Traditional Architecture: House Form of Bohras in Gujarat*.

one can observe every little detail in the *mohallah*, without jeopardising one's *purdah* by being seen from the exterior.

The more modern mid-century interpretation of the traditional Bohra *manzil*, by contrast, is constructed of cement plaster over concrete and decorated in pastel pinks, blues and yellows, containing art deco-shaped ornaments with an Islamic twist (Figures 3.12–3.15). Bohra *manzils* of both traditions have small, gated porches and balconies made of wood with beautifully carved wooden shutters and coloured, stained-glass windows. The entrances of these *manzils* are lavishly decorated with little columns, staircases, vestibules and iron courtyard gates and are often used for minor social encounters and as a backdrop to leisure time spent outside, or, depending on the season, for keeping cattle. As opposed to the hustle and bustle of the street, family life takes place inside the house or in the inner courtyards of these *havelis*, which cannot be seen from the outside.

Figure 3.12 Bohra vernacular architecture (seen here with a *langur* monkey).

Figure 3.13 Art deco with an Islamic twist: a historic *manzil* in the *mohallah*.

Figure 3.14 Wooden façade of a *manzil*, picture taken during Alawi Heritage Walk. Credits: Vadodara Heritage Trust.

Figure 3.15 Another façade of a *manzil*, picture taken during Alavi Heritage Walk. Credits: Vadodara Heritage Trust.

Edward Soja and others have argued that capitalist developments are deeply reflected in the formation of cities.[16] This is certainly the case with the vernacular architecture of Badri Mohallah. The architectural heritage of Bohra *manzils* reflects the daily life in the *mohallah*, which historically was and still is dominated by trade. Traces of mercantile activities are present on the façades of Bohra houses that display plasterwork depicting Arabic calligraphy and arabesques, followed by the date of construction and the name of the *wala* (vendor) who owned the building. The name of the *manzil* refers to the kind of trade the owner practised; for instance, I lived in the *Attarwalamanzil*, the 'house of Attarwala' (perfume seller).[17]

Even though the façades of these houses might indicate otherwise, the Bohra *manzils* of Badri Mohallah are by no means luxurious mansions; in fact, many of these historic houses are deteriorating and dilapidated. Only quite recently, I was told, have

[16] See for more on this discussion Edward Soja's *Postmodern Geographies: The Reassertion of Space in Critical Social Theory* (London: Verso Press, 1989).

[17] See Blank on the introduction of Bohra family names – which were always related to trade – during the British Raj. Blank, *Mullahs on the Mainframe*, 108.

Figure 3.16 Entrance of *manzil*, with a *mu'mina*, her son and a goat, pictured during *eed*.

traditional cow-dung floors been replaced by cement, and before the 1990s many households were not connected to electricity or running water. Moreover, sanitary conditions in the old city of Baroda remain challenging, especially during the monsoon season, which creates health hazards. Another challenge in Badri Mohallah is crowded living-space; most of the Bohra *manzils* host several families on one floor, and sometimes even in one room.

Despite these challenges, the Alawi community is very proud of their historic architecture and have opened up their *mohallah* to the inhabitants of their city during the Alawi Heritage Walk in 2020 (Figure 3.17).[18] The walk, in which fifty heritage enthusiasts participated, included a private tour by the Mukasir Saheb and the Ra's ul Hudood of the *mohallah*, and Alawi arts and craftsmanship, such as *topi* weaving

[18] The Alawi Heritage Walk was organised in corporation with the Heritage Trust of Vadododara. See Alavi Heritage Walk: https://www.alavibohra.org/alavi%20heritage-antique-architecture-culture.htm (last accessed 14 October 2020).

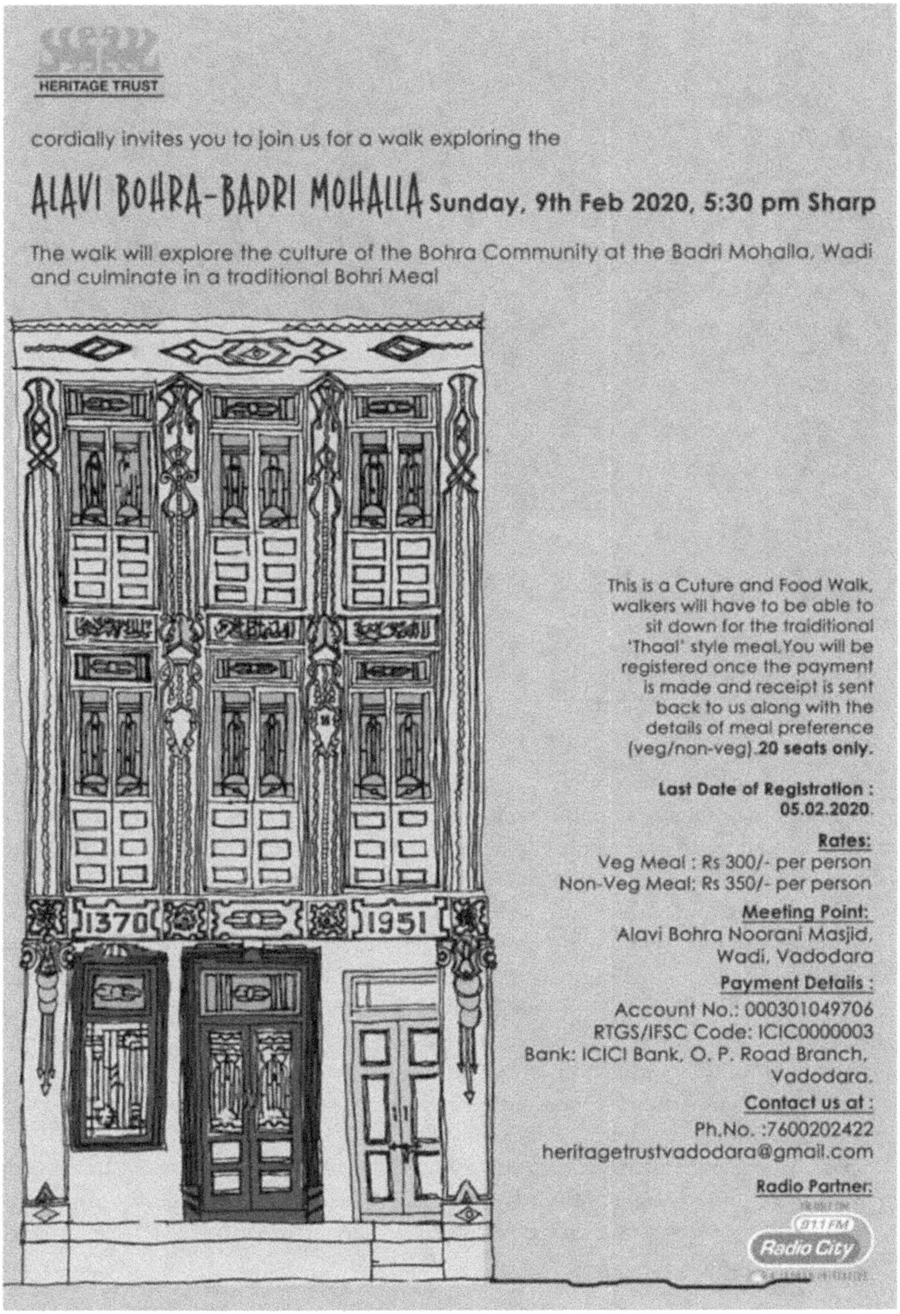

Figure 3.17 Alawi Heritage Walk poster, with drawings of the traditional wooden façades of the Alawi *manzils*. Credits: Shivani Pikle and Vadodara Heritage Trust.

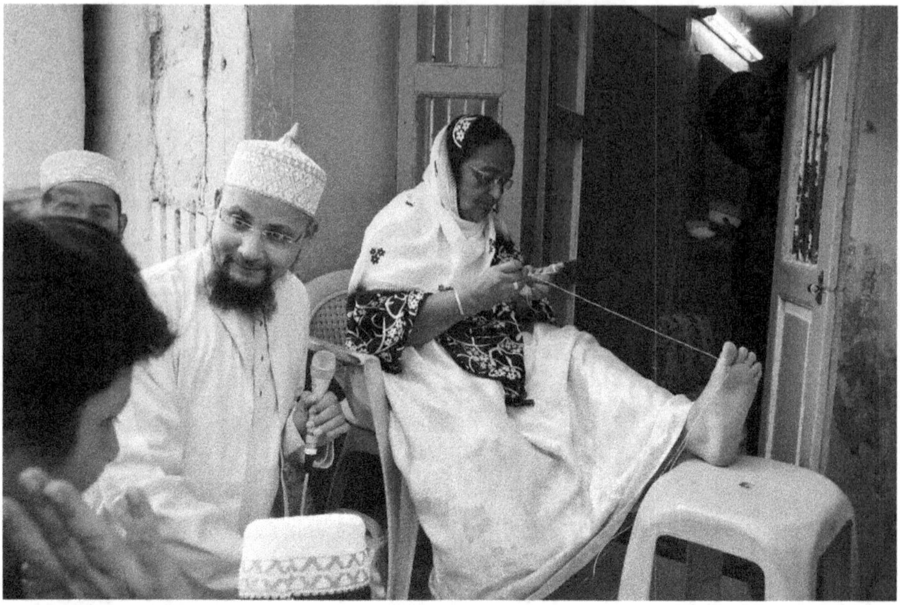

Figure 3.18 *Topi* weaving in the *mohallah*, with the Ra's ul Hudood Saheb with a microphone in his hand. Picture taken during the Alawi Heritage Walk. Credits: Vadodara Heritage Trust.

(Figure 3.18), and Bohra cuisine.[19] Special attention was given to the historic Alawi *manzils* and their interiors, such as their spatial arrangement around a central courtyard and the central room of the house, the *awaas* (galleries that overlook the *mohallah*), the large *otlas* (entrance or vestibule) and broad wooden *khaat* (staircases).

The heritage walk, which was covered in various local newspapers and was featured in a photo exhibition entitled 'Monumental Life of Vadodara', not only provided fellow Barodians with a glimpse into the world of the Alawis but also raised awareness among the people of Badri Mohallah themselves about the historic significance of their *mohallah* as a heritage site within the larger urban context of Baroda. In other words, they came to understand that, in addition to the *khizana* and its old manuscripts, the community's *ʿamma* spaces, including the historic *manzils* in which families have lived in for generations, were heritage sites as well.

Yet the evanescent aura of the Neo-Fatimid *khizana* is never far away. In a recent post on the official website of the Alawi *daʿwa*, the Mukasir Saheb links this new consciousness of the Alawis as heritage custodians in the urban setting of Baroda directly back to the Fatimids:

> We always remember our Forefathers A'immat of Cairo and Du'aat of Yaman, when we see such type of Heritage buildings . . . By seeing all these things we should always remember our Faatemi Imaams who were the pioneers of conceptualizing

[19] Ibid.

> and building the Smart City. In the tenth century AD itself has thrown open the arena of the splendor of Islamic Architecture and shaping the future of Egypt as a Marvelous Heritage and Legacy. We too have a rich Heritage and History and must always encourage our new generation to protect and preserve our Heritage and never forget our roots and origin.

Returning briefly to the modes of access to the profane (access I) and the sacred (access II), one can thus be an Alawi Bohri living in a historic Gujarati *manzil* in Baroda that others can visit and admire during heritage walks, while at the same time being part of a sacred universe, practising 'the Faatemi way of life' that is only accessible to one's fellow-initiated Bohri *mu'minin* and *mu'minat*. In other words, by walking along the Bohra lane, the heritage enthusiasts thus entered the *mohallah* through access I as they were given a tour by the Alawis of the profane infrastructure of Badri Mohallah only. As such, the Alawis kept intact their social practice of *taqiyya* and the scared infrastructure of their universe (access II).

Through the lens of access I, the vernacular architecture of Badri Mohallah and its unique features may be seen within the larger urban landscape of Baroda, and of Gujarat as a whole. The way in which the *mohallah* is structured, its spatial particularity, is clearly a metaphor for the economic and social organisation and hierarchy of the community. The ideas of a Bohra universe and architectural 'togetherness' are made literal by the placement of the houses: there is literally no space in between them, as the *manzils* all together form one organism, which is oriented inwards, away from the rest of the city.

The *mohallah* is thus structured in such a way that the *manzils* together form a tightly-knit collective entity around the *khizana*, the *masjid* and the *jamaat khana*, protecting the community from the outside world while enhancing security and ensuring social control. I observed that literally nothing is private – let alone secret or inaccessible – in Badri Mohallah, except for the esoteric truths stored in the books of the *khizana*. Gaston Bachelard writes, in his *Poetry of Space*: 'In a society where nothing is secret, the one secret thing becomes more secret.'[20] This idea illustrates the psychology of *ʿamma* and *khassa* spaces very well. In *ʿamma* spaces, *everything*, including the domestic spaces, is communal. Social conventions of privacy and the idea of invading one's personal space, as we have seen in the reflexive chapter, are of secondary importance. In contrast, *khassa* spaces represent the exception to the rule and are therefore intriguingly inaccessible. These spaces are not secret; they are known and visible, yet inaccessible. They are the available unknown.

Badri Mohallah encompasses a tightly-knit domestic realm: the lack of space in between the *havelis*, combined with the thinness of the walls, makes it impossible to keep family life and its intricate details private (Figure 3.19). An example of this would be my first faux pas in the *mohallah* – when I took a bath not in the morning but in the evening, when all the men in the building were at home, which was considered *haram*. This fact was immediately reported to the Mazoon Saheb, who lived down the street from me; he called to reprimand me soon after I had finished my bath. The next day my ill-timed bath was the talk of the *mohallah*.

[20] Gaston Bachelard, *The Poetics of Space: The Classic Look at How We Experience Intimate Spaces* (Paris: Presses Universitaires de France, 1969), 40.

Figure 3.19 Painting entitled 'Telephoon' by Abbas Batliwala (undated), depicting communication in the *mohallah*. Credits: https://www.dawoodi-bohras.com/news/1311/107/An-artist-true-to-himself-true-to-his-soil/d,pdb_detail_article_comment.

Despite the strong social cohesion and strict social control, Badri Mohallah should not be regarded as one homogeneous zone. Architecturally, a clear distinction exists between domestic and communal, official and unofficial, and clerical and non-clerical – elaborate façades with intricate wooden carvings veil domestic life, reception rooms for guests versus the rest of the house, balconies on the street side that are never used versus the more hidden courtyards and terraces at the back of the house. Male and female spaces are separated as well: the reception and the gentleman's room versus the kitchen and knitting room. In domestic spaces, despite personal aesthetics and taste, every room of every Bohra *manzil*, whether lavishly decorated or almost empty, has three items that are always present: traditional built-in wooden cupboards, a fan, and a framed picture of the Dai. As noted, with the exception of swing matrasses and the occasional antique Gujarati wooden bed, furniture is uncommon in Badri Mohallah as life – dining, sleeping and working – mainly takes place on the floor.

As mentioned, Bohra domestic architecture, structured around the concept of a secluded or enclosed *mohallah*, is rooted in the regional landscape of vernacular architecture in Gujarat. One can trace very strong similarities with Jain and Hindu architecture in the traditional city centre of Baroda and Ahmedabad, which is organised in enclosed communal urban living spaces known as '*pols*'. These *pols* enclose groups of *havelis* belonging to a certain trader's caste or family and are constructed in such a way that they form a secluded space with only a few entrances.[21] Their structure is strikingly similar to Bohra vernacular architecture. Furthermore, the *pols* of Ahmedabad contain traditions of intricate woodwork on their façades that are very similar to the vernacular Bohra architecture of Baroda.[22]

Accessing the Khizana: the Royal Haveli

Thus far I have argued that the inaccessibility of Badri Mohallah as a Bohra space is built into the vernacular architecture of Alawi Bohra houses and the structure of the *mohallah* in its entirety. The *khizana* is well-camouflaged, although it is easily accessible. Located in the royal *haveli*, it has no locks or keys and is merely a room like any other in that building.

To reach the *khizana* from outside the *mohallah*, an outsider has to enter the alley of Badri Mohallah, passing by the office of the Mukasir Saheb and the *masjid* (Figure 3.3). Before reaching the royal *haveli*, however, the outsider would pass the house of Ali Bhai. Ali Bhai, who refers to himself as 'born to run', is the trusted personal assistant and handyman of the royal family. In a way he is the male equivalent of Amina, the secretary of the Mukasir Saheb. Even though Ali Bhai and Amina are not educated and have no direct say in the decision making of the royal family (as other confidants of the royal family do), they are the eyes and ears of the community.

Without Amina and Ali Bhai the Bohra universe would fall to pieces, not only for practical reasons but also because they know everything about everyone in the community (as opposed to the royal family, who only very rarely interact with the *ʿamma*). Ali Bhai is in charge of everything to do with the public and private lives of the royal family – whether it is opening locks, handling termite infestations, making photocopies of sermons, taking care of the little Bhai Sahebs and Bhu Sahebas, repairing generators, taking the Dai to the doctor or administering religious gatherings and processions: he manages every single thing from his '*masha' Allāh*' scooter. Ali Bhai and Amina are the intermediates between the *ʿamma* and the royal *khassa* not only organisationally but also spatially, for they are the first individuals believers encounter when approaching the royal family and their domain.

Another important assistant of the Mazoon Saheb is Ibrahim Bhai, a very short and slender man who is in charge of the financial affairs of the *daʿwa*. Ibrahim

21 Some of these historic *pols* are secret and were built to enable one to escape from the British during riots, as explained to me on a heritage walk in Ahmedabad in 2011. See Pierre Lachaier, 'Une étude sociologique d'un quartier communautaire ou pol d'Ahmadabad par Ashok Patel. Présentation et traduction' (BEI, N° 28–9 (2010–11), 2013), 205–50.

22 James Burgess, *The Architectural Antiquities of Northern Gujarat, More Especially of the Districts Included in the Baroda State* (London: Bernard Quaritch, 1903).

Bhai lives at the other end of the Bohra lane with his wife and two children. When looking at the map of the *mohallah*, it becomes clear that the management and social control of Badri Mohallah are thus supervised by the assistants to the royal family situated at what are geographically very strategic points in the street; Amina and Ali Bhai at the entrance to the *mohallah*, and Ibrahim Bhai at the end of the lane.

The *khizana* is situated in one of the Bohra *havelis* in the middle of the *mohallah*, known as the 'royal *haveli*'. From an architectural point of view – the access I perspective – the exterior of the *haveli* does not radiate an aura of majesty. In fact, it is very likely that one would pass the building by without noticing the sacral importance of this particular *haveli*. One could argue that, perhaps unwittingly, this is a form of architectural *taqiyya*, safeguarding the location of the *khizana*, a practice that I observed with several Nizari Isma'ili *jamaat khanas* and mosques in the Indian subcontinent. In this case, however, the humble nature of the royal *haveli* is due to the fact that the Alawis as a community have only limited financial means. The Bhai Sahebs and their families live modest lives, and they are supported financially by the community. In addition, the majority of the community's capital is invested in the construction of devotional infrastructure outside of Baroda, such as a new Badri Masjid and *jamaat khana* that recently opened in Mumbai.

The *haveli*, as I briefly touched on in the previous chapter, is officially known as *al-Vezaraat al-Alaviyyah* (Ar. '*al-Wizārat al-ʿAlawiyya*', lit. 'the Alawi government'), but it is usually referred to by the community as *Devdi Mubarak*.[23] The term *Devdi Mubarak* literally means 'the blessed mansion' or 'the circle', which is a spatial reference to the Isma'ili model of cyclical time and space as described in Chapter 1. As the blessed circle, *Devdi Mubarak* is considered the *qutb* (pole) or *jawhar* (essence) of the spatial narrative of the Bohra universe, both on a *batin* cosmic level (access II) and a *zahir* geographical and architectural level (access I).

Devdi Mubarak is the space where all communal affairs are governed. It is, however, by no means a communal place. *Devdi mubarak* is the permanent private residence of the Mazoon Saheb and his extended family, and the second residence of the Dai. The royal *haveli* has been the residence of the Bohra clerical establishment for more than three hundred years. The dual function of the royal *haveli* as a domestic private domain and a communal space becomes apparent when entering the building. The building has one entrance but two stairways: one for the royal household, the *khassa*, and one for the *mu'minin* and *mu'minat*, the *ʿamma*. There is also a secret entrance at the back of the building, which ends in the Sunni *mohallah* and is therefore only used for emergencies. The Mazoon Saheb and his family members occupy most floors and chambers of the *haveli*, which are strictly private. The first floor of the *haveli* serves both domestic and communal functions. It is where the Mazoon Saheb and his family live, but it also includes a reception-cum-waiting room, an official, more extravagantly decorated room meant for receiving the Dai, and his private office, which includes the *khizana*.

[23] One finds interesting parallels here with the Nizari Isma'ilis, who consider their Imamate to be a state, expressed through symbols such as the Nizari flag.

Accessing the Khizana: the Office of the Mazoon Saheb

Mapping Badri Mohallah through the physical lens of access I, let us put aside the notion of the *khizana* as a treasury of books for a moment and analyse its physical space instead. What does this space look like? What are its interior features, and how do these features reflect the function of the space as a treasury of books?

The *khizana* in its entirety, as we have seen, is situated in one room comprising the office of the Mazoon Saheb, who is considered the personal guardian of the *da'wa* manuscript collection. The most prominent objects in the office of the Mazoon Saheb are the iron cupboards, decorated with Qur'anic stickers and mirrors, which store the manuscripts. Just as the office of the Mazoon Saheb has no guards, vaults, doors or thresholds, the actual cupboards of the *khizana* have no locks or keys. From a material perspective, the lens of access I, one could thus theoretically access the *khizana* and its holdings freely without physical obstacles.

All activities in the office, such as paying one's *salams* (respect), asking for *du'a* (invocation) or requesting *fatwas* (legal advice), as well as communal religious gatherings and ceremonies, take place on the floor. The Mazoon Saheb is the only individual who is allowed to sit on a Mughal-style pillow roll, which physically elevates him above his subjects. The Mazoon Saheb's sitting space is situated in the middle of the room; placed in front of him is a small desk that contains his sermons and work in progress. A throne covered in golden fabric behind his sitting space is the Dai's ceremonial *takht*, which is seldomly-used (Figure I.3, *Inside the Treasury of Books*). The pile of books on the right-hand side of the little table (covered with the Mazoon's prayer mat) contains academic reference works (such as Hans Wehr's Arabic English Dictionary, Poonawala and Daftary) and several manuscripts that are being copied by hand. The pile on the left-hand side (covered with a piece of cloth) is a tray containing the Mazoon Saheb's stationery, including calligraphy tools, handkerchiefs, coloured pens and different ink pots.

Jahangir's peacock throne, from which I carried out my tasks, can be found on the left side of the Mazoon Saheb's sitting area, beneath the neoclassical pillar with the fan. On the peacock chair my tools are displayed (rulers, stickers, official *da'wa* vignettes [see Figure I.5, *Inside the Treasury of Books*], glue, pencils, a calculator, etc.), together with several manuscripts that are waiting to be catalogued. The walls of the office are plastered to make them look like marble: all devotional Alawi Bohra spaces such as mausoleums and the *jamaat khana* are made of marble, but I was told that there was never enough communal money to build the royal *haveli* out of marble. The ceilings, covered with fans, are decorated with golden rosettes and Arabic calligraphy that is 'carved' into the upper walls and the Moorish-style niches.

In terms of aesthetics and interior design, the Middle Eastern-inspired style of decoration of the Mazoon's office is a clear reference to the Alawis' identification with their Islamic, Fatimid past. In addition to the Moorish niches, there are other Middle Eastern accents in the space. The floor is covered with 'Oriental' carpets that are in turn mostly covered in sheets. The office is extensively decorated with portraits of the late Dais (note the gigantic painted portrait of the previous Dai hanging right behind the peacock throne) and various kinds of sacred relics from all over the Middle

East that have been donated to the royal family by believers, such as a colossal framed *tasbih* from the holy city of Karbala (to the right of the Andalusian niche, to the left of the windows) and various kinds of items from Damascus, Mecca and the mountainous regions of Yemen. Because the Mazoon Saheb and his brothers are constantly travelling to fulfil their clerical duties, their ceremonial regalia, such as turbans, handkerchiefs and *tasbihs*, are also kept in the *khizana*. Their meticulously white overcoats hang over the doors of the iron manuscript cupboards.

Through its arabesques, Arabic calligraphy, and Islamic relics and souvenirs, it is clear that the office of the Mazoon Saheb is, as described in Chapter 2, a shrine representing the history and heritage of the community. As an outsider, one would never suspect that the collection of the *khizana* is stored in these very utilitarian cupboards. After all, and I cannot emphasise this enough, these cupboards have no locks and keys, and devotees frequent this space on a daily basis. To make sense of this state of affairs, which seems paradoxical at first, let us rethink this space through the lens of access II.

3.3 Access II: A Sacred Geography of the Bohra Universe

As noted throughout this study, the *khizana* is considered the most inaccessible *khassa* space in the community, yet we have seen that it has no gates and its manuscript cupboards have no locks and keys. 'It is not just a matter of keeping things well guarded, it is the psychology of the lock', Bachelard writes[24] – or in the case of the Alawi universe, a matter of the absence of a lock. In this section, we transcend the materiality of locks and doors of the *khizana*, of access I, and move towards the sacred space of access II and the enshrined world of the treasury of books.

In what follows, we anatomise the sacred geography of the *mohallah*. Through this lens, the *khizana* becomes a shrine, both ideographically – through the notion of a repository of texts that becomes a treasury of books – and materially, through its manuscript culture and scribal traditions. Through access II the central building of the Bohra *mohallah* becomes a royal *haveli*, domesticating and enshrining the *khizana* as a treasury of the community, a holy shrine that is governed by an infallible royal genealogy of religious authorities, also known as the *hudud*. While, via the access I perspective, a manuscript leaf is considered merely a piece of paper, inside the Alawi universe and the sacred eulogised space of access II a *waraq* (leaf) of the highest level of a *haqa'iq* work is considered an object of the utmost sacredness and a talisman. The material power attributed to books, both manuscripts and documents, thus becomes apparent through this lens. In the same manner, through access II, the caretaker of the *khizana* becomes a Bhai Saheb: a semi-infallible religious authority and custodian of both the community and its Neo-Fatimid identity.

Instead of walking through the various *ʿamma* and *khassa* spaces of Badri Mohallah using the lens of access II, let us focus on what is so clearly materially absent from the *khizana*: doors, locks and keys. From an access II perspective, rituals and etiquette are the invisible but crucial doors, locks and keys that provide access to the sacred

[24] Bachelard, *The Poetics of Space*, 81.

geography of Badri Mohallah. These unwritten rules and rituals are all part of a larger Bohra habitus or code of conduct to which we were introduced in Chapter 1: the attitude of *taqiyya*. It is thus crucial to first gain an understanding of the Bohra notion of what I call *spatial taqiyya* as a social practice in relation to questions of space. This understanding will not only help contextualise rituals of access but will also provide insight into the ideography of the Bohra secret universe and what secrecy means from an emic perspective.

Again, we work from the outside inwards by first analysing the larger picture: the sacred geography of the Bohra universe in its entirety, and practices of secrecy and initiation into this space, focusing on rituals, initiation and oaths of allegiance. Then, we delve into the sacred world of the treasury of books and its specific rituals of access. Just as this chapter began with reflexive notes from the field, this section concludes with a discussion of gender negotiations and conditions of access.

Spatial Taqiyya: Secrecy in Neon Colours

As noted in the first chapter, as a community or *daʿwa*, the Alawi Bohra universe transcends the borders of Badri Mohallah. Alawi and Dawoodi Bohras, especially the *mu'minat*, instantly stand out in the streets of Surat, Mombasa, Doha or Cairo in their *ridas* consisting of brightly coloured capes and matching long skirts decorated with patterns of lace (Figure 3.10).[25]

The history of the *rida* as a sartorial symbol and marker of identity of the Bohras is fascinating. In contrast to what is often assumed, the *rida* is not a historic Bohra dress as it was invented only in the 1970s by the Dawoodis.[26] Other Shi'i Muslim communities in South Asia, such as the Twelver Khojas, gradually replaced their *saris* with *chadors* after the Iranian Revolution, but there are several narratives about why the Dawoodis introduced the *rida*. Some Dawoodis told me that the *rida* was designed by the Dawoodi Ma Saheba herself as a symbol of modernisation, to make Bohras stand out from other Muslim communities in South Asia. Others, however, said that the *rida* was made compulsory by the Syedna to distinguish 'mainstream' Dawoodis from progressive Dawoodi Bohras, also known as the Reformists. It should be mentioned that during this reform, Bohra men too were urged to change their attire and to wear white *shalwar kameez*, golden *topis*, and trimmed beards.[27] I was unable to trace when exactly the white colour of the *shalwar kameez* for men became linked to the colour of

[25] Eva Paul, 'Die Dawoodi Bohras. Eine Indische Gemeinschaft in Ostafrika'. *Beiträge zur 1. Kölner Afrikawissenschaftlichen Nachwuchstagung* (PDF online), 2006.

[26] Prior to these reforms Bohra women wore the *sari* or the *hijab*. See Hollister, *The Shia of India*, 294 and Blank, *Mullahs on the Mainframe*, 189.

[27] See also Iqbal Akthar, *The Khōjā of Tanzania: Discontinuities of a Postcolonial Religious Identity* (Leiden: Brill, 2015), 158, 159. Akthar also describes how the Dawoodi Bohras of East Africa adopted the *rida* in the late 1970s, *The Khōjā of Tanzania* 161, 162. See for news articles on the *rida*: 'Bohra Women: Cut from the Same Cloth. Wrapping Fashion and Tradition in a Colourful Embrace – the Dawoodi Bohra Rida', *The Express Tribune*, Sunday Magazine, 15 September 2013. 'A Veil with a Rida' Touch', *Mumbai Mirror*, https://mumbaimirror.indiatimes.com/opinion/columnists/manoj-r-nair/a-veil-with-a ridatouch/articleshow/15656398.cms?utm_source=contentofinterest&utm_medium=text&utm_campaign=cppst (both last accessed 14 October 2020).

the Fatimids. Following this Dawoodi sartorial turn, the Alawis adopted the same dress code for their community.[28] Interestingly, the ceremony of the *ʿahd* and the wearing of the *rida* are closely linked. It is only after taking the oath of allegiance that the wearing of the *rida* by women and the pious dress code for men become obligatory.

Even though the Bohras have recently made attempts to show their fellow Indians a glimpse of the life of their *mohallahs*, such as through heritage walks and President Modi's appearance during a Dawoodi Muharram ceremony in 2018, an attitude of secrecy is strongly cultivated.[29] As a result, the Bohras remain the ultimate *other* in India, in the global Muslim *umma*, and even to *each other* after schisms within the Dawoodi community. They are proudly Indian, but not Hindu, Sikh or Jain; a contemporary Muslim mercantile 'caste', yet at the same time not adhering to an interpretation of local or transnational Sunni or Twelver Shi'i Islam, nor linked to Sufi inclinations widely practised in the subcontinent; Isma'ili, but not following the Agha Khan; and Gujarati, from the hinterland but identifying themselves with a cuisine that is distinctly 'Bohra'. They have social practices of the sea and the vast space of the Indian Ocean and use an 'Arabised' sociolect of Gujarati known as *Lisan al-Dawa*. They trace their clerical genealogy to the Haraz mountains of medieval Yemen and their books to the royal libraries of Fatimid Cairo. Finally, they shape their modern identity through a manuscript culture transmitted in Arabic, secret alphabets and esoteric discourse.

It becomes clear that, to understand what it means to be Bohra in the larger context of South Asian society, applying essentialising categories such as 'Sunni', 'Shi'i', 'Isma'ili', 'Muslim' or 'Arabophone', 'Indo-Persianate', or even 'South Asian', is not at all helpful. Nor are notions such as citizenship, ethnicity, caste, gender, cultural capital, empire, or models of religious authority, necessarily useful in making sense of the Bohras, either as a contemporary Muslim community or as a historical phenomenon. Time and time again I observed that Bohras, wherever they live in the world of the Indian Ocean and beyond, consider their communities a 'universe'. As such, the *Weltanschauung* of the Bohras, I argue in this book, is neither defined by the boundaries of any modern nation-state nor, as becomes apparent through this emic access II perspective, the mundane notion of 'community'. Instead, one is part of the *daʿwa*.[30]

Time and space within the universe of the *daʿwa*, are, according to the Alawi interpretation of Isma'ili knowledge, cyclical and not linear. Geography, especially the geography of the here and now (that of places, cities and continents), plays a secondary role.[31] Certain cities and regions might have a special sacred meaning, such as the architecture of Fatimid Cairo, the graves of the prophet, the *ahl al-bayt*, the Imams in Medina, Najaf and Karbala, or the Yemeni mountains of Haraz. Given that the Alawis currently find themselves in the cycle of the Prophet Muhammad, these sacred spaces indeed have great significance for their identity as Neo-Fatimid Isma'ili Muslims and the world of *ʿilm al-zahir*. Yet in the larger *batini* context of cyclical time and space,

[28] The Indian Sulaymani Bohras, I was told, have adopted a secular dress code.

[29] Abantika Ghosh, 'PM Modi to Address Dawoodi Bohra Event Today', *The Indian Express*, 14 September 2018.

[30] See for an interesting parallel among the Dawoodi Bohras of Madagascar: Gay, *Les Bohras de Madagascar*, 118–20.

[31] Pilgrimage is an exception here.

these are merely moments in linear history, which are part of the much vaster progress of the turning wheels of cyclical time.

Returning to the practice of wearing the *rida* and its function as a statement piece in the public sphere, one might not suspect that behind these lavish colourful outfits, which are so unmistakably Bohra, lies a strong orientation to *taqiyya*. And yet, according to my observations, this notion of *taqiyya* is a core element in the Bohra universe and its day-to-day life. We are already familiar with the historical notion of *taqiyya* as described in the first chapter. In day-to-day practice Bohra *taqiyya* is translated into an extremely closed attitude to anyone who does not belong to the realm of the *daʿwa*. Nevertheless, *taqiyya* should not merely be seen as a veil used to keep the outsider world out; it forms an integral part of the Bohra knowledge system, dividing the universe into two spaces: the *dār al-taqiyya* – the Alawi Bohra *daʿwa* (which excludes all other Bohra castes) – and the 'rest': the non-Bohra realms, which are also known as *al-kharij* (see the fieldwork map of Badri Mohallah, fig. 3.3).

Ignaz Goldziher and others have argued that the concept of *taqiyya* should be regarded as something much more profound than merely a passive solution to protect oneself in times of danger.[32] Instead, they argued that *taqiyya* should be seen as a fluid concept that developed over time. To quote Kohlberg: 'What began as a prudential reaction was elevated into a tenet of faith, and severed from the causes which had originally brought it into being.' He continues, 'This development was facilitated by the view (common to esoteric religions) that divine knowledge can only partially be revealed, and even then only to the elect.'[33] Even though these studies are mainly based on the intellectual histories of Twelver Shi'i traditions and not Isma'ili communities per se, the latter point of re-inventing *taqiyya* as a device to keep the *batin batin* is very fitting for the Bohras and, in fact, for many other Shi'i minority communities, such as the Druze.[34]

On the basis of my participant observation in the *dar al-taqiyya*, I would take further Kohlberg's argument of the re-invention of *taqiyya* as a means to further safeguard access to the *batin* by arguing that *taqiyya* in the Bohra context is omnipresent in the community, especially in social practice. And I claim that, as a social practice, the Bohra notion of *taqiyya* has a strong spatial dimension. On the one hand, *taqiyya* strongly defines the dialectics between inside and outside – the Bohra universe versus the 'rest' – and is practised as a veil designed to safeguard access to Bohra religious knowledge and to the Bohra universe at large. Language is crucial in this regard, as the

[32] Ethan Kohlberg, 'Some Imāmī-shīʿī Views on Taqiyya', *Journal of the American Oriental Society* 95 (1975): 395–402. Strothmann, R.; Djebli, Moktar. 'Taḳiyya'., in P. Bearman, T. Bianquis, C. E. Bosworth, E. van Donzel and W. P. Heinrichs (eds), *Encyclopaedia of Islam* (Brill Online, 2015), 2nd edn, http://referenceworks.brillonline.com/entries/encyclopaedia-of-islam-/takiyya-SIM_7341 (last accessed 21 March 2014). Ignaz Goldziher, 'Das Prinzip der taḳiyya im Islam', *Zeitschrift der deutschen morgenländischen Gesellschaft* 59 (1906): 213–26.

[33] Ethan Kohlberg, 'Taqiyya in Shīʿī Theology and Religion', in H. G. Kippenberg et al. (eds), *Secrecy and Concealment: Studies in the History of Mediterranean and Near Eastern Religion* (Leiden: Brill, 1995), 345–80.

[34] M. Tayyib Gökbilgin, 'Durūz', in P. Bearman, T. Bianquis, C. E. Bosworth, E. van Donzel and W. P. Heinrichs (eds), *Encyclopaedia of Islam* (Brill Online, 2015), 2nd edn, http://referenceworks.brillonline.com/entries/encyclopaedia-of-islam2/duruz-COM_0198 (last accessed 21 March 2014).

community's ceremonial language, *Lisan al-Da'wa*, is only spoken and printed in the *da'wa* and not understood outside it.

On the other hand, *taqiyya* is a social instrument used *within* the community itself, preventing the Bohra *'amma* from gaining access to the esoteric manuscripts in the *khizana*. Here too, we see the Bohras' multi-layered culture of secrecy, which is based on interpretations of Shi'i-Isma'ili theology and its implications in the absence of the hidden Imam; these are combined with local Gujarati and South Asian traditions, such as the structure of a clerical sacerdotal royal family whose members, and the objects they are associated with, are seen as sacred. Going beyond the realm of theology and the dissimulation of one's Shi'i identity, the notion of secrecy is thus practised and institutionalised on different levels in the *da'wa*.

In addition to the spatiality of *tayiyya* within the *da'wa*, *taqiyya* also has a strong material dimension among the Alawis. I called this the *materiality of secrecy* in the Introduction, and it also can be traced on these two levels. As for the dialectics of outside and inside, Alawi vernacular architecture can be seen as a material expression of spatial *taqiyya*; for instance, in the way the *mohallah* is built in a *pol* or beehive-like structure within the city, and how the Alawi *manzils* are oriented inwards and organised around a central courtyard. The *rida* is another striking example of the way Bohras express their *taqiyya* through material culture outside their *mohallah*. In the public space, it signals 'we are Bohra, please do not interact' in neon colours, a social code that is widely understood in the societies they live in. As for keeping *'ilm al-batin* from being disclosed within the community, secrecy refers to the materiality of the treasury of books: the many facets of its manuscript culture; codicology; traditions of enshrinement and access; the use of Arabic as a language of non-access; scripts, such as secret alphabets, curses and spells; and scribal practices and traditions. I discuss the materiality of the *khizana* and its manuscripts in detail in the following chapters. Let us first examine the spatial dimensions of *taqiyya* in the Alawi *da'wa*, its treasury of books, and conditions of access.

Initiatory Practices to the Bohra Universe: Taqiyya and the 'Ahd

We start by taking a closer look at *taqiyya* and the dialectics of inside and outside. The Alawi Bohras' strong 'taqiyyatude', the attitude of precautionary dissimulation, as discussed in the previous chapter, is the legacy of constant anxiety about external enemies who threatened the existence of the Alawi Bohra universe. Whether this collective angst is rooted in the historical Shi'i narrative of persecution by the Abbasids, looting and plundering under the Zaydis in Yemen, Mughal rule in India personified in the reign of Aurangzeb, inter-communal schisms, or much more recent events such as the Gujarat riots of 2002, the idea of a threat from outside is constantly present.[35]

The Bohras' 'taqiyyatude' is a habitus taught to Bohra children from an early age and is institutionalised in the oral ceremony of the *'ahd* or *mithaq*. According to the Mukasir Saheb, there are two kinds of oaths of allegiance: the explicit and the inexplicit

[35] See for a parallel in the Gupti community Shafique Virani, 'Taqiyya and Identity in a South Asian Community', *The Journal of Asia Studies* 70 (2011), 99–139, 107.

ʿ*ahd*. As I described in the story of the girl from Pune, in the explicit *mithaq* Bohra children are initiated into the tenets of the Bohra faith, which are to remain undisclosed, and pledge their wholehearted loyalty to the Dai. The Mukasir Saheb explained this rite of passage as follows:

> They are guided to keep numb, to keep silence to people who are not eligible for this knowledge. If he [or she] goes or stands among the people who are not in the *mithaq* of *dawat*, if he talks to someone, if he sits with someone, if he goes in the house of someone who is *kharij*, who is outside the *bay'at* of *dai-e zaman*, he is fired.[36]

By 'fired', the Mazoon Saheb means another practice related to the Bohras' taqiyyatude: excommunication. This bring us to the inexplicit ʿ*ahd* or *mithaq*, which is an oath that does not have a fixed text. Instead, it is designed 'as per requirement for the time, as per the person'. In case of non-pious behaviour, *mu'minin* and *mu'minat* are either asked to retake their oath of allegiance or they are put under *bara'at* (excommunication).[37] Excommunication is considered a very severe social sentence, for in reality it translates into social death and shame upon the *persona non grata* and his or her extended family. The excommunicated family members become outcasts; they no longer have access to the Alawi universe, the *da*ʿ*wa* and its services, such as *nikah* (who will marry my daughter or son to an outcast?) and burial (where will I be buried? who will lead my soul to the afterlife?). *Bara'at* often also results in economic boycotts and bankruptcy, as commerce is tightly knit to the social structures of the *mohallah*.

In other words, once one is excommunicated, surviving in the Alawi universe is impossible. Yet life outside of the *da*ʿ*wa* and its social norms often proves to be unsustainable as well, and many outcasts eventually return, often under pressure from their relatives. This is a phenomenon that is not unique to the Bohras but is common among other tightly-knit communities, such as the Hasidic Jews or the Mormons. Whereas, among the larger Dawoodi community networks, critically-minded 'reformists' do indeed exist, this is, as far as I was able to determine, not the case among the Alawis, which makes survival outside the *da*ʿ*wa* even more challenging.

The tradition of taking the ʿ*ahd* is thus much more than a festive ceremony for Bohra adolescents. Instead, it is a tool for establishing social order, which keeps the hierarchies in the *da*ʿ*wa* in place and reinforces norms of piety and gender segregation. It is for this reason that Denis Gay, who observed the ritual among the Bohras of Madagascar, describes it as a rite of institution, instead of a rite of passage.[38] The only way to get out of one's *bara'at* is to retake the oath of allegiance, as the Mukasir Saheb explains:

> If he (or she) makes a mistake opposed to our *raza* (permission), such as conducting *nikah* or *ziyarat* as per convenience, not as per rules and regulations of *dawat*, we cut the *izn* (Ar. *idhn* 'permission') for one month to one year, as per his (or her) mistake. They get three chances, after [that] they are permanently stopped in

36 Interview with the Mukasir Saheb in his office, Badri Mohallah. 20 October 2012.

37 See, for a similar practice among the Dawoodis, Blank, *Mullahs on the Mainframe*, 61–3.

38 Gay, *Les Bohras de Madagascar*, 145.

> entering our spiritual *dawat* gathering . . . as per entering the *dawat*, they cannot enter unless and until they come in our fold again by taking oath. Per one hundred families one or two happens like this, the majority does wholeheartedly *ta'at* (Ar. *ṭāʿat* 'obedience'): they follow as per our *firman*.[39]

The spatial dimension of the *mithaq* becomes apparent in the last two sentences of the Mukasir Saheb's statement. He argues that it is insufficient to be born into the sacred geography of the Badri Mohallah (access I): one has to take and retake the oath to become and stay part of the Bohra universe, the *dar al-taqiyya* (access II). The world is thus divided between *mu'minin* and *mu'minat* who have taken this oath (access II), who have 'entered the dawat', which he also refers to as 'our fold', and those who have not (access I). The outside, '*al-kharij*', includes not only Hindus, Jains, Christians and Jews, but also Muslims, Sunni and Shi'i alike.

The initiatory practice of the *ʿahd* – as an institutionalised vehicle of *taqiyya* – is not a recent Bohra invention. As mentioned at the beginning of this chapter, the Bohras trace their *ʿahd* tradition back to the Fatimids; this genealogy is also confirmed by Vladimir Ivanow and others.[40] Whereas the modern *ʿahd* formula is recited in *Lisan al-Daʿwa*, the original text or a version of it was transmitted in Arabic in contemporary Fatimid Isma'ili sources and is even the subject of anti-Fatimid treatises.[41]

These sources should be read in the context of initiation and conversion practices of the Fatimid (or pre-Fatimid) Dai missionaries, who were sent to the various corners of the empire to convert people to Fatimid Isma'ilism. With the exception of polemical works, most of these texts are of the 'code of conduct' genre and were transmitted several centuries after their composition in the Tayyibi period by Yemeni and Indian '*muhajir*' scholars. One example is Aḥmad Ibn Ibrahīm al-Naysābūrī's *Risāla al-Mūjaza al-Kāfiya fī 'Adab al-Duʿāt* (A Concise Treatise on the Code of Conduct of the Dai. fl. fourth/eleventh century), which mentions a version of the *ʿahd* formula; this work has come down to us in manuscript form in al-Bharuchi's *Kitāb al-Azhar*.[42] The practice of initiation, or taking the *ʿahd*, did not merely constitute secrecy by letting the subject swear to adhere to *taqiyya*; the *Risala* also reports that the ceremony itself was considered a secret affair between the two parties.[43] A version of the formula of the *ʿahd* is also recorded in the Tayyibi Dai Ḥātim Ibn Ibraḥīm al-Ḥāmidī's (d. 557/1162, no. 2) *Tuḥfat al-Qulūb wa Furjat al-Makrūb*.[44]

39 Ibid.

40 Vladimir Ivanow, *A Creed of the Fatimids* (Bombay: Qayimmah Press, 1936), 13–17. Hollister, *The Shia of India*, 282. See also Gacek's earlier-mentioned catalogue of Isma'ili Manuscripts for the following manuscript: '*ʿahd nameh*' , ms no. 3 (p. 2); and Cortese's *Arabic Isma'ili Manuscripts*, ms no. 140/881. I unfortunately did not have access to these manuscripts.

41 Heinz Halm, 'The Ismaʿili Oath of Allegiance and the "Sessions of Wisdom"', in Farhad Daftary (ed.), *Mediaeval Ismāʿīlī History and Thought* (London: I. B. Tauris, 1996), 91–8. See also James Morris, *The Master and the Disciple: An Early Islamic Spiritual Dialogue: Arabic Edition and English Translation of Jaʿfar b. Manṣūr al-Yaman's 'Kitāb al-ʿĀlim wa'l-ghulām* (London: I. B. Tauris, 2001).

42 See for a facsimile and study of Aḥmad Ibn Ibrāhīm an-Naysābūrī's *Risāla al-mūjaza al-kāfiya fī adab ad-duʿāt* Verena Klemm, *Die Mission des fāṭimidischen Agenten al-Mu'ayyad fī ad-dīn in Shirāz*.

43 Klemm, *Die Mission des fāṭimidischen Agenten*. Klemm and Walker, *A Code of Conduct*, 60–1, ٤٧-٤٥.

44 Hamdani, 'The Dāʿī Ḥātim Ibn 'Ibraḥīm al-Ḥāmidī', 258–300.

To the best of my knowledge, the *Risāla al-mūjaza* is one of the few, if not the only contemporary Isma'ili source in which at least parts of the formula (and thus not the description of the practice) of the Fatimid *ʿahd* are transmitted. In addition, several polemical pamphlets produced in anti-Isma'ili milieux have survived, as identified by Halm in his article on the Fatimid *ʿahd*. These falsely describe the Isma'ili oath of allegiance with the aim of discrediting it.[45] Thus, they may not provide an accurate depiction of the practice of the *ʿahd* or of its content, yet they do prove that such a practice existed. This is important, as sceptics could argue that the Bohra *ʿahd* practice could be a recent invention of a tradition as the earlier-mentioned Isma'ili treatises only survive in their own *khizana*.

Ivanow claims that the *ʿahd* quoted in one of the polemical sources produced by the Egyptian historian al-Nuwayrī (d. 733/1333) in post-Fatimid Syria, titled *Nihāyat al-'Arab fī funūn al-adab* (The Aim of the Intelligent in the Art of Letters), matches almost word for word the modern Dawoodi Bohra *ʿahd*.[46] According to my observations, the *ʿahd* transmitted in al-Naysaburi's *Risala* may not contain the exact same formula as the modern Bohra variant. The *Lisan al-Daʿwa* version, does, however, contain a strikingly similar content and structure, with a strong emphasis on loyalty to the Dai in the Bohra variant, whereas in al-Naysaburi's variant this is reserved for the Imam, who was still alive at the time. Observing their tradition of *taqiyya*, the Alawis' formula of their present-day *ʿahd* is considered secret and is therefore not disclosed in this study.

It is very likely that this oath of allegiance was also practised by the early Fatimid and later Tayyibi missionaries in Gujarat as a means of conversion. One elderly Dawoodi gentleman once told me that the legendary missionaries were so successful in taking people's *ʿahd* that at the end of each day they were surrounded by heaps of sacred threads, taken off by the new converts who were formerly Brahman Hindus.[47] Today, conversion occurs only very rarely in the Alawi community, as, according to the community's interpretation of *fiqh*, it is seen as the prerogative of the hidden Imam. Under exceptional circumstances, however, people from other Muslim 'castes', mostly adolescent women who are asked their hand in marriage, take the *ʿahd* as a way of conversion. I once observed such a conversion *majlis*, where a Sunni woman from Bihar took the *ʿahd* in front of the Mazoon Saheb and her future mother-in-law. In contrast to the other *ʿahd* ceremony I observed earlier, which took place in a festive setting in the presence of the community, this *majlis* took place behind closed doors in the *khizana*.

In addition to other ritual practices, such as the revealing of bifurcation rolls during *ziyara* as a proof of the *nass* of the Dai, and the writing of the *ʿalama* as a seal of approval, the Alawis' tradition of the *ʿahd* is a striking example of social codicology in which Fatimid manuscripts, both textually through their content and ritually in their material form, play a fundamental role in the community's Neo-Fatimid identity. The

45 Halm, 'The Ismaʿili Oath of Allegiance and the "Sessions of Wisdom"', 94–8.

46 Ivanow, *A Creed of the Fatimids*, 13–17.

47 The taking off of the sacred thread is a popular trope, which can also be traced in Bohra historical literature. For instance, in *Mawsim-e Bahar* Rampuri makes this symbolic claim: 'So many people were converted that the weight of sacred threads (taken off by Hindu converts) taken off that day was not less than 260 Arabic pounds.' Translation by Engineer, *The Bohras*, 107.

social practice of taking an oath of allegiance, I argue, has not changed over the course of ten centuries. Instead, it has been ritually preserved and linguistically adjusted by the Bohras and still plays a central role in the daily lives of believers today. Furthermore, the practice of initiation through the *ʿahd* is an example of how Fatimid sources, transmitted in manuscript form and enshrined in Bohra *khizana* today, describe and validate traditions that constitute *taqiyya* as a social practice.

Keeping the strong spatial relevance of the *ʿahd* and the dynamics of outside versus inside in mind, how does one become part of the Alawi Bohra universe as a *dar al-taqiyya*; that is, without converting? Most unusually, in my case the clerics designed a special oath of trust for me as a non-Bohra, which I had to take every day before I started my work. The '*Ollybehn oath*' (tr. 'sister Olly oath') was an oath of trust, and not an oath of allegiance as such, which meant that through this oath I would not convert and become a *mu'mina*. Instead, the focus of the *Ollybehn oath* was on keeping the secret content of certain manuscripts undisclosed; it represented my agreement to honour my conditions of access and handling of the manuscripts, as discussed in the reflexive section of this study.

Taqiyya and the Treasury of Books

Thus far I have argued that as a social practice, *taqiyya* prevents non-initiates from accessing the Alawi Bohra universe or at least its sacred geography (access II). In a similar construction, *taqiyya* is also used *within* the Bohra universe as a mechanism for veiling and safeguarding divine esoteric knowledge, *ʿilm al-batin*, and obstructing the *ʿamma's* access to the treasury of books in the absence of the hidden Imam. This idea is common in Twelver Shi'i societies too, where '*the duty of keeping secrets (taqiyya)*' is considered a canonical obligation.[48] As was shown in Chapter 1, the Bohra *batini* tradition maintains that the past, present and future are embedded in a parallel universe: a history of the universe and humankind, revolving around cycles of *zuhur* (manifestation) and *satr* (concealment) of Prophets, Imams, and the esoteric truths they reveal and transmit. This complex model forms the basis of the entire Bohra knowledge system, or at least the Alawi interpretation thereof, as recorded and safeguarded in the *khizana*.

As an institution, the *khizana* divides the community between those with access to these esoteric truths (access II): the privileged *khassa* elite – the highest layers of the clerical establishment (the Dai, and the Mazoon, Mukasir and Ra's ul Hudood Sahebs), who are masters of both *zahir* and *batin*. The rest are the *ʿamma* – the common believers who are only equipped to digest *zahiri* knowledge – and only on the level of access I.[49] The *ʿamma/khassa* paradigm is strongly reflected in Bohra reading and writing culture and the culture of access to the *khizana*, as explored in Chapter 6.

The Dai and his close entourage are the only individuals in the community who have access to the *khizana* and its manuscripts. *Batini* texts are only available in

[48] Amir-Moezzi, Mohammad Ali, 'Sirr.?', in P. Bearman, T. Bianquis, C. E. Bosworth, E. van Donzel and W. P. Heinrichs (eds), *Encyclopaedia of Islam* (Brill Online, 2015), 2nd edn, http://referenceworks.brillonline.com/entries/encyclopaedia-ofislam2/sirr-SIM_8901 (last accessed 21 March 2014).

[49] See also Hodgson, M. G. S., 'Bāṭiniyya', in P. Bearman, T. Bianquis, C. E. Bosworth, E. van Donzel and W. P. Heinrichs (eds), *Encyclopaedia of Islam* (Brill Online, 2015), 2nd edn, http://referenceworks.brillonline.com/entries/encyclopaedia-of-islam2/bāṭinī yya-SIM_1284 (last accessed 21 March 2014).

manuscript form, and, as we have seen, take up most of the space in the iron cupboards of the *khizana*. All *batini* texts are written in Arabic, the 'original language of the Fatimids' as was often quoted to me, which is a language that is almost completely alien to the Gujarati-speaking Bohra believers. A process of vernacularisation of the *batini* genre has been completely absent in the Bohra scholarly tradition (more about this in Chapter 5). I argue that this absence is another mechanism for keeping the *batin* scholarly tradition *batin* (access II), enhancing its *taqiyya*. In Alawi Bohra manuscript culture, Arabic has thus been elevated to the special rank of a language of secrecy as the *lisān* (tongue) of the treasury of books. As a language of non-access it thus functions as the invisible locks and keys. The inaccessibility of these texts is thus built into the text through language and script; even if the *ʿamma* gained physical access to the esoteric truths of the treasury of books, and could see, touch, smell, and attempt to decipher its script (access I), yet they would still not access its esoteric meaning, let alone embody it (access II).

From the Office of the Mazoon Saheb to the Treasury of Books

The *ʿamma* does have access to the office of the Mazoon Saheb (access I), which is considered a semi-*khassa* space. This office is not a static space but a flexible one, which changes depending on who is accessing it: a *mu'min*, cleric, royal, non-royal, doorman, doorwoman, man, woman, cleaning lady, rich, poor, old, young, insider or outsider. As a space, it is perceived differently by the *ʿamma* (as the office of the Mazoon Saheb), the *khassa* (as the treasury of books), and by me as a researcher (both), and on the basis of how the space is perceived there are different sets of etiquette. However, what every visitor has in common is that it they know they have accessed a sacred space, a treasury of the community.

Witnessing the day-to-day life of this space from the peacock throne, I observed that the office of the Mazoon Saheb is popular with visitors not only because they are seeking legal advice and spiritual guidance but also because they consider the space a shrine of books from Egypt and Yemen, a sanctuary of the history of the infallible royal family. As noted in Chapter 2, the sacredness of this space is based on the idea that for centuries, generations of Dais and their family members resided in the royal *haveli*, ruled the community, and gave birth to generations of Bhai Sahebs.

The sacrality of the royal *haveli* is enhanced by the fact that, as the office of the Mazoon Saheb, it is part of the memory of virtually every believer; every Alawi Bohra has been blessed as a new-born in this very office, has taken his or her oath of allegiance as a child in front of the Dai, and has requested the Dai's permission for marriage, travel, study, family planning and the like. Moreover, it is held by the community that the *ruh*, the souls or spirits of the late Dais, are still present in the royal *haveli*. It is as if the *royal haveli* has stored not only their physical but, more importantly, also their spiritual aura. In the Alawi *mohallah* it is the energy of these Dais that still dwells within the space of the royal *haveli*, an aura that is considered pure and infallible even after death. While the Dai is still alive, his *ruh*, as we have seen in Chapter 1, is believed to have a transformative effect on believers via the blessing of objects, such as coconuts and bottles of water, which attain a sacred materiality (Figure 3.20).

Figure 3.20 The Dai is seen blowing his *ruh* into a coconut during the public royal birthday party of his grandson Luqman Bhai, held in the *jamaat khana.*

The belief that the spiritual energy and charisma of previous generations of Dais are still present in the royal *haveli* is not only a popular notion among the people of Badri Mohallah but is also the strong conviction of the royal family. The idea of the *ruh*, or *rūḥāniyya*, which travels through different realms of time and space, is very prominent in Isma'ili esotericism, for it is believed that the soul of every believer goes up to the realm of the spirits, known as *al-ʿalam al-rūḥāniyya*, enhancing the light of the fire temples of the Imams.[50] These *ruhaniyyat*, whether royal or *ʿamma*, not only transcend the spiritual realm but their auras also dwell in the psychical world, the here and now. The Mazoon Saheb told me that there are specific spaces in the royal *haveli* where he feels more calm and grounded. In the treasury of books, agency is thus attributed not only to manuscripts but also to spaces. There is one particular corner in his office where the Mazoon Saheb always copies his manuscripts and sermons and where he sits and meditates on a problem or concern. This corner is the exact place where his father and grandfathers performed these sacred acts, and he told me that while 'bathing' in the spiritual energy of his forefathers he always finds his prayers answered.[51]

[50] These ideas can for instance be traced in *Adwār al-Akwār* by the Tayyibi scholar ʿAlī b. Muḥammad b. al-Walīd (d. 612/1215), in manuscript form. See also: Daftary, *The Ismāʿīlis*, 269–75.

[51] Badri Mohallah, 29 October 2012.

Rituals of Access: Bohra Adab

Embedded and shaped through social relationships, gender, time and place, etiquette has a strong spatial dimension in the Alawi Bohra universe. By being subjected to these etiquettes, and attempting to adopt them myself during my stay in Badri Mohallah, I experienced how the various sacred *ʿamma* and *khassa* spaces in the Alawi Bohra universe are respected through this habitus and how its modes of access are negotiated and cultivated.

The royal *haveli* is considered an explicit *khassa* space, in the sense that it represents the clerical establishment, and therefore the heritage and history of the Alawi Bohra *daʿwa*, yet it is a flexible one because it is open to believers under certain conditions. Access to these spaces is based not only on whether one belongs to the clerical establishment or the *mu'minin* and *mu'minat* but also on various more subtle social codes and unwritten rules and regulations, which together form the Alawi Bohra *adab*, or proper code of conduct. Spatial *taqiyya* is central to Bohra *adab*, both in relation to outsiders of the community and with regard to the *khizana*. The *ʿamma* are aware that there is a sacred domain they cannot access; therefore, they behave accordingly to avoid de-sacralising the treasury of books and thereby violating their oath of loyalty as orally contracted through the *ʿahd*.

As there are different sets of rituals for the different spatial dimensions of the office of the Mazoon Saheb, there are also different codes of Bohra *adab* depending on one's identity and reputation, 'caste' (royal or common), level of initiation, piety, gender, marital status, family (and *their* reputation), socio-economic status and social relationships. In addition, but not less importantly, there are specific rules related to one's appearance and observance of orthopraxy, which include bodily cleanliness, dress codes (religious dress) and hair-styles (men, minimal or bald plus trimmed beard; women, long hair, dyed with *henna* and worn in a French braid but not visible outside the house), how one conducts oneself through language (*Lisan al-Daʿwa*, Urdu, Gujarati) and speech (humble), and finally, *tahara* (ritual purity) and spiritual purity (for ritual and spiritual purity see Chapter 6). Even though these social codes are unwritten and considered self-evident, they are all imperative when it comes to the question of access and limits in the Alawi universe. The *khizana* can be seen as an institution through which these limits of non-access are performed and legitimised, thereby maintaining social order, as I argued in the previous chapter.

To grasp the significance of these limits, let us walk through the several steps that believers have to take to access the royal *haveli* and subsequently the treasury of books. First, special permission is required by the Ra's ul Hudood Saheb and the Mukasir Saheb, who, as described earlier, have separate offices in Badri Mohallah. These offices are relatively accessible to believers and are therefore semi-open spaces. Believers are expected to discuss their personal problems and concerns (usually family-related matters) with the Ra's ul Hudood Saheb and the Mukasir Saheb first before consulting the Mazoon Saheb. Access is only granted to believers who seek spiritual guidance or legal advice, who wish to pay their *salams* (respect), or receive blessings for a certain life-decision. If granted permission, visitors are admitted by the Mazoon Saheb's doorman and secretary upon entering the royal *haveli*. Upon entering the reception office of the Mazoon Saheb, believers are expected to make a small donation to the *muḥtasib* (accountant) of the *daʿwa* and to wait their turn in the waiting room.

Just as the vernacular architecture is embedded in the sacred space of Badri Mohallah, the royal *haveli* is built in such a way that it facilitates these greeting rituals and etiquette of access. Similarly, the physical body is affected by space. For instance, one has to be ritually and spiritually pure to enter the royal *haveli* and the office of the Mazoon Saheb. According to the tradition of the community, spiritual purity, which is based on piety and a strict set of devotional practices, can only be achieved by keeping the body ritually pure through *tahara*. A crucial aspect of ritual purity is circumcision, which is mandatory for both genders. Female genital mutilation is performed on young girls in the Alawi Bohra community and involves the total removal of the female genitalia.[52] Despite undergoing female circumcision, the 'women folk', according to the Mazoon Saheb, only have limited spiritual purity, because they menstruate, which – according to this interpretation – makes them ritually impure by definition. It is reasoned that the impure blood of menstruation attracts evil spirits to the women. It is for this reason that Alawi Bohra women are shunned during their menstruation and that no women, including the royal Bhu Sahebas, are allowed to be near, let alone touch, the books of the *khizana*. As described in the reflexive introduction, despite my being a non-Bohri, similar rules applied to me, and a as 'lady' scholar I was subjected to questions about my female ritual purity and periods of social seclusion each month.

In addition to ritual and spiritual purity, which is considered obligatory in *fiqh* and therefore applicable to the entire Bohra community, there are different sets of etiquette for the royal *khassa* and the non-royal *ʿamma*. Upon entering the royal *haveli*, the *ʿamma* is expected to show humility towards the *khassa* with a ceremonial greeting (and to everybody else in the room): it entails bowing while putting the right hand to the chest, followed by kissing of the hands and sometimes the feet. Posture and body language are extremely important in this regard. To give an example, one's legs and feet should always be turned away from the *khassa*, and one's focus should be towards the floor. Visitors are required to wear the traditional Bohra dress (*rida* for the women and *shalwar kamiez* and *topi* for the men), remove their shoes, and present themselves in an utterly modest and pure (bodily and spiritually clean) manner to the Mazoon Saheb, the other Bhai Sahebs and their assistants. As with all other devotional sacred spaces, pregnant and menstruating women do not frequent the royal *haveli* at all, to avoid the possible de-sacralising of these spaces.

Even though the conditions for entering the royal *haveli* are self-evident to everybody in the community, they are also written on a large board in front of the entrance of the *haveli* that reads 'No admission without permission', followed by a long list of regulations written in Gujarati. This set of etiquettes elevates the royal *haveli* above other spaces of worship where the *ʿamma* and *khassa* meet, such as in the

[52] With the exception of several newspaper articles and Facebook posts, to the best of my knowledge no sources exist on this topic, due to the extremely sensitive nature of the ritual of FGM in Bohra communities. What is described on the topic in this study is based on interviews with Alawi Bohra clerics. Due to the taboo on FGM and my delicate position in the community as an outsider and woman, I was not able to interview Alawi Bohra women about the topic. See for more news article sources: http://www.hindustantimes.com/mumbai/bohra-women-go-online-to-fight-circumcision-trauma/article1-779782.aspx and http://www.npwj.org/content/Uproar-over-Female-Genital-Mutilation-Bohra-Muslim-Woman-Activist-Launches-CampaignFacebook

masjid, the *jamaat khana*, or on *ziyara*. The Mukasir Saheb described these etiquettes as follows:

> How to stand. How to sit. When the Dai Mutlaq ascends the *takhat-e tayyebi* [throne]. When he comes out from *Devdi Mubarak* [the royal haveli]. When [the] Dai Mutlaq goes to some special lunch or dinner, how to greet him . . . the *adab al-majalis*.[53]

As for the royal code of conduct of the *khassa*, one of the most important forms of etiquette is the display of piety (through dress and personal grooming), humbleness and *purdah*: social seclusion and distance between the royal family and the rest of the community, both in a spiritual and a physical sense, have to be respected at all times. Royal domestic life is strictly private. The community approaches the *khassa*, with the permission of the *hudud*, and *never* the other way around. Women of the royal *haveli* only leave the house on very rare occasions; the men may leave the house at times for walks, but the people of Badri Mohallah would never approach them, let alone talk to the Mazoon Saheb or even make eye contact. The Mazoon Saheb and his wife, even though they are married, are never seen together in Badri Mohallah. Taking a *rikshaw* together would, for instance, be considered improper, and even if the royal family goes on 'outings' outside Baroda they never sit together in the same car. Any sense of marital togetherness, let alone any display of affection, stays within the walls of the royal *haveli*. The same rules of social distance apply to the royal children, who do not interact with their *ʿamma* peers and often are tutored in the *haveli*.

The social segregation of the royal family and their entourage vis-à-vis the rest of the community is also clearly visible during official ceremonies. The space of the *masjid* can only be accessed by the *ʿamma* after it has been officially entered by the Dai and his sons, who are at the head of an elaborate procession with fans, umbrellas and percussion, followed by the rest of the royal family. The great prayer area, the *masjid*, is not only divided between *mu'minin* and *mu'minat*, but there is also an inner royal and an outer non-royal circle (Figure 3.21). The Mukasir Saheb explained, 'A common lady cannot sit on the first row of the *majlis*. She has to take the *raza* [permission] of the Ma Saheba. Can I sit here?' Only the Bhai Sahebs and the Bhu Sahebas, the close confidants of the royal family, are allowed to sit in the royal demarcation of the *masjid* next to the Bhu Saheba, which is in close proximity to the throne of the Dai.

The spatial dimensions of this social demarcation and of royal privilege are clearly visible in Figure 3.21; this photograph was taken during the official ladies' *majlis* in the *masjid*. Sitting in the royal demarcation on the large thrones are the Dai in the middle, the Ma Saheba on the left with the Bhu Saheba and the wives of the Mukasir Saheb and the Ra's ul Hudood on the floor next to her, and the Mazoon Saheb, who is to the right of the Dai on a smaller throne, with the Mukasir Saheb next to him. The other royal Bhu Sahebas are seated on the carpeted floor within an inner *khassa* space marked by white barriers. Three of them are reciting the *marsiyya* in the middle through microphones. The researcher, in pink *rida*, is sitting in the upper left part of

[53] Interview conducted in the office of the Mukasir Saheb, Badri Mohallah, 20 October 2012.

Figure 3.21 Ladies' *majlis* in the *masjid* with the author sitting on the upper left of the 'royal' square. Credits: Alawi *daʿwa*.

this royal square. The majority of the *mu'minat* are seated on the floor around this royal square in their designated *ʿamma* space.

This particular spatial arrangement and its boundaries are observed in similar fashion during male-only *majalis* (Figure 3.7). They are a given among the Alawis, and modes of non-access versus privilege are never questioned. My sudden, unexpected presence in this multi-dimensional system of space and social order in the Alawi universe, including my access to the *khizana* as a woman and reserved spot in the demarcated *khassa* spaces as a non-royal during ceremonies, had a disruptive effect on the Alawi *ʿamma*. Let us end this chapter by exploring this disruptive effect and reflect on the voices of discontent in the Alawi universe as a reaction to my presence in these spaces.

3.4 Gender, Etiquette and Access

In the reflexive section of this study, I provided a detailed account of the complex process of how I, as an outsider, was granted authorised access to the community and the many facets of its sacred universe, rituals and spaces, and how I eventually was allowed to enter the treasury of books and see and touch its esoteric manuscripts. I did not, as we have established, enter the Alawi universe as a believer and thus was never spiritually part of its sacred geography; yet I did not remain an outsider as I had taken a special oath of trust in front of the Dai and agreed to live in the *mohallah* and distance myself socially completely from my personal life so as to dedicate myself to the community.

Spaces, we established, change depending on who dwells in them, moves through them or visits them through the presence of individuals and their auras. I described this phenomenon in relation to the *majlis* of the *ʿahd*, where the modest living room of a family turned into a space of ceremony and ritual once the Dai and his entourage entered it. Similarly, my presence in Badri Mohallah as an accidental ethnographer changed the space of the *mohallah* and its social structures.

While my presence in the *daʿwa* was a *fait accompli* to the Dai and his clerics, this was not automatically the case for the rest of the community, who suddenly had a white, European, non-Muslim, unmarried woman as their neighbour. From the moment I arrived in Badri Mohallah, I spent my days working in the royal *haveli*, entering it and exiting from it on a daily basis. The people of Badri Mohallah observed me entering the royal *haveli* every day on what seemed to them my own special conditions. Their conditions of access as believers, to their surprise, did not seem to apply to me.

I subsequently became part of the inner circles of the royal household, spending my time between two separate domains in the same household: gossiping while rolling *chapatis* and peeling custard apples with the women in the kitchen, and talking about manuscripts and politics with the men in the *khizana* upstairs. After gaining the full trust of the Bhai Sahebs, I was even allowed to work in the treasury of books when members of the royal family were asleep in the afternoon. From the perspective of the *mu'minin* and *mu'minat*, I was breaking boundaries of clerical and non-clerical, royal and non-royal categories, and unspoken and unwritten rules, rituals and etiquette that had always seemed so fixed and eternal were suddenly distorted. My living and working in what was considered a privileged position resulted in discontent and silent protest from the people of Badri Mohallah.

Analysing my presence from the community's emic perspective, these reactions were understandable and perhaps not surprising. One can imagine the believers' astonishment when they were finally granted an audience with the Mazoon Saheb, and they encountered me – a non-Bohri in a *rida*, being part of an entirely masculine domain – sitting next to him. To my great surprise, what often happened was that the attention of the entire session was shifted to me instead of the clerics, because the devotees often came from outside Baroda and had never witnessed someone outside of Gujarat or Mumbai. The Mazoon Saheb was generally amused by this reaction, as he proudly explained to the believers that I was a researcher who had come from abroad to study the community. In his office, my presence thus did not remain unnoticed by its visitors, and, often it had the unwanted side-effect of being disruptive to the order of the day.

On one occasion there was a meeting of the eldest Bhai Sahebs in the office of the Mazoon Saheb. While I was working quietly from my peacock throne in my designated corner, trying to attract as little attention as possible, the committee of Bhai Sahebs discussed the revenues of the goat skins, which were collected after *'eed* and would pay for the salaries of the *madrasa* teachers. Soon, however, the elders were intrigued by my activities, to such an extent that the meeting was interrupted as they stopped to ask me questions, and never managed to discuss the revenue issue.[54] My presence in the office of the Mazoon Saheb, where visitors would behave according

[54] Badri Mohallah, royal *haveli*, 30 October 2012, late afternoon.

to a specific protocol under 'ordinary' circumstances, thus changed the space. Only very rarely did my presence in the office of the Mazoon Saheb go unnoticed. I believe that my poor command of Gujarati actually served me rather well in these situations, because as soon as people realised that I did not understand a word of what they were saying, they would speak freely about their (often very private) personal problems.

Observing the daily life of Badri Mohallah from the peacock throne gave me a unique insight into the otherwise undisclosed world of the *da'wa* and its people, as well as of its treasury of books. Once I had become part of this universe, my presence was non-negotiable to the community, because it was ordered and legitimised by the Bhai Sahebs. Their acceptance of my status in the community was part of the believers' obedience and loyalty to the Dai and their *'ahd*. The more I gained proximity to the royal family, the more believers started to see me as an extended part of the family of the Dai. This somehow extended the royal protocol during ceremonies to me. In some instances, people tried to kiss my feet in the mosque and even offered me little envelopes with money to make a *du'a* in their name, a practice usually performed by the Bhai Sahebs and their wives. These situations caused a real ethnographic dilemma, as I felt great unease as believers reached for my feet, being well aware of my privileged status as a white European researcher in a supposedly post-colonial world. The Mazoon Saheb, however, said that in these situations I could not protest or refuse the envelopes for *du'a*, as this would be seen as disrespectful and a possible humiliation. As these signs of respect were directed to me, and not the other Bhai Sahebs, they did not accept the envelopes from me either. What was I to do? In the end, I donated the tiny envelopes to the *faqirs* of the *mohallah*, hoping that, through their prayers, the believers' *du'as* would be heard.

My presence in Badri Mohallah was thus tied to the royal family and their authority, which strongly linked my own to *their reputation*, and I was expected to behave accordingly. As for the social hierarchy of the *da'wa*, the example of kissing the feet illustrates how the believers associated physical proximity to the royal family, in whatever form, with notions of sacrality. However, as I was living in a non-royal *manzil* in the middle of the *mohallah*, I was not part of the royal household in the domestic sense, which caused tensions. At first, I was not aware of the royal etiquette because it was not spoken of or explained to me: it was considered self-evident. I would have tea with my neighbours, joke around with the kids in the street, admire people's cattle, and commit my biggest faux pas of all: enthusiastically wave at the Mazoon Saheb in the street, the man with whom I had intimate conversations in the privacy of his home every day. My social missteps were silently frowned upon and at times became the subject of gossip and ridicule. They were carefully registered by the people of Badri Mohallah, either because of a sense of fascination or, in some cases, because my behaviour was seen by some as a disgrace upon the royal family and the community at large.

This example demonstrates that the *mu'minin* and *mu'minat* of Badri Mohallah were not always as understanding and inclusive as the clerics would have hoped. Unwillingly, I had disrupted the social order of the *mohallah*, and my presence was often not understood. They could not get their heads around the fact that I could enter these sacred and inaccessible spaces without any restrictions and without performing the

Figure 3.22 The researcher observing an all-male *ʿurs* commemoration at the *maqbara* in Baroda. Credits: Alawi *daʿwa*.

rituals they had to perform, while they, the actual believers who would do anything to get a glimpse of the holy royal family and receive their divine guidance, could not.

In addition to the issue of access to the royal family, the *mohallah*'s social order was also a highly gendered affair, and it was often my presence as a woman in these masculine spaces (Figure 3.22) that was contested. It was mostly the women – and not the men – of the community who were most critical of my presence and code of conduct in the *mohallah* and who did not always tolerate my participant observation in the mosque of *jamaat khana*. This discontent, however, could never be articulated in the domestic space of the royal *haveli* where I was always among the Bhai Sahebs and their loyal assistants. When I was outside the royal realm, however, their hostility on some occasions became apparent.

Because of some of these negative sentiments, the women of the royal family advised me to keep a *rupee* coin close to my heart to protect me from *al-ḥasad* (the evil eye). What we see here is a the close link between the talismanic qualities attributed to objects in relation to the body, their sacred materiality, and rituals and notions of purity and protection, a structure that is not only present in the social codes of the community, the *khizana* and its manuscripts, but is also, as we have seen in this chapter, strongly embedded in the spatial geography of the Bohra universe and its vernacular architecture.

Following this exploration of the material and spatial features of the Alawi universe (access I) and their relation to the community's perspective of the *daʿwa*, its sacred universe and social order (access II), how can my access be best understood? As noted in the introduction to this chapter, initially I was granted permission to access the *khizana* by taking the *Ollybehn oath*, which enabled me to access the *dar al-taqiyya* through an access I perspective. At first, I merely entered and observed the physical space of Badri Mohallah and did not penetrate its sacred universe. Yet the longer I was part of its space, taking my place on the peacock throne and gaining proximity to the royal family, the more I became more than merely spatially present in *Devdi Mubarak*. Instead, it felt as if I had transcended the space of the profane realm of access I into the sacred realm of access II, dwelling between the two in some kind of 'third space', to borrow Edward Soja's terminology, a liminality that was unique to the time and space of my social-codicological fieldwork.[55]

While accessing the community and the treasury of books via a mode in between access I and II, I was exempted from certain parts of the *khizana*-related etiquette, invisible barriers and limitations of the *'amma*. However, forms of etiquette that were specifically related to gender, also known as *purdah*, were applicable to me. Interestingly, restrictions of movement did not (as is explained later) necessarily limit my access to the treasury of books. In fact, I would argue that my gender was the decisive factor in enabling my access to the community and the *khizana*, simply because the clerics felt responsible for my safety and well-being. The Mazoon Saheb told me that if I had been a man I would never have been taken into the community, let alone into the private space of the royal family, and I would not have had the chance to prove my trustworthiness. As a man, I would have found it impossible to negotiate access to the treasury of books, because there would have been no opportunity to gain trust or credibility while being among the women of the community and respecting their *purdah* at the same time.

So how exactly did my gender enable access? Gaining the trust of the clerics was based on two conditions. The first, as I discussed previously, was intelligence ('information is power'), which entailed checking my credentials and reputation as an outsider, scholar and woman, through social media, local networks and, to my surprise, interviewing of my male relatives and close friends. For instance, I was only shown manuscripts after the Mazoon Saheb had spoken to my father. The second condition of access was related to more specific issues of gender. I was expected to integrate all 'ladies'' etiquette related to *purdah*, meaning social and sartorial seclusion: exercising behavioural piety at all times, both in public and private realms, by keeping a modest appearance – wearing a *rida*, using *henna* on hair, hands and feet, and using no make-up; having no communication (either verbal or through body language) or interaction with men except for 'the three brothers', as well as not speaking about my research with anyone; and restricting my movements – I would live inside the *mohallah* and would not move outside the Bohra universe. The formative stages of my stay in Badri Mohallah resembled a probation period or trial, and I was constantly reminded by the clerics that if they detected anything untrustworthy or disrespectable, I would be 'fired'.

Once I passed through the trial period, the *khizana* negotiations of reciprocity and exchange began: I traded certain of my codicological skills, such as preparing a catalogue and giving advice on the preservation of manuscripts and contact information, for scans of manuscript copies and books and slightly more space and presence in the *khizana*. I thus moved from having no access at all to the sacred community to touching the manuscripts of the *khizana* (see the discussion of reciprocity and exchange in the previous chapter). My academic network turned out to be a crucial asset in my negotiations to gain access. Again, we see here the relative flexibility of the *dar al-taqiyya*, as the

[55] Edward W. Soja, *Thirdspace: Journeys to Los Angeles and Other Real-and-Imagined Places* (Malden: Blackwell, 1996).

cleric's agenda to be represented in academic scholarship took precedence. My gender even played a very central but delicate role in sharing my professional network. What I could not do as a woman was make direct demands in the negotiation process. Instead, I would always phrase my request in terms of my male peers and their authority, and preferably people the Bhai Sahebs respected; my male academic professors, my father, and even the Dutch ambassador played a role in the ongoing negotiation process.

For instance, to enable me to gain access to *ʿilm al-haqa'iq* manuscripts, my PhD supervisors at the time would write requests to the Mazoon Saheb suggesting I should take up this study. I learned that this construction was crucial, because while dealing with a delicate topic such as the *haqa'iq* I was always uncertain how far I could go in my demands or what was a faux pas and what was still considered acceptable. When I – via my male colleagues – sometimes overstepped the boundaries of the clerics (something that was inevitable given that so little was known about the community), the faux pas would not be directly attributed to me.

This is how I navigated my gendered presence into Badri Mohallah and the treasury of books. The lobbying process itself, together with my socially distancing myself completely from my private life at home, was the most challenging aspect of my stay in Baroda. On some days nothing seemed negotiable; on others there was room for rose milk and 'discussion'. However, as noted in the reflexive chapter, there was one issue that was impossible to change and therefore difficult to negotiate: my gender in relation to ritual purity and touching the manuscripts. In the end, no male academic peer or authority could mediate in a discussion involving ritual purity. Pragmatism on the side of the Bhai Sahebs, combined with the urgent need to catalogue their *khizana*, turned out eventually to be the deciding factor. While I was preparing the catalogue I would enter the royal *haveli* each day as a woman to the outside world, fully covered in a *rida*; as soon as I entered the treasury of books, I was allowed to take off the *rida* and be dressed like the men, in *shalwar kamiez* and *dupatta* that I wore underneath. As soon as I left the space of the *khizana*, or if someone from outside the royal household entered the office of the Mazoon Saheb, I would be transformed back into the realm of the *rida*, a mode of being that was acceptable to all.

Final Notes to Chapter 3: Locks and Keys of the Alawi Universe

This chapter has addressed questions of secrecy and the two modes of access to the Alawi community and its *khizana*: access I, to the profane geographical realm of the *mohallah*, and access II, to the *daʿwa* or sacred universe. Through the oral contract of the *ʿahd*, a certain habitus of *taqiyya* is institutionalised in the community through various rituals, practices and material manifestations. Considered a central element in the Alawi universe and thus more than a theological notion, the habitus of *taqiyya* divides the world between the *dar al-taqiyya* (access II) and *al-kharij* (access I), the 'rest'.

Yet the spatiality of secrecy, as we have seen, is also practised within the *daʿwa* on the level of the politics of access to the *khizana*. The Fatimid-Tayyibi esoteric truths enshrined in the treasury of books, according to this narrative, must remain undisclosed at all costs in the absence of the hidden Imam, dividing the Alawi universe into the majority of uninitiated *ʿamma* and the clerical, royal *khassa* and their respective spaces.

The space most inaccessible to the *ʿamma*, the treasury of books, has no material locks and keys (access I), yet remains a ritually inaccessible space to the *ʿamma* (access II): it is a space of initiation, limitations and secrecy. The royal *haveli* and the *khizana* are thus also spaces of pilgrimage with treasures and relics, where believers come to pay their respect to the clerics *without* disrespecting the laws of access, de-sacralising the *haqa'iq* or entering the treasury of books. The politics of the *khizana* negotiate a delicate balance between spaces of sacrality, power and access and who occupies them.

One could argue that without the habitus of *taqiyya*, there would be no *daʿwa* or treasury of books. The *khizana* plays a crucial role in the organisational infrastructure of the Alawi Bohra community, representing and legitimising the power of the clerics and maintaining the social order of the *daʿwa* as the *Wezarat al-Alawiyya*. It is a transitional space between the realm of the office of the Mazoon Saheb and the headquarters of the *daʿwa* and the treasury of books and esoteric truths. The two realms could not exist without each other, as they form the backbone of the *daʿwa* and its unique spatial narrative in Baroda.

Finally, the realm of the *khassa* and the sacred books of the *khizana* may be the *qutb* in the community's sacred geography, yet the world of the *ʿamma* and its material manifestations of *taqiyya*, such as vernacular architecture and dress, are central in the Alawi Bohra identity and the dialectics of inside and outside. Together, they form the Alawis' unique fabric of secrecy to their universe in Baroda and beyond.

Chapter 4

Manuscript Stories

Two Bibliophiles in the Treasury of Books

Court historian of the *Daʿwat al-hadiyya*: this was my official title in Baroda, a title that was easy neither to obtain nor to live up to. As I described previously, my entry into the community, its *mohallah* and its treasury of books was a complex process, with various obstacles unforeseen by neither the Bhai Sahebs nor me. It took endless rounds of *thalis* before the alchemical interaction that ethnographers mention so frequently occurred and a relationship of trust was built through the manuscripts of the *khizana* and their stories.

It was not that the Bhai Sahebs were displeased about my arrival. They had, in fact, welcomed me with great enthusiasm, but they simply had no idea what to do next with their court historian. The initial encounters could be described as awkward at best. Being very aware of the community's tradition of secrecy, I was overly conscious of my behaviour, while at the same time uncertain of how to sit, dress or behave appropriately, which made the Bhai Sahebs cautious.

On my first day in the *mohallah*, after my first official audience with the Bhai Sahebs, I was sent directly to accompany the Bhu Saheba, the wife of the Mazoon, on a journey to a lake outside Baroda. She had come all the way to the lake by *tuk tuk* to buy sweet water fish for dinner. I learned that, according to Fatimid law, the fish not only had to have scales and be fresh upon purchasing but also had to be alive. And thus, instead of doing deep philological work, I spent my first afternoon among the Alawis in the pouring monsoon rain, watching a dozen Indian carp being blessed through the recitation of the *basmala*, while being filetted alive.

From buying *halal* fish in the rain to finally earning a seat in the *khizana* on Jahangir's peacock throne was a lengthy process. For weeks I had felt like those carp on dry land, as I struggled with termite infestations, ill-fitting *ridas*, the self-imposed quarantine of the *mohallah* that I could no longer leave without permission, fevers, social codes I did not understand and general monsoon malaise. To make matters worse, it felt like my mishaps, such as when a rotten papaya fell out of my window and landed on someone's head instead of the garbage pile, had made me the source of ridicule in the *mohallah*. It took me weeks before I developed a sense of the rhythm of Badri Mohallah and grasped its etiquette.

My *tarjumān* (translator or guide) in this quest was the Mazoon Saheb, a friendly but at times stern middle-aged gentleman with a long, grey beard: scholar, father of four, chief *qadi*, *khizana* custodian, and designated *mansus* of the community. Following the classical pupil–disciple trajectory, he had first attempted to initiate me into reading a *batini* manuscript. It was a disaster. To be disappointment of the Mazoon, I was not used to the sophisticated and complex Arabic terminology of his Fatimid-Tayyibi manuscripts, and instead of listening, I let my curiosity get the better of me and I asked too many questions. I learned that it was not my place to speak unless I was told to do so, and thus the idea of an 'interview' was impossible.

There was one thing, however, that the Mazoon and I had in common: our love for manuscripts, and, as it is still called in India, the field of *manuscriptology*. And thus, as two bibliophiles we developed a routine where we would come together every afternoon in the treasury of books to talk about manuscripts. We would meet right before the afternoon *namaz*, when the busy life of the *khizana* had quietened down, its secretaries had gone home and phones would stop ringing. It was just the Mazoon, the manuscripts and me.

The Mazoon, who had performed his 'Mazoon duties' all day long with great charisma and ceremony, would kneel down, take off his *pagri*, and pray right next to me on the rich, carpeted floor. This ritual would take place every day and, to me, was deeply humbling. Even though our worlds could not be more different, this time of the day became a liminal space, a ritual where we found a common language: the language of handwritten books. It was the poetics of manuscripts – the smell of leather bindings, the sound of cracking spines, the tactileness of handmade paper, the joy of discovering rare watermarks and of deciphering cryptic marginalia and colophons, and the excitement of finding a date, holograph, secret alphabet, or the occasional unexpected visitor – that became our common language. In other words, we grew closer around aspects of the written word and its social life that cannot be reproduced in printed books. Being among manuscripts and appreciating their codicology are rare privileges, something the Mazoon and I as bibliophiles immediately recognised.

One can perhaps best compare this specific type of bibliophilia, or manuscript fever, to the psychology of the collector's mind and to his or her tireless expeditions to the local flea market or antique fair.[1] In contrast to the hoarder who is aspiring towards an abundance of items and the accumulation of objects, the collector is hunting for unique items, or for rarest and finest object of its kind. To the bibliophile-cum-codicologist, manuscripts are what rare stamps, ancient Ming vases or forgotten Birkin bags are to their collectors: objects that keep on giving and that open up an entire universe to their admirers.[2] Just as my heart would skip a beat when encountering secret alphabets or *neem* leaves, the Mazoon's eyes would light up when he opened a codex or unrolled a *sijill*.

I learned that the Mazoon was not only a scribe and custodian of the *khizana* but also an avid manuscript collector, something which is explored further in this chapter. To the Mazoon and I, the poetics of the manuscripts of the *khizana* became the basis of an alchemical exchange that lasted until the end of my fieldwork. These manuscript sessions had an informal character and, as such, became the space where we could converse freely and sometimes even crack jokes. What I did not realise at the time was that the gentleman with whom I spent so many afternoons in the *khizana* was the indeed

1 Buskens describes collecting as a social process. Léon Buskens, 'From Trash to Treasure', 203.

2 See Kratchkovsky's *Among Arabic Manuscripts* and Buskens' 'From Trash to Treasure'.

the *mansus*: the Mazoon Saheb would eventually become the Dai of the community. Had I arrived in Baroda several years later, after the Mazoon Saheb succeeded his father as Dai, these informal conversations would not have been possible. Although these sessions were initially meant to improve the manuscript catalogue I was preparing for the late Dai, they became the basis of the personal relationship between the Mazoon and me. The Mazoon taught me everything he knew and I listened, and these conversations became the foundation of this study. More importantly, they made all the previous differences, awkward encounters, termite infestations, and misunderstandings fade into the background.

This is how I acclimatised to the life of Badri Mohallah and learned to speak the language of the treasury of books, its shelves and sanctified secrets, and the poetics of its manuscripts – its rolls, tomes, talismans, *kutub*, *makhtutat* and *sijillat*. This was a language we both understood, and from a guest and complete outsider I became *Ollybehn*, a sister, or almost daughter of the Mazoon and his family.[3] A true privilege, which was not without its challenges, nor seen as uncontroversial or unproblematic by the *mohallah*, yet was crucial in every respect. As we conversed our way through heaps of manuscripts together, I began to grasp the social codes and hierarchies of Badri Mohallah, adopt the royal etiquette of the Mazoon Saheb's family, and see patterns in the choreography of the many ceremonies I participated in. Slowly, I began to understand what it meant to be part of the *daʿwa* and live the Alawi 'Faatemi way of life'. Before I knew it, I moved with ease through the *mohallah* as if it were my own, armed with my *rida* and the key to the *khizana*.

Theoretical Considerations

Having spent most of his scholarly years in the company of manuscripts, Kratchkovsky writes, in his *Among Arabic Manuscripts*, that, without exception, books and men have the tendency to mingle in 'fanciful' and 'unexpected' ways. As a social codicologist *avant la lettre*, he argues that the two worlds cannot be separated.[4] The state libraries Kratchkovsky frequented in St Petersburg and Damascus could not be more different from the social reality of the Alawi treasury of books. Yet in Baroda too, I observed how the social and personal, the written and the codicological, were inextricably linked. This fits into my earlier argument that given the social role of the treasury of books in Badri Mohallah, there is no *khizana* without the community and no community without its *khizana*.

The Mazoon Saheb taught me that each manuscript in the treasury of books had its unique biography, with its life cycles and stories of survival, travel, material circumcision and loss. Through the manuscripts of the *khizana* I learned more about the life story of the Mazoon Saheb himself and that of his family; his hopes, dreams, and disappointments; his mind as a collector, as a cleric and, most of all, as a person. I document these, together with the stories of the *khizana*, both its custodians and its

3 This is a common phenomenon in cultural anthropology. See for instance, for a classic ethnographical example, Abu-Lughod, *Veiled Sentiments*, Ch. 1, 'Guest and Daughter', 1–38.

4 Kratchkovsky, *Among Arabic Manuscripts*, 20, 21.

manuscripts, and of the people of Badri Mohallah and beyond, in this chapter. I have done so not only with the aim of showing that they are intrinsically linked but also because I believe that they are of paramount importance for understanding the social role of the treasury of books and the history of its collection. As we will see, manuscripts, without fail, come with unexcepted surprises which do not necessarily fit into the narratives that are built around them. Such is also the case in the *khizana* and its collection history. To make sense of the manuscript stories of the *khizana* and their codicological surprises, let us start with some theoretical considerations regarding the social meaning of manuscripts, their circulation and spatial embeddedness, materiality and immateriality, and the Alawis' emic perspective on codicology.

Circulation, Space, Commodities

The Alawis' emic perspective of space, which I illustrated in the previous chapter, is crucial for understanding the social role of the treasury of books and its manuscripts. As the various manuscript stories that are explored in this chapter demonstrate, within the universe of the Alawi *daʿwa*, a manuscript from the *khizana* is considered a sacred object and is surrounded by practices of secrecy, veneration (see the next chapter) and non-access. Yet once circulating outside the *mohallah* and its sacred geography, these manuscripts, consisting of simple cloth bindings and cheap paper, lose their value as sacred commodities and turn into old dusty handwritten Arabic books. At best, they end up at the stalls of book sellers or, even worse, are collected by paper recyclers or discarded as trash.

Miraculously, as we see, several manuscripts of the Alawi *khizana* were saved from garbage piles in Mumbai. Accidentally discovered by an Alawi *mu'min* who purchased the books and returned them to the *daʿwa*, these manuscripts changed from worthless into sacred objects as soon as they were brought into Badri Mohallah, where they were repaired and enshrined in the treasury of books. This storyline, from trash to treasure, shows how the value of manuscripts of the *khizana* as commodities is thus determined by their spatial context.[5] The displacement of these manuscripts beyond their 'natural habitat', however, can also add to their value as commodities. If these manuscripts had been discovered by a specialist who was aware of the rarity of Isma'ili manuscripts, he or she would be able to sell these discarded books for a fortune on the international manuscript market to certain museums, academic libraries, auction houses or private collectors.

The manuscripts that survived the garbage dumps of Mumbai are just one of the many examples of collecting stories for the treasury of books. Collecting, in this sense, is thus not always pursued by one individual; on many occasions, manuscripts found their way into the *khizana* through others and their networks, often transcending spatial boundaries and sectarian affiliations.[6] Through the lens of social codicology,

[5] Arjun Appadurai, 'Introduction. Commodities and the Politics of Value', in *The Social Life of Things: Commodities in Cultural Perspective* (Cambridge: University of Cambridge Press, 1986), 3–63. Buskens, 'From Trash to Treasure'.

[6] See for further ethnographic studies on collecting practices: Paul van der Grijp, *Passion and Profit: Towards an Anthropology of Collecting* (Berlin: Lit Verlag, 2006) and Markus Schindlbeck, 'The Art of Collecting: Interactions between Collectors and the People They Visit', *Zeitschrift Für Ethnologie* vol. 118, no. 1 (1993): 57–67.

I recorded the collection practices of the *khizana* by both scrutinising the manuscripts and their rich world of marginalia and, at the same time, listening to the histories of the people who rescued, gifted, donated, endowed, preserved and at times even ingested them.

The Social Meaning of Codicology

The importance of the written word in the Alawi Bohra community, as enshrined in the treasury of books, can hardly be overstated. The manuscripts in the *khizana* form the sacred backbone of the *da'wa*, as they are seen as the legitimisation of the clerical organisation of the community and its Neo-Fatimid identity. Whereas, thus far, the treasury of books and the *da'wa* were the main focuses of this study, in this chapter and those that follow, the materiality and social role of these manuscripts are explored.

Before discussing the social lives of the manuscripts of the *khizana*, it is necessary to carry out the philological groundwork of mapping out and defining the manuscript culture, or perhaps even manuscript cultures, of the *khizana* in detail. This chapter begins with this approach for the simple reason that, due to the inaccessibility of sources, not much is known about Isma'ili book culture, let alone Bohra manuscript culture. For decades, Isma'ili manuscripts and their content have been the *subject*, rather than the *object*, of study. Starting with the contributions to the field made by scholars such as Hussein Hamdani, Vladimir Ivanov, Asef Fyzee and Ismail Poonalawa, the academic focus has predominantly been – and still is – on the content of these texts instead of their codicological and material features, which are rarely discussed in relation to the milieux in which they are produced, read, and enshrined. Yet this problem is not only inherent in the field of Isma'ili Studies. It is symptomatic, as I argue elsewhere, of the way we look at books and manuscript cultures in general.[7]

Although in the last several decades the idea of the 'archaeology of knowledge' has made us rethink the historiography of thought and discursive traditions, the 'archaeology of the book' has remained the lens through which medieval and pre-modern manuscript cultures are traditionally studied in Muslim contexts.[8] Yet, in the case of the Bohras, pre-modern book culture is as much alive today as it was five hundred years ago, and therefore speaking of 'archaeology' in the context of manuscripts as inert objects is not very fitting, especially as among the Alawis the opposite is true. As I observed time and time again, although the manuscripts and documents of the *khizana* are considered secret, they have rich social lives in the community, serving as objects of talismanic healing, as material evidence of schisms and authority, and as commodities.[9]

In the previous chapters, I discussed the social role of documentary practices of the *khizana*, such as the revealing of the secret of the *nass sijill* in Ahmedabad and the writing of the *'alama* by the Dai (Chapter 1), and the ceremonial value of the *'ahd* roll during the ritual of the oath of initiation (Chapter 3). In the following chapters,

7 Akkerman, 'The Bohra Manuscript Treasury', 197–200.

8 Adam Gacek, *Arabic Manuscripts: A Vademecum for Readers* (Leiden: Brill, 2012), x.

9 See for a more detailed discussion on the social lives of manuscripts Akkerman, 'The Bohra Manuscript Treasury', 193–4.

I demonstrate that the manuscripts of the *khizana*, too, have many social lives that include but are not restricted to reading. As such, this study is thus an argument in favour of taking manuscripts seriously as objects, rather than focusing on their content alone, which requires investigating the social practices that surround them as much as the intellectual histories and *khizana* traditions of which they are historically part.[10]

I investigate those social practices by combining the basic principles of manuscript studies regarding scrutiny, dating and identification with the emic perspective of the community by humanising its custodians, readers and copyists: I give a voice to the people who have the ceremonial right to access the *khizana* and those who do not – those who write, read, collect, collate, venerate and consume the sacred materiality of its manuscripts. In the opening vignette of this chapter, I describe how the detailed study of the manuscripts of the treasury of books not only took place under the strict supervision of the Bhai Sahebs but actually would have been impossible without their presence, explanations, oral transmission and family histories. Only through this perspective was I able to understand what the books of the *khizana* meant to them and how the scribal traditions they preserve, the codicology they practice and the way they read and transmit knowledge constitute a larger Alawi Bohra manuscript culture, unique to the *khizana* of Baroda.

Reconstructing a 'Medieval' Manuscript World in Baroda

The notion of 'manuscript culture' in the context of the treasury of books is explored in this study using the broadest definition of this term: it includes the historical and the contemporary, the social and the material, which I argue are equally important. John Dagenais's definition of manuscript culture is a starting point for the analysis. In his *Ethics of Reading in Manuscript Culture*, Dagenais argued that it is impossible to study manuscripts without considering their horizon: the world in which manuscripts are produced, consumed, circulate, are 'turned into another', and, most importantly, read and consumed. This horizon is thus an entire universe *an sich*, including a multitude of activities and practices; as he states, it is 'where the most important part of medieval literature happens'.[11] Dagenais emphasises that philologists must stop studying manuscripts through the paradigms of printed books or fixed texts. He argues that, instead of the focusing on authorship, readership and craftsmanship should be the lens of investigation of manuscripts, emphasising their fluidity and codicological uniqueness. Dagenais constructs the horizon of the medieval manuscript world by focusing on what he calls the *rough edges*: the marginalia and the paratexts of manuscript copies.

However, there is nothing 'medieval' about the contemporary Alawi Bohra community in Baroda, which is why I refer to the modern community as 'Neo-Fatimid'. Yet the Alawi clerics, through their *khizana*, are also reconstructing a medieval manuscript world, that of the Fatimids and later Tayyibis, which is central to this identity. The link with their Fatimid past is thus not only cultivated by transmitting Fatimid and

[10] See also Buskens, 'Paper Worlds', 5.

[11] John Dagenais, *The Ethics of Reading in Manuscript Culture: Glossing the Libro de Buen Amor* (Princeton: Princeton University Press, 1994), xvi.

Tayyibi authors and their works but also by preserving a *khizana* tradition in South Asia. Preserving this *khizana* tradition entails maintaining specific politics of access, according to traditions of *batin* and *zahir* and hierarchies of the *da'wa*, and cultivating what one could call their interpretation of a *Neo-Fatimid manuscript culture*. According to my observations in the treasury of books, cultivating this Neo-Fatimid manuscript culture 'happens' on three levels: collecting and collating practices (Chapter 4); social usage, including how manuscript cultures from the past, whether from Yemen or Egypt, are translated to the present through materiality and marginalia (Chapter 5); and copying practices and scribal traditions, specifically of an Isma'ili tradition in Gujarat that is distinctly Arabic (Chapter 6). These practices are all described with active verbs, as they are constantly 'happening' – adapted, negotiated and changed by generations to keep Alawi Bohra manuscript culture alive.

As for the manuscript culture of the *khizana*, we are in the fortunate position that we are able to study this manuscript world, including its material features, through social codicology. This perspective, as we have seen, is not restricted to the historical but also takes into account the social, contemporary, active and participatory present. In fact, I call one aspect of this approach *codicological participant observation*: the study of living archives or book collections and of the culture of book production and consumption through classical anthropological methods, such as participant observation in which the ethnographer actively takes part in certain practices and rituals with the permission of the community, combined with the philological and codicological hands-on work of reading manuscripts and identifying their material features; for example, reading the manuscripts of the *khizana* *with* the Mazoon Saheb, learning how the Bhai Sahebs compose colophons and preserve manuscripts through local techniques, and participating in their ritualised copying practices. The aim of this method, as elaborated elsewhere, is to understand mechanical and social practices of book copying, consuming, venerating and preserving from an emic perspective.[12]

In short, I, as a scholar, am not reconstructing the medieval Fatimid past of the Alawi Bohras through their manuscripts, or at least, not directly. Instead, I am observing how the Alawis themselves reconstruct and cultivate this medieval manuscript world in Baroda, which constitutes the material evidence for their Neo-Fatimid identity by preserving an Arabic manuscript culture from the past and adapting it to the Indian Ocean surroundings of Gujarat.

Texts as Objects: Materiality and Immateriality

From the perspective of social codicology, one could argue that there are no coincidences in the codicology of manuscript cultures.[13] Setting aside mistakes and natural disasters, nothing is left to chance in the Alawi *khizana* and the cultivation of its Neo-Fatimid book culture. After all, the manuscripts of the Alawi *khizana* did not survive to the present day as an afterthought; they were not 're-discovered' recently

[12] Akkerman, 'The Bohra Manuscript Treasury', 190.

[13] Akkerman (ed.), *Social Codicology: The Multiple Lives of Texts in Muslim Societies*.

under the roof of a collapsed mosque or in a *geniza* storeroom, nor were they ever considered lost by its community. Instead, travelling across the Indian Ocean, they have been preserved, and painstakingly so, for a reason, despite climatic conditions and social-political contexts that can be described as hostile at best.

Similarly to how the *khizana* is not an inert repository of books but is a sacred space constructed by its custodians, so Alawi manuscripts are handcrafted, mostly by men: they are handwritten, bound and collated by hand, and produced with the utmost care. As custodians of the books and the sacred traditions, the Bhai Sahebs not only try to preserve their manuscript tradition to the best of their abilities but they also must make editorial choices, codicological and aesthetic changes and scribal interventions. In other words, as custodians, scribes, readers, collectors and collators, they have agency in this process and preserve and reconstruct an uninterrupted chain of Fatimid–Tayyibi manuscript transmission according to what they consider to be pure and authentic.[14]

Thus, the materiality of manuscripts – their shape, appearance, script and palaeography – should not be taken for granted. Of course, additional factors influence their materiality; for example, prevailing traditional values, which may differ depending on their geographic context;[15] the geographical availability of materials, which differed between the mountainous regions of Yemen and the monsoon climate of Gujarat; or the availability of men with technical or linguistic skills. Yemen housed native speakers of Arabic; Gujarati speakers must have had a different relationship to the texts than did believers in South Asia. As I argued in Chapter 2, the social meaning of Isma'ili books changed as they moved from Cairo to Gujarat via Yemen – from being royal manuscripts stored in palace libraries (Cairo) to being carriers of intellectual history (Yemen) and to serving as sacred artefacts enshrined in specially designated treasuries of books (Gujarat).

In addition to the influence of geography and climate, the materiality of manuscript cultures largely depends on personal interventions and choices and the introduction of new rituals, traditions and meanings, instead of there being one timeless and fixed tradition. For instance, as we see in the next chapter, there is a strong correlation between the way certain manuscripts are ceremonially used among the Bohras in Gujarat and their appearance; for example, consider the vertical roll of the *sijill*. Social practice and materiality thus cannot be separated.

The notion of materiality, as proposed by Daniel Miller, is extremely valuable in tackling the question of what social roles the manuscripts of the *khizana* play in the *daʿwa*. Material cultures – 'things', 'objects', 'products' or 'artifacts' – represent and materialise immaterial ideas.[16] Even objects that are considered extremely holy,

[14] The idea of scribes as agents in manuscript cultures has gained momentum in the last decade. See, for instance, the edited volume *Scribes as Agents of Language Change*, ed. Esther-Miriam Wagner, Ben Outhwaite and Bettina Beinhoff (Berlin: De Gruyter, 2013) and Tino Oudesluijs, 'Scribes as Agents of Change: Copying Practices in Administrative Texts from Fifteenth-Century Coventry', in Margaret Tudeau-Clayton and Martin Hilpert (eds), *The Challenge of Change* (Zurich: Gunter Narr Verlag, 2018), 223–48.

[15] Gerald W. R. Ward, *The Grove Encyclopedia of Materials and Techniques in Art* (Oxford: Oxford University Press, 2008), 355.

[16] Daniel Miller, 'Materiality: An Introduction', in *Materiality: An Introduction* (Durham: Duke University Press, 2005), 4.

untouchable and therefore immaterial are still commonly expressed through material culture not only in material forms but also as practices and rituals.[17]

How does this notion of materiality of the sacred translate into the *khizana*? Bohra manuscripts, inaccessible yet at the same time very present in believers' daily lives, are the *material manifestations of the immaterial*, eternal and untouchable esoteric truths. Immaterial ideas are thus expressed through material forms: in the culture of the *khizana*, manuscripts are the manifestation of this immateriality. They are tangible objects that, in turn, shape the community because they play such a central role in the dialectics between clerical and non-clerical, royal and non-royal, the *khizana* and the 'rest'. This is exactly how materiality, as Miller puts it, 'remains foundational to people's stance in the world'.[18]

In addition, in the cultivation of an esoteric system of thought that is so foundational to the Bohra knowledge system, yet so incomprehensible and inaccessible to the *ʿamma*, the daily practice of religion, through the form of rituals and pious conformism, becomes even more important in the community. Through its manuscripts, the divine can be apprehended by the scholarly *khassa*, and the circulation of the esoteric truths within the community can be restricted and controlled, thereby maintaining the sacred geography of Badri Mohallah.

Miller emphasises that material forms or artefacts are not stagnant 'things' or 'objects'. Moreover, some can be more material than others, depending on how they are framed in a specific context or the authority and power attributed to them. Material culture, as the powerful foundation for everything in society, should be considered in terms of networks or orders of things.[19] Mapping and defining Alawi material culture thus helps us understand not only why the manuscripts of the *khizana* look the way they do, why they are produced the way they are and why they are used the way they are, but also their social meaning in relation to power dynamics. In the case of the Bohra community, power is clearly connected to access to and custodianship of the *khizana*, as already demonstrated in Chapters 2 and 3. There can thus be plural forms of materiality through the medium of manuscripts.

At the other end of the spectrum, there is immateriality: the absence of material culture, which can be the result of destruction or decay, or a deliberate absence based on the idea that immateriality is spirituality in its highest form.[20] This idea is especially relevant in relation to the languages of Bohra manuscript culture and the absent processes of venularisation of this literary corpus, which are discussed in Chapter 5. The notion of immateriality is also related to the question, what has survived and what has perished and why? This question, which is central to this chapter, is especially relevant to the highly cultivated Arabised nature of Bohra manuscript culture, which, according to the Bhai Sahebs, has been transmitted from Egypt and Yemen and is considered a 'pure' Arabic tradition. Yet, as we see in Chapter 6, manuscripts in the *khizana* contain

[17] See, for an in-depth discussion on the materiality of the sacred, Birgit Meyer, 'Introduction: Material Religion – How Things Matter', in Dick Houtman and Birgit Meyer (eds), *Things: Religion and the Question of Materiality* (New York: Fordham University Press, 2012), 1-23.

[18] Miller, 'Materiality: An Introduction', 2.

[19] Ibid., 3, 15–20.

[20] Ibid., 20–9.

many 'Indian', subcontinental features, such as the use of Persianised scripts, which do not fit into this narrative of a 'pure' Arabic Fatimid–Tayyibi manuscript culture.

4.1 Secret *Khizana*, Social Manuscripts

As described in the previous chapters, Bohra manuscripts in the *khizana* are considered the material form of the eternal sacred Isma'ili truths that have been, according to the narrative of the community, transmitted in their exact and perfect form from God to the community through the uninterrupted chain of the prophets, the infallible Imams, the Tayyibi Dais of Yemen and the Bohra Dais of India. One could argue that this is the immaterial route of knowledge transmission, in which Bohra clerics are a crucial chain: it is via their authority that believers' souls transmigrate to the afterlife, keeping the processes of cyclical time and space going and eventually hastening the return of the hidden Imam on earth. Through their genealogy and custodianship of the *khizana*, the Bhai Sahebs thus play a central role in the immaterial social lives of the esoteric truths from one generation to another.

Alongside this immaterial chain of transmission of knowledge is a material route of transmission, which is the geographical travel and circulation history of Bohra manuscripts and *khizana* culture (see appendix, Figure 4.14). In Chapter 2, we reconstructed the *khizana* history of the Bohras from Fatimid Cairo to Tayyibi Yemen, and from Tayyibi Yemen to Bohra Gujarat, including Ahmedabad and later Baroda. Yet the story of the circulation of Bohra manuscripts and their material social lives as objects does not end there. In fact, focusing on the individual manuscripts of the Alawi *khizana* we encounter dates, names of infallible men and women, scribes and lay persons, structures of authority and power, traces of theft and plunder, (violent) conflicts, natural disasters, relocations of entire collections, and, in the specific case of the Bohras, bifurcations and schisms within the community.

Throughout their material existence, as I argue elsewhere, Bohra manuscripts have rich social lives through their interaction with people and communities over time and space.[21] The material forms of manuscripts and their world of production, circulation and consumption are thus part of the story, and I would not do justice to the Bohra universe in Baroda without covering their multiple social lives that I observed from my peacock throne. Manuscripts are not just vehicles of knowledge; in fact, they have biographies. These biographies reveal not only histories of composition and circulation, but also 'what people do' with their handwritten books and why.[22]

What is the past, present and future of their manuscripts? How did they travel physically or materially as vehicles of Isma'ili knowledge, both on a macro level, connecting intellectual histories of the Arabophone world with the Indian subcontinent, and on a micro level, within the universe of Badri Mohallah or, on an even more confined level, within the space of the *khizana*? And what do the biographies of *khizana* manuscripts tell us about the immaterial travel and consumption of Alawi Bohra manuscripts as sacred objects?

21 Akkerman, 'The Bohra Manuscript Treasury', 182.
22 Ibid., 183.

Every manuscript has its story to tell that, in the case of the *khizana*, begins with its provenance, followed by its commissioning, producing, owning, storing, enshrining, consuming, venerating and, finally, preserving or discarding. Although some manuscripts provide us with valuable information about how they were produced in the Alawi community itself, others were gathered from a wide variety of places such as bazaars, hostels, mausoleums and, as we see, even bathroom cupboards. Storing manuscripts in the extremely humid climate of Gujarat often proves to be extremely challenging, resulting in the dramatic material decay of these vehicles of sacred knowledge. This raises questions about how to dispose of the materiality of sacred manuscripts in a respectful and lawfully permitted way, without discarding the sacred immaterial, esoteric properties of the text. As we see, reconstructing the past of these manuscripts is not only important in understanding the history of the collection of the *khizana*. The biographies of *khizana* manuscripts discussed are also intertwined with the private lives and personal histories of those who administer the domain of the *khizana*: the Bohra clerics and their families but also the community at large.

A Note on Provenance

The Alawi *daʿwa*, as we have seen, can be considered a universe on its own that is extremely closed to outsiders, including the other Bohra communities. No official relations exist between the Alawis in Baroda and the Dawoodis in Surat and Mumbai. Both communities share the mausoleums of their forefathers in Surat and Ahmedabad and tolerate each other's presence, but beyond this limited interaction the two groups are separate. Given the conditions of access to the Alawi *khizana*, one would expect that the manuscript collection would contain exemplars of Alawi provenance only.

However, on scrutinising the manuscripts of the *khizana*, it became clear that a section of the collection is not, in fact, of Alawi provenance, meaning the manuscripts were not all produced or copied by members of the Alawi Bohra community. Many of these manuscripts were obtained from the other Bohra communities, namely the Dawoodis, and the Sulaymanis to some extent, and have been integrated into the collection of the Alawi *khizana*. Together with a corpus of manuscripts and documents of distinctly Alawi provenance, several non-Isma'ili titles in Arabic and a large collection of printed Arabic books, these Dawoodi and Sulaymani manuscripts are part of the composite collection of the *khizana*.

As I described previously, the Alawi Bohra community has always been smaller and less prosperous than the Dawoodi Bohra community. Dawoodi manuscripts are commissioned and produced on a much larger, if not mass-scale through official clerical institutions, with the result that many Dawoodi manuscripts circulate inside and even outside the community (more about this in the following sections). The output of Alawi manuscripts, by contrast, is much more modest in numbers, as manual copying is carried out by the royal family only. Subsequently, its manuscript culture at present it thus a strictly royal manuscript culture and *makhtutat* are accessed by a much smaller audience, simply because the upper clerical establishment of Bhai Sahebs is smaller than that of the *Qasr-e Ali* (the Dawoodi Bhai Sahebs).

Being produced in different communities, Alawi, Sulaymani and Dawoodi manuscripts contain distinct features and therefore represent different Bohra manuscript cultures (for the technical aspects of Bohra manuscript cultures, see Chapter 5). But let us first look at how manuscripts with various provenances were distributed and circulated. How did these texts end up in the Alawi *khizana* collection if no official relations existed between the communities? In what kind of institutions were they copied? How exactly did they circulate? How and in what circumstances did these texts reach the treasury of books? How did they become part of the collection, and how was the material appropriated to the new context? How is a sacred manuscript 'owned', both in the material and the immaterial sense, if it was not written in one's own community? And finally, does an 'alien' Bohra manuscript have the same sacred materiality as a manuscript written in the Alawi universe?

To answer these questions, I divided the *khizana* collection and its manuscript biographies into three categories: (1) manuscripts of Alawi provenance, including 'royal' copies written by the clerical establishment and manuscripts of non-royal provenance, written or stored by the *mu'minin* and *mu'minat* of the Alawi community; (2) manuscripts of Dawoodi provenance; and (3) manuscripts that reached the treasury of books via external routes. The manuscript stories described next are based on two sources: analysis of the marginalia of these manuscripts and oral histories of their collectors. In comparison to manuscripts, the documents of the *khizana* have different materialities, social roles and biographies, and are therefore discussed in the next chapter.

4.2 Manuscripts of Alawi Provenance

The majority of manuscripts of the *khizana* collection are of Alawi provenance.[23] They are titles that were commissioned, copied and circulated within the realm of the Alawi community only, either within clerical circles or, in rare cases, among the people of Badri Mohallah and their family collections. As the sacred Fatimid-Tayyibi heritage and cultural capital of the community, manuscripts of Alawi provenance are considered more sacred than 'imported' manuscripts, because they were transcribed by the 'forefathers' of the community: the semi-infallible pedigree of the Dais. It is strongly believed that the materiality of their *khaṭṭ* (script) has protective and healing powers. I was told that, because of these properties, Alawi Bohra manuscripts have a sacred status that comes close to, but is not the same as, the Qur'an's. Chapter 6 provides a detailed description of the technical aspects that make a manuscript a 'royal' copy and a book hand a 'royal' script. In this section, we focus on the mobility and circulation of manuscripts of Alawi provenance.

Royal Manuscript Stories: A Discovery at the Mausoleum

The Mazoon Saheb confided in me that a few years ago, he visited the mausoleum of his grandfather to offer his *fatiha*, his prayer for his deceased ancestor. While reciting the formula, his attention was drawn to something in the corner: 'heaps of books lying

[23] For reasons of confidentiality, I cannot provide specific numbers.

on the floor of the mausoleum, among them were many cheaply printed Qur'ans, *madrasa* books and some fifteen to sixteen handwritten works!'. The Mazoon Saheb had the piles of 'sacred trash' moved to the *khizana*, where they were restored extensively; he then discovered that many of these manuscripts – which he had never seen before – were written by his grandfather and great-grandfather.[24] These manuscripts were thus not any kind of popular scribbles cast off in the mausoleum, but were actual 'royal' copies. Interestingly, the Mazoon Saheb was clearly surprised by his 'discovery' in the mausoleum, which implies that he himself was initially not aware of the practice of discarding manuscripts. When I asked him why people disposed of their family collections at the mausoleum, he gave the following answer:

> 'They [believers] do not go for throwing specially, but [the manuscripts apparently] went into the mausoleum because it is a holy place. What we do now, we collect every year discarded Quran al-Karim and other books, which are old and of cheap quality and they have to be replaced every ten to fifteen years, from the mausoleum and just put [the] heaps of these things thrown in the lake or buried in *qabaristan*, we bury, bury!'
>
> 'Really?' I asked. 'But why?'
>
> 'See Olly', the Mazoon Saheb answered, 'why will you keep these things [as non-clerics], how many cupboards do you require? Also, we [Alawi Bohras] throw in unused well; we throw it.'
>
> 'But throwing [the manuscripts] in water is not haram?' I asked.
>
> 'No no no!' the Mazoon Saheb said while shaking his head. 'Because you are just keeping in that place which will not cause its disrespect.'
>
> 'I see, and the lake is a respectful place?' I asked.
>
> 'Yes', he nodded.
>
> 'And [what about] burning?' I asked.
>
> The Mazoon Saheb answered while shaking his head: 'No, no we don't burn.'

As it so happened, a week before I had this conversation with the Mazoon Saheb, the city of Baroda had been preparing for Ganpati Dussehra, the Hindu festival in honour of Ganesha that is celebrated widely in South Asia. Gujarat is especially known for its elaborate Dussehra celebrations of Ganpati, and every year cities such as Baroda and Ahmedabad are full of makeshift shrines dedicated to the elephant deity. Towards the end of the week, the Ganpati idols, some small and some very large, are taken on processions, accompanied by music and chants, to the nearest body of water in which they are ritually immersed and slowly dissolve (Figure 4.1). Whereas in cities such as Mumbai the Indian Ocean is near, in Baroda the nearest body of water is Sursagar Lake, which is in the middle of the Old City. While under the watchful eye of Ali Bhai and among thousands of believers, I observed how the giant elephant idols were hoisted into the water with cranes, amid chanting and the explosion of firecrackers.

24 Adina Hoffman and Peter Cole introduced the term 'sacred trash' in the context of the Cairo *geniza*, a term that seems to be extremely fitting for the manuscript material found at the mausoleum. Adina Hoffman and Peter Cole, *Sacred Trash: The Lost and Found World of the Cairo Geniza* (New York: Schocken, 2011).

Figure 4.1 Dissolving the sacred: pictures taken during the Ganpati Dussehra, 2013, in Baroda. Left: boys in Mandvi carrying a small Ganesha idol, while chanting, on their way to the Sursagar Lake. Right: another Ganesha idol is lifted by a crane into the water of the lake.

I also encountered a similar practice when I visited a Shi'i *roza* (shrine) in Hyderabad where discarded authoritative books such as *Nahj al-Baldgha*, al-Kāfī's *Kulaynī* and other old books with pictures of Khomeini and other *mullahs* were thrown into what looked like a small *geniza*, shaped in the form of an unused well, next to the shrine building (Figure 4.2). The term '*geniza*' (archive, repository for old religious items) is derived from the Hebrew verb '*ganaz*', meaning 'to hide', 'to retain', 'to guard' and 'to place in safekeeping'. The best-known repository is the Jewish *geniza* in the old city of Fustat, Cairo, which is not only a repository of Judaeo-Arabic sources on the social history of the Jewish community but is also linked to the shared Arab past of the Bohras, since it holds a great number of Arabic Fatimid documents.[25]

Having witnessed the practice of immaterialising the divine, especially in the context of the Ganpati idols, I could not help but wonder whether there was a link with the Alawis' practice of disposing their sacred manuscripts in lakes, rivers and wells. The Mazoon Saheb nodded his head in agreement and said, 'Yes, it is possible', muttering something about his forefathers. Then he showed me the manuscripts he had rescued at the mausoleum with a proud smile. The majority of the manuscripts were more than a hundred years old; all were written by 'royal' hands, such as by his great-great-grandfather Sy. Naẓar ʿAlī (no. 40, d. 1296/1879) and great-grandfather

[25] See for the latest research on the Cairo *geniza* documents: Rustow, *The Lost Archive: Traces of a Caliphate in a Cairo Synagogue*.

Figure 4.2 Discarding sacred trash. Pictures of the Darul Shifa Jama Masjid and *roza* in Hyderabad, including its small *geniza* well with discarded books.

Sy. Fakhr al-Dīn (no. 41, d. 1347/1929). These manuscripts were written in very sophisticated hands, and contained royal doxology, elaborate readers' notes, transmission statements, copy-statements and (circular or octangular) owner statements, and stamps in Arabic. Some of the manuscript titles were extremely rare and were added to the *khizana* collection.[26] However, most manuscripts found at the mausoleum were popular titles, such as *Niṣf al-Layl, Khatm al-Qurra, Ṣaḥīfāt* (prayer books), and several

[26] For reasons of confidentiality, I cannot elaborate on the titles of these rare works.

manuals on the holy month of Muharram. Even though all the works were written in Arabic, several codices contained elaborate translations in the margins in Gujarati. These popular manuscripts were also used as diaries and personal notebooks, as could be traced in the paratexts. The margins, inside covers, flyleaves, bindings, colophons and incipits were full of personal notes, multi-lingual writing exercises, phone numbers, cartoon stickers and other 'treasures'. These marginalia of the collection of manuscripts found at the mausoleum showed clearly that it was a common practice to note down personal matters in manuscripts during the time before manufactured paper was widely available in Badri Mohallah.

Sacred Dust: The Story of the Water Tank

As the lake, well and mausoleums stories illustrate, the material circulation of manuscripts ends when parts of the treasury of books are discarded as sacred trash or, following Carolyn Steedman, turn into dust.[27] It is for this reason that the collection of the *khizana* is in a constant state of flux. Although at times its holdings are enriched with fresh material or older royal copies that are accidentally discovered, Bohra manuscripts also cease to exist due to the humid climate of Gujarat, which causes fungi and mould, especially during monsoon season. Another major problem is created by termites, which tend to attack the manuscripts in great numbers. Termites in Gujarat, I experienced first-hand, come in many different shapes and sizes. Whereas some prefer living on human beings, others lay their eggs in manuscripts (usually in the spine), anticipating that the larvae have enough food to grow, as they eat away the spine, binding and paper. This, however, is quite a slow process that usually only affects the outer corners and sometimes the margins of the manuscript leaves, but does not harm the text itself. However, there are more aggressive termite species that are capable of eating away entire houses, furniture and libraries in a matter of hours, chewing their way through entire codices, as the following manuscript story illustrates.

The Mazoon Saheb told me that the royal *haveli* was once besieged by this feared termite during the *ʿaṣr* (reign) of his great-grandfather, Sy. Fakhr al-Din, in the 1950s. At that time, termites 'ate' a very large part of the royal wooden *haveli*, together with most of the manuscript collection, including some of its oldest and most valuable works. The manuscripts were damaged so severely that that they could no longer stay in the *khizana*, but since they were sacred objects they also could not be burnt or thrown away. The Bhai Sahebs decided that, instead of opting for a lake far away from the *mohallah*, the most respectful way to get rid of the manuscripts would be to pulverise them and dissolve the 'sacred dust' in the water tank of the mosque. It was believed that for years believers were blessed by drinking water from this tank, literally drinking the sacred book hands of the late Dais.[28]

The clerics still refer to the collection of the treasury of books 'before the attack' and 'after the attack'. Even though there is little one can do to prevent these extensive

[27] The term 'dust' was introduced by Carolyn Steedman, *Dust: The Archive and Cultural History* (Brunswick, NJ: Rutgers University Press, 2002), ix.

[28] The talismanic function of manuscripts is discussed in more detail in Chapter 5.

termite attacks, several precautions have been taken by the clerics. Since the 'attack' all manuscripts are stored in iron cupboards instead of wooden ones and are dusted and inspected every week for termites. Moreover, the floors of the royal *haveli*, which used to be made of cow dung (which attracts termites), have been replaced by cement. In addition to the *kabikaj* formulae (See Chapter 5) written in the incipits of the codices, local preservation techniques are used, such as placing *neem* leaves between manuscript leaves (mostly between the first folios and two between the second folio) to protect the paper (Figure 2.5). The usage of *neem* leaves is a rather recent development because the Bhai Sahebs were hitherto unaware of their protective properties; the Mazoon Saheb told me that he instituted the practice after finding the leaves in Dawoodi manuscripts that were in surprisingly good condition.

Mothballs and pouches stuffed with rice (against humidity) are also placed in the cupboards to protect the manuscripts. These precautions, however, seem to have had little effect. Chemicals and technology to treat the manuscripts properly (such as fumigation boxes) are either not available or are too costly. Several institutions, such as representatives from the India Manuscript Centre in Delhi, have visited the *khizana* and offered to treat the manuscripts with chemicals and restore them free of charge in exchange for microfilms of the material. The Bhai Sahebs refused the offer because, they reasoned, it would be against 'our *taqiyya*'. 'Our *taqiyya*', as noted, is the social glue of the community and enables the clerics to keep Alawi Bohra manuscript culture alive. Yet, if the Bhai Sahebs keep refusing help from outside their universe, the Alawi Bohra literary heritage will slowly vanish.

Recently, the question was revisited by the Bhai Sahebs of how to get rid of the remains of destroyed manuscripts in a respectful way. According to the clerics the Isma'ili legal tradition does not provide guidance on this issue; it merely prescribes rules on how to store the Qur'an. As noted, Bohra manuscripts enjoy a sacred status close to that of the Qur'an since they were once composed and copied by the holy men of the community. Simply throwing manuscripts outside the window with the rest of the trash, which is a common practice in Badri Mohallah, is thus out of the question. The clerics decided that similar rules applied to manuscripts as to the Qur'an, and so they ruled that the residues of the codices be discarded in the water tank of the *jamaat khana*, basing this on the reasoning that all believers who would drink from the water tank would be blessed with the sacred words (the ink) of the texts. This practice has been continued by the clerics ever since. When I heard this story, I realised that – without knowing its properties – I too had drunk the sacred dust of the manuscripts on my many visits to the *jamaat khana*. The story shows strong similarities with widespread traditions of Qur'anic healing, in Muslim contexts and beyond, where patients literally drink and digest the ink of the words of the holy book prescribed by a *sheikh* or a *ḥakīm* (local physician).[29]

[29] These practices are often carried out by drinking water mixed with paper with Qur'anic verses written on it, or drinking the ink itself, which is washed from a tablet or other object. See, for more information on Islamic healing in the African context, Lisa Mackenrodt, *Swahili Spirit Possession and Islamic Healing in Contemporary Tanzania* (Hamburg: Kovac Verlag, 2011), or, from a historical perspective, Seema Alavi, *Loss and Recovery of an Indo-Muslim Medical Tradition: 1600–1900* (Palgrave: Macmillan, 2008).

Family Collections: The Story of the Bathroom Cupboard

The following manuscript story is another example of sacred trash. A few years back, a student of the Mazoon Saheb brought in a manuscript leaf of a rare *sahifa* work to the *majlis*. The Mazoon Saheb, intrigued by this mysterious folio, asked him if he had more leaves, but the boy said no. After the *majlis* ended, the Mazoon Saheb accompanied the boy to his family *manzil* where they discovered an entire manuscript scattered in a mouldy bathroom cupboard. Due to the humidity of the bathroom, the folios were in a very bad condition, for the house owner had left them there for generations, not realising their value. With the permission of the owner, the leaves were taken to the royal *haveli* where 'ample time was put in restoring it to its former glory'.[30] It took the Mazoon Saheb, the Mukasir Saheb and the Mazoon Saheb's wife three years to re-arrange all the leaves according to the catchwords that were mentioned in the margins (the work, like most manuscripts, was neither paginated nor foliated). According to the Mazoon Saheb, the most difficult task was to identify the title of the work, since the title page and colophon were missing.

After comparing the leaves to several other manuscript copies, the Arabic words '*ʿalā kulluhā* ', which were written on the first surviving folio, were an important clue that revealed the title in the end.[31] After solving this codicological riddle, the Mazoon Saheb was able to copy the title page and the other missing pages and complete the manuscript. To ensure that the work would never be lost again, the Mazoon Saheb prepared another 'fresh' exemplar by hand.

According to the Mazoon Saheb, since so many members of the royal family were engaged in restoring the manuscript, it was 'a great family project' and they 'took great pride in restoring the work in its original glory together'. It is known that in Dawoodi families – the Hamdanis and the Qutbuddins, for example – women are involved in manuscript reading, collation, and even manual copying.[32] This practice is unheard of in the Alawi community. The ''*ala kulluha* manuscript', however, seems to be an exception in this regard for it was the only Alawi Bohri manuscript restoration project in which an Alawi Bohri woman was involved. However, the Mazoon Saheb's wife's involvement in manuscript preservation was only short-lived. Very soon after the restoration, she died a very sudden death. The Mazoon Saheb told me that he has rather mixed feelings about the '*ala kulluha* manuscript because, on the one hand, it represents the success of his attempts to preserve Bohri manuscripts (with very limited means), but on the other it reminds him of his late beloved wife every time he comes across it.

This story shows how much personal lives and histories are connected to the manuscripts in the *khizana*. The manuscripts of Alawi provenance in particular have a very personal significance for the Bhai Sahebs since they were written by generations of people who were not only considered charismatic leaders of the community but were also their own grandfathers, uncles, brothers and sons – their loved and often lost ones, such as Bhai Sahebs who were severely injured or killed during the Gujarat riots

30 Conversation with the Mazoon Saheb, Badri Mohallah, 23 October 2013.

31 It is the wish of the Bhai Sahebs that the actual title of the work remains undisclosed.

32 Although rare, the Hamdani catalogue lists female copyists. De Blois, *Arabic, Persian, and Gujarati Manuscripts*, xiv.

in 2002. The Mazoon's story revealed his sense of immense pride and competition as a collector and heritage custodian. He reasoned that even though the Alawis are a small and not very wealthy community (as the Dawoodis are), the Mazoon Saheb himself was able to restore the heritage of the community with very humble means.

Furthermore, the story also justifies the *daʿwa* policy of obtaining manuscripts from private Alawi collections and enshrining them in the treasury of books. The Alawi Bohras do not carry out the practice, however, of confiscating (without the permission of the family) private manuscripts after a community member dies, as is customary among the Dawoodis.[33] Yet, community members are strongly encouraged by the Bhai Sahebs to donate their handwritten books to the *khizana* where the manuscripts are then stored and preserved. 'This is better', Mazoon Saheb said, 'because our *mu'minin* and *mu'minat* do not know what to do with the manuscripts since they cannot read the Arabic.'

The donation of their manuscripts, he further explained, gives believers *thawwab*, a reward in the afterlife. This is an interesting social fact: the gifting or perhaps even endowing of manuscripts to the treasury of books as commodities thus guarantees a spiritual reward in exchange. The tradition of generating merit by having sacred manuscripts copied and donated to libraries can also be historically traced among Hindu, Buddhist and Jain communities.[34] In Badri Mohallah, manuscripts are thus either donated voluntarily or (rarely) sold by community members, sometimes even 'entire suitcases' of them.[35] The condition of these manuscripts when they reach the *khizana*, however, is often very poor because they are found in the most extraordinary places, such as bathroom cupboards or, even worse, in the trash. Many of the manuscripts that make their way (back) into the treasury of books are often in such a bad condition that it is impossible to identify, let alone use them.

Circulation of Alawi Manuscripts

The stories of the Mazoon Saheb's discoveries of manuscripts raise questions in relation to the hypothesis of the inaccessible treasury of books and the '*taqiyyafication*' of Bohra manuscripts. For instance, how did manuscripts of 'royal' orthography come into circulation outside the *khizana*? Were they taken from the *khizana*, or were they produced elsewhere and therefore never part of its collection in the first place? Why was there such a great demand for Arabic manuscripts in the community, and from whom? The Bhai Sahebs explained to me that a century ago the transmission of religious knowledge only occurred via two channels: the Bohra *madrasa* system, and via popular handwritten books. The Mukasir Saheb explained, 'Around that time there was no education system in Baroda; the only institutionalized education believers received was their *"taʿlīm"* [*zahiri* education] in the *madrasa*.' As a result, believers were versed in all languages that were written in the Arabic script, including Arabic, Persian, Urdu and *Lisan al-Daʿwa*. With the exception of poetry, which was written in Urdu and *Lisan al-Daʿwa*, all religious books that were meant to be read (thus *not batini* texts) were written in Arabic. Popular family manuscript collections must thus

[33] Anonymous interviews conducted with members of the Dawoodi Bohra community.

[34] Wendy Doniger, *The Hindus: An Alternative History* (London: Penguin, 2010), 220.

[35] Conversation with the Mazoon Saheb, Badri Mohallah, 28 November 2013.

have consisted of several standard religious *zahiri* works in Arabic that were consulted frequently on matters of daily religious life.

This, however, was before the introduction of the printing press in colonial India in the early nineteenth century (see Chapter 5.1 for the impact of the printing press on manuscript culture), when popular religious books were only available in manuscript form.[36] The only individuals in the community who were authorised to copy these popular texts (and were trained to do so) were the sons of the Dais, who earned their living by copying parts of Bohra popular literature. *Al-Ṣaḥīfat al-ʿAlawiyyat al-Ṭayyibiyya* – the Bohra interpretation of the *Ṣaḥīfa al-Sajjādiyya*, the famous Shi'i prayer book attributed to Imam Zayn al-ʿĀbidīn (the great-grandson of the Prophet Muhammad) – is an example of a popular text that circulated within the community. Until recently, Arabic, *Lisan al-Daʿwa* and Urdu were to a certain extent the Bohra devotional languages, and manuscripts were the only vehicle of Bohra popular religious knowledge. The Mazoon Saheb once explained, 'For one or two rupees they [the Bhai Sahebs] were writing heaps of pages in Arabic, earning their bread; for instance, each and every family had a copy of the *Sahifat* copied by the son of a Dai.' One may speculate that the copying of manuscript titles on demand was in some cases not always restricted to *zahiri* texts and that some clerics would have been more than happy to copy *batini* material for a few extra rupees.

The introduction of the printing press and secular education to the Indian subcontinent brought an end to the high demand for popular handwritten Bohra manuscripts. The handwritten word lost its significance for the younger generation of believers who did not read Arabic. Private manuscript collections were therefore no longer seen as accessible or practical sources of religious knowledge. This is how many Bohra handwritten Arabic texts ended up in bathroom cupboards, lakes and mausoleums, or were sold for a few rupees to *pastiwalas* (vendors of discarded newspapers and books). Another factor that played a role in the disposal of manuscripts was the lack of physical space for community members to store their collections at home. The demand, and therefore the tradition, of manuscript production of popular Bohra works died out entirely.

Handwritten popular Bohra texts lost their significance even more as soon as these *zahiri* titles were edited, translated and printed into the vernacular Gujarati and, in some cases, even Hindi by the Dawoodi Bohras in Mumbai in the early nineteenth century. For instance, the Hindi translation of *Daʿa'im al-Islam*, the main compendium of Isma'ili *fiqh*, can be found in every Bohra home today. Younger generations of Alawi Bohras preferred printed editions that were not only cheaper and widely available but also much easier to read. Vernacular languages, such as Gujarati and a simplified version of *Lisan al-Daʿwa*, became the new popular devotional language of the Bohra communities. The disappearance of Arabic as the main language of Bohra popular religious discourse, both in printed literature and oral ceremonies, is part of a larger development in the Indian subcontinent in the twentieth century in which vernacular languages replaced traditional languages (more about this in Chapter 5).[37] This is, however, not

[36] A vernacular press in Gujarati was established in 1812 in Bombay. See Horace I. Poleman, 'Serial Publications in India', *Quarterly Journal of Current Acquisitions* 1 (1943): 23–30.

[37] For a more in-depth study on this development, see for example Farina Mir, *The Social Space of Language: Vernacular Culture in British Colonial Punjab* (Berkeley: University of California Press, 2010).

the case with *batini* manuscripts and the manuscript culture of the *khizana*, where Arabic is still the only language of writing, reading and the transmission of knowledge.

4.3 Manuscripts of Non-Alawi Provenance

In addition to producing manuscripts in the Alawi community, generations of Alawi Bhai Sahebs have devoted their lives to enriching the collection of the *khizana* by importing Bohra Isma'ili manuscripts via external and informal scholarly networks. 'Alien' manuscripts, either of Dawoodi or Sulaymani Indian provenance, are, with a few exceptions, always transmitted in Arabic. Whereas manuscripts of Dawoodi provenance are plentiful, Sulaymani manuscripts are rare.[38] All manuscripts of Sulaymani provenance in Baroda contain 'royal' autographs and colophons ending either with '*min ra'īs Sulaymānīyya*' (Ar.; 'from the head of the Sulaymanis') or '*min al-firqat al-Sulaymānīyya*' (Ar.; 'from the community of the Sulaymanis'), in the hand of the Mazoon Saheb. The paratexts of these manuscripts do not give any indication of how exactly they became part of the treasury of books. It should be noted that ties between the Sulaymani and Alawi Bohras have recently been re-established after the Mazoon Saheb and the Mukasir Saheb visited the Sulaymani clergy in Hyderabad. The Sulaymani clerical establishment are aware that their Alawi colleagues possess some of their manuscripts and they do not object to this.

The presence of manuscripts of Dawoodi provenance came about quite differently. The difference in attitude towards Sulaymani and Dawoodi manuscripts in the treasury of books can be traced back to the relations between the communities and their social-political position in Gujarat. The Alawis have nothing to fear from the Sulaymanis since they are a small community, their headquarters are not in India but in Yemen, and they are not extremely wealthy, which means their political influence is only minimal: both communities are on good terms. Relations with the Dawoodis, in contrast, have been strained, especially since the recent destruction of the tomb of Sy. Ali Shamsuddin by the Dawoodis in Ahmedabad (see Chapter 1). The Alawis also claim that the Dawoodis were responsible for looting their manuscripts in the decades following the bifurcation in the eleventh/seventeenth century. There are no official relations between the two communities, and thus Dawoodi manuscripts made it into the Alawi *khizana* through unofficial channels.

The presence of Dawoodi and Sulaymani manuscripts in the collection of the treasury of books does not fit into the Alawis' narrative of there being separate universes since they were separated by earlier schisms. The materiality of these manuscripts and the manuscript cultures they represent show us a different picture of fluidity, connectedness and exchange between these three Bohra *da'was*; they also indicate what Anne Stoler calls 'the uncertainty of the archive' or, in this case, the uncertainty or perhaps the 'anxiety of the *khizana*'.[39] How do the Alawi Bhai Sahebs deal with the somewhat contested provenance and biographies of these manuscripts in their collection, both epistemically and materially?

[38] The exact number of Dawoodi manuscripts cannot be disclosed, for reasons of secrecy.

[39] Stoler, *Along the Archival Grain*, 4, 37.

Before we can answer this question, we must first understand the social context in which Dawoodi manuscripts are produced and consumed. The Dawoodi community is much larger than the Alawi one, and thus there are more initiated clerics who read and are authorised to access *batini* manuscripts. Therefore, the number of Dawoodi manuscripts in circulation is larger and is officially regulated by the Dawoodi *daʿwa*. Manuscripts are produced and distributed in the Dawoodi community via two authorised channels: the *Jamea tus Saifiyah*, and official Dawoodi Bohra copying and publishing houses.

The official institution of higher religious education for the Dawoodi Bohras is the Jamea tus Saifiyah in Surat (also known in Arabic as the *al-Jami'at al-Sayfiyya*), established in 1814, which also has branches in Karachi and Nairobi.[40] As part of their religious training, Dawoodi students, both male and female, copy *zahiri* manuscripts by hand at the Jamea tus Saifiyah. Only those students who are granted special access to *ʿilm al-batin* by the Dai are allowed to copy esoteric books by hand. I was told that, upon completion, the manuscript copies are donated to the school *khizana*. However, many exemplars ended up in private collections and reached the Alawi *khizana* via this channel. The incipits of Jamea tus Saifiyah manuscripts often read '*kutiba fī Daras Sayfiyya*' (Ar.; 'written in the Daras Sayfiyya') and contain a square-shaped Jamea tus Saifiyah stamp.[41] Even though the Jamea tus Saifiyah is considered an accredited institution of education by the Indian state, the university is not accessible to non-Bohris: only Dawoodis who have taken the *ʿahd* and thus have become *mu'minin* and *mu'minat* can receive an education there. According to the Mazoon Saheb, the Jamea tus Saifiyah has secret 'cells' where manuscripts of the highest *batini* level are stored and are only accessible to the Dai.

Professional Dawoodi manuscript copies, by contrast, are copied by authorised *daʿwa* scribes. The Dawoodis have institutionalised the copying of manuscripts by establishing regulated headquarters where professional and 'trustworthy' scribes continuously copy both lower level *batini* and *zahiri* works in Arabic. Treatises copied by these professional scribes are available to believers, who are granted authorised access via a card system (according to their level of initiation). These cards, I was told by my Dawoodi interlocutors, which function as an electronic identity card system, are registered and controlled by local *ʿamils* (cleric of the local *mullahs*), who only grant access to believers belonging to 'trustworthy' families who are initiated to read these texts.[42] Community members, let alone those outside the fold of the Dawoodi *daʿwa* (excommunicates and non-*mu'minin and mu'minat*), do not have access to these texts. Since the number of Dawoodi believers who read these texts (and have a good command of Arabic) is much larger than the number of Alawis similarly situated, it is impossible to provide all believers with manuscript copies. Yet, because the Dawoodis also wish to keep their handwritten book culture alive, they have come up with a clever codicological solution to avoid printing materials. The manuscript copies of

[40] Qutbuddin, 'Bohras', 62. For more information, see the official website of the Jamea tus Saifiyah: http://www.jameasaifiyah.edu/ (last accessed 22 March 2015). Mustafa Abdulhussein, 'Al-Jāmiʿah al-Sayfīyah', in John Louis Esposito (ed.), *The Oxford Encyclopedia of the Modern Islamic World* (New York, Oxford University Press, 1995), Vol. 2, 360–1.

[41] *Daras Sayfiyya* is the old name of the Jamea tus Saifiyah.

[42] Access to the various layers of the Dawoodi *da'wa*, as its *batini* texts, is, in fact, arranged through this ID card system. See Blank, *Mullahs on the Mainframe*, 180–3.

the *da'wa* scribes, including their incipits, stamps, catchwords, and colophons, pagination and footnotes, are photocopied by an official Dawoodi publishing house and then bound and published in beautiful editions. The Dawoodis could easily have had these texts digitised and printed, but the fact that they remain faithful to manuscript copies, even though printed as facsimiles, highlights the importance of the materiality of the handwritten word over the printed, especially for *batini* texts. The *khatt* of these publications is so consistent that one would never suspect these publications are handwritten (Figure 4.3).[43]

The system of access and identity cards is thus designed to control the circulation of *batini* texts and restrict the mobility of these books outside the initiated circles of the Dawoodi community. There is, however, a great demand for these editions outside the Dawoodi universe, for three reasons. Firstly, according to the Mazoon Saheb, the editions are of excellent quality, as is evident in both the penmanship and the editing. Secondly, the Dawoodis publish a wide range of rare esoteric treatises that otherwise would not be available. Thirdly, the handwritten editions are considered authoritative by Alawi clerics because they are copied from manuscripts that are often extremely

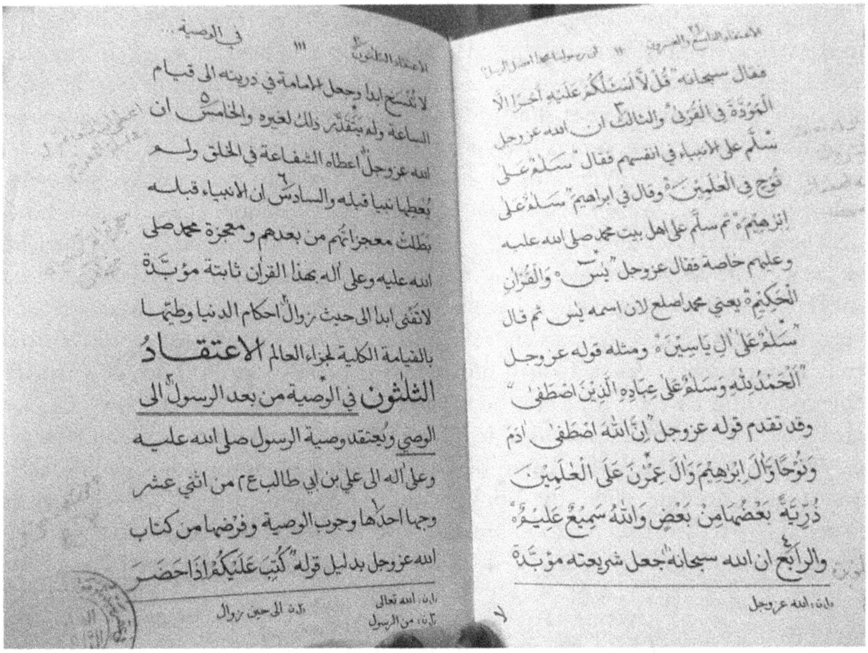

Figure 4.3 Hand-copied yet photocopied Jamea tus Saifiyah edition, including catchwords, pagination and footnotes, with an Alawi *khizana* stamp on the left folio and marginal notes by the Mazoon Saheb in pencil.

[43] A similar discussion is highlighted by Brinkley Messick in *The Calligraphic State*, where he describes the Ottomans' initial refusal in the early eighteenth century to print sacred texts such as the Qur'an and hadith, for they would no longer be considered *scriptures* if not transmitted by hand. Messick, *Calligraphic State*, Ch. 6, 'Print Culture', 115–16.

old. The older the text is in the manuscript culture of the Bohras, the more authoritative it is considered to be, especially when it dates to the Yemeni period. However, a critical apparatus of some kind, including information on the editorial choices made by Dawoodi scribes and on which manuscripts are used as the mother texts for these editions, does not exist. Even though there is a strict Dawoodi policy of accessing (meaning buying) these editions, there are ways to acquire these texts via non-official channels, and many of these Dawoodi editions entered the Alawi *khizana*.

In addition to the Jamea tus Saifiyah, the royal house of the late Dawoodi Dai *Sy.* Burhan al-Din also has its private *khizana* in Surat, which has a similar, if not stricter, policy of access; this *khizana* supposedly houses ten thousand manuscripts.[44] According to insiders who would like to stay anonymous, the collection contains many unknown Isma'ili treatises that would – if made public – turn 'everything we know so far of the history of the Fatimids and Isma'ili history completely upside down'. Unfortunately, absolutely nothing is known about this private *khizana*, and Dawoodi clerics try their absolute best to maintain the policy of *taqiyya*. Manuscript copies of royal Dawoodi provenance never leave the royal family *khizana*, or at least not Dawoodi clerical circles, and access to manuscripts is given to scholars only under the rarest of circumstances.

Manuscripts of Dawoodi 'non-royal' provenance, by contrast, have been reproduced extensively and represent the majority of Dawoodi manuscripts in the Alawi *khizana*. Another source of Dawoodi manuscript production in the past was the private collections of scholarly families. The most famous example is that of the Hamdani family. Many Hamdani manuscripts 'paved the way' into the Alawi treasury of books. As noted in the previous chapter, most Bohra family collections in South Asia were either donated to academic institutions or confiscated by the Dawoodi clerical establishment.

So how exactly did these Dawoodi manuscripts enter the *khizana* 'under the table'? The answer the Mazoon Saheb gave me was very simple: 'many have been bought from Dawoodi Bohras, but others have been gifted'. According to the Mazoon Saheb, several times Dawoodis donated entire suitcases of works to the Alawi *khizana* completely unexpectedly. When I asked him why these Dawoodis had not donated these manuscripts to their own Mazoon, he replied that since the Dawoodi Bohra *daʿwa* is such a large bureaucratic institution, it is impossible to even get an appointment with the Mazoon or the Mukasir. These believers wanted to donate their family collections to an institution where the books would be preserved with care, and so they donated them to the Alawi Mazoon or Mukasir instead. Finally, a substantial number of Dawoodi manuscripts were purchased via the personal network of the Mazoon Saheb.

The Life Story of the Mazoon Saheb

The biographies of *khizana* manuscripts are not merely anecdotal histories: they are deeply entangled with the life stories of the Bhai Sahebs not only as clerics but also as manuscript collectors. Furthermore, as the following story illustrates, they also reveal inter-communal manuscript networks and encounters.

[44] Qutbuddin, 'The Da'udi Bohra Tayyibis', 343. Following the schism in the Dawoodi community, it is currently unclear what the state of affairs is concerning the royal *khizana*.

One afternoon, the Mazoon Saheb and I sat together discussing the colophons of several manuscripts, when he offered me a glimpse into his personal archive. As mentioned in the introduction to this chapter, we could literally sit for hours together 'talking manuscripts', a passion that he had developed not only while virtually growing up in the treasury of books but also as an Islamic Studies scholar, or 'Orientalist' as he refers to himself. When the Mazoon Saheb was a child, he told me, there was no institutionalised Alawi training programme for the sons of the royal family. It was therefore decided by the his father that the Mazoon Saheb, who bore the name Bhai Saheb Valiullah Taiyeb Ziyauddin at that time, was to be trained outside the community, in a discipline that would complement his future position in the ranks of the *daʿwa*. It was decided that at the age of nineteen (which was thirty-five years ago) the Mazoon Saheb would be sent off to Mumbai to pursue his studies in Arabic and Islamic Studies at Mumbai University.

It is customary in the Alawi royal family that the sons of the royal household, and thus possible future Dais, leave their privileged royal lives as teenagers and are sent far away from Badri Mohallah to study; there are given very little money and live under modest circumstances. The Mazoon Saheb told me that he lived on only a few rupees a day. Because the curriculum of Islamic Studies did not cover any Isma'ili topics, the Mazoon Saheb also received training in secret from a Dawoodi *ʿamil* in Mumbai who was willing to introduce him to *ʿilm al-haqa'iq* in exchange for a small tuition fee. It was during his Mumbai years that the Mazoon Saheb composed a list of Isma'ili works and secondary literature that one day he wished to acquire for the *khizana* of his father. The Mazoon Saheb showed me his list, which he still carries with him wherever he goes today, together with all his primary school, high school and university documents (Figure 4.4).

Figure 4.4 The personal archive of student identity cards of the Mazoon Saheb.

Despite the hardships in Mumbai, the Mazoon Saheb became so enthralled by his courses in Islamic Studies that he wrote to his father that he wished to pursue an academic degree abroad. Even though he succeeded in obtaining a PhD offer from an American university (which was a dream for the Mazoon Saheb, who had never left the subcontinent), he was not able to pursue his ambition because nobody in the community was willing to sponsor his trip to the USA. The Mazoon Saheb was thus forced to return to Badri Mohallah where his royal training was taken over by the Dai himself, who taught him 'everything he knew'. After finishing his training, Bhai Saheb Valiullah Taiyeb Ziyauddin was appointed the Mazoon Saheb and was granted the title Ḥātim al-Khayrāt Rabīʿal-Barakāt Ma'dhūn (Mazoon) Mawlā Sayyidī Ḥātim Zakī al-Dīn Sāḥib (Saheb). The Mazoon Saheb in turn trained his brothers, the current Mukasir Saheb and the Ra's ul Hodood, in classical Arabic. As for training the next generation of Bhai Sahebs, instead of sending his eldest son, the *mansus*, Saʿīd al-Khayr to Mumbai, the Mazoon Saheb decided to send him to Qum to study Arabic and Islamic Studies.[45]

After listening to the life story of the Mazoon Saheb, I realised that his biography as a scholar and cleric is of great relevance to the history of the *khizana*: it provides unique information on the making of the treasury of books. Disappointed by not being able to pursue an academic career, the Mazoon Saheb shifted his focus entirely to the *daʿwa*'s treasury of books; he was able to track down Bohra manuscripts all over the subcontinent. Today, the list he once composed in Mumbai as a student has almost been completed. In addition, a very large number of manuscripts reached Badri Mohallah via the Mazoon Saheb's Dawoodi teacher from Mumbai, which is a story in itself.

At a certain point during his training, the Mazoon Saheb was asked by his Dawoodi teacher to hide several manuscripts from Dawoodi clerics who had found out about his collection and were planning to 'loot his property'. The Mazoon Saheb did as he was told, and after hiding the texts for a couple of days in his boys' hostel, the *ʿamil* decided to sell his collection to his pupil. This set of Dawoodi manuscripts was the Mazoon Saheb's first contribution to the collection of the *khizana*, which has grown extensively ever since. To honour the memory of his teacher, the 'Mumbai manuscripts' can be recognised by the presence of his name and the donation statement in Arabic on the first flyleaves and the endpapers of these manuscripts.

Hamdani Manuscripts

The Alawi *khizana* contains an extensive collection of Dawoodi manuscripts produced by the Hamdanis, the influential scholarly family from Yemen described earlier in Chapter 2. This eminent Bohra scholarly family traces its roots to the Hamdan tribe in the region of Haraz, the mountainous stronghold of Tayyibi Isma'ilism in Yemen. The

[45] It is impossible for Bohras to study Arabic or theology at religious institutions in the the Sunni-Arab world, such as al-Azhar University or the Islamic University of Medina, due to their Shi'i-Isma'ili denomination.

family emigrated from Yemen to Gujarat in the mid-eighteenth century, taking along with them their extensive private manuscript collection.[46] The more recent generations of Hamdanis – Sumaiya Hamdani, her late father Prof. Abbas Hamdani and his father the late Husayn F. Hamdani (1901–1962) – have made important contributions to the field of Isma'ili Studies in their own right by publishing critical editions and monographs and by opening their private *khizana* to researchers, such as Vladimir Ivanow and Paul Kraus.[47]

Of all the Bohra manuscript cultures we discussed thus far, the Hamdani manuscripts have had most eventful social lives, ending up all over the world in academic institutions and in the royal Dawoodi and Alawi *khizana*.[48] The majority of these manuscripts were officially donated, but others were taken, as I was told, 'without authorization' from the Hamdani family *khizana* and disappeared for decades.[49] A small number of these manuscripts were rediscovered by Abbas Hamdani upon a visit to the Tübingen University library. The questionable circumstances under which these manuscripts had been procured, however, were not known by the university at the time of acquisition. Instead of reclaiming the manuscripts, the Hamdanis decided to donate their heritage to Tübingen University for research.[50]

In addition to being subjected to theft and donation, manuscripts from the Hamdani *khizana* were also sold in economically dire times. The Manzoon Saheb told me that, since he was a child, he had been in close contact with the uncle of the earlier-mentioned Abbas Hamdani, who at some point sold him 'heaps of manuscripts' for 3,000 rupees (about 35 euros). Because the Alawi clerics actually know exactly where these manuscripts came from, and they were copied by a family of very good reputation, Hamdani manuscripts are considered to be extremely authoritative and valuable.

Hamdani manuscripts are easily distinguishable from other Bohra manuscripts of the *khizana* collection by their exquisite deer-hide gilded bindings; beautiful, clean and neat hands; paper and ink of very good quality; elaborate owner stamps and marginalia (in Arabic); and clear colophons and incipits (Figures 4.5–4.7). Their unique features constitute a subdivision of Tayyibi-Bohra manuscript culture in the *khizana*. Moreover, the Hamdani copies remain in mint condition due to the quality of the materials used.[51] As mentioned, what is also an interesting feature of the Hamdani manuscript tradition is that they are the only Bohra manuscripts that were also sporadically copied by female scribes.[52]

[46] Abbas Hamdani, 'History of the Hamdani Collection of Manuscripts', in De Blois, *Arabic, Persian, and Gujarati Manuscripts*, xxvi.

[47] See, for instance, Daftary, *Fifty Years in the East*, 26, 32.

[48] For instance, the IIS, Tübingen University, Bombay University, the School of Oriental and African Studies, and many more. See Hamdani, 'History of the Hamdani Collection of Manuscripts', xxvi, xxvii.

[49] Hamdani, 'History of the Hamdani Collection of Manuscripts', xxvii.

[50] Private conversation with anonymous manuscript librarian, 31 August 2013.

[51] See for more codicological and palaeographical specimens: De Blois, *Arabic, Persian, and Gujarati Manuscripts*.

[52] Ibid., xiv.

Figure 4.5 Example of a Hamdani manuscript, dated 4th of *Rajab* 1306 (6 March 1889), with burgundy deer-leather binding and two library vignettes: a recent Alawi *khizana* vignette, including a printed stamp reading *al-Daʿwat al-Hādiyyat al-ʿAlawiyya* in Arabic, and an original Hamdani vignette, which includes the title of the treatise, *al-Jild al-ʿAwwal min Kitāb Jāmiʿal-Ḥaqā'iq*, a signature (left) and manuscript numbers (middle and right), written in black ink. The original Hamdani vignette, in this case, has not been erased, most probably due to its unproblematic provenance.

External Manuscript Networks: The Story of the 'Mumbai Daʿa'im'

As noted in Chapter 1, most of the Alawis living outside Baroda are based in Mumbai, and therefore there is a lot of mobility between the two cities, including the physical movement of manuscripts. As we were talking about the Mazoon's years in Mumbai, he told me the story of how several manuscripts surprisingly reached the *khizana* via non-Bohri networks. From all devotional genres of Isma'ili literature, *fiqh* treatises are the most likely to circulate outside Bohra communities because they are widely available and their content is not considered secret. An example is a very neat and clean copy of the *Daʿa'im al-Islam*, the *magnum opus* of al-Qadi Nuʿman, which we have come across already in the Dar al-Kutub in Cairo. As its name reveals, the 'Mumbai *Daʿa'im*' was discovered in Mumbai by accident by a believer twenty years ago. A *mu'min* from Badri Mohallah found it while going through a mass of discarded newspapers and books at the famous Chor Bazar (lit. 'Bazar of Thieves' in Hindi) of second-hand goods in Mumbai. Since it was a manuscript written in Arabic, he told the *pastiwala* (vendor of wastepaper) to donate it to

Figure 4.6 Inside the same Hamdani manuscript is this first flyleaf with notes, including the title written twice: once in black ink (middle), which seems to be written by the same hand as on the Hamdani vignette on the cover, and once in brown ink (upper left, including erasure of previous failed attempt to write '*ḥaqā'iq*'). The name of the author, *Sayyidnā Shaykh ʿalī* (ligature) *b. Sayyidnā Shams al-Dīn*, is written in blue ballpoint ink by a later hand. Below the title in the middle, which was most likely written by the Hamdani librarian, we see '*khān*' (Ar. 'storehouse', according to the Bhai Sahebs 'cupboard') 2, and '*ṣaff*' (Ar. 'shelf') 3, which gives us insight into the organisation and *khizana* culture of the Hamdanis.

him because 'nobody uses Arabic books any more; what are you going to do with it anyway?'. The *pastiwala*, according to the Mazoon Saheb, was happy to get rid of the mouldy old book.[53]

Upon his return to Baroda, the *mu'min* donated the manuscript to the *khizana* in 1406/1986. Twenty-four years later the Mazoon Saheb finally found the time to identify the work and finish restoring it to its former glory in 1432/2010 by adding several missing folios at the beginning and end of the work and by rebinding it. According to the Mazoon Saheb, the 'Mumbai *Daʿa'im*' is the finest copy of the treatise that is in the collection of the *daʿwa*: it is written in a very neat and clean hand, entirely in green ink, which is an anomaly in Bohra manuscript culture as green pigments used to be very expensive in the Indian subcontinent; this writing is complemented

[53] This story reminded me of one of the adventures of Don Quixote when he accidentally buys an Arabic pamphlet (with marginalia) from a boy who sells discarded books. Miguel de Cervantes, *Don Quixote*, trans. John Rutherford (London: Penguin Books, 2002), Book 1, Chapter 9.

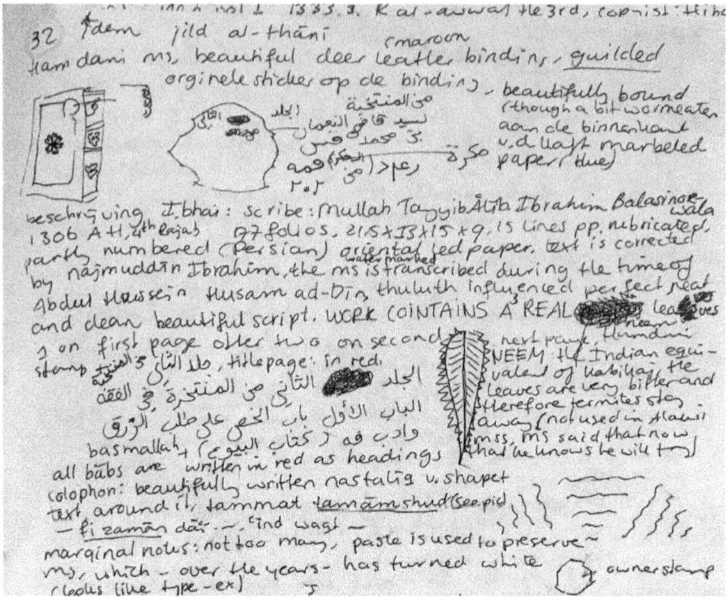

Figure 4.7 Preparation of the catalogue: social-codicological notes taken by the author on the second tome of a Hamdani copy of *Kitāb Jāmi ʿal-Ḥaqā'iq*, with sketches of its codicological features, including the mentioning of a *neem* leaf found between the folios.

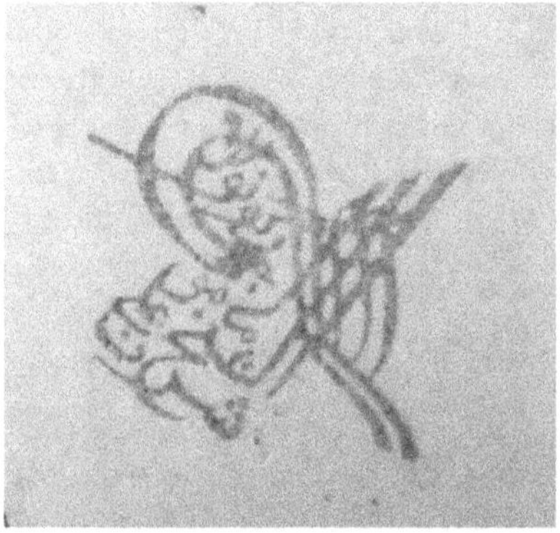

Figure 4.8 The private owner stamp reading *Sharafalisheikhmamujee Rangoonwala*, resembling an Ottoman *tughra* (picture taken from the 'Mumbai *Daʿa'im*' manuscript).

by very elaborate marginalia in Arabic. What is even more interesting is that the colophon contains an ownership stamp of a certain Sheikh Sharaf ʿAlī Rangoonwala (Sheikh Sharaf Ali from Rangoon, the capital of British Burma), which indicates that the manuscript, or at least the family of the owner, was in some way connected to what is today known as the Republic of Myanmar (Figure 4.8). This could very well be possible, as many Bohras historically settled not only along the western Indian

Ocean littoral but also in trade centres in the Eastern Indian Ocean, such as Rangoon, Bangkok and Hong Kong.[54]

The story of the Mumbai *Da'a'im* shows that, even though they are rare, Isma'ili manuscripts still circulate on the market outside Bohra communities and their networks and sometimes surface in the most unexpected places. The chances of encountering Bohra manuscripts today, however, are diminishing, since both the Dawoodis in Mumbai and certain academic institutions are competing in collecting Isma'ili manuscripts in South Asia for their libraries. In fact, I was informed that a large academic institution from Europe at some point requested the Mazoon Saheb to donate his *khizana*, which he naturally refused. I am mentioning this offer because it lays bare the contrasting ways in which the two parties value manuscripts as commodities: whereas academic institutions see the manuscripts as a heritage that needs to be preserved, regardless of its social displacement, the community regards the manuscripts of the *khizana* as sacred, ritualised objects whose materiality and physical presence are crucial for its existence and identity. Despite the renewed interest in Isma'ili manuscripts, these manuscript stories show that, as long as the Mazoon Saheb and his brothers continue to rely on their personal networks, the constant flow of fresh manuscripts will not cease.

4.4 Practices of Borrowing, Lending and Appropriation

In addition to manuscript donation and purchasing, a historic Bohra manuscript copying network continues to exist among the clerics of the respective Bohra communities.[55] This copying network, I was told, functions as follows: manuscript titles that are rare or in danger of perishing in the *khizana* are requested by the Alawi Bhai Sahebs from colleagues and friends outside their respective *da'was* for copying. As part of this intercommunal tradition of manuscript borrowing and lending, the Alawi Bhai Sahebs supply their trusted contacts with a manuscript from their *khizana* in exchange for another manuscript for an agreed period of time. This exchange, I observed, is as much about copying as collecting. Upon their arrival in the *khizana*, the borrowed manuscript is first photocopied before it is copied by hand. This temporary transition from handwritten to printed is a practical solution to the biggest challenge the Bhai Sahebs face in their day-to-day lives: a lack of time to copy. The photocopy is therefore the ideal in-between material storage solution for manuscript projects 'in progress'. Yet when the Mazoon Saheb showed me another cupboard full of photocopies I realised that his collecting fever was in play: piles of photocopied manuscripts, enough for a lifetime of copying, were accumulated on top of each other.

The various Bohra *khizanat* and their living manuscript cultures are interconnected not only through the shared Tayyibi-Fatimid manuscript tradition they enshrine but, perhaps even more so, through these networks of manuscript borrowing and lending.

[54] See for the history of the Bohras in Hong Kong and Bangkok: Anita M. Weiss, 'South Asian Muslims in Hong Kong: Creation of a "Local Boy" Identity', *Modern Asian Studies* vol. 25, no. 3 (1991): 423, 424, and Raymond Scupin, 'Muslim Accommodation in Thai Society', *Journal of Islamic Studies* vol. 9, no. 2 (1998): 245.

[55] See also Ismail K. Poonawala, 'The Contribution of Ismāʿīlī colophons to the Discussion on the Birth and Construction of the Arabic Manuscript Tradition', *Chroniques du manuscrit au Yémen* 8 (January 2019), 74.

These manuscript networks are no recent phenomenon, although the rapidity of circulation seems to have increased sharply in modern times. They remind us of the contacts and networks of manuscript mobility as recorded in the *Qaratis al-Yaman*, where books circulated within the Tayyibi-Bohra networks of the Indian Ocean between Yemen and Gujarat. It is likely that the networks the Bohras rely on are historic ones that continued to exist after the relocation of the *daʿwa* from Yemen to Gujarat and the schisms between the Sulaymanis, Dawoodis and Alawis on the Indian subcontinent. As I mentioned briefly in Chapter 2, this might even be the case in the larger context of the Indian Ocean world today, as the Dawoodis continue to consult manuscripts in Yemen. Another manuscript example of recent Indian Ocean mobility eastwards is the Rangoon manuscript we came across, which is now in the Alawi *khizana* collection.

The *Qaratis al-Yaman* are thus far the only letters that we know of that document these historic networks of manuscript gifting, purchasing and lending. These practices and requests were recorded and have survived because of the official nature of the correspondence between *daʿwa* officials. That inter-communal manuscript borrowing and purchasing often had a more informal, if not a secretive, character explains why these practices are not recorded in documents or letters. Their trajectories and histories are, however, in most cases, present in the 'rough edges' of the manuscripts themselves.

Even though these manuscript and copying networks do not fit into the sectarian narratives of the three Bohra communities, it is important to acknowledge their existence, for two reasons. First, they give us insight into the collecting practices and strategies of the communities, as well as the agency of individual clerics in these exchanges, despite certain hierarchies of power. Second, as much as the stories of individual Dais miraculously copying an entire *khizana* overnight by hand are important to the communities, I argue that, historically, these informal networks have been fundamentally important, both in the past and the present, in building and preserving Bohra treasuries of books in Ahmedabad, Baroda, Hyderabad and elsewhere, as the manuscript stories of the Alawi *khizana* have shown.

The Story of the Missing Royal Basmalas

As much as the manuscripts of the *khizana* have biographies and stories to tell, their individual paratextual features, such as owner statements, stamps, scribal notes, colophons and even *basmalas*, have social lives too that are constantly subject to change. As argued previously, there are no coincidences in the codicology of Bohra manuscript culture, and even in their palaeography nothing is necessarily permanent. In this final section, we look at the ways in which the Alawis appropriate manuscripts of a different sacred provenance from their own, socially and materially, and include them in their treasury of books.

Interestingly, Bohra manuscripts that are 'alien' to the *khizana* are considered authoritative and are used as such. After all, they are the vehicles of the Fatimid-Tayyibi esoteric truths and exoteric knowledge. What, however, about the sacred materiality of these manuscripts? Does the 'alien' codex have the same sacred properties if its text is composed by authorities from the same sacred tradition of knowledge transmission but is copied or authorised by a Dai or Bhai Saheb of a different *daʿwa* genealogy? Can a manuscript of non-Alawi provenance really be 'owned' in the immaterial spiritual sense if it was not written by the Alawi Dai or Bhai Sahebs? And if so, how exactly are these manuscripts 're-branded' for their new *khizana* context? Can a manuscript of a different sacred provenance be stored next to the other manuscripts and consumed (read, quoted and recopied) in the *khizana*?

The answers to these questions can be traced in the paratexts of the manuscripts, which contain valuable information on how these 'alien' texts were appropriated and enshrined in the *khizana*. According to the practice of the clerics, Bohra manuscripts alien to the *khizana* are considered authoritative – after checking of the text and credentials – and are used as such. First, however, the manuscript material must 'become Alawi' before it may enter the treasury of books. As was very clear from the colophons and incipits of these manuscripts, all 'sectarian' features and other traces that could give away the former identity or provenance of the manuscript had to be erased; this included names of copyists, dates, geographic names, owner stamps and statements, reader statements, statements of donation, names and phone numbers (Figures 4.9–4.11). Usually, these features were erased by pen or pencil, but sometimes entire colophons were cut out or the pages were removed and then replaced with a new date and a reader or restoration statement in the colophon. In a way, alien

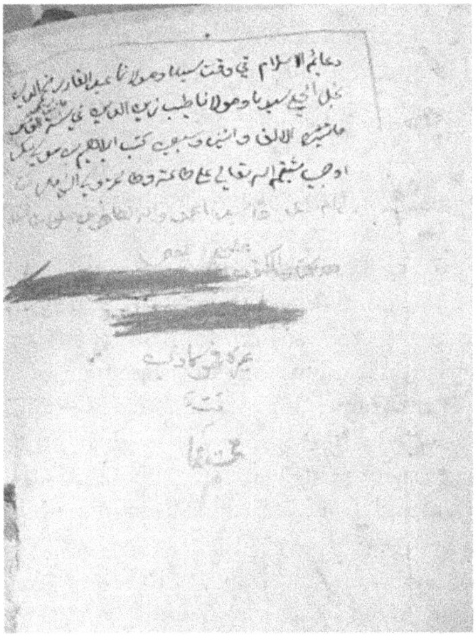

Figure 4.9 Practices of erasure by previous owner in a copy of the *Daʿa'im al-Islam*, a Bohra manuscript of non-Alawi provenance. The colophon, partly erased, is written in red ink. The text following the words '*hadhā 'l-kitāb maktūb* ...' (Ar. 'this manuscript was written ...') is crossed out with a pink pencil, presumably because it includes the information on the *ʿasr* of the Dai (and thus the date) and possibly the name of the scribe.

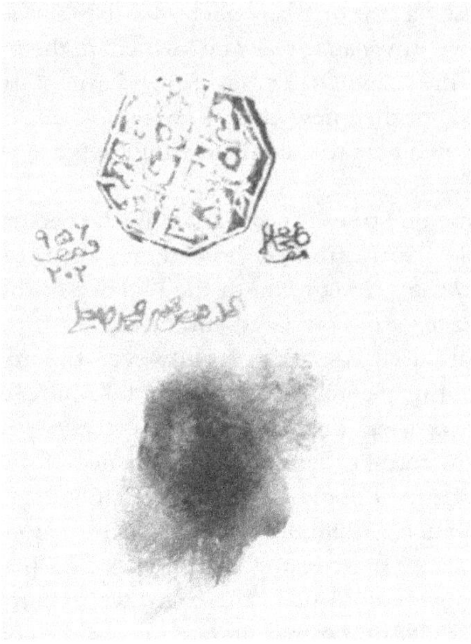

Figure 4.10 Practices of erasure by previous owner: Hamdani manuscript (title must remain undisclosed) with octagonal owner seal of the Hamdani *khizana*, signature (lower right) and manuscript number (lower left), with *taṣliya* (below) and deliberate erasure of the owner stamp by hand (one can still see a fingerprint).

manuscripts thus undergo 'sectarian' changes to become Alawi. It should be noted that the main text of the manuscript is never changed.

Often this practice has already been carried out by the vendor or previous owner of the manuscript. Another sensitive piece of information – the mention of the *ʿasr* of the Dai at the time of copying – is removed from all manuscript copies. The next step in their material appropriation is the writing of a statement of donation or purchase on the first flyleaf or incipit in Arabic. This statement has a standard formula and reads, 'This manuscript was a *hadiyya* [present] gifted by this and that person, on this and this date, in this and this town to the Mazoon Saheb Zaki al-Din of the Alawi *daʿwa*, during the *ʿasr* of this and this Dai.' It makes the transfer of the object between the two parties official.

The new owner statement is almost always followed by the literal 're-branding' of the manuscript with an Alawi *daʿwa* stamp and a *khizana* vignette, which officially makes the manuscript part of the *khizana* collection. While preparing the catalogue of manuscripts for the Dai, I was asked to paste and fill in the information in these vignettes by hand. In a way my cataloging efforts thus became part of the new manuscript stories of the collection. Re-branding the book also means that, in certain cases, a manuscript that was privately owned previously thus changes status, as it becomes the property of the *daʿwa*. There is a certain tension inherent in this transfer, as shown by the history of Bohra family collections versus the narratives of the official *daʿwa khizana*,

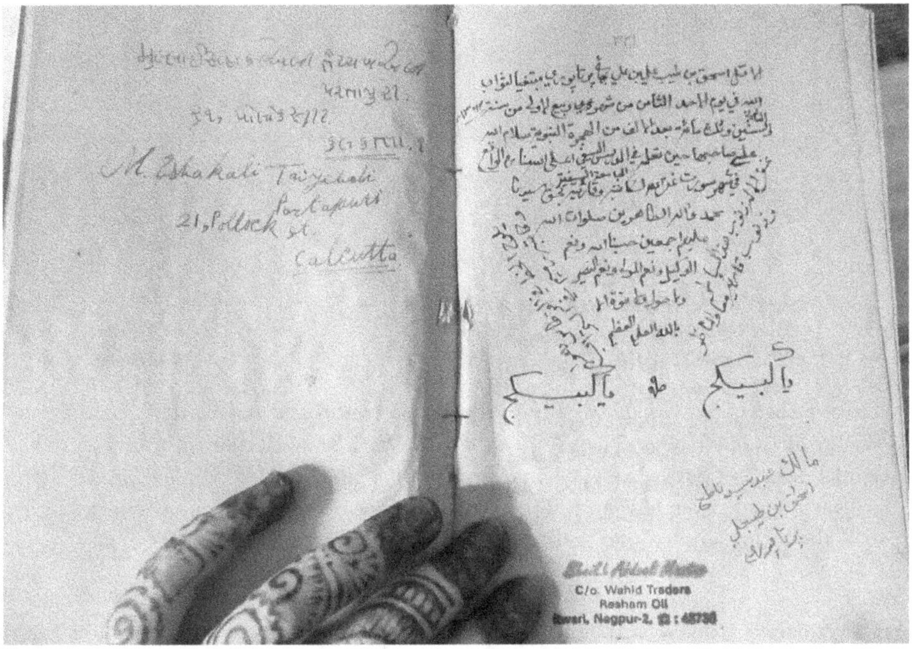

Figure 4.11 Example of a non-Alawi manuscript, dated 8th *Rabīʿal-Awwal*, 1392 (22 April 1972), in which the history of its social life has been preserved beneath the intact colophon and the following folio. The previous ownership was documented in the hand of the Mazoon Saheb (right folio, lower right) in Arabic, which reads '*mālik* [in the possession of] *ʿAbd al-Sayyid Nāṭiʿ Isḥāq b. Ṭayyibʿalī* (ligature) *Partāpūrī*'. Underneath this *mālik* statement we find a stamp of another possible previous owner from Nagpur. The ownership of M. Partapuri is mentioned, most probably by Partapuri himself, on the left folio in both Hindi and English and includes his address in Calcutta.

including the story of the Mazoon Saheb's Dawoodi teacher. These different narratives about the right to private ownership of manuscripts versus the opposite view that handwritten books are considered to belong to the Dai can be traced in the paratextual notes of Bohra manuscripts; for instance, the Persian marginal note that I discussed in Chapter 2 reads: 'One who claims that this book is mine is wrong, it belongs to the *daʿwa*. If you will go to the court of any *Pāshā* he will be the judge of that.' The placing of the Alawi *daʿwa* stamp (Figure 4.12), which should be seen as a statement of private ownership of the Dai, thus marks this transition ritually and materially.

Immaterial features in codicology, too, can tell us a lot about the social lives of manuscripts. Traces of their absence, or even eradication, sometimes provide clues about certain social practices and scribal traditions. The majority of non-Alawi Bohra manuscripts of the *khizana* that I scrutinised had one peculiar codicological feature in common: a large empty space – either the result of careful erasure or a cut-out lacuna at the beginning of the incipit – where traditionally the *basmala* formula is copied. The

Figure 4.12 Alawi *khizana* stamps in English (right) and Arabic (left), reading: *Fī ʿaṣr Sayyidnā Mawlānā Ṭayyib Ḍiyāʾ al-Dīn, Barūdah* (outer circle, trans.: in the reginal period of Sayyidna Mawlana Tayyib Diya' al-Din, Baroda), *al-Dār al-Kutub al-ʿAlawiyya* (inner circle, trans.: The Alawi House of Books) in Arabic. Interestingly, the terms 'library' and '*Dār al-Kutub*' are used here, instead of '*khizana*'.

Mazoon Saheb explained that in Dawoodi manuscript culture the *basmala* is commonly calligraphed by the Dai himself in a specific *dīwānī* script after the completion of each royal manuscript copy. According to the scribal protocol, the copyist thus leaves blank the space where the *basmala* is traditionally written (Figure 4.13).

Yet in the case of many of the Dawoodi manuscripts in Baroda, the *basmala* is either erased and rewritten or cut out from the folio altogether. The rewriting of this 'royal' *basmala*, filled in by the Dai, is another Alawi method of manuscript appropriation and authorisation of 'alien' manuscript copies (more on technical codicological features of 'alien' manuscripts in Chapter 5). The Alawis too, I observed, must have adopted the practice of writing the *basmala* by the Dai, as can be seen in their later manuscript copies. This scribal practice reminds us of the importance of the writing practices of the Bhai Sahebs in the daily lives of believers, as discussed in Chapter 2. As we have seen, the *basmala*, which is part of the *ʿalama* or royal handwritten seal, is written on buildings, talismans and documents by the Dai as a means of authorisation. This writing practice also has pride of place in Bohra manuscript culture, and the rewriting of the *basmala* is thus a form of authorisation.

Yet this scribal practice did not explain the 'circumcision' practices, the rectangular cut-outs in some of the Dawoodi manuscripts of the *khizana*. The Bhai Sahebs mentioned that in some instances these *basmalas* were already cut out from the manuscripts before they reached the *khizana* because they were sold individually as pieces of sacred text. The selling of 'royal' Dawoodi *basmalas*, I was told, is a very profitable (but clandestine) business, since believers are willing to pay many rupees for owning a piece of the sacred handwriting of their Dai. It is no surprise, however, that this practice, which violates the sacred materiality of Bohra manuscripts, is strictly forbidden by the Dawoodi clerics. Whereas the *ʿalama*, the Dais' *basmala* written on documents, as discussed in Chapter 1, is considered a relatively common commodity in the Bohra

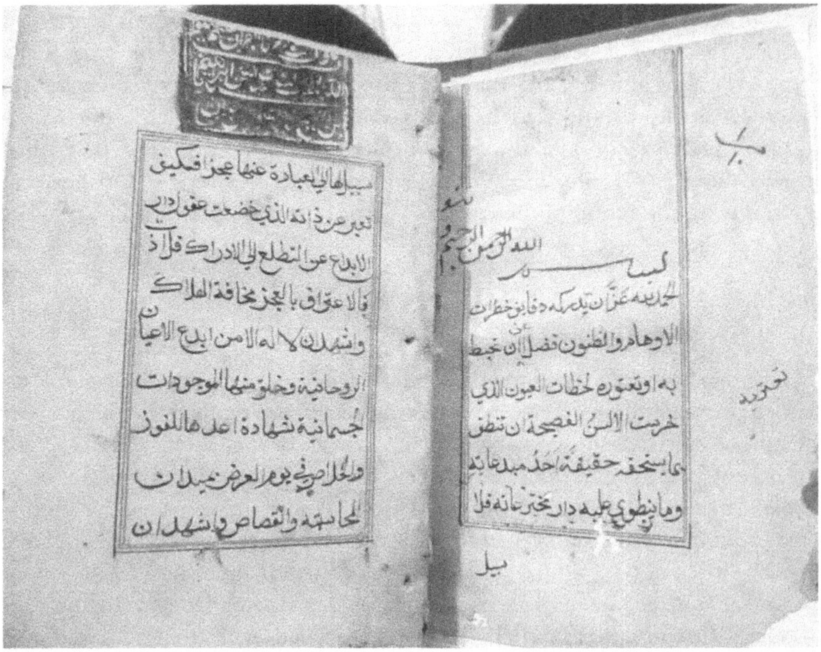

Figure 4.13 Example of blank spaces in a Bohra manuscript. Incipit of a restored manuscript, currently in the collection of the Alawi *khizana*. The *basmala* and the title of the work were supposed to be transcribed by the Dai at a later stage in the blank space of the incipit. The *basmala* was indeed calligraphed, yet not very successfully and most probably by an inexperienced scribe, as we can tell from the poor use of space.

communities, the clandestine trade in 'manuscript *basmalas*' has turned these paper cuttings into highly sought-after objects. So far as I was able to find out, the trade in royal *basmalas* is not practised among the Alawis.

The mobility of manuscripts from one community to another and the practice of rewriting the *basmala* as a means of changing the sacred provenance of a manuscript have strong similarities with how believers enter and move between communities. Given the fact that there is a shortage of marriageable women and men in the Alawi Bohra community, at times *mu'minat* and *mu'minin* from other communities convert in order to marry. In a process rather similar to the manuscript appropriation practices described earlier, these converts undergo rituals of 'sectarian' initiation – including the taking of an oath of allegiance (starting with the *basmala*), change of dress and physical appearance, and circumcision – to become part of the Alawi *da'wa* and its sacred geography.

Let us end this section with the question of how the social lives of manuscripts of non-Alawi provenance continue in the *khizana* after their material initiation, re-appropriation, and circumcision of all traces of their past lives. Having undergone this rite of passage, these manuscripts of non-Alawi provenance carry the same textual authority as Alawi *makhtutat* and are treated, stored and consumed as such. However, the appropriation rituals of the *khizana* have their material limits. An aspect of these manuscripts that cannot be appropriated to their new context is the script in which the treatise is transmitted. Only manuscripts of pure Alawi provenance are considered sacred vehicles of knowledge, because they contain the sacred book hands of their Dais, which are considered to carry healing properties (more on the scribal and scriptural habitus in Chapter 6). In other words, no matter how old or rare an alien manuscript is, in the world of the treasury of books it is thus impossible to change its sacred materiality.

Final Notes to Chapter 4: Bibliophilia in the Treasury of Books

In this chapter, I have documented the stories of the treasury of books, of both its custodians and its manuscripts. Their personal and material biographies, which are intrinsically connected, have shown us that the collection of the Alawi *khizana* is far from homogeneous in its provenance. They have also given us insight into the networks of circulation and collecting of Bohra manuscripts. The stories of handwritten books that were found in mausoleums and in bathroom cupboards, or discarded in lakes and water tanks, force us to re-think the social role of these manuscripts, to go beyond the fact that they are considered material vehicles of sacred knowledge only: they are also commodities that in their material form can be owned, collected, inherited, or even ingested, or cut out and sold. Through collecting, preserving and accumulating these handwritten books as material objects and re-appropriating them to their treasury of books in Baroda, the Alawis thus cultivate a 'medieval' Arabic manuscript culture from the past (see fig. 4.14). It is through this Indian Ocean manuscript culture that they understand themselves as Neo-Fatimids in modern times.

While at times the collecting of manuscripts as commodities went through official channels, in many instances, manuscripts reached the Alawi *khizana* through informal networks or surfaced in unexpected places. This tradition of manuscript borrowing and lending reminds us of the world of the *Qaratis al-Yaman*, where manuscripts circulated within the Tayyibi-Bohra networks of the Indian Ocean. Despite strained inter-sectarian relations, an unofficial Tayyibi-Fatimid manuscript market and copying network continue to exist among the Dawoodi, Alawi and Sulaymani clerics, in which manuscript titles are requested from outside the respective *daʿwas* from other *khizana* and collections for copying. Interestingly, we saw that through these inter-communal encounters, codicological traditions from other Bohra communities were adopted, such as the rewriting of the royal *basmala* and new preservation practices such as the introduction of *neem* leaves. Despite operating in relative isolation, Bohra manuscripts and their material subcultures also influence one another far more than is acknowledged.

Moreover, the scribal traditions and codicological practices that shape these manuscript cultures, together with ideas about the legitimacy of ownership versus custodianship, are subject to change over time. The story of the mausoleum very clearly demonstrated that a century ago popular manuscripts circulated outside of the Alawi *khizana* among believers, or at least *zahiri* manuscripts did. The question remains: How does this story fit into our understanding of the *khizana*? 'Our *taqiyya*', the

Mukasir Saheb explained, which is based on the assumption that all *batini* literature should under no circumstances circulate outside the treasury of books, 'was never endangered because only *zahiri* literature circulated outside the *khizana*.' The appropriation of Bohra manuscripts of a different sacred provenance in the treasury of books did not change this either. In fact, I argue that it contributes to our understanding of the Bohra *khizana* as a treasury of books that is closed and contains a 'clean' manuscript tradition of authorised texts only. 'Alien' manuscripts are indeed enshrined, but before they are merged with the collection these texts are thoroughly re-branded as Alawi manuscripts, as all the material traces of their former social lives are erased. To conclude, the biographies of the manuscripts of the *khizana*, studied through their *rough edges* and unofficial oral histories, have stories to tell that do not necessarily represent the 'official' narrative: they contain traces of cultural and local appropriation; material circumcision; and travel, exchange and circulation across time, space and the highly contested borders of communities.

In addition to the 'secret' status that is attributed to these objects, marginalia reveal that these manuscripts are used in various social contexts for talismanic and healing purposes, which raises questions of the materiality and immateriality of manuscripts as sacred artefacts. This chapter has also addressed questions of materiality and immateriality in relation to circulation. At some point in time and space, the material circulation of manuscripts with even the busiest of social lives comes to an end. As material objects, they inevitably turn into sacred dust or, in the worst case, sacred trash. The transmission of the sacred eternal truths, however, continues through the living manuscript tradition of the *khizana*, as one manuscript is turned into another.

Appendix to Chapter 4: The Transmission Narrative of Bohra Manuscripts

In Chapter 2, the transmission narrative of Isma'ili manuscripts was mapped out according to the Bohra conception of linear history: starting with the period of *kashf* (manifestation of the Imams) during the Fatimid and early Tayyibi period, followed by what is known as the era of *satr* (seclusion of the Imams) and the subsequent relocation of Tayyibi *khizana* to the Indian subcontinent in the ninth/fifteenth century. According to the transmission narrative, the content of this *khizana* was dispersed among the various Bohra communities after their bifurcations. Figure 4.14 provides an overview of how the Sulaymani, Alawi and Dawoodi Bohra manuscript traditions developed in the post-bifurcation period into different *khizana* and textual traditions (royal and institutionalised collections versus non-royal and private collections). It also illustrates the inter-sectarian transmission of Bohra manuscripts and maps out the travel of 'alien' manuscripts into the Alawi Bohra *khizana*.

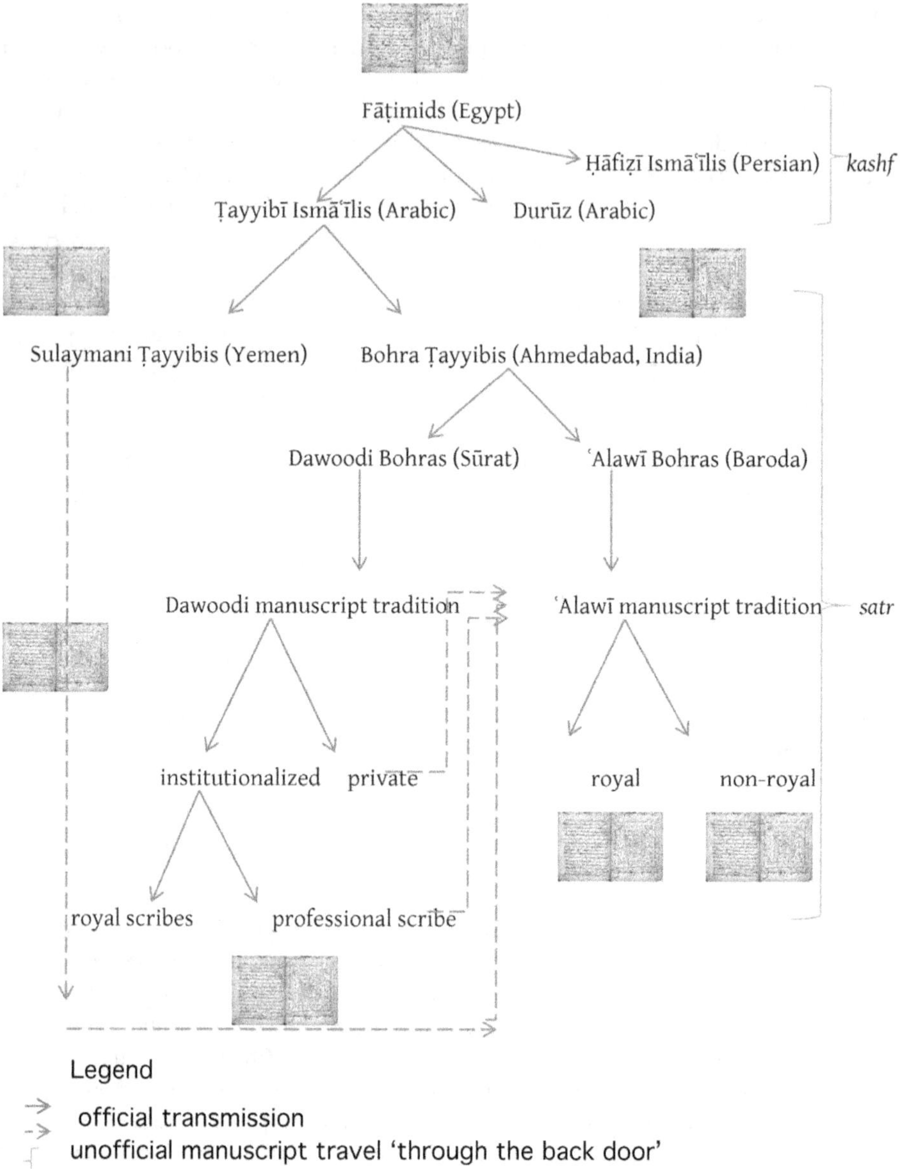

Figure 4.14 Schematic overview of the transmission narrative of Bohra manuscripts. Akkerman, *The Bohra Dark Archive and the Language of Secrecy*, 109.

Chapter 5

Materiality of Secrecy

In the Margins of the Treasury of Books

It was early afternoon in the *mohallah*. It was one of these rare moments when the Bohra lane was deserted, and it was quiet. After having had their family *thali*, the people of Badri Mohallah turned in for a short, or long, afternoon nap, depending on the weather. I, however, felt restless as the tiger mosquitos, the intense humidity and the thought of the daunting piles of manuscripts that were waiting for me in the *khizana* tormented me.[1] The Mazoon Saheb and his family were already used to the fact that I did not take afternoon naps and had, to others' and my own surprise, entrusted me with the key to the royal *haveli* to continue my work in the treasury of books while they were asleep.

The key to the *haveli*, which was essentially the key to the treasury of books, was nothing more than a small padlock, yet carrying it was an extraordinary privilege and an honour. Dressed in my synthetic *rida*, I would quietly sneak into the *haveli*, trying not to wake anyone, enter the *khizana*, turn on the fans (if there was electricity) and get to work. By the time the Mazoon Saheb had woken up and Ibrahimbhai returned to his station, the Bhu Saheba would come upstairs with hot *chai* and biscuits, and the office started to slowly come back to life.

This time, however, it seemed to take forever before the *mohallah* awoke and the *chai* arrived. I had recently finished cataloguing the *batin* and *haqa'iq* section of the treasury of books, and it was now the turn of *zahiri* books, *fiqh* and chrestomathies, in particular. The order in which I was requested to catalogue the treasury of books was a bit peculiar, at least as regards Isma'ili standards of *ʿilm*: I was first tasked with the esoteric treatises, for which one usually needs years of initiation, before scrutinising the less secret, exoteric manuscripts. There was, however, a very practical reason for this order, and soon I was to find out why. There were many more *zahiri* than *batini* manuscripts in the *khizana*, which made them less rare and thus less valuable. Due to their strength in numbers, as material objects, they were less at risk of perishing in the hostile climate of Baroda, and the need to catalogue them was thus less urgent. Qadi Nuʿman, the codifier of Fatimid law whom we already met in Chapter 2, is without a doubt the star

[1] My state of mind reminded me of a passage in Kratchkovsky's *Among Arabic Manuscripts*, where, suffering from fever, he is haunted in his dreams by the manuscripts he worked on: 'They whisper, and gazing at them I recognize them and smile to them. You have not forgotten us? You will come to us? For we have repaid you a hundredfold for bringing us back to life. Do you remember the hours of pain and disappointment, weariness and anxiety, you would seek us out and find in our pages the voices of loyal friends who always welcome you with joy, whom no one can take away from you and over whom death itself has no power?' Kratchkovsky, *Among Arabic Manuscripts*, 9–10.

of the *khizana* collection. As eager as I had been to immerse myself into the realm of *fiqh*, my courage failed when the Mazoon proudly opened his iron cupboard dedicated to *zahiri kutub*. Half of the cupboard, if not more, was dedicated to *Daʿa'im* copies alone. There must have been dozens of them, some fanciful copies, others in tatters, which the Mazoon piled up around my peacock chair with a smiling face.

That afternoon, alone in the treasury of books, I thus found myself in the company of heaps and heaps of copies of the one Fatimid text that seemed to follow me wherever I went: the *Da'aim*. As the towers of *Daʿa'im kutub* sat around me quietly, I was daunted by this new task the Mazooon had set for me. It had taken me weeks to familiarise myself with the peculiarities of *batini* tomes, their authors, spells, secret scripts, cyclical diagrams and other marginalia. *Zahiri* manuscripts, however, were a completely different world that I now had to immerse myself in, despite that fact that I was running out of time in Badri Mohallah and my cataloguing speed was considerably slowed down by the inevitable monsoon fatigue.

While my head was still full of the stories of the *batini* manuscripts and ceremonies that I observed the day before, I randomly opened a modest-looking exemplar that did not seem too daunting at first sight. It was 403 folios long and copied in an elegant *naskh* hand; it had once belonged to Hibatullah Abu b. Ibrahimjee Raj Nagarwala Udaipuri, a Dawoodi gentleman who, as the colophon revealed, finished transcribing the text in honour of his late father in the year 1333 of the *hijra* calendar. The year 1333/1915 was eventful for the Indian subcontinent and for Gujarat in particular, still under British occupation: in that year Mahatma Gandhi returned from South Africa to Ahmedabad to lead the Indian independence movement, and Sy. Muhammad Burhanuddin, heir to the Dawoodi throne as the fifty-second Dai, was born in Surat.[2] Despite these and many other tumultuous events, the tradition of manual copying of the works of Qadi Nuʿman continued uninterruptedly among the Bohras.

Raj Nagarwala Udaipuri's *Daʿa'im* manuscript, it turned out, was full of marginal notes and other paratexts. In fact, it seemed that no space in the codex was left unwritten. Whereas the *batini* manuscripts I was so familiar with were very concise in revealing their past social lives and whereabouts, this copy seemed to me like paratexts on steroids. Among the multitude of magical squares, verses of poetry, stickers, phone numbers, owner statements, dates, *du'as* and other invocations in Arabic, Gujarati, Hindi, Persian, Urdu and *Lisan al-Daʿwa* found in its margins, my eye fell on a few lines jotted down in turquoise ink. The quotation, written in Arabic, immediately inspired confidence. It read, 'Do you think you are only a small insect? But in you is contained a big universe.'

Even though small, this marginal note seemed to urge me to carry on, to not be overwhelmed by the piles of manuscripts and their abundant world of paratexts, nor the actual termites that inhabited them. Its original meaning, the Mazoon Saheb explained to me once the *chai* finally arrived that afternoon, referred to the universes of *batin* and *zahir* and meant that these realms were all within us. Originally perhaps

[2] Bhikhu Parekh, *Gandhi: A Very Short Introduction* (Oxford: Oxford University Press, 2001), 9. Mustafa Abdulhussein, *Al-Dai Al-Fatimi Syedna Mohammed Burhanuddin: An Illustrated Biography* (Surat: Aljamea-tus-Saifiyah Trust, 2001).

not intended as such, the marginal note had the effect on me of what today would be popularly known as an 'inspirational quote'. Suddenly feeling less of a small insect in the treasury of books, I carried on my work, making my way through the piles of the *Daʿa'im* and other *zahiri* works waiting to be catalogued.

As I spent more time with the marginalia of the treasury of books, I learned that the way I had used the quotation I had found in Nagarwala Udaipuri's manuscript to motivate myself was not that far away from its intended usage. In fact, as we see in this chapter, taking omens or predictions from manuscripts and writing handwritten notes in the margins of manuscripts, documents or the holy Qur'an are widely practised in the *khizana* and considered important parts of the daily lives of believers.

In the previous chapter, we gained a better understanding of the rich individual social lives and biographies of the manuscripts of the Alawi *khizana* and the stories behind their mobility, material circumcision and diverse provenances. Each manuscript, as we saw, seemed to tell a unique story of its material survival. Instead of emphasising their uniqueness and individuality, in this chapter we focus on what the manuscripts of the treasury of books have in common, apart from being vehicles of sacred text.

As for my ventures into the *zahiri* manuscripts of the *khizana*, no matter how unusual the provenance of some of the manuscript copies of the *khizana* was or which surprising routes they had travelled before they came into the collection in Baroda, they all had one thing in common: their codicology (material manifestations of the book) and rich marginal traditions were identical, which revealed their social role in the community as books that are regularly taken out and consulted by the clerics during their audience, and possibly by other readers and users before they entered the *khizana*.[3] The opposite phenomenon, I discovered earlier, can be argued for *batini* manuscripts, which codicologically and through their paratexts are made, transcribed and used in such a way that their esoteric contents remain undisclosed to the outside world.

In this chapter, we investigate these two parallel manuscript cultures that coexist in the treasury of books: an esoteric *batini* manuscript culture and an exoteric *zahiri* one. We explore them through their margins and materiality, from spine to cover, head to tail, and from incipit to colophon, and look at their social role, that either veils the esoteric or indeed reveals the future and protects the present. Furthermore, we return to the questions of what it means to the Alawis to practise codicology and how the community reconstructs a medieval Fatimid-Tayyibi manuscript culture in Baroda, translating this tradition to the social reality of modern-day South Asia without vernacularising the intellectual tradition they inherited ritually, ceremonially and materially.

5.1 Codicology of the Treasury of Books

What do the manuscripts of the treasury of books have in common, apart from being vehicles of sacred text? The Alawis' *khizana* collection and the Neo-Fatimid manuscript culture it enshrines are part of the larger phenomenon of Isma'ili book culture,

[3] See for a further discussion and bibliography on codicology: Akkerman, 'The Bohra Manuscript Treasury as a Sacred Site of Philology'.

a field that thus far has remained relatively unexplored.[4] Due to their inaccessibility to scholars, Bohra manuscript culture in particular, or manuscript *cultures*, and their codicology and palaeography are rarely studied.[5] All we know of Bohra manuscript cultures is based on private collections, such as the Fyzee, Zahid Ali and Hamdani collections. Their material features and palaeography have been documented in catalogues but have never been analysed systematically, especially, as I mentioned earlier, in relation to the social role of these manuscripts.[6] These family collections, as we saw in the previous chapter, have very distinct features that show some similarities with but also are very different from the manuscripts produced in Dawoodi, Sulaymani and Alawi clerical *daʿwa* milieux, let alone manuscripts of royal provenance. Although they are part of the larger phenomenon of Bohra manuscript and *khizana* culture, Hamdani manuscripts, for instance, immediately stand out from other Bohra manuscripts codicologically and palaeographically and should therefore be regarded as being part of a unique sub-manuscript culture. Their material features and scribal particularities can be explained by the simple fact that the socio-economic and scholarly environment in which Hamdani manuscripts were originally produced and commissioned was very different from that of other Dawoodi family collections on the subcontinent prior to their dispersal and, as discussed, confiscation, or from that of the official clerical Alawi *daʿwa khizana* in Baroda.[7] As we explore further in this study, the same can be argued for clerical Dawoodi, Sulaymani and Alawi *daʿwa* manuscript cultures.

Bohra documents have not received any sustained academic attention, as communal documents have historically been enshrined in the *daʿwa khizana* of the respective communities. This is not to say that private Bohra collections do not contain documents. In fact, one would expect them to contain documents of a personal nature, authorised by the Bohra *daʿwa*, such as: marriage contracts, wills; inheritance, gift and endowment documents; and proofs of land ownership. Yet access to these documents remains difficult, either because they are still kept in closets and cupboards or becaue they have not been preserved or donated.

Through my immersion in the Alawi treasury of books I was in the privileged position of studying the social role, codicology and, to a certain extent, palaeography (see Chapter 6) of all these communities, as they are uniquely represented in the microcosm of the Alawi *khizana*. This chapter addresses the manuscript cultures of the treasury of books holistically, which include but are certainly not restricted to Alawi handwritten books and other forms of writing. It should be emphasised that the books of the Alawi *khizana*, including its documentary practices, are part of a *living* manuscript culture:

4 Conference, *Before the Printed Word: Texts, Scribes and Transmission. A Symposium on Manuscript Collections Housed at The Institute of Isma'ili Studies*, IIS, 12–13 October 2017, London.

5 Exceptions in this regard are Ismail Poonawala's and Delia Cortese's recent articles: Poonawala, 'The Contribution of Ismāʿīlī Colophons to the Discussion on the Birth and Construction of the Arabic Manuscript Tradition', 74–139; Delia Cortese, 'The *majmūʿ al-tarbiyah* between Text and Paratext: Exploring the Social History of a Community's Reading Culture', in Wafi Momin (ed.), *Before the Printed Word: Texts, Scribes and Transmission* (forthcoming).

6 We have discussed these catalogues of the Hamdani, Zahid Ali and Goriawala collection at length in Chapters 2 and 4.

7 Or, for instance, as Poonawala describes, the private collection of non-clerical, lay individuals, such as the *khizana* of his late father Qurban Husayn. Poonawala, 'The Contribution of Ismāʿīlī Colophons', 108–11.

manuscripts are man-made and manually copied by the scribal hands of the Dai and the Mazoon Saheb. The treasury of books, as we see in the next chapter, can thus be regarded as a *khizana* scriptorium where, in select circles, the Bhai Sahebs copy the esoteric truths of one sacred object into another.

Why manuscripts look the way they do and what people *do* with them are always intentional, especially in the case of the Alawi universe. This is because the manuscripts of the *khizana*, including their codicology and paratexts, are at the centre of what I call the *materiality of secrecy*. Secrecy, as I described earlier, has a strong spatial dimesion. It is expressed materially by the Alawis towards the outside, uninitiated world in various forms, such as architecture, the spatial arrangement of the *mohallah* and sartorial practice. Within the community, however, secrecy refers to the materiality of the *khizana*, which includes codicology and manuscript culture, practices of enshrinement and access, the use of Arabic as a language of non-access, and paratexts, including secret scripts and alphabets. In other words, secrecy is built into Bohra manuscript culture on various levels.

This chapter zooms in on scribal interventions and codicological choices used in Bohra manuscripts to keep Fatimid-Tayyibi *ʿilm al-batin* inaccessible both textually and physically as objects. While, in some cases, these strategies are self-evident, such as the use of secret alphabets, in other instances the relationship between subject and object, and practices of disclosing versus revealing manuscripts as *objects with a social life in a secret khizana*, are more complex. Understanding the intricacies of the materiality of secrecy and its operating mechanisms, I argue, is important, as it is through the manuscript culture of the *khizana* that, indirectly, the social hierarchy of the community in held in place.

Manuscript, Book, Text

Our popular imagination of manuscripts, as produced in medieval Europe or Mediterranean societies or even translated to popular books and movies, envisions them as as handwritten works transmitted in the material form of a codex or in the form of the printed book as we know it today. Nothing could be further from the truth. Manuscripts, as we see, come in all shapes and sizes, and the collection of the Bohra *khizana* is certainly not unique in this regard. In this chapter, we therefore let go of the idea of the codex being the only material form or medium of text and follow the definition of 'manuscript' as proposed by the Center for the Study of Manuscript Cultures in Africa, Asia and Europe (CSMC) in Hamburg: 'A manuscript is an artefact planned and realized to provide surfaces on which visible signs are applied by hand; it is portable, self-contained, and unique.'[8]

To follow this definition, manuscripts, a word derived from the Latin medieval *manuscriptum* ('written by hand'), are the end product of any kind of handmade and

[8] Vito Lorusso, *Searching for a Definition of 'Manuscript'*, 2014, authored with the support of TnT members A. Bausi, D. Bondarev, A. Brita, C. Brockmann, G. Ciotti, M. Friedrich, J. Karolewski, H. Isaacson, R. Samsom, S. Valente, E. Wilden and H. Wimmer. An online version can be seen here: http://www.manuscript_cultures.unihamburg.de/TnT/Definition_of_MS.pdf (last accessed 13 May 2019).

handwritten artefacts, which can be produced on a variety of writing surfaces such as two-dimensional paper or parchment or three-dimensional organic material, such as graffiti inscribed on rocks, walls and glass; *papier-maché*; trees; and palm leaves.[9] As we touched on briefly in the previous chapter, the choice of material used for writing surfaces is strongly linked not only to *geographical availability* and *stages of technological development*, as Gerald Ward argues, but also – and in my opinion this cannot be emphasised enough – to *prevailing traditional values*.[10] These three elements in turn play an important role in the development, shape and material forms, palaeography, and aesthetics of what manuscripts eventually look like. For instance, palm leaves are a commonly-used writing surface in South Asia. However, for the Bohras and other Muslim communities in South and Southeast Asia, notions of what a holy book should look like came from the Arabian Peninsula, where the codex was considered the appropriate vehicle for text.[11]

Some have argued that the definition of 'manuscript' is insufficient because it excludes other forms of writing. Instead, the term 'codicological entity' has been suggested: the intended end product of handwriting on either natural organic material or on handmade paper.[12] As much as I find this term appropriate, in this study I refer to these entities simply as 'manuscripts', or by the Arabic equivalent '*makhtutat*' or '*kutub*', for the simple reason that this is how they are known and referred to within the Bohra universe, both by the clerical *khassa* within the space of the *khizana* and the *ʿamma*.

The Bohra definition of 'manuscript' includes all material forms of handwritten texts produced, accumulated, appropriated or preserved in the *khizana*; thus, it also includes forms of writing such as talismans, *ʿahd* rolls and legal documents.[13] '*Makhtutat*' are also often referred to as '*kutub al-daʿwa*' (books of the *daʿwa*), and 'book' and 'manuscript' are thus used interchangeably. For instance, the Mazoon Saheb would often repeat the sentence 'I'll tell you something: books are the most important holdings of the *daʿwa* on earth'. Books, in this case, are handwritten *makhtutat* and not replaceable printed volumes.

This brings us to the discussion on definitions of the manuscript as a book. A specialist in English manuscript culture, Peter Beal describes how books today are most commonly understood as printed volumes. From a historical point of view, however, he argues, the term 'book' has been used for almost 'any kind of written document, both bound and otherwise'. He explains that the meaning of the book was not so much related to its physicality but rather to 'a sense of authority that the record in question has: i.e. that it is the main or official source of reference or finality'.[14] It is exactly this

9 Colette Sirat, *Writing as Handwork: A History of Handwriting in Mediterranean and Western Culture* (Turnhout: Brepols, 2006), 161. Eltjo Buringh, *Medieval Manuscript Production in the Latin West: Explorations with a Global Database* (Leiden: Brill, 2011), 16.

10 Gerald W. R. Ward (ed.), *The Grove Encyclopedia of Materials and Techniques in Art* (Oxford: Oxford University Press, 2008), 355.

11 See, for instance, Fred Leemhuis, 'From Palm Leaves to the Internet', in Jane Dammen McAuliffe (ed.), *The Cambridge Companion to the Qur'ān* (Cambridge: Cambridge University Press, 2001–6), 145–62.

12 Buringh, *Medieval Manuscript Production in the Latin West*, 16, the advantage of this term being that it is less Eurocentric, as 'manuscript' comes from the medieval European Latin tradition.

13 See, for a more detailed description of this argument, Akkerman, 'The Bohra Manuscript Treasury', 192, 193.

14 Peter Beal, *A Dictionary of English Manuscript Terminology 1450–2000* (Oxford: Oxford University Press, 2008), 43–4.

sense of authority and authenticity, and not so much the physical forms per se, that is at the heart of Bohra manuscript culture and defines Bohra manuscripts.

Before we jump into the manuscript world of inscribed surfaces in the next section, let me offer a final note on the dialectics between book and text. Albert Henrichs makes a very interesting point by suggesting that books were invented for the sake of recording texts, and that became their main function; therefore, books were more dependent on text for their survival than the other way round. In other words, without text there would be no physical books. He further argues that, historically, it was the text that determined the format of the book and not vice versa.[15] Heinrichs thus sketches a book–text relationship in which text dominates the material form of the book.

But is this really true in the case of the manuscript culture(s) of the *khizana*? To a certain extent I would say this is the case. After all, Bohra manuscript culture is based on the authority of the uninterrupted chain of transmission of the Fatimid-Tayyibi eternal truths, the *haqa'iq* and the *makhtutat*, and its scripts are merely a manifestation of the material forms of this process of transmission in the temporal space of this world. From this perspective, it is thus text over the *makhtutat*. However, in Chapters 2 and 4 we witnessed that Bohra manuscripts have been elevated from repositories of written texts to sacred objects: talismanic and other powers of agency are attributed to them as objects written in what are considered the holy auras of the Bhai Sahebs. The dialectics of the Bohra manuscript versus the text it transmits are thus mutually dependent: without manuscript no text exists, since it is the material form of the book that gives the eternal truths of the *haqa'iq* materiality, and vice versa. Text and book are thus both master and slave. On the other hand, without text there is no manuscript surface because there would be no substance to write down.

Yet circulating outside the Bohra universe, these inaccessible, sacred objects of Fatimid-Tayyibi intellectual history lose their social meaning, which is specific to the *khizana* and the space of Badri Mohallah. In other words, in the dialectics between text and the material form of the book, where does the question of the social – *what people do with books* and the relation between *subjects* and manuscripts as *objects* – come in? If we look back at the examples of forms of writing discussed throughout this study, text did indeed impose the format of the codicological entity. An example in this regard is the diplomatic letters of the *Sijillat al-Mustansiriyya*, which were sent to Yemen in the material form of a vertical roll. As things or artefacts, the *Sijillat al-Mustansiriyya* looked a certain way because, as 'things', the letters were used in a certain way:

1. As diplomatic letters (text).
2. Recorded on vertical paper rolls (book form).
3. Meant to ceremoniously unroll and to orate from in public (usage).

Without knowledge of how these manuscripts were used, the textual content of these letters would make no sense in relation to their codicology. For instance, the material format of these diplomatic documents as rolls made them more portable than codices, facilitating their passage from Egypt to Yemen during the Fatimid period.

15 Albert Henrichs, 'Hieroi Logoi and Hierai Bibloi: The (Un)Written Margins of the Sacred in Ancient Greece', *Harvard Studies in Classical Philology* 101 (2003): 207–66.

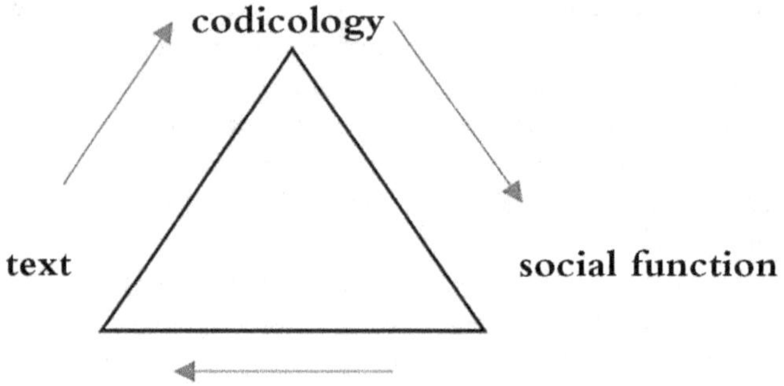

Figure 5.1 Text–codicology–social function triangle.

Writing on materiality and immateriality, Miller states, 'The appearance of the object demonstrates that which must have been responsible for its existence.'[16] In other words, the way an object looks, in this case a manuscript, should be directly connected with what people *do* with it and how it was made. The dialectics between the codicology of books and text, I thus suggest, in practice turn out to be a triangle, its third corner being the social function of the object (Figure 5.1).

The three elements of this *text–codicology–social function* triangle are interdependent and are equally important in understanding handwritten books as objects, text and script and as being part of a larger manuscript culture. As I argued before in the case of the Bohras, there would be no manuscripts and *khizana* culture, and certainly no living chain of transmission of Fatimid-Tayyibi texts, without the community, while at the same time, the community sees its existence in the world as Neo-Fatimids through the material existence of these manuscripts. As we dive deeper into the codicology of Bohra manuscripts, we return to this triangle to better understand the emic perspective on the manuscripts of the *khizana*.

Not All Books Are Books: Scrolls, Talismans and Pocket Notes

Bohra manuscripts come in a great variety of shapes and sizes, and it would be a mistake to assume that the *khizana* merely consists of books in the material form of the classical codex. But what do we mean by a classical codex, and is this term appropriate for the treasury of books? Déroche describes the usage of the term 'codex' as follows: 'Unlike Arabic, which places the emphasis on the aspect of writing (in words such as *kitāb* and *makhṭūṭa*), English, following French and Latin, etymologically refers above all to materials: "book", "codex", and "volume" derive respectively from words meaning "beech tree", "wooden tablet", and "roll of papyrus".'[17] If we follow Déroche, in the context of Arabic manuscripts, practices of writing thus prevail over the materiality of the book. Yet based on ethnographic observation, materiality, together with its social

[16] Miller, *Materiality*, 29.

[17] François Déroche, *Islamic Codicology: An Introduction to the Study of Manuscripts in Arabic Scripts* (London: Al-Furqān Islamic Heritage Foundation, 2005), 11.

usage, plays an equally important role to that of the written word, as I demonstrate in this study. I therefore retain the term 'codex', despite its roots in medieval Latin book culture, which Beal describes as follows: 'the term "codex" (plural: codices) denotes a manuscript volume, comprising quires sewn together at the fold and usually also bound, in contrast to the tablet or scroll of earlier usage'.[18]

Even though there are a rich variety of material forms of the *khizana* manuscripts, the most popular – and practical – medium is without exception the classical codex (Figure 5.2); its codicological features – such as binding, writing surfaces and *mise-en-page* – are examined in the following sections. But let us first take a look at manuscript formats that are not codices. Bohra manuscripts have been recorded and are still manually copied today on scrolls (in Arabic), single-sheet manuscripts (in Arabic), *daftar* account books (horizontal format, mainly used to note down financial affairs such as ledger books, in Gujarati), *safīna* notebooks (vertical oblong format, mainly used for lists, registers, and inventories recorded in Arabic and Gujarati), *qaṣā'id* notebooks (s. *qaṣīda* with classical diagonal text layout, in Urdu and Persian), *awrāq* (s. *waraq*, single-leaf manuscripts in Arabic), personal notes (in Arabic), pocket-sized codices and, finally, as mentioned in Chapter 2, *ta'wiz* or talismans).

Figure 5.2 The Mazoon Saheb proudly presenting a selection of small manuscripts in codex form.

[18] Beal, *A Dictionary of English Manuscript Terminology*, 78.

What is important, however, is to note that these various writing surfaces and formats are not randomly selected. Instead, the different material book forms – which together constitute the material forms of Bohra manuscript culture – are specifically produced for different genres of texts, depending on the social role of these objects. For instance, manuscripts that are used during public functions – and are thus meant to be *portable* and to be *witnessed* – are recorded on large ceremonial scrolls. Texts that require an overview, such as highly detailed charts of inheritance, are written on single-sheet manuscripts in poster format. *Haqa'iq* treatises, at the other end of the spectrum, are explicitly *not* meant to be seen because they fulfil a specific *khassa* role. It is because of the esoteric nature of *haqa'iq* texts that they are recorded in the sheltered classical codex, consisting of bifolios, which are nested to form quires sewn into a cover with a flap, thereby protecting the text from the initiated world outside and within the *khizana* itself. Let us take a closer look at the various book formats of the *khizana*.

Scrolls. A rather extraordinary manuscript format found in the *khizana* is the *rotulus* or vertical roll, as it is referred to in the specialised literature, or 'scroll' or '*sijill*' as Bohra clerics call it.[19] As a writing surface, the scroll has a long history in Mediterranean societies, in Yemen, as well as in Mughal India. It is therefore not surprising that this material form found its way into the Bohra *khizana*. As we have seen, for the Alawi Bohra community, *sijillat* are produced for one purpose only – for public use – and as a medium they are meant to be *orated from* and to be *witnessed by* the *mu'minin* and *mu'minat* during large ceremonies. The scrolls, which are all handwritten and contain a strict layout, are produced either in the shape of the classical *rotulus* (which one rolls up) or a foldable accordion-sized scroll. The *khizana* scrolls are fragile and lightweight and are therefore stored horizontally on top of the codices in the cupboards. The collection of the *khizana* contains scrolls that have been copied by different generations of Dais and are re-copied every decade due to the rapid deterioration of this material form and their intensive usage. Their material life cycles are thus considerably shorter than that of the classical codex.

As a manuscript form, scrolls have one big disadvantage in their day-to-day usage – they have no covers to protect the text – and this makes *rotuli* fragile objects not ideal for intensive use. Scrolls are relatively rare in the treasury of books, which can be explained by the fact that as a book form they are less practical to use than the classical codex. A codex is easier to copy from and can be opened at any page, allowing easier access and consultation, browsing, commenting and glossing. The classical codex also is a much more economical form of writing, for more text fits into less space: both sides of the paper or parchment of a codex are used, which is not the case with the format of the scroll in the *khizana*.[20]

The majority of the *khizana* scrolls are *ʿahd* or *mithaq* scrolls, discussed in Chapter 3, containing the entire formula of the oath of allegiance. These scrolls are frequently used

[19] Not to be confused with the horizontal book format of the *volumen*. See Déroche, *Islamic Codicology*, 12. Thus far, I have used the term 'roll' to refer to the codicological book form (see Chapter 1 on 'the materiality of *nass*'). From this chapter onwards, as a category, however, 'scroll' will be used in accordance with the terminology used by the community.

[20] Lorusso, no. 4, *Manuscript as a Codex*, point 2.

Figure 5.3 The Mazoon Saheb unrolling a scroll in his hands (left and right).

for the ceremony of the *ʿahd* and are therefore laminated and folded, instead of rolled up. In some cases, the scrolls are made by glueing sheets of paper together on the edge, which are folded while storing, leaving fold lines. During my participant observation of these ceremonies, I saw that not only is the scroll a practical format to recite from, since one does not have to turn any pages, but its codicological format also adds to the sacred nature of the ceremonial ritual: it is impressive to watch the Dai read the text of the oath from the scroll ceremonially, opening the scroll and letting the text slip through his fingers until the end when the paper roll covers the entire floor (Figure 5.3). Because of their public social role, scrolls often contain lavishly decorated title panels. Decorative elements are often simple floral patterns and arabesques in colour (not illuminated).

The Mazoon Saheb and his brothers confided in me that using the scroll during this ceremony is essential, because this is how the *majlis* was conducted during Fatimid times when the Dais carried out their secret *daʿwa* missions to the *jaza'ir* outside the empire to convert people. As we saw in Chapter 3, after the fall of the Fatimid Caliphate the practice of oral conversion from the scroll was continued in Tayyibi Yemen and travelled to Gujarat via the Indian Ocean. Without the presence of the handwritten scroll (often copied by the Dai) the ceremony is considered invalid, and one does not become part of the *dar al-taqiyya*. The material format of the scroll is thus linked to this specific ceremony.

Scrolls also fulfil another public function, namely as *awqāf* documents (s. *waqf*, 'pious endowment'). The Mazoon Saheb once showed me a very lengthy scroll that was prepared as a *waqf* document for the opening of the Badri Mohallah mosque (Figure 5.4). The scroll contained a description of the mosque in Arabic, built in the name of God and the Dai, followed by a passage in *Lisan al-Daʿwa* and the signatures

Figure 5.4 Historic *waqf* scrolls.

of the Bhai Sahebs, the contractors and the beneficiaries. The small colophon of the document was closed by official stamps of the *daʿwa*. As I demonstrated in Chapters 1 and 2, scrolls were also used for the proclamation of *nass*, a tradition which can be traced back to Fatimid times. I was told that in former times, these *nass* scrolls were carried around through the entire *mohallah* while the name of the new Dai was publicly announced.[21] Historically, small scrolls were also used for recoding registers and lists, such as marriage and pilgrimage registers. It should be noted that scrolls are also used in this way in the Dawoodi and Sulaymani communities. Poonawala lists several exemplars in his *Biobibliography*, including scrolls for the usage of correspondence and death announcements among the Dawoodis.[22]

Single-leaf manuscripts. Quite an extensive number of manuscripts of the *khizana* are neither codices nor scrolls: they are texts recorded on single sheets of paper. These manuscripts should, however, not be seen as loose folios belonging to greater works; the different formats of these single-sheet manuscripts, even though they only consist of one page, can accommodate entire treatises or sermons. Single-leaf manuscripts exist in their own right and are therefore considered a separate category of book format in this work. This category of manuscripts includes *awraq*, *taʿwiz* and single-sheet charts.

Single-sheet chart manuscripts. Single-sheet chart manuscripts are produced in poster format and serve the purpose of giving the reader an overview of official matters, such as genealogy or inheritance. The content of these posters is meticulously put together according to a very strict geometrical layout, which allows the reader to

[21] See for a similar practice during Fatimid times: Klemm, *Memoirs of a Mission: The Ismaili Scholar, Statesman and Poet, Al-Mu-ayyad Fi'l-Din Al-Shirazi*, 92.

[22] Poonawala lists several of scrolls in the Dawoodi context. Poonawala, *Biobibliography*, 213, 214, 216, 218.

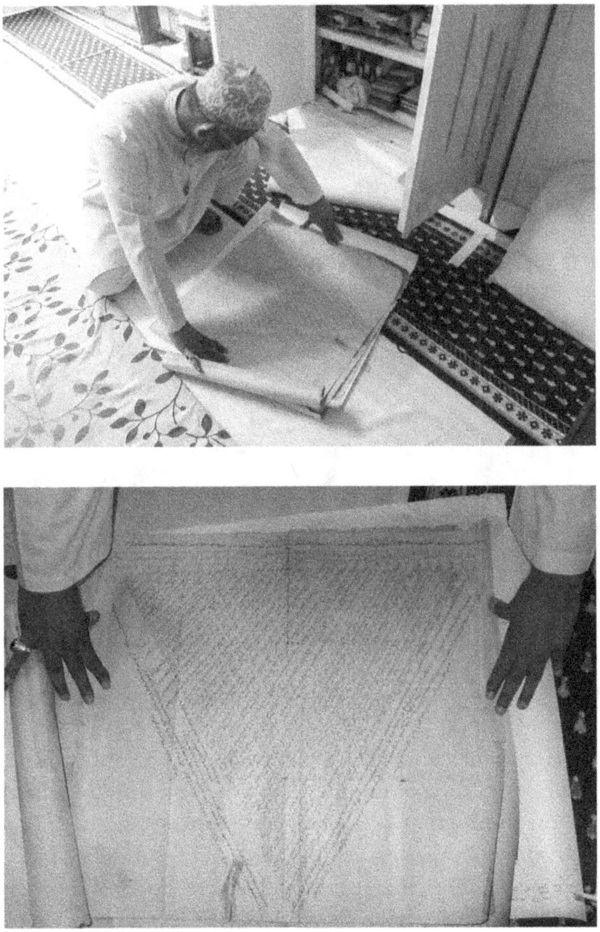

Figure 5.5 Single-sheet inheritance manuscripts laid out on the carpeted floor of the *khizana*.

browse through the numerous tables (Figures 5.5 and 5.6). The text in these posters is written in the form of an inverted triangle. First, the graphical layout of the poster is copied with classical rulers (not with *miṣtaras*, see Chapter 6), then the content of the table is filled in, and finally the chart is rolled up and stored horizontally in the lower stacks of the *khizana* cupboards.

The material form of the single-sheet poster is an example of how prevailing traditional values and day-to-day life shape the form of the manuscript, as the reading and interpreting of these charts take place on the floor. A poster format makes much more sense than the classical codext in this context, because copying or reading a codex on the floor puts stress on its spine. Moreover, this codicological format is meant to be read or consulted by several people at the same time. As a communal object, the reading of the inheritance chart, which I witnessed several times in the *khizana*, has

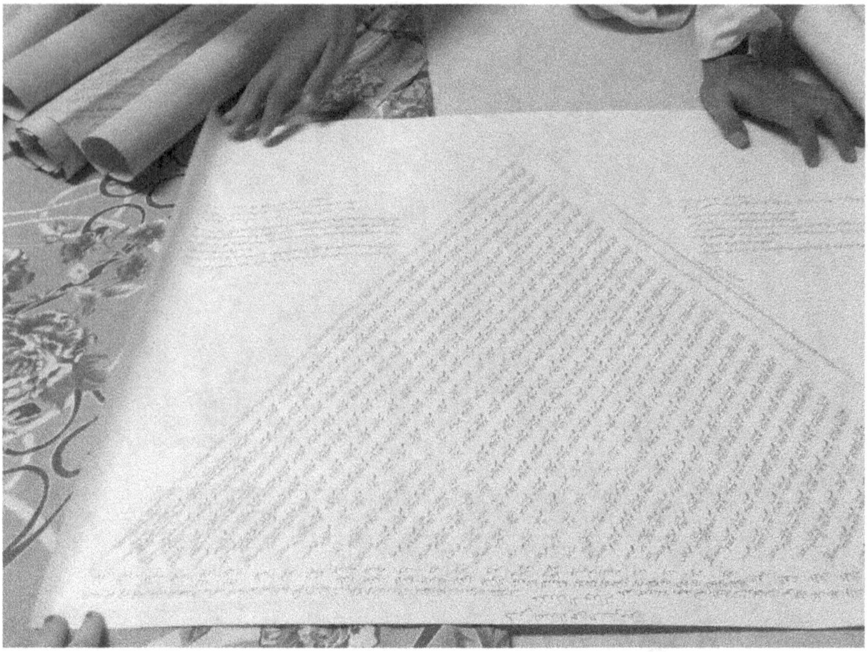

Figure 5.6 Further example of a modern single-sheet inheritance manuscript.

an inauspicious or even macabre feel to it, because it is only rolled out and interpreted when a member of the community has died (and thus the inheritance has to be assessed). In addition to inheritance charts, poster-sheet manuscripts are also used for construction plans and blueprints of the building of mosques and shrines.

The remaining single-sheet manuscripts, the *awraq* (personal notes) and the *taʿwiz* (talismans), share the same material form (A5-size paper) and are therefore stored in a similar way – in plastic bags, which are kept in small plastic transparent pouches like compact packages. They are arranged according to topic and stored in a dedicated cupboard in the treasury of books (they are thus not stored together with the *haqa'iq* treatises). The *awraq* and *taʿwiz* are an intermediate material form between the textual worlds of the *ʿamma* and the *khassa*, because as texts they dwell between the two domains. They do, however, have very different social functions.

The awraq. The *awraq* can be considered the personal scholarly archives of the Dai, the Mazoon Saheb and his brothers. They are collections of small single-leaf manuscripts containing personal study notes of the Bhai Sahebs and the Dai, written on a very wide range of religious and literary topics. As opposed to the *kutub al-daʿwa*, the *awraq* collections are private property of the (royal) owner and therefore have a more personal character. Personal note collections include *sūras*, *āyāt* and *aḥadīth* quotations, which are used to complement citations, speeches, comments, and glosses taken from the *kutub al-daʿwa* collection of the *khizana*. The Mazoon Saheb granted me access to his private *awraq* collection, consisting of massive piles of well-organised plastic pouches (Figure 5.7). He consults his collection daily for private use and for making

Figure 5.7 Left, the Mazoon Saheb stores his *awraq*. Right, the handwritten talisman collection of the *khizana*.

notes for his *bayanat* (speeches), *majalis* (ceremonies), and special sermons for Ramadan and Muharram.

Occasionally, *awraq* leaves contain only a single Qur'anic verse; fragments of literature and Arabic poetry; scribbles in *Lisan al-Daʿwa*, Hindi and Gujarati; or English translations of certain terms (not necessarily religious terms, but very common words such as 'mother', 'guide' or 'battle'). The *awraq* also contain devotional *shiʿr* (poetry), which is traditionally recorded in Urdu. The public performance of this genre of devotional poetry is an integral part of all religious ceremonies. *Shiʿr* is recited in the *masjid* by both the Bhai Sahebs and the Bhu Sahebas from the royal inner circle of the mosque (Figure 5.8). The written poem is ceremonially presented or gifted to the Dai by the reciter, who kneels in front of the Syedna. The poem is then recited, after which the Dai waves his royal hand. Thus, the poem is officially received by His Royal Highness. These devotional poems are personally composed by the Bhai Sahebs and the Bhu Sahebas for special public occasions of the *daʿwa*, such as birthdays of the royals, and performed only by those members of the royal family with the purest (and highest) voices. During my work in the treasury of books, I learned that the Mazoon Sahebs' sisters in particular are true masters in composing and reciting these poems, and activities in the *khizana* were often brought to a halt by spontaneous breathtaking poetry rehearsals, recited by the Mazoon Saheb and his eldest sister, who would compose and practise out loud in the middle of the room.

The *awraq*, whether serving as records for *bayan* or poetry, are thus written texts that are meant to be recited. As texts, they are therefore the material transition between the strict written world of the *khassa* and the oral world of the *ʿamma*. What makes the *awraq*

Figure 5.8 Royal ladies reciting poetry from the *awraq* in the *masjid* in honour of the Dai.

a type of manuscript is that they are handwritten by generations of Dais and Mazoons as self-contained objects (to return to the earlier-mentioned definition of 'manuscript') and are treated as such. They fulfil a less ceremonial role than other book formats and do not contain esoteric truths; therefore, they are allowed to leave the treasury of books. As they are often brought along to the mosque for use during sermons, the *awraq* should be portable and come in a practical pocket format, so that they can be used as a memory aid if necessary (Figure 5.9). The Dai and every Bhai Saheb have their own collections of personal *awraq*, which are inherited from generation to generation. It is for this reason that *awraq* collections contain various scripts from different hands and times and are recorded on different kinds of paper (both watermarked and non-watermarked). To preserve the older, more fragile *awraq* (which may be hundreds of years old), many folios are laminated, and others are preserved according to traditional methods (paper is pasted onto the damaged sides; see Chapter 2). The *awraq* also serve the purpose of avoiding having to consult and remove the *makhtutat* from the cupboards.

The Mazoon Saheb has also managed to collect *awraq* from the Dawoodi community, which he incorporates into his personal *bayanat*. While working on his *bayan* for the holy day of Ghadir al-Khumm, he explained why he collected Dawoodi *awraq*: 'They are very good and useful, plus very important since the Dawoodis are the only Bohra community which has access to the oldest manuscript copies in Yemen: they have the bloodline, the *silisila*, to the spiritual heritage.' For the Alawi

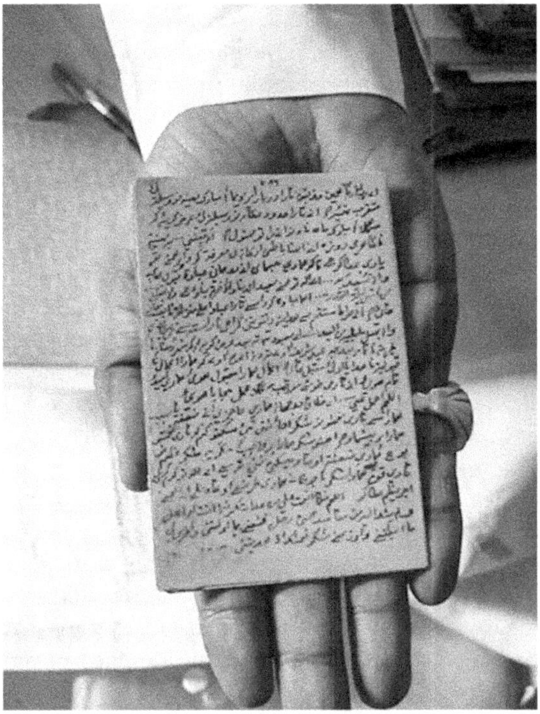

Figure 5.9 A historic *waraq* held in the palm of the Mazoon Saheb.

daʿwa, only the Dai, the Mazoon, the Mukasir and the Ra's ul Hudood Saheb produce the *awraq* for the *bayan*; their limited output is appropriate to the quite small size of the community in Baroda. The Dawoodis, by contrast, produce *awraq* collections for *bayanat* on a much greater scale, and therefore the output and circulation of *awraq* are controlled with a seal of the Dawoodi *daʿwa* (reading 'Saifee Mahal'). The watermarked paper (reading 'Madrasat al-Sayfiyya') also indicates the Dawoodi provenance of these *awraq*.

Every *bayan* written by a Dawoodi *ʿamil* needs to be authorised before he can deliver it to the *mu'minin* and *mu'minat*. This is exactly according to the tradition in Fatimid times, as the Mazoon explained, when the missionaries left for the *jaza'ir* with their *bayan*, verified by the Imams, with the aim of converting the masses. Just like the royal *basmalas*, *awraq* too are commodities in the Dawoodi community. Dawoodi *awraq* are transmitted from *ʿamil* to *ʿamil*, in word and in paper. According to the Mazoon Saheb, there is also a network of trade in and exchange of these *awraq* between the *ʿamils*, who are trying to make their collections as complete as possible and who 'ask around if their colleagues have something new'. *Awraq* produced by Alawi clerics, based on the *kutub* of the *daʿwa*, generally do not circulate outside the *khizana*. As a matter of verification, the three brothers check each other's *bayan*, but, as the Mukasir Saheb put it, there is no need for authorisation of the *bayan* because of their closeness to the Dai.

The layout and material forms of the *awraq* are as follows. Most are written in Arabic in blue or black ink and contain headings and underlining in red. The title of the quoted *kutub al-daʿwa* is mentioned on the upper left corner of the leaves of the *awraq*. The quality of the paper depends on the time and place it was produced and may be watermarked paper, 'Oriental' paper, modern paper with printed lines, blank pages or bleached paper. Both *makhtutat* and *awraq* have sophisticated systems of abbreviations and marginalia.

The taʿwiz. As noted earlier, *taʿwizat*, or talismans, are also recorded on single-leaf manuscripts. The social production and role of talismans are discussed later in the section on paratexts, but now let us consider their relevant codicological aspects. First, *taʿwizat* are an important example of two points made by this chapter: not all manuscripts are codices, and a manuscript's material form strongly depends on the text's social function. Talismans are small pieces of paper containing Qur'anic verses inscribed by the Mazoon Saheb that he gives to a believer seeking guidance. These pieces of paper are rolled up and put in a pouch worn close to the heart, or the script is dissolved in water.

Keeping this explicit immaterial quality of talismans in mind, could *taʿwizat* be classified as proper manuscripts? I would argue that they are, because they fit the elements of our definitions – as artefacts they are *portable*, *self-contained* and *unique*, and are created to *provide surfaces on which visible signs are applied by hand*. Secondly, categorising talismans as manuscripts challenges our understanding of manuscripts even more in relation to materiality versus immateriality. After all, talismans lose their material form after consumption, meaning that they are dissolved in water and taken in by the body by being eaten or drunk. Furthermore, as material objects, talismans are, just like all other manuscript book forms, perishable; not only are their (im)material healing powers embodied by believers but as physical objects they are also eaten away by termites. It is exactly this immaterial quality of manuscripts of the *khizana*, whether in the form of *haqa'iq* codices, talismans, scrolls or poetry books, that turns these sacred artefacts into worldly objects, even though the esoteric message these texts carry is considered eternal. The Dai's *ʿalama* (see Chapter 1), written in his sacred book hand and to which powers of agency are attributed, can also be considered a talismanic manuscript practice of the *khizana*.

Bohra Bookbinding: From Spine to Cover

We have seen that not all books of the *khizana* are codices and its manuscripts come in a wide variety of forms and sizes. As for the manner in which these manuscripts are bound and held together, a clear distinction can be made between book forms that are codices – that is, they are shielded and hugged by a book cover – and material book forms that consist of one folio only, such as scrolls, poster sheets, personal notes and talismans, which are objects that operate and dwell in the cupboards of the treasury of books without a protective outer shell. Hence not all manuscripts are bound, as Déroche rightly notes in his *Islamic Codicology*.[23]

Scrolls and poster sheets have no protective covers. Instead, they are rolled up and held together with simple white cotton strings, and are, as mentioned above, stacked

[23] Déroche, *Islamic Codicology*, 253.

on top of each other in a horizontal fashion. *Ta'wizat* and *awraq* also lack any kind of binding and are instead stored in small plastic bags, and sometimes small cardboard boxes. They are not bound, and do not have flaps, covers or strings.

The codex is a complete different story, and one could dedicate an entire study to the world of book covers, bifolios, quires and flaps, and the various materials and techniques used when binding manuscripts of the *khizana*. The classical codex of the *khizana*, leaving aside *daftar* account books, *qasa'id* volumes and *safina* notebooks, consists of bifolios that form quires, which are sewn into a binding with a front cover, a back cover, a spine, and often a protective flap. The diverse histories and travels of the *khizana* codices can be traced through their covers. It therefore makes sense to indeed judge these books by their covers, because they often have interesting stories to tell. Let us first examine the classical anatomy of the Bohra codex.[24]

As a book form, the classical Bohra codex comes close to what to what Déroche describes as the archetypal type of book binding in the Islamic world.[25] Bohra manuscript covers consist of a paper pasteboard, which is covered either with leather (fine goat- or even deerskin, which is very rare in Arabic manuscript traditions[26]) or with cardboard wrapped in layers of very colourful sheets of paper or cloth, which are often re-used by placing them on top of each other and glueing them together. In the broader Islamic world, book bindings were often replaced when manuscripts ended up in collections of a different nature or different cultural environments by means of cultural appropriation.[27] This does not occur in the Bohra *khizana*, for the simple reason that the book covers of external manuscripts are often more refined – made of expensive and rare kinds of leather – than manuscripts of Alawi provenance, which are made of inexpensive paper and pasteboard bindings.

The layout and decorative devices of Bohra book covers depend on the provenance and quality of the manuscript codex. The more fanciful and luxurious book bindings are all of Dawoodi provenance, bound in very delicate leather or deerskin. Bindings of Dawoodi family collections are often closed with the classical *lisān* (tongue) or envelope flap, which is an extension of the lower cover of the codex, placed either above or under the upper cover of the binding (see Figure 5.10).[28] These *lisan* flaps, which protect the volume when closed, generally contain floral decorations (applied to the cover through panel stamping) and the name of the scholarly family the codex belonged to in Arabic calligraphy (a script that comes close to *thuluth*). Book bindings of a more modest nature are prepared with materials such as cardboard or plastic covered with a cotton cloth or paper, which is garnished with patches of quarter-leather (the edges of the book are covered) at the corner of the book and half-leather at the spine. All manuscript codices of the *khizana* are wrapped with a string of white cotton, tied in a small knot on the fore edge of the codex. Particularly fragile manuscripts are stored in protective cotton slip-covers, which look like envelope pouches with a flap (Figure 5.11).

24 See also Karin Scheper, *The Technique of Islamic Bookbinding Methods, Materials and Regional Varieties* (Leiden: Brill, 2015), 47.

25 Déroche, *Islamic Codicology*, 289.

26 Gacek, *Vademecum*, 141.

27 Déroche, *Islamic Codicology*, 253.

28 Gacek, *Vademecum*, 103.

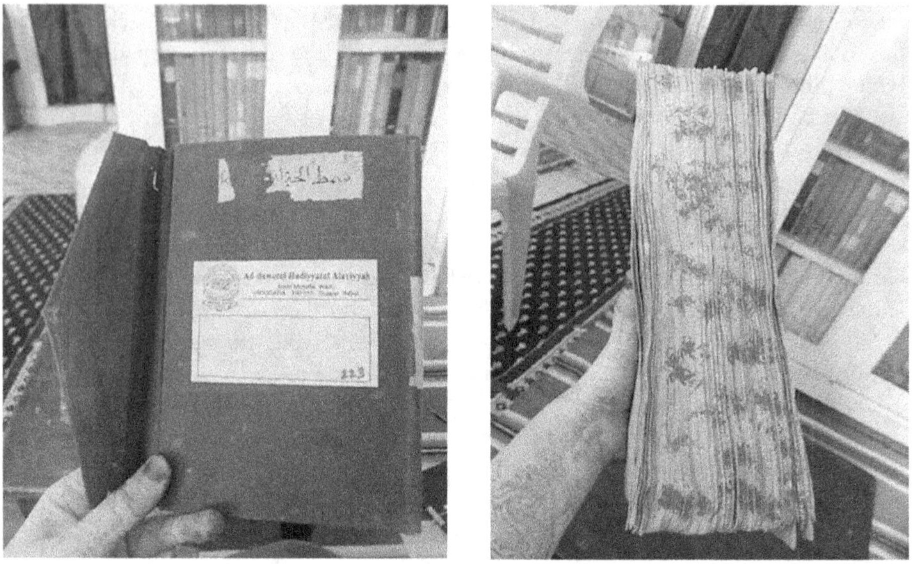

Figure 5.10 Left, book cover with *lisan* binding. Right, fore edge of a classical codex decorated with spray paint.

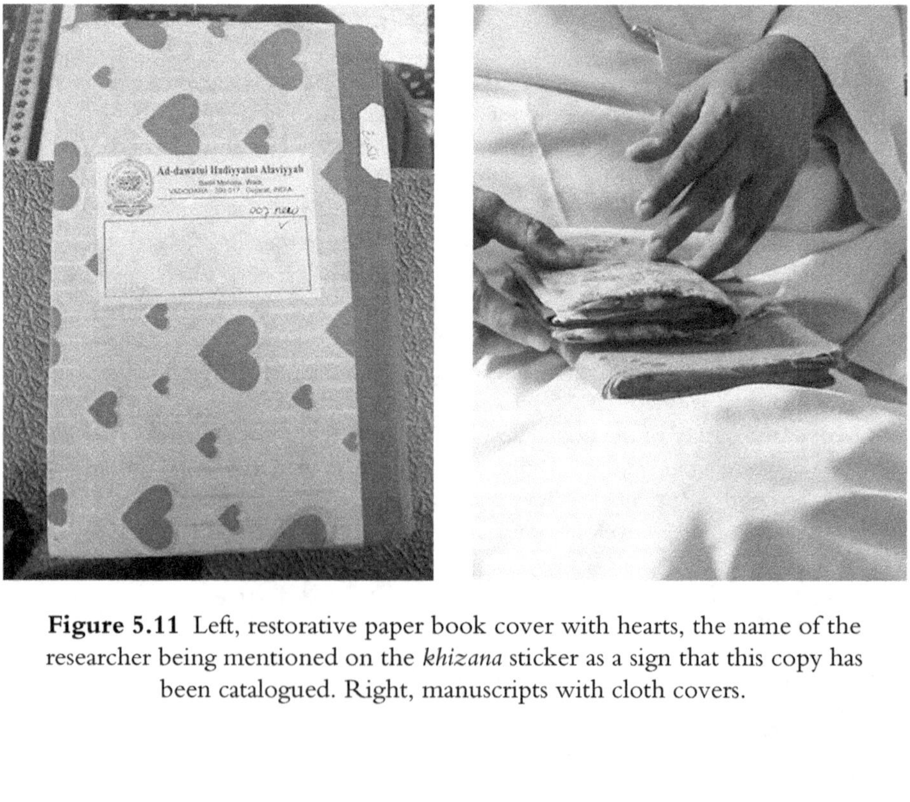

Figure 5.11 Left, restorative paper book cover with hearts, the name of the researcher being mentioned on the *khizana* sticker as a sign that this copy has been catalogued. Right, manuscripts with cloth covers.

Decorative devices are only applied to leather-bound manuscripts. The front covers of these manuscripts often contain small almond- or flower-shaped ornaments, also known as *mandorlas* in specialist literature, which are applied to the cover through panel stamping (they are not gilded).[29] Apart from the *mandorla*, other parts of the book that are decorated are the upper and lower covers and the flap of the book cover, which are decorated in the same floral pattern style, containing simple but elegant floral doublures. As mentioned in Chapter 4, in addition to decorative devices the front covers and spines of the book covers contain labels, mentioning the date of the manuscript and occasionally the *saff* and the *khana* numbers of its previous owners. The fore edges or 'belly' of Bohra *khizana* manuscripts are often decorated with colourful bright pink and yellow 'spray decoration', which is an inexpensive way of giving the manuscript a fanciful touch resembling marbled paper (see Figure 5.10).

Recent 'millennial' manuscript exemplars, copied from the 1980s onwards, are recorded in ready-made notebooks made with a hardcover spine. Because of the challenging climatic conditions of Gujarat, many manuscripts have restorative (modern) covers (see Figure 5.11). The re-binding of these manuscripts is outsourced by the Bhai Sahebs to the official bookbinder of Badri Mohallah, Mister Murmurwala. The craftmanship of Mister Murmurwala – whom I once accidentally met when he was doing a consultation for the preparation of a talisman – is mentioned on a special sticker on the inner cover of all codices of modern book bindings produced in Badri Mohallah.

Bohra manuscripts are characterised by a round back 'Oriental' binding, meaning that the text block is directly sewn into the spine (the spine of the codex has no hollow back). Furthermore, the endpaper of manuscripts of the *khizana* is glued to the cover, strengthening the cohesion between binding and book blocks. The endpapers of Alawi Bohra manuscripts are often re-used as writing surfaces from other codices or documents. Very old pieces of paper often contain large portions of texts and, in some rare cases, paper palimpsests: folios from which the original writing has been erased or washed. Quires are the gathering of a number of folded sheets in a codex.[30] The most commonly used paper quire in codices of the treasury of books is a *quaternion* (four bifolia or eight leaves), which was the dominant model in the seventeenth- and eighteenth-century Persianate world and in India.[31] Quite commonly, Bohra manuscripts contain loose quires that are incorporated or re-bound into the codex.

Writing Surfaces and Watermarks

The manuscripts of the treasury of books are recorded on a wide variety of paper writing surfaces; from very thick and fibrous to very thin and fragile paper, from expensive thin to inexpensive thick paper, from locally handmade paper produced in Ahmedabad to imported British watermarked paper.[32] Roughly, these writing papers can be

[29] Ibid., 151–2.

[30] Ibid., 210–15.

[31] Ibid., 213.

[32] See, for an overview of paper making and usage in the Islamic world, Evyn Kropf and Cathleen Baker, 'A Conservative Tradition? Arab Papers of the 12th–17th Centuries from the Islamic Manuscripts Collection at the University of Michigan', *Journal of Islamic Manuscripts* 4, 1–48.

divided into two categories: 'Oriental' pattern-less paper and 'European' paper containing watermarks and chain and laid lines. The distinction between 'Oriental' and 'European' is slightly problematic, however, in the sense that most of the 'Oriental' pattern-less paper in India was imported and made available from Europe during the British Raj, and the European watermarked paper was less popular in the Alawi Bohra *scriptorium*, for economic reasons.[33]

Let us start with 'Oriental' paper, which is the dominant writing surface used for manuscripts of the *khizana*, especially with exemplars of Alawi provenance. Most of these Alawi manuscripts are copied on rather thin, glossy Oriental paper containing no chain or laid lines, frames or watermarks. The older manuscripts in this category consist of quires made of what Gacek calls 'chaotic patterns': woven paper (meaning paper of a more 'robust' nature) with visible undissolved fibres.[34] As opposed to the more fragile and basic paper mentioned before that was imported by the British, this strong and rather thick paper, made of mulberry bark, was locally sourced and produced in the paper mills of Ahmedabad.[35]

Before the paper would be ready for consumption – and this is especially so for the thick Ahmedabad paper – its folios would first be carefully burnished or polished with a material designed to reduce its roughness. Paper was – and still is today – finished into 'butter paper' and given a glossy appearance by rubbing a wax stone over it that is melted and put into a piece of cloth. This procedure, carried out by 'the forefathers', took place *before* the writing process to make the paper capable of receiving the ink without blemishing or leaking.

European paper is often, but not always, used in manuscripts that are alien to the treasury of books: the manuscripts of (private) Dawoodi provenance (such as the Hamdani and the Fyzee collections). This de luxe type of paper has a very glossy touch and a very creamy appearance. The paper is thin but very strong and occasionally contains laid and chain lines. Interestingly, several manuscripts of this kind contain watermarks (and laid and chain lines) of clear British provenance. Even though I did not encounter them in the *khizana* in Baroda, Anne Regourd has documented several types of watermarked papers commissioned by influential Dawoodi merchants in England in the colonial period, which were distributed over the Indian Ocean via Bombay and found in libraries today from Harar, Ethiopia, to Zabid, Yemen.[36]

The watermarks found in Baroda are impressed watermarks (and thus not imitated), which are crucial in dating manuscripts and determining their sectarian provenance. These watermarks depict dates, names of companies, coats of arms and crescents in full detail (Figures 5.12). A common watermark in these manuscripts is the *Foolscap Universal* watermark. Distinguishable as a belt-decorated lifebuoy with a laureate reading 'Foolscap Universal', the watermark refers to the traditional paper size (8½ x 13½ inches; 21.6 x 34.3 cm) that was standard in the British Commonwealth before the

[33] Categories followed by Déroche, *Islamic Codicology*, 49–64, and Gacek, *Vademecum*, 86–193.

[34] Gacek, *Vademecum*, 190.

[35] See also Anne Regourd, 'Papiers "indiens" de manuscrits éthiopiens (fin xixe–début xxe siècle)', in Anne Regourd (ed.), *The Trade in Papers Marked with Non-Latin Characters* (Leiden: Brill, 2018), 175.

[36] Anne Regourd, 'Papiers "indiens" de manuscrits éthiopiens (fin xixe–début xxe siècle)', 176–80.

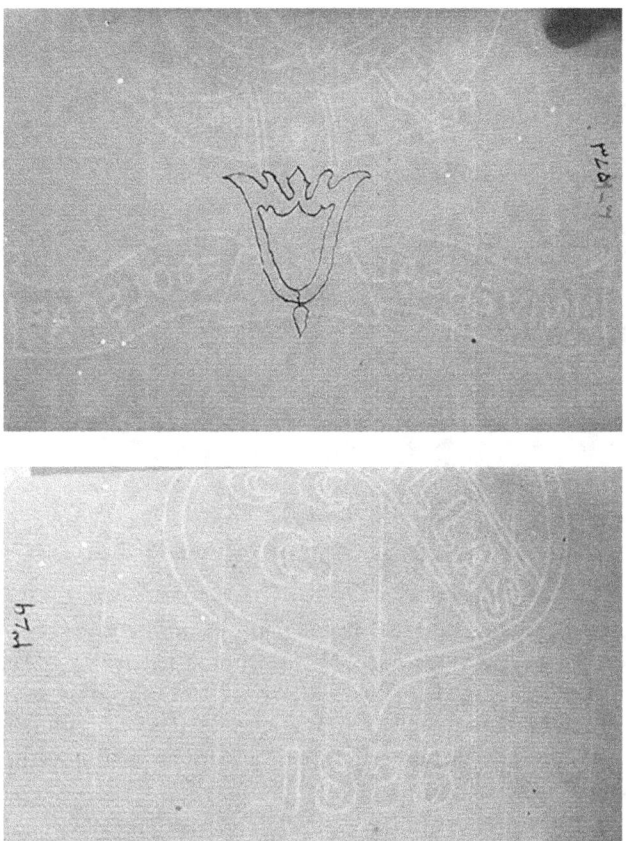

Figure 5.12 Above, Bohra watermarks: *Foolscap Universal*, with depiction of a lifebuoy. Below, a shield with three crescent moons dated 1875.

introduction of A4-sized paper.[37] The full sheet of the foolscap paper is folded *in folio*, meaning folded only once (half of the full sheet is thus one folio), so that the watermark is divided over two pages divided by the spine of the book. Another popular British-made watermark produced for the Indian market has a shield with three crescent moons, dated 1875, reading 'Extra Superfine *Miftāḥ al-Hind* '(Ar.; 'the key of al-Hind') calligraphed in Arabic with two interlocking keys underneath (Figure 5.13).

The archetypal *khizana* codex is relatively small in size in comparison with paper sizes of Arabic manuscripts produced in other bookish Muslim milieux, according to Gacek and Déroche: the size of the paper per folio varies from 12.5 x 14 cm to 15 cm x 25 cm.[38] I suggest that, in addition to economic reasons, the reasonably modest size of the Bohra manuscript codex is strongly related to its social function, which is *secret* and *sacred*. The social role of these codices as secret manuscripts is not meant

[37] Ibid., 180. See also http://en.wikipedia.org/wiki/Foolscap_folio.

[38] Gacek, *Vademecum*, 193. Déroche, *Islamic Codicology*, 53.

Figure 5.13 Another watermark: *Extra Superfine Miftāḥ al-Hind* (Ar.; 'the key of al-Hind') with two interlocking keys.

to be ornamental (lavish decorations or calligraphy require more space on the paper), but to be practical and not to serve a public function: the codex is meant to carry text only. As the material form of the sacred, the content of the Bohra codex is not to be changed or commented upon, which explains the absence of a tradition of glosses and commentary cultures (which also require space in the *mise-en-page* of the paper) in Bohra manuscript culture.

5.2 Anatomy of Bohra Manuscripts: Paratexts from Head to Tail

Now that a better understanding has been gained of the codicology of the Alawi treasury of books and the relationship between text and its social role, the second part of this chapter is devoted to the margins of the treasury of books. As I described in the previous chapter, every afternoon the Mazoon Saheb and I studied the 'rough edges' found in the manuscripts of the *khizana*: marginal notes, glosses, unidentifiable scribbles, poetry, magical squares, and so on. Although most of these manuscript marginalia were used by the Mazoon himself, others were as unknown to him as they were to me, and we would sit and disentangle scribbles, curses and magic tables together for hours. The Mazoon did not have a term to describe the rich world of these marginalia, nor did we find one in his manuscripts. To use the most inclusive term possible, I refer to these and many other scribal phenomena found in the margins of the *khizana* as paratexts or rough edges.

The term 'paratext' was introduced by Gérard Genette, who describes it as follows:

> Paratexts are those liminal devices and conventions, both within and outside the book, that form part of the complex mediation between book, author, publisher, and reader: titles, forewords, epigraphs, and publishers' jacket copy are part of a

> book's private and public history . . . a text without a paratext does not exist and never has existed.[39]

Paratexts thus include all 'undefined zones', 'thresholds', or 'vestibules' of the printed book as Genette calls them, both textual and material, from cover to cover. One could argue that since Genette's all-encompassing definition is meant for commercial printed books, it cannot be used for manuscript cultures. Yet what I find productive about this term is that it considers the materiality of the book, including its binding, tassels and dust covers, as much paratexts as its extra-textual features. As codicology and paratexts are both mutually important and in conversation with another, I have therefore paired them in this chapter.

Focusing on textual elements only within the realm of pre-modern Islamic book cultures, Konrad Hirschler and others use the term 'manuscript notes' to describe paratexts: 'any written material that is found on a manuscript that does not belong to the main text(s), irrespective of whether it refers to the main text and the legal status of the manuscript or is entirely unrelated to text and manuscript itself'.[40] Although this definition is all-inclusive on the textual level, it does not touch upon other dimensions of paratexts, such as the material aspects mentioned by Genette and their social dimensions. Dagenais, a scholar who covers textual, material and social aspects of paratexts in the context of medieval European manuscript culture, introduced the term 'rough edges':

> [The manuscript] had rough edges, not the clean, carefully pruned lines of critical editions; and these edges were filled with dialogue about the text – glosses, marginal notes, pointing hands, illuminations. I began to see that it is at the edges of manuscripts and in the various activities by which medieval people transformed one manuscript into another – commentary, translation, adaptation, reworking, and the 'mechanical' act of copying – that the most important part of 'medieval literature' happens.[41]

With this statement, Dagenais suggests that without the rough edges, there is no manuscript culture, and vice versa, which corresponds to the text–codicology–social meaning triangle presented in this chapter. As we see, the tradition of rough edges in Bohra manuscript culture is very rich, regardless of the genre of manuscripts, and paratexts can even be read as separate texts. Margins and glosses also have aesthetic

[39] Gérard Genette, *Paratexts: Thresholds of Interpretation*, trans. Jane E. Lewin and Richard Macksey (Cambridge: Cambridge University Press, 1997), first flyleaf and Introduction, 4.

[40] Andreas Görke and Konrad Hirschler, *Manuscript Notes as Documentary Sources*, ed. Andreas Görke and Konrad Hirschler (Beirut: Orient-Institut, 2012), 9–10 , 141–62. See also the special issue of the *Journal of Islamic Manuscripts*: Boris Liebrenz, 'Preface', *The History of Books and Collections through Manuscript Notes. Journal of Islamic Manuscripts* 9 (2018): Issue 2–3 (October 2018), 105–7; Adam Gacek, 'Ownership Statements and Seals in Arabic Manuscripts', *Manuscripts of the Middle East* 2 (1987): 88–95; Ayman Fu'ād Sayyid, 'Les marques de possession sur les manu-scrits et la reconstitution des anciens fonds des manuscrits arabes', *Manuscripta Orientalia* 9 (2003): 14–23; Boris Liebrenz, 'Lese- und Besitzvermerke in der Leipziger Rifāʿīya-Bibliothek', *Manuscript Notes as Documentary Sources*, 141–62.

[41] Dagenais, *The Ethics of Reading in Manuscript Culture*, xvi.

dimensions as paratexts were often used as ornamentation.[42] According to my observations, however, paratexts used as ornamentation do not play an important role in Bohra manuscript culture and are therefore left out of the analysis.

Paratexts, or the rough edges in manuscript cultures, by no means randomly end up in codices. In contrast, as I argue, different genres have very distinct traditions of paratexts. The previously mentioned CSMC in Hamburg proposes a different definition of paratexts in manuscripts:

> 'Paratexts' are parts of texts, musical notation or images in manuscripts, usually comprising textual elements. The functions of these elements concern primarily the content, but often the manuscript as a physical object, too. Main categories are: structuring and guiding (both content and object), explicating the content, and documenting the usage of the manuscript. In this respect paratexts depend on the main text, that is, the part of a text which can be transmitted independently. Beyond the functions mentioned, the usage of paratexts is closely related both to the given type of the main text (genre) and the format and layout of the manuscript. Fostered by the material conditions of manuscripts, paratexts are dynamic and subject to change, both in function and form, according to the way manuscripts are produced, transmitted and used.[43]

The conclusion that literary genres have very distinct traditions of paratexts also supports Genette's argument that paratexts are constantly changing, depending on the time and space they are produced in and the audience they are meant for. I would even go further by arguing that, although paratexts constantly change, as rough edges they also shape manuscript culture in its entirety: the Bohra manuscript culture of the *khizana* is a clear example.

In what follows, I examine the 'anatomy' of Bohra manuscripts and the specific paratexts they accommodate: head (incipit), body (margins) and tail (colophon). By doing so, we will gain a better understanding of the dialectics between text and paratext. Furthermore, I demonstrate how the genre of the manuscript shapes its paratexts and how paratexts in their turn shape and re-shape the social function of the manuscript within the space of the *khizana*.

Bohra Manuscript Culture and Paratexts

Bohra manuscripts give materiality to the sacred, immaterial, Fatimid-Tayyibi esoteric truths and are therefore considered the central element in the community's Neo-Fatimid identity in the present. As these esoteric truths are seen as eternal and unchangeable, royal Alawi scribes have copied this heritage from the past by the letter, attempting to stay as close to the Yemeni manuscript exemplars as possible. Adding commentaries or glosses, or any other kind of novelties to the 'mother text', was therefore by no means allowed, nor was introducing changes in the codicology permissible.

[42] See, for instance, the excellent blog on medieval illuminated manuscripts named *Sexy Codicology*: http://sexycodicology.net/blog (last accessed 13 May 2017).

[43] Quotation courtesy of Prof. Dr Michael Friedrich, spokesperson of the Sonderforschungsbereich 950 Manuscript cultures in Asia, Africa and Europe. SFB internal working paper, 2015.

Although, in theory, Bohra copyists have tried to stay as close as possible to a kind of *Urtext*, actual writing practices illustrate an opposite tendency. A discrepancy thus exists between the official narrative of transmission of a 'pure' Tayyibi-Fatimid manuscript culture in Arabic and the practice of consumption and transference in day-to-day life. Flyleaves, inside covers, incipits and margins reveal that, over the course of the centuries, many profane features and traditions have seeped into Bohra manuscript culture.[44] These features, however, know their place in the manuscripts, as they remain in the margins and do not interfere with the 'naked' body of the text.

There are only a few spaces in Bohra codices that allow room for paratexts: the margins, incipits, flyleaves, title pages, colophons, cover and spine. These paratexts have a specific function: they are meant to order, understand, read, translate, brand (own or re-own) or copy the 'original' text, for instance by vocalising the Arabic text in the margins or by adding instructions on how to translate certain sentences. Simply put, the Bohra manuscript as an untouchable secret vehicle of knowledge needed extra features, albeit subtle ones, to be comprehended by the Indian clerical reader and copyist.

Bohra scholarship is thus not at all concerned with innovating or commenting on the 'original' text. After all, during the seclusion of the hidden Imam all knowledge, especially *ʿilm al-batin*, must remain hidden. Instead, it is the art of preserving and transmitting the Bohra philological tradition in its most perfect form that is considered the most pious religious deed and clerical duty for which one receives *baraka* (blessings). Apart from this religious obligation, the extremely humid climate of Gujarat contributes to the culture of re-production instead of production of knowledge, since manuscripts are often prone to either mould or fungi or are eaten away by termites, especially in the monsoon season.

I argue that it is as much the Fatimid-Tayyibi mother text as the paratextual traditions that define Bohra manuscript culture. In fact, it is the unique rough edges that make these manuscripts stand out from other Arabo-Islamic manuscript traditions. Paratexts are what keep Bohra manuscript culture alive, for they bridge the secret content of cyclical time and space with present-day life; the social-codicological, subject to time and space, with the eternal textual. Instead of focusing on separate categories of paratexts, I propose a more holistic approach, browsing through the material from head to tail. By doing so, I not only provide an overview of the kind of paratexts found in Bohra manuscripts but also am able to differentiate between the functions of specific paratexts, especially in relation to their place in the codex and their larger social usage in the community.

Keeping in mind the question of how paratexts shape manuscript culture, I start with two spaces in the manuscript where there is actually room for paratexts: the head (the incipit, including the first flyleaf) and the tail (the colophon, including the last back leaf) of the codex. Then I discuss paratexts situated in the body of the codex – that is, marginalia – and by doing so I intend to demonstrate that within one manuscript culture different marginal traditions are used, depending on the genre of the text.

[44] See for an in-depth description of flyleaves and inside covers in Arabic manuscript cultures: Franz Rosenthal, *The Technique and Approach of Muslim Scholarship* (Rome: Pontificium Institutum Biblicim, 1947), 20–2.

The Tail of the Manuscript: Colophons

Whereas a philologist of European medieval manuscripts would start analysing a codex with its head, known as the *incipit*, in Arabic manuscripts one starts with the tail, known as the 'crowning touch', *khatm* (Ar.; 'seal') or *colophon*. Colophons of Arabic manuscripts often – but not always – contain crucial clues for identifying the codex and its stemma (the genealogy of transmission), such as the title and author of the treatise, ownership statements, the name of the copyist and place of composition, and, if one is fortunate, the date of copying. Figure 5.14 depicts two standard Bohra colophons.[45] Written on the last folio of the codex in an informal non-vocalised book hand, Bohra colophons are commonly shaped in a V-form – an upturned triangle shape – which is a standard feature in Arabic manuscripts. According to Gacek, Arabic manuscripts can have several colophons or none at all, and their content varies from one manuscript to the next.[46] This is not the case in Bohra manuscript culture. Bohra manuscripts only

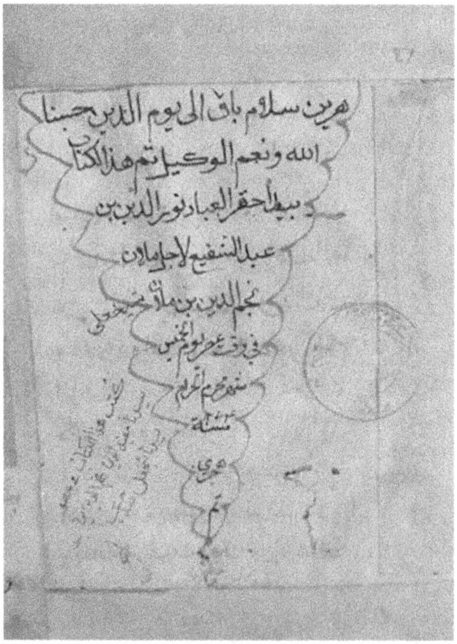

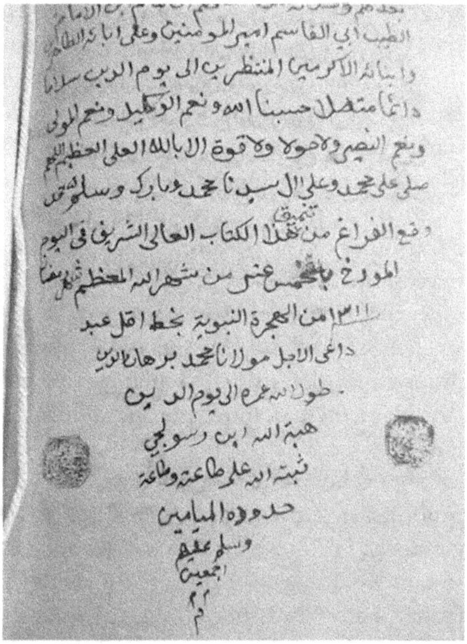

Figure 5.14 Two V-shaped colophons found in Bohra manuscripts. Left, *khatm* of Alawi provenance, written during the *ʿasr* of Sy. Mufīd al-Dīn Najm al-Dīn Nūḥ Shaykhʿalī (no. 39, d. 1274/1857), copied on a Friday, during the month of Muharram 1274/1857. Right, *khatm* of Dawoodi provenance, written during the *ʿasr* of Sy. Muhammad Burhan al-Din (no. 49, d. 1323/1906), dated Ramadan fifteenth, 1311/1893.

[45] See, for more examples of Bohra colophons, Poonawala, 'The Contribution of Ismāʿīlī Colophons', 112–31.

[46] Gacek, *Vademecum*, 71–6.

have one colophon, which is never re-copied by the scribe, because, as a paratext, it is considered a man-made and not a sacred textual element. It is therefore considered unproblematic, as we have seen in Chapter 4, that colophons of previous owners are at times erased and replaced by new information.

In comparison to colophons found in Arabic manuscript cultures of the Middle East, Bohra colophons are generally elaborate, taking the space of an entire folium or more, and carry a rich variety of information, which is not randomly presented to the reader. Instead, colophons display uniformity in style, expression and content, as the scribe follows a fixed template (more on the practical aspects of colophons in Chapter 6).[47] The standardised Bohra colophon, regardless of its provenance or time of composition, contains the following paratextual features:

1. The opening of the colophon with introductory formulae stating the completion of copying, such as:
   - Figure 5.14 (right), fifth line from above: '*qad waqaʿa al-farāgh min tanmīq hādhā 'l-kitāb al-sharīf . . .*' ('the completion and embellishment of this honourable book were completed . . .').
   - Figure 5.14 (left), second line from above: '*tamma hādhā 'l-kitāb bi-yadd aḥqar al-ʿibād*' ('this book was completed by the hand of the lowest of God's servants').[48]

   The statements often include adjectives of self-abasement and humiliation, such as *al-faqīr* (Ar. 'the pauper'), *al-aḥqar* (Ar. 'the most miserable'), or al-*ḍaʿīf* (Ar.; 'the weakling'), followed by pious invocations and pleas for the forgiveness of sins and scribal mistakes made.[49] In addition, Bohra colophons often contain certain mottos or scribal verses in which the scribe begs the reader for his or her prayers (see Chapter 6).[50] Here we see a scribal leftover from Tayyibi Yemen as Ariana D'Ottone argues that the style, form and formulae of these expressions are very specific to Yemeni manuscript culture.[51]
2. Bohra *taṣliyāt* (invocations, see Chapter 6).
3. The date of copying, both written out in full in Urdu numerals (often in superscript above the word *sana'* meaning 'year').
4. The dating by regnal years: the *ʿasr* of the Dai, depending on the lineage followed (Alawi/Dawoodi/Sulaymani), presented in the formula '*bi-khaṭṭ*' or '*bi-yadd ʿabd al-Dai al-ʿajl Mawlanā*' (in the script/hand of the servant of the Dai, the present Mawlana), followed by the name of the Dai and his blessings. In this manner every manuscript copied in the *daʿwa* is written not only in honour of the Dai but also, indirectly, in his hand. When a date of copying is not mentioned, has been

[47] This is also what Poonawala concludes, 'The Contribution of Ismāʿīlī Colophons', 104.

[48] See for an exhaustive list: Poonawala, 'The Contribution of Ismāʿīlī Colophons', 104, f.122.

[49] See Poonawala, 'The Contribution of Ismāʿīlī Colophons', 105, f.124, and Gacek, *Vademecum*, 239–40.

[50] Gaceck, *Vademecum*, 237–8.

[51] Arianna D'Ottone, 2015. 'The Pearl and the Ruby: Scribal Dicta and Other Metatextual Notes in Yemeni Medieval Manuscripts', in David Hollenberg, Christoph Rauch and Sabine Schmidtke (eds), *The Yemeni Manuscript Tradition* (Leiden, Brill, 2015), 82–100. Poonawala, 'The Contribution of Ismāʿīlī Colophons', 107, f.127.

erased or is not readable in a colophon, the mention of the *'aṣr* of the *Dai*, which is always present, is a good indication of the (approximate) date of copying. This paratextual feature is also ideal for determining the provenance of the manuscript. As described in Chapter 4, the dating by regnal years is often removed when manuscripts move from one Bohra sect to another.

5. The name of the scribe: these names are without exception common Bohra compound names, characteristically ending with honorific suffixes such as *bhai*, *bhai saheb* (meaning 'revered brother', which, in the Alawi context, indicates that the scribe was a Bhai Saheb) or *jee* (respected); for instance, Aliabbasjee or Tayyebsayuddinbhai. In case of non-royal (Dawoodi) scribes, the suffix *wala* (man) is preceded by either their profession or *laqab* (place of residence); for instance, Nagpurwala (man from Nagpur) or Attarwala (perfume seller). The place in which the manuscript was copied is rarely mentioned in colophons. This information is, however, easy to deduce due to the *laqab* of the copyist (such as Nagpurī, a person who is from Nagpur).
6. The closing of the colophon with *tasliyat* and other finishing formulae in which God's blessings are invoked on the Prophet and the pure Imams. The standard *tamma* (it is finished) is replaced by *tamma tamamshud* (more about this Persianate feature in the context of Arabic manuscript culture in Chapter 6), which appears in abbreviated forms in the shape of a *mīm* or three *mīms* (Figure 5.14, right).

Since colophons are copied in book hands of a more informal nature, strong influences of *nasta'liq* are visible in the *naskh* of Bohra scribes.

A feature that is present in all Bohra colophons, regardless of their time and place of composition, is the dating by regnal years of the Dai. According to Adam Gacek, the *ta'rīkh bi 'l-julūs*, or the dating in regnal years, in colophons was a common writing practice in pre-modern subcontinental Arabic writing culture.[52] In the Alawi *khizana*, this practice, which seals the manuscript, is even found in clandestine manuscripts copies that were not officially commissioned or authorised by Bohra clerics. Why is the *'asr* of the Dai considered of such vital importance that it is mentioned at the end of *every* Bohra manuscript copy? The answer to this question can again be found in the Bohras' unique conception of time and space, based on the Isma'ili narrative of cyclical hiero-history. The mentioning of the *'asr* of the Dai fits into this model because it is not only a way to refer to linear time periods in history but is also a strong reference to the abstract sense of time in this cyclical model: it is a way of marking or situating the manuscript in the cyclical process.

Poonawala observed that, whereas the commendation of the Dai was indeed also part of Tayyibi Yemeni colophons, it did not include the 'high-flown language or verbose eulogies' one finds in Bohra manuscripts of Indian provenance.[53] This paratextual evolution thus supports the argument I made in Chapter 2 of the metamorphosis of clerical authority, as the community moved from Tayyibi Yemen to Bohra India, from a clerical elite to a sacerdotal royal family, and the consequent changed role of manuscripts as sacred objects.

[52] Gacek, *Vademecum*, 88.

[53] Poonawala, 'The Contribution of Ismā'īlī Colophons', 105.

Head of the Manuscript: Incipits

The second step in identifying Arabic manuscripts is to analyse the head of the codex, the incipit (Lat. 'here it begins'). As is the case with colophons, incipits of Bohra manuscripts are copied according to a fixed template that contains the following paratextual elements (Figure 5.15):

1. The title of the treatise (including the *jild* or section), followed by the complete name of the author, written in the head piece in red ink.
2. The *basmala*, occasionally ending with '*wa bihi nastaʿīn*' (Ar.; 'and it is from Him alone that we seek help'). The space of the *basmala* is intentionally left blank and is reserved for the Dai as a means of authorisation (see Chapter 4 for a description of scribal politics of the royal *basmala*).
3. The *hamdala* (marked with an accolade in red): the first words of the text block, followed by the beginning of the text.
4. Bohra *tasliyat* (invocations), including the *'a'imma al-tahirin* (pure Imams).

Although these paratextual features and layout of the incipit are not unique in the context of Arabic manuscripts, some 'rough edges' are very specific to Bohra manuscript culture. These pre-paratextual features are all linked to the space of the manuscript in which they are recorded. First, there is the practice of leaving the space of the *basmala* blank for the Dai. Second, Bohra incipits contain a variety of paratexts written in the margins of the folio, such as *khizana* stamps on the right rule-border of the

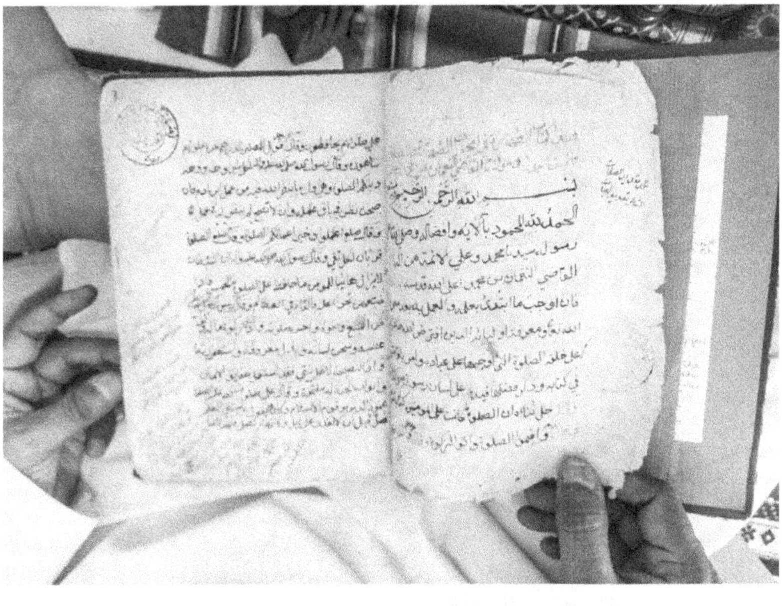

Figure 5.15 Standard Bohra incipit with marginal notes, royal *basmalas* and owner stamps.

folium, next to the head piece. The practice of using these stamps, containing Arabic calligraphy, is common in all three Bohra communities in both official *da'wa* contexts and in private family collections. Due to the rich social lives of these manuscripts and their inter-communual mobility, it is not uncommon for one manuscript exemplar to contain stamps of the different communities and scholarly families (which are often erased; see Figure 5.16 and 5.17).

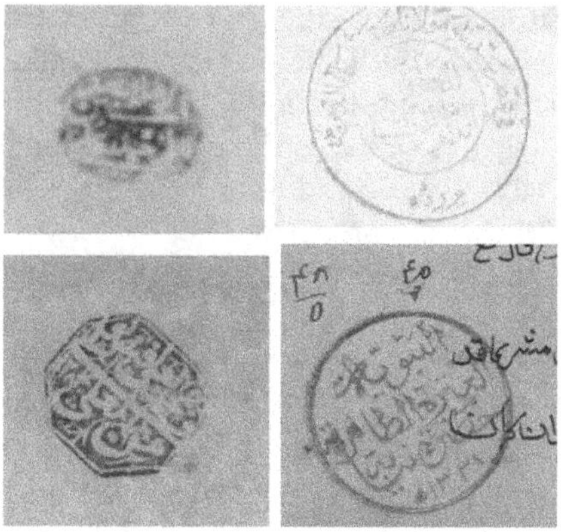

Figure 5.16 A sectarian overview of Bohra owner stamps, including the Alawi royal stamp (top right) and the Hamdani family *khizana* stamp (bottom left) that we have seen in the manuscript copy of the Qaratis al-Yaman (Figure 2.8).

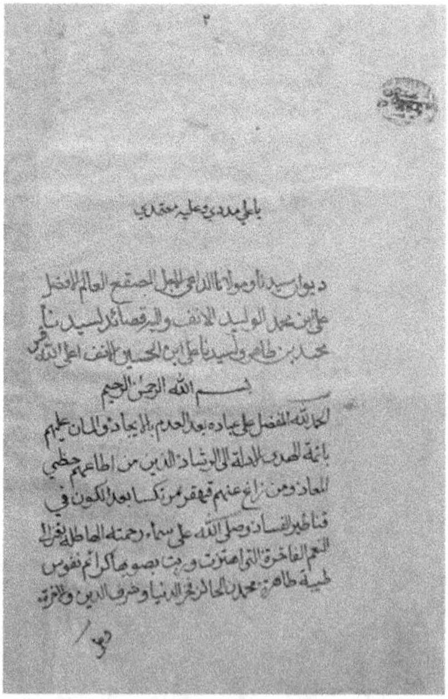

Figure 5.17 Ownership stamp, incipit.

Manuscripts that are donated or 'gifted' to the treasury of books as a '*hadiyya*' (present) or are acquired by the Mazoon Saheb contain notes (in English or Arabic) mentioning the date, place, time and nature of exchange. Some incipits and first flyleaves contain private ownership statements, either in the form of octangular owner stamps and seals (Figure 5.16) or noted in the margins, followed by the name of the Dai, the name of the owner and his *laqab*, and the date of the transfer (in Urdu numerals). Cortese and Triton mention that, in the case of Bohra family collections, inheritance statements were also noted down in the first flyleaves of the codex, especially in the case of multiple-volume manuscripts that were divided among the heirs after the death of the original owner.[54] Through these statements we learn that the inheritance of manuscripts as symbols of family scholarly pedigree and cultural capital, as Cortese argues, was deemed more important than keeping the multiple volumes of a treatise together. She writes: 'In such cases the manuscript becomes an object with agency in that its endowment was intended to reinforce familial bonds and community attachment where its possession bestowed in turn on each new owner the role of keepers of secret knowledge and heritage.'[55]

Additional marginal paratextual features are pagination (and occasionally foliation), which starts with the incipit, and readers' notes: marginal glosses explaining the main text (often written diagonally), references to other texts, and dates of reading that are marked in the upper-left corner of the folium with the *sana* (year), followed by the year in Persian numerals and the letter *hā'* (which stands for *hijra*; see Figure 5.18). In addition to mentioning the years of reading in the incipit, more specific dates of reading, mentioning the day and sometimes even the time of day according to the prayers, are jotted down throughout the entire manuscript. These readers' notes give a unique insight into scholarly reading culture, including practices and reading aids: one can exactly trace *when* a text was read, by *whom* and together with *which other texts*, and at

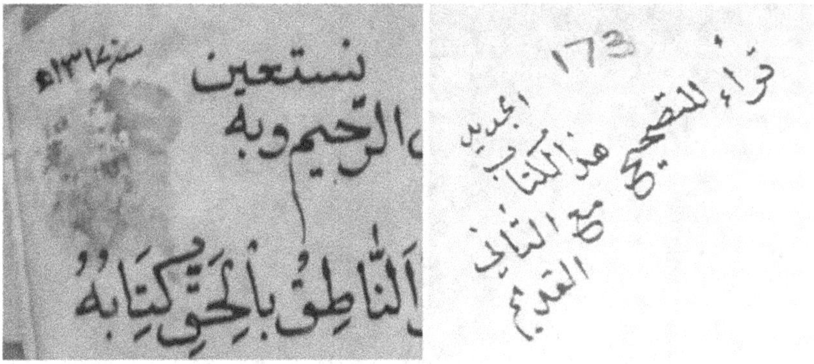

Figure 5.18 Reader notes. Left, a note in Arabic mentioning the year 1317/1899 (note the Urdu numeral for seven) in the upper-left corner of the folio. Right, the note reads 'In order to correct it, this new book was read with another, older copy' in Arabic. See Chapter 6 for more discussion on manuscript collation.

[54] Cortese, 'The *majmū' al-tarbiyah* between text and paratext', 5. A. Tritton, 'Notes on some Isma'ili Manuscripts', *BSOS*, vol. 7 (1933), 35.

[55] Ibid., 35.

what *speed*.[56] These notes also reveal that old and new copies of the same text were often read together (Figure 5.18). Occasionally, incipits contain the personal reading lists of Dais, which mention the title of the manuscript and date of reading.

Although one can thus speak of a great abundance of Bohra paratexts, there are also certain features related to reading, writing and transmission commonly found in Arabic manuscripts that are absent in Bohra manuscript culture. The most striking example is the absence of transmission statements, such as *ijaza* and *sama'a* certificates and notes: I did not come across any examples in any of the manuscripts of the Alawi *khizana* collection. According to Poonawala, these statements are not permitted due to traditions of secrecy.[57] I address the question of the absence of these transmission statements further in Chapter 6.

The Body

Now that we have covered the head and tail of Bohra manuscripts, let us examine the remaining 'borderlands' where there is room for paratexts: the margins or ruled borders, which can be found in the body of the codex, and the front and back free endpapers. Rich traditions of marginalia are a central part of Bohra manuscript culture, and codices often contain almost archaeological layers of historical marginalia, written down by generation of Bohra copyists and readers. An important codicological feature in Bohra manuscript culture, as Poonawala pointed out, is the *juz'* (fascicle, see Figure 5.19). He describes the *juz'* as a codicological unit that functions autonomously from the main text

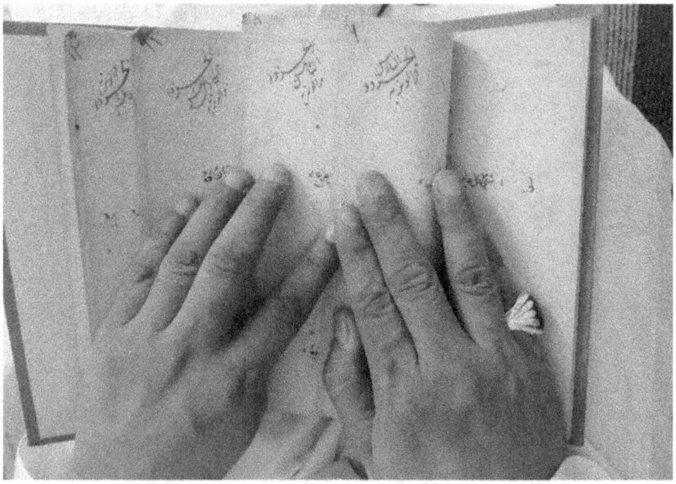

Figure 5.19 The codicological unit of the *juz'* of the text, mentioned throughout the manuscript on the upper left side of each folio.

[56] In her study of manuscript copies of the *majmū 'al-tarbiya*, Cortese argues that these aids and other paratextual features were added by readers to establish a sense of order in the text. Cortese, 'The *majmū' al-tarbiyah* between Text and Paratext', 4, 9.

[57] Poonawala describes a similar phenomenon, with copies of the *Da'a'im al-Islam* as an exception. Poonawala, 'The Contribution of Ismāʿīlī Colophons', 97.

as an intermediary between the quire and the codex.[58] Interestingly, Poonawala mentions that the division of the *juz'* can mostly be found in the works of Qadi Nuʿman and authors of the Fatimid period. I observed the same phenomenon in Fatimid in manuscript titles in the Alawi *khizana*, which seems to indicate that this paratextual feature is an ancient codicological leftover dating back to the pre-Tayyibi period.[59] Further codicological features, including layout, are discussed in the next chapter.

From a material perspective, the margins, or *ḥāshiyāt*, are the most fragile part of the codex: more often than not the outer margins are severely worn and damaged due to frequent use and termite assaults.[60] *Khizana* manuscripts clearly contain traces that indicate that in the past marginalia were considered of minor importance by Bohra copyists and collectors, for they were never re-copied and were even trimmed with no mercy for the purpose of restoration. In fact, the 'circumcision' of the unrepairable rotten or eaten parts of the folios was often done so drastically that it affected the quality of the manuscript, both because large parts of the texts were cut away (especially the endings of sentences) at the inner margins and because the codices were bound so tightly that it is impossible to open them properly without damaging the book.

In a similar fashion, the outer margins on the other side of the folios were cut away, either damaged by termites or made fragile by use. Both margins of the manuscripts shown in Figure 5.20 were partly removed, causing the loss of their unique paratextual traditions. This cutting away of the margins of these manuscripts shows

Figure 5.20 Material 'circumcision' of marginalia.

[58] Poonawala, 'The Contribution of Ismāʿīlī Colophons', 104; Poonawala, 'The Chronology of al-Qāḍī al-Nuʿmān's Works', 2018, 106–7, n. 78.

[59] Ibid.

[60] See for this phenomenon Déroche, *Islamic Codicology*, 177.

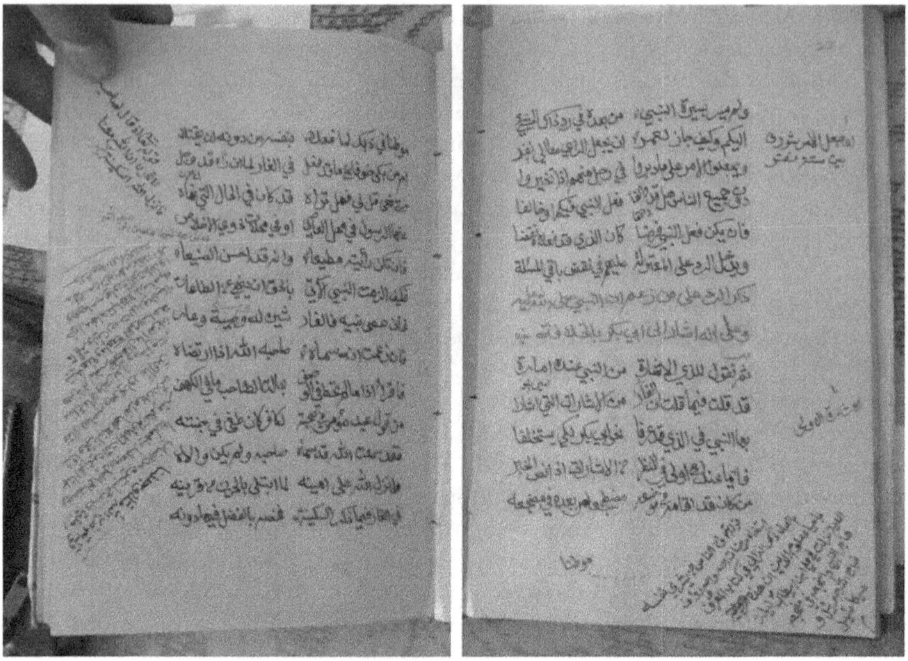

Figure 5.21 Left, paratextual reading features found in a *zahiri* manuscript: explanation of a term on the verso folio – note the dotted line. Right, explanation of a Qur'anic verse on the recto folio.

that in former times the rough edges were seen mainly as a residue that did not belong to the manuscript, or at least was not considered important enough to be preserved. However, the scholarly attitude of the clerics towards marginalia is changing, as are their codicological and preservation practices. In fact, I learned that the reading of marginalia 'of the forefathers' is often of great help to the clerics in understanding and copying treatises properly. As the Mazoon Saheb once said, 'Marginal notes reflect related matters' (Figure 5.21).

Paratexts as Carriers of Baraka

After cataloguing the holdings of the treasury of books, it became clear to me that the powers of *baraka* in Bohra manuscripts are not only attributed to the secret content of the text and the sacred materiality of the book hands of Bohra Dais. As objects, thus including all their codicological features, manuscripts are also considered to have strong talismanic qualities. Moreover, talismanic features can be traced in the manuscripts in the form of individual paratexts. Their powers are believed to function on two levels: to protect, guide or heal the person in need and to safeguard the manuscript itself from readers who are not supposed to access it.

Although the genre and the type of paratext are strongly and uniquedly linked, these marginal practices of writing seem to function completely independently as literary traditions from the manuscripts to which they belong. They can be read and written down as such and can be removed without interfering with the mother text. According to my observation, Bohra manuscripts thus have two very distinct social functions, secret as esoteric books, and as carriers of *baraka*. As carriers of *baraka*, paratexts are not just 'things' passively written down. Once written in the manuscript, their individual social lives begin. As we see in the following section, depending on the type of paratext, they serve a particular purpose as they are consulted, recited from, used as historical sources and even re-used into new paratextual traditions that come to life.

5.3 Occult Paratexts: *Batini* Manuscript Culture

For the codicologist researching and cataloguing Bohra manuscripts, paratexts are an ideal companion in identifying unknown manuscript titles and classifying these texts into genres. I observed that the *zahiri* and *batini* manuscript genres of the *khizana* contain distinct paratextual cultures that vary to such an extent that one can speak of separate manuscript cultures. As we will explore in this section, esoteric texts contain a great variety of paratexts that enhance the secret character of the text or hinder access through curses and spells. Manuscripts belonging to the exoteric genre, in contrast, contain paratexts whose function is so paratextual that they actually transcend the codex because they are used for popular magic and healing.

Let us start with manuscripts of an esoteric nature, which would be classified as *batin* and into which only the highest Bohra clerics are initiated. Esoteric manuscripts contain a rich tradition of 'occult' paratexts that enhance the secret character of the text. Common occult paratexts include traces of numerology, secret alphabets, magical seals (also known as the Seal of Solomon), encoded inscriptions and *kabikaj* formulae (see the later discussion) to protect the manuscript from both readers and floral and faunal inhabitants, and secret tables and diagrams. The function of these marginalia is to hinder access to the uninitiated reader, either by coding the text or through curses and spells.

There are different ways in which esoteric texts are coded through paratexts. The most common paratext in the context of *khizana* manuscripts and Isma'ili book culture is the use of secret alphabets. As described in Chapter 1 in the context of the *nass sijill*, these secret alphabets are collated from signs and referred to as *kitab sirriyya* (Figure 5.22).[61] The coding of esoteric or occult knowledge in script is a common practice in South Asia among Hindu and Muslim communities, and Gacek confirms that, as a written tradition, *kitab sirriyya* is very specific to Isma'ili manuscripts in India, both Bohra and Khoja.[62] *Kitab sirriyya* has two functions: veiling secret knowledge and coding the cursing of certain historical figures in early Shi'i history, such as the rightly-guided Caliphs ʿUmar, Uthman and Abu Bakr.

In the case of the latter, manuscript culture and social practice overlap. The tradition of *laʿn* (Ar.; 'cursing') is carried to the present day in an oral form among the Alawis and other Bohras: it is practised during all ceremonies, especially during the holy month of Muharram. In the old city of Baroda, the practising of the *la'n* out loud is so popular

[61] De Blois, *Arabic, Persian and Gujarati Manuscripts*, xxii.
[62] Gacek, *Vademecum*, 245.

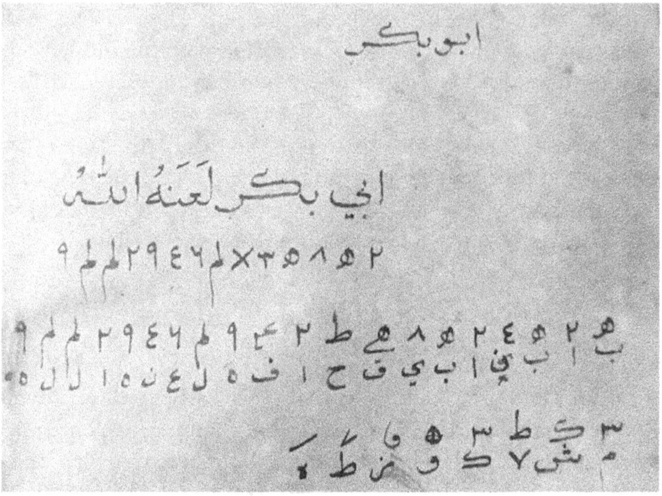

Figure 5.22 The 'Rosetta stone' of one of the variants of *kitab sirriyya*, reading *Abū Bakr la'nahu Allāh* (Ar. 'Abu Bakr, may he be cursed by God'). It is written on the first flyleaf of a *batini* manuscript.

among Twelver Shi'i and Bohra communities that it has become part of the highly contested soundscape of the city, causing inter-communal violence and riots. There are various versions of secret alphabets that operate in the treasury of books, which reflects what Rudolf Strothmann and others have argued for in Isma'ili manuscripts in general.[63] Only some of these scripts have been deciphered, and it is only through academic literature that the Mazoon Saheb and his brothers are able to decipher the codes themselves.

Another coded paratextual inscription is the Seal of Solomon, the coded *basmala*, which can be found on the first flyleaves, colophons and incipits. According to the scribal tradition of the Bhai Sahebs, it protects the manuscripts against evil spirits, termites and, most importantly, uninitiated readers. The Seal of Solomon is a very commonly used paratext that is often written in the margins of incipits and underneath colophons (see Figure 5.23).

A paratext with the same protective function that is not coded is the '*ya kabikaj*' formula (*oh kabikaj!*; see Figures 5.24 and 5.25). The '*ya kabikaj!*' phenomenon has an interesting social life within the history of Bohra manuscript culture and the Alawi *khizana*. In the context of Arabic book cultures found in the Middle East, North Africa and beyond, the *kabikaj* was a type of plant whose leaves were put between the bifolios of the manuscript to discourage termites because of their bitter taste.[64] Since the *kabikaj* plant was not widely available, the formula '*ya kabikaj*' is written instead throughout

[63] Strothmann, *Gnosis-Texte der Isma'iliten*, 60, 61. Akkerman, 'Documentary Remains of a Fatimid Past in Gujarat', 300.

[64] See Gacek, *Vademecum*, 199 and Adam Gacek, 'The Use of "kabikaj" in Arabic Manuscripts', in *Manuscripts of the Middle East* I (1986), 49–53. James W. Pollock, 'Kabikaj to Book Pouches: Library Preservation Magic and Technique in Syria of the 1880's and 1980's West', *MELA Notes* 44 (Spring 1988) 8–10. Akkerman, 'The Bohra Manuscript Treasury as a Sacred Site of Philology', 195.

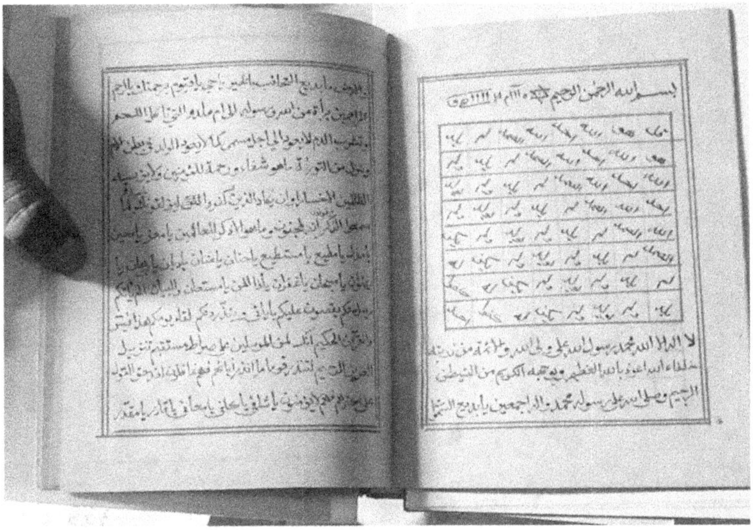

Figure 5.23 The seal of Solomon written above a *buduh* square.

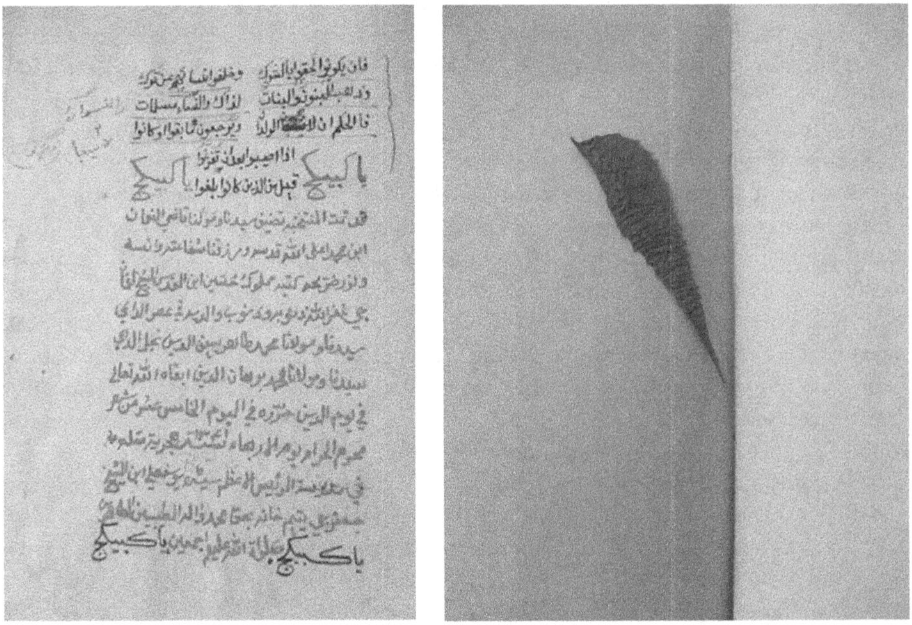

Figure 5.24 *Ya kabikaj*: paratextual practice versus preservation practice. Left, four ya *kabikaj* invocations, marking the corner edges of the colophon. This example seems to indicate that, by protecting its edges, the *kabikaj* formulae are metaphorically protecting the entire book. Right, dried *neem* leaf found in the empty flyleaves of a manuscript.

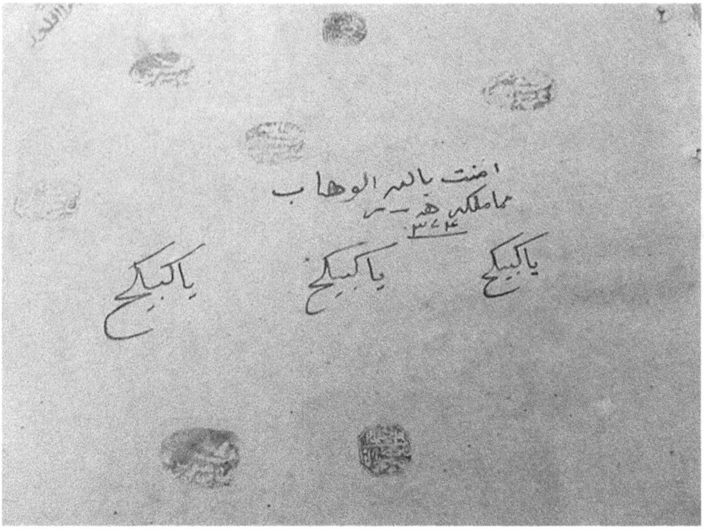

Figure 5.25 Ownership statement plus stamps and *kabikaj* formulae, followed by the formula 'I am faithful with God the all-giving from what he owns', and numerals.

the codex, a tradition practised throughout the Islamic world. The *kabikaj* expression could thus refer to a botanical species, as well to a kind of *jinn* or, as Gacek describes, a 'patron angel of reptiles'.[65] Uniquely, in the Bohra philological tradition *kabikaj* is not known as a plant but as the 'king of termites', which, according to legends, is such a nasty beast that just invoking its name is enough to terrify insects and creepers.[66]

The fact that the *neem* plant was indeed widely available on the Indian subcontinent did not stop the Bohras from copying the '*ya kabikaj*' formula from Yemeni manuscripts into their tradition.[67] As I briefly touched upon in Chapter 2, Dawoodi scholars and book collectors, however, did add actual *neem* leaves to their manuscripts, in addition to writing the formula to reinforce their protective powers. Upon finding dried *neem* leaves in Dawoodi manuscripts that entered their *khizana*, the Alawis took over this preservation practice. Both the leaves and the written formula thus protect Bohra manuscripts, which have a similar function to that of the *budūḥ* square (magical square) and the Seal of Solomon (Figure 5.23).[68]

In addition to secret alphabets made up of signs, alphabets coded in numerals can also be traced in the margins of Bohra manuscripts. I encountered these *abjads* on several occasions at the end of colophons (following '*tamma tamāmshud*'): they coded a list of the *adwar* (the prophetic cycles) and the names of the *nutaqa'* (the 'speakers'; that

[65] Gacek, *Vademecum*, 49.

[66] Interestingly, Gacek also mentions 'king of cockroaches'. Gacek, 'The Use of "kabikaj" in Arabic Manuscripts', 49.

[67] I consulted a copy of al-Kirmani's *Kitāb Tanbīḥ al-Hādḥ wa'l-Muhtadḥ* ('The Book of Exhortation to the Rightful Guide and the Rightly Guided') from the Hamdani collection, which is dated 1202/1787 and possibly of Yemeni provenance, which contains a *kabikaj* on the title page. De Blois, *Arabic, Persian, and Gujarati Manuscripts*, 66–7 (Ms. 160).

[68] Gacek comes to the same conclusion: Gacek, 'The Use of "kabikaj" in Arabic Manuscripts', 49.

is, the prophets, see Figure 5.26 and Chapter 1).[69] These *abjad* numerals are one of the very few paratextual features in Gujarati script found in *batini* manuscripts. Numerical alphabets are also used to bless official documents that circulate among the Bhai Sahebs, such as *awraq*, sermons and *awqaf*. As mentioned earlier, there is a yearly ceremony in which members of the royal family bless the new account books of businessmen of the community for a prosperous year by signing them with the numerical equivalent of the *basmala* (Figure 5.26). Moreover, official written invitations to community functions, such as weddings and birthdays, also contain this formula in Gujarati *abjad* numerals.

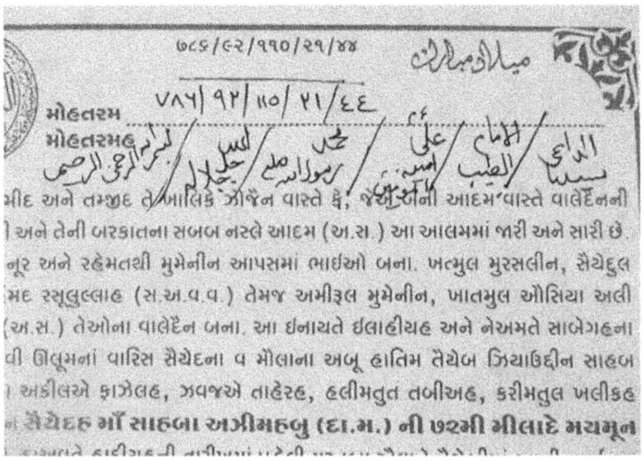

786/110/92/21/44 (Arabic and Gujarati numerals):	
	Bismillahu al-Raḥmān al-Raḥīm
786	Allāh Jalla Jallāluh
110	Muḥammad Rasūl Allāh
92	ʿAlī Amīr al-Muʾminīn
21	al-Imām al-Ṭayyib
44	al-Dāʿī Sayyidnā

Figure 5.26 Picture of an official *daʿwa* invitation to the communal celebration of the birthday, the *mīlād mubārak*, of one of the royal princes. The *abjad* numerals are printed in Gujarati numerals, which are converted into Arabic numerals and their *abjadi* equivalent in the book hand of the Mazoon Saheb to explain their meaning.

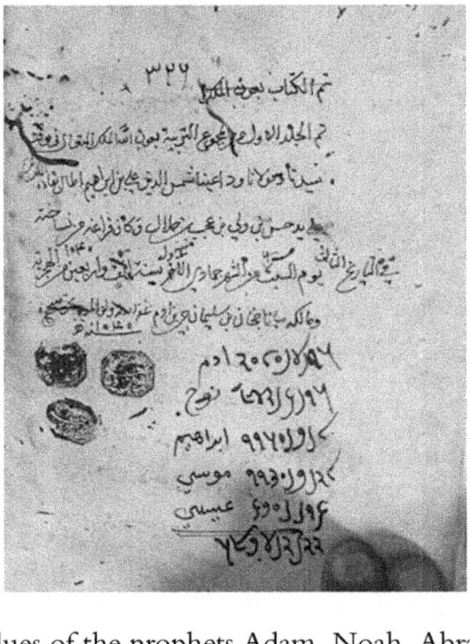

Figure 5.27 *Abjad* values of the prophets Adam, Noah, Abraham, Moses and Jesus, written in Gujarati numerals, found below the colophon of a *batini* treatise.

[69] Gacek, *Vademecum*, 11–13.

Figure 5.28 Diagram found in a *batini* manuscript.

Secret alphabets, whether coded in numerals or abstract signs, are written in the first flyleaves, incipits, colophons and margins of manuscripts and are therefore not re-copied or re-edited by scribes. Only occasionally are these paratexts are written within the main body of the text, such as is the case with *kitab sirriyya*. Finally, elaborate and abstract circular and rectangular diagrams are paratextual features commonly found in *batin* manuscripts, *haqa'iq* treatises in particular (Figure 5.28).

5.4 Magical Marginalia: *Zahiri* Manuscript Culture

As with the genre of *batini* books, manuscripts belonging to the exoteric *zahiri* genre, such as *fiqh* manuals, *ta'rikh* works or polemic treatises, contain paratexts that are so extra-textual that they essentially go beyond their social role as secret books and are used for popular healing practices. *Zahiri* manuscripts of the *khizana*, and the paratexts that they carry, are used for popular magic, healing, and divination, thus transcending the physical book. Discussing these paratexts is of great importance because it shows that they are frequently used as sacred material objects, even though these manuscripts are not meant to be accessed (they are less secret than *batini makhtutat* yet remain inaccessible). *Khizana* manuscripts, no matter how secret, are thus part of the daily lives of the people of Badri Mohallah. As argued in Chapter 3, it is exactly this tension of the secret manuscript that is *seen* and *noticed* by the layperson during these sessions of healing, but that cannot be accessed, which defines the culture of the treasury of books.

Just as much as *khizana* manuscripts play an important social role in the Bohra *da'wa* as secret objects, so are practices of popular magic and healing of equal significance to the daily private lives of believers. Carried out by the Mazoon Saheb and his brothers in the space of the *khizana*, these practices are considered entirely in accordance with Islamic principles. To my surprise, I was invited to observe these practices while cataloguing the manuscripts of the *khizana* in the office of the Mazoon Saheb.

Paratexts for the purpose of healing and popular magic vary greatly in terms of what they are used for: planetary pregnancy pies (Figure 5.32), magical squares and spells, and descriptions and explanations of magical knots, amulets, *'ilm al-fāl* (the taking of Qur'anic omens) and *'ilm al-ḥurūf* (magical letters). The paratexts of these manuscripts, some of which are centuries old, are still used extensively today by the Bhai Sahebs to assist people with their personal problems. These 'historic' marginalia, some of which come from Dawoodi and Sulaymani manuscripts, thus have rich individual social lives in the Alawi treasury of books. For this reason, these manuscripts are more worn out than the esoteric ones that are not accessible to everyone.

'Ilm al-fal (Qur'anic Omens)

Apart from regulations stipulated in Islamic law, how do the people of Badri Mohallah deal with questions of a more personal yet universal nature, such as the following: Is he or she the right partner for marriage? Should I invest in this property? Is it time to switch career? The answer is: through the marginalia of the treasury of books.

Paratexts that are widely present in *zahiri* manuscripts on *fiqh*, as well as in printed Qur'ans, are descriptions of how to perform *'ilm al-fal* and *'ilm al-huruf* (Figure 5.29). It should be mentioned that *'ilm al-fal* is widely practised in Muslim milieux in South Asia, Iran and Turkey.[70] For instance, I observed this practice at home among the Twelver Khojas in East Africa as '*istikhāra*'. In the Alawi Bohra context, *mu'minin* and *mu'minat* visit their Dai and Mazoon Saheb frequently to have their 'Qur'anic omen' taken. The ritual is carried out as follows: the omen taker visits the Mazoon Saheb in a ritually pure state of mind, and he or she recites the *fāṭiḥa* (1), *sūrat al-ikhlāṣ* (112), *sūrat al-falaq* (113) and *sūrat al-nās* (114), starting with a *basmala*, followed by the recitation of a *du'a*. The omen taker is, as the Mazoon Saheb explained, 'urging *Allāhu ta'āla* in his or her heart that I am just taking omen so that it should be lucky, predestined and in my favour'. With this intent he or she opens the Qur'an with his or her right hand and hands it over to the Mazoon or Dai, who then turns the pages seven times to the left (from the right side), searching for the first *ḥarf* (Ar.; 'letter', pl. *ḥurūf*) of the seventh *āya* (Figure 5.30). It is this specific letter that is then looked up in the marginal notes on *'ilm al-fal*.

All *huruf* of the Arabic alphabet, from *alīf* to *yā'*, carry a predestined message. For instance, the letter ج (*jīm*) reads (tr. from Arabic): 'When in your *fāl* the *ḥarf jīm* comes, then be effortful and endeavourful, what is hidden in your intention, it will be in your fortune.' This predestined message means that the omen taker should have a proactive

70 Annemarie Schimmel, *Calligraphy and Islamic Culture* (London: I. B. Tauris, 1990), 84.

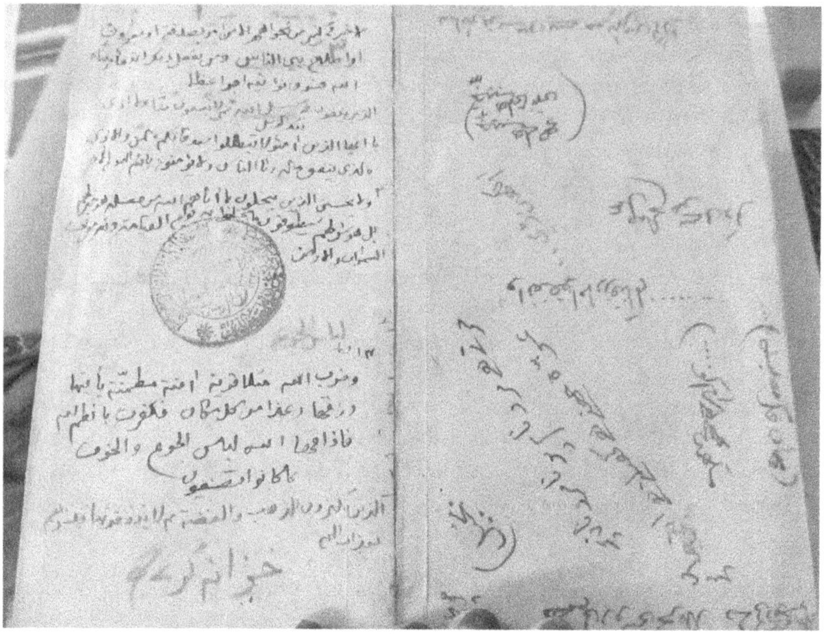

Figure 5.29 The paratexts: *ʿIlm al-fal* and *huruf* description written in blue and red pencil, including non-Alawi *khizana* reference, and owner stamp, found in a *fiqh* manuscript.

Figure 5.30 The social practice: *ʿilm al-fal* in action.

attitude to solve whatever predicament he or she is facing in life. The importance of Qur'anic omens for Bohra believers should not be underestimated. According to my interlocutors, these omens – together with the personal advice of the Mazoon Saheb and observing auspicious and inauspicious days – are the basis on which believers make their life decisions. The importance of *ʿilm al-fal* is reflected in the number of paratexts in Bohra manuscripts explaining the procedure.

The paratext, however, cannot function on its own in the Alawi universe. Its powers can only be accessed and mediated through the intercession of the Dai or Bhai Sahebs, who do not only interpret and write the magical marginalia but also are the ones attributing agency to them. The magical marginalia of the treasury of books are therefore an excellent example for demonstrating the complex relation between people as subjects and manuscripts as objects, and what *people do with books*. To return to the triangle of text–codicology–social meaning, the text thus relies both on the human, social interaction for its social life and on its material, codicological form to exist and survive as a codicological entity within manuscripts.

Taʿwizat *(Talismans)*

In addition to paratexts that are consulted and actively used during audiences and ceremonies, *zahiri* marginalia also generate other writing practices in the treasury of books. One of the most commonly used paratexts in the *khizana* are the *taʿwiz*. 'Let me show you one thing', the Mazoon told me during one of our afternoon manuscript sessions. 'This is my spiritual file; these are my *taʿwiz*, my talismans. When somebody comes with a fever, headache, bad dreams, I do not do *ḥifẓ al-ʿilm* (Ar.; 'from memory'), I do not remember each and everything. This is my handbook of spiritual things; it is my gospel.'[71]

As discussed previously, the tradition of talismanic healing, carried out by the Dai, Mazoon Saheb and the Ra's ul Hudood, is a popular practice in Badri Mohallah. Talismans are Qur'anic verses, *du'as*, and magical squares, known as *buduh* squares, that are written in Arabic on a piece of paper.[72] To the outsider, the *taʿwiz* may appear a humble piece of scribbled paper, yet to believers they are sacred commodities due to the Qur'anic verses they contain and because they are handwritten by the holy men of the community. The objects are kept close to the heart, underneath the pillow or in the suitcase, depending on the malady of life they are prescribed for. In addition, the ink of talismans is dissolved in water, blessed by the *ruh* of the Bhai Sahebs, and then drunk by the patient. I described the story of the water tank of the *jamaat khana* and the termite plague in Chapter 4, when believers ingested the manuscript dust of the *khizana*. In these cases, the power attributed to these talismans, or the 'talismanic sacred trash' of manuscripts, is two-dimensional: both the authority of the text it carries and the handwriting of the clerics constitute its sacred nature.

[71] Conversation with Mazoon Saheb, Badri Mohallah, 26 October 2013.

[72] See also Jean-Charles Coulon, 'L'ésotérisme shi'ite et son influence sur le corpus magique attribué à al-Būnī', in M. A. Amir-Moezzi, M. De Cillis, D. De Smet and O. Mir-Kasimov (eds), L'ésotérisme shi'ite, ses racines et ses prolongements (Paris: Brepols, 2016), 509–38.

The practice of drinking the sacred written word, especially the Qur'an, challenges ideas of the materiality of sacred texts, since in these instances script is intentionally removed and internalised throughout the body of the patient. In the case of water-dissolvable *ta'wizat*, it is therefore more apt to speak of the immateriality of manuscript and script. The idea behind this practice of immateriality is that the blessings of the talismanic water will reach the heart of the believer directly, instead of going through the ear to reach the brain.[73]

Ta'wizat are an important genre of texts in the *khizana*: they are scattered all over the cupboards of the *khizana*, and *zahiri* manuscripts contain plenty of depictions of talismans and paratextual descriptions of how to prepare and use them. In a similar vein to *'ilm al-fal* and *'ilm al-huruf*, through the Dai and Mazoon Saheb, certain powers are thus attributed to these practices and, in the case of the *ta'wiz* and other forms of writings, to material artefacts through their mediation (Figure 5.31). This phenomenon, as I described in Chapter 1, is not uncommon in South Asia among various denominational communities, such as Muslims and Hindus, and shows the Bohras' Gujarati roots.

Figure 5.31 The Mazoon Saheb is writing a *ta'wiz* in his office.

[73] See, for an in-depth study of drinking sacred scripts, the anthropologist Hannah Nieber's *Drinking the Written Qur'an: Healing with Kombe in Zanzibar Town* (PhD diss., Utrecht University, 2019).

These rituals of healing and divination are practised throughout the Middle East, East Africa and South Asia among all social layers of society.[74] What is unique, however, to Bohra practices is that they have both a strong ritual and a (para)textual dimension in the space of the *khizana*. The examples described in this chapter demonstrate that practices thus transcend the barriers of the secret manuscript. To conclude, without manuscript, there is no ritual, and without ritual, there are no paratexts.

Saints, Miracles and Planetary Pregnancy Pies

Visiting the Mazoon Saheb's office for guidance, I observed, is certainly not a gendered affair. I noticed, however, that one paratext was particularly popular among women. In this case, the same manuscript, a dusty *fiqh* compendium, was taken off the shelves each time, containing what I can best describe as the *planetary pregnancy pie*: a diagram for predicting pregnancy. This unusual paratext consisted of a circular diagram depicting the names of the sun, moon and planets in Arabic, noted down on the first flyleaf of the hefty tome. Even though not dated, the manuscript and paratext must have been transcribed around a hundred years ago, at a time when birth control and other forms of modern contraception were not available. The Mazoon was able to extract from the marginal notes that the circular diagram was used for women to ascertain whether they were expecting; if so, the diagram would reveal the sex of the unborn child. All the *mu'minat* had to do was to visit the Mazoon or Dai in a ritually pure state of body and mind, recite the *fatiha*, and place their fingers randomly on the planetary pregnancy pie; the result would then be interpreted by the clerics. Despite the availability of medical tests to determine pregnancy today, the planetary pregnancy pie remains in use among the people of Badri Mohallah, who consider all aspects of the cycle of life, including conception, a matter of the divine (Figure 5.32).

Another popular marginal feature that can be found in the flyleaves of exoteric manuscripts is stories of saints and their miracles. Figure 5.33 depicts a description of a miracle performed by a Bohra saint at the graveyard of Saraspur; it is five folios long and is written in *Lisan al-Daʿwa*. The details of this story, however, remain hidden. When I asked the Mazoon Saheb to translate this story to me, he said with a very stern tone in his voice: 'No, no! Maybe it is a good one, and I will use it for myself.'

Finally, manuscripts also paratexts of a less sacred kind, such as literature and poetry fragments, including *ghazals* (love poetry), telephone numbers, addresses in Hindi and Gujarati, writing exercises, children's drawings, even cowboy stickers, and pictures of action figures (Figures 5.34 and 5.35). Even in the treasury of books, no matter how sacred the text of its Fatimid-Tayyibi manuscripts, the profane inevitably seeps into the margins. While documenting these and the many more magical marginalia, I realised there is a certain beauty to this dichotomy. as it is through the margins of the *khizana* that the *makhtutat* remain connected with the profane, day-to-day life of Badri Mohallah, textually and through social practice.

[74] Particularly exciting examples that address this topic are Joyce Burkhalter Flueckiger's *In Amma's Healing Room: Gender and Vernacular Islam in South-India* (Bloomington: Indiana University Press, 2006) and Ali Reza Doostar's dissertation titled *Fantasies of Reason: Science, Superstition, and the Supernatural in Iran* (Harvard University, 2013).

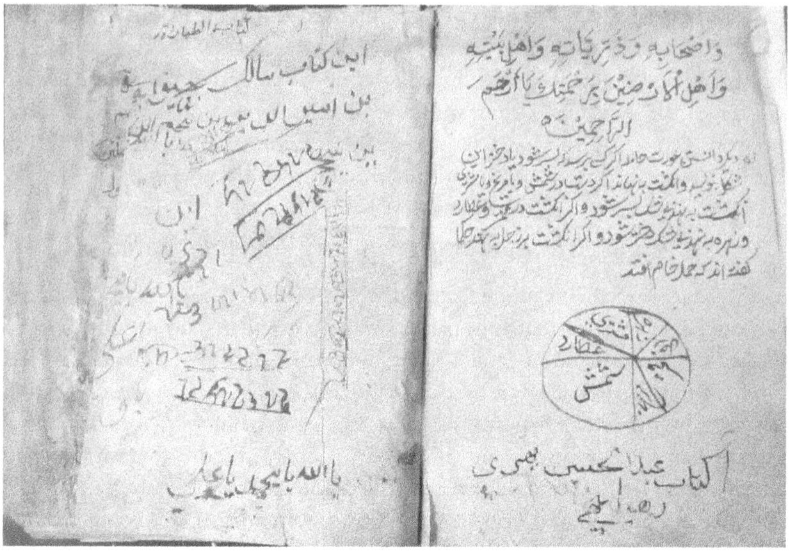

Figure 5.32 The planetary pregnancy pie on the right folio, with a description in Persian above.

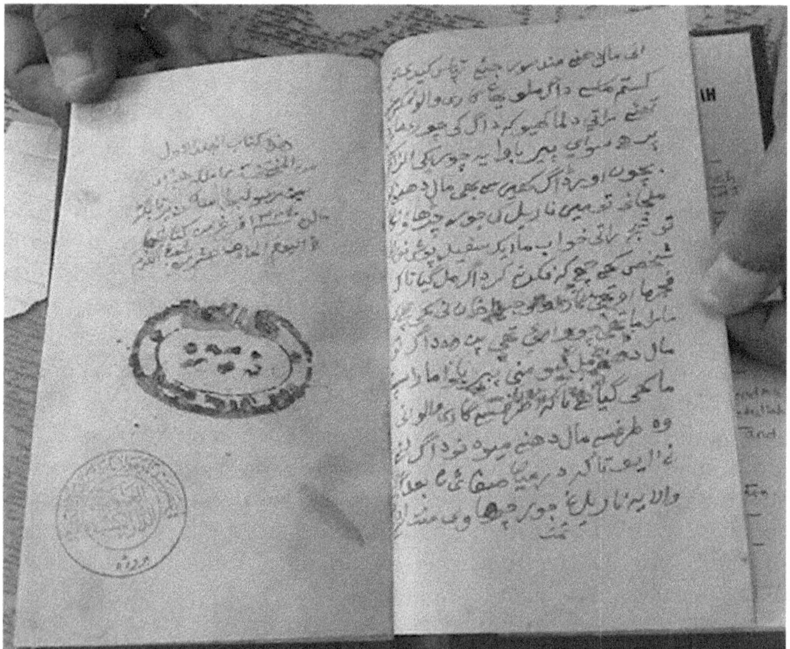

Figure 5.33 Paratext on the miracles of a Bohra saint in Saraspur, written in *Lisan al-Daʿwa*.

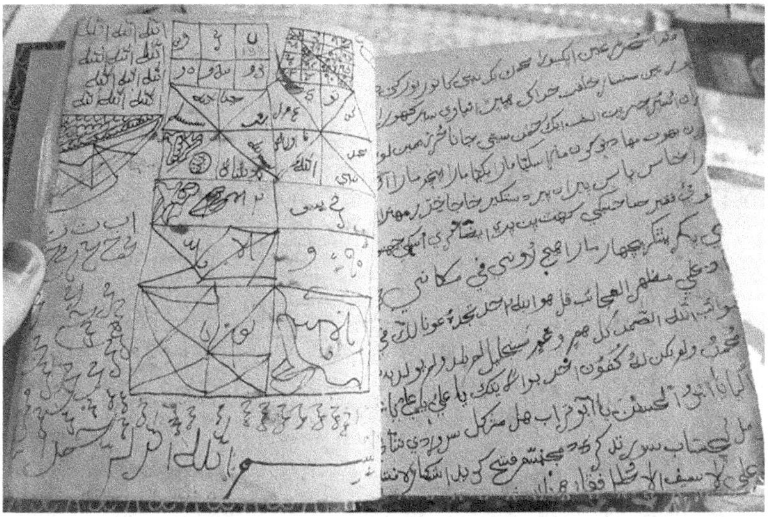

Figure 5.34 Various scribbled notes and writing exercises.

Figure 5.35 Various marginalia on the final flyleaves of a *zahiri* manuscript, containing cowboy stickers along with a glossary in the form of a small dictionary giving the definition of the words *talkhīṣ*, *takhlīṣ* and *taṣnīf*. Interestingly, these notes were written by Kalsum al-Najafi, the wife of the tutor of the Mazoon Saheb (she and her husband were born in the city of Najaf).

Final Notes to Chapter 5: The Power of Books

After dwelling in the margins of the *khizana*, spending time among its scrolls, *awraq*, notebooks and codices, I became aware of the importance of the Alawis' notion of the 'power of books', as well the social meaning of codicology and paratexts in Bohra manuscript culture and the community in its day-to-day life. Ironically, it is these aspects of book cultures and the question of their materiality and social role that, with few exceptions, often remain peripheral in Manuscript Studies. In this chapter, I have demonstrated the need for a codicology of manuscripts that is concerned with the question of *what it is that people do with books.*

In the case of the Bohras, the notion of secrecy and the inaccessibility of the manuscripts of the *khizana* is built into the materiality of their manuscript culture. I call this the *materiality of secrecy*. It is not the books themselves that are secret, as they are known to exist to the community. What is important is how secrecy is attributed to them through their material form or codicology and the social practices of revealing and disclosing through their paratexts.

The various social roles of these different manuscript forms are shaped by and, in turn, transform their physical appearance. In the treasury of books, one finds manuscript forms such as the *awraq* that function as the material 'liminal' transition between the secret *batin* codices and the strictly written word or the *khassa*, and public documents such as the scroll and the oral realm of the *ʿamma*. It is, however, not only the physical appearance, as we have seen, that constitutes the significance of the manuscript. Instead, it is the authority that is ascribed to it, as well as the place it occupies in the chain of transmission of the Bohra eternal esoteric truths. Text, codicology and social function are intrinsically connected and equally important in understanding the meaning of Bohra manuscript culture from an emic perspective. A manuscript, in whatever material form, we can conclude, looks the way it does because it is used in a certain way.

Moving from the material forms of the *makhtutat*, we delved into the rich tradition of paratexts, asking the question how paratexts have shaped manuscript culture and have made this living Isma'ili book culture distinctly 'Bohra'. A striking feature of Bohra manuscript culture is that the Dai is omnipresent in every form of writing, whether it be a codex or a scroll: from head to tail, beginning with the incipit, where the writing process is authorised by the royal *basmala*, and ending with the colophon, which is sealed in his name and with his royal regnal year. Another unique characteristic of Bohra manuscript culture is that different paratextual traditions exist along each other, depending on whether books belong to the *batin* or *zahir* genre. Whereas *batini* paratexts enhance the secret character of the manuscript and are meant to obstruct its access, *zahiri* rough edges are indispensable for the daily practice of healing and popular magic, regardless of the main text of the manuscript. The power of talismanic paratexts is two-dimensional: it is both the authority that is attributed to the object – that is, the manuscript and its secret content – and the materiality of the sacred handwriting of the clerics that constitute its sacred nature.

The codicology and paratexts of Bohra manuscript culture, it should be emphasised, are part of a living *khizana* tradition. Manuscripts and their rough edges are constantly produced, consumed, consulted, and turned into other manuscripts in the Alawi universe and its materiality of secrecy. On an individual level, historic paratexts too, as we have seen, have rich social lives in the treasury of books, some of them being inherited from the genealogy of Alawi Dais and others coming from the outside. In the case of the latter, new paratextual traditions and marginalia are added to existing social practices in the community.

Without the mediation of the clerics, however, the codicology of *khizana* manuscripts and their rough edges lose their social meaning and their place in the spotlights of the community. The deep meaning of a diagram written on a dusty flyleaf of a manuscript remains abstract and undisclosed to most believers, yet it comes to life for the people of Badri Mohallah during an audience with the Mazoon Saheb as a planetary pregnancy pie. At the same time, it is only the paratexts of these manuscripts that are revealed to believers, a strategy of access we have discussed earlier in the context of the social role of the treasury of books. Paratexts are thus much more than a few incidental scribbles. As an important part of the materiality of secrecy, they play a central role in the dialectics of the secret *khizana*, which maintains the social hierarchy of the community. As such, they thus truly function, to borrow Genette's terminology, as the *thresholds* of something, in this case, to 'almost' accessing the esoteric truths.[75]

I claim that it is the tradition of paratexts, in their own minor but significant way, that has kept and continues to keep Bohra manuscript culture alive; it is the link between the sacred domain of text, script and the community, between the Tayyibi-Fatimid esoteric truths and the here and now. Paratexts are not only what uniquely distinguish Bohra manuscripts, whether Alawi, Dawoodi or Sulaymani, from other Arabic manuscript cultures, but their rough edges also have a deeper meaning as they connect the Bohra Isma'ili narrative of cyclical time and space with linear time, and translate a historic Fatimid-Tayyibi book culture from the past to the social reality of Gujarat.

[75] Genette, *Paratexts: Thresholds of Interpretation*, 2.

Chapter 6

Script and Scribal Politics

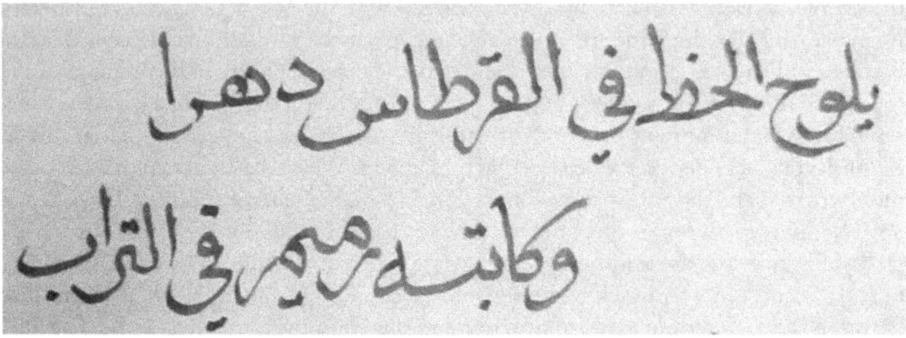

Figure 6.1 Marginal note found written on the end flyleaf of a *khizana* manuscript.

An Exercise in Palaeography

EARLY ONE MORNING, I WAS having a session with the Mazoon Saheb in the *khizana*, asking for permission to photograph a pile of *zahiri* manuscripts, when we stumbled upon a very old codex. 'And this', the Mazoon Saheb said, 'is the oldest copy, four hundred years old. 'Look', he said with a stern tone as if I were taking an exam in palaeography, 'did you find a difference between this Arabic script and this one?' as he pointed to a modern copy of the same text. Reluctantly, I confessed to the Mazoon Saheb that I had not looked at the script properly, for I was afraid to open the codex due to the fragile state it was in. Moreover, following the recent discussion we had on ritual purity and touching the *makhtutat* as a 'lady scholar', I had become even more cautious. Before I could answer the Mazoon's question, our conversation was overshadowed by the *sabziwala* downstairs, who loudly offered his vegetables for sale from his cart in the street.

The Mazoon then said, 'Look, look, I will open it, you see.' He opened the binding of the manuscript with the utmost care, as if it were a fragile butterfly, and uttered the words '*al-ḥamdu lillāh rabb al-ʿālamīn*'. While doing so, he seemed to enter a different, more pure state of mind, as he greeted the folios with great respect and humility. It was a liminal moment that only lasted for a second as Ibrahim Bhai, the secretary of the *daʿwa*, hesitantly entered the room while his office phone, attached to a long plastic wire, kept ringing in his hands. '*Salam aleikum konbhai* (*Salāmu*

ʿalaykum, who is it?)?' the Mazoon Saheb asked in a distracted tone. After dealing with an urgent financial issue raised by Ibrahim Bhai, the Mazoon gave me a palaeographical assignment: 'So you just collate these two manuscripts, not a difference of a word you will find, just collate two pages. And find out, is it identical?' Our conversation ended as abruptly as it started after the Mazoon's cousin came in for an audience, asking for advice on a family-related issue. While providing marital advice in Gujarati, in a lowered voice the Mazoon quickly said to me. 'I will show you two (manuscripts) tomorrow *inshallah*.'

As the Mazoon continued with the affairs of the day, I retreated to my corner and began to compare the two Fatimid manuscript titles, the details of which I was requested to keep undisclosed. In terms of their codicology, the two *makhtutat* could not have looked more different. The handmade paper quires of the older copy, which was possibly of Yemeni provenance, were held together by a worn-out, thick leather binding with a *lisan* (envelope) flap, in which even older, recycled fragments of text were pasted inside. The 'millennial' manuscript, by contrast, a copy prepared by the Mazoon Saheb in the 1990s, consisted of a modern, machine-made notebook, its Arabic copied in fountain pen on chemically bleached paper.

Despite being part of the same chain of textual transmission and manuscript culture, palaeographically these two *kutub* differed greatly: the world of the book hand of the Mazoon, which scripturally could best be described as resembling a modern printed *naskh*, seemed to contrast sharply with that of the archaic, sixteenth-century flamboyant *naskh* of the Yemeni manuscript, carefully transcribed with a reed pen and brown ink. Yet despite differences in their material appearance, the text, copied sometime between these four centuries, was virtually identical. In fact, as I spent the rest of the week expecting to find textual variants among the other manuscripts in the *zahiri* pile, I was surprised to find almost none. Here it was, right in front of me: the Bohra scribal tradition of a Fatimid treatise stretching over 400 years, possibly starting in Yemen and ending in Badri Mohallah, Baroda.

6.1 A Modern Isma'ili Manuscriptorium

Throughout the previous chapters, we have become familiar with the community's narrative of the transmission of the Tayyibi-Fatimid intellectual tradition, in which the Bohras place themselves as both the saviours and the custodians of the eternal esoteric truths that form the basis of their Neo-Fatimid identity in the present. Today, the Alawi *khizana* functions not only as a centre of power and governance and as a treasury of books, enshrining what I called the materiality of secrecy, but also, as I mentioned in Chapter 2, as an Isma'ili *manuscriptorium*.

Commonly referring to the place of manuscript copying in monastic communities of medieval Europe, the term *scriptorium* is rarely used in the context of Arabic or Islamic book culture.[1] Michael Carter has argued that, in contrast to in medieval Europe, in the Arab world the production of manuscripts was considered a predominantly secular practice, carried out by the *warrāq* (scribe, pl. *warraqūn*). The *warraqun*

[1] 'Scriptorium', Encyclopedia Britannica.

were often craftsmen and men of letters at the same time, as well as vendors of paper and books, who operated their small businesses from their *ḥānūt* (workshop or stall) in mostly urban settings, such as the market-place and libraries, and in authors' homes.[2] As such, they were the link between the men of letters of these bookish societies and the general public.[3]

Even though the Bohras identify their scribal tradition with the culture of the *warraqun* in the 'bookish' societies of the medieval Arab world, the socio-economic position and status of the Bohra scribe could not be more different. To the Bohras, the copying of manuscripts has historically been an explicitly non-secular affair, which today is confined to and enshrined in the ritualised space of the treasury of books and, in the case of the Dawoodis, the Jamea tus Sayfiyya seminaries. Poonawala thus refers to the Bohra scribal tradition as a 'private and confidential service' that had to be kept secret from the hostile, uninitiated Sunni world. He argues that, in the Bohra context, there was never a professional class of *warraqun* such as in the medieval Arab world. Instead, Bohra scribes were *ulama*, who, initiated into the *ʿulum al-daʿwa*, learned the practice from their *mufīd* (spiritual master). The scribal efforts of these *shaykhs*, *mullahs* and *ʿalims* were seen as acts of religious devotion in the *khidma* (service) of the *daʿwa*, which, God willing, would be a way of receiving forgiveness and *baraka* in the hereafter.[4] I found that this is still the case today among the Alawis, where the class of learned scribes consists of the elite group of the Dai and the Bhai Sahebs, including the Mazoon, the Mukasir and the Ra's ul Hudood Sahebs.

As such, the treasury of books can be considered an Isma'ili manuscriptorium, where the production, copying and restoring of handwritten books are restricted to a class of clerical scribes. These and other Bohra manuscriptoria in Gujarat, as we see in this chapter, are not merely spaces where text is copied blindly by scribes. Instead, they are spaces of sacred knowledge transmission, enshrining scribal traditions that are deeply rooted in the culture of the sacerdotal *daʿwa* families of the Alawis, Dawoodis and Sulaymanis.

These highly ritualised scribal traditions connect one manuscriptorium – in this case the Alawi *khizana* of Baroda – historically, materially and spiritually with the Indian Ocean world of Hasan al-Bha'ruchi, the manuscriptoria of Tayyibi Yemen and the palaces of al-Mustansir and Mu'ayyad fi Din al-Shirazi and other Fatimid Caliph-Imams and their Dais. Through this lens, the position of the scribe thus changes from a humble copyist serving the demands of the manuscript market of bookish societies into the Dai who, as the divinely appointed custodian of this sacred past, is responsible for the existence of an entire universe.

Yet as a humble *kātib* (scribe) of the *daʿwa*, the Dai is only a vessel of transmission in this greater scheme of the continuation of cyclical time. The following popular

[2] Michael G. Carter, 'Arabic Literature', in David C. Greetham (ed.), *Scholarly Editing: A Guide to Research* (New York: Modern Language Association of America, 1995), 556. See also Ayman Fuad Sayyid, 'Le rôle des conservateurs des ḫazāʾin al-kutub dans la reproduction des manuscrits arabes', in Judith Pfeiffer and Manfred Kropp (eds), *Theoretical Approaches to the Transmission and Edition of Oriental Manuscripts* (Beirut: Orient Institut, ser. 'Beiruter Texte und Studien', 207), 197–201.

[3] Poonawala, 'The Contribution of Ismāʿīlī Colophons', 89.

[4] Ibid., 93.

scribal verse (Figure 6.1), found in Alawi and other Bohra manuscripts, illustrates the scribe's position:[5]

> *The writing on the paper continues to glitter for long, while its scribe is rotting in the dust.*
>
> يلوح الخط في القرطاس دهرًا
> وكاتبه رميم في التراب

This statement, which I encountered several times, either at the end of colophons or written on the first flyleaves of manuscripts, should be read in the larger context of Islamic manuscript cultures, where practices of self-abasement of the scribe are common, if not the norm. However, in Bohra manuscript culture, this scribal verse has an additional, deeper meaning as it refers to the evanescent character of the Tayyibi-Fatimid tradition. This tradition will carry on, despite the demise of empires, the seclusion of Imams, the inevitable mortality of the Dais, or even the material demise of the *khizana* and its manuscripts. The *katib* will rot in his grave, and even his *makhtutat* will turn to dust at some point in their material life, yet the essence of *ʿilm al-batin*, the scribal verse seems to indicate, will never get lost and will continue to shine.

When I asked the Mazoon what this scribal responsibility meant to him, both in his capacity as the designated *mansus* and personally as a bibliophile, he answered, 'The copying of makhtutat is a *jihad*'.' For months I had observed the intense physical labour and deep concentration with which the Mazoon Saheb, and occasionally the Dai and the Mukasir Saheb, would copy manuscripts. In awe, I witnessed how they sat patiently on the floor of the treasury of books transcribing word for word in their beautiful *naskh*. While cataloguing, I became intimately familiar with their personalised book hands, each of them individual and uniquely reflecting their personality. Yet until the moment I participated in this tradition myself, including its rituals of purity and scribal initiation, copying alongside the Bhai Sahebs, I could not fully understand why the Mazoon considered this task a *jihad*, a *jihad* of the *nafs* to be precise – of the struggle with the self, the ego – also known as the *jihād al-kubrā* (the greater *jihad*).[6]

In this chapter, we will tackle the question of the Alawis' *scribal jihad*, palaeography, and the social life of book hands and scripts of the *khizana* manuscriptorium. We look at Bohra manuscript culture as a scribal tradition and practices of manual transmission: the material forms of script, typologies and techniques of writing, book hands, and inks. As opposed to classical Arabo-Islamic book features that I identified previously, in this chapter questions of script and its relation to text and access are addressed through both the lenses of classical palaeography and social practice. Attention is given to the unique position of Arabic as a language and script, questions of access, and the presence or absence of regional and trans-regional features and traditions.

5 Poonawala has documented the same scribal verse, which he translates as follows: 'The written word on [a piece of] paper shines for a long stretch of time While its scribe's [bones] are decaying under the earth.' Poonawala, 'The Contribution of Ismāʿīlī Colophons', 107.

6 As opposed to the *jihād al-sughrā*, the lesser *jihad*, which, as the Mazoon Saheb explained, is not limited to but does indeed include holy war.

How do the Alawis understand the notion of script in the treasury of books? Can it merely be restricted to a medium of transmission of sacred texts, or are matters such as aesthetics and social, political and sacral dimensions equally important? Which script typologies are appropriated? Is there scriptural hegemony in the *khizana*? Are there encounters, or even competitions, between vernacular scriptural practices and imported ones, and do we observe appropriation processes over time? In terms of writing practices, can we detect scriptural hegemony over minor practices of writing? And what does this tell us about the history of the community, especially in relation to its larger social and political surroundings?

To answer these questions fully, I carry out a comparative palaeographical analysis in this chapter, with the aim of providing a history of Bohra book hands from Yemen to Baroda, covering a period of roughly 450 years. This will not only provide a better understanding of what the book hands of the *khizana* look like and how they evolved over time, but also, more importantly, the scribal practices from the past will help us understand why Bohra manuscripts are still copied by hand today.

Having gained a better understanding of Bohra manuscript culture as a living manuscript tradition, in the second section of this chapter I map out strategies of writing, focusing on the agency of the scribe within this tradition and the practices, choices, interventions and experiences of writing – a tradition I call *scribal politics*. I also analyse what the Mazoon Saheb called the '*jihad*' of the scribe, both through the perspective of the Bhai Sahebs and through the lens of my own participation in this tradition, thus inscribing myself in the treasury of books.

6.2 Script and the Language of Secrecy

In the Indian subcontinent, the use of Arabic as the sacred scriptural, ritual and calligraphic language of Islam is almost as old as Islamic civilisation itself: since Umayyad commanders conquered the west Indian province of Sindh in the first/eighth century, Arabic has been the religious *lingua franca* of a long list of Muslim dynasties ruling the subcontinent, such as the Ghaznavids, the Ghurids, the Delhi Sultanate, the Sultans of the Deccan, Kashmir and Gujarat, and the Mughals.[7] While Persian was adopted as a devotional language of mysticism, as well as the language of administration and high culture under the rule of the Mughals (1526–1858/932–1274), Qur'anic scripture and *tafsir*, calligraphy and epigraphy were primarily expressed in Arabic.[8] Qutbuddin notes that whereas the use of Persian gradually died out after the fall of the Mughal Empire, the role of Arabic has remained unchanged as a Muslim scholarly language, up to the present day.[9]

For centuries, Islamic literature was produced by the scholarly elites of Indian Muslim milieux in Arabic in manuscript form, a tradition that died out gradually

[7] Schimmel, *Calligraphy and Islamic Culture*, 66.

[8] Tahera Qutbuddin, 'Arabic in India: A Survey and Classification of Its Uses, Compared with Persian', *Journal of the American Oriental Society* vol. 127, no. 3 (2007): 315–37. See for Persian in South Asia: Muzaffar Alam, *The Languages of Political Islam in India: c. 1200–1800* (Chicago: The University of Chicago Press, 2004).

[9] Qutbuddin, 'Arabic in India', 315, 320.

after the introduction of the printing press in the early nineteenth century.[10] It was during the same period that philological traditions of Muslim communities were translated, re-worked, and re-adapted into local languages or high languages such as Urdu.

In his *Rise and Development of Arabic in Gujarat*, Baqirali Tirmizi describes how Gujarat maintained strong cultural and commercial relations with the Arab world during, after and even before the advent of Islam; patronage of Islamic scholarship in Arabic was especially cultivated during the Sultanate of Cambay (793–991/1391–1583).[11] In contrast to the strong Turkic and Persian influences in the north of the subcontinent, the hegemonic position of Arabic in Gujarat was strongly reflected in Islamic literature and institutionalised in Arabic academies, *madrasas* and libraries in Ahmedabad, Surat, Bharuch and Nahrwala. Furthermore, Gujarati *ulama* were well known for their treatises on *tafsir*, *hadith*, *taṣawwuf* and Arabic grammar and philology and for their calligraphic hands.[12]

Jyoti Gulati Balachandran describes how Gujarat, as a commercial centre of the Indian Ocean world, attracted learned-men-cum-merchants from overseas, who, as native Arabic speakers, established themselves as key figures in local Muslim communities, serving as religious scholars and judges.[13] The Bohras, as I demonstrated in Chapter 2, relied on their own Indian Ocean scholarly and mercantile networks with Yemen to legitimise their genealogy. As a Muslim community from Gujarat, however, they were not the only ones to have strong ties with Yemen, as the work of Elizabeth Lambourn has shown. Lambourn's contribution on the *khuṭba* networks between Yemen and India in the seventh/thirteenth century is especially relevant in this regard. *Qadis* (judges) and *khaṭībs* (preachers), she argues, appointed by the Rasulid Sultans of Yemen were sent across the western Indian Ocean to Muslim trading communities of the south-western and south-eastern Indian littoral to spread their message, reading the *khutba* in their name.[14]

In this light, it is neither surprising nor unique that an Arabic-Isma'ili tradition of learning and knowledge transmission existed as part of a larger Muslim scholarly milieu of medieval Gujarat. Nevertheless, the hegemonic position of Arabic, so specific to the social context of Gujarat, came to an end during the post-Aurangzeb period

10 Poleman, 'Serial Publications in India', 23–30. See for the historic role of Arabic among Muslim elites in South Asia: Christopher Bahl, 'Creating a Cultural Repertoire Based on Texts: Arabic Manuscripts and the Historical Practices of a Sufi in 17th-Century Bijapur', *Journal of Islamic Manuscripts* vol. 9, nos 2–3 (2018): 132–53, and 'Arabic Philology at the Seventeenth-Century Mughal Court: Sa'd Allāh Khān's and Shāh Jahān's Enactments of the Sharḥ al-Raḍī', *Philological Encounters* vol. 5, no. 2 (2020): 190–222. See for print in the colonial context in Sindh: Michel Boivin, *The Sufi Paradign and the Makings of Vernacular Knowledge in Colonial India: The Case of Sindh (1851–1929)* (London: Palgrave Macmillan, 2020).

11 Tirmizi, *Rise and Development of Arabic*, 49.

12 Ibid. See also Sheikh, *Forging a Region*, 6–9.

13 Jyoti Gulati Balachandran, *The Making of a Muslim Community in Gujarat, c. 1400–1650* (Oxford: Oxford University Press, 2020), 44.

14 Elizabeth Lambourn, 'India from Aden' and 'Khutba and Muslim Networks in the Indian Ocean (Part II) – Timurid and Ottoman Engagements', in Kenneth Hall (ed.), *The Growth of Non-Western Cities: Primary and Secondary Urban Networking, c. 900–1900* (Lanham, MD: Lexington Books, 2011), 55–97 and 131–58. See also Mahmood Kooria's forthcoming study *Ocean of Law* (Cambridge University Press).

(after 1119/1707) due to severe political turmoil.[15] As a result, Sunni and other Shi'i communities in the subcontinent gradually stopped producing literary works in Arabic. The Bohras, self-isolated from society due to *taqiyya*, were one of the few communities, if not the only community, able to continue the tradition of textual transmission in Arabic. This observation is confirmed by Tirmizi: 'The Isma'ilis [Bohras] made use of Arabic to the entire exclusion of Persian for every purpose because of their direct contact with Yemen and their isolation from the main current of the religious and literary life of the Muslims of Gujarat.'[16] The fact that Arabic is cultivated as a living scriptural language of the treasury of books up to this day is therefore a rare phenomenon in the context of the Indian subcontinent.

Arabic is the dominant scholarly *lingua franca* of any Bohra *khizana*, and *naskh* is its undisputed *khaṭṭ* or scriptural form of transmission. Jan Just Witkam argues that, as a book hand, *naskh* is a script of convenience for the palaeographer because it is too broad a category in the absence of precise typologies.[17] Although this may apply to manuscripts produced in Middle Eastern or native-speaking Arabic milieux, the situation could not be more different in the context of Gujarat, where, historically, regional variants of *nastaʿlīq* had scriptural hegemony over *naskh*. In addition to the special status of Arabic in the *khizana*, the position of *naskh* as a minor scriptural form of transmission in the context of the socio-political history of the subcontinent is therefore unique (more about this later).

As the dominant script of the Alawi *khizana*, variants of *naskh* are found in roughly 90 per cent of *khizana* manuscripts, followed by *nastaʿliq* (roughly 5 per cent of the *khizana*) and other scripts (the remaining 5 per cent); these other scripts are mainly hybrid scripts of *naskh* with strong *nastaʿliq* and possibly *bihārī* influences. For reasons of aesthetics, manuscripts often consist of various scripts; in practice, this means that *naskh* is the dominant script used to write the main text, the colophon and marginalia, and *thuluth* or *diwānī* script is applied for writing the *basmala*, *tasliyat* and the title of the treatise (see Chapter 5). As a script, *naskh* thus has a strong scriptural hegemony over all forms of writing, even documents and talismans.

It should be noted, as shown in the section on book hands, that the broad categories of *naskh* and *nastaʿliq* are problematic in the context of the *khizana*, since a wide variety of hybrid forms and encounters are commonly used. Yet, I use the term *naskh* throughout this chapter because of its special meaning as a 'Middle Eastern' script, as the Bhai Sahebs would refer to it. Another reason to use the classification '*naskh*' is that the Bhai Sahebs refer to all their book hands of the *khizana* as *naskh*. In fact, according to the narrative of the community, the script of transmission of the eternal truths or *haqa'iq* can and should only be transmitted in the form of *naskh*, since this was according to the written courtly culture of the Imams and Dais of Fatimid Cairo and Tayyibi Yemen. The cultivation of *naskh* as the Bohra book hand of transmission *par excellence* is considered a sacred practice and a continuation of the uninterrupted thread of knowledge transmission, as described in Chapter 2. With few exceptions, processes

15 Tirmizi, *Rise and Development of Arabic*, 49. See also Sheikh, 'Aurangzeb as seen from Gujarat'.

16 Ibid., 53. By 'the Isma'ilis' he means the Bohras and not the Isma'ilis from Multan.

17 Jan Just Witkam, *Seven Specimens of Arabic Manuscripts Preserved in the Library of the University of Leiden* (Leiden: Brill, 1978), 18.

of appropriation of vernacular scripts, such as Sindhi script in the case of the Khojas, are absent from the treasury of books for this particular reason.

Inks and Scripts

A crucial codicological element in the transmission of script is ink. Black and red inks are the main colours in which *khizana* manuscripts are recorded and transmitted and are used in accordance with classical Arabic manuscript traditions: black ink transmits the main body of the text, and red ink is applied to mark titles and *tasliyat* or to jot down secondary textual features such as vocalisation, diacritical marks and orthoepic signs.

As we have already seen in the previous chapter, economic factors shaped, and continue to shape, Bohra manuscript culture in terms of book binding and the selection of paper. This is also true when it comes to ink. Most manuscripts analysed contain lacunae intended for red ink. These open spaces were intended to be filled in later, during more prosperous times, as pigments used to produce red ink were more expensive than black ink. The *khizana* manuscripts, those of Alawi provenance in particular, show that often the more prosperous times anticipated by the scribes never came, and these lacunae are either left blank or have been cautiously filled in with pencil.

Some de luxe manuscript exemplars, mostly those of Hamdani provenance, contain rarer ink colours such as emerald green and turquoise blue. I have not come across any manuscripts containing golden ink. The tradition of manuscript copying and use of specific inks, which is addressed in the second section of this chapter, has been adapted to modern times. Modern millennial manuscript copies, produced by the Bhai Sahebs in the last two decades, are copied in fountain pen in dark-blue colours and are complemented by the classical textual additions in red fineliner pens.

Glosses and commentaries are written in often-casual *naskh* hands, which implies that *naskh* is used not only as a formal script but also as an informal book hand for minor or peripheral practices of writing. Paratexts, however, of a less formal or intellectual nature, such as stories, addresses and magical squares, are commonly jotted down in *nasta'liq* in Urdu and Persian, or Hindi and Gujarati. Pagination (not foliation) seems to have been absent in older manuscript copies (those more than two decades old) and was systematically added later in pencil to the lower outer margins of the folios. According to Gacek, this feature is specific to Arabic manuscripts of the subcontinent and to Isma'ili manuscripts, in particular.[18] Interestingly, pagination is marked in Persian or Urdu numerals (noticeable by differences in the numerals 0, 6 and 7), and not in Arabic ones, which is a clear subcontinental feature and possibly a remnant of the Mughal past. Only in very rare cases are quires of Bohra manuscripts of the *khizana* foliated or both foliated and paginated.

The Lisan of the Treasury of Books

Bohra manuscript culture is, as we have seen, characterised by the fact that as a script, *naskh* has a strong hegemony over language, and not vice versa. Script and language, I observed, are not necessarily fixed: they operate independently from each other. For

[18] Gacek, *Vademecum*, 107.

example, although the great majority of *khizana* manuscripts are transmitted in Arabic, a very small number of non-religious *makhtutat* have been transmitted in Persian, but are nevertheless written in *naskh*.

One very hot afternoon during a session with the Mazoon Saheb in his office, we were discussing the specific role of *naskh*. 'See, if you look at this manuscript, see how the Arabic words are written in the Persian style', the Mazoon Saheb said. 'Would you say this is *nasta'liq*?', I asked. The Mazoon replied: '*Nasta'liq, nasta'liq* yes, hmm.' He continued: 'It means that this *Seyyedna* was very well-versed in Persian, as well as Arabic, and his Persian poetry was splendid, splendid.' I continued the conversation by asking the Mazoon when one uses *nasta'liq* and when *naskh*. He replied, while shaking his head: 'No, there is no, hmm, hmm, I cannot say when they were using this, hmm, they used to write Persian in *naskh-e shareef*, in *naskh-e* these things, *naskh-e* script.' This anecdote shows that, even though strong influences of *nasta'liq* can be traced in the palaeography of the *khizana*, there is no awareness or knowledge of this scriptural form among Bohra clerics today. I suggest that this absence or scriptural break reflects certain larger political processes, which are discussed at length in the following sections.

An exception in this regard is poetry in Urdu, which in the Bohra community is strongly linked to a specific genre of written and oral poetic texts known as *shi'r*, including the *marsiyya* recited at *Ashura*. *Shi'r* is always recorded in informal hands in the scriptural form of *nasta'liq*. Another small collection of *khizana* manuscripts illustrates the opposite scriptural phenomenon: Arabic manuscripts written in the scriptural form of *nasta'liq*. This indicates that, in addition to Arabic, Urdu and Gujarati, the Dais of the seventeenth and eighteenth centuries who produced these manuscripts must have been well-versed in Persian and its scriptural variants. However, it should be noted that these manuscripts represent very few of the holdings of the *khizana*.

The Bohra philological tradition – even though secret and closed – thus connects Gujarat with the Arabophone world of Egypt, Yemen and the Indian Ocean through the medium of script, both historically and in the present time. From the perspective of the uninterrupted chain of esoteric Isma'ili knowledge transmission, once produced in medieval Tayyibi Yemen or Fatimid Cairo, the cultivation of Arabic as a scholarly and sacred language of the *khizana* and *naskh* as its main script seems to be perfectly plausible. But what about its larger surroundings: the social space of Badri Mohallah and the Bohra universe at large? What place does '*khizana* Arabic' have in the sociolinguistic universe of the Alawis in contemporary Baroda? And what does Arabic mean to the *mu'minin* and *mu'minat*?

As a scholarly Bohra *lingua franca*, '*khizana* Arabic' seems to be an opaque linguistic element in Badri Mohallah. To the outsider, it seems surprising that a process of vernacularisation of the treasury of books – into the locally spoken Gujarati – is absent. The social space of Badri Mohallah is certainly a literate society, and according to my experience believers are without exception well-versed in Gujarati, Hindi and English, and often also in Urdu. Arabic, the language of the sacred scripts, is a different and complex matter.

The Mazoon Saheb's take on the historical development of Arabic in the community is that, during pre-colonial times, believers' command of Qur'anic Arabic and knowledge of *namaz*, *akhbar* and *wudu'* (and thus not of *'ilm al-batin*) were very good, and its learning was encouraged in local *madrasas*. The vernacular Gujarati, by contrast, was hardly used as a written language. According to the Mazoon, it was during the advent of the British hegemony of the subcontinent that *madrasas* were replaced with secular education, which brought about the decline of Arabic and the rise of Hindi and Gujarati as the new more accessible *lisans* (languages). This development, however, was only reflected in the popular literary tradition of the *ʿamma* of Badri Mohallah. The manuscript tradition of the *khassa* continued in Arabic.[19]

Today, the command of 'the sacred language of Islam' of the *mu'minin* and *mu'minat* is restricted to basics in Qur'anic Arabic only, taught at the Tayyibi *madrasas*. Further learning of Arabic is not offered, and in fact is actively discouraged by the clerical establishment. This active policy of Bohra clerics to limit Arabic to circles of the royal family has turned Arabic into an inaccessible and abstract language for the *ʿamma*. Even if esoteric sources circulated outside the *khizana*, the layperson would never be able to access those texts due to language barriers, leaving aside the multi-layered vocabulary of Bohra Isma'ili esotericism.

On the basis of my observations, I argue that, as a language alien to native speakers of Gujarati, Arabic has been elevated to a language of esotericism (genre) and secrecy (practice), and it is actively used as a tool to inhibit access to and circulation of esoteric sources to the uninitiated: it is thus a linguistic tool of *taqiyya*. Or as the Mazoon Saheb puts it, 'Without Arabic, no access', and 'even then they would not understand it; we don't want to confuse them'. In former times, Arabic used to be taught by the Mazoon to interested believers. However, after taking these classes, some *mu'minin* and *mu'minat* started to interpret Isma'ili or polemical texts found on the internet by themselves, 'illegally, without our *raza*', which, according to the Mazoon Saheb, led to instances of 'transgressions' and even cases of excommunication.[20]

If sources in Arabic are not available to the *mu'minin* and *mu'minat*, what religious literature do believers read? The Mazoon Saheb stressed one morning that 'apart from the Isma'ili tradition recorded in the manuscripts, this [the vernacular literary tradition of the Bohra *ʿamma*] is the other tradition which is keeping our *adab* (etiquette)'.[21] He explained that, to fill the linguistic gap of Arabic, popular religious works, advice literature and newsletters have been made accessible by the *daʿwa* by providing translations in *Lisan al-Daʿwa*.[22] *Lisan al-Daʿwa* publications are mostly excerpts derived from original *zahiri* treatises in Arabic, and their content is adapted to the local socio-religious context of contemporary Baroda. These texts are printed and therefore circulate widely in the community and are part of the Alawi Bohra *madrasa* curriculum (Figure 6.2). It should be noted that the Qur'an has not been translated into *Lisan al-Daʿwa*, for doing so would violate the sacred character of the Arabic text.

[19] Conversation with the Mazoon Saheb, Badri Mohallah, 30 October 2013.

[20] Conversation with the Mazoon Saheb, Badri Mohallah, 10 November 2013.

[21] Ibid.

[22] See for a publication of the Alawi *daʿwa* on *Lisan al-Daʿwa*: Asma Barodawala Attarwala, 'Alavi Bohra Language: Languages in Contact', presented at the Linguistic and Language Development in Jammu and Kashmir with Special Reference to Tribal Languages, Department of Linguistics (University of Kashmir), 14–16 November 2011, http://alavibohra.org/lisaan%20dawat%20research%20paper%2011-2011.pdf (last accessed 21 December 2020).

The vernacular literary tradition of the Bohra *ʿamma* of 'keeping the etiquette' includes the following elements:

1. *Diwāns*: compilations of devotional *qasa'id* composed by the Dais in Urdu, which are recited during religious functions such as the *ʿurs*.
2. *Sayfat* (Ar. '*al-ṣaḥīfāt*'): booklets on different kinds of *namaz* in *Lisan al-Daʿwa*, with occasional passages in Arabic.
3. *Munājāt*: midnight prayers that are recited during the month of Ramadan (in Urdu, *Lisan al-Daʿwa*, and occasionally in Arabic [Qur'anic verses]). The *Munājāt* are recited according to 'a specific Bohra style' (both Dawoodi and Alawi) and are recorded on CD. According to the Mazoon, listening to these CDs (and his personal CD, and his 'tune' in particular) brings believers *baraka*.

These and other literary genres of the Bohra *ʿamma* written in *Lisan al-Daʿwa* deserve scholarly attention. Books and newsletters, however, are only one small aspect of religious life in Badri Mohallah. According to my observations, it is the oral text during rituals, ceremonies such as *nikah* and the *mithaq* and sermons that play a much larger role in the daily lives of believers. As an oral religious language of the people, *Lisan al-Daʿwa* is considered by all to be a ritual and ceremonial *Lisan*, and only secondarily is it a language of the written word.

Interestingly, notions of access and non-access, and vernacular versus non-vernacular languages, vary greatly for insiders and outsiders of the community, including the researcher. For Bohras, the non-vernacular Arabic is a language of secrecy in the context of the treasury of books, and *Lisan al-Daʿwa* is the accessible devotional and ceremonial language of their universe (Figure 6.2). Paradoxically, for outsiders of the community, however, it is the other way round: Arabic, as the universal language of revelation of Islam, is accessible, and *Lisan al-Daʿwa* is a language of secrecy that only insiders of the community and initiates are able and meant to have access to and understand.

Overview of status of languages

Arabic	All *kutub al-daʿwa*: *zahiri* and *batini* holdings of the treasury of books, read by the *khassa* only, with the exception of the Qur'an, talismans, *nass sijillat*, *awraq*, and documents, including *awqaf*.
Lisan al-Daʿwa	Sociolect of Gujarati with Arabic influences, ritual and ceremonial language of the *daʿwa*: orally and written (in Arabic alphabet), popular devotional and advice literature, certain historiographic works, communal newsletters, *madrasa* books (meant to be read by the *ʿamma*), ceremonies (*nikah*, *mithaq*, etc.), sermons.
Urdu	*Sahifat*, *Diwans*, *Munajat*, devotional *'Ashura* poetry, written and performed during special occasions, such as *muharram*, *ʿurs*, *ziyara* and festive ceremonies, occasionally: paratexts in manuscripts.
Persian	Language of historical literature (rare), not a religious language: occasionally paratexts in manuscripts (popular culture).

Gujarati	Non-religious literature, spoken language of communication, occasionally paratexts in manuscripts.

Note. Secret languages also form an intrinsic part of Bohra manuscript culture or, to be more precise, secret scripts and alphabets and numerical script (see Chapter 5.2 on paratexts).

The materiality of secrecy is thus also expressed through the active cultivation of the language of transmission only available to the Bhai Sahebs, Arabic, versus vernacular languages accessible to all believers. Moreover, the choice of script, *naskh*, especially handwritten, also obscures manuscripts even more, as it is considered difficult to read for the native-speaking Gujarati *mu'minin* and *mu'minat*, who are accustomed to reading Qur'anic Arabic in more cursive *nasta'liq* forms of typography.

Similarly to how the codicology of *khizana* manuscripts is linked to the content of the text and determines social usage, palaeography, script typologies, book hands and

Figure 6.2 Collation of *da'wa* publications in *Lisan al-Da'wa* and Gujarati, including a Gujarati translation of the *Da'a'im al-Islam* (second row on the left). Note the jubilee issue of the Dai in the middle (with ribbon).

choices as to how language is transcribed into script fulfil very specific social roles in the community. The hegemony of Arabic as the *lisan* of the *khizana*, and *naskh* as its *khatt*, thus demonstrates that, in addition to codicology, palaeography too is key in understanding text and manuscripts as objects and their being part of a larger manuscript culture. As such, I argue, it is an important additional element in the text–codicology–social meaning triangle I discussed earlier (Figure 5.1).

6.3 *Khizana* Scripts

Now that we have gained an understanding of the importance of Arabic as a sacred and secret language of the Bohra scribal tradition, and *naskh* as an inaccessible category of script of the treasury of books, we move to how this ideal model of script translates into practice. What do the book hands of the *khizana* look like? How did the book hands of the *khizana* evolve over time? And, contrary to the narrative of a 'pure' Arabic manuscript culture, what regional features do these manuscripts and book hands carry?

Script Dichotomies

Manuscripts are manual copies of script that, in turn, are book hands of individual scribes and their personal signatures, preferences and respective skills, while following scribal protocols and traditions. Although book hands are strictly personal, they are not as arbitrary as one would think. Just as in codicology, there are no coincidences in palaeography: book hands look the way they do for a particular reason. The *khizana* manuscripts provide the palaeographer with a vast ocean of book hands. To organise this material, the following four scriptural dichotomies are distinguished:

1. Royal hands versus non-royal hands.
2. Alawi versus non-Alawi hands.
3. Paratext versus main text.
4. The solo scribe versus multiple book hands.

A short note on these categories: when mapping out typologies of script, ideally one would start with the genealogies of script and look at how script has evolved diachronically over time. However, on the basis of my sources (manuscripts) and experiences in the *khizana* (with clerics), I came to the conclusion that, scripturally speaking, it is primarily the divide between the royal clerical and the rest of the community that shapes scripts of the archive; only secondarily do other factors, such as time and sectarian provenance, come into play.

Royal versus non-royal hands. The hierarchy of the royal *khassa* and the lay *ʿamma* is spatially omnipresent not merely in the *mohallah* and in all temporal and religious matters, but also in the realm of script. With the exception of *kutub* of non-Alawi provenance and copies of popular historic works by amateur copyists (Chapter 4), the majority of Bohra manuscripts are produced by *khassa* royal hands. The quality of these royal hands is strongly influenced by one's position in the hierarchy of the royal family: the higher the rank, the more professional and refined the book hand. Without exception, royal hands of Dais are very sophisticated and can therefore easily be distinguished from book hands of the lower ranks of the *daʿwa*, let alone the occasional amateur scribe. After all, the Dai is a professional copyist, and it is he alone who has the ceremonial right to copy manuscripts in the name of God and the hidden Imam and to authorise others to do so. Every Dai I observed has a signature *naskh* book hand. As the history of manuscript production is often well-documented in elaborate colophons, one can observe the personal development of royal scribes and their book hands over the course of their lives and how scripts evolve from scribbly schoolboyish *naskh* to steady, sophisticated, royal book hands. The greater the Dai's authority, the more grand and imposing his hand becomes.

Let us take as an example the royal book hand of Sy. Fakhr al-Dīn Jīwābhāʾī b. Amīr al-Dīn (no. 41, d. 1347/1929; see Figure 6.3) from Baroda, who was responsible for copying an extensive collection of manuscripts. His book hand can be classified as a large and cursive variant of *naskh*, containing grand pointed-head *serifs*, slanted strokes and a limited number of lines per page. It is clear that the unique Fakhr al-Din hand is a book hand of a Dai, for its script is stable, mature, sophisticated, faultless, and completely identical throughout the entire manuscript. This is especially the case in manuscripts copied towards the end of his life. The Fakhr al-Din hand seems to be *kāmil* (perfect) and *ka ʾl-maʿsum* (close to infallible), just as was its master.

The book hand of the late Dai, His Royal Highness Sy. Tayyib Diyaʾ al-Din, could not be more different. Tayyib Diyaʾ al-Din's book hand is characterised by a much smaller, conservative Arabic *naskh* that can best be described as very clear,

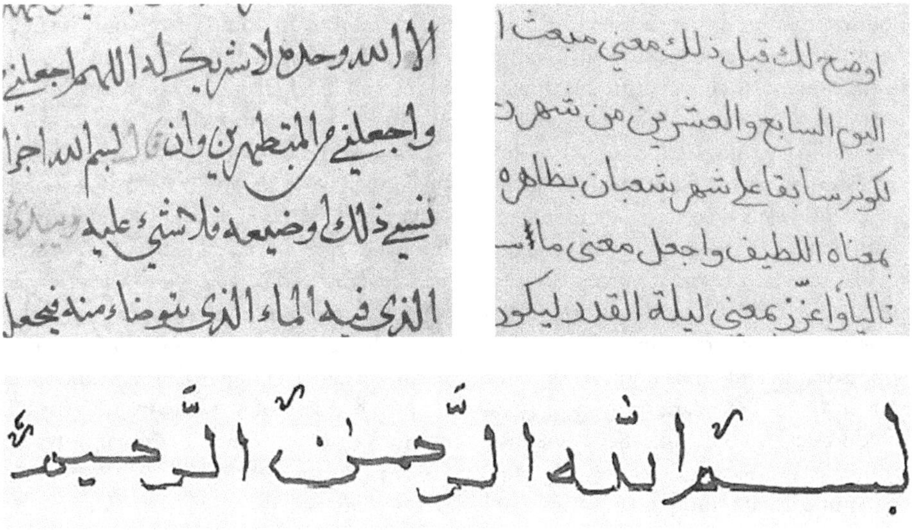

Figure 6.3 Above left, writing samples of the late Dai Fakhr al-Din Jiwābhaʾi b. Amir al-Din in comparison to (above right) the early writing of the late Dai Diya al-Din, and (below right) recent copies.

confined and 'clean' (containing hardly any elements of other script typologies), with modest head *serifs* and a relatively high number of lines per folio. It is said that one's personal characteristics are reflected in one's handwriting, or, in the case of professional scribes, in one's book hand. I had the pleasure of getting to know His Royal Highness as a very humble, pious, self-confined and introverted man – qualities one can clearly trace in his signature *naskh*.

Interestingly, although Sy. Tayyib Diya' al-Din did not have the opportunity to copy manuscripts on a large scale – due to political turmoil in the community at the beginning of his *ʿasr* – his humble but strong style of handwriting, resembling printed *naskh*, has been extremely influential in shaping the script of the next generation of Bhai Sahebs: the late Mazoon, and the current Mazoon, Mukasir and Ra's ul Hudood Sahebs. From a palaeographical point of view, it is clear that these royal men are trained by their father and that their scriptural orientation is on keeping *khizana* book hands as standardised as the talent of the scribe in question permits it. I consider this development to be a strong appropriation of *naskh* script, corresponding with the larger process of Arabising Bohra traditions as a legitimation of the Fatimid past, on the one hand, and of being part of the greater Islamic *umma* on the other (see Chapter 1).

Alawi versus non-Alawi hands. As described in Chapter 4, a substantial part of the *khizana* collection comprises manuscripts of non-Alawi provenance. From the perspective of script and book hands, these manuscripts, which are mostly produced by Dawoodi scribes, do not show substantial discrepancies in writing culture. As seen in the following section, the politics of sectarianism have surprisingly had a limited impact on script. There is no such thing as 'script othering' by attempting to make script more distinguishable as belonging to one group. However, there is one category of manuscripts that stands out in terms of script but for reasons other than sectarian politics: manuscripts produced by the Hamdani family. In addition to sophisticated book bindings, as discussed in Chapter 4, manuscripts of Hamdani provenance are unique due to their signature book hands, which can be characterised by a very clean, neat and thick *naskh* with strong *nastaʿliq* influences; very round, slanted strokes; and extraordinary inks, such as ochre yellows and emerald greens.[23]

Paratext versus main text. Even though paratexts were already discussed at length in the previous chapter, I include here a short note on the scriptural dichotomy of main text versus paratext. In Islamic codicology, a distinction is made between official formal scripts (the main text), also known as *chirodictic* scripts, and *composed* scripts in personalised, casual handwriting.[24] These scripts have very different scriptural features to serve their different functions. Although chirodictic scripts of the *khizana* are often sophisticated and clean book royal hands, composed casual scripts – found in the margins of the codex – are often non-royal and comprise scribbles and hasty notes, such as addresses, account numbers, telephone numbers or dates. These marginal notes do not have to look good, as they are often texts of a profane nature.

While cataloguing manuscript copies, I encountered many of these composed informal scripts. This was especially the case with the piles of copies of the *Daʿaʾim* I

23 See for more details De Blois, *Arabic, Persian, and Gujarati Manuscripts*.

24 Octave Houdas, *Essai sur l'écriture maghrébine*, Nouveaux Mélanges Orientaux (Paris: l'Ecole des Langues Orientales Vivantes, 1886), 105, 110.

mentioned earlier, which contained many undecipherable notes, such as attempts to write the name '*Allāh*'. When the Mazoon Saheb saw my surprise, he said, 'The scribbles have no meaning, students were just sitting around the Dai taking these things and these books were lying there, writing like this.' I asked him if the students were not punished for this: 'Neey, punished neey, this is how they learned, the *mawlanā* was not scolding them, this was the tradition.'[25] In his appreciation of paratexts, the Mazoon Saheb thus clearly is selective, as he attaches little importance to the these marginal features. According to my observation, however, it is important to recognise the presence of these 'scribbles' and other casual writing practices as an important facet of manuscript culture and not merely vis-à-vis the main text of a codex.

The solo scribe versus multiple book hands. Although these various scriptural dichotomies of the treasury of books bring about order in the sea of individual book hands, these categories prove to not be entirely waterproof. Manuscript copying was, and still is today, often a joint effort. This explains why I have come across numerous manuscript copies consisting of several hands, transcribed at the same time or at a later stage, with very different qualities, provenances and paratextual features. For example, I scrutinised many manuscripts that contained at least five or six different hands; one manuscript was even collated by eleven hands in total. More often than not, the different hands are easily detectible because different *miṣtaras* (ruling boards; see the later discussion) were applied (and thus the number of lines per page varies) and the quality of the script differs.

Reasons for the presence of several book hands vary; perhaps scribes did not live long enough to carry out the copying process in its entirety, and others finished the edition (these manuscripts are often lacking an original colophon and are therefore difficult to date); certain sections of manuscripts were omitted (either by mistake or on purpose); copyists did not have the proper folios at their disposal at the time of copying (and scribes of later periods did); or several separate (smaller) treatises of one genre were copied by different scribes with the aim of collating them into an anthology or multiple-text manuscript. These different scribes were often Dais, and I was told by the Bhai Sahebs that the more royal hands a manuscript contains, the more sacred the materiality of the *makhtuta* is considered to be.

Restoration is another explanation for the presence of multiple book hands in manuscripts. The Mazoon Saheb one afternoon described how he restored a certain manuscript, which was collated by four generations of Bhai Sahebs (thus adding an extra book hand to the codex):

> 'This is how [pause] a work that was omitted [was restored] and made a fresh copy, see how I did', he said, while opening the manuscript carefully. 'I purchased handmade paper similar to the colour of the old paper. This is handmade paper, I re-wrote the text, and I loosened the binding to each page [pauses to show me the binding of the codex]. And now it stopped, ha, the worms.

A manuscript may have multiple book hands because of a lack of time and money; the loss of folios due to natural disasters, such as termite attacks or monsoon flooding;

[25] Conversation with the Mazoon Saheb, Badri Mohallah, 20 October 2012.

or because manuscripts were collated *on purpose*, either as family projects (as we have seen with the '*ʿalā kulluhā*' manuscript in Chapter 4) or for educational purposes (more about this in Chapter 6, section 6.2). The co-production and collating of manuscripts by multiple artists or scribes have a long history in South Asia, given the fact that Persian miniatures were traditionally produced in ateliers collaboratively.[26] The same can be said for the production of Sanskrit texts.[27]

As described in Chapter 4, the collating of manuscripts in the social space of Badri Mohallah is thus a (royal) family affair. When I asked whether the Mazoon had copied manuscripts with his father, he remained pensive for a while and then said: 'Ja, ja, *Risālat al-Kāmila*, two pages, I will show you. [pause] See these are my father's writings before five years [silence].'[28] Me: 'Ah, now I see, I catalogued this manuscript yesterday.' The Mazoon replied: 'Yes, yes, but yesterday I did not tell you this is copied by my father [followed by a long silence].' Then he said contemplatively 'So which is the book after this?' and the topic was closed.

Serving an educational purpose, several manuscripts I came across were clearly copied as writing exercises, with the first folios written by a majestic *naskh* book hand that clearly belonged to a Dai or Mazoon Saheb. On the basis of the various inexperienced hands and scribbles written on the following folios, the manuscript must subsequently have been handed over to several pupils, whose book hands return throughout the codex. The presence of these 'exercise' manuscripts shows that as a pedagogical effort manual copying took place in small *silsilas*, instead of in big institutional settings. This is, at least, clearly the case with manuscripts of Alawi provenance. Dawoodi manuscripts of a pedagogical nature, as present in the *khizana* in Baroda, seemed to have been copied on a much larger institutional level, as becomes apparent from the Jamea tus Sayfiyya stamps they bear in the first flyleaves of the *makhtutat*. Whereas Alawi manuscripts are copied in male-only royal circles, the basic teachings of the *jihad* of the scribe are thus part of the curriculum of Dawoodi Bohra students, both male and female.

Due to questions of circulation and secrecy, it is difficult to say anything meaningful about the scribal practices taught at the Jamea tus Sayfiyya, as students customarily donate their manuscripts to the university library upon completion. Manuscripts, even when copied at the Jamea tus Sayfiyya, however, tend to surface in unexpected places. Recently, I stumbled upon several Arabic Jamea tus Sayfiyya manuscript copies, transcribed in the 1980s by different pupils in Surat, that were for sale on eBay India by a seller from Gujarat. The images of these *zahiri* manuscript copies confirmed what I suspected. Even though the institutional context is very different, in terms of their palaeography and codicology the manuscripts showed striking similarities with Alawi manuscript culture. They contained identical colophons, *naskh* book hands, use of *mistaras*, and other layout features, such as the absence of the *basmala* at the incipit,

26 Virginia Whiles, 'Wastelands: Between Art and Anthropology'. Lecture presented at The Museum for Ethnology, Dahlem, Berlin, 22 January 2015.

27 Sheldon I. Pollock, *The Language of the Gods in the World of Men: Sanskrit, Culture, and Power in Pre-modern India* (Berkeley, CA: University of California Press, 2006), Introduction.

28 The manuscript mentioned is *Risālat al-Kāmila fī maʿnā al-thālith al-mayālī* by ʿAlī b. al-Ḥusayn b. ʿAlī b. al-Walīd (d.682/1284). See Poonawala, *Biobibliography*, 166.

and they were copied in similar pre-bound booklets.[29] These similarities in manuscript and scribal culture again show the interconnectedness of the Bohra communities and their scholarly networks.

Khizana Book Hands and the Question of 'Indian' *Naskh*

As discussed in detail previously, *naskh* is the signature Bohra book hand of the *khizana* and is used both for Persian and Arabic, and as both an official and a casual script. The popular book hand, known for its straight *alif* without an initial stroke, is written in a fine reed pen; it evolved into regional styles after the seventh/thirteenth century and was paired with local scripts and traditions of writing that developed according to local artistic tastes.[30] While the travel and transformation of localities of *naskh* from the Arab peninsula to the east (Baghdad: the flamboyant *thuluth*; Damascus and Cairo: the rather stiff Mamluk *naskh*, also known as *muḥaqqaq*; Persia: the elegant *nasta'liq*, mix of *naskh* and *ta'līq*), the north (Anatolia: *thuluth*) and the west (the Maghreb lands: the staccato Maghribi *naskh*) are well-documented, very little is known about the scriptural genealogy of *naskh* on the Indian subcontinent.[31]

Calligraphic styles of *naskh*, and its hanging and slanting cousin *nasta'liq*, came to the Indian subcontinent via Iran in the fourteenth and fifteenth centuries.[32] The scriptural spread of Bohra *naskh* challenges this paradigm, given the fact that, as we have seen in Chapter 4, manuscripts of the *khizana* – and the spread of Tayyibi Isma'ili Islam at large – took the 'Arabic' Indian Ocean route over sea, as opposed to the 'Persian' route over land. Contrary to Persian and Urdu, which have been the main focus of study of South Asianists for centuries, the presence of *naskh* as a script of Islamic devotional literature has been overlooked, even though the script was – and in some cases still is – used in the province of Sindh, the Pashtun-speaking areas, the coast of Tamil Nadu, and in Gujarat.[33] What is intriguing is that similar processes of scriptural dominance of *naskh* can be detected, regardless of the language of transmission, whether Arabic or vernacular languages, both high and low. An example of this is represented by devotional texts on secrecy and initiation produced in Sufi milieux in Pondicherry, which are transmitted in Tamil language and written in Arabic script.[34]

Although the label 'Indian *naskh*' is frequently used in manuscript catalogues to refer to 'South Asian' book hands that are not *nasta'liq*, there seem to be no standards for what this vernacular variant of *naskh* is supposed to look like in reality.[35] Annemarie Schimmel describes Indian styles of *naskh* as follows: 'it is even stiffer (than "Middle

[29] See my forthcoming article on the scribal practices of the Jamea tus Sayfiyya.

[30] Gacek, *Vademecum*, 162–5.

[31] Schimmel, *Calligraphy and Islamic Culture*, 23.

[32] Ibid., 29, 66.

[33] Danesh Jain, 'Sociolinguistics of the Indo-Aryan Languages', in Danesh Jain and George Cardona (eds), *The Indo-Aryan Languages* (New York: Routledge, 2003), 52.

[34] Prof. Dr Torsten Tschacher, private manuscript collection.

[35] Gacek, *Vademecum*, 162–5. See also Adam Gacek, *Strokes and Hairlines: Elegant Writing and its Place in Muslim Book Culture* (Montreal: McGill University Library, 2013).

Eastern" *naskh*), the round endings of the letters being small and perfectly circular so that a page may look very calm and sedate. However, the letters are often too closely crammed together, and someone used to Turkish *naskh* would find a Koran printed in Pakistani style difficult to appreciate.'[36]

'Indian' or 'subcontinental' *naskh* (including the north and south of India, Bangladesh and Pakistan) is simply too large a geographical category for script, because it cannot include all hegemonic and minor practices of *naskh*, nor do justice to local and trans-local scriptural and scribal politics (more about this in the next section). The issue of politics has not been systematically explored, and proper palaeographical research is necessary to do justice to the variety of *naskh* traditions in the Indian subcontinent, separating it from its dominant younger brother *nastaʿliq* and studying it as a scriptural tradition in its own right.

Given that this study is limited to scripts and scribal practices of the treasury of books, it has yet to be seen how the Bohra philological tradition of *naskh* fits into subcontinental traditions and practices of writing. What we can trace in the specific social context of the *khizana* is the evolution of script within this manuscript culture. My aim in this section is not only to define what Alawi Bohra *khizana naskh* looks like, but also, more importantly, to place these unique book hands in their historical and geographical context, taking into account various factors that influenced these scripts. I conducted a comparative palaeographical analysis of roughly 300 (often individual and unique) book hands covering manuscript copies from a period of almost 450 years – from the late sixteenth century/eleventh century to the present day. This comparative analysis of scripts focuses on both the quantity of the writing samples and the quality of the handwritten documentation; that is, whether the manuscripts are of good quality, have a clear provenance, and are dated through a colophon and – if possible – autographs, attestations and owner stamps.

How does a system of classification of Bohra scripts contribute to or challenge our understanding of the *khizana*, and the Bohra universe at large? According to both my observation and the following palaeographical analysis – in addition to the material forms and styles of the scripts – this system of classification involves three broader contexts: (1) local history: how and why the style of scripts changed or was re-invented over a period of 450 years and what those changes indicate about the community; (2) questions of scriptural spread and mobility; and (3) ideals, models, practices, experiences and technologies of manual copying, scribal agency and knowledge transmission.

From Yemen to Baroda: An Archaeology of Bohra Book Hands

After a thorough comparative analysis of scripts, I argue that the Alawi book hands of the *khizana*, meaning those produced in the treasury of books in Baroda, can roughly be classified into three historical periods. This classification is based on their scriptural features – the ductus, letter forms, head-serifs and so on – and not necessarily on the time or place of production, although these palaeographical features are evidently strongly linked:

[36] Schimmel, *Calligraphy and Islamic Culture*, 24.

1. Early Bohra hands of the late sixteenth and seventeenth century, of which the majority was copied directly from archaic Yemeni book hands (dated between 990–1120/1582–1700, if not older).
2. Alawi Bohra hands of the eighteenth century and nineteenth centuries, in which more cursive and majestic-looking book hands developed after the Alawi–Dawoodi schism (dated 1120–1210/1700–1800 and 1210–1320/1800–1900).
3. Contemporary Bohra hands, following a scriptural turn after which book hands resemble modern printed *naskh* (dated 1320/1900–present).

We thus concern ourselves here with the Indian Bohra book hands, as samples from Yemeni manuscripts were not available in sufficient quantities.

The oldest Indian copies present in the *khizana*, however, do resemble features of Yemeni exemplars. This is not surprising, as these manuscripts date back to the early years of the Bohra *daʿwa* in Gujarat, right after the official relocation of the *daʿwa* from Yemen. It is also important to remember that centuries before this relocation, the copying of manuscripts was already part of the curriculum of Bohra students who were trained in the Tayyibi *madrasa* system in Yemen, and they continued these practices upon their return to India. Bohra book hands are therefore thus truly a mix of Yemeni and Gujarati scribal practices and traditions. This is especially true for the formative phase in Bohra *daʿwa* history, when the community, despite its Gujarati Dais, was still very much focused on Yemen until the Sulaymani schism of in 999/1591. After this schism and the Alawi–Dawoodi bifurcation that followed, Bohra book hands developed into their own distinctive styles. Let us start, however, with a few observations on Yemeni-Tayyibi book hands.

A brief note on Yemeni book hands. As discussed previously, the oldest manuscripts in the treasury of books are of Yemeni provenance and pre-date any other Indian book hand in the *khizana*. The survival of these manuscripts is important, because they give us a glimpse into the archaic book hands and manuscript culture of the Yemeni Tayyibis, which forms the basis of all Bohra manuscript cultures and scribal traditions. As it is unlikely that any original Fatimid copies reached or survived in Gujarat, it is the Yemeni exemplars that the Bohras considered the historic 'mother' manuscripts, the ideal model for the Bohra manuscriptorium to which one should aspire in terms of base text, codicology, palaeography, reading and writing.

The Hamdani in London collection contains a unique manuscript that provides an idea of what Tayyibi Yemeni book hands looked like and how they developed into Indian Bohra hands. The manuscript in question is a copy of al-Kirmani's *Kitāb al-Riyāḍ* (The Meadows of the Righteous), which De Blois considers the oldest known 'Fatimid' manuscript copy from Yemen accessible outside Bohra *khizana*.[37] It contains two book hands: (1) an undated Yemeni book hand, copied before 760/1359 by an unidentified copyist, and possibly even dating back to the fourth/tenth century; and (2) an Indian royal book hand, dated 988/1580 and attributed to the twenty-seventh Dai, Sy. Da'ud b. Ajabshah (d. 997/1589).[38] On the basis of De Blois's analysis, the manuscript has been among generations of Dais for centuries,

[37] De Blois, 'The Oldest Known Fatimid Manuscript from Yemen', 1–7. Ms. 1458, Hamdani collection, IIS, De Blois, *Arabic, Persian, and Gujarati Manuscripts*, 60–6.

[38] De Blois, *Arabic, Persian, and Gujarati Manuscripts*, 63.

as it was donated in 760/1359 by the fifteenth Yemeni, Sy. Shamsudīn ʿAbbās b. Muḥammad (d. 779/1377), to one of his followers and at a later stage taken to India; there, its missing folios were recopied in 988/1580 by Sy. Da'ūd Burhānuddīn b. Quṭshāh (no. 27, d. 1021/1612) in Ahmedabad, roughly a century before the Alawi–Dawoodi schism.[39] In Figure 6.4, we see the colophon of the Indian book hand, in which the names of the Dai and the scribe are written in *kitab siriyya*.[40]

This manuscript is of great interest as it contains book hands of both continents, which, as we can see in Figure 6.4, differ greatly. The Yemeni *naskh* is written in a clearly legible, rectilinear hand that is vocalised and pointed; it contains various archaic palaeographic features, such as a tailed *ʾalīf* and Kufi-esque looking *kāf*.[41] According to De Blois, these and other 'striking graphic and orthographic features' are typical of the archaic *naskh* of the fourth/tenth, fifth/eleventh or sixth/twelfth centuries found in the Arab world.[42]

The penmanship of the Indian book hand, by contrast, appears to be much more flamboyant and round. It is unpointed, unvocalised, contains ligatures, and has a lot of roundness in comparison to the angularity of the Yemeni hand: its descenders are curved, combined with more pointy and rectilinear-looking ascenders. The Indian

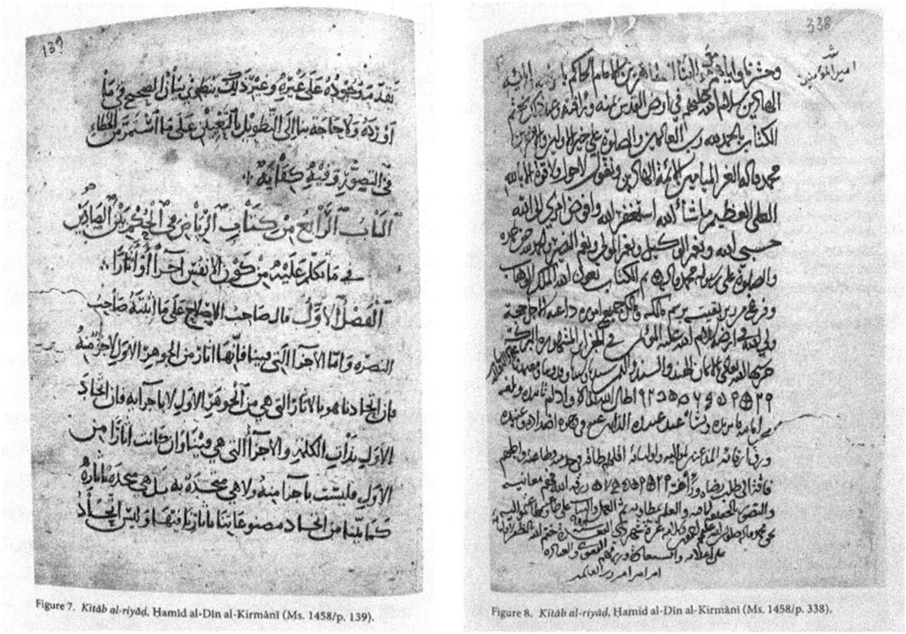

Figure 6.4 The Yemeni (left) and Indian (right) book hands of Ms. 1458. Source: De Blois, *Arabic, Persian, and Gujarati Manuscripts*, 64–5.

[39] Ibid., 60–6.

[40] See for a full transcription of the colophon: De Blois, 'The Oldest Known Fatimid Manuscript from Yemen', 3.

[41] Ibid., 2–3.

[42] De Blois, *Arabic, Persian, and Gujarati Manuscripts*, 62.

hand in some cases has pronounced head-serifs, such as the *kāf*. Whereas the line of writing in the Yemeni hand appears to be straight, in the Indian hand it has a clear slanted baseline that curves down towards the end. In the Indian hand, the tails of the *bā's* and the *nūns* show this very clearly as they slant downwards at an angle, whereas in the Yemeni hand the tails of the *bā's* and *nūns* are at horizontal and reach the base line. Moreover, in the Yemeni hand there is more interlinear space between the lines, whereas the Indian scribe has used a different *mistara*.

It should, of course, be kept in mind that the two book hands compared here are at least two centuries, if not more, apart, and one could thus argue how archetypical the Yemeni book hand is. However, in terms of their angularity and other 'archaic' features, Ms. 1458 shows palaeographical similarities with the book hands found in manuscripts of Yemeni provenance I have seen in Baroda. The more round and curved Indian hand of Ms. 1458, by contrast, is very typical for Bohra book hands, both Alawi and Dawoodi, of the centuries that follow. The scribal traditions and book hands of the Tayyibi and later Sulaymani Yemenis also evolved over time. Through the recent articles of Poonawala and Traboulsi, we get a glimpse into how they evolved in Yemen, after the relocation of the *daʿwa* to Gujarat, into script typologies that are less straight and rectilinear, which can for instance be observed in the twelfth-/eighteenth-century Hamdani manuscripts copied in Haraz.[43]

Early Bohra hands of the sixteenth and seventeenth centuries. The oldest Bohra book hands of the Alawi *khizana* date from as early as the late tenth/sixteenth and early eleventh/seventeenth centuries, following the relocation of the *daʿwa* from Yemen to Gujarat before the Alawi–Dawoodi schism and the subsequent move of the community from Saraspur, Ahmedabad to Badri Mohallah, Baroda. Among the earliest Bohra book hands of the *khizana*, I came across the *khatt* of none other than Da'ud Burhanuddin b. QutbShah, the twenty-seventh Dai whose flamboyant Indian penmanship we have just analysed in the context of Ms. 1458. As the third Indian Dai in Gujarat, he governed the *daʿwa* for twenty-two years in Ahmedabad following the Sulaymani schism. Despite the political turmoil, he remarkably found the time to restore Yemeni manuscripts, such as *Kitab al-Riyad*, and prepare fresh copies from Yemeni titles that at the time must have been widely available, such as the *Risāla al-Waḍiyya* (The Epistle of Custody), of which a script sample can be seen in Figure 6.5. The presence of his book hand in Baroda, in the Hamdani *khizana*, and most likely also in the *khizana* of the Dawoodis shows how interconnected are Bohra manuscripts, and their book hands.

Book hands from the pre-bifurcation period, when the Alawis and the Dawoodis still shared the same genealogy of Dais, are characterised by the continuation of a similarly curvy and flamboyant *naskh* style and ductus, mostly written with thick reed *qalams*. Scripturally speaking, these book hands are dominantly *naskh* with strong cursive characteristics (sloping to the lower left), the ligatures curved and round. Some book hands are more slanted, whereas others are more horizontal, which might be an attempt to write in the archaic or perhaps neo-archaic Yemeni style (Figure 6.6). It

[43] Poonawala, 'Isma'ili Manuscripts from Yemen', 242–3. Traboulsi, 'Sources for the History of the Tayyibi Isma'ili Da'wa in Yemen and its Relocation to India', 270–4.

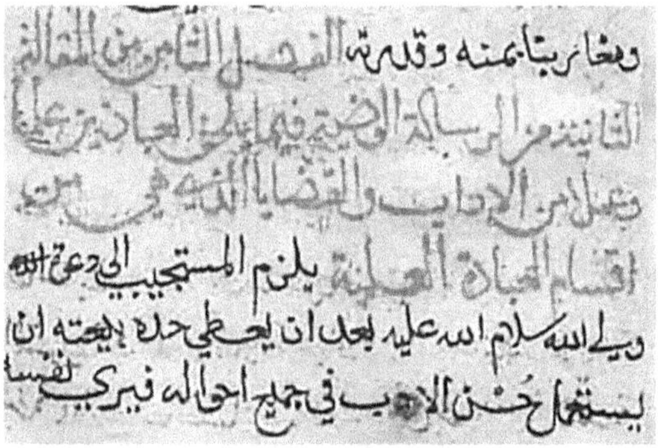

Figure 6.5 Script sample of Sy. Burhanuddin b. Qutb Shah, *Risāla al-Waḍiyya.*

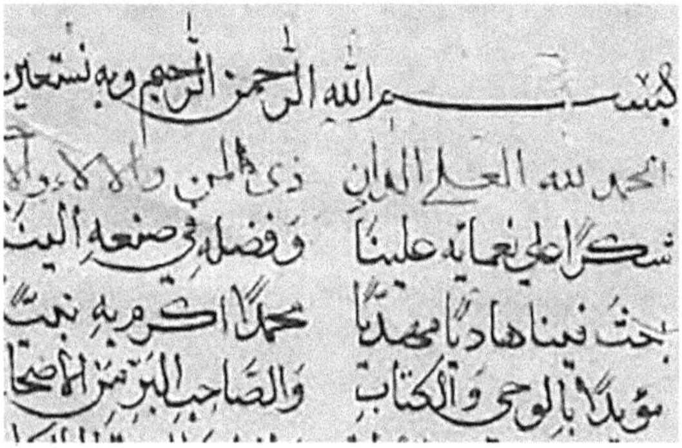

Figure 6.6 Another script sample of Sy. Burhanuddin b. Qutb Shah.

seems that in some cases, copyists, such as Sy. Burhanuddin b. Qutb Shah, were able to write both the more slanted (Figure 6.5) and the more horizontal *naskh* (Figure 6.6).

In this period, occasionally elements of *bihari*, the chancery script of the Delhi Sultanate (602–962/1206–1555), can be found.[44] A 'strange mutation of *naskh* script', according to David James, *bihari* remained popular during the early years of Mughal India and can be recognised by its shortness and emphasis on the sub-linear slanted strokes of letters, which are 'thickened at their centers and chiseled like swords at their ends'.[45] While the deep slanted strokes produced by Bohra hands are not as dramatic as those found in the famous *bihari* Qur'ans of the Delhi Sultanate, there are some major scriptural similarities, such as consonants *sans serif* and emphatic letters and *ʿayns* and *ghayns* with large, flat oval shapes[46] Early Bohra hands seem to be influenced by *bihari* features, whereas the later hands moved away from this *naskh* variant (Figure 6.7).

[44] Gacek, *Vademecum*, 19.

[45] David James, *After Timur: Qur'ans of the Fifteenth and Sixteenth Centuries* (Oxford: Oxford University Press, 1992), 102.

[46] Gacek, *Vademecum*, 19. Schimmel, *Calligraphy and Islamic Culture*, 31.

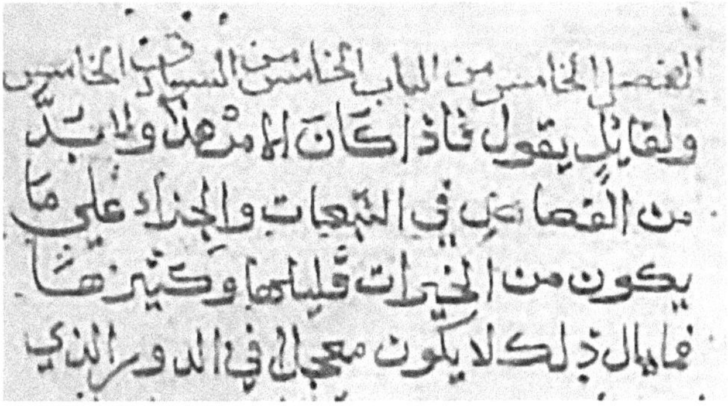
ولقائل يقول فاذا كان الامر هكذا ولا بد
من الفضائل في التبعات والجزاء على ما
يكون من الخيرات قليلها وكثيرها
فما بال ذلك لا يكون معجلا في الدور الذي

Figure 6.7 Script sample of the namesake of the community, Sy. Ali Shamsuddin b. Ibrahim.

Alawi hands of the eighteenth and nineteenth centuries. From the formative phase of the official Bohra *daʿwa* in Gujarat in the late sixteenth and seventeenth centuries, we move to Bohra hands produced in the eighteenth and nineteenth centuries. Manuscripts copied in the eighteenth century are rare in the *khizana*, and there is a clear historical reason for this: this is the period of the long aftermath of the Alawi–Dawoodi schism. Additional factors that contributed to the turmoil of the eighteenth century, as the oral history of the community reports, include severe termite attacks and religious persecution during the post-Aurangzeb period.[47] Manuscripts that survive from this period have a *naskh* variant that seems to be symbolic of the Alawi *daʿwa* at the time: a community in transition. The royal book hands consist of clearly legible *naskh*, without the *bihari* influences of the mid-sixteenth and early seventeenth century. In comparison to earlier scripts, eighteenth-century Bohra hands stand out in terms of height (the script increases in size), resulting in fewer lines per folio, and ductus (less stiff and staccato than seventeenth-century book hands). It is likely that, following the schism with the Dawoodis, in order to reaffirm their claim of *nass* in script and scribal practice, the Alawi Dais adopted their own, more majestic-looking *naskh* variant.

Alawi hands of the nineteenth century can be described as the largest and most imposing variant of the *naskh* hands under consideration, due to their strong rectilinear ascenders and curvy descenders. Even though a more thorough comparison with Dawoodi *daʿwa* manuscripts is necessary, on the basis of the large number of manuscript copies present in the Alawi *khizana*, and their book hands, Alawi scribal practice from this period seems to have come into its own. As a signature feature, the hands have long, sub-linear strokes and characteristic hairlines; they also contain the occasional subcontinental feature, such as the *baṛī yā*'s found in *nastaʿliq* scripts (Figures 6.8–6.10). The script is great in height, descenders and ascenders are long and deep, letter forms contain s-shaped *kāfs*, and its *serifs* are very prominent and dramatically wave leftwards, ending in a hook shape. Letter shapes of separate words are often interlaced closely, resulting in ligatures of a very unconventional nature.

[47] See also Tirmizi, *Rise and Development of Arabic*, 53, 54, and Sheikh, 'Aurangzeb as seen from Gujarat'.

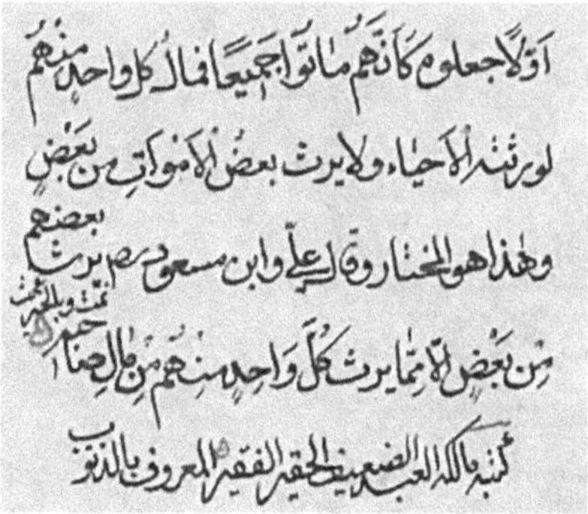

Figure 6.8 Script sample of Sy. Nūruddīn b. Shaykhalī (no. 35, d. 1178/1764).

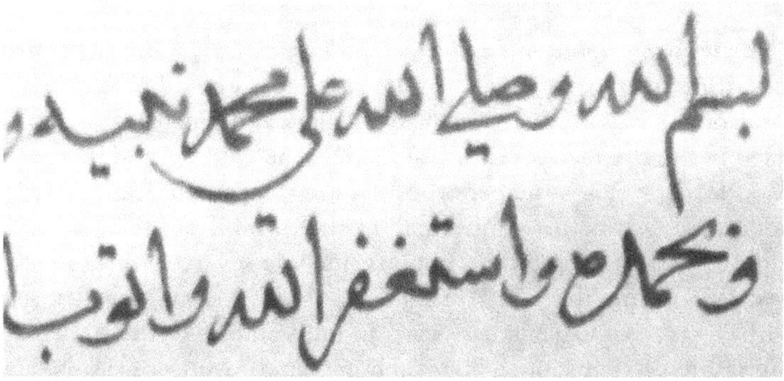

Figure 6.9 Nineteenth-century book hand.

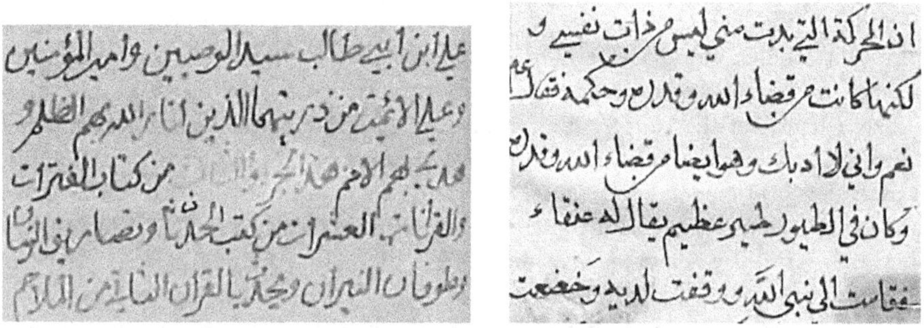

Figure 6.10 Further samples of nineteenth-century royal book hands.

Moreover, Bohra hands of the nineteenth century are stiff and firm, containing deep strokes that sometimes surpass entire words, giving several scripts a very complex, rather inaccessible and theatrical outlook. There is almost no distance between the words, which makes the script difficult to read. A great majority of manuscripts of this period are vocalised (diagonally) with deep slanting descenders to the right. One

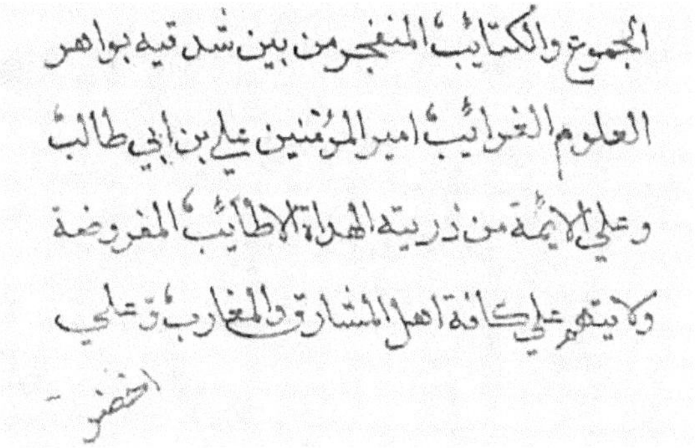

Figure 6.11 Sample of early twentieth-century royal book hand.

can also observe that the later nineteenth-century book hands are already moving towards a more standardised *naskh*.

Contemporary Bohra hands from the twentieth century to the present. When browsing through manuscripts produced during the past century, one can clearly trace a discontinuity or even a scriptural break with the past: the grand *naskh* book hands of the nineteenth century are replaced by a clean and sober script that resembles printed *naskh* variants of the early twentieth century. This 'modern standard Bohra *naskh*' – as far as one can use these terms for individual book hands – seems to be a more unified script without room for individual artistic improvisation. Whereas early twentieth-century book hands still have a cursive character (Figure 6.11), the more modern hands are entirely stripped of the deep slants and cursive descenders that are so clearly present in earlier scripts. They have been replaced by more modest exemplars (more vertical and of lesser height), head-*serifs* are smaller and less elaborate and unconventional ligatures are absent. Moreover, Bohra hands of the twentieth century are more confined, smaller in height, and written in a 'staccato' fashion.

Although a clear discontinuity can be traced from Bohra book hands of the eighteenth and nineteenth century, this development is not entirely abrupt: manuscripts of the *khizana* illustrate that the process of scriptural appropriation was a gradual one. Scripts dated from the late nineteenth century already contain traces of 'modern *naskhification*', a process that continues until the 1920s. It seems that from the 1920s onwards, contemporary book hands are 'cleared' of all strong rectilinear, curvy and subcontinental features, such as *bari* ya's found in *nastaʿliq* scripts (Figure 6.12).

A scriptural turn of Bohra book hands. This palaeographical analysis of *khizana* scripts shows the scriptural diversity and development of Bohra *naskh* hands over a period of four and a half centuries in the Alawi treasury of books. To summarise the evolution of Bohra book hands: manuscript material was first transmitted in an angular form of archaic *naskh* from Yemen, with round letter forms with curved descenders and deep tails, a slanted base line and occasional *bihari* influences (late sixteenth and early seventeenth centuries). These early Bohra hands went through a period of transition in the centuries that followed, developing into the flamboyant and dramatic *naskh* book hands of the late eighteenth and early nineteenth centuries, which were

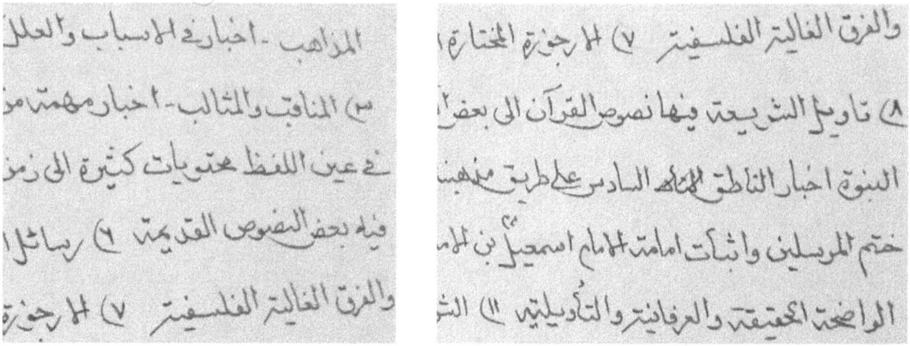

Figure 6.12 Examples of late twentieth-century book hands.

gradually replaced by a standard form of Bohra *naskh* up to the present time, in which all non-*naskhi* features were drastically reduced. Although we may conclude that *naskh* dominates Bohra scriptural culture throughout the ages, strong cursive features can nevertheless be traced in all book hands of the *khizana*, which indicates – following Schimmel to a certain extent – the 'subcontinental' context in which these scripts were produced.

This question remains: what greater social, religious and political circumstances does this evolution of Barodian Bohra book hands reflect, either locally in the *daʿwa* of Badri Mohallah or at large? To begin with the oldest handwriting, the presence of *bihari* features in early Bohra scripts might confirm an oral tradition of the community that reports that the Alawi Bohra Dais of the mid-sixteenth and early seventeenth centuries maintained warm political relations with the local governors courts of the Mughals in Gujarat, exchanging manuscripts between them.[48] This information challenges the notion of a *khizana* and the closed scribal culture of Badri Mohallah. Instead, it indicates a scribal exchange of styles that were in vogue at the time, as we have seen in the case of the poetry exemplar of the Dai to the Mughal courtier in Chapter 1.

The elaborate calligraphic style and large output of manuscript copies from the nineteenth century seem to indicate a golden age of Alawi royal book hands. The scriptural turn from these elaborate *naskh* hands to contemporary Bohra 'standard' *naskh* could not be more dramatic and needs elucidation. The Alawis' introduction of closed scriptural categories of *naskh* clearly was related to the introduction of the printing press in colonial India in the early nineteenth century and to new ideas about depicting more standardised forms of writing and connectedness of language and script.[49] Where the scribal practices of the Alawi Bohras remained relatively untouched by this development (at least in their mode of production), the Dawoodi *daʿwa*, as I described in Chapter 4, partly substituted manual manuscript copying in favour of procuring controlled and strictly authorised printed critical editions. In addition, the invention

48 It should be noted that the presence of Mughal manuscripts in the *khizana* remains obscure and manuscripts of this provenance were never revealed to me.

49 A vernacular press in Gujarati was established in 1812 in Bombay. Poleman, 'Serial Publications in India', 23–30.

of the steam engine resulted in an increase in the numbers of people and goods moving between the Indian subcontinent and the Arab world, which increased mobility, trade, travel and, in the case of the Bohras, pilgrimage and access to the holy lands of Saudi Arabia, Egypt, and Yemen, as well as the revival of their old networks of manuscript mobility. This was especially true for Mecca and the performance of the *Hajj*; as a result, as demonstrated by John Slight, numerous Muslims of South Asia remained in the Middle East after their pilgrimages, for reasons of both piety and economics.[50]

Although there is no clear proof that the introduction of the printing press and increased continental exchanges affected script directy, it is evident that the focus of the *daʿwa* westwards to the Arab world and Europe must have had an impact on the ideas, aesthetics of script and politics, and the 'Arabo-Islamisation' of book hands. As the culture of print took root in South Asia and the Middle East in the nineteenth century, the book markets of Bombay and Cairo were flooded with printed editions of what Ahmed El Shamsy calls 'the Islamic classics' in Arabic, Urdu, Persian and vernacular languages. In term of aesthetics, layout and paratexts, these printed editions still resembled manuscripts, by the addition, for instance, of the corrector's colophon and the *taqrīẓ* (endorsement).[51] It is likely that these 'historic' Arabic printed editions, which are widely available in the Alawi treasury of books, and their early script typologies of a standardised, printed *naskh* influenced Bohra scribal culture in the nineteenth and twentieth centuries.

As noted in the historical introduction on the Bohras, their communities prospered in the colonial period, due to their gaining economic monopolies in trade and a relief from Sunni persecution. During the *ʿasr* of the fifty-first and fifty-second Dawoodi Dais, a policy of reform, modernisation and secular education was put into practice, inspired by modernist thought during the late Raj, followed by a programme of Arabo-Islamisation and re-institutionalisation of Bohra religious life during the post-colonial era. Especially after the 1960s, the Alawi and Dawoodi communities invested in representations of a new Bohra Muslim identity, with a strong link to the Arab past of the community in Yemen and Egypt, while strictly adhering to notions of *taqiyya*.[52] There is no doubt that the process of Arabo-Islamisation of the Dawoodi community had an impact on the aesthetics of Bohra Indian *naskh* and its 'de-cursification', which had the effect of removing subcontinental influences. Although these developments are specific to the modern history of the Dawoodis, in terms of the institutionalisation of religious life and *daʿwa* policies the communities are strikingly similar. The earlier-mentioned 'modern *naskh*' script appropriation of the current Syedna is an example of how script is part of a larger process of Arabising Bohra traditions as a means of legitimising the past.

[50] John Slight, *The British Empire and the Hajj, 1865–1956* (Cambridge, MA: Harvard University Press, 2015). See also James L. Gelvin and Nile Green, *Global Muslims in the Age of Steam and Print* (Berkeley: University of California Press, 2014). We know of small Bohra communities that settled in Jeddah during the nineteenth and twentieth centuries, thanks to Prof. Dr Ulrike Freitag's lecture on Jeddah in Leiden, 2014. Ulrike Freitag, *A History of Jeddah: the Gate to Mecca in the Nineteenth and Twentieth Centuries* (Cambridge: Cambridge University Press, 2020), 138.

[51] Ahmed El Shamsy, *Rediscovering the Islamic Classics: How Editors and Print Culture Transformed an Intellectual Tradition* (Princeton: Princeton University Press, 2020), 79–81.

[52] Blank, *Mullahs on the Mainframe*, 52.

6.4 Scribal Politics

Now that we have gained a better understanding of *khizana* scripts and book hands, let us examine the Alawis' scribal tradition in practice. The manual copying of manuscripts plays a central role in Alawi Bohra *khizana* culture – in its materiality of secrecy, knowledge production, textual transmission and preservation, and, as I argued throughout this study, in the community's cultivation of a Neo-Fatimid identity. As the treasury of books, the *khizana* thus not only domesticates and enshrines *makhtutat* from the past as a living manuscriptorium but is also the space in which manuscripts are produced and turned into another.

The Jihad of the Scribe

During my stay in Baroda, I thought that, for me to understand what it meant to be part of this sacred scribal tradition, the ultimate participant observation in the *khizana* would be to copy a *batini* manuscript by hand alongside the Bhai Sahebs. Practising this form of social codicology would allow me, the researcher, to stand in the light of a centuries-old tradition and take part in the uninterrupted chain of secret Isma'ili knowledge transmission, experiencing at first hand its technologies and rituals. Never would I have imagined that the Bhai Sahebs would grant me – a non-believer, a non-royal, a non-Indian and, on top of all of that, a woman – permission to participate, since manuscript copying is considered an exclusive royal practice and sacred act of devotion.

The Mazoon Saheb, however, was under the impression that it would benefit the catalogue to master the mechanics of Bohra manuscript copying. And so it was under his strict supervision that I copied an entire *batin* manuscript, using *mistaras*, inks and pens that had been used by generations of Dais and Mazoon Sahebs. The manual copying of manuscripts in Arabic seems easy at first, but is in fact a long and painstaking ritual, which can only be carried out according to specific rules and etiquette. It was only after days of endless copying – my hands covered in ink and blisters, finding small pieces of old manuscripts in my *dupatta* and not being able to walk straight for days because of the long hours of sitting cross-legged on the floor – that I understood why the Mazoon Saheb had said 'The copying of *makhtutat* is a *jihad*'.

The *jihad* of the scribe, I learned, requires great patience, precision and skill. It takes time, for instance, to get accustomed not only to the text of the mother manuscripts but also, and more importantly, to the individual book hands of the scribes who went before you, their penmanship, ligatures, the rhythm of their hand, the way they often played with the spatial layout of the folios, and other particularities. Moreover, one has to develop one's own personal book hand and penmanship, including ductus, letter forms and head-serifs, which manifest themselves only after the writing of many folios. And, of course, this process entails a great deal of physical labour. Or, as a certain Mir 'Ali of Mashhad describes it, 'The calligrapher needs five things: a fine temperament, understanding of calligraphy, a good hand, the necessary utensils and finally, endurance of pain'.[53]

[53] Schimmel, *Calligraphy and Islamic Culture*, 39.

It is the experience of being a scribe of the Alawi *da'wa* that is central to the following two sections. According to observations I made during this experiment of scribal participation, the manual copying of manuscripts consists of two facets: (1) the social dimensions of the *scribal*, that is, copying as an experience, including rituals, traditions and etiquette; and (2) the *scriptural*, that is, the technical and stylistic practice of manuscript copying. Scribal and scriptural cultures together form what I call *scribal politics*: all choices made by the scribe (whether stylistic or ritualistic) while copying a codex, roll or talisman, which are closely related to the larger social dimensions of the *khizana* and the Bohra universe at large. In this process, the scribe is thus not blindly copying script. Instead, he or she has agency in the process. Even though the scribe is part of a greater tradition of knowledge transmission, it is his or, in rare cases, her scribal *jihad*. Script, social dimensions, and choices of the copyist are thus strongly intertwined in giving shape to the manuscript culture of the *khizana* and to the community's materiality of secrecy.

Scribal Practices: A Rite of Passage

The sacred act of manuscript copying is guided by a long-standing tradition in the bookish societies of the pre-modern Islamic world. Professional scribes received a long training with a private master, and upon completion of their apprenticeship an *ijaza* was granted, after which copyists were allowed to write in their own name, taking on assignments commissioned by scholars or royal courts.[54] The art of calligraphy flourished especially in the context of Sufism in the Indian subcontinent, where scribal traditions were transmitted to its initiated members via spiritual – and often secret – chains known as *silsilas*.[55]

Even though Alawi Bohras do not make use of the term *silsila*, a spiritual chain of or genealogy of transmission between master and disciple does exist, especially in relation to transmission of scribal culture and practices of initiation. From an early age, the Bhai Sahebs of Badri Mohallah are initiated into scribal practices from generation to generation, whether from father to son or brother to brother. Copying is thus a strictly intimate family and royal affair that takes place at home, in the treasury of books. Like the conditions of access to the treasury of books, the scribal transmission holds in place established structures of clerical authority within the community.

Poonawala describes how, before the foundation of the Jamea Sayfiyya, in Dawoodi scholarly milieux manuscripts were copied in the *daras* (classes, s. *dars*) of *shaykhs* or *ulama* or in the larger *ḥalqas* (study circles) of the Dai, where *kutub* were collated, transcribed and corrected.[56] The mobility of Bohra scholars and of their manuscripts from Yemen to Gujarat led to the proliferation of these copying circles in Gujarati

[54] Wadad al-Qadi, 'How Sacred is the Text of an Arabic Medieval Manuscript: The Complex Choices of the Editor Scholar', in Judith Pfeiffer et al. (eds), *Theoretical Approaches to the Transmission and Edition of Oriental Manuscripts*, 13–53 (Wurzburg: Ergon Verlag, 2007). See also: Jan Just Witkam, 'The Human Element between Text and Reader. The Ijaza in Arabic Manuscripts', in Geoffrey Roper (ed.), *The History of the Book in the Middle* East (Farnham: Ashgate, 2013), 89–112.

[55] See for an excellent study on this topic Schimmel's chapter 'Calligraphy and Mysticism' (III) in *Calligraphy And Islamic Culture*, 77–114.

[56] Poonawala, 'The contribution of Ismāʿīlī colophons', 99–103.

cities, such as Surat, Pune, Ujjain, Godhra and Jamnagar. These cities became the centre of *halqas* for the copying of Isma'ili *kutub*, specifically manuscript copies from Yemen, as can be seen from the colophons of Bohra manuscripts in which scribes praise the mother manuscripts they used for copying.[57] A boom in manuscript copying, and especially the transcription of Yemeni manuscript exemplars, can be traced in the twelfth/eighteenth century following the overseas relocation of the Hamdani family *khizana*.[58] Another fascinating Indian Ocean, Isma'ili manuscript network is that of the Fyzee family and the transcription of Sulaymani Yemeni manuscripts in this period.[59] These and several other Bohra networks of intellectual activity can be linked to generations and groups of *ulama* and their *khizana* from these towns in Gujarat, who would travel around with their manuscripts, such as was the case with the Fyzees and the Hamdanis.[60]

Another characteristic of the Bohra scribal tradition is that it is predominantly a male tradition. As noted, on very rare occasions royal female scribes of the Dawoodi Bohra community contributed to the collection of the *khizana* by copying manuscripts, a tradition that was not unusual in the pre-modern Islamic world of scribes.[61] In fact, Schimmel argues that the role of women calligraphers in Islamic history was far more important than has been acknowledged.[62] With the exception of the preservation of manuscripts, however, Alawi 'lady' book hands are not represented in the *khizana*. This fact made my participation in the copying of manuscripts exceptional to say the least, and it was often met with great shock and curiosity from the royal women.

According to the tradition of Bohra scribal culture, manuscript copying does not start with the pen and paper. Instead, it is primarily a matter of etiquette related to mind and body and to ritual purity.

Ritual purity. As discussed in the first chapter, *tahara* or ritual purity – influenced by Vaishya ideas of caste purity – is considered a religious obligation for all *mu'minin* and *mu'minat*, due to the fact that it is one of the seven pillars of faith. Just as every aspect of Bohra religious life has a *batini* and *zahiri* interpretation, the believers' practice of *tahara* is reflected both externally, through ablution and personal hygiene, and internally, through prayer and self-reflection. Ritual purity can therefore best be defined as 'spiritual purity', because, according to my experience, it transcends the body as a state of mind.[63]

Since the written word of the *khizana* carries the eternal Isma'ili sacral truths, which are blessed with *baraka*, transcribing manuscripts is regarded a sacred act. Annemarie Schimmel could not have phrased it more aptly than when she wrote that the 'purity of writing is purity of the soul'.[64] It is astonishing to see the parallels in ideas and

[57] Ibid.

[58] De Blois, *Arabic, Persian, and Gujarati Manuscripts*, xxvi.

[59] Poonawala, 'The contribution of Ismāʿīlī colophons', 102–3.

[60] Ibid., 110.

[61] Poonawala, 'The Contribution of Ismāʿīlī Colophons', 95.

[62] Schimmel, *Calligraphy and Islamic Culture*, 46, 47.

[63] Blank also uses the term 'spiritual purity' for '*tahara*', Mullahs on the Mainframe, 144, 171.

[64] Schimmel, *Calligraphy and Islamic Culture*, 38.

practices of purity between the Bohra philological tradition and the way manuscript copying was carried in the pre-modern period in the Islamic world, such as during the Ottoman, Mughal and Deccan Empires. Schimmel writes: 'Future calligraphers needed certain psychological characteristics, such as an "unassuming disposition" and a "sweet character" and "being not unclean for a single hour" to receive the *baraka* of writing.'[65] Further requirements for the copyist to attain ritual purity, according to Franz Rosenthal, were facing the *qibla* while copying and maintaining the utmost cleanliness of clothes, ink and paper.[66]

So how does one attain bodily and spiritual purity for the specific purpose of manuscript copying? According to the scribal customs of the *khizana*, one starts by performing the large *wudu* for bodily cleanliness, which for the Bhai Saheb includes cutting his nails, trimming his beard and completely shaving his head. These bodily rituals of cleanliness are followed by the three daily prayers for spiritual cleanliness. They are important because they keep the scribe in a pure state of mind and body. Should the scribe need to use the bathroom while copying or has thoughts that are considered impure, the ritual *wudu* has to be performed again. In addition to these prayers, spiritual cleanliness includes only performing pure deeds and engaging in occasional fasts.

Sartorial practices form an important part of bodily purity; the scribe must wear a white *kurta* and *sherwani*, an overcoat and a *topi*. As part of his personal *tahara*, the Mazoon Saheb has a special *topi* for manuscript copying (See Figure 6.13). As discussed in Chapter 4, bodily purity, let alone spiritual purity, is not attainable for women due to their physiological features and their ability to bear children, which are considered to attract impure thoughts and actions, and even evil spirits.

In an attempt to respect the scribal traditions of the *khizana*, I observed the rules of *tahara* as much as I could, performing the *wudu*, and meditating on having pure thoughts and being in good spirits. Even though these rituals did not comply with Bohra standards of *tahara*, the Bhai Sahebs appreciated my efforts, which made me more willing to compromise on aspects of ritual purity I felt less comfortable negotiating. It was my monthly cycle and other gendered notions of *tahara* related to my body that once again were an obstacle in my work.

In addition to the Bohras following very strict interpretations of *tahara* in their day-to-day religiosity, ritual purity plays an important role in many Muslim contexts among both genders, as the ethnographic work of Buskens and others have shown.[67] Buskens describes how, having the status of a *nesrani* in Morocco – as someone from a different cultural world, a non-Muslim and an *ahl al-kitāb* (a person of the book) – he was allowed to enter the restricted networks of manuscript trade of his friend Mostapha; yet he was not permitted to own or buy manuscripts or enter sacred spaces such as mosques and shrines. In his case too, this notion was not so much related to whether he had taken the *shahada* or not, but to questions concerning the purity and impurity of his physical body, based on polluting factors such as eating pork and not being circumcised.[68]

65 Ibid., 36, 37.

66 Franz Rosenthal, *The Technique and Approach of Muslim Scholarship*, 12.

67 Buskens, 'Paper Worlds', 250–3.

68 Ibid., 250.

In Buskens' case, as an outsider *nesrani* he was able to keep a low profile in the manuscript market and remain in the periphery of his interlocutor's network, which allowed him to observe it. In the case of my ethnographic fieldwork, this was not possible as I lived among the community, was at the centre of its *da'wa*, and had obtained the privilege of actively participating in its rituals and traditions. In my scribal *jihad*, some form of reciprocity had to be reached. As in my work as a cataloguer, the Bhai Sahebs and I agreed that I would abstain from copying, touching the manuscripts, or even entering the treasury of books during my period. Through this pragmatic solution I lost a considerable amount of valuable research time, yet in the end, it also made me use my time wisely.

Posture. In addition to spiritual purity, crucial habitual elements of the Alawi scribal tradition are the posture of the scribe, and the time and place of copying. I learned that the best results for the manual copying of manuscripts could be achieved while sitting in a cross-legged position, while the paper or the booklet is resting on the left knee, or sitting sideways (Figure 6.13). In the *khizana* I only saw right-handed scribes; I cannot say whether this was a coincidence or whether it was also related to ideas of *tahara* and the idea that the left hand is seen as impure. Just as the feet of the *mu'minin* and *mu'minat* should not point at the royal family, the soles of the feet of the scribe should never face the mother manuscript or any other sacred text.

Figure 6.13 The Mazoon Saheb at work.

Space. As argued throughout this study, the production, consumption and circulation of manuscripts of the Alawi *khizana* are strictly confined to the space of the *khizana*. The three Bhai Sahebs have special places and corners within the *khizana* where they copy their work. The Mazoon Saheb copies his work on his pillow in the centre of the room, the space where generations of Dais used to sit, govern the community, receive believers and copy manuscripts. The Mukasir Saheb and the Ra's ul Hudood copy their manuscripts on the Mazoon Saheb's left-hand side, with their backs against the manuscript cupboards. According to Schimmel, calligraphers ideally copied their manuscripts on the floor instead of on hard tables, because this would make the paper flexible and the round shapes and endings of letter forms easier to write.[69] In Mughal times, calligraphers occasionally worked on small desks while sitting on a bolster. In the case of the Bohras, the practice is carried out on the floor for very different reasons: life in Badri Mohallah takes place on the floor, 'close to the soil of the earth', as the Ra's ul Hudood used to say; however, 'some places on the floor are better to copy than others'.

Time. In addition to spiritual purity, posture and space, time is a decisive factor in the process of copying. In the universe of Badri Mohallah, time is not a linear concept. Instead, it is considered a cyclical process through which the eternal truths of the *haqa'iq* are manifested and transmitted. The transmission of manuscripts, which are the material bearers of these truths, is therefore crucial, because without it, the cyclical process, leading to salvation and the end of days, comes to an end. This narrative explains the important position the Dai has in the community as a scribe and vice-regent of the hidden Imam. Time in the linear sense, however, is not on the Bhai Sahebs' side because the humid climate of Gujarat is causing the contents of the *khizana* to slowly decay. It has yet to be seen whether the new generations of Bahi Sahebs will be able to copy fast enough to safeguard the *khizana* from further deterioration.

Bohra scribes do not copy manuscripts whenever it suits them. The act of copying can only be carried out on specific hours and days, and only during certain months and years. According to the Mazoon Saheb, Monday evenings are considered best, especially after the holy month of Muharram. Although not much is known as to whether time played a similar role in other Muslim milieux in the pre-modern period, Schimmel quotes Mir 'Ali, who stated, 'At daytime one should practice the small hand, *khafī*; in the evening the large one, *jalī*.'[70] The specific times of manuscript copying are strongly linked to the Fatimid calendar followed by all Bohra communities, which divides the *hijri* years according to the Islamic months, the *'urs* (death anniversaries of the Dais) and *ziyarat*. However, the local Gujarati conception of time, based on the idea of auspicious and inauspicious days, as noted in Chapter 1, still plays a very important role in the daily life of both *mu'minin* and the royal family. According to my observations, manuscript copying simply did not take place on inauspicious days.

[69] Schimmel, *Calligraphy and Islamic Culture*, 38.

[70] Ibid.

Scriptural Practices and Etiquette

This book has been completed, tamma tamāmshud.[71]

Having reached a spiritually sound state of mind through these rituals and taking into account etiquette, such as dress and posture, and larger aspects of the Bohra universe, such as time and space, the act of copying can begin. While being in a state of ritual purity, the scribe's mind and hands are now occupied with the technical and stylistic practices of manuscript copying.

In this context I do not use the term 'calligraphy', since it indicates a focus on aesthetics and the ornamental aspect of manuscript production. These factors should, of course, not be neglected, for the art of manuscript copying is an aesthetic experience as much as it is a scholarly one, even in the treasury of books. However, the Bhai Saheb's *scribal jihad* is, for all, an affair of the textual transmission and preservation of Fatimid-Tayyibi esoteric manuscripts. Therefore, scribal practice is defined here as the act or practice of manual manuscript copying, with the intention of following a model or register of script. As I discussed in Chapter 4, manual manuscript copying is often a process of collation, rather than literal copying from one source only, and choices made by scribes come very close to the critical apparatus of academic critical editions. It is thus fairly common that the scribe, while seated on the floor, is surrounded by several copies of the same manuscript, which he consults in preparing a fresh manuscript copy. Just as is the case with the critical apparatus in manuscript editing, one manuscript is selected as the base text. Marginal notes in the fresh manuscript copy in the first flyleaves often identify this base text and mention which other manuscripts were consulted in the collation.

In addition to *stylistic* and *ritualistic* decisions, scribal politics also includes the choices the scribe makes in selecting manuscripts: which manuscript title is copied and which is not, and which manuscript is used as the base text. In Chapter 4 this matter has already been discussed at length, and I concluded that two factors play a decisive role in the selection of manuscripts: (1) the state of deterioration of the material; and (2) the position of the manuscript in the collection (for instance whether it is deemed a newly acquired, rare or common work). We saw that the copying of esoteric manuscripts has priority over the copying of exoteric titles. As for the selection of the base text, the older the manuscript, the more authoritative it is considered. The quality of the book hand and the identity of the scribe – for instance, a royal versus an amateur copyist – also play an important role in the selection of the base text. If necessary, manuscripts are borrowed from outside the Alawi *daʿwa* to aid the copying process. The copying of documents, such as *waqf* scrolls and talismans, I observed, is less complex as formulae are fixed, the texts are shorter, and collation is often not necessary.

Tools of the Scribe: the Qalam and the Miṣtara. Proper tools are crucial for the successful copying of a manuscript and need to be prepared first. The *qalam* or reed pen (now replaced by fountain pens) is cut in a specific way, followed by the mixing of the different inks (now ready-made); then the (quality of the) paper is selected, which

[71] The closing marginal feature of Bohra colophons, translated by the Mazoon Saheb.

needs to be burnished first with either a big white cowrie shell or a piece of wax to uneven the fibres and to avoid leaking of the ink. Once the paper is made ready to receive the ink, it is rubbed with a *miṣṭara* (rule board) to create lines, rules and borders.

The *mise-en-page* or layout of Bohra manuscripts seems to be relatively rudimentary at first sight. The text block, or '*umm*' (which literally means 'mother'), occupies the centre of the page and is organised in a rectangular shape, which is framed by a passep-artout of rule-borders that enclose the main text, separating it from its marginalia. The aesthetics of a manuscript page and its geometrical construction however, are far from simple in terms of composition, preparation and presentation. The layout of pages does

Figure 6.14 Examples of historic cardboard *mistaras*, including the name of its owner and date of production (below and upper right), and layout raster (upper left) made of recycled paper, reading 'electric bill dewdi' (electricity bill of the royal *havelī*).

Figure 6.15 Preparing the paper: the making of lines with the *mistara*.

not merely serve the purpose of organising the text and producing straight lines; as Déroche argues, the practice of ruling also helps calibrate the length of the text, meaning that often there simply is a limited amount of paper, which influences the number of lines per page (the less paper. the more lines per folio).[72] To the Bhai Saheb scribes, the meticulous geometrical organisation of a manuscript page reflects the aesthetics of a godly order. Furthermore, it reveals the importance of the manuscript copy (only important titles and royal copies are ruled) and the scribe's personal talent and intent.

Manuscript quires and folios of *khizana* manuscripts, whether very old or recent copies, contain visual traces of ruling, so-called furrows, which are very subtle imprints visible to the copyist only, creating a pattern of blind lines. The ruling is applied to the paper with a so-called *mistara* or ruling board. The ruling board contains threads, which are placed underneath the paper page and subsequently the paper is rubbed over the threads manually to create lines (Figures 6.14–6.16). Applying rules to paper with the help of the *mistara* was a very widespread tradition in the world of Islamic bookmaking, and Gacek suggests that the practice dates as far back as the twelfth century, if not earlier.[73] The *mistara*, which is an important aspect of the scribal culture of the treasury of books, is thus a continuation of this practice.

The treasury of books holds a small collection of *mistaras*, some of which are 'antique', which were produced by 'the forefathers': the different generations of

[72] Déroche, *Islamic Codicology*, 160–6.

[73] Gacek, *Vademecum*, 232. Déroche, *Islamic Codicology*, 165, 166.

Figure 6.16 Upper: manuscript copying by the researcher from a photocopy. Lower: corrections by the Mazoon Saheb.

Dais and Bhai Sahebs. Fulfilling the function of a scribal tool, these *mistaras* should be considered historic *khizana* objects in their own right. Each *mistara* is carefully dated, containing the name and the period of the *ʿasr* of the Dai in handwritten *naskh*, followed by a *basmala* and *hamdala*, and in several instances the names of the prophets and the *ahl al-bayt*, which give an esoteric *haqa'iq* touch to these rulers, referring to the notion of cyclical prophetic time. The *hamdala* and the *basmala* are crucial in dating these objects, and a clear evolution in script can be traced in these eulogies: from majestic *naskh* with dramatic pointed *serifs* (the older exemplars) to a more sober and small standardised variant of *naskh* (the modern variants, see Figure 6.14).

The presence of the *hamdala*, the *basmala* and the name of the Dai also fulfils an additional function: the tradition of rulemaking is performed in their name, and each and every time the finger of the Mazoon Saheb or his brothers rubs over the paper to produce these lines, it is carried out in the name of God, the prophets and the *ahl al-bayt*. The simple act of rulemaking in this way is thus an act of piety, forming an integral part of the *jihad* of manuscript making and copying.

Mistaras come in different sizes, and the number of blind lines varies from nine to nineteen lines per folio. The great majority of manuscripts under scrutiny contained either nine lines (for smaller-sized manuscripts) or fifteen to seventeen lines per page (for larger-sized codices). The number of lines per folio does not necessarily correspond with the size of the paper: a limited number of rulings per page on a relatively large-sized manuscript page results in space for a bigger font (and thus less text) or calligraphy, and vice versa. As discussed previously, manuscript codices are often collated from quires from different book hands; therefore, it is common that one codex consists of folios with different numbers of lines per quire (different types of *mistara* thus either ended up in one codex or were used during the copying process).[74]

As noted, the practice of ruling assists in the calibration of the length of the text, and vice versa, depending on the availability of paper. To make a broad generalisation, *khizana* manuscripts vary as greatly in the number of folios as they do in shapes and sizes (from fewer than ten folios for an entire manuscript up to more than 400 folios). An average number of folios would be 150 to 200 per manuscript. *Majmu'at* manuscripts – compendia of any kind of genre, but mainly in the field of *fiqh*, *haqa'iq* and *ta'rikh* – can be extensive in size, having up to and over 400 bifolio per codex (800 pages).

As for pagination or foliation, no proper system seems to apply. Interestingly, even though there does not seem to be a dominant tradition, all Bohra manuscripts in Baroda were either foliated or paginated by the scribes, which is exceptional in the history of Islamic bookmaking.[75] A slight majority of *khizana* manuscripts are paginated (and not foliated). As discussed, pagination is recorded in Urdu and not Arabic numerals (visible through the number '5'). The system of numbering pages through foliation is, with few exceptions, almost always practised in Arabic or Persian numerals in traditions of Islamic bookbinding.[76] Bohra manuscripts are unique in this sense because they are

[74] It would be interesting to research how exactly the size of the *mistara* relates to the size of the paper. Due to the demise of the production of rule boards (the Bhai Sahebs prefer using the old *mistaras* and do not produce new exemplars) and their rare availability, I was not able to look into this properly.

[75] Often, foliation is absent in Islamic manuscript traditions, see Gacek, *Vademecum*, 105, 106. 315.

[76] Ibid., 107.

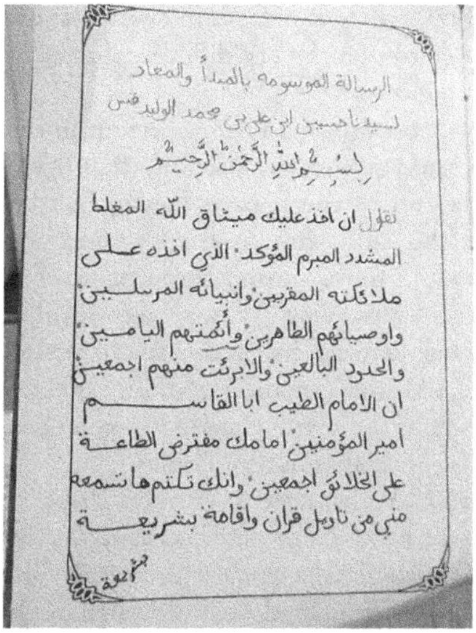

Figure 6.17 The *naskh* of the researcher with the royal *basmala* of the Mazoon Saheb. Note the catchwords on the lower left corner of the folio.

commonly foliated in European (Latin) numerals. It seems that the use of Latin numerals was (and still is today) popular for foliation of pages, recorded on the upper-right corner of the outer margins of the verso of every a-folio, in either black or red ink. The *jild* (section) number of most treatises is written on the outer upper margins of every recto (a-side, for instance '*jild* twenty-nine', written in letters), and the title to the left side of every verso (b-side).

As for the larger *mise-en-page* of the book, the title frame and incipit (which in Bohra manuscripts cover the same page) and chapter headings are rubricated panels (the blind lines of the *mistara* are disregarded in order to draw the frame). These rubricated panels carry the title of the book, a *basmala* and a *hamdala* (as we have seen with the *mistara*), followed by the standard Bohra *tasliyat.* The Mazoon Saheb explained, 'The *basmala* is a must; it is like a talisman for the manuscript, it safeguards it.'[77] Often these *basmalas* are recorded in coded form.

The rubricated panels are plain: they do not contain any decorative elements. Instead, they are written in red ink, often in a majestic calligraphic style that comes close to *diwani* or *thuluth* script as opposed to the simple *naskh* of the main text (this is especially the case with pure copies of a royal pedigree), and the font is bigger than the main body of text. During the copying process, blank spaces (meant for titles, eulogies or diagrams) are intentionally left open by the scribe and filled in after the text is copied with special-coloured inks. These special inks, and especially the pigment for red, were very scarce in former times, which is why these blank spaces frequently were filled in with pencil later on or were never filled in at all.

[77] Conversation with the Mazoon Saheb, Badri Mohallah, 19 September 2013.

The v-shaped colophon, which is present in every manuscript and serves as the tail of both the text and the book, has a very different layout from the rest of the folios and is not prepared with a *mistara*.

Reading Aids. Another feature that is omnipresent in the layout of Bohra manuscripts is the catchword: the last word of the folio that is written diagonally or horizontally in the outer margins of the b-page (verso) below the last line of the text (Figure 6.17). Although the initial function of these catchwords was to ensure the right order of the quires and folios during the process of binding (quires were not bound during the process of copying), I observed during my participation in the process of manual copying that catchwords help the scribe (and the reader of the manuscript) keep track (and even memorise) the text better. Another feature that helps the reader keep track of the text is the satchel (a thin string with a strap), which is present in the more elaborate manuscript copies.

Proofing the Manuscript. A final note to end this chapter concerns the control and authorisation of manuscript production and circulation. As noted previously, manuscripts of the treasury of books are *the available unavailable*: although they are visible to the communal *'amma*, they are produced and consumed by the elite of the *khassa* only, and manuscript copying is thus strictly authorised and commissioned. How does this paradigm translate into Bohra manuscript culture in the codicological sense of the word?

There are various kinds of textual and paratextual mechanisms that authorise, brand or even circumcise manuscripts in the context of the *khizana*. Most either were described in the previous chapters on manuscript stories and circulation – where I demonstrated how 'alien' Bohra manuscripts are appropriated and enshrined into the *khizana* by rewriting incipits and colophons – or are addressed in the next section on paratexts. As for the standard *mise-en-page* of Bohra manuscripts, the word *riḍā* (Ar.; 'approval' or 'consent', pronounced '*raza*') appears on the upper-right side of the a-folio of every first quire. We have already encountered this term in the larger context of the *da'wa*, where '*raza*' refers to the permission believers have to request from their Dai to engage in life-cycle events or to go on *hajj*. In the context of scribal culture, the presence of this catchword, which seems to be small and insignificant at first sight, indicates that the manuscript was commissioned and approved of by an authority higher than the copyist (in the case of the Mazoon, the Dai would authorise the manuscript, and the Mazoon would authorise manuscript copies prepared by the Mukasir and the Ra's ul Hudood). The word *rida* is thus a Bohra form of an *ijaza* throughout the body of the text and can be compared with the '*ṣaḥḥa*' (Ar.; 'correct') validation remark in Islamic documents.[78]

Copying Etiquette. After the preparation of the writing instruments and using of the *mistara*, the *jihad* of the scribe can commence. Before the scribe puts the pen onto the paper, he has studied the mother manuscript in detail, which entails memorising the text, and has prepared exercise sheets to practise the inkstand. He then recites the *basmala*. The first letters the scribe puts on paper are usually not aesthetically pleasing; unless he is very experienced, the first folios of copying are usually messy and unevenly

[78] See, for a discussion of the absence of the *ijaza* in Bohra manuscript culture, Poonawala, 'Isma'ili Manuscripts from Yemen', 97–9.

written. After these folios, the book hand of the scribe usually stabilises. It is for this reason that paratextual features that have a prominent place on the title page, such as the title of the work and the name of the author, are added later in different colours of ink. Nor, as we have seen, is the *basmala* written.

As for techniques of copying, the scribe is supposed to lift his hand as little as possible from the paper, unless he needs to split words. During the copying process many scribal choices have to be made to avoid blasphemy, such as whether and how to split a pious word or not, and how to erase mistakes. The splitting of those words that are considered to have a sacred aura, such as God, the names of the seven Prophets or the seven Imams, is by no means allowed. To avoid splitting, certain letter forms at the ending of sentences are prolonged (Figure 6.17), which gives the book hand of a scribe a calligraphic outlook. The splitting of non-sacred words is circumvented for stylistic reasons. The scribe also has to be economical in his or her writing: due to differences in penmanship, the spatial arrangement of the mother text might turn out differently from that of his or her fresh copy. One has to be sure that, towards the end of the codex, the scribe is not faced with a shortage of paper, which, in the case of ready-bound booklets, should be avoided at all times.

Scribal Errors. Every scribe, no matter how experienced or well-versed, makes scribal errors. These scribal errors are marked with a small cross or v-shaped symbol (x, v) in superscript written on top of the end of the word; the x- or v-system is subsequently repeated in the margins together with the correction or in the text itself above the word. A Bohra scribe would never copy marginalia from the mother manuscript or add his own comments or interpretations, unless the text of the mother manuscript contains omissions. According to my observation, the rich tradition of paratexts found in Bohra manuscripts, as discussed in Chapter 5.2, is more a tradition, as Cortese argued, of ordering the text and economically filling the flyleaves with as much information as possible than of reading, writing and transmission.

***Writing the Colophon and the* Basmala.** Apart from the long hours of sitting on the floor, by far the most challenging component of the *jihad* of the scribe is the writing of the colophon upon the completion of the text. Throughout the entire copying process the scribe should stick to the literal word of the mother manuscript, and the fresh copy can under no circumstances be changed or contain discrepancies. The colophon, however, is the only part of Bohra manuscripts that is composed by the scribe him- or herself and thus is not re-copied. As such, its composition requires effort.

As demonstrated in Chapter 5, colophons are composed according to certain formulae, which are fixed. From what I have seen, the fixed structure of the colophon did not change the fact that the Bhai Sahebs struggled with this part of manuscript copying, and therefore exercise sheets were prepared first (Figure 6.18). The *khizana* is full of these exercise sheets – which cannot be discarded due to their mentioning of the sacred names of God, the prophets, the hidden Imam and the Dai – containing scribal corrections from peer scribes. Instead of ending with the usual *tamma* or the letter *mīm*, Bohra colophons come to an end with the Arabic-Persian phrase '*tammat tamāmshud*' (This book has been completed), or as the Mazoon once said, 'Whether it is an Alawi or a Dawoodi *'alim*, they used to write not *tammat al-risāla* or *tammat qiṣṣa*. [pause] *No, tammat tamāmshud* is a general practice.' The phrase '*tammat tamāmshud*'

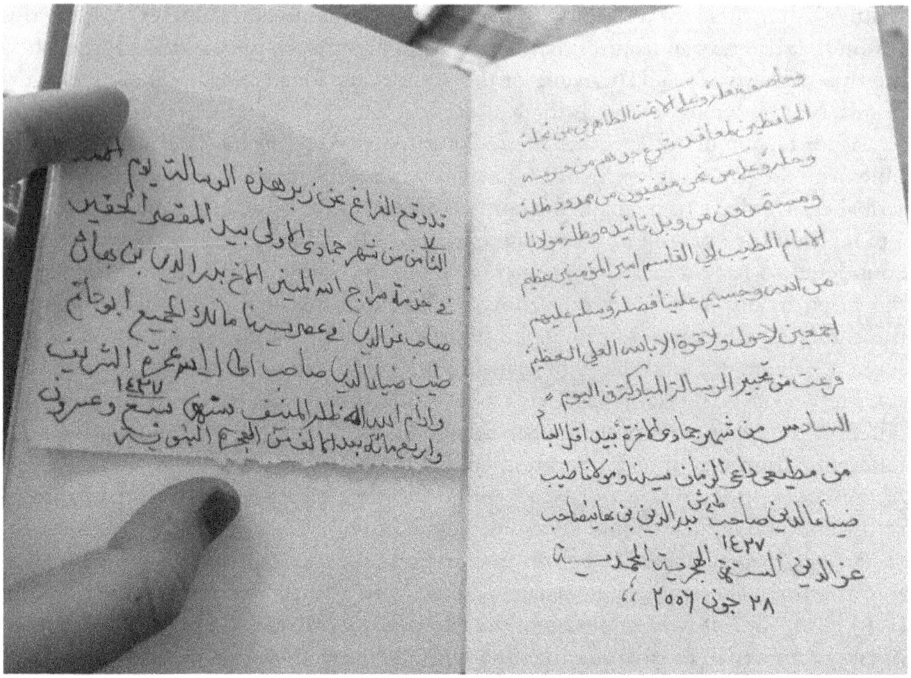

Figure 6.18 The colophon-exercise sheet of the Mazoon Saheb and the fresh manuscript copy in a booklet (henna hands by the researcher).

is often complemented by several '*ya kabikaj*' formulae, which diagonally envelop the colophon and keep the text safe from incipit to tail.

The *jihad* of the scribe ends after the ink of the colophon has dried. The ritual, however, needs to be sealed by the writing of the royal *basmala* by the Dai, which can almost be seen as an *ʿalama* for the manuscript, both authorising and blessing it as an object. In the broader context of Islamic manuscripts, one could argue it fulfils the functions of an *ijaza*. Upon receiving this seal of approval, the manuscript is numbered, catalogued and enshrined in the collection of the *khizana* together with the older *makhtutat*.

To summarise, the sacred act of copying a manuscript includes the following steps:

Attaining spiritual purity.
Preparing the pens and inks.
Choosing the quality of the paper.
Burnishing the paper.
Rubbing the *mistara* to create lines.
Paginating.
Making exercise sheets.
Reciting the *basmala*.
Manual copying.

Practising the colophon on an exercise sheet, writing the colophon. '*tammat tamāmshud*'.
Authorising.
Enshrining into the treasury of books.

Scribal Output. I end this chapter with a final note on the output of the scribe. The transcribing of books and the productivity of scribes, I observed, are highly personal and depend on the scribes' personal skills and the amount of time they have available, as well as on external factors, such as political turmoil or termite attacks. For instance, during his time as the Mazoon Saheb, the Mazoon had ample time to copy *kutub* and *waraq*, and therefore his scribal output is visible throughout all genres and book forms of the *khizana*. After he took on the role of the Dai in 2015, however, his activities as a scribe lessened as he has had other, more pressing *daʿwa* responsibilities to attend to, something that is not easy for a bibliophile such as the Mazoon. We have also seen that within the Alawi *khizana* tradition, certain Dais were more active in manuscript copying than others. In comparison to other smaller Dawoodi family *khizanat*, such as the Zahid Ali and Hamdani collection, and their scribal productivity, however, the historic output of Alawi scribes has been far from modest.[79]

Final Notes to Chapter 6: A Manuscriptorium at Work

The final chapter of this study has been devoted to the Alawis' *scribal jihad*, the politics of palaeography and scribal transmission, and the social life of *khizana* scripts in the treasury of books. Within the specific context of the manuscript copying practices of the Alawis, their *khizana* should be seen as a living manuscriptorium where books are not only read and consumed but also, at a remarkable speed, turned into others by hand.

Despite different temporal and spatial parameters, the manual transmission of Fatimid-Tayyibi manuscripts is as much alive today in Baroda as it was centuries ago. It is through these scribal traditions and ritualised practices of transmission that the Alawi clerics connect their modern manuscriptorium in Gujarat with the historic manuscriptoria of medieval Yemen and Fatimid Cairo. The Alawis' Neo-Fatimid identity is thus derived not only from the survival of manuscript titles and the institution of the *khizana*, but, even more so, through the community's scribal traditions, which are seen as being part of the uninterrupted chain of transmission of the esoteric truths from Fatimid times to the present. In the context of the *khizana* as manuscriptorium, the meaning of the copyist thus changes from that of a modest scribe to that of a custodian and vessel of transmission of this divine heritage. The manual copying of manuscripts is considered a sacred practice, which can only be carried out by the royal Bhai Sahebs, following a strict protocol of secrecy, etiquette and rituals, of which some are related to the more technical aspects of writing while others are linked to the spiritual purity of the body and the self and to the journey of the *jihad* of the scribe.

[79] See, for examples of Bohra scribes in these families and the numbers of manuscripts they copied during their lives, Poonawala, 'The Contribution of Ismāʿīlī Colophons', 95.

Thus, it is not only textual content, codicology and social usage that give meaning to the manuscripts of the *khizana* as sacred objects and its materiality of secrecy. Palaeography and script also form an essential part of the materiality of secrecy of the *khizana*, with Arabic as its *lisan* and *naskh* as its hegemonic *khatt*, illegible to the majority of believers. As such, the scribal tradition of the Alawis thus reinforces established structures of clerical authority within the community, both through the exclusivity of the practice and through the book hands themselves. Although *khizana* manuscripts are subject to a closed philological practice that is uniquely 'Bohra', their sacred book hands and scripts have their own social lives, as they evolved over time, moving from the archaic Yemeni prototype to unique Bohra *naskh* typologies over the centuries.

In addition to the *raisons d'être* for manuscript copying discussed – manual copying as a sacred act of *jihad*, the need to preserve the Fatimid-Tayyibi philological tradition, as well as keeping cyclical going – I would like to end this chapter by arguing that there is a strong element to scribal transmission that is often overlooked: the human element. We should not forget that manuscripts are handmade and that their scribes, in whichever context they operate, are human, make mistakes, have agency and, in the case of the Alawi clerics, themselves are avid manuscript collectors and bibliophiles. It is their dedication to codicology and palaeography, their *jihad for books*, that keeps Bohra manuscript culture, in all its facets, alive.

For a few months, I was privileged to be part of this *jihad for books*, by cataloguing the *khizana*, documenting its manuscript culture and, as discussed in this chapter, participating in the scribal traditions of the manuscriptorium. The Bhai Sahebs were convinced that even though I was not a Bhu Saheba or even a *mu'mina*, my modest yet painstaking scribal efforts were not in vain. On the contrary, they were sure that my copying attempts would be rewarded with *baraka* and *thawwab*. Towards the end of my stay in Badri Mohallah, I completed the copying of my manuscript, including attempting to write a colophon in the name of the Dai. The Mazoon Saheb authorised my manuscript by sealing it with his handwritten *basmala* (Figure 6.18). Following Bohra tradition, I intended to donate the manuscript to the treasury of books as a farewell present and humble symbol of my gratitude. The Bhai Sahebs, however, insisted I kept the manuscript, as it would function as a talisman for my scribal efforts. 'Keep it close to your heart, wherever you travel outside of the *da'wa*', they said, 'and it will protect you for the rest of your life.'

Conclusion: A *Jihad* for Books

It has been eight years since I left Baroda. Badri Mohallah and its people, however, have stayed in my mind. While times have changed and I am no longer physically part of the *mohallah* and its sacred universe, some things remain exactly the same.

It is five o'clock in the morning, and I am woken up by my phone. Given the odd hour of the message, it can only come from one time zone: India. It is a message, I realise, from the Mazoon. The Mazoon, however, is no longer the Mazoon Saheb. He is *Syedna Abu Sa'eed il-Khayr Haatim Zakiyuddin Saheb*, as he has carried the epithet *45th ad-Da'i al-Mutlaq al-Haqq Haatim ul-Khayraat Rabee' ul-Barakaat* since his ascent to the throne in 1436/2015. Despite his new royal title and position in the community, we have kept in touch over the years, continuing our manuscript conversations digitally. Respecting *daʿwa* protocol, the Dai, or 'Syedna' as I call him now, regularly sends me snapshots of his latest scribal achievements, new *khizana* acquisitions and discoveries, and updates on his family and the state of affairs of the *daʿwa*.

On this early morning in April, I receive a special written text from the *khizana* in the inbox of my WhatsApp. It is a talisman, handwritten by the Dai himself for the special purpose of protection against the new threat the world is facing: the coronavirus. The community, I learn, has been hit hard by the pandemic. The Alawi Bohras and their predecessors in Yemen and Egypt, however, have been no strangers to pandemics. In fact, retracing the genealogies of Bohra Dais and their *khizanat*, one encounters a long list of them, from outbreaks of the plague in twelfth-century Fatimid Cairo, to the spread of unknown diseases in sixteenth-century Haraz, Yemen among high-ranking Tayyibi notables and Bohra *muhajirun*, to an influenza eruption in the *mohallahs* of late nineteenth-century colonial Bombay, to the recent Surat plague of 1994.[1]

Whereas I do not remember encountering historic talismans for pandemics such as the plague in the *khizana* in Baroda, they must have existed. Looking at their social role, their physical absence in the treasury of books hints at the fact that these talismans were not the forms of writing that were collected but instead were meant to be used and consumed. Even though it is strictly speaking not a talisman, in the *qasida* verse shown in figure 7.1, written in the hand of the 37th Dai Sy. Ali Shamsuddin, in the same vein the Dai asks God for the protection of his community, the *daʿwat al-ʿAlawiyya*.

[1] Aḥmad ibn 'Alī al-Maqrīzī, *Kitāb al-sulūk li-ma'rifat duwal al-mulūk*, ed. Muhammad Mustafa Ziyada (Cairo: Lajnat al-Ta'lif wa-al-Tarjamah wa-al-Nashr, 1956–73), vol. 2: 772–3; Traboulsi, 'The Ottoman Conquest of Yemen', 53; G. Swetha, V. M. Eashwar and S. Gopalakrishnan, 'Epidemics and Pandemics in India throughout History: A Review Article', *Indian Journal of Public Health Research & Development* vol. 10, no. 8 (August 2019): 1,570–8.

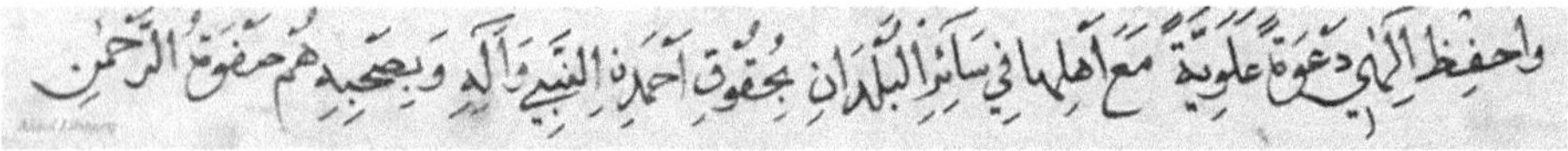

Figure 7.1 *Qasida* verse, written in the hand of the 37th Dai, Sy. Ali Shamsuddin.

A photo of this *qasida* couplet was uploaded to the official Alawi *daʿwa* website as its main banner during the second wave of the COVID-19 pandemic.[2] In addition to its content, which calls for keeping the community protected in times of hardship, it is the handwritten word of the Dai. The sacred materiality and healing qualities that are attributed to it give this manuscript fragment an aura of evanescence and authority. Though now presented in digital form online, it is the sacred materiality of the text, the tangibility of the object, which believers know is stored in the treasury of books in their *mohallah*, that imparts strength and protection.

My fieldwork among the Alawis has taught me the importance of the materiality of manuscripts as 'things', of how people ascribe certain powers to the handwritten word, and how, as such, manuscripts play a central role in people's lives. In the dire times of pandemics, the materiality of the handwritten word of the Dai, enshrined in the treasury of books, has become more significant than ever to the people of Badri Mohallah. Within their *mohallah*, I observed, notions such as time, space, things and people are embedded in a cyclical movement of the universe of death and birth, revelation and concealment, rise and fall, and flourishing and demise. The materiality of manuscripts within the universe, too, is cyclical – from their birth in the manuscriptorium until their burial in shrines of the *qabaristan* or dissolution in sacred lakes or water tanks of mosques. Although the physical decay of manuscripts is inevitable, through practices of ingestion, the esoteric truths *continue to shine and glitter* – in reference to the scribal verse in Chapter 6 – in the bodies of believers, even as the scribe passed away long ago. As the custodian of these esoteric truths in the absence of the hidden Imam, the presence of the Dai in the community is essential. He can be seen as the embodiment of the sacred materiality of the manuscripts of the *khizana*, which he carries and radiates with a certain grace and charisma that believers will do anything to catch a glimpse of. Through his aura and his scribal *jihad*, the Dai essentially *is* the treasury of books.

The longer I spent in the *khizana*, the more a sense of trust and coevalness was established through manuscripts. As I explored their biographies and codicology with the Mazoon Saheb during our manuscript sessions, my initial role as outsider and 'court historian' of the *daʿwa* changed into that of ethnographer of the community and their treasury of books. As a study in social codicology, this book essentially became an ethnography of the *khizana*, in which I documented the social lives of its manuscripts and the way people see their past and communal identity through them. By documenting Bohra manuscript culture in Baroda, cataloguing the Alawis' *khizana* collection and recording its materiality and scribal traditions, this study became part of the Mazoon Saheb's *jihad* for books.

2 https://www.alavibohra.org (last accessed 25 November 2020).

The Mazoon Saheb taught me to look at manuscripts differently: as objects with unique biographies, scribal particularities and ritualised meanings, instead of as inert vehicles of text only. I started to understand, as I described in Chapter 5, how social usage, codicology and text are intrinsically linked and are equally important in understanding manuscripts as things. The encounter between people and their handwritten books, in whichever codicological form of writing as *kutub*, *makhtutat*, documents, *ʿalamat* or *taʿwiz*, I learned, is complex if not paradoxical to the outside world. Handwritten books can be many things at the same time, and their social meaning depends entirely on their emic context and what people choose to do with them.

Books, for instance, can be considered sacred things and secret objects, being part of what I called the materiality of secrecy, yet at the same time be in demand as forbidden commodities, as we have seen in the case of the circumcision of royal *basmalas*. Similarly, they can be considered secret and inaccessible, but nonetheless have busy social lives and, as such, play an important role in the daily lives of the people, as in Badri Mohallah. Manuscripts and the institutions that enshrine them, such as the *khizana*, can help create and reinforce social order and hierarchies of power within communities, yet at the same time divide others, leading to schisms, as is the case in what I have called the materiality of *nass*. They can protect yet curse at the same time, veil and reveal what should remain hidden, and authorise, notarise and legitimise certain practices and traditions. The manuscripts of the treasury of books fulfil a multitude of social roles in the community, which are certainly not restricted to reading alone. Some books of the *khizana* are considered so secret that they are never read, whereas others have been used so extensively that they have become *khizanat* in themselves, enshrining entire histories of paratextual traditions and other 'rough edges'.

Where certain books are used as objects to predict the future, through divination practices such as *ʿilm al-fal*, others shape the way communities see their past through their material survival into the present. As I have argued throughout this study, the Alawis trace the history of their books and themselves back to the Fatimids. They are, however, not alone in making this claim. Whereas other Isma'ili communities, such as the Nizaris, claim their genealogical link to the Fatimids through the presence of a living Imam, the Alawi Bohras legitimise their 'Neo-Fatimid' identity through the survival of a living Arabic Isma'ili manuscript culture. As such, they consider themselves Neo-Fatimids in modern times, on the basis of a chain of manuscript mobility and scribal transmission of Tayyibi-Fatimid manuscripts, enshrined in their treasury of books.

Yet the narrative of the survival of 'forgotten' books, intellectual histories, *khizana* practices and scribal traditions is not only a story of the Caliph-Imams of Fatimid Cairo and the 'lost world' of their royal book treasuries; it is also part of the lesser-studied history of the Indian Ocean and of the mobility of Bohra books, *khizanat*, and entire *daʿwas* across the Arabian Sea through the networks of Yemeni-Tayyibi Dais in Gujarat and the involvement of Bohra *muhajirun*, students and merchant tycoons in Yemen. In Alawi Bohra historiography, it is thus as much the mountains of Haraz and its Tayyibi fortresses and shrines that speak to their Neo-Fatimid identity as the al-Hakim mosque of Fatimid Cairo.

In exploring the Alawis' Neo-Fatimid identity, this monograph has given voice to the Alawis' emic perspective of their community and history, honouring how they read and transcribe their past through their *khizana* and how they practise their 'Faatemi way of life', as discussed in Chapter 1, as descendants of the Fatimids in Gujarat today. Although a philological link between the Bohras, Fatimids and Tayyibis has hitherto been acknowledged to some extent, rituals of secrecy and traditions of initiation, as well as aspects of codicology and social usage in Bohra manuscript culture and documentary practices, have remained unexplored. In analysing these features, I demonstrated that the Alawis claim and reassert their Neo-Fatimid identity through reconstructing practices and re-inventing new traditions, such as through sartorial practices and a 'Neo-Fatimid' turn in architecture. Certain remnants from Fatimid times, I observed, have indeed survived in the community, including the clerical hierarchies of the *daʿwa*, jurisprudence, conditions of access to esoteric texts, and the usage of the *misri* calendar. All these traditions, old and new, are part of the Alawis' Neo-Fatimid identity in the present.

The Alawi Bohras' treasury of books, however, is the central element of the community's Neo-Fatimid identity as it provides undeniable material evidence of the community's historic Indian Ocean, Tayyibi-Fatimid past: first, through the material survival of Fatimid and Tayyibi manuscript titles, which are foundational for the Alawis' practice and transmission of its knowledge system; and second, through its 'composite' manuscript culture, enriched through its various stages of mobility from Cairo to Yemen, over the Indian Ocean, and to and within Gujarat, representing the different Bohra sub-manuscript cultures and their networks of manuscript copying and exchange.

I demonstrated that practices and codicological forms and terminology from the Fatimid chancery continue to survive today in the Bohra community's documentary and manuscript culture in everyday life, such as the ceremonial usage of the *sijill* and the writing of the Dai's *ʿalama* as his royal seal. The Tayyibi Yemenis too, as shown in Chapter 6, have left their imprint on Bohra manuscript culture, through certain formulae used in paratexts such as scribal verses, secret scripts and alphabets, and scribal traditions and models of script that formed the basis for the development of 'Indian' *khizana* book hands. I argued in Chapter 2 that, parallel with the transformation of clerical authority in Gujarat, the social meaning of manuscripts changed from vehicles of text to sacred objects as they moved from Yemen to the Indian subcontinent. The sacred materiality that became associated with manuscripts was derived not only from their esoteric content or Yemeni provenance but also because, as objects, they became associated with the Dai as the head of a new royal, sacerdotal family, as can be traced in colophons from this period. As the influence of Bohra family *khizanat* in Gujarat and their once-flourishing scribal circles slowly faded in the centuries that followed, and new structures of absolute clerical authority asserted themselves, the right to possess manuscripts gradually became associated exclusively with the *daʿwas* of the respective Bohra communities. This transformation would eventually lead to what I called the *taqiyyafication* of Bohra *khizana* culture, in which treasuries of books and their restrictive conditions of access became the centres through which the hegemony of the Dai and social order were established and reinforced.

It is not, however, only within the Bohra communities that manuscripts play a political role; perhaps they play an even more political role beyond the *daʿwa*. Even though the worlds of Badri Mohallah and the royal *khizana* of Fatimid Cairo may seem light years apart, the undeniable fact is, as I argued in the introduction, that authors such as Qadi Nuʿman and al-Sijistani are read and copied among the Bohras in Gujarat today and have been for centuries, as we can trace in the readers' and scribal notes of manuscripts. As such, the Alawi Bohras' chain of manuscript transmission counters the existing paradigm of 'destruction' of Fatimid *khizanat*. Although, to the outside world, the Bohras were seen as the 'saviours' of this long-lost tradition, to the community, this tradition was never lost. Whether stored in private scholarly collections or *daʿwa* book treasuries, Fatimid-Tayyibi manuscript copies have always been part of their *khizana* tradition.

Leaving the material evidence found in the Alawi *khizana* aside for a moment, a question that has remained unanswered in this study is whether the notion of being heirs to the Fatimids has been a central element in the Alawis' and other Bohra communities' identity or is a more recent development. To state this problem directly in terms of the universe of Badri Mohallah and its people, I am asking the question: was the Fatemi General Store I describe in the Prologue to this book always called Fatemi General Store?

It is my hypothesis that the Bohras' emphasis on their Fatimid roots is a relatively recent phenomenon, which should be seen in the specific historical context of nineteenth- and twentieth-century Bombay and Gujarat. Whereas, in the past, Fatimid heritage was a given and was articulated through a Yemeni-Tayyibi manuscript tradition and the succession of Tayyibi Dais, with the advent, however, of colonialism, and its categorisation of communities and their origins in South Asia, the Bohras, parallel to the Khojas and the Agha Khan, increasingly laid claim to the heritage of Fatimid Imamism. This was especially the case following the Agha Khan court cases in Bombay in the mid-nineteenth century, during which Agha Khan I, Hasan Ali Shah (d. 1881), claimed his hegemonic position as living Imam by declaring himself to be of Fatimid-Nizari descent.[3] As the other mercantile Isma'ili 'caste' with a presence in Bombay, the Bohras must have realised that their own Tayyibi-Fatimidism had been enshrined in the form of manuscripts in their *khizana* for centuries, a claim the Agha Khan and his followers were not able to make.

The question of the emergence of Neo-Fatimidism among the Bohras, parallel with and in competition with the claim of the Nizari Aga Khanis, awaits further research into sources and institutions outside the Bohra *khizana*, which, ironically, I was not able to access at the time of my fieldwork. What is clear, however, is that the Bohra notion of Neo-Fatimidism culminated in the second half of the twentieth century with the monumental restoration projects in Fatimid Cairo and Yemen and the 'Neo-Fatimid' turn in Bohra communal architecture that followed. Wittingly or

[3] Green, *Bombay Islam*, 155–78. See also: Teena Purohit, *The Agha Khan Case*; Michel Boivin, *L'âghâ khân et les Khojah Islam chiite*; Amrita Shodan, *A Question of Community: Religious Groups and Colonial Law* (Calcutta: Samya, 2001); Soumen Mukherjee, *Isma'ilism and Islam in Modern South Asia: Community and Identity in the Age of Religious Internationals* (Cambridge: Cambridge University Press, 2017).

unwittingly, this study plays a part in this ongoing new *gestion d'heritage* by highlighting connections between the Bohras and the Fatimids through their book culture. It is what the Bohras have chosen to emphasise and flag as significant that, I thus argue, has changed over time. In other words, the Bohras' articulation of their communal identity has by no means been static or fixed throughout history, as historiographic works from the pre-colonial period have shown. The manuscripts of the *khizana*, however, as this study has demonstrated, have always been there. Future research on the articulation of the Bohras' religious identity and the precise dynamics of their Neo-Fatimid turn, comparable to work on the South Asian Khoja followers of the Agha Khan, will enable us to better trace the roots of the Bohras' Neo-Fatimidism.

This problem, however, is of no direct relevance to the people of Badri Mohallah. The Fatemi General Store is simply the place where one gets *kulfi* ice cream on a hot monsoon day, while the Dai and the Bhai Sahebs uninterruptedly continue their *jihad* for books. To them, their *khizanat al-kutub* is and always has been a Fatimid treasury of books in Baroda.

Epilogue: A Case for Social Codicology

As two bibliophiles, the Dai and I occasionally continue our manuscript sessions over WhatsApp. Yet as fascinating as the Yemeni book hands and magical squares are that come my way, between our screens there is 'something' that gets lost. Being far removed from the treasury of books, I miss the sounds of the creaking spines of codices, the smell of dusty scrolls and the touch of leather bindings. Sitting in my sterile university office, at times I even miss the termites, which despite the many *kabikaj* formulae nonetheless keep invading the books of the *khizana*, finding new homes for their nests in bindings and papers, and dwelling in the nooks and crannies of the office of the Dai. The 'something', I realised, that gets lost in our brief digital interactions is the tangible materiality of objects. Scrolling through a photograph of a handwritten talisman may still have healing benefits to those who ascribe certain powers to it, yet the practice of having it in hand, dissolving its ink and ingesting it creates a different reality altogether.

As the humanities have undergone a digital turn in recent years and new technologies present themselves, the possibilities within the fields of Islamic manuscripts and documents, especially at a meta level, seem endless. Yet the more we acquaint ourselves with databases and other sophisticated tools, the more we run the risk of losing touch with the physical written word, the codicology of manuscripts and the materiality of other forms of writing altogether. The question of the social role of manuscripts, however, and the ways people relate to them, remains.

In the case of the Alawis, we have seen that through the multiple materialities of the treasury of books, such as the materiality of secrecy and the materiality of *nass*, the community gives meaning to the world they live in as modern Gujarati Muslims and heirs of the Fatimids. Had I written this study on the basis of the manuscript microfiches I was provided with at the Dar al-Kutub in Cairo (Chapter 2), this perspective would have been lost entirely.

As a study in social codicology, this monograph has been an argument in favour of bringing the materiality of the book, and the social practices that give meaning to it, to the centre of our enquiry. In times of pandemics, global warming, and the rise of institutionalised anti-Muslim violence and the erasure of their cultural memory in the context of the nation-state, it is not only the people of minority communities such as the Bohras who are under threat. It is also their written heritage, which in the case of the Bohras is almost a millennium old. Even though the digital preservation of living and historic manuscript and documentary cultures is admirable and important, for the next generations, their emic meaning, and thus a sense of community, will be lost on the screen. Manuscripts are political, and if we do not make the effort of understanding why these traditions matter to the people they belong to and take their physical materiality seriously, we will be unable to protect and preserve the cultural memory of those communities that are less known to the world: we run the risk of losing them for good.

Berlin, December 2020
Tammat tamāmshud

Glossary

This glossary contains all the terms (doctrinal and technical terms, honorary titles, etc.) cited in the monograph. It should be noted that the terms contained in this glossary are explained in their specific Bohra context. Abbreviations such as 's.' and 'pl.' refer to 'singular' and 'plural' and 'lit.' to 'literally', and 'q.v.' (*quod vide*) is used for cross-reference in the glossary.

adab: 'etiquette', in this monograph used in the context of the Bohra royal family, the Dai (q.v.) specifically.

ʿahd: oath of allegiance, used both historically as a means of conversion and in contemporary times in the Bohra communities (see Chapter 3.); see also *mīthāq*.

ahl al-bayt: the nucleus family of the Prophet Muhammad, including Ali, Fatima, Hasan and Husayn.

ʿalāma (pl. *ʿalāʾim*): the Dai's calligraphic signature for documents (see Chapter 1); see also *sijill*.

ʿāmil (pl. *ʿāwwamil*): a deputy cleric responsible for the administration of Bohra *mohallahs* in regions and cities that are not the religious headquarters.

ʿāmma: the common non-royal believers, as opposed to *khāṣṣa* (q.v.). Also applied as a category for spaces and conditions of access (see Chapter 3).

ārthī: an Indic *puja* ritual of burning *ghee* and singing devotional songs.

ʿAshūra: tenth day of the holy month of Muharram, on which the death of Imam Husayn is commemorated.

ʿaṣr: reign/regnal years of the Dai, a standard feature in Bohra manuscript colophons.

awrāq (s. '*waraq*', only used in the plural): single leaf manuscripts, used within the context of the *khizana* for the personal notes of the Mazoon Saheb, the Mukasir Saheb and the Ra's ul Hudood.

baraka: blessings for life on earth, which can be earned by good deeds in the *khidma* (service) of the community; see also *thawāb*.

barat: the communal practice of excommunication through social pressure.

bayān: ceremonial speech.

Bhai Saheb: honorary royal title, equivalent of 'prince' of the house of the sacerdotal Alawi family.

Bhu Saheba: honorary royal title, equivalent of 'princes' of the house of the sacerdotal Alawi family.

bid'a: a religious innovation/practice which is considered undesirable for reasons of orthopraxy.

bihārī: script form; see Chapter 6.

Bohrwads: Bohra quarter consisting of several *mohallahs*.

budūḥ: lit. 'square', used in the context of occult practices as so-called magical squares, to be found in the form of paratexts. Furthermore, produced by members of the royal family as popular talismans.

chamal: the royal umbrella, use of which is considered the ceremonial right solely of the Dai.

chauri: the royal fly whisk, use of which is considered the ceremonial right solely of the Dai.

chori: royal attire: a top which is tied asymmetrically and diagonally on the right side of the chest.

daftar: book form, horizontal account format.

Dā'ī/Dā'ī Muṭlaq (pl. '*Du'āt Muṭlaqīn*'): lit. 'absolute Dai'. Bohra honorary royal title, connoting the spiritual, political and temporal vice-regent of the hidden Imam of the community on earth, also referred to as *Sayyidnā* ('our lord/Sayyid', usually spelled '*Syedna*' or '*Sy.*'). For the historical development of the office of the Dai see Chapter 1.

da'wa: in the context of Isma'ili historiography, the Arabic term '*da'wa*' refers to either (1) missionary activities or the propagation of the Isma'ili message, and the organisation of this (see Chapter 1), or (2) statehood or community (in contemporary times for the Bohras, see Chapters 2 and 3).

Dawr (pl. *adwār*): 'prophetic cycle', part of the Bohra interpretation of cyclical time and space; see Chapter 1.

Devdi Mubarak: lit. 'the blessed circle', the clerical headquarters and permanent private residence of the Alawi royal family in Baroda; see Chapter 3.

Diwān: poetry anthology; see Chapter 1.

diwānī: script form; see Chapter 6.

dupatta: South Asian sartorial practice, a shawl worn over the head and shoulders.

Fāṭimids: Isma'ili Shi'i Empire which ruled North Africa and Egypt (296/909–466/1171), overseen by Caliph-Imams. The three Bohra communities trace their religious, literary and historical tradition back to the Fatimid Empire, including their manuscript tradition.

Fatimid calendar: Bohra non-lunar calendar based on calculations dating from Fatimid times, also known as the *miṣrī* (Egyptian) calendar.

genīza: Hebrew term referring to a communal treasury belonging to Jewish communities where religious texts are accumulated because they cannot be disposed of due to their sacred nature.

ghadīr khumm: the historical event during which, according to the Shi'ite narrative, the Prophet Muhammad designated his cousin and son-in-law Ali b. Abu Talib as his legitimate successor.

ghaghra: royal attire, a voluptuous gathered white skirt which is tied at the waist with cotton strings.

ghayba: concealment of the last Imam recognised by Twelver Shi'is. See, for the concealment of Imam Tayyib and his descendants, *satr*.

ḥāfiẓ: memoriser of the Qur'an.

ḥajj: pilgrimage to Mecca.

haldi: turmeric, used to decorate the body and face for wedding ceremonies.

ḥaqā'iq: eternal esoteric truths, highest level of *'ilm al-bāṭin* (q.v.); see Chapter 1.

haveli: the royal palace of Badri Mohallah, housing the *khizana*.

ḥudūd (s. *ḥadd*): the hierarchy of the Bohra clergy, which is considered a sacred hierarchy, including the Dai, the Mazoon Saheb, the Mukasir Saheb and the Ra's ul Hudood; see diagram in Chapter 1.

'ibādāt: Islamic law terminology: 'religious duties', as opposed to *mu'āmalāt* (q.v.).
ilhām: Godly inspiration received by the Dai through the hidden Imam in *satr* (q.v.).
'ilm al-bāṭin: knowledge referred to by the Alawi Bohras as 'esoteric', as opposed to *'ilm al- ẓāhir* (q.v.), 'exoteric' knowledge. *'Ilm al-bāṭin* is considered to be kept hidden in the *khizana* and is transmitted through a secret manuscript tradition. At the highest level of *'ilm al-bāṭin* are the *ḥāqā'iq* (q.v.), which require extra special permission for access (see Chapters 1 and 2).
'ilm al-fāl: popular practice in South Asia known as 'Qur'anic magic'; see Chapter 5.
'ilm al-ḥurūf: the practice of the taking of Qur'anic omens and magical letters, a popular practice in Central and South Asia.
'ilm al-ẓāhir: knowledge referred to by the Alawi Bohras as 'exoteric', as opposed to *'ilm al-bāṭin* (q.v.), 'esoteric' knowledge.
Imām: in the Shi'i/Isma'ili/Bohra context, the divine leader of the community who traces his ancestry back to the Prophet Muhammad through Ali b. Abu Talib. See also *Imāmat*.
Imāmat: the office of the *Imām*. Both Twelver Shia communities and the Bohras consider their last Imām to have gone into concealment. Twelver Shi'i communities refer to this state or event as '*ghayba*' (q.v.); the Bohras use the term '*satr*' (q.v.).
jamaat khana/jamā'at khāna: the central communal space for gathering in all Bohra and Nizari communities, which is directly connected to the *masjid* (q.v.), where all communal affairs and gatherings take place. See also *musafir khana*.
jihād: lit. 'struggle'. As the seventh pillar of Isma'ili Islam (and thus of Bohra *fiqh*), *jihād* refers to the struggle of the *nafs* (q.v.). In addition to the big *jihād*, there is also the small *jihād*, which is the obligation to fight the holy war for the cause of the Imam. In his absence during the period of *satr* (q.v.), the small *jihād* is not permissible (see Chapter 1). See also *scribal jihād* for the special context of the *khizana* (Chapter 6).
jild: paragraph or section in manuscript (see Chapter 5).
jinn: evil spirits which are believed to possess the body and minds of believers. In the context of the Alawi Bohra narrative *jinn* are attracted by impure body fluids.
ka 'l-ma'ṣūm: lit. 'like infallible', status of 'near-'infallibility of the Dai (q.v.); see Chapter 1.
kashf: period of historiography recognised by the Bohras as the manifestation of the Imam, also known as *ẓuhūr*. See also *satr*.
khāṣṣa: members of the (extended) royal family, as supposed to *'āmma* (q.v.); also a category for spaces (see Chapter 3) and conditions of access (see Chapter 2).
khaṭṭ: script; see Chapter 6.
khidma: (services) to the community; see also *mullāh*.
khizāna: (lit. 'treasury') or *khizānat al-kutub*. Term used to refer to the Alawi treasury of books, also combined with the following adjectives: *al-khizānat al-maknūna* (the 'guarded' *khizāna*), *al-khizānat al-khāṣṣa* (the 'special' *khizāna*), *al-khizānat al-mubāraka* (the 'blessed' *khizāna*), *al-khizānat al-amīra* (the 'royal' *khizāna*), or simply *al-khizānat al-'Alawiyya* (the Alawi *khizāna*). The Dawoodi and Sulaymani Bohra sects use similar terminology.
khums: Shi'i/Isma'ili/Bohra tradition of alms payment of one fifth of an unexpected income such as an inheritance.
khuṭba: Friday sermon, followed by the *wāz* (q.v.).
kitāb sirriyya: the tradition of writing secret or discreditable matters (such as the cursing of certain names) in secret script, found in manuscripts (Chapter 5).
kurta: South Asian sartorial practice, traditional upper garment, in the Bohra context mostly worn in white by men.
kutub al-da'wa: lit. 'books of the *da'wa*', term used by the Bhai Sahebs (q.v.) to refer to the manuscript collection of the *khizana*.
la'n: the textual and social practice of cursing the three rightly-guided Caliphs.

lisān: lit. 'tongue', manuscript terminology, envelope flap, which is an extension of the lower cover of the codex, placed either above or under the upper cover of the binding.

Lisān al-Daʿwa: also referred to as 'Bohra Gujarati' by non-Bohris, sociolect of the Alawi and Dawoodi communities, which is a mix of Arabic, Urdu and Gujarati (both oral and written); see Chapter 6.

mahdī: lit. 'the rightly-guided one'; according to the Bohra narrative a descendant of Imam Ṭayyib who will return to the community on the Day of Judgement to restore justice on earth. See also *qā'im*.

majlis: religious gathering, held in the *masjid* (q.v.).

majmūʿa: book form/literary genre, manuscript compendia of any kind of genre; see Chapter 2.

makhṭūṭa: (pl. '*makhṭūṭāt*') manuscript; see also *kutub al-daʿwa*.

mandorla: manuscript terminology, small almond or flower-shaped ornaments sporadically found on Bohra manuscript covers.

manṣūṣ: The designated heir of the throne of the *daʿwa*, upon whom *naṣṣ* (q.v.) has been bestowed; see Chapter 1.

maqbara: graveyard containing the shrines of the forty-four Dais, as opposed to the *qabaristān* (q.v.), which is meant for common believers.

Ma Saheba: 'mother of the community', honorary royal title meant for the wife of the Dai (q.v.).

marsiyya/marthiyya: religious poetry in honour of Imam Husayn recited on the holy day of *ʿAshūra* (q.v.), performed in Urdu.

masjid: mosque; see also *jamaat khana*.

ma'tam: the practice of self-castigation (by hand) carried out either during the holy day of *ʿAshūra* (q.v.) or during the *ʿurs* (death anniversary, q.v.).

Mazoon Saheb: honorary royal title, see *ḥudūd*.

minbar: pulpit in the *masjid* (q.v.), which is absent in Bohra mosques due to the *satr* (q.v.) of the Imām.

miṣrī calendar: see *Fatimid calendar*.

miṣtara: manuscript terminology, tradition ruler device; see Chapter 6.

mīthāq: see *ʿahd* (Chapter 3).

muʿāmalāt: affairs in the daily life of believers, as opposed to *ʿibādāt* (q.v.).

Muḥarram: the sacred month of the Islamic calendar which is marked by collective mourning, and in which the holy day of *ʿAshūra* (q.v.) takes place.

Mukasir Saheb: honorary royal title, see *ḥudūd*.

mullāh: honorary non-royal title, which can be attributed to *mu'minin* (q.v.) as a reward for their *khidma* (q.v.) to the community.

mu'min (s., male pl. *mu'minīn*, female pl. *mu'mināt*): lit. 'believer'; exclusive member of the *daʿwa* (q.v.).

munājāt: midnight prayers which are recited during the holy month of Ramadan in Urdu, in *Lisān al-Daʿwa* (q.v.) and occasionally in Arabic (Qur'anic verses).

musāfir khāna: communal pilgrimage lodge, see also *jamaat khana*; see Chapter 1.

nafs: ego, also referred to as 'the self', used in discussions on *ʿilm al-bāṭin* (q.v.) and *jihād* (q.v.).

namāz: prayer, performed five times a day divided over three moments, also known as *ṣalāt*.

naskh: script form, often (but not necessarily) linked to Arabic as a language; see Chapter 6.

naṣṣ: divine designation of succession by the Dai. The designated heir of the throne of the *daʿwa* is called the *manṣūṣ* (q.v.); see Chapter 1.

nastaʿlīq: script form, often (but not necessarily) linked to Persian and Urdu as languages; see Chapter 6.

nazār al-maqām: alms paid for the absence of the hidden Imam, see *satr*.

Nizāris: Isma'ili community mostly present in Central and South Asia, following the genealogy of Imām al-Zamān Karīm al-Aghā Khān IV.

pagri: royal attire, a ceremonial turban wrapped around a *topi* (q.v.).

pols: architectural terminology, traditional closed-off living quarters linked to specific communities in Gujarat, (often) containing secret entrances.

pastiwala: vendor of waste paper; see Chapter 4.

qabaristān: graveyard of the common believers, as opposed to the *maqbara* (q.v.), which is the space where the shrines of the forty-four Dais are located.

qāḍī: (pl. *quḍāt*) honorary title for judge.

qā'im: according to the Bohra narrative, a descendant of Imam Ṭayyib who will return to the community on the Day of Judgement to restore justice on earth. See also *mahdī* .

qalam: manuscript terminology, (reed) pen.

qaṣā'id: specific book form used for poetry.

Qaṣr-e 'Alī: lit. 'castle/house of *'Alī*', honorary title for the Dawoodi royal family.

quaternion: manuscript terminology, used to refer to four bifolia or eight leaves.

rabbī' al-ākhir: the celebration of the birth of Imam Ṭayyib (see Imām, Ṭayyibis), following the tradition of *rabī' al-awwal*, the celebration of the birthday of the Prophet Muhammad.

rakhi: ceremonial attribute, a shiny piece of cloth used during various ceremonies.

rasm: ceremonial right of the Dai, mostly related to courtly sartorial practices, for instance the wearing of certain *pagris* (q.v.), being fanned by the *chauri* (q.v.) and being ceremonially shaded by the *chamal* (q.v.).

Ra's ul Hudood: honorary royal title; see *ḥudūd*.

rida: traditional Bohra dress for women.

riḍā: 'approval' or 'consent', pronounced *raza*.

Risāla (pl. *rasā'il*): epistle; see Chapter 1.

rotulus: book form, also known as scroll; see also *sijill*.

rūḥ: the spirit of the Dai, the presence of which is considered an auspicious blessing and is therefore transmitted to various objects, such as coconuts or water bottles.

salām: audience with the royal family.

satr: the concealment of Imam Tayyib and his descendants; see for the Twelver Shi'i interpretation *ghayba*.

ṣawm: fasting, which is performed not only during Ramaḍān but also during special

ceremonial days, such as Muharram (q.v.) and *'urs* (q.v.): death commemorations of the Imams and the Dais.

Sayyidnā/Syedna: informal variant of honorary royal title of the Dai (q.v.).

seal of Solomon: paratext with talismanic function (to protect the manuscript) containing a David Star, also known as the coded *basmala* (Chapter 5). See also '*yā kabīkaj*'.

shadi: South Asian wedding rituals, see *haldi* and *ārthī*.

shahīd (pl. *shuhadā'*): martyrs of the community who lost their lives after violent incidents (see Chapter 1).

sayfat (Ar. '*al-ṣaḥīfāt*'): booklets on different kinds of *namāz* (q.v.) in *Lisān al-Da'wa* (q.v.) and occasionally in Arabic.

sherwani: South Asian sartorial practice, coat garment worn over a *kurta* (q.v.).

shi'r: devotional poetry.

sijill (pl. *sijillāt*): official *da'wa* document in the form of a *rotulus* or vertical roll. See also *'alāma*.

Ṣulayḥids: sixth-/twelfth-century Isma'ili dynasty in Ḥarāz (north-western Yemen), initially affiliated with the Fatimids (q.v.), and later with the Tayyibi Isma'ilis (q.v.).

tabla: ceremonial drums commonly used in South Asia for official ceremonies and celebrations.

ṭahāra: *fiqh* terminology: ritual purity, one of the seven Fatimid/Bohra pillars of Islam. *takht*: ceremonial throne of the Dai.

tamma tamamshud: lit. 'it is finished', Persian formula and standard Bohra codicological practice used to close the colophon of a manuscript; see Chapter 5.

taqiyya: the practice of dissimulating one's religious identity, a well-practised tradition among the three Bohra communities; see Chapter 3.

taqlīd: legal terminology, the (unquestioning) adoption of tradition.

tasbīḥ: royal attribute: a rosary made of silver or semi-precious stones.

taṣliyya: written eulogy, found in manuscripts.

ta'wīdh /ta'wiz (pl. *ta'wīdhāt*): talisman, used by the Alawis both as physical object and as paratext in manuscripts; see Chapters 1 and 5.

Ṭayyibis: Isma'ili community that followed Imam al-Ṭayyib (d. unknown) after his *satr* (q.v.) after the year 524/1130 in Yemen (see *Ṣulayḥids*). The term 'Ṭayyibī Ismā'īlis' is often used to refer to the Bohras prior to the moving of the Tayyibi religious headquarters to Gujarat in the twelfth/seventeenth century.

thali: Gujarati communal family meal; see Chapter 3.

thawāb/sawab: reward for good deeds in the afterlife, see also *baraka*.

thuluth: script form; see Chapter 6.

topi: Bohri skullcap, see also *pagri*.

'urs: death anniversary of the Dais (q.v.).

Vaishya caste: Hindu mercantile caste, to which the Bohra communities allegedly belonged prior to their conversion to Islam.

wala: man, vendor; for instance, *sabziwala*, vegetable seller.

walī: honorary non-royal title, assistant to the Dai (q.v.).

waqf (pl. *'awqāf'*): book form: pious endowment, see *rotulus*.

walāya: allegiance to the Imam, his Imamate and his representative in the community, the Dai (q.v.). One of the seven Fatimid/Bohra pillars of Islam.

wāz: the weekly Friday sermon after the *khuṭba* (q.v.).

'yā' Husayn!': 'Oh *ḥusayn*', invocation expressed during *ma'tam* (q.v.).

'yā' kabīkaj': 'Oh *kabīkaj*', paratext with talismanic function (to protect the manuscript). See also *seal of Solomon*.

zakat: alms.

ziyāra: pilgrimage dedicated to an Imam (q.v.) or Dai (q.v.); see Chapter 1.

Bibliography

Secondary Scholarship

Abdul Hussain, Mian Bhai Mullah (1920). *Gulzare Daudi for the Bohras of India* (Ahmedabad).

Abdulhussein, Mustafa (1995). 'Al-Jāmiʿah al-Sayfīyah'. In John Louis Esposito (ed.), *The Oxford Encyclopedia of the Modern Islamic World* (New York: Oxford University Press), 360–1.

Abdulhussein, Mustafa (2001). *Al-Dai Al-Fatimi Syedna Mohammed Burhanuddin: An Illustrated Biography* (Surat: Aljameatus-Saifiyah Trust).

Abu-Lughod, Lila (1986). *Veiled Sentiments: Honor and Poetry in a Bedouin Society* (Berkeley: University of California Press).

Adem, Rodrigo (2017). 'Classical Nass Doctrines in Imāmī Shīʿism: On the Usage of an Expository Term'. *Shii Studies Review* 1: 42–71.

Akkerman, Olly (2016). 'The Bohra Dark Archive and the language of secrecy. A codicological ethnography of the Royal ʿAlawī Bohra Library in Baroda. PhD diss., Freie Universität.

Akkerman, Olly (2019). 'The Bohra Manuscript Treasury as a Sacred Site of Philology: A Study in Social Codicology'. *Philological Encounters* 4: 1–21.

Akkerman, Olly (2020). 'The Bohras as Neo-Fatimids: Documentary Remains of a Fatimid Past in Gujarat'. *Journal of Material Cultures in the Muslim World* 1: 286–308.

Akkerman, Olly, editor (2021). *Social Codicology. The Multiple Lives of Texts in Muslim Societies* (Leiden: Brill).

Akthar, Iqbal (2015). *The Khōjā of Tanzania: Discontinuities of a Postcolonial Religious Identity* (Leiden: Brill).

Alam, Muzaffar (2004). *The Languages of Political Islam in India: c. 1200–1800* (Chicago: University of Chicago Press).

Alavi, Seema (2008). *Loss and Recovery of an Indo-Muslim Medical Tradition: 1600–1900* (London: Palgrave Macmillan).

Aminji, Hussain (1975). 'The Bohras in East Africa'. *Journal of Religion of Africa* 7: 27–61.

Amir-Moezzi, Mohammad (2011). *Le Coran silencieux et le Coran parlant: Sources scripturaires de l'islam entre histoire et ferveur* (Paris: CNRS Éditions).

Appadurai, Arjun (1986). 'Introduction: Commodities and the Politics of Value'. In Arjun Appadurai (ed.), *The Social Life of Things, Commodities in Cultural Perspective* (Cambridge: University of Cambridge Press), 3–63.

Assmann, Aleida (2008). 'Canon and Archive'. In Astrid Erll et al. (eds), *Cultural Memory* Studies (New York: Walter de Gruyter), 97–108.

Bachelard, Gaston (1969). *The Poetics of Space: The Classic Look of How We Experience Intimate Spaces* (Paris: Presses Universitaires de France).

Bahl, Christopher (2013). 'Histories of Circulation – Sharing Arabic Manuscripts across the Western Indian Ocean, 1400–1700. PhD diss., School of Oriental and African Studies.

Bahl, Christopher (2018). 'Creating a Cultural Repertoire Based on Texts: Arabic Manuscripts and the Historical Practices of a Sufi in 17th-Century Bijapur'. *Journal of Islamic Manuscripts* vol. 9, nos 2–3: 132–53.

Bahl, Christopher (2020). 'Arabic Philology at the Seventeenth-Century Mughal Court. Saʿd Allāh Khān's and Shāh Jahān's Enactments of the Sharḥ al-Radī'. *Philological Encounters* vol. 5, no. 2: 190–222.

Balachandran, Jyoti Gulati (2020). *The Making of a Muslim Community in Gujarat, c. 1400–1650* (Oxford: Oxford University Press).

Bang, Anne K. (2003).*Sufis and Scholars of the Sea: Family Networks in East Africa, 1860–1925* (Leiden: Brill).

Beal, Peter (2008). *A Dictionary of English Manuscript Terminology, 1450–2000* (Oxford: Oxford University Press).

Beben, Daniel (2017). 'The Fatimid Legacy and the Foundation of the Modern Nizari Isma'ili Imamate'. In Farhad Daftary and Shainool Jiwa (eds), *The Fatimid Caliphate: Diversity of Traditions* (London: I. B. Tauris), 192–223.

Beben, Daniel, Jo-Anne Gross and Umed Mamadsherzodshoev (forthcoming). *Isma'ilism in Badakhshan: A Genealogical History*.

Behrens-Abouseif, Doris (2018). *The Book in Mamluk Egypt and Syria (1250–1517): Scribes, Libraries and Market* (Leiden: Brill).

Berg, Gabrielle R. van den (2004). *Minstrel Poetry from the Pamir Mountains: A Study on the Songs and Poems of the Isma'ilis of Tajik Badakhshan* (Wiesbaden: Reichert Verlag).

Bhaṭṭa, Somadeva (trans.) (1994). *Kathasaritasagara* (New Delhi: Penguin).

Bhalloo, Zahir (2015). *A Brief Note on the Bohras in Malindi*. Unpublished typescript.

Bhalloo, Zahir (2016). 'Construction et gestion identitaire chez les Lawatiya du Sultanat d'Oman, de Multân à Masqaṭ'. *Journal Asiatique* vol. 304, no. 2: 217–30.

Bhalloo, Zahir (forthcoming). 'Archival Practice in Safavid Iran: The View from the Shrine'. In Paolo Sartori (ed.), *Cultures of Documentation in Persianate Eurasia* (Leiden: Brill).

Bhalloo, Zahir (forthcoming). 'Le culte de l'imam Husayn chez les Khojas ismaeliens aga khanis a la fin du XIXe s'. *Studia Islamica*.

Bhalloo, Zahir and Iqbal Akhtar (2018). 'Les manuscrits du sud de la vallée de l'Indus en écriture khojkī sindhī: état des lieux et perspectives'. *Asiatische Studien/Études Asiatiques* vol. 72, nos 1–2: 319–38.

Bierman, Irene A. (1998). *Writing Signs: The Fatimid Public Text* (Berkeley: University of California Press).

Biran, Michal (2019). 'Libraries, Books, and Transmission of Knowledge in Ilkhanid Baghdad'. *Journal of the Economic and Social History of the Orient* 62: 464–502.

Bishara, Fahad A. (2017). *A Sea of Debt: Law and Economic Life in the Western Indian Ocean* (Cambridge: Cambridge University Press).

el-Bizri, Nader (ed.) (2008). *The Ikhwan al-Safa and their Rasail: An Introduction* (Oxford: Oxford University Press).

Blanchy, Sophie (2007). 'Le "retour" des Bohras au Caire (Egypte): de l'état fatimide à la terre promise'. In Michel Boivin (ed.), *Les ismaéliens d'Asie du sud: gestion des héritages et productions identitaires* (Paris: L'Harmattan), 49–74.

Blank, Jonah (2001). *Mullahs on the Mainframe: Islam and Modernity among the Dawoodi Bohras* (Chicago: University of Chicago Press).

De Blois, François (1984). 'The Oldest Known Fatimid Manuscript from Yemen'. *Proceedings of the Seminar for Arabian Studies* 14: 1–7.

De Blois, François (2011). *Arabic, Persian and Gujarati Manuscripts: The Hamdani Collection* (London: I. B. Tauris).

Bloom, Jonathan (1989). 'The Blue Koran, an Early Fatimid Kufic Manuscript from the Maghrib'. In *Les Manuscrits du Moyen-Orient* (Istanbul: Institut Francais d'Etudes Anatoliennes d' Istanbul).

Bloom, Jonathan (2001). *Paper before Print: The History and Impact of Paper in the Islamic World* (New Haven: Yale University Press).

Boivin, Michel (1998). 'Institutions et production normative chez les ismaéliens d'Asie du Sud'. *Studia Islamica* 88: 141–77.

Boivin, Michel (2003). *La Renovation du Shi'isme Ismaelien En Inde Et Au Pakistan: D'apres les Ecrits et les Discours de Sultan Muhammad Shah Aga Khan* (London: Routledge).

Boivin, Michel (2013). *L'âghâ khân et les Khojah Islam chiite et dynamiques sociales dans le sous-continent indien (1843–1954)* (Paris: Karthala).

Boivin, Michel (2020). *The Sufi Paradigm and the Makings of Vernacular Knowledge in Colonial India: The Case of Sindh (1851–1929)* (London: Palgrave Macmillan).

Bora, Fozia (1984). 'Did Salah al-Din Destroy the Fatimids' Books? An Historiographical Enquiry'. *Journal of the Royal Asiatic Society* vol. 25, no. 1: 21–39.

Bora, Fozia (2019). *Writing History in the Medieval Islamic World: The Value of Chronicles as Archives* (London: I. B. Tauris).

Borgolte, Michael (ed.) (2014). *Enzyklopädie des Stiftungswesens in mittelalterlichen Gesellschaften* (band 1) (Berlin: De Gruyter).

Brun, Christelle (2013). 'De la caste marchande gujarati à la communauté religieuse fatimide: construction identitaire et conflits chez les daoudi bohras (ouest de l'Inde)'. PhD diss., Toulouse University.

Burgess, James (1903). *The Architectural Antiquities of Northern Gujarat, More Especially of the Districts Included in the Baroda State* (London: Bernard Quaritch).

Buringh, Eltjo (2011). *Medieval Manuscript Production in the Latin West: Explorations with a Global Database* (Leiden: Brill).

Burton, Antoinette (ed.) (2006). *Archive Stories. Facts, Fictions, and the Writing of History* (Durham, NC: Duke University Press).

Buskens, Léon (1995). 'Maliki Formularies and Legal Documents. Changes in the Manuscript Culture of the 'Udul (Professional Witnesses) in Morocco'. In Yasin Dutton (ed.), *The Codicology of Islamic Manuscripts: Proceedings of the Second Conference of Al-Furqan Islamic Heritage Foundation* (London: Al-Furqan Islamic Heritage Foundation), 137–45.

Buskens, Léon (2017). 'Paper Worlds: A Nesrani Ethnographer Entering the Manuscript Trade in Morocco'. In M. Almoubaker and Pouillon (eds), *Pratiquer les sciences sociales au Maghreb: Textes pour Driss Mansouri* (Casablanca: Fondation du Roi Abdul-Aziz Al Saoud pour les Etudes Islamiques et les Sciences Humaines), 239–65.

Buskens, Léon (2017). 'From Trash to Treasure: Ethnographic Notes on Collecting Legal Documents in Morocco'. In Maaike van Berkel, Léon Buskens and Petra M. Sijpesteijn (eds), *Legal Documents as Sources for the History of Muslim Societies* (Leiden: Brill), 180–207.

Carter, Michael G. (1995). 'Arabic Literature'. In David C. Greetham (ed.), *Scholarly Editing: A Guide to Research* (New York: Modern Language Association of America), 546–74.

Cervantes, Miguel (trans. John Rutherford) (2002). *Don Quixote* (London: Penguin).

Cilardo, Agostino (2012). *The Early History of Isma'ili Jurisprudence: Law under the Fatimids: A Critical Edition of the Arabic Text and English Translation of al-Qadi al-Nu'man's* Minhaj al-Fara'id (London: I. B. Tauris).

Contadini, Anna (1998). *Fatimid Art at the Victoria and Albert Museum* (London: V&A Publications).

Contractor, Noman (1980). *The Dawoodi Bohras* (Pune: New Quest Publications).

Correa, Charles (1988). 'Spiritual Architecture'. *Mimar: Architecture in Development*= 3: 21–3.

Cortese, Delia (2000). *Ismāʿīlī and Other Arabic Manuscripts* (London: I. B. Tauris).

Cortese, Delia (2002). *Arabic Ismāʿīlī Manuscripts: The Zāhid Alī Collection* (London: I. B. Tauris).

Cortese, Delia (forthcoming). 'The *majmūʾ al-tarbiyah* between Text and Paratext: Exploring the Social History of a Community's Reading Culture'. In Wafi Momin (ed.), *Before the Printed Word: Texts, Scribes and Transmission.*

Coulon, Jean-Charles (2016). 'L'ésotérisme shi'ite et son influence sur le corpus magique attribué à al-Būnī'. In M. A. Amir-Moezzi, M. De Cillis, D. De Smet and O. Mir-Kasimov (eds), *L'Ésotérisme shi'ite, ses racines et ses prolongements* (Paris: Brepols), 509–38.

Dachraoui, Fuad (1975). *Les commencements du Califat Fāṭimide au Maghreb: Un edition critique et analyse du Kitāb Iftitaḥ ad-Daʿwa du Qāḍī an-Nuʿmān* (Tunis: SDT).

Daftary, Farhad (1996). *Mediaeval Ismāʿīlī History and Thought* (London: I. B. Tauris).

Daftary, Farhad (2004). *Isma'ili Literature: A Bibliography of Sources and Studies* (London: I. B. Tauris).

Daftary, Farhad (2007). *The Ismāʿīlis: Their History and Doctrine* (Cambridge: Cambridge University Press).

Daftary, Farhad (ed.) (2015). *Fifty Years in the East: The Memoirs of Vladimir Ivanow* (London: I. B. Tauris).

Dagenais, John (1994). *The Ethics of Reading in Manuscript Culture: Glossing the Libro de Buen Amor* (Princeton: Princeton University Press).

Déroche, François (2005). *Islamic Codicology: An Introduction to the Study of Manuscripts in Arabic Scripts* (London: Al-Furqān Islamic Heritage Foundation).

Derrida, Jacques (1996). *Archive Fever: A Freudian Impression* (Chicago: University of Chicago Press).

Desai, Madhavi (2008). *Traditional Architecture: House Form of Bohras in Gujarat* (Delhi: National Institute of Advanced Studies in Architecture).

Doniger, Wendy (2010). *The Hindus: An Alternative History* (London: Penguin).

Doostar, Ali Reza (2013). 'Fantasies of Reason: Science, Superstition, and the Supernatural in Iran'. PhD diss., Harvard University.

D'Ottone, Arianna (2015). 'The Pearl and the Ruby: Scribal Dicta and Other Metatextual Notes in Yemeni Medieval Manuscripts'. In David Hollenberg, Christoph Rauch and Sabine Schmidtke (eds), *The Yemeni Manuscript Tradition* (Leiden: Brill), 82–100.

Durkheim, Émile (trans. Carol Cosman) (2001 [1912]). *The Elementary Forms of Religious Life* (Oxford: Oxford University Press).

Eickelman, Dale F. and Jon W. Anderson (2003). *New Media in the Muslim World: The Emerging Public Sphere* (Bloomington: Indiana University Press).

El Shamsy, Ahmed (2020). *Rediscovering the Islamic Classics: How Editors and Print Culture Transformed an Intellectual Tradition* (Princeton: Princeton University Press).

Engineer, Ali Asghar (1980). *The Bohras* (New Delhi: Vikas).

Enthoven, R. E. (1920). *The Tribes and Castes of Bombay* (Mumbai: Governmental Press).

Flueckiger, Joyce, B. (2006). *In Amma's Healing Room: Gender and Vernacular Islam in South-India* (Bloomington: Indiana University Press).

Foltz, Richard (2006). *Animals in Islamic Traditions and Muslim Cultures* (London: One World Publications, 2006).

Freitag, Ulrike (2003). *Indian Ocean Migrants and State Formation in Hadhramaut: Reforming the Homeland* (Leiden: Brill).

Freitag, Ulrike (2020). *A History of Jeddah: The Gate to Mecca in the Nineteenth and Twentieth Centuries* (Cambridge: Cambridge University Press).

Fyzee, Asef (1969). *Compendium of Fāṭimid Law* (Simla: Indian Institute of Advanced Study).

Fyzee, Asef (ed.) (1991). *Daʿāʾim al-ʿIslām wa dhikr al-ḥalāl wa ʾl-ḥarām wa ʾl-qaḍāya wa ʾl-ʿaḥkām* (Cairo: Dār al-ʿAḍwā').

Gaborieau, Marc (1983). 'Typologie des specialists religieux chez les musulmans du sous-continent indien, les limites d'islamisation'. *Archives des sciences sociales des religions* 29: 29–52.

Gacek, Adam (1985). *Catalogue of Arabic Manuscripts in the Library of the Institute of Isma'ili Studies*, Vols I and II (London: Islamic Publications).

Gacek, Adam (1986). 'The Use of "kabikaj" in Arabic Manuscripts'. *Manuscripts of the Middle East* I: 49–53.

Gacek, Adam (1987). 'Ownership Statements and Seals in Arabic Manuscripts'. *Manuscripts of the Middle East* 2: 88–95.

Gacek, Adam (2012). *Arabic Manuscripts: A Vademecum for Readers* (Leiden: Brill).

Gacek, Adam (2013). *Strokes and Hairlines: Elegant Writing and Its Place in Muslim Book Culture* (Montreal: McGill University Library).

Gay, Denis (2009). *Les Bohra de Madagascar: Religion, commerce et échanges transnationaux dans la construction de l'identité ethnique* (Berlin: Lit Verlag).

Gelvin, James L. and Nile Green, eds (2014). *Global Muslims in the Age of Steam and Print* (Berkeley: University of California Press).

Genette, Gérard (trans. Jane E. Lewin and Richard Macksey) (1997). *Paratexts: Thresholds of Interpretation* (Cambridge: Cambridge University Press).

Gerholm, T. (1977). *Market, Mosque and Mafrag* (Stockholm).

Ghalib, Mustafa (1971). *Kitāb Kanz al-walad* (Wiesbaden: Franz Steiner).

Ghalib, Mustafa (ed.) (1973–8). *Silsilat al-turāth al-Fāṭimī*, Vols 4–6 of *ʿUyūn al-akhbār wa-funūn al āthār* (Beirut: Dār al-Andalus).

Ghalib, Mustafa (ed.) (1991). *Zahr al-Maʿānī* (Beirut: al-Muʾasassa al-Jāmiʿiyya li-al-Dirāsāt wa-al-Naṣr wa-al-Tawzīʿ).

Ghosh, Amitav (1992). *In an Antique Land: History in the Guise of a Traveler's Tale* (New York: Vintage).

Ginsberg, Carlo (1992). *The Cheese and the Worms: The Cosmos of a Sixteenth-Century Miller* (Baltimore: Johns Hopkins University Press).

Goitein, Shelomo (1987). 'A Portrait of a Medieval India Trader: Three Letters from the Cairo Geniza'. *Bulletin of the School of Oriental and African Studies* vol. 50, no. 3: 449–64.

Goitein, Shelomo and Mordechai Friedman (2007). *India Traders of the Middle Ages: Documents from the Cairo Geniza 'India Book'* (Leiden: Brill).

Goldziher, Ignaz (1906). 'Das Prinzip der taḳiyya im Islam'. *Zeitschrift der deutschen morgenländischen Gesellschaft* 59: 213–26.

Goodman, Richard Lenn E. (2009). *The Case of the Animals versus Man Before the King of the Jinn* (Oxford: Oxford University Press).

Goodman, Zoe (2018). *Tales of the Everyday City: Geography and Chronology in Postcolonial Mombasa.* PhD diss., School of African and Oriental Studies, University of London.

Goriawala, Muhammad (1965). *A Descriptive Catalogue of the Fyzee Collection of Isma'ili Manuscripts* (Bombay: Bombay University Press).

Görke, Andreas and Konrad Hirschler (eds) (2011). *Manuscript Notes as Documentary Sources: Beiruter Texte und Studien, 129* (Beirut: Ergon).

Green, Nile (2011). *Bombay Islam: The Religious Economy of the West Indian Ocean, 1840–1915* (Cambridge: Cambridge University Press).

Griffini, Eugenio (1915). 'Die jüngste ambrosianische Sammlung arabischer Handschriften'. *Zeitschrift der Deutschen Morgenländischen Gesellschaft* 69: 63–88.

Habermas, Jürgen (1991). *The Structural Transformation of the Public Sphere: An Inquiry into a Category of Bourgeois Society* (Cambridge, MA: MIT Press).

Haji, Hamid (2007). *Founding the Fatimid State: The Rise of an Early Islamic Empire* (London: I. B. Tauris).

Halm, Heinz (1996). *The Empire of the Mahdi: The Rise of the Fatimids* (Leiden: Brill).

Halm, Heinz (1996). 'The Isma'ili Oath of Allegiance and the "Sessions of Wisdom"'. In Farhad Daftary (ed.), *Mediaeval Ismā'īlī History and Thought* (London: I. B. Tauris), 91–8.

Halm, Heinz (1997). *The Fāṭimids and their Traditions of Learning* (London: I. B. Tauris).

Halm, Heinz (2001). *Shi'ism* (Edinburgh: Edinburgh University Press).

Hamdani, Abbas (1936). *The Beginnings of the Ismā'īlī da'wa in Northern India*. Hamdani Institute of Islamic Studies, Surat, Islamic Studies Series, 1 (Cairo: Sirovic Bookshop).

Hamdani, Abbas (1979). 'An Early Fatimid Source on the Time and Authorship of the Rasa'il Ihwan al-Safa', Arabica 26 (1979): 62–75.

Hamdani, Abbas (2011). 'History of the Hamdani Collection of Manuscripts', in François De Blois, *Arabic, Persian, and Gujarati Manuscripts. The Hamdani Collection* (London: I. B. Tauris): xxvi–xxxiv.

Hamdani, Abbas (n.d). *Fatimid Literature: Creation, Preservation, Transfer, Concealment and Revival*", http://dawoodi-bohras.com/news/77/97/Fatimid-Literature-Creation- preservation-transfer-concealment-and-revival/d,pdb_detail_article_comment/ (last accessed 2 July 2017).

Hamdani, Hussain (1933). 'Some Unknown Ismā'īlī Authors and their Works'. *Journal of the Royal Asiatic Society* : 359–78.

Hamdani, Hussain (1934). 'The Letters of Al-Mustanṣir bi'llāh', *Bulletin of the School of Oriental Studies* vol. 7, no. 2: 307–24.

Hamdani, Hussain (1955). *Al-Ṣulayḥiyyūn wa 'l-ḥaraka al-Fāṭimiyya fi 'l-Yaman* (Cairo).

Hamdani, Hussain (1974). 'The Dā'ī Ḥātim Ibn 'Ibraḥīm al-Ḥāmidī and His Book Tuḥfat al-Qulūb'. *Oriens* 23–4: 258–300.

Hamdani, Sumaya (2006). A. *Between Revolution and State: The Path to Fāṭimid Statehood* (London: I. B. Tauris).

Hamzali, Taibali (2012). 'The Architectural Heritage of the Lamu Bohra Mosque'. *Kenya Past & Present* 40.

Harre, Dominique (2017). 'Exchanges and Mobility in the Western Indian Ocean: Indians between Yemen and Ethiopia, 19th–20th Centuries'. *Chroniques des manuscrits du Yémen*, special issue *From Mountain to Mountain: Exchange between Yemen and Ethiopia, Medieval to Modern* 1: 42–68.

Hathaway, Jane (2003). *A tale of Two Factions. Myth, Memory, and Identity in Ottoman Egypt and Yemen* (Albany: State University of New York Press).

Henrichs, Albert (2003). 'Hieroi Logoi and Hierai Bibloi: The (Un)Written Margins of the Sacred in Ancient Greece'. *Harvard Studies in Classical Philology* 101: 207–66.

Hiltebeitel, Alf (2001). *Rethinking the Mahabharata: A Reader's Guide to the Education of the Dharma King* (Chicago: University of Chicago Press).

Hirschler, Konrad. *The Written Word in the Medieval Arabic Lands* (Edinburgh: Edinburgh University Press).

Hirschler, Konrad (2016). *Medieval Damascus: Plurality and Diversity in an Arabic Library: The Ashrafiya Library Catalogue* (Edinburgh: Edinburgh University Press).

Ho, Engseng (2006). *The Graves of Tarim: Genealogy and Mobility across the Indian Ocean* (Berkeley: University of California Press).

Ho Engseng (2007). 'The Two Arms of Cambay: Diasporic Texts of Ecumenical Islam in the Indian Ocean'. *Journal of the Economic and Social History of the Orient* 2–3: 347–361.
Hoffman, Adina and Peter Cole (2011). *Sacred Trash: The Lost and Found World of the Cairo Geniza* (New York: Schocken Press).
Hollister, James, N. (1953). *The Shi'a of India* (London: Luzac).
Houari, Touati (2003). *L'armoire à sagess: Bibliothèques et collections en Islam* (Paris: Aubier).
Houdas, Octave (1886). *Essai sur l'écriture maghrébine*. Nouveaux Mélanges Orientaux (Paris: l'Ecole des Langues Orientales Vivantes).
Hugh-Jones, Stephen and Hildegard Diemberger (eds) (2012). 'L'objet livre'. *Terrain* 59.
Hurgronje, Snouck (1888–9). *Mekka* (The Hague: Het Koninklijk Instituut voor de Taal-, Land- en Volkenkunde van Nederlandsch-Indie te 's-Gravenhage).
Ivanow, Vladimir (1933). *A Guide to Isma'ili Literature* (London: Royal Asiatic Society).
Ivanow, Vladimir (1936). *A Creed of the Fatimids* (Bombay: Qayimmah Press).
Ivanow, Vladimir (1939) 'The Organisation of the Fatimid Propaganda'. *Journal of the Bombay Branch of the Royal Asiatic Society* 15: 1–35.
Ivanow, Vladimir (1948). *Studies in Early Persian Isma'ilism* (Leiden: Brill).
Jaaware, Aniket (2019). *Practicing Caste: On Touching and Not Touching* (New York: Fordham University Press).
Jain, Danesh (2003). 'Sociolinguistics of the Indo-Aryan Languages'. In Danesh Jain and George Cardona (eds), *The Indo-Aryan Languages* (New York: Routledge), 173–84.
James, David (1992). *After Timur: Qur'ans of the Fifteenth and Sixteenth Centuries* (Oxford: Oxford University Press).
al-Jarāfī, ʿAbd Allāh b. ʿAbd al-Karīm (1951). *al-Muqtaṭaf min tārīḫ al-Yaman* (Cairo, Dār iḥyāʾ al- kutub al-ʿarabiyya).
Jewell, John H. A. (1976). *Dhows at Mombasa* (Nairobi: East African Publishing House).
Jiwa, Shainool (2017). *The Fatimids: The Rise of a Muslim Empire* (London: I. B. Tauris).
Jones, Justin (2012). *Shia Islam in Colonial India: Religion, Community and Sectarianism* (Cambridge: Cambridge University Press).
Khan, Dominique-Sila (1997). *Conversions and Shifting Identities: Ramdev Pir and the Isma'ilis in Rajasthan* (New Delhi: Manohar).
Khan, Geoffrey (1993). *Arabic Legal and Administrative Documents in the Cambridge Genizah Collections* (Cambridge: Cambridge University Press).
Klemm, Verena (1989). *Die Mission des fāṭimidischen Agenten al-Mu'ayyad fī ad-dīn in Shirāz* (Frankfurt: Peter Lang). [Includes Aḥmad Ibn Ibrāhīm an-Naysābūrī's *al-mūjaza al-kāfiya fī adab ad-duʿāt*.]
Klemm, Verena (2004). *Memoirs of a Mission: The Ismaili Scholar, Statesman and Poet, Al-Mu-ayyad Fi'l-Din Al-Shirazi* (London: I. B. Tauris).
Klemm, Verena and Paul Walker (2011). *A Code of Conduct: A Treatise on the Etiquette of the Fatimid Isma'ili Mission* (London: I. B. Tauris).
Kohlberg, Ethan (1975). 'Some Imāmī-shīʿī Views on Taqiyya'. *Journal of the American Oriental Society* 95: 395–402.
Kohlberg, Ethan (1995). 'Taqiyya in Shī'ī Theology and Religion'. In H. G. Kippenberg and G. Strousma (eds), *Secrecy and Concealment: Studies in the History of Mediterranean and Near Eastern Religion* (Leiden: Brill), 345–80.
Kooria, Mahmood (2018). 'Texts as Objects of Value and Veneration: Islamic Law Books in the Indian Ocean Littoral'. *Sociology of Islam* 6: 60–83.
Kratchkovsky, Ignace, Y. (1953). *Among Arabic Manuscripts: Memories of Libraries and Men* (Leiden: Brill).
Kratli, Graziano and Ghislaine Lydon (2011). *The Trans-Saharan Book Trade: Manuscript Culture, Arabic Literacy and Intellectual History in Muslim Africa* (Leiden: Brill).

Kropf, Evyn and Cathleen Baker (2013). 'A Conservative Tradition? Arab Papers of the 12th–17th Centuries from the Islamic Manuscripts Collection at the University of Michigan'. *Journal of Islamic Manuscripts* 4: 1–48.

Lachaier, Pierre (2013). 'Une étude sociologique d'un quartier communautaire ou pol d'Ahmadabad par Ashok Patel. Présentation et traduction'. BEI, No. 28–9.

Lambourn, Elizabeth (2008). 'India from Aden: Khutba and Muslim Urban Networks in Late Thirteenth-Century India'. In Kenneth Hall (ed.), *Secondary Cities and Urban Networks in the Indian Ocean Realm* (Lanham, MD: Lexington Books), 55–97.

Lambourn, Elizabeth (2011). 'Khutba and Muslim Networks in the Indian Ocean (Part II): Timurid and Ottoman Engagements'. In Kenneth Hall (ed.), *The Growth of Non-Western Cities: Primary and Secondary Urban Networking, c. 900–1900* (Lanham, MD: Lexington Books), 131–58.

Lambourn, Elizabeth (2018). *Abraham's Luggage: A Social Life of Things in the Medieval Indian Ocean World* (Cambridge: Cambridge University Press).

Leemhuis, Fred (2001–6). 'From Palm Leaves to the Internet'. In Jane Dammen McAuliffe (ed.), *Encyclopaedia of the Qur'an* (Cambridge: Cambridge University Press), 145–62.

Lewis, Bernard (1940). *The Origins of Isma'ilism* (Cambridge: W. Heffer & Sons).

Liebrenz, Boris (2012). 'Lese- und Besitzvermerke in der Leipziger Rifāʿīya-Bibliothek'. In Andreas Görke and Konrad Hirschler (eds), *Manuscript Notes as Documentary Sources* (Beirut: Orient-Institut), 141–62.

Liebrenz, Boris (2018). 'Preface: The History of Books and Collections through Manuscript Notes'. *Journal of Islamic Manuscripts* 9, no 2–3: 105–7.

Lorusso, Vito (n.d.). *Searching for a Definition of 'Manuscript'*. http://www.manuscript cultures.unihamburg.de/TnT/Definition_of_MS.pdf

Mackenrodt, Lisa (2011). *Swahili Spirit Possession and Islamic Healing in Contemporary Tanzania* (Hamburg: Kovac Verlag).

Messick, Brinkley (1992). *The Calligraphic State: Textual Domination and History in a Muslim Society* (Berkeley: University of California Press).

Messick, Brinkley (2018). *Sharia Scripts: A Historical Anthropology* (New York: Columbia University Press).

Meyer, Birgit (2012). 'Introduction: Material Religion – How Things Matter'. In Dick Houtman and Birgit Meyer (eds), *Things: Religion and the Question of Materiality* (New York: Fordham University Press), 1–23.

Meyer, Birgit and Annelies Moors (2005). *Religion, Media, and the Public Sphere* (Bloomington: Indiana University Press).

Miller, Daniel (ed.) (2005). *Materiality: An Introduction* (Durham, NC: Duke University Press).

Mir, Farina (2010). *The Social Space of Language: Vernacular Culture in British Colonial Punjab* (Berkeley: University of California Press).

Moncelon, Jean (1995). 'La Daʿwa fatimide au Yémen'. *Chroniques yéménites* 5: 26–37.

Morris, Brian (1987). *Anthropological Studies of Religion: An Introductory Text* (Cambridge: Cambridge University Press).

Morris, James (2001). *The Master and the Disciple: An Early Islamic Spiritual Dialogue: Arabic Edition and English Translation of Jaʿfar b. Manṣūr al-Yaman's* 'Kitāb al-ʿĀlim waʾl-ghulām' (London: I. B. Tauris).

Mukherjee, Soumen (2017). *Isma'ilism and Islam in Modern South Asia: Community and Identity in the Age of Religious Internationals* (Cambridge: Cambridge University Press).

Nadir, Zafir (1935). 'The Origin of the Bohras'. *Islamic Culture* 8: 638–44.

Netton, Ian R. (1996). 'Foreign Influences and Recurring Ismâ'îli Motifs in Rasâ'il of the Brethren of Purity'. In Ian R. Netton, *Seek Knowledge: Thought and Travel in the House of Islam* (London: Routledge Curzon), 27–41.

Netton, Ian R. (2009). 'Private Caves and Public Islands'. In M. Elkaisy-Freimuth and J. M. Dillon (eds), *The Afterlife of the Platonic Soul: Reflections of Platonic Psychology in the Monotheistic Religions* (Leiden: Brill), 107–20.

Neumeier, Emily (2006). 'Early Koranic Manuscripts: The Blue Koran Debate'. *Elements* vol. 2, no. 1: 11–19.

Nieber, Hannah (2019). 'Drinking the Written Qur'an: Healing with Kombe in Zanzibar Town'. PhD diss., Utrecht University.

Nourmamadchoev, Nourmamadcho (2013). 'The Isma'ilis of Badakhshan: History, Politics and Religion from 1500 to 1750'. PhD diss., School of Oriental and African Studies.

Oudesluijs, Tino (2018). 'Scribes as Agents of Change: Copying Practices in Administrative Texts from Fifteenth-Century Coventry'. In Margaret Tudeau-Clayton and Martin Hilpert (eds), *The Challenge of Change* (Zurich: Gunter Narr Verlag), 223–48.

Parekh, Bhikhu (2001). *Gandhi: A Very Short Introduction* (Oxford: Oxford University Press).

Paul, Eva (2006). 'Die Dawoodi Bohras: Eine Indische Gemeinschaft in Ostafrika'. *Beiträge zur 1. Kölner Afrikawissenschaftlichen Nachwuchstagung*, 2006.

Pinault, David (2008). *Notes from the Fortune-telling parrot: Religious Pluralism in Pakistan* (London: Equinox).

Poleman, Horace, I. (1943). 'Serial Publications in India'. *Quarterly Journal of Current Acquisitions* 1: 23–30.

Pollock, James, W. (1988). 'Kabikaj to Book Pouches: Library Preservation Magic and Technique in Syria of the 1880's and 1980's West'. *Middle East Library Association* Notes 44: 8–10.

Pollock, Sheldon, I. (2006). *The Language of the Gods in the World of Men: Sanskrit, Culture, and Power in Pre-Modern India* (Berkeley, CA: University of California Press).

Poonawala, Ismail, K. (1977). *Biobibliography of Isma'ili Literature*. Malibu: Gustave von Grunebaum Center for Near Eastern Studies, UCLA/Undena Publications.

Poonawala, Ismail, K. (1996). 'Al-Qaḍī al-Nuʿman and Ismāʿīlī Jurisprudence'. In Farhad Daftary (ed.), *Mediaeval Ismāʿīli History and Thought* (Cambridge: Cambridge University Press), 117–43.

Poonawala, Ismail, K. (1999). *Al-Sulṭān al-Khaṭṭāb: Ḥayātuhu wa-shiʿruhu* (Beirut: Dār al-ġarb al-islāmī).

Poonawala, Ismail, K. (2014). 'Isma'ili Manuscripts from Yemen'. *Journal of Islamic Manuscripts* 5, nos 2–3: 220–45.

Poonawala, Ismail, K. (2015). 'MAJDUʿ, ESMĀʿIL' In *Encyclopædia Iranica*, online edition. https://iranicaonline.org/articles/majdu-esmail

Poonawala, Ismail, K. (2018). 'The Chronology of al-Qāḍī al-Nuʿmān's Works'. *Arabica* 65: 84–162.

Poonawala, Ismail, K. (2019). 'The Contribution of Ismāʿīlī Colophons to the Discussion on the Birth and Construction of the Arabic Manuscript Tradition'. *Chroniques du manuscrit au Yémen* 8: 74–139.

Poonawala, Ismail. K. and Asef A. A. Fyzee (2002). *The Pillars of Islam: A Translation of al-Qādī An Nuʿmān's Daʿā'im al-Islām* (Oxford: Oxford University Press).

Prange, Sebastian (2018). *Monsoon Islam: Trade and Faith on the Medieval Malabar Coast* (Cambridge: Cambridge University Press).

Purohit, Teena (2012). *The Agha Khan Case: Religion and Identity in Colonial India* (New Haven: Yale University Press).

Qutbuddin, Tahera (2007). 'Arabic in India: A Survey and Classification of Its Uses, Compared with Persian'. *Journal of the American Oriental Society* vol. 127, no. 3: 315–37.

Qutbuddin, Tahera (2011). 'The Da'udi Bohra Tayyibis: Ideology, Literature, Learning and Social Practice'. In Farhad Daftary (ed.), *A Modern History of the Isma'ilis: Continuity and Change in a Muslim Community* (London: I. B. Tauris), 331–54.

al-Qāḍī, Wadād (ed.) (1970). *Iftitāḥ al-daʿwa* (Beirut: Dār al-Thaqāfa).

al-Qāḍī, Wadād (ed.) (2007). 'How Sacred Is the Text of an Arabic Medieval Manuscript: The Complex Choices of the Editor Scholar'. In Judith Pfeiffer and Manfred Kropp (eds), *Theoretical Approaches to the Transmission and Edition of Oriental Manuscripts* (Wurzburg: Ergon Verlag), 13–53.

Rangwala, Normal (2011). *With a Pinch of Salt: An Expression of Bohra Culture and Cuisine* (Mumbai: Create Space Independent Publishing Platform).

Regourd, Anne (ed.) (2018). *The Trade in Papers Marked with Non-Latin Characters: Documents and History* (Leiden: Brill).

Ricci, Ronit (2011). *Islam Translated: Literature, Conversion, and the Arabic Cosmopolis of South and Southeast Asia* (Chicago: University of Chicago Press).

Rosenthal, Franz (1947). *The Technique and Approach of Muslim Scholarship* (Rome: Pontificium Institutum Biblicum).

Rots, Aike Peter (2014). 'The Rediscovery of "Sacred Space" in Contemporary Japan: Intrinsic Quality or Discursive Strategy?' In Liu Janhui and Sano Mayuko (eds), *Rethinking 'Japanese Studies' from Practices in the Nordic Region* (Kyoto: International Research Center for Japanese Studies), 31–50.

Rustow, Marina (2020). *The Lost Archive: Traces of a Caliphate in a Cairo Synagogue* (Princeton: Princeton University Press).

Salvadori, Cynthia (1989). *Through Open Doors: A View of Asian Cultures in Kenya* (Nairobi: Kenway).

Sanders, Paula (1999). 'Bohra Architecture and the Restoration of Fatimid Culture'. In Marianne Barrucand (ed.), *L'Égypte fatimide. Son art et son histoire* (Paris: Presses de l'Université de Paris-Sorbonne), 159–65.

Sanders, Paula (2008). *Creating Medieval Cairo: Empire, Religion and Architectural Preservation in Nineteenth-Century Egypt* (Cairo: AUC Press).

Sawa, George Dimitri (2021). *Ḥāwī l-Funūn wa-Salwat al-Maḥzūn, Encompasser of the Arts and Consoler of the Grief-Stricken by Ibn al-Ṭaḥḥān* (Leiden: Brill, 2021).

Sayyid, Fuad (1988). *Tārīḫ al-maḏāhib al-dīniyya fī bilād al-Yaman ḥattā nihāyat al-qarn al-sādis al-hiǧrī* (Cairo, Dār al-miṣriyya al-lubnāniyya).

Sayyid, Fuad, Paul Walker and Maurice A. Pomerantz (2002). *The Fāṭimids and their Successors in Yaman: An Edition and Translation of ʿUyūn al-Akhbār* (London: I. B. Tauris).

Sayyid, Ayman Fuad (2003). 'Les marques de possession sur les manuscrits et la reconstitution des anciens fonds des manuscrits arabes'. Manuscripta Orientalia 9: 14–23.

Sayyid, Fuad, Paul Walker and Maurice A. Pomerantz (2007). 'Le rôle des conservateurs des ḫazāʾin al-kutub dans la reproduction des manuscrits arabes'. In Judith Pfeiffer and Manfred Kropp (eds), *Theoretical Approaches to the Transmission and Edition of Oriental Manuscripts, Proceedings of a Symposium Held in Istanbul March 28–30* (Beirut: Orient Institut), 197–201.

Scheper, Karin (2015). *The Technique of Islamic Bookbinding Methods, Materials and Regional Varieties* (Leiden: Brill).

Schimmel, Annemarie (1990). *Calligraphy and Islamic Culture* (London: I. B. Tauris).

Schindlbeck, Markus (1993). 'The Art of Collecting: Interactions between Collectors and the People They Visit'. *Zeitschrift Für Ethnologie* vol. 118, no. 1: 57–67.

Scupin, Raymond (1998). 'Muslim Accommodation in Thai Society'. *Journal of Islamic Studies* vol. 9, no. 2: 229–58.

Sheikh, Samira (2010). *Forging a Region: Sultans, Traders and Pilgrims in Gujarat* (Oxford: Oxford University Press).

Sheikh, Samira (2018). 'Aurangzeb as Seen from Gujarat: Shiʿi and Millenarian Challenges to Mughal Sovereignty'. *Journal of the Royal Asiatic Society* 28: 1–25.

Shibani, Roy (1984). *The Dawoodi Bohras: An Anthropological Perspective* (Delhi: D. K. Publishers).

Shodan, Amrita (2001). *A Question of Community: Religious Groups and Colonial Law* (Calcutta: Samya).

Shreen, Kala (2010). 'Socio-Cultural Dimensions of Ritual Objects: Nagarathar Rites of Passage'. *International Journal of Interdisciplinary Social Sciences* vol. 5, no. 5: 79–92.

Sirat, Colette (2006). *Writing as Handwork: A History of Handwriting in Mediterranean and Western Culture* (Turnhout: Brepols).

Slight, John (2015). *The British Empire and the Hajj, 1865–1956* (Cambridge, MA: Harvard University Press).

Soja, Edward (1989). *Postmodern Geographies: The Reassertion of Space in Critical Social Theory* (London: Verso).

Soja, Edward (1996). *Thirdspace: Journeys to Los Angeles and Other Real-and-Imagined Places* (Malden, MA: Blackwell).

Steedman, Carolyn (2002). *Dust: The Archive and Cultural History* (New Brunswick, NJ: Rutgers University Press).

Stetkevych, Suzanne Pinckney (2006). 'From Text to Talisman: Al-Būṣīrī's "Qaṣīdat al-Burdah" (Mantle Ode) and the Supplicatory Ode'. Journal of Arabic Literature 37, No. 2 (2006): 145–189.

Stetkevych, Suzanne Pinckney (2010). *Burda. The Mantle Odes. Arabic Praise Poems to the Prophet Muhammad* (Bloomington: Indiana University Press).

Stern, Samuel M. (1964). *Fatimid Decrees: Original Documents from the Fatimid Chancery* (London: Faber & Faber).

Stoler, Ann (2009). *Along the Archival Grain: Epistemic Anxieties and Colonial Common Sense* (Princeton: Princeton University Press).

Strothmann, Rudolf (ed.) (1943). *Gnosis-Texte der Isma'iliten* (Göttingen: Vandenhoeck & Ruprecht).

Swetha, G., V. M. Eashwar and S. Gopalakrishnan (2019). 'Epidemics and Pandemics in India throughout History: A Review Article'. *Indian Journal of Public Health Research & Development* vol. 10, no. 8 (August): 1,570–8.

Thakkar, Jay (2008). *Naqsh: The Art of Wood Carving in Traditional Houses of Gujarat* (Ahmedabad: Research Cell).

Tirmizi, Baqirali (2011). *Rise and Development of Arabic Language & Literature in Gujarat* (Ahmedabad: Hazrat Pir Mohammad Shah Library & Research Centre).

Traboulsi, Samer (2000). 'Lamak ibn Mālik al-Ḫammādī and Sulayhid-Fāṭimid Relations'. *Proceedings of the Seminar for Arabian Studies* 30: 221–7.

Traboulsi, Samer (2005). 'The Formation of an Ismāʿīlī Sect: The Ṭayyibī Ismāʿīlis in Medieval Yemen'. PhD diss., Princeton University.

Traboulsi, Samer (2009). 'The Ottoman Conquest of Yemen: The Isma'ili Perspective'. In J. Hathaway (ed.), *The Arab Lands in the Ottoman Era* (Minneapolis: University of Minnesota Press), 41–60.

Traboulsi, Samer (2014). 'Sources for the History of the Ṭayyibī Ismāʿīlī Daʿwa in Yemen and Its Relocation to India'. *Journal of Islamic Manuscripts* 5: 246–74.

Tritton, Arthur, S. (1933). 'Notes on Some Isma'ili Manuscripts'. *Bulletin of the School of Oriental Studies* 7: 35–9.

Urban, Hugh (1998). 'The Torment of Secrecy: Ethical and Epistemological Problems in the Study of Esoteric Traditions'. *History of Religions* vol. 37, no. 3: 209–48.

van der Grijp, Paul (2006). *Passion and Profit: Towards an Anthropology of Collecting* (Berlin: Lit Verlag).

Virani, Shafique (2011). 'Taqiyya and Identity in a South Asian Community'. *Journal of Asia Studies* 70: 99–139.

Wagner, Esther-Miriam, Ben Outhwaite and Bettina Beinhoff (eds) (2013). *Scribes as Agents of Language Change* (Berlin: De Gruyter).
Walker, Paul (2009). *Orations of the Fatimid Caliphs: Festival Sermons of the Isma'ili Imams* (London: I. B. Tauris).
Walker, Paul (2016). 'Libraries, Book Collection and the Production of Texts by the Fatimids'. *Intellectual History of the Islamicate World* vol. 4, no. 1–2: 7–21.
Ward, Gerald W. R. (ed.) (2008). *The Grove Encyclopedia of Materials and Techniques in Art* (Oxford: Oxford University Press).
Weiss, Anita M. (1991). 'South Asian Muslims in Hong Kong: Creation of a "Local Boy" Identity'. *Modern Asian Studies* vol. 25, no. 3: 417–53.
Witkam, Jan Just (1978). *Seven Specimens of Arabic Manuscripts Preserved in the Library of the University of Leiden* (Leiden: Brill).
Witkam, Jan Just. (1987). 'Manuscripts & Manuscripts: Research Facilities for Manuscripts in the Egyptian National Library'. *Manuscripts of the Middle East* 2: 111–25.
Witkam, Jan Just (2013). 'The Human Element between Text and Reader. The Ijaza in Arabic Manuscripts'. In Geoffrey Roper (ed.), *The History of the Book in the Middle East* (Farnham: Ashgate), 89–112.
al-Yaʿlāwī, Muḥammad (ed.) (1985). *Taʾrīkh al-khulafāʾ al-Fāṭimiyyīn bi'l-Maghrib: al-qism al-khāṣṣ min Kitāb ʿuyūn al-akhbār* (vols 5 and, partly, 6 of *ʿUyūn al-akhbār wa-funūn al-āthār*) (Beirut: Dār al-Gharb al-Islāmī).
Zahid Khan, Ansar (1975). 'Isma'ilism in Multan and Sind'. *Journal of the Pakistan Historical Society* 22: 36–57.
Zaidi, B. H. (1988). *The Fatimi Tradition* (Mumbai: Dawat-e Hadiyah, Department of Statistics and Information), pamphlet.

Primary Sources

al-Bharūchī, Ḥasan bin Nūḥ (1958). *Kitāb al-azhār wa-majmaʿ al-anwār al-malqūṭa min basātīn al-asrār*, ed. ʿĀdil al-ʿAwwā (Damascus: Muntakhabāt Ismāʿīliyya).
Burhānpūrī, Quṭb al-Dīn Sulaymānjī (1999). *Muntazaʿ al-akhbār fī akhbār al-duʿāt al-akhyār*. ed. Samer F. Traboulsi (1999) (Beirut: Dār al-Gharb al-Islāmī).
al-Hamidi, Husayn (1971). *Kitāb Kanz al-Walad*, ed. Mustafa Ghalib (Wiesbaden: Franz Steiner).
al-Ḥāmidī, Ḥātim (2012). *The Precious Gift of the Hearts and Good Cheer for Those in Distress. A Critical Edition of Risālat tuḥfat al-qulūb wa-furğat al-makrūb*, ed. Abbas Hamdani (London: Dar-al-Saqi).
Imad al-Din, Idris (1991). *Zahr al-Maʿānī*, ed. Mustafa Ghalib (Beirut: al-Muʾasassa al-Jāmiʿiyya li-al-Dirāsāt wa-al-Naṣr wa-al-Tawzīʿ).
al-Maqrīzī, Aḥmad ibn 'Alī (1956). *Kitāb al-sulūk li-ma'rifat duwal al-mulūk*, vol. 2. ed. Muhammad Mustafa Ziyada (Cairo: Lajnat al-Ta'lif wa-al-Tarjamah wa-al-Nashr).
al-Maqrīzī, Aḥmad ibn 'Alī (2010). Ittiʿāẓ al-ḥunafāʾ, Vol. 3, ed. Ayman Fuʾād Sayyid (London: Institute of Isma'ili Studies in association with the Institut français du Proche-Orient).
al-Nuʿman, al-Qaḍī. *Daʿā'im al-'Islām wa dhikr al-ḥalāl wa 'l-ḥarām wa 'l-qaḍā ya wa'l-'aḥkām*. Microfilm no. 49075, Dar al-Kutub Misriyya.
al-Nuʿman, al-Qaḍī (1991). *Daʿā'im al-'Islām wa dhikr al-ḥalāl wa 'l-ḥarām wa 'l-qaḍāya wa 'l-'aḥkām*, ed. Asaf b. Ali Asghar Fyzee (Caïro: Dār al-'Aḍwā').
al-Nuʿman, al-Qaḍī (1948). *Kitāb al-himma fī ādāb atbāʿ al-aʾimma*, ed. Muhammad Kamil Husayn (Cairo: Dār al-Fikr al-ʿArabī).
Rāmpūrī, Muḥammad ʿAlī b. Mullā Jīwābhāʾī (1884–93). *Mawsim-i bahār fī akhbār al- ṭāhirīn al-akhyār* (Bombay: Maṭbaʿat Ḥaydarī Ṣafdarī). [Lithographed, 3 vols].
Qarāṭīs al-Yaman, MS Ma VI 330, Tübingen University Library.

Aṣḥāb al-Yamīn fī dhikr al-du'āt al-muṭlaqīn al-yamāniyīn (Gujarati and English). Historical account published by the Alawi Bohra da'wa, 1432 AH, Baroda.

al-Zubayr, Aḥmad ibn al-Rashīd Ibn (1996). Book of Gifts and Rarities, trans. Ghādah Ḥijjāwī Qaddūmī (Cambridge, MA: Harvard University Press).

Websites and Blogs

Doctrine of Infallibility in Isma'ili Tradition

http://dawoodi-bohras.com/news/66/97/Doctrine-of-infallibility-in-Islamilitradition/d,pdb_detail_article/

Introduction

http://www.alavibohra.org/introduction%20files/intro%20-%20Vadodara%20City%20A%20centre%20of%20Dawat.htm dawoodi-bohras.com (progressive Dawoodi Bohras)

Fatimid Literature: Creation, Preservation, Transfer, Concealment, and Revival

http://dawoodi-bohras.com/news/77/97/Fatimid-Literature-Creationpreservation-transfer-concealment-and-revival/d,pdb_detail_article_comment/

An Artist True to Himself, True to His Soil

http://dawoodi-bohras.com/news/1311/107/An-artist-true-to-himself-true-to-hissoil/d,pdb_detail_article_comment/

Learning Gujarati in Yemen

http://blogs.wsj.com/indiarealtime/2012/09/24/learning-gujarati-in-yemen/

The Intricacies of Succession: Two Claimants Emerge for Dawoodi Bohra Leadership

http://www.huffingtonpost.com/rizwan mawani/the-intricacies-of succes_b_4687546.html

Bohra Women Go Online to Fight Circumcision Trauma

http://www.hindustantimes.com/mumbai/bohra-women-go-online-to-fightcircumcision-trauma/article1-779782.aspx

Uproar over Female Genital Mutilation: Bohra Muslim Woman Activist Launches Campaign on Facebook to Ban Practice

http://www.npwj.org/content/Uproar-over-Female-Genital-Mutilation-BohraMuslim-Woman-Activist-Launches-Campaign-Facebook

September 28: Qubba of Syedna Idris Imaduddin RA (Shibaam-Yemen)

Qutbibohras.blogspot.com/2014/09 (last accessed 16 May 2020).

'Preserving Culture for Posterity' ,Times of India, date unknown

http://alavibohra.org/images/photographs/akhbar/culture.jpg

The Historic City of Thula, UNESCO

http://whc.unesco.org/en/tentativelists/1719/ (last accessed 1 September 2020)

Badri Masjid, Mumbai

https://www.alavibohra.org/Badri%20masjid%20-%20mumbai%20darajaat%20e%20tameer.htm (last accessed 7 November 2020)

Alavi Heritage Walk

https://www.alavibohra.org/alavi%20heritage-antique-architecture-culture.htm (last accessed 14 October 2020)

The Jamea of Africa: A Millennium of Fatemi Learning Comes to Life in Kenya, 2018

https://www.thedawoodibohras.com/2018/02/02/the-jamea-of-africa-a-millenium-of-fatemi-learning-comes-to-life-in-kenya/ (last accessed 1 August 2019)

Newspaper Articles

'A Veil with a "Rida" Touch' (2006). *Mumbai Mirror*, https://mumbaimirror.indiatimes.com/opinion/columnists/manoj-r-nair/a-veil-with-a ridatouch/articleshow/15656398.cms?utm_source=contentofinterest&utm_medium=text&utm_campaign=cppst

'Bohra Women: Cut from the Same Cloth: Wrapping Fashion and Tradition in a Colourful Embrace – The Dawoodi Bohra Rida' (2013). *Express Tribune, Sunday Magazine*, 15 September.

Ghosh, Abantika (2018). 'PM Modi to Address Dawoodi Bohra Event Today', *Indian Express*, 14 September.

Hamdani, Abbas (2008). 'Fatimid Literature: Creation, Preservation, Transfer, Concealment and Revival', http://dawoodi-bohras.com/news/77/97/Fatimid-Literature-Creation- preservation-transfer-concealment-and-revival/d,pdb_detail_article_comment

Johari, Aarefa (2015). 'India's Bohra Muslims Are Back Safely from Yemen but Have Many Reasons to Still Be Anxious', https//scroll.in/article/719205

'Sangh's "Ghar Wapsi" event in full swing in Gujarat' (2014).
https://economictimes.indiatimes.com/news/politics-and-nation/sanghs-ghar-wapsi-event-in-full-swing-in-gujarat/articleshow/45611337.cms

Encyclopaedia Entries

The following entries are from P. Bearman, T. Bianquis, C. E. Bosworth, E. van Donzel and W. P. Heinrichs (eds), *Encyclopaedia of Islam* (Brill Online), http://referenceworks.brillonline.com/entries/encyclopaedia-of-islam-2

Amir-Moezzi, Mohammad Ali, 'Sirr'. http://referenceworks.brillonline.com/entries/encyclopaedia-of-islam-2/sirrSIM_8901

Bazmee Ansari, A.S., 'Barōda'. http://referenceworks.brillonline.com/entries/encyclopaedia-of-islam-2/barodaSIM_1241

Daftary, F., 'al-Ṭayyibiyya'. http://referenceworks.brillonline.com/entries/encyclopaedia-of-islam-2/altayyibiyya-SIM_7472

Gökbilgin, M. Tayyib, 'Durūz'. http://referenceworks.brillonline.com/entries/encyclopaedia-of-islam-2/duruzCOM_0198

Hodgson, M. G. S., 'Bāṭiniyya'. http://referenceworks.brillonline.com/entries/encyclopaedia-of-islam-2/bāṭinī yya-SIM_1284

Mazaheri, Mas'ud Habibi and Farzin Negahban, 'Aḥmad b. ʿAbd Allāh al-Mastūr'. In *Encyclopaedia Islamica*, Editors-in-Chief: Wilferd Madelung and Farhad Daftary.

Poonawala, Ismail, K., 'al-Bharūchī, Ḥasan b. Nuḥ'. http://referenceworks.brillonline.com/entries/encyclopaedia-of-islam-3/bohrasCOM_24020

Qutbuddin, Tahera, 'Bohras'. http://referenceworks.brillonline.com/entries/encyclopaedia-of-islam-3/bohrasCOM_24020

Smith, G. R., 'Ṣulayḥids'. http://referenceworks.brillonline.com/entries/encyclopaedia-of-islam-2/sulayhids-COM_1112

Strothmann, R. Djebli, Moktar. 'Taḳiyya'. http://referenceworks.brillonline.com/entries/encyclopaedia-of-islam-2/takiyya-SIM_7341

The Editors of Encyclopaedia Britannica, 'Scriptorium', *Encyclopedia Britannica*, 8th edn, s.v. 'Internet' (Chicago: Encyclopaedia Britannica, 2009).

Lectures

Attarwala Asma, Barodawala (2011). 'Alavi Bohra Language: Languages in Contact'. Lecture presented at the Linguistic and Language Development in Jammu and Kashmir with Special Reference to Tribal Languages, Department of Linguistics, University of Kashmir, 14–16 November. http://alavibohra.org/lisaan%20dawat%20research%20paper%2011-2011.pdf (last accessed 21 December 2020).

'The Occurrences of the Episodes of Arab History in Isma'ili Literature', private written lecture of the Mazoon Saheb (unpublished).

Whiles, Virginia (2015). 'Wastelands: Between Art and Anthropology'. Lecture presented at Museum für Ethnology, Dahlem, Berlin, 22 January.

Index

abjad numerals, 288, 289
access, 15–17, 21–44, 158–208
adab, 13, 74–5, 113, 152, 201, 309, 353
Ādam, Miyān Nūḥjī b., 138–9
Aden, 6, 45, 132, 135, 137
aesthetics, 84, 90, 162, 184, 187, 254, 304, 306, 327, 334–6
agency, 12–13, 16–17, 20, 34, 103–4, 143, 198, 216, 240, 255, 266, 281, 293, 304, 318, 329, 344
ʿahd, 33, 114, 158–62, 190, 192–96, 199, 203–4, 207, 213, 230, 254, 258–60; *see also mīthāq*
Ahmedabad, 10, 47–60, 75, 80, 94–7, 135–9, 143, 147–9, 156, 165, 172, 185, 213, 218–21, 229, 240, 250, 270, 305, 320, 321
ahl al-bayt, 11, 61, 64, 68, 83, 154, 169, 190, 338, 353
ʿalāma, 83–5, 157, 195, 213, 244, 266, 342, 348; *see also sijill*
ʿAlī (b. Abī Ṭālib), 63, 122
ʿAlī, Sy. Naẓar, 222
ʿāmil, 77, 320, 233–4, 265
Amīr al-Dīn, Sy. Jīwābhā'i Fakhr al-Dīn b., 313
ʿāmma, 75–7, 162–9, 172–6, 182–8, 192, 196–208, 217, 254, 262, 263, 298, 309–12; *see also khāṣṣa*
Arabic, xviii, 3, 7, 10, 12, 16, 44, 53, 55–7, 60, 74, 88, 90, 92, 94, 98–115, 121, 128, 136–7, 142, 156, 169, 176, 197, 216–22, 304–6, 347
archive *see khizana*
ārthī, 88
al-Arwā, Malika al-Ḥurra, 65, 125
Aṣḥāb al-Yamīn, 45–6, 124–43
ʿAshūra, 27–8, 71, 308, 310
ʿaṣr, 57–8, 68, 224, 241–2, 276–8, 314, 327, 338
auspiciousness, 51, 82, 83, 87, 89–90, 125, 170, 175, 262, 293, 333
awrāq, 257–267, 289, 298, 310

Badr al-Dīn, Sy. Nūr al-Dīn Yūsuf b., 169
Badri Mohallah, 21–44, 158–208
baraka, 31, 83, 87, 122, 275, 284–5, 307, 310, 330
barat see excomminication
Baroda, 21–44, 47–8, 55, 62, 75, 80–1, 221, 244, 304, 309, 318
basmala, 240–6, 279, 298, 341
bayan, 55, 263–5
Bhai Saheb, 26–44, 75
Bharuch, 305
al-Bha'rūchī, Ḥasan b. Nūḥ b. Yūsuf b. Muḥammad b. Ādam, 133–56, 194
bhishti, 132

Bhu Saheba, 26–31, 44, 75, 77–8, 175, 209
bibliophilia, 1, 113, 118, 209–11, 246–8
bid'a, 108
bihārī, 306, 322–6
Bohra Studies, 14, 47
Bohrwads, 26, 165; *see also mohallah*
bookbinding, 118, 266–9, 339
book culture, 213, 215, 230, 251, 257, 298–9, 350; *see also* manuscript culture
book hands, 312–27
Brahmins, 90–4
budūḥ, 116, 287–8, 293
Burhānpūrī, Quṭb al-Dīn Sulaymānjī, 90
Burhānuddīn, Sy. Muḥammad, 58, 82, 90, 144, 250, 320–321

Cairo, xviii, 1–9, 45–8, 53, 65, 98–103, 119–29, 145–8, 182, 190, 222, 327, 343–351
Cambay *see* Khambhat
caste, 86–94, 190, 199, 330
chamal, 79
chauri, 71
chori, 78, 80
circumcision, 36, 160, 200, 245; *see also* FGM
coconut, 85–8, 197
codex, 53, 98, 118, 240, 250–61, 267–300, 314–16, 338–41
codicology, 15–17, 192, 210–25, 240–3, 249–99, 351
colonialism, 16–17, 90, 119, 349
colophon, 276–8, 341–2
copyist, 113, 136, 144, 214, 241, 244, 275–8, 282–3, 300–4, 312–50; *see also* scribe
  female, 226, 230, 235, 316, 330
curse, 19, 108, 167, 192, 272, 285–6, 347
cyclical time, 62–7, 97, 109, 121, 163, 186, 191, 218, 275, 278, 299, 302, 333, 338, 344, 346

Da'ā'im al-Islām, 67, 98–100, 116, 152, 228, 236, 239, 241, 282, 311, 314
daftar, 257, 267
dalits, 48, 91, 92
Damascus, 2, 17, 188, 211, 317
Daras Sayfiyya *see* Jamea tus Saifiyah
da'wa
  missionary activities and networks (Fatimids), 9, 124, 148, 151
  al-hādiyya (Bohras), 42, 47, 60, 62, 103, 109, 138, 155, 209, 242
Ḍaw' al-Nūr al-Ḥaqq al-Mubīn, 57
dawr, 65, 68, 69–70, 93
Delhi, 99
Delhi Sultanate, 304, 322
Devdi Mubarak, 186, 201, 206
al-Dīn, Rāja b. Ḥasan Walī al-Hind Shāja' *see* Moulai Raj Bin Moulai Hasan
al-Dīn, Sy. Idrīs Imād, 125, 127, 130–2, 143, 147, 153, 156
divination *see 'ilm al-fāl*
diwān, 55–6, 113, 154, 244, 310
Diwān-e Ḥasan, 56
Diwānī, 244
documents, 47, 72–86
du'ā, 83, 86–7, 96, 187, 204, 291
dupatta, 79, 159, 207, 328

Egypt, 1–4, 8–9, 68, 98–102, 113, 119–26, 151, 183, 195, 197, 215, 217, 255, 308, 327, 345
ethics, 27, 70, 102–5, 214
excommunication, 74, 93, 193, 309; *see also barat*

fātiḥa, 58, 149, 159, 220, 291, 295
Fāṭimids, 1–12, 47, 57, 61–5, 73, 78, 85, 96–104, 119–30, 144, 146, 151, 156–7, 182, 189, 194, 197, 214, 232, 246, 256, 347, 351
  calendar, 70–2, 348
  '*Faatemi way of life*', 18, 47, 60–2, 67, 97, 101, 188, 211
  jurisprudence, 67–70, 209

fatwa, 187
FGM, 36, 93, 200
fihrist, 107, 118, 140
Fihrist al-Kutub wa'l-Rasā'il, 131
fiqh, 36, 64, 67–70, 99, 107, 141, 151–3, 195, 200, 228, 236, 249–50, 290–2, 295, 339
fitna, 13–15, 140
fungus, 115–16, 224, 275
Fyzee, Asaf A., 100, 154, 330

Ganesha, 221
gender, 15–17, 23–4, 34–7, 90, 103, 160, 176, 189–190, 193, 202–7, 295, 331
genīza, 216, 222–3
ghadīr khumm, 71, 264
ghaghra, 295
ghayba, 64, 69
ghazal, 295
ginān, 5
Gujarat, 1–14, 21–2, 26, 28–9, 34, 36, 43, 48, 56, 58, 62, 65, 67, 70, 75, 80, 86, 89, 90, 92, 96–105, 113, 119–57, 195, 203, 215–16, 218–21, 224, 226, 229, 235, 240, 250, 259, 269, 275, 299, 302–8, 316, 319, 321, 323, 326, 329–30, 343, 347–9
Gujarati, 10, 21, 28–9, 43, 46, 62, 67, 74, 82–3, 89–90, 97–8, 101–5, 109, 114–15, 118, 128–9, 133, 139, 143–6, 150–1, 156, 161, 167, 183–4, 190, 192, 197, 199, 200, 216, 224, 228, 235, 250, 257, 263, 289, 294–5, 301, 305, 307, 311, 319, 329, 333, 351

ḥāfiẓ, 94, 96–7
Ḥajj, 68, 71, 76, 327, 340
ḥalāl, 62, 70, 124, 174, 209, 363
haldi, 88
ḥalqa, 329–30
al-Hamdani
  Abbas, 148, 235
  Hussayn, 121, 126, 148
  see also khizana
al-Ḥāmidī, Sy. Ḥātim b. Ibrāhīm, 66, 127, 153, 194
al-Hammādī, Lamak b. Mālik, 124–6
ḥaqā'iq, 15, 19, 64–5, 74, 104, 108–9, 152–4, 164, 188, 207–8, 233, 237, 249, 255, 258, 262, 266, 290, 306, 333, 338–9
al-Ḥaql, 136–7
ḥarām, 33, 36, 62, 69, 175, 183, 221
Ḥarāz, 9, 45–6, 55, 129, 134–5, 140–1, 148, 190, 234, 245, 347
Ḥasan, Amīnjī b. Jalāl b., 68, 154
al-Ḥasan, Sy. Idrīs Imād al-Dīn b., 127, 153
Ḥasan, Sy. Jalāl Shamsuddīn b., 48
al-Ḥasan, Sy. Sulaymān b., 48, 135, 140, 143, 153, 302
haveli, 27, 30, 83, 106, 109–10, 146, 162, 165, 168–9, 176, 185–8, 197–208, 224, 226, 249
henna, 27, 88, 199, 206
heritage, 4, 5, 10, 13, 29, 34, 61, 91, 100, 103, 121, 152, 176, 180, 182–8, 190, 199, 220, 225–7, 235, 239, 264, 274, 281, 343, 349–50, 352
Hindi, 82, 107, 113, 115, 133, 228, 236, 343, 250, 263, 295, 307, 309
Hinduism, 90, 92
Hong Kong, 239
ḥudūd, 26, 69, 73, 77–8, 80, 109, 131, 147, 188, 201
Husayn, 32, 51, 55, 61, 153, 175–6
al-Ḥusayn, Sy. Idrīs Imād al-Dīn b., 153
al-Ḥuṭayb, 45
Hyderabad, 3, 26, 34, 223, 229, 240

ʿibādāt, 62, 67
Ibrāhīm, Sy. ʿAlī Shamsuddīn b., 56
ijāza, 282, 329, 340, 342
ilhām, 53
ʿilm al-bāṭin, 15, 62–8, 70–4, 107, 112, 124, 126, 130–1, 151–3, 186, 190–2, 196–7, 209, 215, 227–31, 249–53, 275, 285–6, 290, 298, 303, 308, 310, 328, 330; *see also ʿilm al- ẓāhir*

ʿilm al-fāl, 291–4, 347
ʿilm al-ḥurūf, 291–2, 294
ʿilm al-ẓāhir, 15, 62–4, 74, 106, 108, 153, 190, 196, 230, 249, 290, 293–4; *see also ʿilm al-bāṭin*
imāmat, 62
immateriality, 212, 215–17, 248, 256, 266, 294
Indian Ocean, 1–20, 25, 45–8, 81, 96, 102, 105, 124–46, 190, 215–16, 221, 239, 240, 246, 259, 270, 302, 308, 317, 330, 347–8
initiation, 11, 15, 24, 27, 36, 61–62, 74, 88, 92, 93, 104–5, 108, 114, 125, 158, 160, 163, 189, 194, 196, 199, 208, 213, 230, 245, 249, 303, 317, 329
ink, 54, 187, 225, 235, 250, 266, 270, 279, 293, 301, 307, 328, 331, 335, 339

jamāʿat khāna, 25, 31, 48, 88, 162, 165, 172–6, 183, 186–7, 198, 201, 205, 225, 293
Jamea tus Saifiyah, 230–2, 250, 302, 316
Jamnagar, 45, 55, 330
Jazīrat al-Hind, 45, 124, 142
Jibla, 45
jihād, 19–20, 32, 68–9, 125, 134, 303–4, 316, 328–9, 332, 334, 240–6
jild, 279, 339
jinn, 36, 228
juz', 282–3

kabīkaj, 115, 225, 242, 285–8, 351
ka 'l-maʿṣūm, 73; *see also maʿṣūm*
Karbala, 172–3, 175–6, 188, 190
kashf, 62, 64–5, 68, 113, 152–4, 248
Khambhat, 45, 124, 133–4, 138, 162
khāna, 118, 237, 269; *see also ṣaff*
al-khārij, 163, 191, 193–4, 207
khāṣṣa, 74, 77, 106, 162–3, 174, 183, 185–6, 188, 196–7, 199, 200–2, 207–8, 217, 254, 258, 262–3, 298, 309–10, 312, 340; *see also* ʿāmma
khaṭṭ, 126, 220, 231, 277, 306, 312, 321, 344
khidma, 77, 132–3, 174, 302; *see also mullāh*
khizanjee, 107
khizāna
  al-khizānat al-ʿAlawiyya, 107
  al-khizānat al-amīra, 107
  al-khizānat al-khāṣṣa, 106
  al-khizānat al-kutub, xix, 1, 12, 55, 100, 106–7, 120–1, 134, 141, 145, 343, 347
  al-khizānat al-maknūna, 106–7
  al-khizānat al-mubāraka, 107
  al-Khizānat al-Muḥammadiyya al-Ḥamadāniyya, 148
  catalogue, 34–5, 38, 41, 103–4, 118, 122, 207, 211, 242, 249, 328
  destruction, 349
  practices, 14, 112, 125, 127–8, 130, 140, 143, 151, 347
Khojas, 5, 7, 58, 86, 90–1, 154, 172, 189, 291, 307, 349
khums, 68
khuṭba; 69, 170, 305, 355, 358; *see also wāz*
al-Kirmānī, Ḥamīd al-Dīn, 3, 66, 152, 288, 319
kitab, 100, 256, 277, 285
Kitāb al-Azhar, 153
Kitāb al-Himma, 75, 152
Kitāb al-Ḥawāshī, 153
Kitāb Iftitāḥ al-Daʿwa, 152
Kitāb Ithbāt al-Naṣṣ, 56, 58
kitāb sirriyya, 54, 285–6, 290
Kitāb al-Ṭahāra, 152, 331
Kitāb Ta'wīl al-Daʿā'im, 152
kurta, 25, 78, 158, 331

laʿn, 285–6
library *see khizana*
lisān, 267–8, 301, 307, 309, 312, 344
Lisān al-Daʿwa, 52, 55, 57, 67, 90, 113, 115, 159, 160, 190, 192, 194–5, 197, 199, 227–8, 259, 263, 295, 310
looting, 129, 141, 143, 149, 192, 229

Madagascar, 11, 14, 190, 193
madrasa, 4, 38, 111, 116, 139, 142, 158, 162, 203, 221, 227, 265, 305, 309, 310, 319
maghrib prayer, 42, 68, 132
mahdī, 64, 78, 83, 133; *see also qā'im*
mahr, 88
al-Majdū', Ismā'īl b. 'Abd al-Rasūl, 131, 147
majlis, 29–30, 52, 58, 71, 76, 132, 155, 170–1, 195, 201–3, 226, 259
majmūca, 282, 339
makhṭūṭa, 75, 113, 115, 118, 211, 219, 245, 254, 255–6, 264, 266, 295, 298, 300–1, 303, 308, 315–16, 328, 242, 347; *see also* manuscript
mandorla, 269
manṣūṣ, 53–4, 58, 74, 76, 108, 119, 209, 211, 234, 303; *see also naṣṣ*
manzil, 165, 176–84, 192, 204, 226
manuscript
  acquisition, 5, 235, 345
  burying, 221
  circumcision, 19, 224, 248, 251, 283, 347
  collation, 226, 281, 311, 334
  commodification, 84
  consumption, 19, 88, 215, 218, 270, 275, 333
  destruction, 2, 124, 140, 217
  discarding, 19, 83, 219, 334
  donation, 13, 51, 68, 100, 114, 227, 234–5, 239, 241–2
  preservation, 103, 116, 129, 226
  theft, 113, 218, 235
  veneration, 16, 88, 212
  see also makhṭūṭa
manuscriptology, 210
manuscriptorium *see* scriptorium
marginalia *see* paratexts
materiality
  of objects, 351
  of *nass*, 58, 347, 351
  of secrecy, 11, 192, 249–99, 301, 311, 328–9, 344, 347, 351
  see also immateriality
maqbara, 205; *see also qabaristān*
al-Maqrīzī, Aḥmad b. 'Alī, 96, 120, 345
marthiyya, 32, 51, 302, 308
Ma Saheba, 37–9, 75, 172, 176, 189, 201
Masār, 133–4
masjid, 27, 48, 71, 163, 165, 169–72, 176, 183, 185–6, 201–2, 223, 263–4
ma'ṣūm, 73
ma'tam, 28, 94, 169, 176, 277–9, 317, 334, 341; *see also 'Ashūra* and *'urs*
Mawsim-e Bahār, 57, 90
minbar, 69, 169, 170
miṣtara, 261, 315–16, 321, 328, 334–6, 338–40, 342
mīthāq see 'ahd
Mombasa, xviii, xix, 4, 96, 169, 189
Moulai Raj Bin Moulai Hasan, 135–8
mu'āmalāt, 63; *see also 'ibādāt*
Mughals, 55, 69, 119, 144, 304, 326
muhājirūn, 132, 134, 139, 142, 144, 194, 345, 347
Muḥarram, 68, 78, 92, 167, 170, 176, 190, 224, 263, 386, 310, 333; *see also 'Ashūra*
al-Mu'izz, li-Dīn Allāh, 53, 67, 99
mullāh, 10, 68, 77
Mumbai, xix, 3, 12, 14, 26, 29, 36, 48, 81, 100, 147, 169, 186, 203, 212, 219, 221, 228, 233–4, 236–9
munājāt, 310
Muntaza' al-Akhbār, 90
musāfir khāna, 4, 49, 51–2, 58–9
al-Mustanṣir, Abū Tamīm Ma'add, 91, 124–6, 302

nafs, 57, 66, 68, 303, 355
Nagoshiyyas, 54, 93
Najrān, 46, 143

Najm al-Dīn, Sy. Jalāl, 54
namāz see *ṣalāt*
naskh, 20, 98, 150, 250, 278, 301–27, 338–9, 344
naṣṣ, 44, 51–59, 69–70, 74, 94, 134, 143, 152, 195, 213, 258, 260, 285, 310, 323, 331, 347, 251
  al-jālī, 58
  see also manṣūṣ
nasta'līq, 278, 306–8, 311, 314, 317–18, 323, 325
al-Naysabūrī, Aḥmad B. Ibrahīm, 75, 194, 195
nazār al-maqām, 68
neem, 115–16, 210, 225, 238, 246, 287, 288; *see also kabīkaj*
nikāḥ, 69, 87–9, 114, 193, 310
Nizāris, 4–5, 172, 347
Neo-Fatimid
  architecture, 48, 110, 169
  identity, xix, 5–6, 9, 16, 47, 67, 75, 97, 100–1, 146, 156, 188, 195, 213, 274, 301, 328, 343, 347–8
  khizana, 19, 182
al-Nu'mān, al-Qāḍī, 3, 5, 67, 69, 75, 98, 100, 116, 124, 152, 156, 236, 249–50, 349
Nuzhat al-Afkār, 127

oral
  ceremonies, 158, 160, 228
  contract, 104, 160, 192, 207
  history, 19, 147, 149, 220, 248, 232
  text, 308, 310
  tradition, 55, 58, 326
  transmission, 119, 214
owner stamps, 129, 235, 238, 241–2, 279–81, 292, 318
owner statements, 98, 223, 240, 242, 250

pagri, 78–80, 158, 210
palaeography, 34, 240, 252, 254, 300, 303, 308, 311–12, 316, 319, 343–4
palimpsests, 269
paratexts, 19, 118, 214, 224, 229, 240–1, 243, 250–3, 266, 272–99, 307, 310–15, 327, 340–1, 347–8
parrots, 94–7
participant observation, 18–19, 24, 73, 174, 191, 205, 215, 259, 328
pastiwala, 228, 236–7
persecution, 9, 11, 55, 59, 69–70, 119, 134–5, 139, 143, 157, 161, 192, 323, 327
Persian, 5, 74, 96, 98, 107, 113–16, 151, 154, 167, 190, 218, 227, 243, 257, 269, 278, 281, 304, 306–8, 310, 316–17, 327, 339, 241
pol, 192
print, 5, 15–6, 20, 115, 119, 231, 305, 327
privilege, 15, 17, 27, 78, 82, 88, 102, 164, 196, 201–3, 210–11, 233, 249, 252, 322, 344
purdah, 76, 177, 201–6
purity
  ritual purity, 11, 27, 35, 76, 89, 93, 199, 200, 207, 300, 330–1
  spiritual purity, 27, 199–200, 330–3, 342, 343

qabaristān; 45, 47–51, 59, 94, 96, 105–6, 162, 165, 221, 346; *see also maqbara*
  destruction, 49, 51, 229
qāḍī, 44, 69–70, 75, 80, 125, 209
qā'im, 8, 15, 19, 25, 57, 62–5, 74, 76, 84, 109, 151–4, 164, 207, 236–8, 255, 258, 266, 290, 306, 333, 345
qalam, 320, 334
Qarāṭīs al-Yaman, 53–4, 128–31, 133–41, 146, 156–7, 240, 246, 280
qaṣā'id, 257, 267, 310
quire, 269, 283, 339–40
Qur'an, 21, 79, 87, 90, 94, 96, 132, 220–1, 225, 251, 294, 322

qur'anic, 83, 85–6, 97, 169, 176, 187, 263, 266, 291, 293, 304, 308–10, 311
Qaṣr-e ʿAlī, 75
Quṭbshāh, Sy. Dā'ūd b., 143, 153, 321
Quṭbuddīn, Sy. Quṭub Khān, 96

Rajput, 91, 144
rakhi, 88
Ramadan, 27, 47, 68, 71, 263, 310
Rāmpūrī, Muḥammad ʿAlī b. Mullā Jīwābhāʾī, 47
Rangoon, 11, 238–40
Rasā'il Ikhwān al-Ṣafā', 66, 96
rasm, 79, 83
reformists, 5, 12, 189, 193
rida, 25, 28–9, 38, 41, 43, 45, 59, 78, 90, 106, 158, 189–92, 200–1, 203, 206–7, 211, 249, 340
risāla, 55, 57
Risāla al-Mūjaza, 194
Risāla al-Ramaḍāniyya, 57
Risāla al-Waḍiyya, 321–2
Risāla fī Ithbāt al-Naṣṣ, 56
rough edges, 214, 240, 272–5, 279, 284, 298–9, 347; *see also* paratexts
rūḥ, 87, 126, 197–8, 293
Rutlam, 99

ṣaff, 118, 237, 269; *see also khāna*
*al-Ṣaḥīfat al-*ʿAlawiyyat *al-Ṭayyibiyya*, 228
safīna, 257
saints, 295
salām, 40, 44, 187, 199
San'a, 140, 141
Saraspur, 47–52, 94–6, 106, 135, 147, 295–6, 321
satr, 8, 61, 64–6, 69, 72, 107, 113, 152–4, 169, 196, 248; *see also ghayba*
ṣawm, 68
sayfat, 310
Sayfuddīn, Sy. Ṭahīr, 48, 82, 84
schism, 25, 42, 101, 119, 141, 145, 192, 213, 218, 229, 240, 347
  Alawi-Dawoodi, 48–59, 149, 319–21, 323
  Sulaymanis-Indian Bohras, 143
  Tayyibi-Hafizi, 8
scribal
  etiquette, 340–1
  jihad, 303, 329, 332, 334, 343, 346
  politics, 19, 279, 300–41
  practice, 244, 323, 334
  rituals, 20, 215–16, 303, 328–9, 331–2, 334, 343
  traditions, 188, 215, 328–9, 331–2, 343, 348
scribe, 19, 23, 84, 136, 210, 241, 245, 276–8, 301–4, 312–16, 320–1, 328–46
  female, 226, 230, 235, 316, 330
  see also copyist
scriptorium, 118–19, 253, 270, 301–3, 319, 328, 343–4
scrolls, 38, 47, 98–9, 256–60, 266, 298, 334, 351, 357
seal of Solomon, 285–88
secrecy, 10–25, 60–9, 102–8, 189–97, 207–12, 301, 304, 309–11, 316–17, 328–9, 343–4, 347–8, 351
secret alphabet *see kitāb siriyya*
sehra, 88–9
self-abasement, 277, 303
shadi, 88
shahīd, 56, 95–6, 357
Shamsuddīn, Sy. ʿAlī, 47–59, 82, 94, 159, 229, 345
sharia, 3, 5, 12, 44, 67, 69, 75, 107
sherwani, 78, 331
shiʿr, 155, 263
Shams al-Dīn, Sy. Shams al-Dīn Shaykh ʿAlī b., 149
Shibām, 129, 132–4, 141, 145
al-Shīrāzī, Mu'ayyad fī Dīn, 125, 143, 152, 260, 302

Sidhpur, 10, 124, 134, 147, 165, 176
Sindh, 10, 114, 119, 124, 128, 304, 307, 317
sijill, 53–60, 85, 114, 124–8, 145, 157, 160, 210, 213, 216, 255, 258, 310, 348
Sijillāt al-Mustanṣiriyya, 124–8, 157, 255
al-Sijistānī, Abū Ya'qūb, 1, 3, 66, 152, 156, 349
Social Codicology, 15–17, 44, 83, 131, 195, 212, 215, 328, 346, 351
social life, 1, 7, 15, 17–20, 44, 70, 88, 94, 100, 141, 210, 243, 253, 286, 293, 303, 343
Ṣulayḥids, 8–10, 125
Sulaymān, Sy. Yūsuf Najm al-Dīn b., 10, 54
Surat, xviii, 3, 6, 26, 45, 55, 121, 138–9, 147–8, 165, 189, 219, 230, 232, 250, 291, 305, 316, 330, 345

tabla, 72
ṭahāra, 35–6, 68–70, 92–3, 152, 199–200, 330–2
talismans, 19, 38, 47, 59–60, 72, 83, 86–7, 101, 188, 205, 211, 213, 224, 244, 248, 254–7, 262–3, 266, 269, 284, 293–4, 298, 306, 310, 329, 334, 339, 344–5, 351; *see also ta'wīz*
takht, 71, 79, 169, 172, 187
tamma, 277–8, 289, 334, 341, 343, 352
taqiyya, 28–9, 33, 62, 69–70, 186, 191, 194–5, 225, 306, 309, 327
  dār al-taqiyya, 191, 194, 205–8, 259
  practice, 9, 11, 23, 55, 99, 142, 149, 160, 183, 196
  spatial, 189, 192, 199, 232, 246
taqiyyafication, 18, 149, 156, 227, 348
taqlid, 69
tasbīḥ, 78, 188
taṣliya, 242, 277, 279, 306–7
ta'wīz, 83, 114, 257, 260, 262, 266–7, 293–4, 347
al-Ṭayyib, al-Amīr b., 8, 313
Ṭayyibis, 8–13, 57, 65, 91, 113, 121, 124–30, 134–6, 139–43, 151, 153, 161, 214, 319, 348; *see also* Ṣulayḥids
Ṭayyibshāh, Sy. Ādam Safīuddīn b., 59
termites, 43, 113, 115–16, 119, 149, 224–5, 250, 266, 275, 283, 286, 288, 351
thali, 28, 31–2, 52, 59, 88, 164, 172–5, 209, 249, 316
thawab, 32
Thūla, 129, 140, 372
thuluth, 267, 306, 317, 339
tijāra, 124, 132, 139
topi, 45, 78, 180, 182, 200, 331
Tuḥfat al-Kirām, 114
Tuḥfat al-Qulūb, 66, 127, 194
Twelver Shi'is, 7, 16, 54, 64, 68–9, 71, 73, 83, 106, 108, 119, 154, 167, 172, 189–91, 196, 286, 291

Ujjain, 45, 55, 131, 330
'ulamā', 73, 148, 302, 305, 329–30
Urdu, 74, 82, 107, 113, 115, 199, 227–8, 250, 257, 263, 277, 281, 305, 307–8, 310, 317, 327, 339
'urs, 51–2, 59–60, 71, 94, 134, 159, 176, 205, 310, 333
'Uyūn al-Akhbār, 127

Vadodara *see* Baroda
Vaishya, 10, 89, 90–3, 330; *see also* caste
Vehwar see Vaishya

Wajīḥ al-Dīn, Sy. Ibrāhīm, 148
wala, 82, 179, 278
walāya, 67–8, 74, 122, 124
walī, 64, 88, 131
Walī al-Hind, 132, 137
waqf, 1, 114, 116–17, 259–60, 334
watermarks, 210, 264–6, 269–72
wāz, 71, 76
wizārat, 76
  al-wizārat al-'Alawiyya, 186, 189

Yūsuf, Sy., 54, 135
Yūsuf, Sy. Abū Ḥātim Ṭayyib Ḍiyā' al-Dīn b. Nūr al-Dīn, 44

Zabīd, 45, 270
al-Ẓāfir, 91, 96
Zahr al-Maʿānī, 153
zakāt, 10, 68, 77, 114
Zakī al-Dīn, Sy. ʿAbd al-Ṭayyib, 57
Zakī al-Dīn, Sy. Abū Saʿīd al-Khayr Ḥātim, 26, 44
Zaydis, 134–5, 137, 139–41, 143, 192
ziyāra, 28–9, 38, 45, 47, 49, 51, 68, 76, 124, 193, 195, 201, 310, 333

EU representative:
Easy Access System Europe
Mustamäe tee 50, 10621 Tallinn, Estonia
Gpsr.requests@easproject.com

www.ingramcontent.com/pod-product-compliance
Lightning Source LLC
Chambersburg PA
CBHW060348250426
43667CB00051B/2482
* 9 7 8 1 4 7 4 4 7 9 5 7 8 *